THE DEVIL'S HANDWRITING

CHICAGO STUDIES IN PRACTICES OF MEANING
Edited by Jean Comaroff, Andreas Glaeser, William Sewell, and Lisa Wedeen

The Devil's Handwriting

PRECOLONIALITY AND
THE GERMAN COLONIAL STATE
IN QINGDAO, SAMOA,
AND SOUTHWEST AFRICA

George Steinmetz

THE UNIVERSITY OF CHICAGO PRESS : *Chicago & London*

GEORGE STEINMETZ is professor of sociology and German studies at the University of Michigan and the author of *State/Culture: State Formation after the Colonial Turn, The Politics of Method in the Human Sciences: Positivism and Its Epistemological Others,* and *Regulating the Social: The Welfare State and Local Politics in Imperial Germany.*

The University of Chicago Press, Chicago 60637
The University of Chicago Press, Ltd., London
© 2007 by The University of Chicago
All rights reserved. Published 2007
Printed in the United States of America

16 15 14 13 12 11 10 09 08 07   1 2 3 4 5

ISBN-13: 978-0-226-77241-7 (cloth)
ISBN-13: 978-0-226-77243-1 (paper)
ISBN-10: 0-226-77241-1 (cloth)
ISBN-10: 0-226-77243-8 (paper)

Library of Congress Cataloging-in-Publication Data

Steinmetz, George, 1957–
  The devil's handwriting : precoloniality and the German colonial state in Qingdao, Samoa, and Southwest Africa / George Steinmetz.
      p.   cm. — (Chicago studies in practices of meaning)
  Includes bibliographical references and index.
  ISBN-13: 978-0-226-77241-7 (cloth : alk. paper)
  ISBN-13: 978-0-226-77243-1 (pbk. : alk. paper)
  ISBN-10: 0-226-77241-1 (cloth : alk. paper)
  ISBN-10: 0-226-77243-8 (pbk. : alk. paper)
  1. Germany—Colonies—History. 2. Germany—Foreign relations—1888–1918. 3. Germany—Colonies—Race relations. 4. Qingdao (China)—History. 5. Germany—Foreign relations—China. 6. China—Foreign relations—Germany. 7. Samoa—History. 8. Namibia—History—1885–1915. 9. Imperialism. I. Title.
  JV2017.S74 2007
  325′.343—dc22

                                        2006019664

To Julia and to the memory of my mother

CONTENTS

ILLUSTRATIONS

The phrase "the devil's handwriting" comes from the title of the memoirs of Paul Rohrbach, *Um des Teufels Handschrift,* published in 1953. Rohrbach is an emblematic figure in the story I tell here. He shows up repeatedly in the German colonies in Africa and China and other spheres of German imperial interest. Rohrbach served as the official "commissary for settlement" in Southwest Africa between 1903 and 1906, during the war between the German colonizers and their indigenous subjects. He visited the German colony in Qingdao (Kiaochow), China, in 1908–9 as an unofficial "cultural missionary," and there he helped to create a high school for Chinese girls.[1] In addition to his practical involvement in German imperial settings, Rohrbach was a prolific travel writer and colonial propagandist. He was a producer of *ethnographic discourse.*[2] More specifically, Rohrbach contributed to the armory of images of Germany's own overseas subjects, images that profoundly shaped the formation of "native policy" in those colonies.

1. Rohrbach also recommended that Turkey deport the Armenians, although, as Hull notes, the Ottoman Empire's rulers in the Committee of Union and Progress (CUP) "hardly needed" Rohrbach and German staff officers "to give them the idea for mass population removal," and it remains unclear whether German officers "helped precipitate the shift in CUP policy . . . to mass murder via deportation" (2005, pp. 273, 278). On Rohrbach's activities before World War I see Mogk 1972; Bieber 1972 focuses on the period after 1918.

2. The words *ethnography* and *ethnographic discourse,* as I use them here, are not restricted to professional or scientific texts but include travel accounts, fiction, visual images, and any other representations that claim to represent the culture or character of a community defined variously as an ethnic group, race, nation, community, or people. This does not mean that I reject the idea that sociocultural descriptions vary in their adequacy or accuracy. But questions of the truth or accuracy of precolonial or colonial ethnographic perceptions are not relevant to the causal connections explored in this book.

Ethnographic representations were also partly responsible for the physical genocide and the destruction of indigenous ways of life ("ethnocide") that characterized Germany's activities in Southwest Africa—the precursor of contemporary Namibia. The idea of the devil's handwriting therefore condenses a central argument in this book.[3] Ethnographic discourse cannot entirely explain the contours of colonial native policy or the shift to massacre and genocide in certain settings. Nonetheless, the inherited archives of precolonial ethnographic representations provided the ideological raw materials for almost everything that was done to colonized peoples in the modern era. Rohrbach's career brings together both sides of this equation— the production of ethnographic discourse and the elaboration of colonial policy.

As a member of the middle-class educated German-speaking elite, or *Bildungsbürgertum*,[4] Rohrbach also exemplifies a social type that played a prominent role in governing many of the overseas German colonial states. Rohrbach had a university education and a considerable stock of internalized cultural capital, but he lacked inherited wealth and aristocratic titles. Many nineteenth-century *Bildungsbürger* strove to attain social recognition within a class system that continued to accord more prestige to members of the traditional nobility, a system that increasingly recognized commercial and industrial capitalists as well. The fragmented German elite's internal struggle for status and power was played out inside the metropolitan German state and, as I show here, was transposed from the metropole to the overseas colonial political field. Even as they were trying to control the lives of their colonial subjects, Germans on the overseas stage were drawn into these imported dynamics of intraelite class conflict. More specifically, German colonizers competed with one another for a particular form of "symbolic capital" (in the words of social theorist Pierre Bourdieu) that characterized the modern colonial state field. They demanded from one another recognition of their *ethnographic capital,* of the acuity of their perception and judgment with respect to exotic cultures and indigenous subjectivities. German colonizers jockeyed with one another within the intersubjective ambit of

3. In defense of Rohrbach it should be noted that he opposed General von Trotha's exterminationist policy against the Namibian Ovaherero, arguing that the "Herero people with its huge cattle herds and its labor potential should be saved for the colony for economic reasons" (Nuhn 1989, p. 300; see Rohrbach 1909b). All translations in this book are my own unless otherwise noted.

4. Rohrbach was actually a "diaspora German," or *Volksdeutscher,* from the Baltics, but after his university studies in Dorpat (Tartu) his career was focused on Germany and Germany's imperial and colonial peripheries.

the colonial state, drawing from the stock of inherited ethnographic materials in order to make claims and counterclaims to possess a superior understanding of the native Other. So-called native policy was framed, propelled, and constrained by these ethnographic position takings. The received library of ethnographic ideas was the medium in which officials competed for the type of cultural capital that was specific to the colonial state field.

The idea of the colonizers' ethnographic discourse as an infernal one resonates with the ubiquitous return of satanic tropes in the history of European and German colonial engagements. Cotton Mather referred to colonial America as "the *Devil's* Territories."[5] A similar language was used to describe the inhabitants of Southern Africa, Polynesia, and China, the regions examined in this book. German Catholic missionaries in Shandong called China the "land of Satan" and a "bulwark of the devil."[6] Missionaries, colonial soldiers, and officials saw the Southwest African Ovaherero as "black devils" controlled by a "demonic power."[7] Even the putative tropical paradise, Samoa, was sometimes described in these terms, although Edenic tropes were more common. One nineteenth-century European visitor depicted Samoa as "l'inferno," as "a weird, strange, intoxicating scene" that combined "the sublime and the grotesque." It was "a nightmare, a tale of Hoffmann, a vision of Dante!"[8] Lest we assume that this hyperbolic language was heard only on the side of the colonizers, we should recall that some nineteenth-century Chinese referred to Europeans as *fan gui* or *yang guizi* (or in a dialectical variant, *guizi*), meaning "foreign demons," or more literally, "foreign ghosts."[9] There was sometimes a devil's calligraphy, as it were, alongside the European devil's handwriting. I do not want to suggest, however, that all transactions between colonizer and colonized took place

5. Mather [1692] 1950, p. 14. Cornelius de Houtman, the first traveler to the East Indies for the DEIC, claimed to have encountered in Madagascar a native population with devil-like horns; see plate 10 in Rouffaer 1925, facing p. 10.

6. Missionaries Wewel and Anzer, quoted in Rivinius 1979, p. 90 n. 8, and Mühlhahn 2000, p. 331.

7. Quotes from Erffa 1905, p. 70; Beiderbecke 1875, p. 273.

8. Hübner 1886, vol. 2, p. 407. The American explorer Wilkes (1845, vol. 2, p. 82) discussed the towns on the southern coast of Tutuila as "devil's towns"; along similar lines see Colvocoresses [1852] 1855, p. 88.

9. These Chinese terms were usually mistranslated by Europeans as "foreign devils," raising the possibility that the colonizers were at least dimly aware of the "diabolical" character of their own activities. Lydia Liu reminds us that the Chinese concept of *gui* (ghost, spirit) has "a much broader semantic reach than the English notion of 'devil,' ranging from the occult, fantastic, or repulsive to the spiritual, the exotic, and the playful" (2004, p. 100; see also Hua 2000).

in a mutually demonizing register. Indeed, many of the representations and interactions I describe in this book were affectionate, and some were even respectful. The dialectics of demonization underscore the blindness of most European perceptions of non-Europeans during the precolonial and colonial eras, their imperviousness to evidence that contradicted existing stereotypes.[10]

The protoconcept of the devil's handwriting in Rohrbach's text has additional layers of meaning. Rohrbach claimed to have discovered the phrase in George Kennan's 1951 book *American Diplomacy*. In the relevant passage, however, Kennan was not describing colonialism or religion but the Treaty of Versailles, which, he wrote, had "the tragedies of the future written into it as by the devil's own hand."[11] Because Rohrbach was publishing his autobiography in the aftermath of the Holocaust and the downfall of Nazism, it is difficult to disentangle his reliance on Kennan's formula from apologetic motives concerning the more recent German atrocities.[12] Rohrbach's phrase "the devil's handwriting" seems like an attempt to shift the reader's attention first from colonialism to Nazism, and then to the putative external determinants of Nazism.

In light of Rohrbach's long-lasting involvement with international affairs, an additional cluster of meanings suggests itself, having to do with the figure of the *writing devil* in medieval European literature and art. This demon, who frequently bears the name Tutivillus beginning in the thirteenth century, records idle words, unprofitable speech, and the names of sinners.[13] Whether consciously or not, Rohrbach was gesturing toward a

---

10. Anticolonialism and decolonization changed "northern" perceptions of the global South. Colonial rule required homogenizing and unitary portraits of the colonized, for reasons discussed in the next chapter. But while most cultural anthropologists no longer find it plausible to identify a single, stabilized essence for every culture (Ortner 1999), others continue to pursue this chimerical goal (e.g., Huntington 1996).

11. Kennan 1951, p. 69.

12. Rohrbach's use of Kennan's phrase may have anti-Semitic resonances as well. Hitler had described the Versailles Treaty as part of a "Jewish conspiracy," and according to Michael Camille (1989, p. 358 n. 15), mediaeval depictions of satanic scribbling in an unknown language may have been meant to suggest Hebrew. Bieber (1972, pp. 199ff.) discusses Rohrbach's gradual accommodation to Hitler. On the links between the Holocaust and colonialism in the anticolonial imagination of the 1950s and early 1960s see Rothberg 2004; Fanon [1952] 1967; Césaire [1950] 2000; and H. Arendt [1950] 1958.

13. M. Jennings 1977, pp. 10, 16. As Camille (1989, p. 356) notes, Tutivillus appeared in a "great variety of materials from the fourteenth through the twentieth centuries"—in literature, theatrical plays, works of art, and church decoration; see Halm 1952; Wildhaber 1955; and Rasmussen 1972, for other examples.

dense web of associations linking demons to the pagan Other and to the act of writing itself. His implicit endorsement of the idea of a satanic mode of writing indirectly acknowledges the role played by writers like himself in helping to conjure up and to propel the phenomenon that Hannah Arendt called "colonial imperialism."

Without succumbing to any intellectualist illusions, it can also be argued that the German colonial state was an especially writerly one.[14] The British argument after 1918 that the Germans had failed as colonizers because of their inexperience is belied by the colonial statecraft evident in some of the earliest German interventions in places like Qingdao and Samoa. When the Germans annexed Kiaochow in 1897, translators had already prepared instructions in Chinese for local inhabitants.[15] In the course of administering the Kiaochow colony the Germans compiled and translated legal codes of the Qing dynasty in an effort to devise a dualistic legal system. By 1914 hundreds of Germans had been trained in colonial law, theory, and languages at the Seminar for Oriental Languages at Berlin University (founded in 1887) and the Colonial Institute in Hamburg (founded in 1907).[16] If the mass killing of the Ovaherero people in 1904 occurred partly beyond the reach of record keeping, detailed records were kept on the murderous concentration camps and forced labor that came afterward. The archival documentation from the German colonies, which lasted just a little over three decades (1884–1918), is voluminous. This does not mean that *Bildungsbürger* were automatically elevated into leading positions in the colonies, but they were in a stronger position than in the metropolitan field of power. This relative advantage of the writerly classes was due to the colonial state's reliance on translators and its emphasis on policies aimed at stabilizing indigenous culture.

A short piece of fiction by Arthur Schnitzler on the European campaign against the Boxer Rebellion captures the central place of writing in German

14. The written material concerning the Chinese colony of Kiaochow in the Freiburg military archive alone constitutes a "small mountain of documents, approximately a good truckload" (B. Martin 1994, p. 384). When we consider the intensive photographic and cinematographic activities of the German colonial state, it must also be considered a scopophilic one; see, for example, the enormous photographic collection of the German Colonial Society at the Stadt- u. Universitätsbibliothek Frankfurt. The photographic records of the Namibian National Archives fill an entire room. On the role of photography in German colonialism see Geary 1988; and Blanton 1995; on German colonial cinematography see Fuhrmann 2003.

15. German district commissioners in Kiaochow were not required to record the protocols of criminal trials or even to take testimony, but they did record the punishments they imposed.

16. See Sachau 1912; and Universität Hamburg, Allgemeiner Studentenausschuss 1969.

imperialism. In this story a German lieutenant frees one of his seventeen Chinese captives awaiting execution, who is engrossed in reading a novel and making notes in the margins of his book. This act of mercy is motivated by the lieutenant's concern that his prisoner might not be able to finish reading the novel, which seems to him a "monstrous" (*ungeheuerlich*) possibility. After some pleading with his commander the lieutenant is allowed to pardon the reader, and the order is put "in writing." The venerable European image of the urbane and literate Chinaman becomes the focus for the lieutenant's identification across the imperial-racial boundary. Since the sixteenth century, educated Europeans had admired the Chinese literati for their combination of erudition and power. As the bookish Boxer rises and recedes "slowly into the distance," the lieutenant comments laconically: "I wanted to follow him."[17] Where militaristic Sinophobes insisted that "every Chinaman in certain regions is a Boxer in the clothing of a citizen," Schnitzler reveals a citizen in the clothing of a Boxer.[18]

Schnitzler's story touches on two additional determinants of colonial policy that I will explore in this book alongside ethnographic representations and intraelite class conflicts inside the colonial state. The first of these is cross-cultural identification. In a surprising number of instances, German colonizers identified across the seemingly unbreachable cultural boundary with an imago of their colonized subjects. Sometimes this cross-identification reinforced the policy preferences that flowed from the colonizer's efforts to display his ethnographic sagacity. In other cases cross-identification led colonizers to interact with the colonized in ways that were counterproductive from the standpoint of garnering social recognition and symbolic capital. Only in rare circumstances was the imago of cross-identification a "satanic" one. More typically the colonizer identified with an image of the colonized that promised some sort of phantasmagoric pleasure or dreamlike upward mobility. The imagos used for identification were not invented from whole cloth. Like the raw materials wielded in competition for ethnographic capital, these imagos were culled from the ethnographic reservoir.

If we stopped at this point, the explanation of native policy would seem to be focused almost entirely on the colonizers. Although European

17. Ibid., pp. 92–94. Schnitzler was Austrian, and the Austrians had troops in the allied campaign against the Boxers, so the lieutenant in the story may actually be Austrian, not German. But he is probably a German, as suggested by the story's third line: "His Majesty had commanded that no mercy be shown" (kein Pardon gegeben werden), which alludes to the infamous speech by Kaiser Wilhelm, discussed in chap. 1.

18. The quote is from the memoirs of a participant in the German East Asian Expeditionary Force, Captain Georg Friederici (n.d., p. 57).

representations of the colonized related to indigenous cultural realities in oblique and highly mediated ways, this does not mean that the indigenous subject was absent from such image making. I am concerned in this book with the effects of ethnographic discourse rather than its production, but there will be examples of indigenous realities inflecting European discourse and of observed subjects resisting or actively coauthoring European ethnographic representations. Colonial native policy was also a dialogic process insofar as colonized populations responded to European expressions of paternalistic affection or demonization in ways that influenced the success or failure of a given policy. The fourth determinant of native policy is therefore the entire array of practices ranging from resistance to cooperation by the colonized. This nexus has been explored in great detail in the recent colonial historiography. Indeed it has sometimes been overemphasized, in a well-intentioned but epistemologically naive attempt to redress historians' earlier analytic bias toward the agency of the colonizers. Acts of resistance and collaboration by the colonized were able to frustrate or sanction colonial policies, but they were typically reactive rather than proactive. Resistance did not usually set the colonial agenda, as it were, but mediated its success or failure. The colonized were not the authors of their own native policy, even if they sometimes revised it or selectively reinforced certain parts of it. Native policy depended on the colonized agreeing to play their assigned roles. Where this did not occur, colonizers felt compelled to look for an alternative approach or to move away from native governance altogether, abandoning the colony or annihilating its inhabitants.

A final set of determinants of colonial native policy relates to capitalism and geopolitics. The nineteenth-century literature on imperialism and colonialism emphasized the pressures of capitalist overaccumulation and the quest for new markets, cheaper labor, and raw materials. But the actual centerpiece of modern colonialism, at least in these German colonies, was native policy, not economic extraction or trade. The initial conquest was often justified in economic terms, of course, and metropolitan discussions turned repeatedly to economic goals. But in the daily governance of the overseas colonies, motives of stabilization and order often overshadowed and even contradicted such publicly proclaimed goals. Neo-Marxists pointed to "modes of production" as determinants of state formation, but such society-level arrangements of property and labor were often the result of decisions taken for reasons that were not primarily "economic." The devastation of the Ovaherero in Southwest Africa, for example, led to the massive mobilization into the postgenocide colonial economy of the northern Ovambo people. The resulting "articulation" between precapitalist Ovambo village life and migratory labor in the copper and diamond mines was the result of an "antieconomic" decision to annihilate the colony's previous workforce. The fact that additional acres of land were *not* put under plantation agriculture in German Samoa after the colony's founding resulted from deliberate government decisions to halt or reverse the processes that had been turning Samoans into proletarians and consumers since the 1860s. Native policy in Kiaochow was decisively shaped by German geopolitical considerations, but European economic interests in the colony were partly sacrificed after 1904 in order to maintain internal order and improve German relations with China.

My goals in this book are theoretical, historical, interpretive/explanatory, interdisciplinary, and political.[19] With respect to the first of these, I focus on three bodies of theory whose compatibilities and incompatibilities have not yet been carefully explored. In *Orientalism* Edward Said codified the argument concerning the effects of precolonial ethnographic representations on colonialism—I call this the "devil's handwriting" thesis. This fits into a much broader set of arguments in the human sciences concerning the constitutive role of culture, language, semiosis, or meaning making on patterned social interactions and institutions.[20] The second theoretical framework addressed here derives from Pierre Bourdieu, whose writing has been extremely fruitful for thinking about the state and the "field of power" more generally but whose importance for analyzing colonial forms of governance has not been discussed.[21] My third theoretical resource is the analysis of colonial subjectivity adumbrated by Homi Bhabha, whose central point of reference is Lacanian psychoanalysis. Put rather crudely, we can say that these three theories emphasize three somewhat distinct ontological levels or objects: the *discursive,* the *social,* and the *psychic.* Rather than simply combining these three levels or lumping together Said, Bourdieu, and Bhabha, my aim is to reconstruct all three approaches and to track the ways in which the levels of the discursive, sociological, and psychic were intertwined in

19. Interpretation (*verstehen*) and explanation (*erklären*) have been described as distinct and even opposing types of activity both by positivist philosophers of science and phenomenologists like Martin Heidegger ([1927] 1996, sections 31-32). Against this view I have argued that social knowledge or social science is simultaneously interpretive and explanatory (Steinmetz 2004a; 2005d).

20. For some foundational statements along these lines see Wittgenstein 1969; Foucault 1980; and Laclau and Mouffe 1985; for an overview of some of these approaches see Steinmetz 1999b.

21. I have sketched the lineaments of a Bourdieuian analysis of the colonial state in Steinmetz 2002 and 2003b.

the determination of colonial native policy. This reconstruction tries to enrich each of the theories by specifying their central arguments, revealing their weaknesses, and excavating their hidden strengths. For example, I will argue that the cogency of Bourdieu's social theory rests on a specific model of the psychic that Bourdieu himself fails to elaborate and that can be best understood through Lacanian psychoanalysis.[22] Similarly, Said's "discursive" ontology needs to be regrounded in social and psychic processes. This reconstruction of theory sheds light on the modern colonial state, on the divergent history of these three colonies, and by implication on other colonies and on social practice in general. Readers who are less interested in theory can bypass the latter sections of chapter 1 and skip ahead to the historical narratives that start in chapter 2.

With respect to historiography, this book deals with three precolonial ethnographic contexts and with the colonial states that emerged in the same geocultural sites after 1884. These spaces are Southwest Africa, where I examine the fate of the Ovaherero, Witbooi, and Rehoboth peoples; Qingdao (Kiaochow); and the western part of the Samoan archipelago in Oceania. The time frame is the three decades after the onset of the European "scramble" for colonies with the Berlin West Africa Conference (1884–85). All three accounts are based on primary archival documents as well as published primary and secondary sources.[23] The extant secondary literature is most extensive for German Southwest Africa and much smaller for Kiaochow and German Samoa. This difference in attention corresponds roughly to the physical size and population of the colonies but also to the grievousness of German atrocities committed in the three settings. This emphasis in the historical literature on the most genocidal of the colonies introduces various sorts of bias into the study of colonialism. Although the present book does not aim to relativize the horrors and humiliations of colonialism, the juxtaposition between differing experiences serves as a corrective to hasty generalizations about colonialism per se.

In methodological terms, my aims are interpretive and explanatory. I propose an *interpretation* of precolonial ethnography and an *explanation* of colonial native policy.[24] Chapters 2, 4, and 6 reconstruct the layered archive

22. See Steinmetz 2006b; and, for a Freudian reading of Bourdieu, Fourny 2000.

23. See app. 1 for a note on sources.

24. Although my main goal is not to unearth new facts, some of the events narrated here have not been discussed in previous historical literature. There has not been a sustained historical treatment of the Rehoboth Basters of Namibia since Eugen Fischer's infamous 1913 monograph. The current book also provides the first sustained interpretation of German representations of Samoa.

of ethnographic meanings that were available to colonizers at the dawn of colonial annexation. Here I present readings of precolonial ethnographic texts that are relatively familiar even today, such as Robert Louis Stevenson's Pacific writings and Theodor Fontane's *Effi Briest,* and other texts that are nowadays obscure but that were widely read in their time, such as the travel narratives of John Barrow on China and South Africa, Louis-Antoine de Bougainville's descriptions of Tahiti, and Eugen Fischer's eugenic-cultural analysis of the Namibian Rehoboth people. I do not try to explain the rise of these discursive formations, since this would require an additional set of analyses that are not required for the project at hand. For example, in chapter 6 I reconstruct the emergence of European Sinophobia starting in the mid-eighteenth century and establish its availability to late-nineteenth-century German colonizers, but I do not offer a detailed explanation of the reasons why this Orientalist framework appeared at this moment. By contrast, my aim in chapters 3, 5, and 7 is mainly explanatory. Here I ask why native policy in German Southwest Africa, Samoa, and Kiaochow took varying forms and changed in particular ways over time.

This book is also an argument for *comparison,* even if this is not a comparative study in the pseudoscientific "experimentalist" format that was preferred by an earlier generation of historical sociologists.[25] I compare colonies that were linked to one another in the minds of Germans and German colonial subjects and via the circulation of officials and military,[26] rather than look for colonies exhibiting the specious quality of "independence" of "cases." My approach is similar to the method recommended by historian Marc Bloch, who argued that "there is no true understanding without a certain range of comparison; provided, of course, that that comparison is based on differing and, at the same time, *related* realities."[27] The relation-

25. See Sewell 1996 for an authoritative critique of this approach. I have argued elsewhere that comparative historical research can and usually does follow a critical-realist approach (Steinmetz 1998, 2004a); see also Lawson 1998, 1999.

26. These German colonies were also compared to other European colonies at the time, and colonial officials like Governor Solf in Samoa traveled to neighboring colonies to compare notes. The German colonial archives are replete with systematic comparisons to the policies in other powers' colonies. This internalized politics of cross-cultural comparison (Stoler 2001) does not necessarily mean that we should avoid comparison ourselves, although we have to be careful to provide lessons *about* empire rather than lessons *for* empire (Steinmetz 2004b, 2005c).

27. Bloch 1953, p. 42 (my emphasis). See Sewell 1967 for a methodological discussion of Bloch. As Sewell (1985, 1996) notes, Skocpol's (1979) celebrated account of the French, Russian, and Chinese revolutions actually relies on the fact that these three "events" were intrinsically related to one another, even if she describes her own method as pseudostatistical.

ship between the realities in question guarantees that we are not comparing apples and oranges.[28] This is crucial since the mechanisms that produce
social events (as opposed to the causal mechanisms studied by the natural
sciences) vary across space and over time, meaning that there can never be
a general law or theory of human practice. Explicitly thematizing the connections among related realities is also crucial because some of the most
powerful mechanisms shaping human practice, such as memory, mimicry,
learning, disavowal, projection and the return of the repressed, are predicated on the connectedness of, and comparison among, events rather than
their independence. This book compares empirical events (native policies)
that are broadly similar to one another as types and also compares the effects of particular causal structures or "mechanisms" such as precolonial
discourse and symbolic competition.

This book is also a political intervention of sorts, even if the events described here are a century old. Colonial history continues to resurface in
the former metropoles and in the postcolonies, from the German apology
for the 1904 Namibian genocide in 2004 to the suburban riots in France in
2005.[29] And more than ever before, people living in the United States or in
countries whose destiny is deeply entangled with the United States need to
understand the forces that shaped modern colonialism and the differences
and similarities between colonialism and other forms of imperial domination.[30] I began writing this book during the years of the Clinton administration and after the release of Namibia from South African domination
and rule. Postcolonialism at that time seemed more like a chronological
concept rather than a term for the persistence of the colonial past in an
uneasy present. The only major episodes of decolonization during the 1990s
involved Hong Kong and South Africa. Colonialism had become an almost
antiquarian concept, quaintly redolent of a Victorian age and serving at best
as a warning for future generations. During the 1990s, the few remaining
imperialists sounded like nostalgic curmudgeons and cold war relics. Defending colonialism seemed as outlandish as advocating cancer or nuclear
war. A widely discussed book at the end of this decade redefined "empire"

28. Steinmetz 2004a.

29. On the former see Steinmetz 2005b.

30. For the distinction between colonial and imperialist styles of foreign intervention, see
Osterhammel 1995; Steinmetz 2003a, 2005e. A related distinction is made by Gallagher and
Robinson (1953) and more implicitly by world-systems theorists (e.g., Bergesen and Schoen-
berg 1980), but it has been rejected by Marxist theories of imperialism. Mann (2003) refers to
"territorial imperialism" rather than colonialism. As Grosse (2006) demonstrates, Hannah
Arendt's work on imperialism ([1950] 1958) uses a shifting and unstable terminology.

as no longer having anything to do with nation-states. According to Michael Hardt and Antonio Negri, the world had become a centerless network of overlapping partial sovereignties and nodes of power.[31] It was impossible to anticipate that by the time I completed this book the dominant policy debate in the United States would pit champions of longer-term colonial-style occupations of foreign countries against advocates of something closer to the nineteenth-century "imperialism of free trade" in which a hegemon bolsters friendly regimes without actually governing them directly. In the foreign policy world of George W. Bush, empire changed from a dirty word into a dominant paradigm.[32] As in the colonial stories I tell here, U.S. military and civilian policymakers went into Iraq in 2003 primed with "ethnographic representations" of their new subjects. For example, Captain Josh Rushing, the central command press officer representing the U.S. Marines to the outside world on the war in Iraq in 2003 and 2004, claimed to have based his interventions on books by Bernard Lewis (including *What Went Wrong? Western Impact and Middle Eastern Response*) and on a tract entitled *Iraq for Dummies*.[33] A much more influential student of Lewis was Vice President Dick Cheney, who "immersed himself in a study of Islam and the Middle East" after September 11, 2001, "meeting with scholars such as Bernard Lewis and Fouad Ajami."[34] Similarly, we could think of the precolonial ethnographic texts on China and Southwest Africa that German officials read before arriving in those colonies as bearing titles like *What Went Wrong? Western Impact and Chinese Response* or, perhaps, *Namibia for Dummies*.

31. Hardt and Negri 2000.

32. See C. Johnson 2004 for an overview. For one blunt use of the term see the interview with a senior adviser to President Bush the Younger who says, "We're an empire now, and when we act, we create our own reality. And while you're studying that reality—judiciously, as you will—we'll act again, creating other new realities, which you can study too, and that's how things will sort out. We're history's actors . . . and you, all of you, will be left to just study what we do" (Suskind 2004).

33. *Fresh Air* from WHYY, National Public Radio, October 29, 2004. I have found no record of a publication entitled *Iraq for Dummies*. Captain Rushing may have read *The Middle East for Dummies*, by Craig Davis (Hoboken, N.J.: Wiley Publishing, 2003), or Joseph Tragert's *The Complete Idiot's Guide to Understanding Iraq* (Indianapolis: Alpha Books, 2003); he may also have been pulling the interviewer's leg.

34. Daalder and Lindsay 2003, p. 130. See also John Diamond, Judy Keen, Dave Moniz, Susan Page, and Barbara Slavin, "Iraq Course Set from Tight White House Circle," *USA Today*, September 11, 2002; and Juan Cole, "All the Vice President's Men: The Ideologues in Cheney's Inner Circle Drummed Up a War: Now Their Zealotry Is Blowing Up in Their Faces," *Salon.com*, October 28, 2005.

ACKNOWLEDGMENTS

This book could never have been written without the inspiration and support of a number of friends and colleagues. I received initial encouragement more than a decade ago at Chicago from David Laitin, John Comaroff, Prasenjit Duara, Martin Riesebrot, and William Julius Wilson. Moishe Postone and Bill Sewell have been close friends and theoretical interlocutors for years. The other members of the Chicago social theory group, including Craig Calhoun, Jean Comaroff, Nancy Fraser, Ben Lee, Ed LiPuma, Tom McCarthy, Leslie Salzinger, Lisa Wedeen, and Eli Zaretsky, all contributed in various ways to this project. Three of my students, all of whom have since gone on to careers of their own, completed dissertations on colonial and imperial topics during that period: Suk-Jung Han, Julian Go, and Sean Hsiang-lin Lei. And I am eternally grateful to Jeremy Straughn and Neil Brenner, who plowed through colonial documents for me as research assistants while working on their dissertations.

At Michigan I have had the great fortune to move into an interdisciplinary space between history and sociology, a space prepared almost four decades ago by Charles Tilly and further developed by Bill Sewell during his time at Michigan. As chair of sociology Howard Kimeldorf has presided over the emergence of Michigan as the leading center in the United States for historical sociology. I have also greatly appreciated the efforts of Michigan's Dean of Letters, Sciences, and Arts, Terry McDonald, to protect and nurture historical sociology and the interpretive social sciences against powerful countertendencies. I have benefited from interactions with my colleagues in the sociology, history, anthropology, German, and comparative literature departments at Michigan and in the Comparative Studies in Society and History editorial committee. As a member of the "Eley-Blackbourn School" of German history I have had the great pleasure of having Geoff Eley as my colleague. I would also like to single out several other people associated with Michigan: Peggy Somers, for her constant intellectual provocations; Webb Keane, with whom I have carried on an extremely stimulating exchange; Lydia Liu, whose interests overlapped so strongly with my own, and who helped me find my way into the Chinese studies field; John Lie, who was an invaluable interlocutor during his short stay here. Ann Stoler and Larry Hirschfeld provided intellectual and culinary nourishment. Others at Michigan who have contributed in one way or another to this project include Vanessa Agnew, David William Cohen, Fred Cooper, Mamadou Diouf, Nancy Hunt, Kader Konuk, Tom Trautmann, Johannes von Moltke, and Ernie Young. A number of my students, especially those working on colonialism and imperial topics—Ou-Byung Chae, Andy Clarno, Claire Decoteau, Daniel Goh, Chandan Gowda, Kim Greenwell, Asli Gur, Seth Quartey, Besnik Pula, and Sadia Saeed—have contributed in more ways that they can imagine. And my special gratitude goes out to Julia Adams, whose own quirky and brilliant work, and constant enthusiasm, has been an inspiration for me.

Other debts are more difficult to categorize. My Ph.D. adviser Erik Olin Wright has provided me with moral and intellectual support over the years. My former adviser Ron Aminzade shifted his own research focus from France to Tanzania around the same time I was starting work on colonialism, encouraging me to move ahead. Ann Orloff has been a wonderful friend, and she invited me to present my work at her department on several occasions. I received invaluable comments from Ralph Austen, Jean-François Bayart, Richard Bernstein, Michael Burawoy, Christophe Charle, Yves Dezalay, Paul Gilroy, Francine Muel-Dreyfus, Emmanuelle Saada, Ann Stoler, Tom Trautmann, Loïc Wacquant, and Jürgen Zimmerer. Romain Bertrand and Gisèle Sapiro translated my work into French and discussed it with me at length. Michael Chanan convinced me to shift my attentions away from this book project for several years to collaborate with him on a documentary film, for which I am grateful. Beth Povinelli and Jeff Paige read the entire manuscript and gave me stimulating comments. I am not sure who the other anonymous reviewers of the book manuscript were, but I would like to thank all of them for taking time out of their busy schedules.

Many others have reacted to specific parts of the manuscript in lectures and seminars. Although I cannot thank them individually, that does not mean that I did not heed their advice. I presented parts of this book at the Centre de Sociologie Européenne and the Centre d'Études et de Recherches Internationales (CERI) in Paris, the University of Namibia in Windhoek, Qingdao Oceanic University, the University of the West of England in

Bristol, Ghent University (Belgium), the Center for German and European Studies at the University of Minnesota, and the Graduate Faculty of the New School for Social Research. I also presented parts of this work to the sociology departments at the universities of California–Berkeley and Los Angeles, Pennsylvania, Western Ontario, Texas, Chicago, and Michigan, and at Northwestern, Yale, and Lancaster University (U.K.).

I received indispensable aid for the Namibian part of my research from Caspar W. Erichsen, Robert Gordon, Dr. Volker Harms, Patricia Hayes, Malvern van Wyk Smith, Ulrich van der Heyden, and Joachim Zeller. Reinhart Kössler showed me around Okahandja and Katatura and translated an article of mine into German. Peter Hempenstall and Damon Salesa gave me advice on the Samoan part of the research.

Three people who have helped me enormously with the Chinese part of my research are Thomas Lahusen, Michael Dutton, and especially Lydia Liu. For the Qingdao section of the book I am grateful to my Chinese language tutors, especially Min Zhou, a recent Michigan Ph.D. in German. During my first visit to Beijing, Ethan Michaelson was kind enough to serve as guide and translator. My Chinese translations were carried out or checked by Xiaoxi Tong and Lijun Chen (both of them former University of Chicago sociology graduate students), Arbin Liu of Qingdao Oceanic University, and Yufen Chang of the University of Michigan. Professor Aili Mu of Iowa State University translated some of my research into Chinese. During the summer of 2005 I enjoyed the hospitality of Prof. Wang Zhongchen of Tsinghua University in Beijing, Prof. Zhu Ziqiang, director of the Humanities Institute at Qingdao Oceanic University, and Qingdao professors, including Prof. Sun Lixin of the German department. Ms. Zhu Jianjun was generous enough to spend several days helping me locate sites and documents in Qingdao. Ms. Fuxiang Gu of Qingdao was kind enough to take a picture of the dragon on the roof of the Qingdao Governor's mansion for me.

Without the expert advice of archivists and librarians this book could never have been completed. I would like to thank the dedicated staff of the German Federal Archives in Berlin, Freiburg, and Koblenz; the archives of the Foreign Office (Berlin); the Namibian national archives (especially Dr. Werner Hillebrecht); the municipal archives of the city of Qingdao; Beijing Library (Beijing Tushuguan); the Staatsbibliothek in Berlin; the Municipal and University library of Frankfurt (especially Dr. Irmtraud D. Wolcke-Renk of the Africa and Asia Department); Harvard University's Yenching Library; and the James Ford Bell Library at the University of Minnesota. Mr. Wolfgang Apelt at the Archiv- und Museumsstiftung Wuppertal has been extraordinarily generous. I received assistance from Mr. Maarten P.

Bakker, *assistent-conservator* at Museum Huis Doorn in the Netherlands, and Dr. Dag Henrichsen of the Basler Afrika Bibliographien. The University of Michigan librarians have been unstintingly generous, particularly the staff of the Interlibrary Loan and Special Collections departments and the William L. Clements Library, and bibliographer Beau Case.

Financial support for this project came from the John Simon Guggenheim Foundation; the German Academic Exchange Service; the American Sociological Association/NSF Fund for the Advancement of the Discipline; the University of Chicago Social Sciences Division; and the Institute for the Humanities, Chinese Studies Center, Sociology Department, and Office of the Vice President for Research at the University of Michigan.

Doug Mitchell at the University of Chicago Press encouraged this project from the start, Timothy McGovern helped shepherd it through, and Erik Carlson did an extraordinary job editing it. Rob Haug made the maps. Rick Smoke solved numerous computer emergencies. Sun-Young Lee helped enormously with the final editing and read most of the book out loud to me. Kim Greenwell also helped with the reading, and Claire Decoteau sprang into action in the midst of all of her other obligations and did a tremendous job creating the index.

I owe most pleasurable debt of all to Julia Hell. Over the course of writing this book she has taught me about Lacan, visual theory, and ruins; I have responded with tales of Lothar von Trotha and Ku Hung-Ming. The mix of humanities and social science presented here is the result of this microscopic transdisciplinary relationship.

ABBREVIATIONS

Ausw. Amt: Auswärtiges Amt (Foreign Office)
BA-Berlin: Bundesarchiv Berlin (German Federal Archives, Berlin-Lichterfelde)
BA-Koblenz: Bundesarchiv Koblenz (German Federal Archives, Koblenz)
BA-MA-Freiburg: Bundesarchiv-Militärarchiv Freiburg (German Federal Archives–Military Archives, Freiburg im Breisgau)
DBC: Deutsche Botschaft China (German Embassy in China)
DEIC: Dutch East Indies Company
DHPG: Deutsche Handels- und Plantagen-Gesellschaft der Südsee-Inseln zu Hamburg, or German Trade and Plantation Society for the South Sea Islands in Hamburg
DSWA: Deutsch Südwest Afrika (German Southwest Africa)
LMS: London Missionary Society
NAN: National Archives of Namibia (Windhoek, Namibia)
NZNA AGCA: New Zealand National Archives, Archives of the German Colonial Administration
PA-AA: Politisches Archiv des Auswärtigen Amts (Political Archives of the German Foreign Office)
r: recto
RKA: Reichskolonialamt (Imperial Colonial Office)
RMA: Reichsmarineamt (Imperial Navy Office)
RMG: Rheinische Missionsgesellschaft (Rhenish Missionary Society)
RT: Reichstag
SOS: Seminar für Orientalische Sprachen (Seminar for Oriental Languages)
SWA: South West Africa
SWAC: South West Africa Company
v: verso
VEM: Vereinigte Evangelische Mission (United Evangelical Mission, Wuppertal)

MAP 1
Southwest Africa

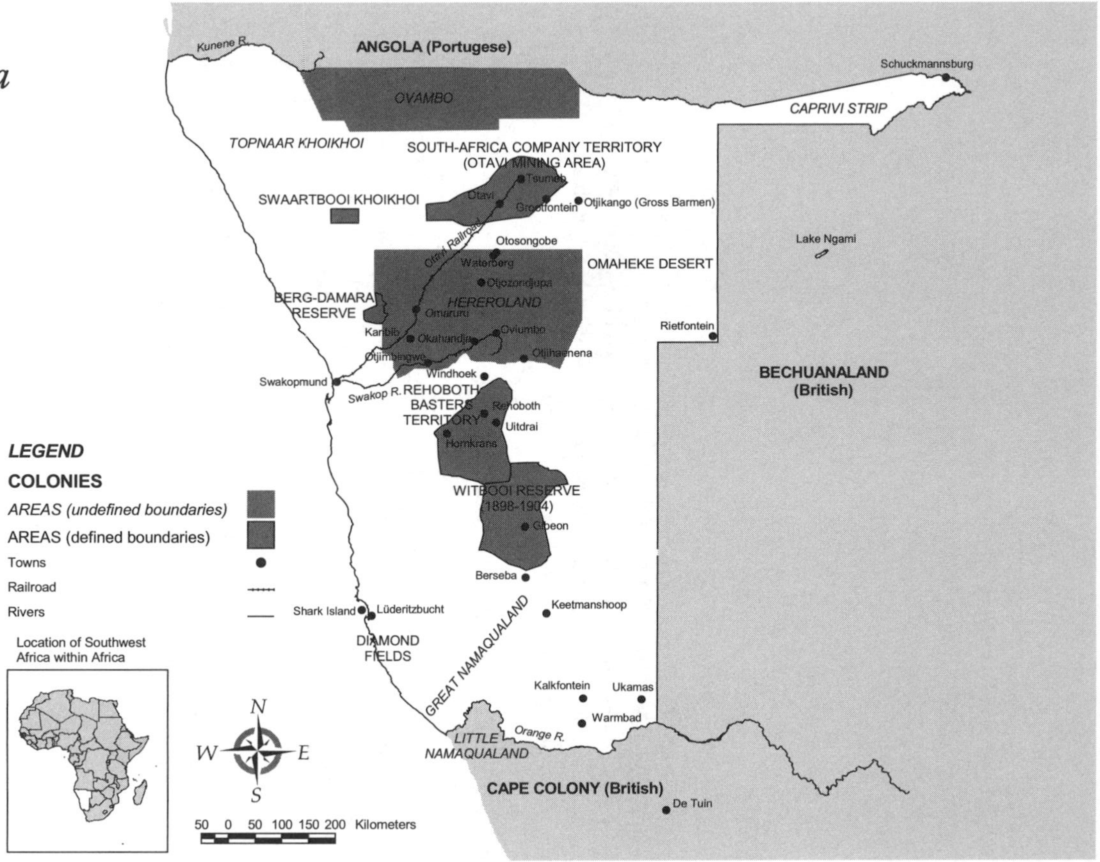

LEGEND

COLONIES

AREAS (undefined boundaries)

AREAS (defined boundaries)

● Towns

----- Railroad

—— Rivers

Location of Southwest
Africa within Africa

50 0 50 100 150 200 Kilometers

N W E S

ANGOLA (Portugese)

OVAMBO

TOPNAAR KHOIKHOI

SWAARTBOOI KHOIKHOI

Kunene R.

SOUTH-AFRICA COMPANY TERRITORY
(OTAVI MINING AREA)

CAPRIVI STRIP

Schuckmansburg

Lake Ngami

BECHUANALAND
(British)

OMAHEKE DESERT

Rietfontein

Otjikango (Gross Barmen)
Barmfontein
Otavi
Tsumeb
Waterberg
Otosongobe
Otjozordjupa
Onsaruru
Okatjandja
HEREROLAND
Otjimbingwe
Okahandja
Windhoek
Karibib
BERG-DAMARA
RESERVE
Omburo
Otjihaenena

REHOBOTH
BASTERS
TERRITORY
Rehoboth
Uitdrai
Hornkrans

Swakop R.

Swakopmund

Shark Island
Lüderitzbucht

WITBOOI RESERVE
(1898-1904)
Gibeon

Berseba

Keetmanshoop

DIAMOND
FIELDS

GREAT NAMAQUALAND

LITTLE
NAMAQUALAND

Orange R.

Kalkfontein
Ukamas
Warmbad

CAPE COLONY (British)

De Tuin

MAP 2
Oceania
(contemporary)

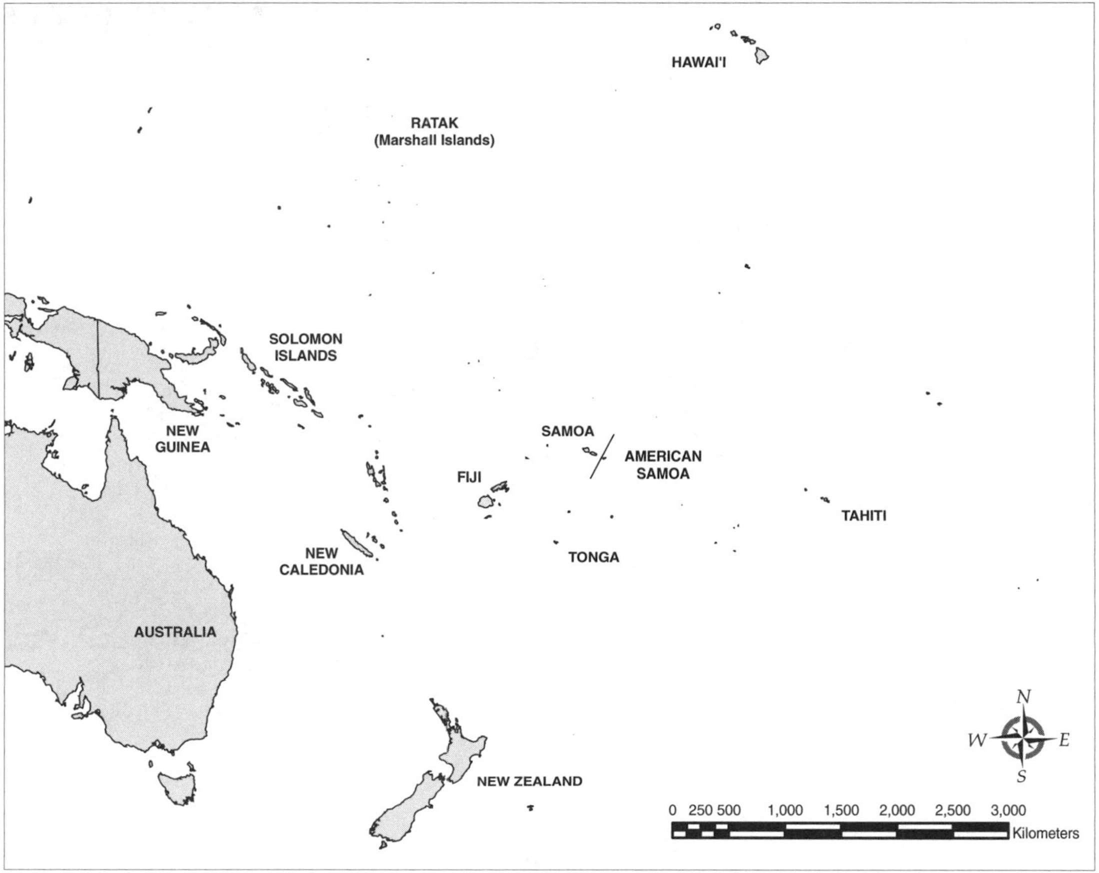

HAWAI'I

RATAK
(Marshall Islands)

SOLOMON
ISLANDS

NEW
GUINEA

NEW
CALEDONIA

FIJI

SAMOA

AMERICAN
SAMOA

TONGA

TAHITI

AUSTRALIA

NEW ZEALAND

N
W   E
S

0 250 500 1,000 1,500 2,000 2,500 3,000
Kilometers

MAP 3
Samoa

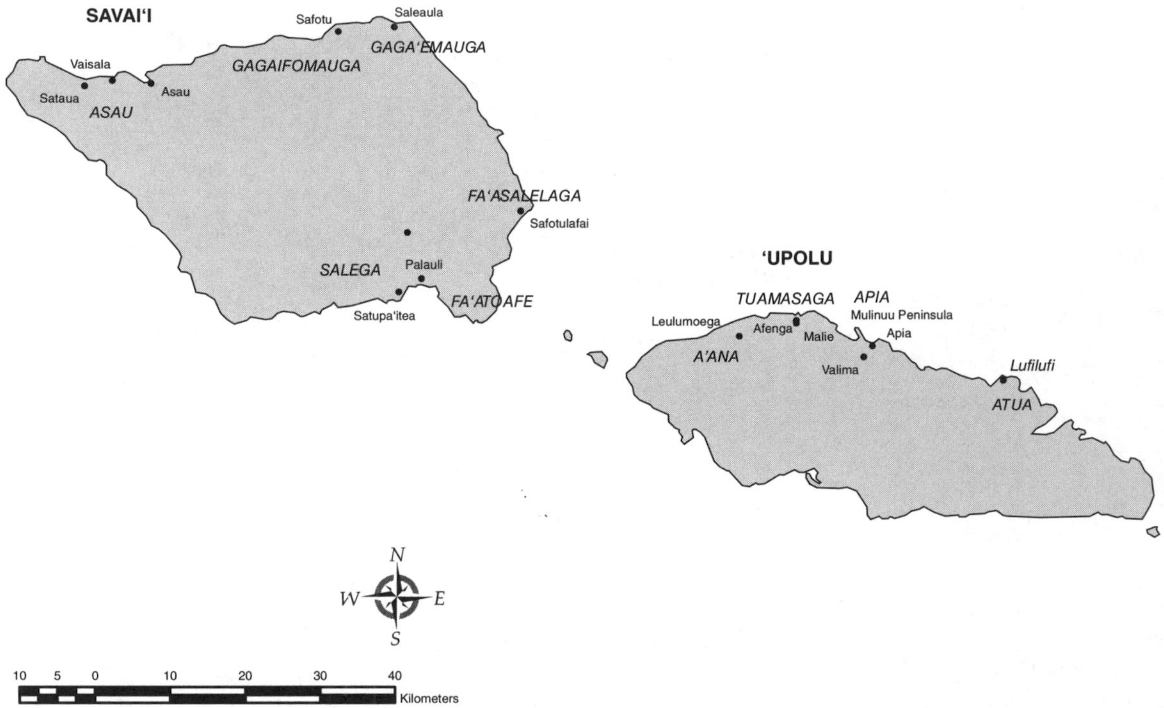

SAVAI'I

Vaisala
Sataua
ASAU
Asau
GAGAIFOMAUGA
Safotu
Saleaula
GAGA'EMAUGA
FA'ASALELAGA
Safotulafai
Palauli
SALEGA
Satupa'itea
FA'ATOAFE

'UPOLU

TUAMASAGA
A'ANA
Leulumoega
Afenga
Malie
Vaiima
APIA
Mulinu'u Peninsula
Apia
ATUA
Lufilufi

N
W E
S

10 5 0 10 20 30 40
Kilometers

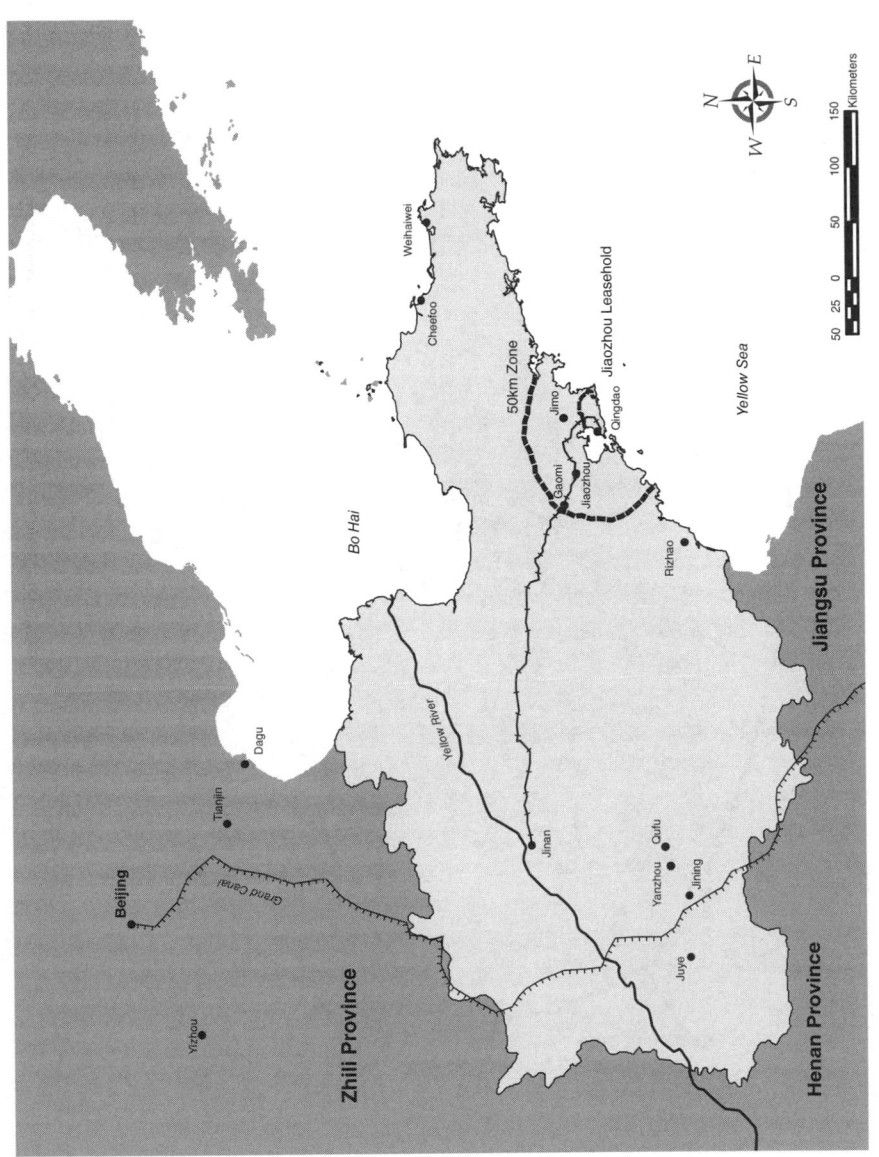

MAP 4
*Shandong
Province
(1897–1914)*

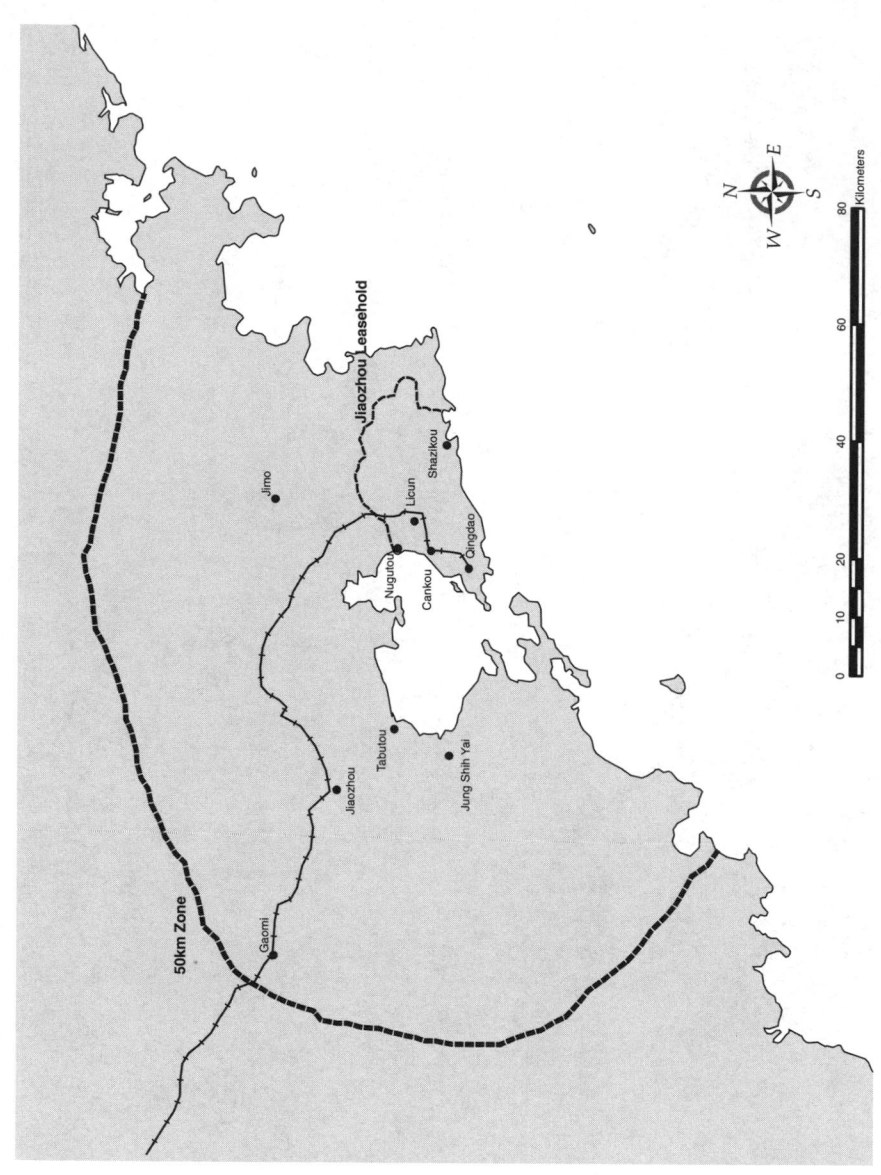

MAP 5
German colony of Kiaochow

MAP 6
Qingdao (ca. 1911)

ONE

Introduction &
Ethnography and the Colonial State

Social theorists have often treated colonialism as a monolithic object, a uniform condition. Yet even a cursory overview of the historical literature indicates that colonialism is actually an extremely capacious category, encompassing everything from pillage and massacre in the Spanish conquest of the New World to the peaceful coexistence between British rulers and Chinese subjects in late colonial Hong Kong.[1] The colonies that made up the German overseas empire, which lasted from 1884 until the end of World War I, exemplify the enormous variability even within the more delimited category of modern colonialism. This specifically modern variant of European colonialism, as opposed to the early modern (or earlier) forms, is my focus in this book. I have selected three colonies to illustrate the wide spectrum of colonial native policy, which, I will argue below, was the core activity of the modern colonial state. These colonies are German Southwest Africa, forerunner of modern-day Namibia; German Samoa, precursor of the contemporary nation-state of Samoa; and Kiaochow, a colony that consisted of the city of Qingdao and its surrounding hinterland in China's Shandong Province.[2] These three cases also represent three of the main

1. For general overviews of colonial history see Fieldhouse 1966; Reinhard 1996; and Ferro [1994] 1997; a comparative history of early modern colonialism from America to Macao by way of Goa is provided by Bitterli 1989; Albertini 1982 and Gustav Schmidt 1989 are comparative histories starting with the late-nineteenth-century scramble; Osterhammel 1995 is an excellent general overview of theoretical and conceptual issues. On late colonial Hong Kong see Chiu 1997.

2. Gründer 2004 provides the most comprehensive overview of the German colonial empire and the current state of historical research; see also Eckert 2003. Other comparative treatments of the German overseas empire are Townsend 1930; Brunschwig 1957; Gann and Duignan 1977; W. Smith 1978; and Henderson 1993. The essays in Gifford, Lewis, and

zones of intensive European colonial activity in the worldwide "scramble" for colonies that started in the 1880s—sub-Saharan Africa, Oceania, and (after 1897) the Chinese coast. Germany did not have any colonies in South Asia, Southeast Asia, or the Near East.[3]

In order to evaluate the claim that precolonial ethnographic representations shaped colonial native policy it is important to compare colonies whose inhabitants were defined in divergent ways by nineteenth-century Europeans. This criterion is already met by the single case of China, since the Chinese were discussed in increasingly Sinophobic ways in the nineteenth century but also continued to be regarded through the lenses of early modern European Sinophilia. Southwest Africa allows for internal comparisons, given the multiplicity of ethnic groups and communities. I examine the colonial treatment of three Southwest African peoples: the Khoikhoi (known as "Hottentots" in colonial jargon); the Ovaherero (or "Herero"); and the "Basters," a population descended from Boers and Khoikhoi and classified by Europeans as a "mixed race." Variability is further enhanced by the inclusion in the analysis of "Polynesians," who were perceived by many nineteenth-century Europeans as the ultimate noble savages living in an earthly paradise.

The central problem that I try to account for in this book—my "explanandum"—is colonial native policy. Four determining structures or causal mechanisms were especially important in each of these colonies: (1) precolonial ethnographic discourses or representations, (2) symbolic competition among colonial officials for recognition of their superior ethnographic acuity, (3) colonizers' cross-identification with imagos[4] of the colonized, and (4) responses by the colonized, including resistance, collaboration, and everything in between. Two other mechanisms influenced colonial native policy to varying degrees: "economic" dynamics related to capitalist profit seeking (plantation agriculture, mining, trade, and smaller-scale forms of business) and the "political" pressures generated by the international system of states.

Smith 1967 and Gifford and Louis 1971 are useful but often apologetic. The most valuable earlier overview is Hempenstall 1987, p. 94, which reads German colonialism as unsystematic, with no consistent "structures of administration" or uniform national model. This diagnosis should hold for *all* modern colonial empires, for reasons elaborated in this chapter.

3. On German imperial interventions in the Near East before 1914 see Trumpener 1968, chap. 1; and McMurray 2001.

4. *Imago,* suggesting a culturally and psychically constructed image, rather than *image,* which suggests a more direct "mirror of nature." See Laplanche and Pontalis 1973, p. 211; and Liliane Fainsilber, "Le pouvoir des 'imagos': Notes de lecture sur les premiers textes de Lacan psychanalyste," online at http://perso.wanadoo.fr/liliane.fainsilber/pages/imagos.htm.

This book does not attempt to identify any singular, general model of colonial rule. Indeed, general theory and general laws are widely recognized as implausible goals in the social sciences. Historians have always preferred complex, overdetermined, conjunctural accounts, but sociologists and some other social scientists have been reluctant to abandon the chimerical goals of parsimony and "general theory."[5] Rather than attempt to use colonial comparisons to fabricate a uniform model of the colonial state, I will seek instead to identify a limited set of generative social structures or mechanisms and to track the ways they interacted to produce ongoing policies. Even though each instance of colonial native policy was shaped by a different constellation of influences, the four primary mechanisms named above were always present and efficacious to varying degrees.

Three Colonies

The beginnings of the German overseas empire are shrouded in historical mist, even if colonial propagandists attempted to invent a coherent tradition during the 1870s in order to fortify their argument that the newly unified German nation should embark on colonial adventures. The Great Elector of the state of Brandenburg, Frederick William, had established a trading post on the Danish-owned Caribbean island of Saint Thomas in 1685, but operations ended in 1731. He had also founded a Brandenburg-African trading company, which built a slave-trading fort called Großfriedrichsburg on the West African Gold Coast in 1682. The fortress was sold to the Dutch West Indies Company in 1721.[6] The next official German colonial endeavor began in 1879, when Germany signed a "friendship treaty" with Samoa that initiated two decades of informal, quasi-colonial influence on those islands by Germany, Great Britain, and the United States. The conventional date marking the beginning of the formal German colonial empire is April 24, 1884, when Southwest Africa was declared a "protectorate." The full extent of the German colonial empire at the beginning of the twentieth century is shown in figure 1.1. At this point the empire encompassed nearly one million square miles of territory. The empire came to an end three decades later, when the German colonies fell to the invading armies of France, Britain,

5. The implausibility of general laws is due to ontological peculiarities of the social world—above all, to its *openness*, in the sense of containing a multiplicity of irreducible causal mechanisms (Bhaskar 1986). See also the essays in Steinmetz 2005f.

6. Van der Heyden 2001; Schück 1889; Grosser Generalstab für Kriegsgeschichte 1912; Durchhardt 1986. We can disregard the Prussian territorial gains in the eighteenth-century partition of Poland, which were primarily of a noncolonial character, at least according to the definitions proposed below.

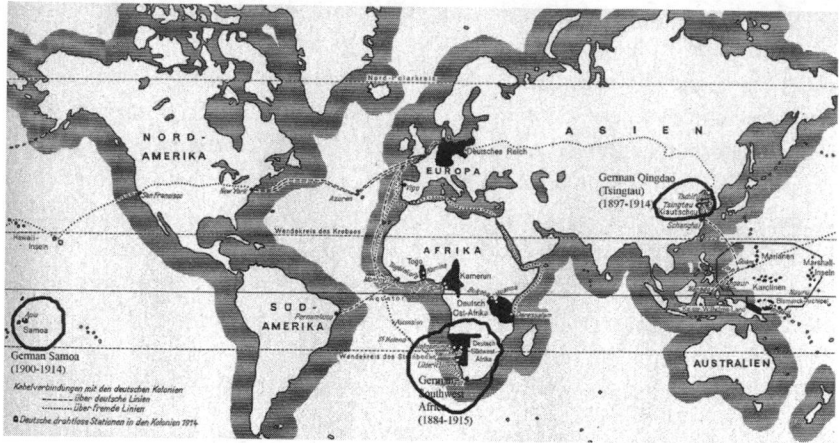

FIGURE I.I   The German colonial empire in 1914, with circles showing locations of
Samoa, Southwest Africa, and Kiaochow and black patches showing all colonies.
From *Deutsche Kolonien* (Dresden: Cigaretten-Bilderdienst Dresden, 1936).

Japan, Belgium, South Africa, and New Zealand. The last German colony
to capitulate was East Africa, where a mixed African and German force led
by Paul von Lettow-Vorbeck surrendered to Allied forces on November 25,
1918, more than two weeks after the armistice in Europe.[7] Although the fate
of the empire was still uncertain through 1918 and it remained possible that
Germany would regain at least partial possession of some of its colonies, the
Versailles Treaty of 1919 deprived Germany "of all her rights and titles over
her overseas possessions." The colonies were distributed to their new owners under article 22 of the League of Nations Covenant, which established
the mandates system.[8]

Despite the relatively short life span of this colonial empire, there was a
longer history of German *protocolonial* machinations in each of the regions
examined in this book. German missionaries entered Southwest Africa in
the first half of the nineteenth century and paved the way for the region's
annexation in the 1880s. German merchants and political envoys dominated

7. Iliffe 1979, p. 245. On the 1914–18 military campaign in East Africa see Hordern and
Stacke 1941; and Louis 1963, chap. 19.

8. The German colonial successors were Belgium in Ruanda-Urundi, Japan in Qingdao
(until 1922) and on the islands north of the equator in the western Pacific, and Britain in East
Africa/Tanganyika. Togo and Cameroon were divided between France and Britain, and con-
trol over of the other mandate colonies was assumed by Britain's southern dominions: South
Africa in Namibia, Australia in New Guinea and Nauru, and New Zealand in Western Samoa.
See chap. 8 for a discussion of the mandate system.

precolonial Samoa starting in the 1860s. German Catholic missionaries were active in Shandong Province beginning in 1880.

It was relevant for the colonized populations that Germany was the *first* formal colonial ruler in their territories, though not because German colonialism took the same form in each colony. The colonizers who succeeded the Germans after 1918 in Namibia, Ruanda-Urundi, Samoa, and Tanzania preserved many of the basic structures of colonial administration and native policy that had been introduced by their predecessors.[9] In older historiography colonialism was usually described as taking nationally specific forms: the British practiced "indirect rule," the French preferred "direct rule" and later "associationism," the Americans engaged in "democratic tutelage," and the Germans pursued a colonial style that was described variously as "scientific," "economic," "emigrationist," or exceptionally brutal.[10] The sheer variability among the colonies of the German empire should immediately lay to rest any hypothesis of a national colonial style, even if there were nationally specific processes that combined with more general, pan-European ones and with local forces to give each colony its specific characteristics. Any putative "German effects" played themselves out differently in each site. Specifically, configurations of elite class conflict based in Germany were transferred to the colonies, where they were transformed according to the logics of the colonial field of power.

The German overseas empire has sometimes been dismissed as being unworthy of serious historical attention. This empire was unprofitable, except for a few particular investors. The German colonies had smaller military forces than other colonies in Africa and attracted a relatively small number of settlers, with the exception of Southwest Africa. The German empire emerged later than the British, French, Dutch, Spanish, and Portuguese empires and was short lived; and its officials lacked the competence that supposedly came with centuries of colonial experience. This view ignores the global political situation in the decades before World War I, which was one in which disputes over faraway places like Samoa or Morocco could escalate into conflicts among the great powers, transform alliances, and shift the international bal-

---

9. One reason for continuity revolved around the fact that the colonies had been "mandated" rather than conquered or annexed. British legal advisers determined that German law should remain in force in formerly German East Africa "until altered by the Mandatory power" (Callahan 1999, p. 41). The entire German administrative structure was preserved until 1925 (Iliffe 1979, p. 318). The New Zealanders broke with the German model in Samoa in certain respects (Field 1991) but also retained some of the key institutions of native policy, such as the Land and Titles Commission.

10. See Knoll 1978, p. 4; W. Smith 1978; and Union of South Africa 1918.

ance of power.[11] This view also ignores the fact that Bismarck triggered the first phase of the scramble for Africa among the European powers with the Berlin West Africa Conference and that Germany initiated the scramble for Chinese coastal colonies in 1897 by seizing Qingdao.[12] Another reason to reexamine this history is related to arguments that trace the Holocaust and German techniques of government in occupied Poland during World War II to pre-1918 colonialism.[13] But these justifications for focusing on German colonialism are still Eurocentric. For the colonized, the salient facts were subjugation, exploitation, and loss of sovereignty, not the merits or demerits of Germans relative to other imperialists. It matters little to a mugging victim whether his assailant has a bad haircut or speaks a provincial dialect. The populations that were harrowed by German colonizers cannot be assuaged by the fact that their conquerors were inexperienced latecomers or early leavers or that Europeans found their lands less lucrative or beguiling than, say, Sri Lanka, Tahiti, Brazil, or New England. Contemporary Namibians and independent Samoans are acutely aware of the fact that it was Germany and not some other power that first deprived them of their liberty. According to Marshall Sahlins, the "moment of domination" that is "most marked in historical consciousness" in the global peripheries is the "advent of the colonial state."[14] But what exactly did this momentous transition entail?

COLONIAL GROTESQUE:
GERMAN RULE IN SOUTHWEST AFRICA

The boundaries of Southwest Africa during the German era were almost identical to those of contemporary Namibia (map 1).[15] The Namibian population encompassed numerous Khoikhoi communities that were differentiated

11. On the international crisis around Samoa in 1898–99 see P. Kennedy 1974; on the 1911 Agadir crisis see most recently Meyer and von Kiderlen-Wächter 1996.

12. Förster, Mommsen, and Robinson 1988.

13. See Zimmerer 2003. For a similar argument focused on French colonial atrocities in Algeria and their relationship to "total war" and French "state anti-Semitism" culminating in the Vichy government's law on the "statut des Juifs," see Le Cour Grandmaison 2005, p. 337–38.

14. Sahlins 1993, p. 16. Some historians have insisted that British colonial rule in India entailed a sharp and discontinuous break, even if South Asians were not supine victims of exterior powers and even if some Indians profited from the Raj; see Chatterjee 1993, pp. 27–32.

15. Southwest Africa included the areas known to nineteenth-century Europeans as Damaraland (later "Hereroland") in the center, the southern regions inhabited mainly by Nama and Orlams, part of Ovamboland along the northern border, and the arid Kalahari in the east. An exchange of territories with Britain in 1890 added the Caprivi Strip in the northeast. When referring to the colonial state and its territory I will use the term "Southwest Africa." "Namibia" indexes the contemporary postcolonial nation-state as well as the historical region.

from one another mainly by the identity of their leaders. The nineteenth-century Namibian Khoikhoi were also subdivided into Nama (Namaqua) communities that had long been present in the region and various Orlam (or Oorlam) communities that had migrated overland from the Cape Colony into the areas called Greater Namaqualand, north of the Orange River.[16] Orlam typically spoke a mixture of Cape Dutch and Khoisan languages, were partly integrated into European markets, and relied on commodities like guns and textile clothing. Their mode of life (or "mode of production") was pastoralism; some engaged in livestock rustling from other Namibian communities and from white settlers. In the next two chapters I focus on one particular Orlam "commando group" that was politically dominant over other Namibian Khoikhoi during the first two decades of German colonial rule: the Witbooi, or /Khobesin people. These chapters also analyze ethnographic representations and native policies concerning two other Namibian nations, the Rehoboth Basters and the Ovaherero. The region designated "Hereroland" on map 1 was the nineteenth-century center of Ovaherero habitation, but Ovaherero extended northward all the way into Portuguese Angola. Some escaped into British Bechuanaland during the 1904 war, establishing Ovaherero communities there as well.[17] The Rehobothers were mixed descendants of Khoikhoi and European (mainly Dutch) settlers, and in the late nineteenth century they were the largest of several "Baster" communities north of the Orange River. Another ethnic group was the Berg Damara, who were also called "Hill Damara" or "Bergdama" at the time, and nowadays simply "Damara." They resembled the Ovaherero physically and were often enserfed by them during the nineteenth century but spoke a Khoisan language rather than Otjiherero or another Bantu tongue. Other ethnic groups included the Ovambo (Ambo) in the northern regions along the Angolan border, the Bushmen, and various communities in the northeastern Caprivi Strip. The Germans devised specific policies for most of these groups, but their administrative and military energies were focused on the Ovaherero, Witbooi, Rehobothers, and other Orlam and Nama populations.[18]

16. The five main Orlam groups in nineteenth-century Namibia were the Afrikaners, Witbooi, and the Bethany, Khauas, and Berseba peoples; see Dedering 1993a, p. 55 n. 4.

17. The eastern Ovambanderu spoke a different dialect of Otjiherero and also differed from other Ovaherero in terms their kinship system and clothing (Henrichsen 1997, p. 15). They are still considered a branch of the Ovaherero nation (Sundermeier, Tjituka, and Lau 1985). On the post-1905 Ovaherero community in Botswana see Durham 1993; 1995, p. 184; on the Angolan Ovaherero, see Estermann 1981.

18. The Caprivi Strip remained a distant outpost and was never effectively brought under the colonial state's control before 1914 (Fisch 1999). The Ovambo were employed in the

The Rhenish Mission Society (Rheinische Missionsgesellschaft, abbreviated RMG) was founded in 1828 and based in Barmen, Germany, modeling itself on the London Missionary Society (LMS).[19] The first missionaries sent abroad by the RMG worked in the Cape Colony. During the 1840s the RMG began expanding northward into the regions that were incorporated four decades later into the German colony. This close correspondence between the missionaries' field of operations and the boundaries of the Southwest African colony was no mere coincidence. The mission played a central role in the 1863 "war of liberation" in which Ovaherero freed themselves from the Afrikaners, or //Aixa//ain, who at the time were the most powerful Orlam group in central Namibia. The immediate result of this uprising was seven years of continuous warfare between the two groups, until the missionaries brokered a peace treaty in 1870. In 1864 the RMG created a "mission colony" of white artisans and shopkeepers at Otjimbingwe, in the center of Ovaherero territory, adumbrating the formal colonial process that started two decades later. In 1869 the RMG founded a "mission trading company" in Namibia, further blurring the boundaries between missionaries and settlers. Hugo Hahn, founder and head of the "Herero mission," became a practicing merchant at this time.[20] In 1879 the director of the RMG in Germany, Friedrich Fabri, published his manifesto for the nascent colonial movement, *Does Germany Need Colonies?* His answer was a resounding yes: Germany "must no longer hesitate to *resume* its colonising vocation."[21] When fighting broke out again between Ovaherero and Orlams in 1880 the RMG called on the German government to extend protection to its missionaries.

Three years later a representative of a Bremen trading firm owned by Franz Adolf Eduard Lüderitz met with tribal leaders and began collecting signatures on treaties that granted the German company a monopoly on trade along the coast and the right to create "factories, farms, or plantations" in exchange for an annual tribute and the German government's promise of protection.[22] In April 1884 Bismarck agreed to extend German "protection"

---

colonial copper mines and after 1908 in the diamonds mines. This led to increasing scrutiny of Ovamboland by the colonial state and the beginnings of native policy there (Eirola 1992).

19. See Strassberger 1969; and Rohden 1888.

20. Lau 1987b, p. 93; Esterhuyse 1968, pp. 12–13; Vedder [1938] 1966, pp. 400–401. The formation of a trading company was a technique used by other German mission societies in Africa; see, for example, Quartey 2004 on the Basel Missionary Society's trading company on the Gold Coast during the nineteenth century.

21. Fabri [1879] 1998, p. 181 (my emphasis). Fabri went on to become the leader of the German colonial movement (Bade 1975).

22. Külz 1909, p. 8.

to the territories claimed by Lüderitz. The colony was initially called Angra Pequeña after the bay and town of the same name (later renamed Lüderitz-bucht, or Lüderitz Bay).[23] These "protection treaties" stipulated that the Namibians would not sign treaties with any other foreign government or alienate land to "a different nation or members thereof" without the German emperor's consent.[24] Lüderitz eventually gained tenuous title to the entire coastal area stretching from the Orange River to the Kunene River and reaching inland twenty geographic miles. Just one year later, however, a bankrupt Lüderitz sold his entire interest to a chartered company, the German Colonial Society for South West Africa, which had been created by leading financial interests at Bismarck's behest. In May 1885 the first German government official, "Imperial Commissary" Heinrich Göring, or Goering (father of Nazi Reichsmarschall Hermann Goering), accompanied by two assistants, was dispatched to oversee the new protectorate. Goering's official charge was to administer justice, issue proclamations, train African constables, and conclude protection treaties with the remaining Namibian communities. During the next five years German sovereignty existed mainly on paper. Only after 1890 did the Germans begin extending effective control over the colony's inhabitants.

The German massacre of the Ovaherero in 1904 is widely recognized as the first genocide of the twentieth century.[25] Ovaherero grievances against their colonial overlords had increased steadily in the decade leading up to the 1904 war due to ongoing expropriation of land and livestock, railway construction through tribal lands, mounting indebtedness to German traders, and an accumulation of incidents of violence and humiliation at the hands of German settlers and the *Schutztruppe* (colonial army).[26] Most of the soldiers and officers in the *Schutztruppe* and most German settlers were opposed to the government's plan to set aside land for Ovaherero reservations (*Reservate*)—fixed territories restricted to members of a particular "tribe."[27] Rumors of an imminent Ovaherero uprising began circulating at the end of 1903. The Ovaherero-German war effectively started when German troops opened fire on Ovaherero at Okahandja on January 12, 1904,

23. Külz 1909, p. 11; Rohlfs 1884.

24. W. Werner 1993, p. 137.

25. See Samuel Totten and William S. Parsons, introduction to Totten, Parsons, and Charny 1995, p. xv; and Bridgman and Worley 1995.

26. Bley [1971] 1996; Drechsler [1966] 1980; Krüger 1999.

27. "Foreigners," a category that included other indigenous Southwest Africans, were generally prohibited from settling within reservations, with the exception of missionaries (Sudholt 1975, p. 151).

although missionaries and military writers contributed afterward to the myth of a long-planned revolt.[28] The ensuing war was devastating for the Ovaherero in physical and cultural terms. Estimates of Ovaherero deaths in the actual fighting and its aftermath in an archipelago of "concentration camps" (*Konzentrationslager*) run as high as 80 percent of the population, although there are no exact figures. Following their decisive military defeat at the battle of Hamakari (Waterberg) on August 11, 1904, most of the surviving Ovaherero fled with their livestock into the Omaheke (Kalahari) Desert, where countless numbers died of thirst.[29] General Lothar von Trotha, the commander of the German military campaign, issued a "proclamation" to the Ovaherero on October 2, 1904—his infamous "annihilation order"—which declared that every Ovaherero man, woman, and child had to leave the colony or face death. Ovaherero men were executed by public lynching, sometimes stripped of their clothing, in a manner reminiscent of the American South during the same period (fig. 3.12). Ovaherero survivors who remained in the colony or returned after the extermination order was lifted in December 1904 became prisoners in the concentration camps and were used as forced laborers until the end of 1907 (figs. 3.8–3.11). The most devastating blow, for a pastoralist people whose community and spiritual life revolved around their cattle, was the ban on ownership of land and livestock. In the decade after the 1904 genocide the government focused on transforming the Ovaherero into an abject proletariat. Individuals and small groups of Ovaherero were attached as workers to German employers. By 1913, 90 percent of adult males living in the so-called Police Zone—the majority of whom were Ovaherero—were engaged in wage employment.[30] Various writers have used Southwest Africa as an illustration of Hannah Arendt's thesis concerning the colonial roots of European totalitarianism and Nazism. This argument is implicit in Thomas Pynchon's novels *V* and *Gravity's Rainbow*.[31]

28. See Gewald 1999, p. 154. Settlers also opened fire on Ovaherero, ignoring protestations of their loyalty, in Otjimbingwe. The term "Ovaherero-German war" is preferred to names like "Herero uprising" or "Herero revolt" by historians who see it as a defensive war against German aggression.

29. Pool 1991, pp. 251–81; Steinmetz 2005b.

30. W. Werner 1993, p. 140. The Police Zone, officially designated in 1907, encompassed "those areas which fall within the sphere of influence of the railway line or main roads" (W. Werner 1993, p. 139). It included most of the colony with the exception of "the northern regions of Kaoko, Ovambo, Kavango, and Caprivi" (Prein 1994, p. 103).

31. Bley [1971] 1996; Olusoga 2004. Of course, Arendt's argument in *The Origins of Totalitarianism* deals with South Africa, not with German Southwest Africa. More important,

The Witbooi people, whose leader Hendrik Witbooi (!Nanseb Gabemab) rallied many of the colony's Khoikhoi against their Teutonic oppressors in mid-1904, were also decimated by the colonizers' violence. Witbooi soldiers had been been integrated into the *Schutztruppe* after their defeat in 1894 at the hands of colonial governor Theodor Leutwein. In the decade that followed the Witbooi were described by German officials and writers as noble savages and heroic warriors and were frequently compared to Native Americans. In October 1904, however, Witbooi soldiers fighting in the *Schutztruppe* against rebellious Ovaherero were cunningly disarmed before they were able to learn of their leader's decision to change sides and declare war on the Germans. These Witbooi members of the *Schutztruppe* were deported to German Togo and were subsequently moved to German Cameroon. Most of them succumbed to the harsh conditions of imprisonment and drastic change in climate. Other Witbooi prisoners were dispatched to the concentration camp on Shark Island, which soon became known as "Death Island" (fig. 3.6).[32] Prisoners' conditions there were so atrocious that the commanding officer protested in 1907 that he was reduced to playing the role of a "hangman."[33] All land and property belonging to the Witbooi were expropriated by the colonial government. In proportional terms the devastation of the Witbooi was even greater than the vengeance wreaked upon the Ovaherero. The size of the Witbooi community fell from more than two

---

it does not actually connect *colonial policy* to totalitarianism. Rather, Arendt describes the descent of the Dutch Boers to the allegedly precivilizational level of African natives as prefiguring the rootlessness, antistatism, racism, and hordelike behavior of the European "pan" movements that spawned fascism. She characterizes Africans as "vegetating" "savages" who lack not only "a culture and history of their own" but even a "specifically human character" (Arendt [1950] 1958, pp. 194, 190, 186, 192). The Boers' failing, according to Arendt, was to have moved *outside* the ambit of the colonial state. Indeed, colonialism for Arendt *contributed* to the civilizing process by changing "the country into a normal producing part of Western civilization" ([1950] 1958, p. 205), even if imperialism more generally was symptomatic of the dissolution of the European nation-state (Grosse 2006). The connection between South Africa and totalitarianism for Arendt is therefore not so much causal as comparative. Nonetheless, by depicting colonies as breeding grounds for race thinking and as the sites of ubiquitous massacre, Arendt opened up the possibility for readings of overseas colonialism as the seedbed of Nazism, elaborated by writers like Schmitt-Egner (1975) and Theweleit ([1977-78] 1987-89) and continued into the present by Zimmerer (2003).

32. The most complete study of the German concentration camps in Namibia between 1904 and 1908 is Erichsen 2004; Hull 2005 also discusses Shark Island but did not access the Namibian archive sources.

33. Telegram from Oberleutnant Estorff to Foreign Office in Berlin, April 10, 1907, BA-Berlin, RKA, vol. 2140, p. 88v.

thousand people before the fighting to a mere thirty-eight in 1913—a loss of almost 98 percent.[34]

Not all of the colony's subjects were the targets of this murderous wrath. The Rehoboth Basters received preferential treatment throughout the German colonial period. They supported the Germans steadfastly during the Ovaherero and Nama wars (1904–7) and broke with them only when troops of the Union of South Africa marched into the territory in 1915. In return for their loyalty the Basters were allowed to remain self-governing and to keep the land they had claimed after their migration to Namibia from the northern Cape in 1870–71.[35] Many settlers saw Rehoboth as one of the most desirable pieces of real estate in the colony, and by 1910 officials were beginning to argue that the Basters would eventually have to be separated from their homeland.[36] But no significant moves had been made in this direction prior to the outbreak of World War I. The Rehobothers' ability to ensconce themselves in their "ancestral" territory reflected their favored status within the colonial system of rule.[37]

SAMOA: THE "LOTOS ISLANDS" AND SALVAGE COLONIALISM

For Robert Louis Stevenson, writing in the late 1880s, Samoa represented the "lotos islands": The lotus of Greek legend, described by Homer, was so delicious that those who ate it "left off caring about home and did not even want to go back."[38] Samoa, German's prize possession in Polynesia, consisted of the western islands of 'Upolu, Savai'i, Apolima, and Manono. Taken together these islands make up the present day nation-state of Samoa, known until recently as Western Samoa (maps 2–3). Samoa was the site of the first modern German overseas plantation economy, created by the Hamburg firm Godeffroy in the 1860s and 1870s (the firm was reorganized in 1880 under the name German Trade and Plantation Society for the South

---

34. Jod 1961–62. The Nama and Orlam peoples of Southwest Africa counted perhaps twenty thousand people in 1904 before the fighting began and ten to thirteen thousand people in 1911 (A. Bühler 2003, pp. 337–38).

35. On the historical origins of the Rehoboth community, see missionary Heidmann, "Gemeindechronik der Bastardgemeinde Rehoboth," VEM, RMG 3.538b.

36. Hoffmann 1911, p. 59; Zwergern 1911; Rohrbach 1907, p. 144; and Hölscher to State Secretary of the Colonies von Lindequist, "Report on the Mood and Situation in Bastardland," November 30, 1910, BA-Berlin, RKA, vol. 2124, p. 129.

37. See Kurd Schwabe 1899, pp. 38–39; Bayer [1906] 1984; and chap. 3.

38. Stevenson [1890] 1998, p. 33.

Sea Islands in Hamburg, or DHPG).[39] Samoa was also often referred to as Germany's "first colony" because of the 1879 "friendship treaty" between the two countries. In 1887–88 there had been a short-lived attempt to take control of the islands by Eugen Brandeis, a former Bavarian cavalry officer and DHPG employee. The following year a conference in Berlin involving Germany, Britain, and the United States concluded that consuls from those three powers and a selected European or American chief justice would administer the port city of Apia, where most Europeans and Americans lived, and advise the Samoan king, who would retain sovereignty over the rest of the country.[40] Germany became the sole ruler of the western islands in 1900, raising the flag at Mulinu'u Peninsula in Apia on March 1. The United States took over the eastern islands, which remain in a state of semicolonial limbo to this day.[41]

Some historians have described German Samoa as a living ethnographic museum in which the colonizers protected traditional culture from the depredations of capitalist modernity. The truth is more complicated. On the one hand, the colonial regime attacked any aspect of Samoan culture that threatened German authority. The German rulers were less concerned with immoral behavior than the missionaries, but they did try to suppress customs that were repellent to European mores.[42] On the other hand, many of the colonial government's interventions attempted to stabilize an imagined corpus of Samoan custom and to protect Samoans against induction into a culture-leveling version of capitalist modernity. In this respect the German colonial project in Samoa can be described as a form of *salvage colonialism*.[43] For example, the colonial government created an office whose job was to distinguish between heirloom-quality fine woven mats and mats that were used as currency and to affix an official stamp on the latter. This intervention worked against the incipient mingling of monetary and sacred value systems—a mixing that did not make sense from a European perspective and that threatened the project of preserving a tropical utopia alongside the modernized sector. The government tried to coax Samoans back into traditional customs that were being abandoned. For example, Samoans were urged to use traditional roofing materials on their houses rather than

39. P. Kennedy 1974.

40. Gilson 1970, chap. 16.

41. "Hoisting of the Flag," *Samoa Weekly Herald,* March 3, 1900; Shaffer 2000.

42. See BA-Koblenz, Nachlass Solf, vol. 20, p. 45, for one example of a ban on a "bad custom," namely, the power of Samoan elites to drive people out of their homes. The text of the order of September 1901 is in NZNA AGCA XVII A 1, pt. 2, p. 183.

43. I proposed this concept in Steinmetz 2004b.

corrugated metal.[44] Reliance on manufactured materials would limit the legendary mobility of Samoans, since Western-style houses involved greater sunk costs than a traditional *fale* (house).[45] Colonial governor Wilhelm Solf (fig. 5.1) is somewhat notorious for his opposition to intermarriage between Samoans and *papalagi* (whites), a stance that led eventually to an outright ban on mixed marriage. But this did not necessarily stem from racial animus against Polynesians. The policy also "prohibited Chinese labourers from setting foot in Samoan houses as well as forbidding Samoan women from entering Chinese quarters."[46] In light of Solf's well-documented disdain for the white settlers in Samoa and his fondness for Samoans, which led him to form an imaginary identification across the cultural boundary with an imago of a Samoan chief and to give his children Samoan names, his rejection of mixed marriage seems to have flowed mainly from a concern to defend the islanders against the sort of "racial" corruption that he believed was occurring in Tahiti and elsewhere in the Pacific.[47] Settlers in Samoa, like those in Southwest Africa, demanded that the colonial state alienate native-owned land and compel Samoans to work for wages. Instead, the government imported Chinese laborers to meet the plantations' needs.[48]

Samoan uprisings against the German state prompted settlers to call repeatedly for increased security. In contrast to Southwest Africa, however, the government positioned itself against the settlers and refused to strike an aggressive military pose. There were no colonial troops or German policemen in Samoa, and punishment by flogging was never considered appropriate for Samoans. A movement against German rule, the Lafoga 'Oloa, arose in 1904 among the chiefs of the Mālō which was the highest institution of nominal Samoan self-government at the time. The movement's aim was to start an independent copra-marketing company that would bypass European middlemen and generate the resources that would permit Samoans to free themselves from German control.[49] In response, the Mālō was disbanded and replaced with a body of salaried officials appointed by the

44. NZNA AGCA XVII A 1, pt. 6, p. 145.

45. See Salesa 2003 on the Samoan "love of travel."

46. Shankman 2001, p. 129.

47. See Solf's "Report on Mixed Marriage," September 15, 1907, BA-Berlin, RKA, vol. 5432, p. 29.

48. NZNA AGCA VII 14; also Moses 1972; and Tom 1986.

49. See Hempenstall 1978, chap. 1; "Statement by Lauaki FK. before Imperial Amtmann Williams of Savai'i, as to the Origin of the 'Oloa," BA-Koblenz, Nachlass Solf, vol. 30, pp. 148–75. Also "Bekanntmachung" concerning "Die Selbstverwaltung der Samoaner," in *Samoanisches Gouvernements-Blatt* 3 (4, September 5, 1900): 15–17.

governor. One of the rebels, Lauaki (fig. 5.4), was placed on probation; another was deported. These punishments were less harsh than in Southwest Africa, since Samoans were familiar with the German practice in the South Seas of banishing rebels only to repatriate them as soon as they were needed for political purposes.[50]

Samoa was still a colony, however, not an ethnographic nature park. The government's aim was to *stabilize* Samoan custom rather than simply allow it to exist and evolve undisturbed. The German regime introduced subtle changes by translating and codifying Samoan customary law.[51] They introduced more dramatic changes by banning certain institutions, including the position of Samoan king, or *tupu*. The Germans' overarching assumption of Samoan difference and "savagery"—even if that savagery was "noble"—prevented the colonized from being construed as legal equals suited for genuine self-government. The idiom that Governor Solf adopted for his relations with Samoans was explicitly paternalistic. In contrast to Kiaochow, the Germans never expressed any interest in civilizational exchange with Samoans. Within the dominant German and European racial imagination the Samoans never escaped from the category of *Naturvolk* (natural or primitive people) into the category of the *Kulturvolk* (cultural or civilized people).[52] But in contrast to the systematic demonization of the Ovaherero, German officials followed the ethnographers in idealizing Samoans. This provided the colonized with some measure of protection from aggression and gave a very different cast to colonial rule.

QINGDAO (KIAOCHOW): FROM SEGREGATION TO SYNCRETISM

In 1879 the first German missionaries from the Societas Verbi Divini, the Steyl Mission, arrived in Hong Kong, moving from there into southern Shandong Province, which became their base of Chinese operations. The head of the Steyl Mission in China was Johann Baptist von Anzer (fig. 6.10). A decade later the German navy began to search for a base on the Chinese coast for use as a coaling station and as the launching point for carving out a German sphere of influence in China. In 1882 geographer Ferdinand von Richthofen (fig. 6.7) called Jiaozhou Bay the "biggest and best ocean harbor

50. Hempenstall 1978, p. 47.

51. Translations by Schultz-Ewerth (1905, 1911).

52. The opposition between *Kulturvölker* and *Naturvölker* was ubiquitous in German ethnological writing during the second half of the nineteenth century, even if the terms were given varying definitions (compare, e.g., Klemm 1843–52, vol. 1; and Vierkandt 1896).

in all of northern China" and emphasized its "past and *future* importance."[53] Bishop Anzer's repeated provocations of Chinese officials led to a series of attacks on missionaries and Chinese Christians in Shandong. The murder of two Steyl missionaries in 1897 provided Germany with its eagerly awaited pretext for seizing Qingdao.

The German coastal colony in Shandong, Kiaochow (maps 4–6) was not identical to the treaty ports like Canton and Shanghai which were jointly administered by Chinese and foreigners, even if Kiaochow did begin sliding in that direction in the years leading up to World War I.[54] Rather, it was a formal colony under European rule, like Hong Kong, which tolerated only minor infringements by China on its sovereignty. The Germans referred to the leasehold as the Kiautschou protectorate. To avoid confusion I will use the older English-language transliteration Kiaochow (rather than Jiaozhou) to designate the German leasehold in the 1897 boundaries. I will use Jiaozhou (the transcription of 胶州 in the contemporary Pinyin system of Romanization) when referring to the city that fell inside the fifty-kilometer zone but outside the boundaries of the Kiaochow leasehold (see map 5).[55] The name Qingdao (青岛) refers here not to the entire colony but rather to the city where the colonial government was headquartered, which was the place of residence for most Europeans in the colony (see maps 6 and 7). The Germans called that town Tsintau during the first year of their leasehold and Tsingtau later on; in English it is known as Tsingtao. The colonial city was located on Jiaozhou Bay and was constructed on the site of an ancient Chinese village (also called Qingdao) and of a recently built Chinese army barracks. The village and the barracks were razed by the Germans.[56]

Qingdao was invaded by the German navy in 1897, and the Kiaochow colony was coercively leased from China for ninety-nine years. Germans retained full sovereignty over Chinese inhabitants within the leasehold. They also had the right to intervene in a fifty-kilometer buffer zone surrounding the leasehold, to build two railroads through Shandong Province, and to mine for coal along the railway lines.

53. Richthofen 1877–1912, vol. 2, p. 262 (my emphasis). Von Richthofen had traveled extensively in China during the 1860s and 1870s and played a major role in shaping German perceptions of China and official colonial policy there; see chap. 6.

54. Fairbanks [1953] 1969, p. x. Fairbanks's pioneering analysis of the assault on Chinese sovereignty in the nineteenth century has been criticized for its reliance on a "modernization" framework; see Barlow 1997.

55. The city known as Jiaozhou in the colonial period is now called Jiaoxian.

56. On the history of the Chinese army base at Qingdao, which had been built after 1892, see Zhang Shufeng 1991.

Colonial interventions in Kiaochow and Shandong Province during the first seven years of German rule unfolded under the sign of segregation and anti-Chinese hatred, recalling the treatment of the Namibian Ovaherero. The preexisting Chinese settlements in Qingdao were demolished to make room for the planned colonial city, which was laid out in quasi-apartheid fashion, with segregated districts for Europeans and Chinese. A dualistic legal system was crafted, in which the Chinese were subject to harsh punishments for violating both German and Chinese laws. Their sentences were determined by a German district commissioner, or *Bezirksamtmann,* who acted single-handedly as policeman and judge.

After establishing themselves in the colony the Germans quickly took advantage of the treaty's fifty-kilometer clause in ways that signaled their intention to establish a permanent presence in that zone.[57] Almost immediately they began construction of the railway that would eventually reach the provincial capital of Ji'nan and connect to the north-south line running up to Tianjin. Villagers began erecting reinforced walls around their towns, sabotaging the railway tracks, harassing railroad employees, and opening fire on railway company workers. During the next three years the Germans responded by burning and sacking temples and villages, seizing local mandarins as hostages, massacring villagers, and installing garrisons in towns lying outside the leasehold boundary.

All of this took place against the backdrop of the uprising of the Yihetuan (Boxers) secret society, a movement that emerged in Shandong and other northern provinces in the 1890s and began attacking Western missionaries and Chinese Christians at the end of the decade. This rebellion was provoked partly by the German missionary and colonial presence in Shandong.[58] Germany was heavily involved in the joint expedition of the great powers against the Yihetuan, eventually dispatching twenty thousand troops to China, and the Kiaochow colony was directly involved in this campaign. The German Third Naval Infantry Battalion that was stationed permanently in Qingdao sent divisions to Tianjin and Beijing, where the main battles against the Yihetuan were being fought. There were also expeditions against Boxers and alleged Yihetuan supporters in Kiaochow's hinterland. Sinophobic ideology that positioned the Chinese under the sign of the generic racial inferior had been gaining power since the second half of the eighteenth century, and it reached its apogee with the anti-Boxer campaign, just as the German colonial regime was taking shape in Qingdao.

57. Schrecker 1971; Stichler 1989; Mühlhahn 2000.
58. Esherick 1987; Cohen 1997.

German Sinophobia was epitomized by Kaiser Wilhelm's *Hunnenrede* (Hun speech) to the East Asian Expeditionary troops being dispatched from Bremerhaven to China on July 27, 1900. The emperor called on his soldiers to emulate "King Etzel's Huns of a thousand years ago" and vowed that "no Chinese will ever again dare to look askance at a German."[59] He had already declared in a June telegram to the Foreign Office that Beijing should be "razed" to the ground.[60]

By 1905, however, German policy in Kiaochow had become less violently expansionist and segregationist. German troops pulled back into the lease-hold and stopped provoking the provincial government. New colonial institutions embodying a program of cultural rapprochement and exchange with China were superimposed on the preexisting apartheid foundation, although they never entirely displaced it. This shift was alluded to in a speech in November 1904 by a German bank director in Qingdao who praised the governor for giving the Chinese *Bürger* (citizens) "their civil rights" and involving "them in the affairs of the colony."[61] Indigenous Southwest Africans and Samoans were referred to as subjects (*Untertanen*) but never as citizens (*Bürger*). Although Chinese elites in Qingdao never gained legal rights that were fully equal to those of Europeans in the colony, many wealthier Chinese were allowed to participate in elections to a mixed European-Chinese council of advisers to the governor. Other German colonies had advisory boards or elected assemblies of European settlers, as well as institutions of native "self-government," but nowhere else did colonizer and colonized work together in the same council.

The ban on Chinese residence in the European district was partially lifted due to the influx into Qingdao of Chinese elites associated with the deposed Qing dynasty during the 1911 republican revolution.[62] The colonial government worked with a progressive missionary society, the Weimar Mission, to create Chinese schools at all levels with a mixed Chinese and European curriculum. The culmination of this educational policy was the

---

59. The actual text of this speech, quoted here, was suppressed by the German government at the time but has been verified and reconstructed by Soesemann (1976).

60. Quoted in P. Fischer 1996, p. 351.

61. "Festive Speech of Bank Director Homann on the Occasion of the Onset of Governor Truppel's Vacation, November 6, 1904," BA-MA-Freiburg, Nachlass Truppel, vol. 59, p. 3.

62. The expansion of the Chinese population and Chinese-owned business is another indicator of the difference between Qingdao and Southwest Africa. Southwest Africa suffered proportionately huge population losses between 1904 and 1908, while Qingdao continued to grow, from just a few hundred inhabitants in 1897 to over fifty-five thousand in 1913 (Matzat 1998a, p. 106).

Qingdao German-Chinese college. This college had German and Chinese teachers and granted degrees that were recognized by the Chinese government for admission to examinations at the national university in Beijing. Within the college's Department of Law and Political Economy, students studied Chinese and European law and the faculty encouraged a process of transculturation in which the Chinese would fill German legal forms with Chinese contents and Germans would learn from Chinese legal traditions.[63] Middle-class translators and Sinologists working inside or together with the colonial administration and the German foreign service in China tended to admire and even identify with Chinese mandarins. Such educated, middle-class Germans became more influential within the Kiaochow administration in the decade before 1914. These changes were encouraged by the German Foreign Office, the navy, and the Beijing Legation, all of whom agreed that Germany should move away from direct colonialism in China and toward less obtrusive methods of influencing rather than bullying that potential ally.

Making Sense of Colonial Variations

The patterns of variation among these three colonies are as puzzling as is the sheer degree of heterogeneity. The German depredations in Namibia might not seem so paradoxical if one believed that colonialism always leads to massacre, or if one subscribed to the theory that German colonialism was singularly hideous. But the comparison with Samoa and Kiaochow instantly refutes both of these simple accounts. This is not to deny that massacre was always a possibility in a system predicated on the intrinsic inferiority of the Other, but it was by no means the norm, at least in the period after 1884. Indeed, the Germans' genocidal actions against the Ovaherero and Witbooi stand out as exceptionally brutal even in a century of "racial" slaughter and ethnic "cleansing."[64] But there was no singular German approach to colonial governance.[65]

These three cases pose a series of puzzles that cannot be resolved by the leading theoretical approaches. Current explanations of colonialism in sociology, political science, and history tend to focus on broadly socioeconomic or material determinants: a colony's location in the global economy, colonizers' economic interests, or environmental conditions. But not even the

---

63. See Romberg 1911, p. 25.
64. Steinmetz 2005b.
65. Gann and Duignan (1997, p. 74) agree.

economic policies that were promoted by colonial states—policies concerning the kinds of export products, modes of production, and existence and power of settler economies—can be derived from metropolitan economic interests or socioeconomic conditions in the colony. World-system theory locates the causally relevant social classes in the global "core" and derives political structures from economic functions. This approach is too coarse grained to account for variations among different parts of the raw-material-producing periphery. If colonies are all the same, a uniform category, the difference between the slaughter of the Ovaherero and the paternalistic protection of the Samoans becomes invisible. This is not to say that individual world-system theorists are indifferent to colonial genocide, but that their theory makes no room for these fateful differences.

Neo-Marxist theorists expect states to correspond broadly in their form and function to the interests of dominant social classes. Structuralist versions of neo-Marxism attribute a sort of capitalist omniscience to the state, which is seen as balancing or mediating among competing class fractions or groupings.[66] But it is not clear which classes are relevant in the colonial context, that is, whether it is the classes dominant in the metropole or in the colony that are structurally dominant.[67] Indeed, the reason this cannot be determined "economically" is that such dominance is assigned politically, that is, by the central and colonial states. Structuralist neo-Marxism is unable to make sense of the fact that overseas colonies *created* their own European class structures and were not mere transmission belts for preexisting metropolitan power configurations.

Even if we were able to define the relevant ruling classes or "historical blocs" in the colonies, these configurations would not necessarily explain colonial state policy. Colonial rulers in German Samoa, Qingdao, Southwest Africa, Togo, and Cameroon often disregarded or directly flouted the demands of European investors, capitalists, and settlers.[68] One problem, as with structural Marxism more generally, is that it is impossible to identify any mechanisms that would be responsible for adjusting policy to the needs of capitalist development in a given colony. Most German colonial states

66. See Berman and Lonsdale 1992 for an application of a structural Marxist state theory to colonial settings.

67. Poulantzas 1975, 1978.

68. On German officials' opposition to "the very European merchants whose interests they presumably [in a Marxist view] represented" in Cameroon, see Austen and Derrick 1999, p. 130. On the preference given to indigenous farmers on small plots in Togo, against the plantation model preferred by German capitalist interests, see Erbar 1990, pp. 63–67, 97; and Sebald 1988, p. 258.

relied heavily on revenues from the metropolitan government. There was no guarantee that these resources would be used in ways that benefited capitalist investors or European property owners. In this respect, colonial states were more akin to despotic "Third World states," insofar as their structural ability to *ignore* the interests and demands of their own dominant social classes, including local economic elites, was rooted in the availability of resources from sources external to their own territory.[69]

Another class-analytic or Marxian approach suggests that *settler colonies* are especially brutal because competition for land is a zero-sum game.[70] One empirical problem with this account is that there were actually *more* white settlers in Samoa than in Southwest Africa at their respective moments of colonial annexation (1900 and 1884). This situation was reversed after a decade of German rule in the two colonies, pointing to the fact that colonial policies shaped modes of production and class structures as much as they reflected them.[71] A focus on settlers would expect policy to have been harsher in Samoa than in Southwest Africa, but the opposite was actually the case. Agrarian settlers may be prone to brutal displacement and repression of indigenous landholders, but the German colonies remind us that settlers' interests were not necessarily translated into policy. Settlers were quite peripheral to colonial government in several instances, including German Togo, Kiaochow, and Samoa.

69. Tilly 1990, chap. 7. Nor was there any systematic articulation between the colonial state and the needs of metropolitan German capital. The institutional structure that might have promoted such an alignment was the Kolonialrat, an advisory board to the government consisting of economic, political, and scientific elites that was created in 1890. But the Kolonialrat was never more than just one among many competing agencies with a voice in central colonial policymaking. The German Reichstag had a surprising degree of influence on national-level colonial policy as compared to its weakness in other areas, but the kaiser was constitutionally granted a much greater say in colonial than in domestic policymaking (Hoffmann 1911, pp. 11, 37–39).

70. Osterhammel 1995, p. 48; Bley 1995; Büttner 1885c.

71. There were 137 Europeans in Southwest Africa during the 1870s (Esterhuyse 1968, p. 13). In the western islands of Samoa on the eve of annexation there were 400–800 white settlers. The number of whites in Southwest Africa in 1884 was well below the 498 recorded in the same colony in 1891, which included about 100 traders (Walther 2002, p. 58; "Excerpt from Annual Report, 1900–1901," NZNA AGCA, G.S.A. IV 5.a, p. 21; Bochert 1980, p. 38). By 1912 there were 500 whites (294 Germans) in German Samoa and 14,816 whites (12,135 Germans) in Southwest Africa (*Die deutschen Schutzgebiete in Afrika und der Südsee*, 1911/12, Statistischer Teil, pp. 7, 22, 33). This reversal was the result of the aggressive promotion of settlement in Southwest Africa and antisettler politics in Samoa, and of the fact that many soldiers who fought in the German-Namibian war (1904–7) stayed in the colony.

A related theoretical approach suggests that the direction of colonial policies is determined by ecological or environmental considerations.[72] This is broadly correct with respect to the sorts of export products that characterize a given colony: Southwest Africa was too arid and Kiaochow too cold in the winter for plantation agriculture; Samoa was unsuited for ranching, and so on. It is also correct that the economies of modern European colonies emphasized the production of raw materials rather than manufacturing, and that indigenous manufacturing was often suppressed. And it is correct that colonial agriculture tended to become less diverse and more monocultural due to its alignment with the needs of the core. But ecological preconditions cannot predict the contours of the indigenous class relations that emerge under colonial rule. The comparison among the German colonies forces us to ask why some colonies became sites of European settlement while others emphasized plantation agriculture or indigenous smallholder farming. Looking forward from 1880, an ecologically inclined historian would expect Samoa to continue developing along its earlier path toward a plantation economy, with Samoans increasingly drawn into employment as agricultural laborers. The same historian would also predict an increase in the number of settlers, since Europeans obviously found the islands appealing in the second half of the nineteenth century. And she would expect Southwest Africa to remain a barren desert populated by indigenous herders and a few missionaries and scattered white traders, with a desultory copper-mining industry.[73] The fact that the colonial economy actually became *less* oriented toward proletarianization and raw material extraction in Samoa than in Southwest Africa suggests that the colonial state's selection of models for economic development and class relations did not flow automatically from environmental conditions. Samoa's precolonial copra sector was much more profitable than Southwest Africa's precolonial copper mines. The alienation of Samoan soil had proceeded apace from midcentury until 1889, when the Berlin Conference on Samoa halted all further land sales outside Apia. After 1900 the new German administration reasserted the 1889 Samoa Act and the ban on long-term land leasing and land sales to foreigners. In Southwest Africa, by contrast, the colonial state pushed for maximal expropriation of land and cattle from the Ovaherero starting

72. See W. Smith 1978, p. 53; and Emmett 1999, pp. 39–41, for examples of this; Sahlins 1958 provides a strong statement of the ecological-determinist model (one that his more recent work has abandoned).

73. Even the RMG Trading Company that was created in 1870 had a difficult time and eventually "died a natural death" (Vedder [1938] 1966, p. 401).

in the 1890s. Samoa and Southwest Africa were both initially understood as having suitable climates for European settlement, but it was Southwest Africa that came to be seen as the primary target for emigration. Fanon was thus correct in writing that "in the colonies the economic infrastructure is also a superstructure."[74]

It would be absurd to deny that capitalism shaped German colonialism. Adolf Lüderitz was motivated by expectations that he would discover precious minerals. Even if the chartered companies and settler societies were originally creatures of the German state, they immediately voiced "private" interests. Yet even where the colonial state consisted of little more than a chartered company—that is, where state policies were *identical* with the interests of "capital," as in early German Southwest Africa, New Guinea, and East Africa—we still need to reconstruct the ways in which company officials defined their own interests. One cannot assume that these interests were narrowly "economic" in any conventional sense.[75] The investors in the company that bought Lüderitz's land in 1885 were motivated at least in part by a desire to please Bismarck and to prevent the colony from falling into British hands. At its first meeting, that chartered company concluded cautiously that the "possibility of profitability" should *not be excluded altogether*. The investors described their money as being spent in "fulfillment of patriotic duty, in a certain sense as a sacrifice." An exhaustive study of all of the land-speculating and mining companies in Southwest Africa finds that only three of them produced dividends, and only after 1900.[76] This does not mean that we should dismiss the German Colonial Society for South West Africa as unimportant, even if it did little more than sit on its property holdings for two decades.[77] Starting in 1904 the company suddenly became very profitable by supplying consumer goods to the thousands of German soldiers who were brought to the colony for the war and to the masses of workers building the Otavi railway line.[78] Economic interests and pressures

74. Fanon [1961] 2004, p. 5.

75. Adams (1994, 2005) shows that the leading figures in the Dutch East Indies Company understood their interests in ways that led them to define their time horizons in much longer terms than simple economic or class-based models would expect.

76. Sander 1912, pp. 20-21, quoted by Dreschsler (1996, p. 21); Dreschsler 1996, pp. 274-77.

77. In 1892 the Colonial Society got involved in promoting the earliest wave of German settlement in the colony, but this enterprise was underfunded and unprofitable.

78. Esterhuyse 1968, pp. 171-79. The SWAC, founded in 1892 by Dr. Julius Scharlach and soon purchased by Cecil Rhodes's agents, had a more exclusively economic focus; see Drechsler [1966] 1980, p. 47; 1996, pp. 56ff. and chap. 2.

were certainly important, but even in a colony like Southwest Africa their impact on policy was indirect. And the colonial government's emphasis on native governance often trumped calculations of profitability and reframed economic considerations.

If broadly socioeconomic and materialist theories cannot make sense of the main patterns of variation in native policy, what about the perspective that emphasizes colonialism's cultural determinants, including the role of ethnographic discourse? Here the foundational text is Edward Said's *Orientalism* (1978), which established two central hypotheses. First, Said followed Michel Foucault in suggesting that Orientalist discourse should be defined quite broadly, rather than being restricted to the writings of professional historians of the Orient. As Michel-Rolph Trouillot notes, we often "claim to distinguish clearly between travelers' accounts, colonial surveys, ethnographic reports, and fictional utopias . . . [but] the line between these genres was not always clear-cut" in the past.[79] Second, Said accepted the distinction between discourse and practice that structures most of Foucault's work (contrary to the view of some of his epigones), a distinction that underlines his vision of psychoanalysis creating the neurotic body or Jeremy Bentham's ideas helping to forge the panoptical society. The relevant field of discourse for Said is the Orientalist "library of *idées reçues*." The effects of this "library," he suggests, include Napoleon's Egyptian expedition and later colonial endeavors. In Said's succinct formula, "from travelers' tales . . . colonies were created." Said thus posits not only an "absolute unanimity" between Orientalism and empire but also a causal relationship between the two. When he writes that "an observation about a tenth-century Arab poet multiplied itself into a policy towards . . . the Oriental mentality in Egypt, Iraq, or Arabia," the verb "multiplied" points to a determining connection between an order of discourse and an order of political practice.[80] Orientalism preexisted the colonization of the "Orient," or Near East, and gave it form. By extension we should expect early modern Sinology to provide the lineaments of nineteenth-century efforts to penetrate China, we should trace the connections between accounts of early explorations and missionary endeavors in Africa and subsequent systems of colonial rule, and we should examine the effects of eighteenth- and nineteenth-century narratives of Oceanic exploration and tropical romance on late-nineteenth-century colonization of Polynesian islands.

Said's intervention marked an important break with the so-called handmaiden of colonialism thesis, which emphasized the effects of colonialism

79. Trouillot 1991, p. 23.
80. Said 1978, pp. 123, 104, 96, 94, 117.

on anthropology rather than focusing on causal arrows running in the opposite direction. After being introduced to the English-speaking world by Talal Asad and the contributors to his *Anthropology and the Colonial Encounter* (1973), this idea became something of a commonplace in anthropology.[81] Said hewed more closely to Foucault than to the sociology of knowledge in this respect. I refer to this claim that colonies were created from "travelers' tales" as the "devil's handwriting" hypothesis.

Writing inspired by Said and Foucault has emphasized the effects of European representations of the non-West on subsequent colonial and imperial activities. In *Colonizing Egypt,* Timothy Mitchell argues that a generic European modern consciousness was replicated in the self-modernization of nineteenth-century Egypt and other parts of the Near East. In *The Cunning of Recognition,* Elizabeth Povinelli suggests that the ways in which early anthropologists in Australia situated "the indigenous . . . within extant discourses of the wild and reasonable and the civil and savage" shaped the subsequent "formulation of state policy in relation to Aboriginal persons and white settlers." In *Colonial Fantasies,* Susanne Zantop portrays German myths about overseas colonization in the eighteenth and earlier nineteenth centuries as giving form to practical German colonial activities in the late nineteenth century.[82] Blueprints for colonialism were prepared not so much in Europe's official foreign ministries as in the scholar's study, the traveler's diary, and the playwright's tale of Oceanic shipwreck and African adventure.

How does this thesis fare with respect to the German colonies? In chapters 2, 4, and 6 I will demonstrate that the Germans who established colonial states in Samoa, Kiaochow, and Southwest Africa did, in fact, come equipped with well-wrought images of the colonized cultures, images that were derived from earlier writers and artists. In Qingdao the German colonial founders established an actual library of *idées reçues* during the first year of the colony. That library's Asia section was stocked with European classics on China ranging from Marco Polo to Karl Gützlaff.[83] During the thirty years of colonial rule examined in this book native policy rarely went beyond suggestions that were already present in precolonial ethnographic discourse.

At first glance there also seems to be a strong correlation between the dominant precolonial representations of Samoans, Chinese, and Southwest

---

81. Stocking 1991, p. 4; Leiris (1950) and Leclerc (1972) had already analyzed the connections between anthropology and colonialism.

82. Mitchell 1988; Povinelli 2002, p. 77; Zantop 1997, p. 203.

83. *Buecher-Verzeichnis der Kiautschou-Bibliothek* 1898.

Africans within each of the relevant discursive formations and the policies that were subsequently imposed on them. The Germans' assault on the Ovaherero in 1904 seems almost to leap off the pages of the missionary and traveler accounts from the middle decades of the nineteenth century. A society that had been regularly defamed as cruel and brutal was dealt with in a commensurately cruel and brutal manner; a culture that had been dismissed as lacking value and destined for extinction was immorally annihilated. Along parallel lines, the Germans' expressed desire to preserve the Samoans in a pristine "natural" condition appears to flow directly from prevailing nineteenth-century European depictions of Samoans as noble savages. Said's thesis thus receives some initial support at the level of these crude empirical correlations between precolonial ethnographic perceptions and the contours of colonial native policy.

This simple model falters immediately, however, once we turn to German Kiaochow, and it stumbles if we examine the history of colonial Namibia or Samoa in more detail. German thinking about China at the end of the nineteenth century was extremely heterogeneous and protean, even if Sinophobia had been gaining strength for over a century (chap. 6). Late-nineteenth-century writers revised their view of China from one book to the next, or combined contradictory tropes within a single narrative. Without further investigation it is impossible to understand why colonial policy expressed one of these visions of China rather than another. Even where the ethnographic archive was relentlessly repetitive and monolithic, as with the Ovaherero, the linkages between precolonial discourse and colonial practice need to be specified in more detail. We need to know why colonizers acted in accordance with received ethnographic wisdom rather than developing novel approaches in response to ongoing events. Without further specification of the links between "travelers' tales" and colonial policy, Said's thesis becomes as reductionist as the socioeconomic approaches that it was meant to supplant.[84] More specifically, it is reductionist in its causal imagery and its lack of attention to social and psychic levels of causality, and even in its textual interpretation of Orientalist discourse. Following the lead of Foucault in *The Archaeology of Knowledge,* Said argues that Orientalism in its entirety was derived from a common set of premises. But this is belied by European discourse on China, which was radically heterogeneous. Said's claim that Orientalism after the eighteenth century "could never revise itself" is contradicted by the overarching change from Sinophilia to Sinophobia as the leading approach.[85]

84. Comaroff and Comaroff 1991–97, vol. 1, p. 9.
85. Said 1978, p. 96.

It follows that Orientalism's effects on colonial practice must have been complexly mediated and not simply the execution of preexisting scripts.

I define *ethnographic discourse* as any representation, textual or visual, that claims to depict the character and culture of a given sociocultural collective, regardless of whether that collective is described as a race, a culture, a society, an ethnic group, a community, or something else. Said is correct in suggesting that precolonial ethnographic discourse often contained explicit or implicit recommendations for the practical governance of the people being represented. What he failed to acknowledge was that many if not most formations of ethnographic discourse are multivocal or multiaccentual. Within some of these formations, competing authors painted radically differing pictures of the non-Western Other and thus suggested differing techniques of colonization. European observers of China ranged from those who reviled it as the source of a "yellow peril" suited only "to be sliced up by the different powers" to those who believed that Europe needed "missionaries from the Chinese who might teach us the use and practice of practical religion."[86] There were diametrically opposing visions of the Khoikhoi and Samoans as well. Only in exceptional cases were Orientalist or ethnographic discourses seamless and uniform. We need to discover how and why one particular strand of precolonial discourse rather than another was mobilized in colonial policy.

There were at least three crucial links in the chain of determinations leading from ethnographic representations to native policy: (1) patterns of resistance and collaboration by the colonized, (2) symbolic competition among colonizers, and (3) colonizers' imaginary cross-identification with images of their subjects. Before discussing these three mechanisms, however, I want to step back for a moment and define the modern colonial state and justify the focus in this book on native policy.

The Specificity of the Colonial State

The fact that most extant states are descendants of colonies suggests that the colonial state needs to be integrated into theoretical discussions of organized forms of political domination. But theorists and historians have been slow to recognize the uniqueness or even the existence of the colonial form of the state.[87] There is no generally accepted definition of the colonial state. Some writers reduce it to an appendage of the metropoli-

---

86. Heyking 1926, p. 199; Leibniz 1994, p. 51.

87. For recent exceptions see the special issue "L'Etat coloniale" of the journal *Politix: Revue des Sciences Sociales du Politique* (Paris: Presses de la Fondation nationale des sciences

tan state, a conveyor belt carrying out tasks formulated at the center.[88] Yet colonial governors often enjoyed a great deal of independence from their metropolitan supervisors in elaborating and executing day-to-day policy.[89] Some writers deny that colonial regimes are really states at all, and Hannah Arendt described nineteenth-century "colonial-imperialism" as the antithesis, even the "suicide," of the European nation-state.[90] From a strictly legal standpoint, colonial regimes do lack sovereignty, which is the defining feature of stateness.[91] Colonial governments were dependencies of metropolitan states and were not recognized as autonomous entities within the international state system. They did not send diplomatic or consular representatives to other states or to international bodies and did not represent themselves in international negotiations. European powers frequently entertained the possibility of trading entire colonies or parts of colonies, treating them as chess pieces in a global game with much greater stakes. Colonial governors and officials typically had no voice in such deliberations.[92] Colonial governors were not elected or appointed locally by the settlers or natives of a colony but were chosen by the metropolitan state and could be discharged at will. Indeed, any regime whose heads of state are selected locally, by local residents, has already exited from colonial status by definition.

In other respects, however, these colonial regimes were eminently statelike. One of the defining features of colonialism was that it involved a *transfer* of sovereignty from indigenous inhabitants to foreigners. Of course, if one considers sovereignty from a strictly legal standpoint, power was transferred to the metropole, not the local European administration. But we also need to consider the effective, ongoing exercise of power when locating sovereignty. As Carl Schmitt argued, "Sovereign is he who decides on the exception" or the emergency.[93] Colonial governance consisted of an endless,

---

politiques), vol. 17 (66, September 2004); Trotha 1994; Bertrand 2005; and Le Cour Grand-maison 2005.

88. Carl Schmitt interprets the Belgian Congo in strictly legal terms as being fully assimilated into the Belgian state after its 1908 "annexation" ([1950] 2003, pp. 221–26).

89. This independence is demonstrated not only in the three cases explored here but also in British Malaya and the U.S. Philippines (Goh 2005).

90. H. Arendt 1945/1946; Grosse 2006.

91. C. Young 1994, p. 10.

92. An exception was the South African minister of defense Jan Smuts, who "played a major role in determining British policy in Africa" during World War I as part of the British War Cabinet (Yearwood 1990, p. 317).

93. Schmitt [1922] 1985, p. 5.

even a permanent series of exceptions and emergencies, and the responses to these emergencies were usually formulated by the governing authorities *sur place*. Metropolitan governments, at least in this period, did not attempt to micromanage daily activities in the colonies, due to the long distances and relatively crude communication and transportation technologies. It was common practice to allow a great deal of leeway to the local governor even after telegraph communication became available to colonial governments— something that happened very late in the period examined in this book (for example, in 1914 for Samoa).[94] The governor of Kiaochow was required to get prior approval from his superiors in Berlin only for "the most important and far-reaching regulations," and in fact, none of his regulations were ever overturned.[95] The German Colonial Department minuted in 1900 that "it would not be appropriate for the Foreign Office to determine the further details of native policy given that conditions are really only visible on the spot."[96] Only once, at the height of the war in Southwest Africa in 1904 and after months of battle and the death of scores of German civilians, did the metropolitan government decide to assume direct control of the ongoing affairs of a colony.

Beneath the administrative level of the governor, effective sovereignty resided with the legendary "men on the spot," the "real chiefs of the empire," or "little governors," who were in direct contact with indigenous leaders and communities.[97] In the German colonial empire these "little governors" included the district commissioners (*Berzirksamtmänner*), military commanders, policemen, and judges. The local power of the district commissioners was so extensive than in German Togo one of them replaced all 544 chiefs in his district during his twenty years in office.[98] The district commissioners in Kiaochow adjudicated most legal cases involving Chinese defendants and could send a Chinese subject to jail for life without consulting anyone else. They needed the governor's authorization only when recommending the death penalty.[99] The autonomy of colonial officials from

94. Klein-Arendt 2001, 189–90.

95. The navy administration and Foreign Office overruled colonial governor Truppel's opposition to the German-Chinese university and eventually replaced him (Seelemann 1982, p. 87, 106 n. 123; Schrecker 1971, p. 60).

96. Ausw. Amt to Solf, May 31, 1900, NZNA AGCA XVII.A.1, vol. 1, p. 90.

97. See Delavignette 1939; and Trotha 1994, pp. 109–10.

98. Trotha 1994, p. 268. Of course, each Togolese chief had an average of only 320 subjects (ibid., p. 270), but this still meant that a single district commissioner appointed the indirect rulers of approximately 174,080 people.

99. Crusen 1914.

the metropolitan state was coupled with a significant level of independence from the local "civil society," including the European propertied class.[100] A governor's autonomy extended to long-range planning for his colony and did not simply concern daily crisis management. The leading officials in a given colony were sometimes able to "colonize" the responsible section of the Colonial Department, further diminishing control from the European center. For example, the Southwest African "native ordinances" of 1907 (discussed in chap. 3) were drawn up in Berlin by veterans of Southwest African politics, all of whom later returned to the colony to occupy key administrative roles.[101] The officials in the Foreign Office in Berlin who were in charge of overseeing German Samoa were former envoys to those islands.

The Reichstag was empowered to discuss colonial politics and to interpellate colonial administrators in the course of its annual budget negotiations and to influence colonial policy in broad terms. But the Reichstag did not participate in naming colonial officials or in the daily activities in the colonies. The emperor was legally empowered to dissolve the Reichstag, and he exercised this power in December 1906 in response to the Reichstag's refusal to appropriate funds for the ongoing "Hottentot" war in Southwest Africa.[102]

The central government pressured the colonies to increase the revenues they raised locally and demanded that they become self-sustaining. But Berlin could generally be counted on to pay for ongoing operations. This

100. In Southwest Africa before the 1904 war colonial governors could largely ignore the demands of the settlers; after the war a Gouvernementsrat (later called the Landrat) was created which allowed for advisory input from the settlers. The main legislation on native policy was drawn up by von Lindequist and other officials and presented to the Landrat for commentary. See "Verhandlungen des Gouvernementsrats in Windhuk, 1906," BA-Berlin, RKA, vol. 2174, for discussions with the Governing Council; and Eingeborenen-Verordnungen etc. (1907–14), BA-Berlin, R. 1002, vol. 2597, p. 3.

101. These officials were von Lindequist, Hintrager, and Golinelli (Zimmerer 2001).

102. When the Social Democrats and the Catholic Center Party refused to approve funds to continue operations against the Nama rebellion, the chancellor dissolved the Reichstag. The so-called Hottentot elections that were held afterward, in January 1907, resulted in a new bloc favorable to the government and a reduction in the number of Social Democratic seats from eighty-one to forty-three (Crothers 1941; Reinhard 1978). The Social Democrats' opposition to colonialism was usually tepid in any case, focusing mainly on "the current negative rentability of the colonies and the disproportionately high public outlays for them" (Mergner 1988, pp. 76–77) and on instances of egregious brutality or sexual abuse by colonizers (Schröder 1968, 1973; Hyrkkanen 1986). There were important exceptions, and occasionally the Social Democrats and Center Party challenged some of the worst abuses (see chap. 3 on the 1913 Reichstag resolution on the Witbooi prisoners in Cameroon). In general, the circles within the Social Democratic Party that were prepared to cooperate with the government on colonial questions became stronger after the 1907 electoral debacle.

exempted the colonial state from the sorts of structural constraints and censoring effects to which even the most centralized modern European states were exposed due to their reliance on economic growth and tax revenues.[103] Colonial governments were therefore better positioned than governments in Europe to resist demands from European civil society. The colonized populations did not participate directly in making the policies that were imposed on them, even if they inflected these policies through the "subaltern" political logics discussed below.

Colonial states' dual independence—from metropolitan and local interests—was extremely consequential for the formation of native policy. A typical colonial state was staffed by a tiny number of European officials and had an undemocratic, even despotic constitution. The result was that a single official could have an enormous impact on the direction of policy. The colonial state's dual autonomy enhanced the *agency* of individual colonial officials relative to the efficacy of officials operating within the confines of metropolitan states. This is not to say that colonial officials were unconstrained in their decision making, but that a much smaller group of actors was involved in the process and that the familiar constraints and pressures were attenuated. The colonial state was able to resist structural pressures of the sort that often force metropolitan states to align their policies *grosso modo* with the perceived needs of capitalist development and the expressed interests of economic elites.

Salaried colonial state officials and civil servants were not completely immune to colonial civil society or separate from it. What is needed is a more *sociological* account of the colonial state as a *field* in Pierre Bourdieu's sense—specifically, as a state field that was itself located within an environing colonial field of power. This suggests that colonial officials were engaged in a competitive struggle with one another and with other Europeans in the colony.[104] Emphasizing the colonial state's "fieldness" is compatible with the argument about the state's relative autonomy, since the logic of any social field is irreducible to that of other fields. At the same time, the definition of the actors within the colonial state field was homologous to that of the German metropolitan state field. I will return to this redescription of the colonial state as a field in a moment.

What about the colonial state as a material "apparatus"? Most colonial states, including the ones discussed here, were extremely weak in terms of material resources and their ability to penetrate indigenous society.[105] The

103. Block 1988; Offe 1984.

104. Especially, but not exclusively, with others of the same nationality: colonial fields were exceptionally and paradoxically national despite their location in transnational contact zones.

105. Mann 1986–93.

German colonial regimes had only a small number of full-time officials and employees. In Southwest Africa in 1912, for example, there were 824 civil servants (a number that included 488 employees of the police force) and 2,172 members of the *Schutztruppe*, covering a territory that was larger than Germany. There were fewer than 40 civil servants in the Samoan colony in 1912.[106] In Togo the "entire German personnel—from the Governor down to the last of the assistant gardeners—numbered less than ninety men," in a country almost as big as the former German Democratic Republic.[107] There were not enough resources to refashion the entire colonial landscape or to confront each colonial subject with a direct European presence in an ongoing way. As Anthony Appiah remarks, "the experience of the vast majority of [the] citizens of Europe's African colonies was one of an essentially shallow penetration by the colonizer."[108] This was also true of the Asian and Pacific colonies, outside the main cities.

Nonetheless, the colonial state was usually able to put its stamp on the annexed territory and to broadcast its presence widely. It met Max Weber's criteria of stateness by wielding coercion and operating permanently. One guarantee of the *permanence* of the state's operations was the written rules specifying who was to assume the office of the governor when he was absent from a colony.[109] The colonial state tried to gain control over the means of violence, even if it was never able to monopolize the means of coercion completely (but neither were metropolitan states). In Samoa, where German coercion was minimal, the government's first act in 1900 was to conduct a largely successful campaign to disarm Samoans by offering to buy their guns. In Southwest Africa the colonial government issued decrees in 1888, 1890, 1892, and 1897 making the sale of arms without a license punishable by fines or imprisonment. Every gun in the colony was to be stamped and registered, and the widespread English Martini-Henry rifles had to be exchanged for the German M71 in order to give the colonizers "a better idea of how much ammunition was actually in the possession of Africans." Africans were required to pay "double the price for guns and ammunition that Europeans were required to pay." These policies were not entirely suc-

106. There were 31 civil servants in Samoa in 1912, according to *Die deutschen Schutzgebiete in Afrika und der Südsee*, 1911/12, Statistischer Teil, pp. 22, 32. A larger number of civil servants (37) is given in a memo of 1912, BA-Berlin, RKA, vol. 5432, p. 105. These numbers do not include indigenous leaders who were paid a salary by the colonial state or native policemen, soldiers, and employees.

107. Gann 1987, p. 10.

108. Appiah 1992, p. 7.

109. This was codified in a series of national regulatives and laws, such as the Law on the Substitute Representation of Civil Servants from May 31, 1901.

cessful, but the Cape government cooperated by stopping arms imports via British Bechuanaland.[110] Charles Tilly's formula for the state in general is applicable to the colonial state: it exercised "clear priority *in some respects* over all other organizations within substantial territories."[111]

Colonial states often had a strong *symbolic* presence, even if this presence did not necessarily meet another Weberian criterion for stateness, "legitimacy."[112] None of the states examined made a serious effort to gain legitimacy in the eyes of its subjects, but all of them made a socio-ontological claim on locals' beliefs. The colonial state demanded acknowledgment of its existence and its distinctness from other institutions, especially indigenous ones. The state's symbolic self-construction took various forms. The effort to define a bounded territorial space already rendered the state visible, even if it involved an injury to indigenous understandings of space in those places where absolute private property in land was unknown before the arrival of Europeans.[113] In China, where permanent political boundaries and private land ownership were well entrenched long before the colonizers arrived, the cultural affront involved the very act of carving colonies like Kiaochow out of the Chinese geobody in ways that ignored or destroyed preexisting roads and structures (see maps 4–5 and plate 9). Shandong Province contained some of the most significant Chinese national and religious sites, including the birthplace and temple of Confucius at Qufu (曲阜) and the holiest of the Daoist sacred mountains, Taishan (泰山). The Germans placed physical markers around the borders of the Kiaochow colony. These acts of resculpting settled space and containerizing state territory contributed to the colonial "state effect."[114]

Despite its institutional weakness the colonial state succeeded in liberally distributing symbols of its presence. Roads and railways brought the colonial state into remote villages and sutured territories that had been arbitrarily cobbled together. Transportation routes and hubs signaled which locations were considered most important by the colonial overlords. In Togo the simple act of posting a sign in German at the entrance to every village

110. Bochert 1980, pp. 99, 106, 133.

111. Tilly 1990.

112. For his "mature" definition of the state see M. Weber 1978, vol. 2, p. 909; [1919] 1958, p. 78.

113. See Trotha 1990.

114. On the state as "container" see Giddens 1985; Brenner 1999; Lefebvre 2003; Taylor 2003; and for Southwest Africa, Noyes 1992. On the "state effect" see Mitchell 1991. The Royal Museum for Central Africa in Tervuren, Belgium, displays a boundary stone erected in 1910 between Kisenyi (Gisenyi) in Rwanda (German East Africa) and Goma (Belgian Congo).

reminded inhabitants of the colonizers' presence and intention to stay.[115] The colonial state in Togo created a network of district "stations" and mandated the creation of a network of rudimentary shelters, spaced at one-day intervals throughout the country, for traveling German officials. Local inhabitants were required to keep these shelters clean.[116] The annual birthday celebrations for the German kaiser that were held in all of the German colonies arranged the subject populations around the figure of the emperor, as in the infamous cover illustration from the German colonial newspaper *Kolonie und Heimat* captioned "The people of the German colonies pay homage to the kaiser" (fig. 1.2). Legalism was another crucial component of the colonial state's self-elicitation. This involved drawing up treaties, writing legal codes, appointing judges, delegating judicial power to selected indigenous figures, and holding court hearings in the most remote corners of the land. Currency and postage stamps were issued bearing the name and symbols of the colony. Colonial space was permeated with signifiers of modern stateness and foreign sovereignty. Some of the larger colonial towns, including Windhoek, Swakopmund, and Lüderitzbucht in Southwest Africa, Apia in Samoa, and Qingdao, were physically reconfigured and outfitted with a modern infrastructure of roads, sewers, telephones, and the like. Each colonial state tended to become an independent reality in the eyes of its subjects, settlers, and administrators.

Naturally we cannot assume that all colonized subjects were prepared to read these state signifiers in the way they were intended. John Iliffe's discussion of the dances performed in German East Africa on the occasion of the kaiser's birthday celebrations underscores this point: "One circle performed *robata*, a dance from the north-east which imitated the actions of decorticating and bailing sisal. Another danced *bom*—from the Swahili *bombom* for a cannon or machine-gun—which was doubtless one of the many dances imitating German military drill."[117] One visitor gave an account of Samoans performing a night dance that mimicked and mocked the visit of a German naval officer to a native village.[118] The state's ability to project itself was also limited by the minimal levels of investment in many of the colonies. When Heinrich Goering landed in Southwest Africa in May 1885

---

115. Sebald 1988, p. 207.

116. Trotha 1994, p. 123; Sebald 1988, p. 206. Von Trotha 1990 extrapolates from the German West African experience, calling the "station" *the* "original unit of the colonial state." Colonial states actually grew out of different sorts of institutions, ranging from mission stations—in Southwest Africa, for example—to mercantile settlements, as in Samoa.

117. Iliffe 1979, p. 238.

118. Churchill 1902, p. 76.

FIGURE I.2   *The People of the German Colonies Pay Homage to the Kaiser* (1913). Cover illustration from *Kolonie und Heimat,* vol. 6, no. 28, Ausgabe A.

with a single adjutant, for example, he was poorly positioned to put any sort of mark on the immense territory claimed by Germany. Ovaherero leaders effectively expelled Goering from the colony in 1888.[119] Yet it is equally remarkable that Goering had succeeded in getting most Namibian leaders to act as if the German "protection" treaties were valid before there were any German troops in the colony. At a minimum, the sheer presence of signs of alien sovereignty and the reputation of European powers led the colonized to orient their own activities toward the foreigners' presence and their obvious intention to stay. By acquiescing at this minimal level and by continuing to participate in daily interactions within the new colonial

119. Esterhuyse 1968, p. 138.

space rather than assaulting it frontally, or exiting from it, nominally colonized people helped to will the colony into existence.

At the opposite pole from theorists who deny the stateness of colonial regimes are those who suggest that *all* states or states in formation are somehow colonial in nature. The creation of ancient, medieval, and early modern states involved the annexation of culturally distinct regions by a core power. Some historians have therefore described these states, as well as crusading states and the expanding states of the nineteenth century, as colonial.[120] Historian Eugen Weber argued that French statesmen at the beginning of the Third Republic viewed the mass of Frenchmen as uncivilized wildmen, even as a different race, which contrasted unfavorably with colonized peoples in North Africa and the New World. French Continental state making, even in the nineteenth century, therefore seemed to be a sort of colonialism.[121]

Against this inflation of the concept of colonialism, we should keep in mind the specific ways in which modern invaders justified *to themselves* their subjugation of the colonized. Partha Chatterjee has convincingly argued that the assumption of the essential difference and incorrigible inferiority of the subject population is structurally inherent in the modern colonial state. Barriers are erected against recognizing the colonized as civilizational or human equals. Along with the seizure of sovereignty by a foreign power, this so-called rule of difference is a defining characteristic of modern colonialism. Modern colonial states were permeated by the assumption of an unbridgeable difference between themselves and their subjects and of the ineradicable inferiority of the colonized.[122] The rule of difference explains why "assimilation taken to its extreme meant, quite simply, the ending of colonialism," as Sartre commented.[123]

120. See Given 1990, p. 251; Bartlett 1993; and the forthcoming dissertations by Lenny Ureña (University of Michigan) on late-nineteenth-century Germany's colonial treatment of its eastern Prussian provinces and by Markus Roth (Bochum) on the General Government of Nazi-occupied Poland (also Roth 2004).

121. E. Weber 1976, pp. 3, 6, 7.

122. The colonial versus noncolonial distinction is less useful for the premodern period. Feudal ruling classes tended to understand themselves in protoracialist terms as fundamentally different from their "own" peasantry, such that a homogenizing (national) identity was often the furthest thing from their minds (Foucault 1980). To the extent that early modern politics was permeated by Christianity, there was also less insistence on the inextinguishable otherness of conquered non-Christian peoples, who were amenable to conversion. Thus, the crusading Teutonic Knights of the *Deutscher Ritterorden* converted and assimilated the people they conquered in Prussia, for instance.

123. Sartre 2001, p. 46.

Chatterjee's thesis is mainly descriptive, however, and does not explain the *necessity* of a rule of difference. It seems to me that without this ubiquitous "rule"—a rule that was often bent or broken, like all other rules—modern colonial domination ran the risk of appearing arbitrary to the colonizers and to the metropolitan populations who were being asked to pay for the colonies' budget. From the mid-eighteenth century onward it became necessary in Europe to actively defend conquest, subjugation, and the establishment of conditions of permanent domination and inequality. These concerns were linked to discourses of democracy, political secularism, cultural relativism, abolitionism, and even explicit anticolonialism.[124] As Hannah Arendt wrote (exaggerating only slightly), no nation state by the nineteenth century could "try to conquer foreign peoples" "*with a clear conscience,*" much less keep foreigners in a permanent state of unequal rights, unless it could define those peoples as inherently inferior. Arguments for treating the colonized this way drew on concepts of biological race, civilizational decline, social underdevelopment, and cultural shortcomings such as the absence of "this-worldly asceticism," which was Max Weber's criterion of civilization.[125] International conventions in the sixteenth and seventeenth centuries limiting aggression had excluded the "noncivilized" states.[126] But by 1896 the governor of German Southwest Africa felt compelled to defend the *nonapplicability* of the first Geneva Convention of 1864 to colonial warfare, thereby demonstrating that the applicability of such conventions outside Europe had entered the realm of the thinkable.[127] Colonies were given euphemistic labels like "protectorate" or "mandate" (after 1919), and colonialism was disguised as an educational or civilizing mission, implying that the foreign rulers would leave as soon as they had accomplished their pedagogical task.

The rule of difference was expressed in dual structures for the governance of Europeans and "natives." Although colonial strategists frequently tried to fragment their subject populations by emphasizing internal ethnic differences, a strict dualism was usually imposed on top of this fissured population. However great the number of invented tribes, ethnicities, and races within a given colony, all of the indigenous inhabitants were typically gathered together under a common heading of tradition, custom,

124. The fact that the same period saw the rise of scientific racism and allied theories illustrates the general point about the multiaccentuality of social-cultural fields.

125. Arendt [1950] 1958, p. 126 (my emphasis). See K. Marx 1969; Mandair 2006; and Zimmerman 2006. Mosse 1985 is a pioneering treatment of modern theories of "race."

126. Schmitt [1950] 2003.

127. Leutwein to Chancellor Hohenlohe-Schillingfurst, June 8, 1896, BA-Berlin, RKA, vol. 1489, pp. 35v–36r.

backwardness, or racial inferiority, counterposed to the colonizer's modernity, rationality, development, and racial superiority. As the acting governor of German Southwest Africa wrote in a memo in 1905, the "natives" had to be treated as a "unified mass."[128] Over and above the proliferation of petty chiefdoms in a colony like German Togo or Cameroon, racial dualism was reasserted every time the chiefs from a given district were called together by the district officer for a meeting. At the banquets that were held in official headquarters the Germans sat together upstairs and the African chiefs downstairs.[129] At the so-called fraternization parties that took place at the end of British rule in India, according to the journalist Gupta in Paul Scott's novel *Six Days in Marapore*, "at one end of the lawn there will be gathered the representatives of the Raj, and at the other those of us who have passed some test of whose nature we are not aware but the reward for which is the invitation to the party. . . . Then, at a signal, perhaps that of a raised eyebrow from the Sahib to his Memsahib, the Raj will cross the lawn *en bloc* and they will then—I am thinking the expression is *mingle*. . . . After the mingling has gone on for, say, half-an-hour . . . the Raj will return across the lawn."[130] Even in the colonies that relied most heavily on strategies of divide and conquer, indirect rule, and enforced tribalism, the *legal system* revealed an overarching binarism. An imported, unified German legal code applied to all Europeans and others defined as "foreigners" or "whites" and existed alongside one or more systems of customary or newly minted "native" law.[131] Non-Europeans who were integrated into the society of the colonizers, such as Japanese businessmen in Asia and the Pacific or Samoans who married Europeans, were usually lumped into the "foreigner" or "white" category rather than being fitted into some third, in-between status. Colonial cities bore the physical stamp of this binary logic, even though tribal or religious distinctions were sometimes allowed to complicate this pattern. The capitals of German East Africa, Cameroon, and Togo were all characterized by residential segregation and distinct building styles and

128. Thus, when a white settler was in debt to a member of one native group but was owed something by a member of another, he could pass his debt on to the second (Tecklenburg to RKA, July 17, 1905, BA-Berlin, RKA, vol. 1212, pp. 34r–v).

129. Trotha 1994, p. 301.

130. P. Scott [1953] 2005, pp. 57–58.

131. German colonial law typically distinguished between natives, who were usually defined in racial terms, and nonnatives, a category that included groups like the Christian Goanese in German East Africa, "half-castes" in early German Samoa (Salesa 1997; Wareham 2002, chap. 5), and the Japanese in all German colonies.

codes for the European and non-European districts.[132] No matter how many distinct "tribes" were said to exist in the hinterlands of German East Africa, all of the Africans were clustered in the same neighborhoods in the capital city of Dar-es-Salaam. A 1911 regulation in Swakopmund required natives "to leave the sidewalk when they encountered a European."[133] The planners of German Qingdao designed separate neighborhoods for the Chinese middle-class and laborers, but none of the Chinese were allowed to live in the European quarter except for servants. Combined with the assault on native sovereignty, these practices of legal and institutional dualism defined the colonizer and colonized as opposing blocs. Although recent scholarship on colonial societies has focused on the "fragile and porous character of the binary identities . . . on which the colonial order depended," the state's continual efforts to reinforce this simplifying logic set the parameters for much activity in the colony.[134]

In contrast to this colonial pattern, modern *noncolonial* states usually try to turn their conquered and subjected internal Others into assimilated national subjects. The Third Republic's Parisian elites may well have regarded the French peasantry as savages, but Eugen Weber's book is concerned precisely with efforts to turn those "savages" into Frenchmen. By contrast, even those colonized subjects who came to believe that they were fully French were almost never treated as equals, as French, by their colonizers.[135] The fact that individual colonial subjects could sometimes move into the colonizer category through marriage, education, or economic success does not gainsay the argument for an overarching binarism. Or rather, once the trickle of isolated individuals across the colonizer-colonized boundary becomes a flood, the political situation is already becoming noncolonial. Colonial rule is perfectly compatible with partial or pseudoassimilation and with forms of acculturation that retain indelible signs of ascriptive inferiority, as in the German treatment of the Ovaherero after 1904 as abject partial copies of their colonizers. British-occupied Ireland in the nineteenth century seems to be more colonial under this definition than, say, the former East German provinces (*Bundesländer*) in postunification Germany. Even if many East Germans experienced unification as a "colonial" takeover, their

132. Sometimes in the African colonies there were additional districts for Indian, Lebanese, or Hausa traders. The residential distinctions among non-European groups, such as the separate Hausa quarters in Lomé and other West African colonial cities, were often holdovers from the precolonial era.

133. Gaydish 2001, p. 68.

134. The quote is from Saada 2002, p. 363.

135. Fanon [1952] 1967; also Memmi [1965] 1991.

legal rights immediately became almost identical to those of former West Germans.[136]

Colonial and noncolonial forms of rule are the extreme poles on a fluid continuum. Some colonial states moved toward the noncolonial form by violating one of the two criteria—foreign sovereignty or the politics of enforced hierarchical difference. Indeed, some colonial states shared power with locals or moved toward legal and social equality.[137] Kiaochow toward the end of the German colonial period saw a transition toward some sort of noncolonial partnership. In 1913 the Germans "voluntarily" renounced their right to build any more railways in Shandong Province, and in August 1914, after war had broken out in Europe but before the Japanese had conquered Qingdao, the Germans offered to return Kiaochow to China in exchange for "compensation."[138] Sometimes the period of foreign sovereignty was defined from the start as brief, as in U.S.-occupied Iraq in 2003.

In sum, the modern colonial state was a permanently operating, coercion-wielding apparatus exercising effective sovereignty—"clear priority over all other organizations" with respect to law and policymaking—within a substantial territory. Like other states, it existed not just as apparatus but as "idea"; it inscribed its existence on the landscape, minds, and bodies; it broadcast its presence through legal texts and political rituals. Compared to metropolitan states, the colonial form often achieved a greater degree of independence from dominant interests in "civil society"—in this case, from the interests of the local European colonials. Its independence from the metropolitan state was also typically greater than that of regional and municipal governments within the metropole. The modern colonial state is defined by (1) foreign sovereignty and (2) state institutions and practices that define, express, and reinforce a cultural difference and fundamental inferiority of the territorial natives. This second definitional criterion is linked to the colonial state's emphasis on native policy, to which I will now turn.

136. Put differently, a Samoan or Cameroonian could never have become governor of German Samoa, much less German chancellor, during the colonial era, but a former East German became chancellor of the Federal Republic in 2005. German unification recalls familiar processes of state expansion via incorporation of new territories, processes that may be imperial but are not colonial. For the relations among the terms *empire, imperialism,* and *colonialism* see Steinmetz 2005e. Present-day uses of the term *colonialism* frequently draw on an older stock of meanings having to do with tilling the soil and settling on reclaimed agricultural lands.

137. See, for example, Belmessous 2005 on an early modern case of assimilationism in French Canada.

138. Kirby 1984, p. 12. French colonialism in Africa was also beginning to shift away from a politics of difference after World War II, and it was partly for this reason that it could not sustain itself as colonialism; see F. Cooper 1996; and Wilder 2005.

Precolonial Mimicry and the Centrality of Native Policy

Native policy encompasses the core activities that differentiate the modern colonial state from other state forms. The masthead of a German colonial journal called *Die deutschen Kolonien* (The German Colonies) proclaimed as its "motto" that "colonial policy is, above all, native policy."[139] Although native policy is a political and folk category (and perhaps a racist one), it can also be defined *analytically* as the site at which the colonial state identifies, produces, and reinforces the alterity that is required by the rule of hierarchical difference. Because of the uncertainties and difficulties for the colonial state in this process, due especially to the code-switching abilities of the colonized and their resistance to being defined by the outsider, native policy came to be concerned specifically with the *stabilization* of the culture, subjectivity, and activities of the colonized on the basis of clear definitions.[140]

By projecting Homi Bhabha's concept of colonial "mimicry" backward into the *pre*colonial context we can see why modern colonizers were compelled to look for ways to stabilize their new subjects from the moment they laid claim to a foreign territory. Bhabha situates the condition he calls mimicry within colonial and postcolonial settings.[141] But mimicry was also a precolonial paradox that confronted would-be colonizers, at least in the modern period, from the later eighteenth century onward. The colonialisms that emerged from the scramble for Africa and the Pacific in the last third of the nineteenth century confronted populations that had already been exposed to Europeans for decades and even for centuries.[142] Even for the most "remote" cultures it was nearly impossible to remain untouched and unobserved by the legions of restless missionaries, explorers, traders, and pioneer ethnologists who were released by the expanding Euro-American capitalist core. By the time the Berlin West Africa Conference ratified Germany's entry into the colonial game, many of the people in Africa, Oceania, and Asia who were destined to become German subjects were already familiar with Europeans and sometimes even with Germans. The Namibian Ovaherero, Khoikhoi, and Rehobothers had interacted with Rhenish missionaries for decades prior to the hoisting of the German flag; Samoans had gotten to

139. See *Die deutschen Kolonien* 1 (1, 1902): 1.

140. By contrast, noncolonial imperialist powers sometimes pursue *destablization* for its own sake; see T. Mitchell 2002 for an example of this in American foreign policy.

141. See Bhabha 1994a, 1994b, 1994c.

142. Needless to say, this prior familiarization with Europeans was even more pronounced in the case of the former Ottoman territories of the Middle East that became European colonies after World War I.

know the managers of the German Godeffroy firm after 1860 and various German consuls and would-be rulers starting in 1879; and the Chinese residents of Shandong Province had encountered German missionaries from the Societas Verbi Divini since the 1880s.[143] The victims of modern colonial conquest were rarely as mistaken about the identity of their Western conquerors as the Aztec ruler Montezuma.[144] In an effort to ward off colonial takeover, societies in Africa, Asia, and the Pacific developed new concepts of statehood and national sovereignty, adopted Western religious practices and beliefs, studied European military strategies and weapons, and created written languages.[145] Many non-Westerners learned to move fluidly between indigenous and European cultural codes. As Marshall Sahlins writes, in the era "before the flag" "western commodities and even persons could be encompassed within [the] 'development schemes'" of traditional cultures.[146]

European conquerors and their candidates for subjection related differently to this condition of precolonial familiarity with the invading culture. The would-be rulers tended to view partially "Westernized" people as threateningly ambiguous, shifting between similarity and strangeness. One German specialist on Southwest Africa warned that "the Hottentot knows us better than we know him."[147] Nineteenth-century European depictions of not-yet-colonized Africans, Asians, and Pacific islanders referred frequently to a putative disjuncture between essence and appearance, words

143. Spanish Franciscan missionaries had worked in Shandong during the eighteenth century; see Willeke 1947; and Maas 1932.

144. See Todorov 1984. Whether or not Todorov is correct about the role of literacy in the fall of the Aztecs, they failed to recognize Cortés as a conquistador rather than the Aztec god Quetzalcoatl. Captain Cook's reception at Hawai'i does not refute the idea that modern colonial subjects are rarely confused about the identity of their conquerers. Even if Cook and the sailors of the *Resolution* and *Discovery* were misidentified by the Hawai'ians (Sahlins 1981), the Hawai'ians had plenty of time to get to know Europeans and Americans and their commodities before they were formally colonized. A significant amount of time elapsed between first contact and colonial annexation in all of the Pacific islands. See Linnekin 1991a for a comparison between Hawai'i and Samoa that emphasizes the lasting impact of "first contact."

145. For Africa, see Bley 1995; Samoans' defensive deployment of practices of kingship and Christianity are discussed in chaps. 4 and 5. King Njoya of Bamum in German Cameroon created a written language starting around 1895, wrote a history of the kingdom, and created forty-seven schools to teach the Bamum syllabary, and "in 1913 he commissioned a member of his court to prepare a printing press using it." Although this development occurred during the German colonial period, it was clearly an effort on Njoya's part to expand his independence. See "Bamum," *Encyclopaedia Britannica Online*, http://search.eb.com.proxy.lib.umich.edu/eb/article-9012088 (accessed September 16, 2005); Geary 1988.

146. Sahlins 1993, pp. 16–17.

147. Schultze 1907, p. 335.

and deeds, ostensible and hidden meanings. The recurrent complaints by European merchants and missionaries about lying, cheating, dissimulation, and mimicry index the perceived chasm between a partly Westernized "exterior" and a recalcitrant and unfathomable "interior." The act of lying was made out to be an intrinsic part of Samoan culture while truth telling was said to be "un-Samoan."[148] Sinophobic commentators returned incessantly to the tropes of Chinese "cunning," "forked-tonguedness" (*Doppelzüngigkeit*), and double-dealing. Chinese society was allegedly more concerned with saving "face" than with telling the truth.[149] The South African Khoikhoi were described in the nineteenth century as being "cultivated in deceit" and afflicted by a disturbing "talent for mimicry."[150]

Colonial states were "contact zones," fields of interaction between radically different cultures.[151] Europeans perceived the ability of the colonized to move suddenly and strategically between positions of cultural similarity and stark difference as a menace to colonial hegemony. The overarching goal of native policy, therefore, was to arrest the mobility of the colonized within this slippery cultural space, to put an end to the maddening oscillation between local and European signifying systems. Native policy was an attempt to identify a uniform cultural essence beneath the shimmering surface of indigenous practice and to restrict the colonized to this unitary identity. Native policy can thus be defined as any official intervention directed toward stabilizing a colonized group around a particular definition of its culture, character, and behavior.[152]

148. Werner von Bülow, "Die Verwaltung der Landgemeinden in Deutsch-Samoa," NZNA ACGA XVII A 1, vol. 3, p. 32; also NZNA AGCA XVII A 1, pt. 3, p. 32. According to a very recent study of Samoa, "one of the first things a stranger notices about Sāmoans is they may not mean what they say" (Love 1991, p. 1).

149. See BA-MA-Freiburg, Nachlass Diederichs, vol. 24, p. 39; chap. 8; and, above all, Anson [1748] 1974; and Hevia 1992, p. 316, for a discussion of the European theory of the Chinese understanding of "face."

150. "German South-West Africa," *Owl*, November 18, 1904, p. 11; second quote from Friedrich Müller 1873, p. 79.

151. On the concept of the (pre)colonial contact zone see Pratt 1992.

152. It is not relevant to this definition whether colonizers actually used the phrases *native policy, politique indigène,* or *Eingeborenenpolitik*. The core problem for the modern colonial state—uncontrollable code switching by the subject population—was identified by Europeans before this terminology emerged. It would be a nominalist methodological mistake to proscribe the use of concepts that were not available to the historical actors in question. Moreover, the concept did eventually emerge in situ. Social science concepts typically ply the waters between everyday and conceptual language; see Bourdieu, Chamboredon, and Passeron [1968] 1991.

Native policy was not just a program of enforced cultural essentialism but was also premised on the inferiority of the governed. Complete identity and genuine assimilation were incompatible with the rule of difference. Colonial programs ostensibly geared toward assimilation were usually organized around a second-class or degraded version of likeness. Identity with the colonizers was held out as a deferred promise. At the same time, colonial rulers could not tolerate incommensurable difference, which eluded their understanding and control. Even in the most hands-off versions of indirect rule based on "tradition" and "customary law" the colonized were expected to present an unchanging, recognizable version of their own culture. In order to stabilize the subject culture it had to be translated, codified. Colonizers needed to find some basis of agreement with indigenous leaders about cultural categories. Native policy attempted to lock the colonized into a position located somewhere along the spectrum running from absolute difference to complete identity. Between these extremes there was a wide range of possible policy approaches. The colonized could be framed as an earlier version of one's own culture, as in social-evolutionary perspectives,[153] or as children; as a degenerate or fallen civilization; or as permanently inferior, a suggestion that was backed by theories of polygenesis and scientific racism.[154]

Colonial massacre marks another boundary condition on native policy. For Joseph Conrad, massacre was not just the most extreme face of colonialism, but its essence.[155] Sartre claimed that colonialism was a contradictory system that "wills simultaneously the death and the multiplication of its victims."[156] But the German governor Theodor Leutwein protested General von Trotha's 1904 annihilation order with the argument that colonialism without the colonized was a contradiction in terms. Another contemporary emphasized the incongruity between Southwest African settlers' desire to exterminate the Africans and their complaints about labor shortages, writing, "As long as there are only a few white 'masters' in the land—and this situation will last for a long time—and as long as the European, even if he was only a serf back home—refuses all menial labor as unsuited for a member of the master race, we will be unable to forgo the colored laborer."[157] As Leutwein had warned, the postwar colonial economy struggled for a decade

153. E.g., J. Forster [1778] 1996; Fabian 1983.

154. See Stocking 1987.

155. Trotha 1994, p. 42. On colonial massacre as a general category see Lindquvist 1996; Cocker 1998; Palmer 2000; and Le Cour Grandmaison 2005.

156. Sartre quoted in Memmi [1965] 1991, p. xxvii.

157. Spectator Germanicus 1913, p. 251. For a similar formulation by a more recent historian see Eckert 2003, p. 234.

with severe labor shortages.[158] Colonialism may make massacre more likely, but it does not follow that massacre is the inevitable telos of colonialism.

Toward an Explanation: The Colonial State as a Social Field

We can now return to the empirical conundrum presented by the three German colonies. On the eve of colonial annexation, Southwest Africa seemed less hospitable to European settlement and less economically promising than Samoa, but it was transformed into the main target of German colonial settlement.[159] The German government in Samoa consistently repelled settler demands and worked to fortify its chosen version of traditional native culture. The number of foreign residents in Samoa actually fell from about 800 to 347 during the first two years of German rule and barely rose between 1902 and 1912.[160] In Samoa the indigenous population was handled mildly, while Southwest Africa became the stereotypical settler colony, marked by displacement, ethnocide, and genocide. This difference seems explicable at first glance in terms of divergent precolonial representations of Samoans and Southwest Africans, but the Kiaochow case undermines the straightforward "devil's handwriting" explanation. Precolonial German representations of the Chinese were heterogeneous, and colonial policy in Qingdao was mercurial. There was no simple circuit running from "travelers' tales" to colonialism.

To make sense of this historical puzzle we need to theorize the colonial state as a *field* and to situate it in relation to the metropolitan field of power. In addition to offering the tools for constructing a theoretical account of the colonial field of power, Bourdieu's framework explains why ethnographic discourse is usually multivocal, pace Said. Social fields are organized around differences—differences of perception and practice. It is difficult to imagine what sorts of materials actors could use in their efforts to carve out

---

158. Other sources of labor were available, from Ovamboland in the north and from the British Cape Colony, requiring the state to develop new forms of native policy. But these alternate sources proved unsatisfactory to many employers in the colony; see *Jahresbericht der Windhuker Handelskammer* (1913).

159. So was the difference due to a German colonial emphasis on emigration and settlement, as W. Smith (1978) argued? Smith's argument that German colonialism was driven by a desire for outlets for settlement has not stood the test of historical scrutiny. It cannot explain why Samoa and the South Sea islands did not become sites of settlement after 1900, or why many German colonial officials disliked and disadvantaged settlers.

160. There were 400–800 foreigners in Samoa in 1900 (NZNA AGCA, "Excerpt from Annual Report, 1900–1901," G.S.A. IV 5.a, p. 21) and 347 in 1902 (*Die deutschen Schutzgebiete in Afrika und der Südsee*, 1911/12, Statistischer Teil, p. 7); see note 71.

hierarchies of cultural distinction if they were faced with cultural formations as flat and uniform as Saidian "Orientalism." According to Said, there
were diverse "idioms" at the surface of Orientalist discourse but a homogeneous "layer of doctrine about the Orient" underneath, "*converging* upon . . .
essential aspects of the Orient."[161] If this were true, Orientalism would not
have been able to organize itself around differences of status distinction, as
a hierarchical field. But social theorists and researchers have shown that
heterogeneity and stratification complicate even the most apparently unstri-
ated discursive formations.[162]

Writers inspired by Mikhail Bakhtin/Valentin Volosinov look for associations between particular voices or "accents" within a linguistic formation and specific social groups or classes.[163] Once we locate ethnographic
discourse within social fields, our attention is drawn to these sorts of fili-
ations between particular tropes or ways of speaking and specific social
groups. European discourse on the Southwest African Ovaherero was indeed monotonously repetitive, so much so that colonizers were unable to
deploy its tropes against one another in demanding recognition of their superior ethnographic taste. But portrayals of the Namibian Ovaherero were
located at a univocal extreme. Most ethnographic formations, including the
ones concerned with Samoa and China, were much more multivocal.

The linkages between ethnographic visions and social divisions are contingent and historically variable. In the chapters that follow I will trace
various examples of the forging and reforging of linkages between European social classes and representations of non-European cultures. Between
the sixteenth and mid-eighteenth centuries, for example, Sinophilia was
dominant in Europe and was associated with the educated middle classes
and Jesuit missionaries, while Sinophobia was correlated with the merchant
capitalists operating along the Chinese coast. In the second half of the eighteenth century, however, the educated middle classes began to lose their affinity for Sinophilia and to gravitate toward the "merchant" view of China.
This is evident in the writings of Montesquieu, Herder, Cornelius de Pauw,
Hegel, and even Karl Marx, all of whom paraphrase or quote directly from
the merchant accounts. At the end of the nineteenth century Sinophobia
again became less attractive for educated middle-class Europeans, many of
whom began to realign themselves with an updated version of Sinophilia.[164]

161. Said 1978, p. 203 (my emphasis).

162. Bakhtin 1981; Volosinov 1985.

163. E.g., S. Hall 1983; Bell and Gardiner 1998.

164. German examples of this neo-Sinomania include Paquet 1911, 1912; Boerschmann
1911–14; Schmitz 1924; Keyserling 1925; Hesse (see Hsia 1974); and R. Wilhelm 1926.

Thus, while ethnographic images often had a well-defined social base in any given time and place, such correlations were rooted in changing constellations of political, ideological, and economic processes rather than some omnihistorical logic of social class and its impact on mentalities.[165] The evolving connections between social divisions and ethnographic visions can be illuminated by reconstructing the social fields in which social actors expressed their contending representations of the colonized Other. These affinities reflected the dynamics of intraelite class struggle that were imported into the colonies, where they underwent patterned transformations. This transposition of metropolitan class configurations is one reason why modern colonial empires actually did vary according to the national identity of their European colonizer: dominant classes were organized differently in the European metropoles, even if all of them worked with roughly similar pan-European precolonial ethnographic discourses once in the colony. For example, the *Bildungsbürgertum* was an unusually powerful social group in imperial Germany, not simply a theoretical "class on paper."[166] The hereditary nobility had a greater political presence in Germany and Britain than in France at this time, and it was nonexistent in the United States.[167] Articulations between social location and ethnographic posture

165. There is another unspoken but necessary condition for the causal link between Orientalism and colonial policy. A particular ethnographic or Orientalist perspective could not influence colonial policy unless its bearers were represented within, or at least recognized by, the colonial administration. The colonial state was thus a determinant of its own policies. Given the undemocratic and autonomous nature of these states, those Europeans located in the colony but outside the governing apparatus were in a very weak position to influence policy.

166. See Bourdieu 1987 for the notion of "classes on paper" and Steinmetz 1992 for further elaboration of this point.

167. The formation of social classes or groups should not be understood in objectivist terms as a function of preexisting resource distributions, but neither should it be understood in subjectivist terms as entirely a product of ideological interpellations (e.g., in Laclau and Mouffe 1985). Instead, it involves "material," corporeal, ideal, and psychic dimensions. "Materialism" and "idealism" make sense only as analytical abstractions or in a purely synchronic analysis that freezes historical time. Social class, expressed as patterned practices and identifications, is indeed built upon a foundation of different sorts of "capital" (Bourdieu 1987). But the values of cultural *and* economic capital are set and reset continuously in the course of ongoing conflicts within an interactive and intersubjective social context, rather than determined in advance by material conditions. Because the present analysis begins with formations of ethnographic discourse, which appear as a "cause" of colonialism, it might seem to be privileging the "ideal" over the "material." But ethnographic discourse was itself a material process located in specific social "fields" such as Sinology or travel literature. My decision to treat ethnographic discourse as a given rather than tracing its formation is a heuristic choice, since my main goal is explaining native policy. As Hedström and Swedberg observe, "Faced with a world consisting of causal histories of nearly infinite length, in prac-

varied partly in line with these metropolitan arrangements of dominant social classes and groups.

But what is a field? It is only possible to speak of social practices and perceptions as arranging themselves into a patterned social field when all of the "practitioners" recognize the same stakes of competition and the same criteria of distinction or signs of honor. A precondition for the existence of a field is that all social actors share the same *illusio,* that they all perceive the same perceptions (tastes) and practices as markers of field-specific cultural capital. It is this mutuality of perception, this web of mutual recognition (*erkennen* and *wiedererkennen*) of status differences, which transforms cultural capital into symbolic capital.[168] Recognition of hierarchies of distinction may not be fully conscious, and it may be accompanied by a defiant embrace of one's own dominated taste, that is, by a "taste for necessity" or *amor fati,* a love of ones fate. The field should best be thought of as a variable and not as an either-or condition. Spheres of activity in which participants disagree about what counts as distinguished are less fieldlike than others.

Was the colonial state characterized by common perceptions of distinction and stakes of conflict? German colonial administrators did in fact compete for a specific form of cultural distinction within the ambit of the colonial state, and this struggle guided each individual toward particular kinds of native policy. More specifically, officials within the colonial state competed for recognition of their *ethnographic acuity,* their discernment in understanding "natives." Colonial officials demanded recognition from one another of their ethnographic perceptiveness. Given the colonial state's inbuilt emphasis on finding a way to stabilize native culture, it is clear why this particular talent would be so highly valued. Every official was compelled by the force of the situation to develop an ethnographic vision, however rudimentary, in order to develop a course of action and to legitimate his presence as a foreign conqueror. The ability to understand the natives, to judge their character and gauge their responses, became a widely recognized criterion of value among members of the colonial elite. Ethnographic acuity was structurally comparable to notions of good taste in art, a "musical ear" in classical music, or "soul" in popular American music. This does not mean that the dominant actors in the colonial state field

---

tice we can only hope to provide information on their most recent history" (1998, pp. 12–14). A separate analysis that took ethnographic discourse as its central object would need to reconstruct precolonial contact zones.

168. Bourdieu 1985. I discuss the role of recognition in the Bourdieuian concept of symbolic capital in Steinmetz 2006b.

actually had a superior grasp of the colonized; ethnographic perceptions and representations were wielded as markers of distinction regardless of their fictiveness, offensiveness, or even absurdity.

Control of the field of the state in Wilhelmine Germany was precariously balanced between three elite classes or class fractions, each of them rooted in a different social source of status: the modern economic bourgeoisie, based in wealth and property; the nobility, based in titles and land; and the middle-class intelligentsia or *Bildungsbürgertum,* based in educational culture. Each group struggled to impose its definition of the "dominant principle of domination."[169] Discussions of so-called German exceptionalism have tried to determine which of these social elites was *generally* dominant within the imperial German state. In fact, no particular source of capital was all-powerful. Urban government was dominated by the liberal bourgeoisie and its values. The aristocracy remained well entrenched in the army and the diplomatic corps. Middle-class intellectuals prevailed in most of the cultural fields, and they were also well represented in the overseas colonial administrations. This was partly because these posts were considered relatively unimportant, but in some instances middle-class "academics" were preferred because of the emphasis on understanding foreign cultures.[170] This does not mean that *Bildungsbürger* were always able to dominate the colonial elite class struggle. Compelling claims to "native expertise" could also be made by noblemen, military officers, settlers, and even capitalists. But university-trained philologists or lawyers were sometimes able to attain a level of political power in the colonial states that was inaccessible to their class in metropolitan national politics.

The colonial stage thus became an exaggerated version of imperial Germany's three-way intraelite class struggle. Given the structural pressures that pointed to ethnographic sagacity as the common coin of the colonial state field, officials were virtually compelled to emphasize the excellence of their understanding of indigenous ways. As a result, each group selected tropes and narratives from the ethnographic archive that promised to showcase its socially constructed strengths, its existing holdings of capital. Thus, university-educated colonial officials tended to emphasize interpretations

169. Bourdieu [1989] 1996, p. 376.

170. For the foundational critique of the thesis of German exceptionalism, see Blackbourn and Eley 1985; for its genealogy see Steinmetz 1997. I discuss the power of the Wilhelmine bourgeoisie in municipal politics in Steinmetz 1993; for class relations inside the army see Craig 1955, p. 235; on class and the German diplomatic service see Philippi 1985, p. 63; and Preradovich 1955.

of the colonized that relied on hermeneutic and linguistic skills and that were distant from motives of money and violent military domination, which they dismissed as undignified and unrefined. Many of the officials who took this broadly "hermeneutic" approach had been trained as Orientalists, Sanskritists, philologists, translators, or lawyers.[171] Career military men tended to describe the colonized using martial categories, and their preferred native policies emphasized the arts of coercive command, which was the traditional specialty of the German nobility. Nonetheless, they too claimed a superior grasp of the natives. As General Lothar von Trotha wrote, "My *exact knowledge* of so many central African tribes, Bantu and other, has always demonstrated to me with absolute necessity that the Negro never bows to treaties but only to raw violence."[172] This suggests that von Trotha was swimming in the same social waters as his more "humanistic" opponents, seeking recognition in the same register. Settlers and investors typically wanted to transform the colonized into interchangeable laborers or versions of *Homo economicus* and were therefore attuned to evaluative categories like idleness and usefulness. Although they were relatively uninterested in extant indigenous culture, they too claimed insight into it.[173]

171. The ethnographic tendencies of missionaries were extremely heterogeneous. Some show evidence of a broadly hermeneutic approach, but they were usually discouraged from being curious about non-Christian cultures except where it would facilitate their educative campaigns and help diagnose barriers to conversion (Gewald 1998b, p. 140). Todorov (1984) argued that missionaries like Las Casas were poor ethnographers because they saw all humans as potential Christians. This applies to a subset of the missionaries discussed in this book. Most of the Rhenish missionaries were indeed poor ethnographers, but this was not necessarily because they sympathized with the Ovaherero. The more alert missionaries, like Gottlieb Viehe, Philipp Diehl, and Jakob Irle, provided invaluable historical information on Ovaherero culture, even if one has to disentangle the useful parts of their writing from stereotypical formulas. Missionary Viehe (1879, p. 372) wrote that most Europeans were too impatient to find out about Ovaherero customs and assumed that native practices were simply random (*Willkur*), whereas in fact custom was "regulated in the smallest details, and when you ask several Hereros they will give you the same details in almost the same words." This passage is interesting not just for its precocious anthropological "structuralism" but also because it demonstrates that missionaries were themselves involved in making claims to ethnographic acuity. Missionaries like Richard Wilhelm in China (see chap. 7) immersed themselves in the local culture for quite different reasons, but they also tended to frame their pronouncements in terms of ethnographic expertise.

172. Von Trotha to Schlieffen, October 4, 1904, BA-Berlin, RKA, vol. 2089, p. 5v (my emphasis).

173. See, for example, the report "Education of Samoans to Industriousness," by Herr A. Kraus, a member of the opposition to Governor Solf in Samoa, in BA-Berlin, RKA, vol. 3065, pp. 174ff.

Of course, there were countless exceptions to these sociological regularities. Ethnographic preferences were not stamped like number plates on the backs of European actors, even within a particular historical and geographic context. The peculiar sense that an individual made of her personal social position and class dilemma could lead her away from what might have been the more strategically astute approach in terms of the schematics of symbolic capital. Many colonizers were located in *contradictory* class positions. Others were more interested in *changing* their class status than in capitalizing on their current one. The German writer and traveler Count Hermann von Keyserling enthused about Asia and China in ways that were more typical of the intellectuals and artists with whom Keyserling associated in the "School of Wisdom" that he created in Darmstadt after the war—men like Rabindranath Tagore, Thomas Mann, Carl Jung, Leo Baeck, Leo Frobenius, and Alfred Adler—than of his aristocratic class of birth.[174] Keyserling described China as possessing an ideal form of government and advanced aesthetic sensibilities.[175] Richard Wilhelm introduced Keyserling to his own circle in Qingdao, the Confucius Society, and wrote that his "old men of Qingdao" were "not a little impressed" with Keyserling, who was "very earnest about learning something of Chinese culture."[176] But Keyserling had transformed himself, as he later wrote, from a dueling member of the fraternity at the University at Dorpat (Tartu) into an "aesthete,"[177] rather than easing into the role of state official to which he was destined as a member of the Courland aristocracy with family connections to the upper reaches of the German nobility. An opposing example is the middle-class professor Max Weber, who held sociologically anomalous views of China. Weber argued that Confucianism was oriented toward "adjustment to the world" rather than "rational transformation of the world," a cultural handicap preventing rational capitalism from emerging in China.[178] This argument closely followed the Sinophobia that was more typical of German military and business elites than of the *Bildungsbürgertum*, but it corresponded to Weber's racism with respect to

174. Boyer 1979, pp. 142-49, 545; Gahlings 1992, pp. 89-96; 2000. Georg Lukács attacked Tagore as a colonial apologist in 1922 in a review in *Die rote Fahne;* Thomas Mann disparaged Tagore as effeminate (Kämpchen 1999).

175. Keyserling enthused about the writer Ku Hung-Ming (see chap. 7) as "a man of such wit and such a fiery temperament that I am sometimes reminded of a Latin" (1925, vol. 2, pp. 106-7).

176. R. Wilhelm 1928, p. 183.

177. Keyersling 1926, p. 32; Boyer 1979, chap. 1.

178. M. Weber 1964, pp. 235, 242.

Poles.[179] In many biographies, however, there were pervasive associations between social class and ethnographic posture.[180]

Attending to social "distinction strategies" takes us part of the way toward understanding how colonial officials selected from a preexisting array of ethnographic and policy options. Native policymaking was directed not only toward the colonized but was intended to signal something to other Germans, both at home and in the colony. The fields of ethnographic perception and overseas colonial rule were not sweepingly dominated by any of the elite class fractions vying for power in states Germany. Because of the unsettled nature of the German colonial state field and the German "field of power" more generally, such struggles were pervasive and intense.

Postcolonial theorists have argued that metropolitan dynamics are imported into the colony, and vice versa.[181] Contrary to the "mirror" of Europe that some used as a description of overseas colonies,[182] however, the colonizers' social field was not a simple replica, or even a reversed mirror image, of the metropolitan one. Nor was the overseas colonial realm a garbage can for the detritus of elite European society. The colonial state field, unlike

179. Zimmerman 2006.

180. Settlers constituted the other European social group in the German colonies, but they were rarely able to do more than inflect or comment on existing native policies. Nonetheless, it is important that they too framed their policy preferences in terms of their superior "knowledge of the native" (see, e.g., Deeken 1901; Gordon 1998).

181. The German overseas colonial empire was too small and short lived to decisively shape "metropolitan" society or culture in the Kaiserreich in the ways usually discussed by colonial and postcolonial theorists (Kiernan 1980; Said 1993; Spivak 1988; Ashcroft, Griffiths, and Tiffin 1989; McClintock 1995). The significant German literary texts from this period that are structured by the colonial margin, such as Gustav Freytag's *Soll und Haben* (1855), Wilhelm Raabe's *Stopfkuchen* (1891), and Theodor Fontane's *Effi Briest* (1895) integrate a more generic *pan-European* colonial mentality or culture with metropolitan German themes. Writers from the Kaiserreich who *were* explicitly oriented toward German colonies, such as Frieda von Bülow (see Wildenthal 2001) and Elisabeth von Heyking (see chap. 6), are less convincing examples of the argument that the *canonical core* of European culture is constituted by the imperial margin. Most of the writers discussed by Noyes (1992), for example, were virtually unknown in Germany during the colonial era and never became part of the German canon. Some trivial German colonial literature was extremely popular, of course, including the novels of Friedrich Gerstäcker, Karl May, Gustav Frenssen, and Hans Grimm, but their texts were partly constituted vis-à-vis a pan-European imperial outside, rather than a specifically German one. Indeed, not a single novel by Gerstäcker or May is concerned with a *German* colony. The only German colony that significantly influenced metropolitan German culture was Southwest Africa.

182. E.g., Kiernan 1980; and Cannadine 2001.

the metropolitan one, was compelled to focus on native policy, and this placed a premium on claims to ethnographic acuity. This in turn enhanced the power of the educated middle class, or *Bildungsbürgertum,* which could make a reasonable claim to be best suited for penetrating the world of the colonized. Thus, a solidly middle-class governor like Wilhelm Solf, a trained Sanskritist and lawyer, could describe a group of discontented settlers in Samoa as being too uneducated to "find their way into" (sich hineinfinden) the Samoans' peculiar "logic" and "foreign ways of thought."[183] Sinologist Otto Franke, who was involved at two decisive moments in policymaking in the Kiaochow colony, was extremely respectful of China and crossidentified strongly with Chinese mandarins. Franke disparaged Europeans who adopted the discourse of the "yellow peril" or exhibited an "artificially heightened race feeling." Franke translated during the negotiations over the leasing of Kiaochow, and his superior was the aristocratic German envoy to China, Baron Edmund von Heyking. According to Franke, von Heyking and his novelist wife, Elisabeth von Heyking, arrogantly positioned themselves "beyond good and evil" and regarded their Chinese counterparts in the Zongli Yamen (Chinese Foreign Office) as "dirty, cowardly, retarded, and disgusting."[184] Setting aside the question of the accuracy of these judgments, they throw into sharp relief the churning cultural class struggle within the German elite in the overseas imperial milieux. Because both Solf and Franke achieved major successes in their colonial settings against representatives of the ethnographic views they despised,[185] their cases illustrate the ways in which the structural peculiarities of the German colonial state could allow members of the "dominated fraction of the dominant class" to triumph against the dominant sectors. This was less true in Southwest Africa. Theodor Leutwein, an official of middling social origins, was forced out of power after a decade as governor by a representative of the old German aristocracy, General Lothar von Trotha. One reason for von Trotha's success in this epic battle was that inherited German visions of the Ovaherero were too monolithic to allow Leutwein to apply an appreciative hermeneutic approach to their culture. The monotonous negativity of Ger-

183. BA-Koblenz, Nachlass Solf, vol. 27, p. 66. Solf's social position is discussed in chap. 7, and in Hempenstall and Mochida 2005.

184. O. Franke 1911a, p. vi; 1954, p. 98. Indeed, both Baron von Heyking and his wife described their Chinese government counterparts as barely human (see chap. 6).

185. Franke's main success came while conducting negotiations with the Chinese Ministry of Education over the creation of the Qingdao German-Chinese university (see chap. 7). Against vehement resistance by Qingdao's colonial governor, Franke accepted that the Chinese would become coequal partners in running the school.

man ethnographic views was itself a function of Ovaherero resistance to being culturally penetrated, to "confessing"—but that story will not figure centrally in this book.[186]

We can often begin to understand why one strand of precolonial discourse rather than another guided colonial practice once we know who was put in charge of a given colony. As it happens, German Samoa was run by middle-class intellectuals with advanced degrees in Sanskritology and law (Erich Schultz, the second governor, was a trained lawyer). This does not mean, however, that we should actually be studying the processes by which governors were appointed rather than the ongoing creation of polices in the colonies. As noted above, the relevant sections of the Foreign Office (or, later, Colonial Office) bureaucracy in Berlin were often synchronized with the dominant views in the foreign colonies that they supervised. The specialists in the Foreign Office who appointed Solf as governor of Samoa in 1899 were oriented, like him, toward a "salvage" colonialism organized around an ethnographic discourse of noble savagery, and they knew exactly what they were getting with Solf.[187] But they could not anticipate how Solf would translate this generic vision into specific policies. It was not a foregone conclusion, for example, that Solf's liberal "hermeneutic" approach would lead him to embrace what seemed to be a jarringly racist stance on the question of mixed marriage. Moreover, officials' ethnographic postures were often transformed by interactions in the colony.

---

186. On this entire problematic of ethnographic confession see Goh 2005.

187. This is not to say that the field within the metropolitan Foreign or Colonial Office was constructed around the same stakes and forms of cultural capital as the overseas colonial state. Questions of ethnographic "taste" did surface inside the colonial and foreign service bureaucracy, and many of the same officials circulated between overseas postings and the bureaucracies in Berlin. But for the most part these metropolitan battles were carried out in a different register. The conflict over the conduct of the Ovaherero war in 1904, for example, pitted supporters of a genocidal course—the General Staff (von Schlieffen) and the kaiser himself—against the chancellor and some in the Foreign Office who advocated a more conciliatory and "colonial" course with a longer time horizon and an emphasis on native policy. But this was a struggle over broadly differing German goals for the colony, not over differing interpretations of Ovaherero character. The language of von Trotha and Leutwein, both of whom claimed superior knowledge of the "natives," did not structure these internal discussions in Berlin. Similarly, the debate over the creation of the Qingdao German-Chinese university pitted the colony's governor, Truppel, against a broad front (the Foreign Office, navy secretary, and the German envoy in Beijing), but the discussion never involved opposing interpretations of the Chinese. In debates with his metropolitan interlocutors Truppel never insisted that the Chinese were not culturally suited for treatment as equals but instead argued that treating colonial subjects as equals was contrary to colonialism. Those inside the Berlin ministries who hoped to cultivate China as an ally ignored discussions about Chinese cultural decline or civilizational greatness.

A central determinant of native policy was conflict among officials for reciprocal recognition of individual ethnographic discernment. The cultural raw materials for these battles were the formations of ethnographic discourse that had been handed down from the precolonial era.[188] The theories of Said and Bourdieu are essential for the explanation of modern colonialism. But there are two more stages in the explanation. The first one overdetermines colonizers' gravitation toward specific framings of the colonized, while the second is concerned with the reproduction and revision of native policies once they are introduced.

Symbolic and Imaginary Identifications

Both Bourdieu and Said ignore or marginalize the psychic level of analysis, which has been at the heart of Homi Bhabha's pathbreaking interventions in postcolonial theory. Said alludes to a deeper level of colonial discourse which he labels *latent* Orientalism and describes as analogous to dream-work, but he never develops this idea in any detail.[189] Bhabha draws heavily on Jacques Lacan in reconstructing the ambiguous identifications that take place across the colonizer-colonized boundary.[190] What Bhabha does not fully explain is why colonizers, in addition to rejecting fundamental cultural difference and channeling it into more palatable forms, might also *partly identify* with their subjects, that is, why they might also desire difference, even while continuing to keep it at arm's length.[191] Nor is Bhabha

188. Needless to say, these raw materials were not a neutral "toolkit." This metaphor implies that the materials contained in the "kit" are neutral in both semiotic terms (carrying denotations, but no connotations) and social terms (i.e., they are not *always already* located within intersubjective communities of speakers). The connotations of the ethnographic raw materials were already established before any individual German colonist reached for them. It is necessary to return to Wittgenstein's *Philosophical Investigations* to recover this more sociological, historical, and "structuralist" sense of the "tool" metaphor.

189. Bhabha 1994b, p. 71; Said 1978, pp. 201–25. On this psychic problematic see Fanon [1952] 1967; Bhabha 1994b, 1994c; Sieg 1998; and Macey 2000, chap. 5.

190. Bhabha suggests that colonizers are threatened by the cultural difference that they seek to contain, and that the structure of colonial mimicry resembles Freudian fetishism in both disavowing and acknowledging this difference. The colonized are therefore urged to become similar to the colonizer, but at the same time they are allowed only to become "almost the same, but not quite" (Bhabha 1994c, p. 86).

191. Cannadine (2001) suggests that British colonizers sought a "mirror" for their own grandeur in the colonies. But he fails to elaborate any theoretical account of cultural, sociological, or psychic practice and therefore does not shed light on the nature of cross-identification with the colonized. Cannadine's "mirror" trope refers to simple reflection and lacks the elements of wish-fulfillment, distortion, paranoia, and misrecognition that Lacan introduced with his analysis of the mirror stage (Lacan [1949] 1977).

interested in the ways colonizers' cross-identification might be related to colonial governance.

Although Bourdieu argued forcefully for the role of *habitus* in lending a tentative coherence to human practice, he was relatively uninterested in the psychic forces that motivate practice or generate the unity of the habitus. Bourdieu's avoidance of this area seems to reflect the overarching epistemological-ontological division of labor between psychoanalysis and the social sciences.[192] The reasons for the exorcism of the unconscious from the social sciences have been discussed elsewhere.[193] In recent years, however, a rising chorus of voices scattered across various disciplines has called for reintegrating the unconscious and psychoanalysis more generally into social theory and socioanalysis. Bourdieu's work has been justly celebrated for breaking down untenable divisions between mind and body, language and practice, and sociology and cultural anthropology. Psychoanalytic terminology appears repeatedly in Bourdieu's work, although it is often hedged about with defensive comments. Bourdieu slowly began to acknowledge the similarity between his own thought and psychoanalysis in his later years, but he never deployed its categories systematically.[194] The status of psychoanalysis in Bourdieu's work is extremely uneasy, suffering from denegation (*Verneinung*) or disavowal (*Verleugnung*) of its relevance for and contributions to his own approach.[195] And as Slavoj Žižek remarks with respect to another contemporary social theorist on the other side of the Rhine, there is a "curious detail concerning Lacan's name" in Bourdieu's writing: it is mentioned only rarely and usually in the context of puns or anecdotes. In *Homo Academicus*, Lacan figures only as a data point, and elsewhere in Bourdieu's writing he is studiously avoided.[196]

192. We can see this in the deference to Lacan by both Lévi-Strauss and Althusser, and in Lacan's reciprocal delegation of the realm of the social to those theorists (Althusser 1996). In the United States, psychoanalysis was becoming central to social science around the middle of the twentieth century but later was almost completely suppressed or presented in a truncated, oversocialized version centered on superego control.

193. See Jacoby 1983; and Steinmetz 2006b.

194. See de Gaulejac 2004, p. 83. The most explicit discussion of psychoanalysis occurs in Bourdieu's *Masculine Domination* ([1998] 2002, p. 17). See also the interview with Jacques Maître (1994) and Bourdieu (1980) for earlier explorations of the relations between psychoanalysis and Bourdieu's theory. I am grateful to Francine Muel-Dreyfus for bringing these texts to my attention.

195. Fourny 2000; Muel-Dreyfus 2003; de Gaulejac 2004; and Steinmetz 2005a.

196. One of the peculiarities of Bourdieu's relationship to psychoanalysis is that when he actually engages with its internal logic (as opposed to borrowing its terminology), he tends to draw on Anglo-American ego psychologists rather than Freud or the Lacanian school. As

Bourdieu's theory has been criticized for the vagueness of some of its central concepts. Indeed, the categories of habitus and cultural capital make sense only when their psychoanalytic understructure is made explicit. Specifically, the concepts of cultural and symbolic capital, on the one hand, and habitus, on the other, become more compelling and precise once they are articulated with the Lacanian concepts of symbolic and imaginary identification. Rather than a mechanical combination of the Bourdieuian and Lacanian approaches, however, the former has to undergo a thorough theoretical reconstruction. Symbolic and imaginary identification then turn out to be fruitful categories for making sense of the practices of colonial officials.

The most significant aspect of Lacanian theory in the present context is that it allows us to reground Bourdieu's concept of symbolic capital in Lacan's notion of the symbolic order and in the related dynamics of recognition and misrecognition that are so central to symbolic identification for Lacan. The symbolic in Lacan is the realm of language, difference, metonymy, and the law—the realm of socially sanctioned, official ego ideals. The *ego ideal* for Lacan is the "position of the subject within the symbolic, the norm that installs the subject within language." Subjects seek to *recognize* the normative injunctions of the symbolic order, and they seek *to be recognized* by those who issue these injunctions.[197] Symbolic identifications are linked to the construction of an ego ideal (*Ichideal*) which "constitutes a model to which the subject attempts to conform."[198] In Lacan's later writings, symbolic identification is understood more specifically as identification with *the place from which we are observed:* the "demand of the *Ichideal* takes up its place within the totality of the demands of the law."[199] The first symbolic identification, for the young boy, is with the father. Given the Oedipal structure, however, this identification is in a fundamental way

---

Bertrand Geay remarks, Bourdieu is generally closer to psychology than to psychoanalysis, and his notion of the unconscious is similar to the *preconscious* in Freudian terms, rather than *the repressed* (*le refoulé*). Bourdieu came much closer in *Weight of the World*, his systematic study of individualization using actual individual cases, to a psychoanalytic analysis of the habitus as stemming partly from the "repression of the image of the father and contradictory injunctions tied to parental images" (Geay in Corcuff 2004, pp. 96–97).

197. Julien 1994, p. 167. This is *recognition* in Hegel's sense, as *Anerkennen* or *Wiedererkennen*, rather than simply *Erkennen* (or knowledge). In his Jena *Realphilosophie* Hegel observes that "in recognition, the Self ceases to be this individual, it exists by right in recognition. . . . Man is necessarily recognized and necessarily gives recognition. . . . He *is* recognition" (Hegel 1983, p. 111). See Siep 1979; Honneth 1995.

198. Laplanche and Ponatalis 1973, p. 144.

199. Žižek 1989, p. 105; Lacan 1991, p. 134.

an impossible one: "There issues forth an impossible double command: to be like the father, but not to be like the father with respect to his sexual power."[200] Symbolic identification is thus structured by the desire for recognition but is forever undercut by difference. Identification is the attempted "resolution of desire."[201] At the same time subjects seek to be recognized by those agencies issuing the injunctions to identify.

Along parallel lines, Bourdieu's notion of symbolic capital is based on the premise of the reciprocal recognition by all actors in a field of the cultural positions, the habituses and tastes, of all the other actors. Without mutual recognition by all actors of the value of differing forms of cultural capital there is no guarantee that they will all misrecognize the arbitrariness of these values and thereby ratify their own social domination. Without this dialectic of recognition and misrecognition there would be no reason for Bourdieu's theoretical "stuttering," that is, his doubling of the concept of cultural capital (which is a sort of "capital on paper") by symbolic capital—capital as it is interactively lived and socially understood.[202] It is only by attending to processes of symbolic identification that we can understand the source of the desire for recognition that motivates cultural competition in Bourdieu's framework.

200. Bryson 1994, p. 233; see also Freud [1923] 1961, p. 34.

201. Butler 1997, pp. 86, 102.

202. Symbolic capital, Bourdieu says, represents cultural capital insofar as it is recognized by others in the field, that is, insofar as it is "doxic." A well-structured, or doxic field thus resembles Lacan's symbolic order. A doxic field is hierarchically differentiated. All actors in the field, including the dominated, acknowledge a common definition of cultural capital and develop a taste for their own domination. Bourdieu's understanding of symbolic capital is thus akin to Lacan's notion of the symbolic, which is dominated by the law of the father. Indeed, Lacan often uses the same terms as Bourdieu (*champ, enjeu*) in describing the operations of the symbolic. By desexualizing the Oedipal crisis and reframing it as the entry into language and culture, Lacan makes the parallels between the law of the father and the doxic structure in Bourdieu's field even more evident. What Bourdieu's theory lacks is an account of the ontogenesis of this constantly repeated subjection to doxa, and of the motivation underlying competition for distinction (although Bourdieu did seem to recognize the need for such an account; see his comments in Bourdieu [1997] 2000, p. 166). Just as the foundation of imaginary identifications and "habitus" lies in the mirror phase, the foundation of symbolic identifications and "subjection to doxa" lies in the Oedipal crisis. Lacan's theory can of course be subjected to a parallel critique: it is a sociologically generic account that cannot name the "name of the father" as a specific social class or class fraction (a problem that Althusser [1971a, 1971b] addressed but failed to resolve). Although it may once have been useful heuristically for Lacan and Lévi-Strauss to allocate the psychic and the social objects to distinct human sciences, this division of labor has since become an intellectual hindrance.

If misrecognition for Bourdieu means misrecognition of social inequality, what does it mean for Lacan? To answer this we need to attend to the other two dimensions of Lacan's tripartite ontological division: the imaginary and the real. The subject's fundamental ontological separation from the real begins with the mirror phase, when the fragmented consciousness identifies with its own reflected image, alienated but satisfyingly totalizing.[203] Such primordial identifications are located in the realm of the imaginary, the realm of plenitude and wholeness. Imaginary identification is identification with an image that Lacan (following Freud) calls the ideal ego, or *Idealich* (as opposed to ego ideal, or *Ichideal*). This is an image that represents "what we would like to be."[204] The earliest imaginary identifications in the mirror phase thus provide a psychic template for a whole series of future images of bounded and embodied selfhood similarly characterized by a striving for wholeness and unity, including those body images that are central to Bourdieu's notion of habitus.[205] The misrecognition in the mirror stage, then, involves misrecognition of the fundamentally fictional character of this ur-identification (the image is reversed in the reflection, it presents a subject who is already in control of its boundaries and bodily functions, etc.) and of all of the further identifications that are constructed on the model of this roughcast. Unlike symbolic identifications, which work through difference or metonymy, the specular operations of the mirror phase function via sameness or metaphor.[206]

Whereas the symbolic is the sphere of the law, the imaginary, according to Julia Hell, is the realm of "illegal identifications," identifications that are forbidden from the standpoint of the present social-symbolic order.[207] The imaginary is "preoccupied" with and "structured by the law" but it does "not immediately obey the law." For example, Hell analyzes non-Jewish German writers' identification with the victims of the Holocaust as a form of symbolically illegal imaginary identification. Daniel Lagache points out that the ideal ego serves as the basis of "heroic identifications" with "great personalities from history or contemporary life characterized by independence,

---

203. Lacan [1949] 1977; Hell 1997, pp. 160–62, discusses the notion of an "acoustic mirror" that may precede the (visual) mirror stage described by Lacan.

204. Žižek 1989, p. 105; also Lagache 1961; Lacan 1991, pp. 134–48.

205. Freud already recognized that identifications need not involve explicitly erotic cathexes (Freud [1921] 1955; Padel 1986).

206. Saussure [1915] 1986.

207. Hell 2002.

pride, success."[208] Of course, not all imaginary identifications are "illegal"; the culture industry encourages an incessant stream of such identifications, harnessing them to the needs of capital, while the public machinery of official patriotism generates imaginary identification with national founders and leaders. But these identifications are still illegal from the standpoint of the symbolic (as opposed to the imaginary) order: I cannot appear before the law as George Washington or George Clinton or Bill Clinton without suffering repercussions, even if I am encouraged to identify with them in the movie theater or the concert hall.

The psychoanalytic emphasis on the doubling of conscious processes and motives by unconscious ones opens up a line of political analysis that is distinct from the Marxist, Saidian, and Bourdieuian ones. Lacan suggests an explanation for the widespread phenomenon of the colonizer's cross-identifications with the colonized. The categories of the imaginary, imaginary identification, and ideal ego are central here, although they are always working simultaneously with the symbolic. In the colonies, however, identification with the colonized *was* culturally forbidden, due to the racist rule of colonial difference—the colonizers' insistence on the irrefragable inferiority of colonized subjects—which prohibits the *metaphoric* logics of the imaginary. Such identifications were illegal from the standpoint of the prescriptions of the social-symbolic order of empire, which insisted on the inferiority of the colonized. Hence the many derogatory terms for "going native" in German colonial discourse: *Verkaffern* (going Kaffir), *Verchinesung* (going Chinese), *Verkanackern* (going Kanak), and *Verniggern* (going nigger).[209]

Lacan recognized that the contents of imaginary identifications later in life are provided by suggestions coming from the symbolic order. Similarly, colonizers' choices for imaginary identifications make sense only in terms of

208. Lagache 1961, pp. 41–42. The notion of imaginary identification can also be connected to the overarching psychoanalytic concept of fantasy, which has been used to great avail by theorists of nationalism, communism, totalitarianism, and postfascism (see Žižek 1989; Silverman 1992; Hell 1997; J. Rose 1998). Fantasy scenarios express a conscious or unconscious wish. Imaginary identification is one site for such wishful scenarios. For a recent overview see Levy and Inderbitzin 2001.

209. These phrases are discussed in the relevant chapters. Needless to say, the symbolic order of the colonized was structured differently. While the German traveler and geographer Ferdinand von Richthofen objected to the adoption of Chinese clothing, food, and other customs by European missionaries as a "descent into the customs of a lower race" and insisted that missionaries should "assume a superior standpoint to the native in every respect" (1907, vol. 2, p. 140), Chinese officials were encouraging European missionaries to wear Chinese clothing.

the broader repertoire of ethnographic discourses. How else can we understand that Wilhelm Solf identified with a Samoan chief and Bishop Anzer with a Chinese mandarin, rather than with native commoners, or for that matter with European settlers? These identifications were also corporeal. Solf commented on the fact that his own corpulence, which he sometimes experienced as an embarassment in European contexts, actually enhanced his status in Samoan society. Similarly, Bishop Anzer was extremely awkward in European society,[210] but in his mandarin masquerade he appeared self-assured (see fig. 6.10). This points to the way in which imaginary identifications are organized at the level of the body and body images.

This argument needs to be distinguished from the Conradian view of the colonizer as actually becoming decivilized—"going troppo"—and of the colony as a laboratory of European madness.[211] It is also necessary to distinguish the argument that Europeans cross-identified with imagos of the colonized from the claim that German colonial officials' *tastes* for specific ethnographic viewpoints (and hence for different native policies) were guided by their socially acceptable symbolic identifications with socially prestigious positions. Colonizers engaged in both symbolic projects and narcissistic, imaginary ones.

This doubling of symbolic and illegal identifications is not specific to "offstage" or colonial settings but is characteristic of subjectivity in general. Nonetheless, the peculiarities of overseas colonialism encouraged the proliferation of imaginary identifications by colonizers. The subjugated status of the colonized made them appear to be particularly available for mobilization as props in colonizers' fantasy scenarios. A colonial official in Africa or Oceania was better positioned than a city councilor in Berlin or Hamburg to engage his subjects in scenarios linked to imaginary identifications. The built-in power imbalance between colonizers and the colonized made it easier for Europeans to imagine themselves as omnipotent. And anything the colonial official did that involved the colonized became de facto part of native policy. Interactions with colonized people were viewed by many Europeans as lying outside the rules of behavior that held sway in the metropole. As Jürgen Osterhammel notes, colonial wars were understood

210. Rivinius 1979.

211. See Césaire [1950] 2000, p. 35; H. Arendt [1950] 1958, p. 193; and most recently, Fabian 2000. "Going troppo" is used to describe someone adopting a "primitive" lifestyle or succumbing emotionally to the pressures of a tropical climate. *Tropenkoller* is the title of a novel by Frieda von Bülow based on the case of Carl Peters, the German explorer of Africa who paved the way for the German annexation of East Africa and was dismissed from his post as district commissioner for Kilimanjaro in 1897 due to his "mad" abuse of Africans.

as being fought against "an enemy who did not seem to adhere to the same cultural code."[212] In European eyes this legitimated techniques that would be disdained in "civilized" warfare. Many Europeans regarded "primitive people" as less than fully human, and, in Freud's words, as being "led almost exclusively by the unconscious."[213] Of course, there are also contexts in metropolitan life in which the defense mechanisms that normally limit the expression of wishful fantasies are attenuated and a dreamlike sense of omnipotence is encouraged. What is distinctive about modern colonies is that for many colonizers, especially those in the most powerful positions, *all* of these conditions were present, almost all of the time. Colonial contexts were therefore particularly conducive to the acting out of imaginary identifications whenever a psychologically useful imago or framing of the colonized was available.[214]

Struggles among German elite groups shaped the contents of German colonizers' imaginary identifications. The army and the foreign service, especially the diplomatic corps, were arenas in which the venerable cultural capital of the aristocracy was still dominant, if increasingly embattled, in the German Kaiserreich.[215] This was true even though capitalist modernity

212. Osterhammel 1995, p. 50.

213. Freud [1921] 1955, p. 77. For a more redemptive reading of Freud on Africa see Berman 1998; for the standard "postcolonial" critique see Brickman 2003.

214. No German or European before 1915 seems to have identified with the imago of the "Baster." Even if the Basters were generally regarded as a reliable colonial ally, their very name focused attention on their extreme illegitimacy (see Kjæret and Stokke 2003). European men in Southwest Africa who sought indigenous wives were often drawn to Rehobother women, but this followed different psychic rules from those of cross-cultural identification.

215. The upper echelons of the German army continued to be dominated by traditional noble values, even as officer recruitment was becoming more bourgeois. Middle-class officers were admitted under the condition that they display a "nobility of temperament" (*Adel der Gesinnung*), in Kaiser Wilhelm's revealing phrase, which underscored the sorts of symbolic identifications that were officially encouraged (Craig 1955, p. 235; Kehr 1977). The administration of colonial affairs was located until 1907 within the German Foreign Office, and was initially closely tied to the diplomatic service. The first imperial commissary for Southwest Africa, for example, Goering, came from the diplomatic corps and reentered it after he left the colony for Jamaica. Diplomacy had always been a thoroughly aristocratic arena, but in Prussia and Germany, as elsewhere in Europe, the number of educated nonnoble experts within the diplomatic corps increased over the course of the nineteenth century. Yet the most important positions, those of the representational diplomats, remained largely in the hands of nobles. The German diplomatic service in 1909 was said to have seventy officials from the ancient nobility (*Uradel*), twenty-five from the old *Briefadel* (nobility by letter-cachet), thirty-five from the modern *Briefadel,* and nine bourgeois (Philippi 1985, p. 63; Preradovich 1955). The growing influence of the translating branch of the Foreign Office within the Qingdao colonial administration was resisted and resented by the more aristocratic representational

had come to dominate most aspects of everyday life and even domestic policymaking in imperial Germany. As a result many middle-class Germans continued to focus on the nobility as an object of imaginary identification even as a different set of symbolic identifications urged them to compete with and displace those same aristocrats. Wilhelm Solf discovered a means of dealing with both of these imperatives by openly attacking German settlers, military men, and aristocrats while forming an imaginary identification with Samoan notables. This provided an attractive, if realistically unworkable, solution to the social dilemma of the German *Bildungsbürger*. Samoan elites were seen as attaining their noble status through merit and struggle rather than mere inheritance—a sort of *noblesse de robe* (nobility of the gown) whose titles were not necessarily passed on to their biological heirs. The Chinese mandarins had a similar status, since they had risen to the pinnacles of state power by passing university examinations rather than being born to power. Numerous Europeans identified with this imago. Bishop Anzer wore Chinese clothing and led a partly Chinese lifestyle, and was eventually able to attain the rank of first-class mandarin, which allowed him to use the Chinese title "Excellence" and to use the "green state sedan-chair with a retinue of ten riders and bearers of his insignia."[216] While serving as a translator for the German consular service in China, Otto Franke requested permission to publicly wear a badge signifying his promotion by the Chinese state to the rank of the "Third Stage of the Second Class of the Order of the Double Dragon."[217] Richard Wilhelm, who headed part of the school system in colonial Kiaochow, did not dress in Chinese clothing, but he apprenticed himself to a distinguished member of the Qing dynasty literati and was described by contemporaries Carl Jung and Hermann Hesse as having acquired the bodily habitus of a Chinese mandarin.[218] The most famous example of German cross-identification in this period is Eduard Schnitzer, who began his career as a medical officer in the Ottoman army in 1865 and then served the Ottoman governor of northern Albania (1870-74), at which time he adopted a Turkish lifestyle and name. Schnitzer received an administrative post at Khartoum in the British Sudan in 1876 and was

---

branch. See von Kemnitz to Foreign Office, March 12, 1917, PA-AA, R 2167 (discussed in chap. 7), in which von Kemnitz rails against these inferiors.

216. H. Gründer 1982, p. 288.

217. Franke to Chancellor Hohenlohe, June 19, 1889, PA-AA, Personnel Documents, Otto Franke, vol. 3905 (no pagination).

218. See chap. 8. In German Togo, the district commissioner and novelist Richard Küas wore Hausa shoes and gown (Küas 1939, p. 85).

appointed governor of Equatoria (southern Sudan) in 1878, with the Ottoman title of bey. Eventually he was elevated to the rank of pasha. Mehmed Emin Pasa (or Emin Pasha), as Schnitzer was now known, was "rescued" from the Mahdist uprising by Stanley in a famous expedition in 1888.[219]

Threatened by the onslaught of political modernization, the nobility also pursued imaginary identifications across the colonial boundary while waging defensive rearguard campaign to slow down the sweeping shift of societal power to the bourgeoisie. Nondemocratic systems of rule—of which colonial administration was a prime example—had been the nobility's traditional stronghold. But this was not the case in Germany's colonial empire, whose officials were drawn more or less equally from the nobility, bourgeoisie, and *Bildungsbürgertum*. This did not mean that aristocrats formed imaginary identifications with the rising middle classes, but it did create the preconditions for strange identifications across cultural boundaries, including ethnic ones. A member of the German nobility like Ferdinand von Richthofen might unconsciously identify with a positively coded image of the Chinese mandarin elite, as Jürgen Osterhammel has suggested,[220] while another aristocrat, Lothar von Trotha, in his struggle against the middle-class upstart Leutwein, could form an imaginary identification with a negatively coded imago of the ferociously cruel Ovaherero.

Attention to processes of imaginary identification sheds some light on the spiral of seemingly hysterical violence in von Trotha's discourse and conduct of the war. Von Trotha used the term *Vernichtung* deliberately in his *Vernichtungsbefehl* or "extermination order" against the Ovaherero, issued on October 2, 1904. Von Trotha relished the dual resonance of *Vernichtung* with traditional German military language, in which the *Vernichtungskrieg* referred to a "war of annihilation," and with the specifically colonial connotations of massacre, which he emphasized with his lurid language of "rivers of blood and rivers of money" and exerting "violence with blatant terrorism and cruelty." Von Trotha's conflict with Leutwein was fueled by the class hostility that arose "naturally" in Wilhelmine Germany between a Prussian aristocrat and a pastor's son who flaunted his classical education.[221] The tension between the two men was heightened by the way in which von Trotha entered the colonial arena as usurper of power from Leutwein, who had himself replaced Curt von François as the colony's head administrator

219. Caillou 1974; Kraft 1976. As a German Jew in anti-Semitic Germany Schnitzer/Emin Pasha was doubly driven to overcome his symbolic domination.

220. Osterhammel 1987.

221. Quotes from BA-Berlin, RKA, vol. 2089, p. 100v; and Pool 1991, pp. 243-44.

in March 1894. (Von François was a member of the nontitled nobility and the son of *Generalmajor* (Major General) Bruno von François, a hero of the Franco-Prussian War). Von Trotha was therefore reasserting the authority of the traditional Prussian nobility and its specific cultural capital, its specialization in the arts of violent domination. His aggressive identification with an imago of the Ovaherero was directed as much against "liberal" adversaries like Leutwein who opposed his annihilation order as against the putative African enemy. Soon after arriving in the colony von Trotha wrote that if Leutwein did not agree with his plans he would "make short work of him."[222] And indeed, von Trotha did make short work of the governor, bringing his career to an abrupt and ugly end.[223] Von Trotha seems to have taken seriously Kaiser Wilhelm's injunction to emulate "King Etzel's Huns," becoming as barbaric as the received image of the Ovaherero. This should not be understood as a wallowing in fantasies of downward social mobility, however, but as an identification connected to terrorizing the would-be challenger from the middle class.

Such imaginary identifications were more closely related to daydreaming than to any real bid for power, and indeed they were sometimes symbolically counterproductive, inviting sanction or ridicule. Bishop Anzer wore his mandarin costume publicly and crafted a hybrid self-presentation using Catholic and Chinese symbols, seeking respect in the eyes of the Chinese elites, but he was correspondingly disrespected by Europeans. Wilhelm Solf was ridiculed by German settlers for his evident identification with Samoan chiefs.[224] Psychoanalysis helps to make theoretical sense of the psychic enjoyment, the otherwise inexplicable energy dedicated to identifications that promised little in the way of symbolic recognition from relevant actors in the field. And if such identifications failed to yield any fungible cultural capital, they could reinforce or contradict the ethnographic leanings that were produced by the field of competition for symbolic capital. Because they could involve large numbers of real people as supporting actors, they were sometimes directly relevant for native policy.

222. Von Trotha diaries, quoted by Pool 1991, p. 247.

223. Leutwein's conflict with von Trotha is discussed by Bley ([1971] 1996) and in chap. 3. Von Trotha and his supporters marginalized Leutwein in the colony, forcing him to give up his position and return to Germany. Having fallen from grace, Leutwein was never again able to work for the colonial administration (P. Leutwein 1934, p. 42) and was reduced to begging the government for access to reports on his earlier performance (see letter from Leutwein to chancellor from February 17, 1909, BA-Berlin, RKA, vol. 2119, pp. 90–91). In 1909 Leutwein was still seeking "restitution of his official honor" (ibid., p. 92v).

224. Tyszka 1904.

Resistance, Cooperation, and Inflections of Native Policy by Its Addressees

The selection of particular native policies was a result of precolonial ethnographic representations, the symbolic positioning of colonizers vis-à-vis one another, and imaginary identifications with the colonized—in addition to economic considerations and international relations. The relative importance of each of these mechanisms varied from place to place and from moment to moment. But in every instance, responses by the colonized shaped the ability of a particular framework of native policy to be implemented and perpetuated. On the one hand, the entire theater of native governance could not even exist without a rudimentary willingness on the part of the colonized to play their assigned parts. Foot-dragging and recalcitrance—the miniature tactics of the weak analyzed so trenchantly by James C. Scott—were rarely sufficient to eliminate a given regime of native policy.[225] The mere act of showing up at work or agreeing to pay a "hut tax" meant that a colonial subject was colluding in native policy and colonial rule. The "half-castes" in Samoa who applied for legal status as "foreigners" or "whites" ratified the colonial state's dualistic racialism.[226] Locals who accepted official functions within the colonial state as "tribal leader" or "native policemen" fortified the existing native policy system. This also suggests that the term *cooperation* should probably be used instead of *collaboration*. Indigenous cooperation was a necessary condition for the success of any regime of native policy, but it had little to do with the initial selection of one policy rather than another by the colonizers.

Resistance is located on the opposite side from cooperation. Colonized peoples were able to modulate and revise native policies. By signing up as a native policeman one might be able to temper colonial abuses of power. More frontal forms of resistance could bring a regime of native policy to an abrupt halt and force the colonial state to seek a new approach. In Qingdao in 1912 the students at the German-Chinese university changed the school's policy by threatening to resign if they were not allowed to meet with republican leader Sun Yat-sen (Sun Yixian), who was opposed to both colonial rule and the traditionalist Qing government elites to whom the Germans had granted refuge in Qingdao. The students' protest nudged official German policy even farther away from the "rule of difference," as they were granted rights of assembly and political expression. The differing ef-

225. J. Scott 1985.
226. See Laitin 1986 and Comaroff 1987 on individual strategizing with regard to ethnic or racial reclassification.

fects of indigenous cooperation and resistance are illustrated sharply by the
changing strategy of the Witbooi people. After the Germans defeated the
Witbooi militarily in 1894, they were allowed to keep their horses and rifles
and were enlisted as trackers and sharpshooters in the colonial army. As a
result of their cooperation the Witbooi were no longer described as abject
"Hottentots" or deculturated mimic men but were equated with James Fenimore Cooper's noble Mohicans. When the Witbooi broke their pact with
the Germans and rebelled in 1904, however, they were ultimately unsuccessful.[227] This does not mean that unsuccessful uprisings always resulted
in harsher policies. Although the rebellions in Shandong in 1899–1900 and
in Southwest Africa in 1904–7 were followed by a sharp increase in repression, this was not the case after the defeated uprisings in Samoa in 1904
and 1908–9. Colonizers' reactions cannot be understood independently of
the cultural context. In the metropolitan German setting, the effects of ex-
traparliamentary resistance on social policymaking were mediated by the
interpretative frameworks of the men in charge of the local and central
states,[228] and the same was true in the colonies.

Collective resistance was more often a response to heightened repression
than a stimulus to it. Groups that had peacefully cooperated with colonial
rulers sometimes suddenly found themselves the targets of state violence.
The Maji-Maji rebellion in German East Africa (1905–7) was triggered by
grievances connected to a new scheme of the colonial government to grow
cotton using forced labor.[229] The colonial state expropriated the land of the
Duala people in Cameroon in the 1910s despite their moderate and collaborative stance, resulting in bitter protest and petitioning of the German
Reichstag by the Duala.[230]

227. The agency of the colonized affected native policy indirectly in other ways, just
as the pressure of the "native" can be detected within ethnographic discourse. The ethnographic representations that shaped native policy were a coproduction of the observer and the
observed. Because ethnographic discourse is treated here mainly as a determinant of native
policy, I do not systematically reconstruct the processes that Raymond Firth (2001) called
the "creative contribution of indigenous people to their ethnography." Many of the ethnographers discussed in this book had "native informants" who effectively coauthored their work,
even if their contribution was disavowed or minimized. Perhaps the most egregious example
is Lao Naixuan, a "neo-Confucian scholar and Government official known for his scholarly
account of the Boxer movement" (Forsman 1979, p. 102), who worked with Richard Wilhelm
on his famous translation of the Yi Jing but whose full name was not given in Wilhelm's published account of his Qingdao years (1924).

228. I provide statistical and qualitative evidence for this claim in Steinmetz 1993.

229. Iliffe 1967; Seeberg 1989, chap. 4; Sunseri 1993.

230. The German decision to seize this land in the center of the city of Douala did not
occur in response to an uprising but actually sparked the first open movement of anticolonial

Imperial Germany and the German Empire

One of this book's historiographic interventions concerns the supposed peculiarities of metropolitan Germany. As in most other areas of German studies, the history of German colonialism and colonial discourse has been strongly informed by theories of German exceptionalism. Rather than arguing that any particular fraction of the German elite was dominant I will show that all fractions were engaged in the same struggle for supremacy and that none was "structurally" more powerful than any another. Indeed, the orientation of the colonial field to the criterion of ethnographic acuity helps explain why the educated middle classes were able to compete culturally in a sphere ostensibly dominated by the Foreign Office and the army, which were still strongholds of the traditional nobility. These *Bildungbürger* presented themselves as uniquely possessed of the qualities needed to understand exotic cultures, such as cultural sensitivity, subtlety of judgment, and familiarity with literary and scientific sources. They tended to drape their ethnographic pronouncements with the markers of a "hermeneutic" sensibility. This does not mean that other groups of colonizers agreed that the educated middle classes were the most discerning ethnographers. Although most colonizers acknowledged the common currency of the colonial state field, they disagreed vigorously on what counted as ethnographic discernment. But the *Bildungsbürger* at least had some chance of political success here, whereas they were *hors compétition* in political fields defined as mainly military or economic.[231] Historians who have focused on specific German colonies (post-1904 Southwest Africa, Qingdao before 1904, New Guinea in the first several years of German rule, or the Marshall Islands) have overestimated the military and capitalist character of German colonialism.[232]

The other reason educated middle-class Germans were more influential in overseas colonial government than in national politics was the centralized

---

resistance among the Duala. See Ralph Austen 1977, Eckert 1999, and Austen and Derrick 1999, pp. 128–37.

231. It is important to note that the fact that German Southwest Africa was dominated at all levels before 1907 by military men does not mean that the state was a military field. The position of colonial governor was defined as a "personal union" of civilian and military functions. Leutwein's struggle with von Trotha in 1904 made this dualism visible, and as a result the post-1904 colonial state had more clearly defined military and civilian offices. A police force distinct from the colonial army was created. The post-1904 governors von Lindequist, Schuckmann, and Seitz were not career military men.

232. On the thoroughgoing exploitation of the Marshall Islands by the Jaluit-Gesellschaft see Treue 1976.

and quasi-despotic structure of the colonial state. Middle-class statesmen like Solf seized the opportunity to defy the settlers, commanders, and capitalists and to translate their disdain for these groups into policy.[233] The non-democratic political structure could also boost the authority of men from the nobility or the bourgeoisie, of course, once they were placed in power by the national authorities. As commander in chief and ruler of the Southwest African colony Lothar von Trotha was able to implement his ultraracist vision of Africans to devastating effect. Only after the Ovaherero had been massacred was von Trotha reigned in by his superiors in Berlin. Yet he stayed in power for almost another year and issued an equally threatening proclamation to the rebellious Nama in 1905.[234] The constitution of the colonial state and its position in the overall German political structure put great power in the hands of the colonial governor and a small number of officials.

A different exceptionalism argument concerns the nature of German colonialism per se. Some writers have identified nationally specific styles of colonization.[235] But the stark differences among the three colonies examined here and in the treatment of different communities within Southwest Africa cautions against placing too much weight on the national factor. The theme of German *colonial* exceptionalism dates back to the campaign to justify the post–World War I British takeover of the German colonies.[236] Even earlier, British and American writers had described German colonialism as especially brutal and militarized, but this did not yet influence official publications or policy.[237] Yet the differences between French, British, and German colonial policies directed at populations that Europeans categorized as culturally similar were less striking in any given historical period

233. After governing the colony for an entire decade Leutwein was replaced, but this was due to the disastrous turn of the Ovaherero war and the mobilization of metropolitan opinion due to the murder of German settlers, as well as von Trotha.

234. Reprinted in Kriegsgeschichtliche Abteilung 1 des Grossen Generalstabs 1906–7, vol. 2, p. 186.

235. E.g., Miles 1994. See J. Go 2000 for an analysis of the supposed exceptionalism of U.S. overseas colonialism.

236. See Union of South Africa 1918. As Yearwood (1999, p. 316) notes, before 1914 "Africa appeared as a continent where deals might be struck to appease the Anglo-German antagonism or create precedents for Anglo-German co-operation." This was illustrated in the stance of the South African government during the 1904–7 Namibian war. Top-level British discussions during World War I about the future of the German colonies demonstrate that statements of concern about German brutalism were motivated by the desire to wrest the colonies, above all Southwest Africa, from Germany's grasp (Callahan 1999).

237. See, for example, Bigelow 1900.

than broader patterns of similarity.[238] A study of British colonies located in areas construed as culturally similar to these three German colonies—say, British policy in Fiji, British treatment of the Khoikhoi in the Cape Colony, and British practices in Hong Kong—might well discover a similar pattern of variations. Indeed, British policy in Fiji was studied by the first governor of Samoa, British practice in Hong Kong was examined carefully by the architects of Kiaochow, and the Cape Colony and Union of South Africa were looming precedents for German administrators in Southwest Africa. It would be a mistake to attribute any similarities to German mimicry of the British colonies, however, without investigating the possibility of a shared source in European-wide ethnographic and racial ideologies and comparable class conflicts within colonial state fields.

The one colony that may indeed have been a "deviation from the normal"[239] is Southwest Africa. Of course, the colonial massacres by Spain and the United States in the Americas, the British in Tasmania and Kenya, the Belgians in the Congo, the Italians in Libya, and the French in Madagascar and Algeria are too familiar to permit any serious argument about a uniquely German colonial brutality.[240] What is unique, perhaps, at least for twentieth-century colonialism, is the German attempt in 1904 to exterminate an entire people—the men, women, and children of the Ovaherero nation.[241] This decision was related to the nationally specific constellation of elite class structure and struggle discussed above, as well as to the ethnographic representations of the Ovaherero that may have been uniquely hateful (due to characteristics of the Lutheran-dominated Rhenish Mission and their frustrating and largely fruitless efforts in the six decades leading

238. Of course, solid evidence for this hypothesis has to await further comparative research. One of the few explicitly comparative colonial studies is Miles 1994, which explores the long-term effects of French and British colonialism in Niger and Nigeria, respectively. But Miles's excellent study does not demonstrate that French and British colonial practices *in general* fell into these patterns.

239. Bley [1971] 1996, p.xvii.

240. On the massacres in the Americas see Todorov 1984; Jennings 1975; and Stannard 1992. Clendinnen 1987 is an exemplary study of Spanish "totalitarianism" among the Mayans in the Yucatan. On the Pequot War as genocide see M. Freeman 1995. On Tasmania and the United States see Cocker 1998, pt. 2; and Palmer 2000. On the scope of the 1919 massacre at the Jallianawala Bagh in Amritsar see Rai 2000, p. 28. On Italy's slaughter of Libyans between 1912 and 1942 see J. Wright 1982; and Mack Smith 1976. On Kenya and the Mau Mau see the essays in Odhiambo and Lonsdale 2003. On the Belgian Congo see Vangroenweghe 1986; Hochschild 1999; and Marchal 1996. On Madagascar see Rabemananjara 2000. On Algeria see Le Cour Grandmaison 2005. On Kenya see Odhiambo and Lonsdale 2003.

241. Steinmetz 2005b.

up to the genocide to convert Ovaherero). This array of factors was perhaps uniquely German, but it was at best a necessary and not a sufficient condition for pushing a colony toward genocide.[242]

This book also provides a new narrative of the history of three colonies. Chapters 3, 5, and 7 reconstruct the (sometimes implicit) theoretical and analytic claims informing historical writing on these colonies. The debate on German colonialism in Southwest Africa, for instance, has been largely structured around the genocidal war against the Ovaherero in 1904; there has been less interest in the other ethnic groups in the colony, such as the Khoikhoi and especially the Rehoboth Basters. There has been very little research on precolonial ethnographic representations of Southwest Africans, and nothing on the relationship between these discourses and the subsequent activities of German rulers. German Samoa has been described both as ethnocidal and as a benevolent and protective regime.[243] Both approaches fail to capture the colony's distinctiveness. Very little has been written about precolonial European representations of Samoa, and nothing at all about the German literature on those islands.[244] As for Kiaochow, historians have agreed that native policy began to change around 1904 but they have disagreed about the reasons for this shift. None of them has connected this change to precolonial representations of China or to intraelite symbolic struggles. There is an enormous literature on European images of China from the Middle Ages to the present, most of which identifies a transition from Sinophilia to Sinophobia between the early modern and modern eras. I will show that Sinophobia had not completely replaced Sinophilia even by the end of the nineteenth century but that it was in abeyance, a dominated discourse. As a result Sinophilia could quickly reemerge after 1904.

In the following chapters I will reconstruct precolonial ethnographic representations of the Southwest African Khoikhoi, Ovaherero, and Basters (chap. 2), of Samoans and Polynesians more generally (chap. 4), and of the Chinese (chap. 6). These chapters do more than provide "backstory," since precolonial ethnography was one of the main determinants of colonial native policy. The analyses of precolonial discourse are followed in each case by chapters focused on the German colonial era.

242. The argument that the Southwest African genocide and German colonialism more generally laid the groundwork for Nazism and the Holocaust (Roth 2004; Zimmerer 2003) seems to exaggerate the impact of one causal strand for the sake of historiographical novelty.

243. For the former, see Meleisea 1987a, 1987b; for the latter, see Hiery 1995.

244. See Linnekin 1991b, Harms 1991, and Blanton 1995.

PART ONE   *Southwest Africa*

"A World Composed Almost Entirely of Contradictions" ⁊ Southwest Africans in German Eyes, before Colonialism

This chapter reconstructs the emergence of a vast and repugnant repertoire of European, and particularly German, images of the three indigenous populations that attracted the most attention from the colonial state in Southwest Africa after 1883. These were the Ovaherero people; the Witbooi, or /Khobesin, a group of Orlam Khoikhoi who migrated northward from the Cape in 1863; and the Baster community that migrated from De Tuin in the northern Cape to Rehoboth in Greater Namaqualand in 1870–71. My aim in returning to these abstruse and often offensive ethnographic descriptions is to be able subsequently to investigate the ways they shaped the German colonial state's treatment of the three communities.

There was not, in fact, a sharply delineated transition from precolonialism to colonialism in Southwest Africa (or in either of the two other colonies treated in this book). Starting in 1864 the Rhenish Mission created a "mission colony" at Otjimbingwe, and Great Britain dispatched a "special commissioner to the tribes north of the Orange River" from the Cape. Prior to formal colonialism in Samoa there were two short lived foreign regimes (1873–76 and 1887–89) and a German-American-British tridominium that lasted from 1889 to 1900.[1] In China, systematic European infringements on sovereignty through military pressure and in the treaty ports began with the First Opium War in 1842.[2] German missionaries and envoys based in Beijing forced the Chinese to accept limitations on their sovereignty inside Shandong Province even before the annexation of Kiaochow in 1897. In

---

1. The first of these was the American regime headed by the American Albert Steinberger; the second, the German "Brandeis" regime; see Gilson 1970.

2. The classic study is Fairbank [1953] 1969; more recent treatments of the treaty ports include Hevia 2003; and Wood 1998.

such instances we can distinguish between precolonial and protocolonial situations, just as the last chapter developed criteria for differentiating colonial and noncolonial conditions. Of course, these categories should not be seen as a linear sequence or even as cyclical: protocolonial conditions in some places, like Shanghai in the early twentieth century or U.S.-occupied Iraq in 2003–4, never led to formal colonies, and in other places there was no protocolonial prologue to colonialism but rather an abrupt transition from freedom to colonial servitude. Under protocolonial conditions, technologies of foreign rule are elaborated in advance of any claim to sovereignty over a territory. The ethnographic productions of the British "special commissioner" were not colonial, strictly speaking, since Britain was still hesitating to annex the territories of the "tribes north of the Orange River." But neither were these textual activities part of precolonial discourse, since they were interwoven with practical efforts to control those "tribes" and were premised on assumptions of the natives' inferiority. The topic of the generative relationship between ethnographic discourse and colonial technologies of domination is thus already broached in this chapter (and in chaps. 4 and 6) before the colonizing flag is even hoisted.

There are two goals that I do not pursue in this chapter. First, I do not try to *explain* the formation of European precolonial ethnographic representations; this would require an additional book. Nor do I attempt to reconstruct the actual social practices or beliefs of the precolonized communities. This too would lead us off on tangents. The present book concerns forms of cultural and material domination exerted over non-European peoples by modern colonizers, and the changes that resulted among colonizers and colonized. This is a history, or sociology, or anthropology, of the colonial encounter. The reality of Ovaherero or Samoan culture is not at issue. This is not to say that I adhere to an epistemology of incommensurability that would bar any access to the realities of a foreign culture.[3] I will refer occasionally to actual indigenous practices, to actual social life and subjectivity among the precolonized, and contrast these realities with European misperceptions, in order to point out the fictional nature of the latter.[4] Only by distinguishing between African, Chinese, and Samoan realities and

---

3. Steinmetz 2004a.

4. Calling attention to the effects of ideological discourse on political history does not necessarily entail an idealist epistemology. Ethnographic discourses were just as real, material, and socially effective as land tenure patterns, stock prices, or copper mines. Discourse is not independent of material conditions, although the opposite is not true—material objects are not necessarily signified. The pervasive opposition between discursive and materialist explanations in the human sciences is extremely misleading (see Hacking 1999).

European renderings of them can we distinguish among different European observers and identify those who were less trapped by stereotypes. I will try to signal these unusual Europeans, especially when their textual productions had a lasting impact on broader European ethnographic discourse or colonialism. But the realism of ethnographic texts or images was less important historically and causally than their actual contents.

Precolonial and Protocolonial Imagery of Southwest Africans

The three formations of ethnographic discourse considered in this chapter differ in several important ways. One relates to historical depth: the Khoikhoi were described repeatedly by Europeans starting in the sixteenth century. Representations of the Namibian Orlams and Basters in the nineteenth century were directly continuous with earlier depictions of those groups at the Cape. But there were no Ovaherero communities at the Cape before 1860.[5] With the exception of a few scattered Portuguese travelers in southern Angola and northern Namibia along the Kunene River, the Ovaherero remained all but invisible to Europeans until the nineteenth century.[6]

These three formations can be differentiated with respect to their substantive contents—their images, tropes, and rhetorical formulas—and with respect to their relative level of internal homogeneity, that is, their domination by one particular way of framing the group in question. The founder of eugenics, Francis Galton, wrote in 1853 that the various cultures he encountered in Southwest Africa were basically identical, differing only in terms of their "polish."[7] But most Europeans made distinctions. Most formations of ethnographic discourse also exhibited some degree of internal structure. Certain figures of speech were repeated more often than others, and some were deployed with a greater rhetorical sense of their prima facie obviousness. The routine description of the Basters as superior to other groups of Namibians because of their partial acculturation and their admixture of

---

5. Around 1860 groups of Ovaherero began arriving in the Cape as migrants or refugees from the north, and they formed several independent communities. These groups seem to have barely registered in European colonial writing of the time, however (Silvester 2000, pp. 477–81).

6. On Portuguese observations of the northwestern Ovaherero (Himba) starting in the seventeenth century see Estermann 1981, chap. 1; and "The Ovaherero: A Radically Simplified Ethnographic Discourse," below. These early descriptions were untranslated and virtually unknown in northern Europe until the late nineteenth century.

7. Galton 1853, p. 68.

"white blood" contrasted with the even more routine treatment of the Ova-herero as cruel, secretive, primitive, and destined for extinction. Native policy targeting these two cultures during the colonial period was broadly consistent with these portraits. Conversely, the shifting treatment of the Witbooi during the German colonial period was predicated in part on the greater diversity of precolonial opinion concerning the Khoikhoi.

As noted in the previous chapter, a central paradox at the heart of all late-nineteenth-century colonialisms was the familiarity of the recently colonized peoples with their conquerors. As a result, the colonized were able to bewilder their colonizers by switching between codes, feigning ignorance and incomprehension, and remaining inscrutable. Southwest Africa was perhaps distinctive with respect to this complex of mutual (mis)understanding. Other early colonies shared with Namibia a long pre-history of interactions with Europeans. But many of the indigenous Namib-ian groups on the eve of colonialism were emigrants from another colonial setting and were in that respect "precolonized." Such communities posed an unusually difficult problem for their colonizers.

Nowhere in the German empire did missionaries dominate the field of precolonial ethnographic discourse to such an extent as in Namibia, even if they also played a weighty role in the Chinese and Samoan precolonies. Most of the missionaries who served in nineteenth-century Namibia were associated with the Protestant Rhenish Missionary Society (Rheinische Missionsgesellschaft, or RMG), which began its operations in 1828.[8] The RMG was not affiliated with any particular Protestant denomination, al-though the founders of the Namibian mission were Lutherans. The RMG's monthly *Berichte* (Reports) were widely distributed to its contributors and members and contained a wealth of "ethnographic" material from mission-aries in Namibia. Conditions in the precolony led non-African visitors to rely heavily on the Rhenish missionaries for shelter, information on local cultures, translating services, and access to aboriginal leaders and inhabit-ants.[9] Many of the men who helped lay the foundations for the colonial state after 1883 were former Rhenish missionaries, or relatives of missionaries. During the colonial era academic anthropologists and policymakers relied

8. The earliest missionaries to Great Namaqualand had been sent by the London Mission-ary Society. During the first half of the nineteenth century the Rhenish Mission competed with the Methodist Wesleyans for influence in central Namibia. In the 1870s Catholic mis-sionaries also began operations in Hereroland.

9. See, for example, the story of a trader, Mr. Nelson, whose interactions with the Namib-ian Red Nation were mediated by Rhenish missionary Friedrich Weber: "Hoachanas," *Berichte der Rheinischen Missionsgesellschaft* (cited hereafter as *Berichte der RMG*) 10 (1, 1860): 23.

heavily on these early missionary reports. In Namibia, missionary discourse was the fount of "white writing."[10]

The Khoikhoi: The Path to Precolonial Mimicry

The Khoikhoi are storied figures in the sordid history of European racism, where they long figured as "Hottentots." According to historian Richard Elphick, they were the "most frequently observed of all nonliterate people in the Eastern hemisphere,"[11] and they "became the symbol of all that is raw and base in mankind."[12] There was a morbid fascination with the allegedly grotesque and monstrous sexuality and corporality of the Khoikhoi. Discussions of sexual grotesquerie were part of a broader discourse concerning the "indescribable habits of the Hottentots," which were in fact described ad nauseam.[13] The European production of the "Hottentot" culminated in the infamous exhibition of Saartje Baartman, the "Hottentot Venus," in early-nineteenth-century European salons.[14]

The historical literature has ignored the anomalous moment of "enlightened" perceptions of the Khoikhoi, however. This framework was particularly associated with the French naturalist François Le Vaillant, and was echoed in the writings of leading French enlightenment philosophers, including Rousseau, Voltaire, and Diderot.[15] Here the Khoikhoi figured as "noble" rather than as "ignoble" savages. Europeans at the Cape provided a powerful ethnographic framing of the Khoikhoi that was transferred almost unchanged to Southwest Africa (even if some Europeans differentiated between the Namaqua north of the Orange River and those to the south). The noble savagery paradigm thus reemerged during the middle decade of German colonialism in Southwest Africa (1894-1904) with regard to the Witbooi. The secondary literature has also overlooked the fact that dominant European representations of the Khoikhoi changed in important ways during the nineteenth century. The prevailing view in Southern Africa in the decades

---

10. Coetzee 1988.

11. Elphick [1975] 1985, p. xvi. See also Mielke 1993.

12. Elphick [1975] 1985, pp. xvi, 196. Elsewhere Elphick discusses Europeans' focus on sexual grotesqueness and concludes that the prevalent attitudes were hate and fear (1977, p. 196-200).

13. Bhabha 1994a, p. 112.

14. The literature on the Saartje Baartman episode is enormous; see especially Gilman 1985.

15. Tcherkézoff (2003, p. 185) repeats the common misconception that the French Enlightenment philosophers "felt nothing but revulsion" for the "Hottentots."

before German colonialism figured the Khoikhoi as unreliable mimic men, the epitome of unstable cultural indeterminacy. They were seen as fluctuating unpredictably between European customs and their older traditions—as having "two souls" in their breasts, in Theodor Leutwein's emblematic formulation.[16] Historians have concentrated on the earlier, more corporeal images, but the appalling Saartje Baartman episode was not representative of the dominant mid-nineteenth-century images of the Khoikhoi in the southern African contact zones.[17] The following section reconstructs the earliest European images of the Khoikhoi, the images that defined the "traditional" half of their allegedly divided souls. I will then trace the emergence of the portrait of a schizoid Khoikhoi mimicry in which their "partially Europeanized" and "ignoble" countenances were jarringly combined.

EARLY IMAGES: THE KHOIKHOI AS IGNOBLE SAVAGES

What occurs among [the Hottentots] can in no way take place among other peoples, such as ourselves.

CHRISTIAN WOLFF (1721)[18]

During the two centuries between the late 1400s, when Portuguese explorers began rounding the Cape of Good Hope, and the late 1600s, after five decades of Dutch colonial rule, most European observers agreed in their descriptions of the Cape's indigenous inhabitants, whom they associated with lack, perversity, and abjection.[19] At the very beginning of this period the Khoikhoi were described with a catalog of negative traits familiar from early modern descriptions of other "savages."[20] Soon the Khoikhoi started to be dehumanized to an even greater extent than Amerindians and other Africans.[21] Early writers echoed the visitor to the Cape in 1604 who wrote

16. T. Leutwein 1907a, p. 305.

17. Indeed, it is likely that Baartman was understood by most of her European viewers as a generic African and not specifically as a "Hottentot." Europeans in South Africa and in precolonial Namibia had more distinct images of Khoikhoi and Bushmen than of other groups of Africans.

18. C. Wolff [1721] 1975, p. 335, par. 369.

19. More recent anthropological literature refers to these people as "Khoikhoi" or "Khoikhoin," a Nama word meaning "men of men." This was the word they used to designate themselves. See T. Hahn 1881; Boonzaier et al. 1996, p. 2.

20. On the early modern categories of the barbarian and the savage see Bitterli 1976.

21. One exception is the people of Tierra del Fuega, who were regularly described as "debased"; see J. Forster [1778] 1996, p. 169.

that the Khoikhoi were "the most savage and beastly people as ever . . . God created."[22] Two centuries later the French zoologist Jean-Baptiste Bory de Saint-Vincent argued that the Khoikhoi were "an intermediate genus between the genera 'homo' and 'gibbon.'"[23]

This discursive formation was structured around a series of contrasts between Khoikhoi and Europeans, with the latter figuring as the norm, or indeed as the human rather than animal. A sugeon with the British East India Company described the Khoikhoi in 1612 as "bruitt and sauadg, without Religion, without languag, without Lawes or gouernment, without manners or humanittie, and last of all withoutt apparell."[24] Early discussions of Khoikhoi savagery emphasized their supposed lack of religious beliefs.[25] But over time European observers were confronted with plentiful evidence of Khoikhoi religious practices. It was difficult to overlook the signs strewn across the physical landscape, such as the cairns dedicated to the Nama deity Heitsi-Eibib. Europeans occasionally noticed that Nama huts and graves were oriented toward the east, where Heitsi-Eibib was thought to have lived.[26] Others commented on Khoikhoi ritualistic practices directed toward the full moon or a particular type of mantis. Yet even these observers managed to preserve their stereotypes by classifying such practices as "superstition" rather than religion. The diaries of Georg Schmidt, the first missionary to the Khoikhoi in South Africa, are typical in this respect, in their insistence that Khoikhoi practices directed at the moon were "not worship."[27] Eduard Kretzschmar's 1853 *South African Sketches* (*Südafrikanische Skizzen*) insisted at one point that the Khoikhoi had possessed "no religion [*Gottesdienst*]" at all before their conversion to Christianity. Kretzschmar referred in the next sentence to their "special *worship* of a large grasshopper" known as the "God of the Hottentots" without noticing the inconsistency.[28] Like Orientalism in Said's account, observations of Khoi culture seemed impervious to empirical counterevidence.

22. An unknown writer aboard an English ship in 1605, whose journal is reproduced in Raven-Hart 1967, p. 32. A German caller in 1671–76 remarked that the Khoikhoi appeared "more like monstrous apes than genuine human beings" (Raven-Hart 1971, vol. 1, p. 161).

23. Quoted in Mucchielli 1996, p. 211.

24. From the journal (1612) of Ralph Standish, surgeon on the *Hosiander* (Foster 1934), reproduced in Raven-Hart 1967, p. 57.

25. See, for instance, "Die Groß-Namaquas," in *Unterhaltungen aus der Länder- und Völkerkunde* (Hirschberg: Verlag Carl Krahn Jr.), 2 (9, 1818): 67.

26. T. Hahn 1881, p. 65.

27. Georg Schmidt 1981, p. 320.

28. Kretzschmar 1853, p. 208 (my emphasis).

Language was another valued marker of civilization, and it was sometimes claimed that the Khoikhoi lacked it altogether. Linguistically challenged Europeans complained about their "incomprehensible" language, which was described as resembling the "clucking of turkeys" or the "screaming of cocks" rather than any "human tongue." Khoikhoi speech was said to be "apishly [rather] than articulately sounded" and was compared to farting.[29] The word "Hottentot" itself was sometimes said to have come from a Frisian or Dutch word for the quacking of a duck. One German visitor who asserted in 1686 that the Khoikhoi "have no language at all" (haben gantz keine Sprach) conceded that they were "still able to understand one another."[30] But while Europeans expressed frustration at being unable to learn the local tongue,[31] Khoikhoi picked up English or Dutch very quickly. Europeans seemed incapable of reaching the obvious conclusion that the locals had more linguistic talent than their foreign visitors.

The earliest representations of Khoikhoi emphasized lack. In addition to language and religion, Europeans insisted for centuries that the Khoikhoi lacked government, law, and the will to work.[32] Another object of horrified fascination in the early modern literature was the ritual circumcision of one testicle among Khoikhoi men and the custom of removing the first joint of the woman's finger at marriage.[33]

The "Hottentot" was not simply "representative of the essence of the black" during the early centuries of European colonial contact but was a more elaborate and grotesque image.[34] In addition to lack, representations

29. Khoikhoi speech was also compared to the clumsy speech of "the folk in Germany" (various sources, reproduced in Raven-Hart 1967, pp. 18, 179; 1971, vol. 1, pp. 52, 63, 161, 204; 1971, vol. 2, pp. 233, 259).

30. Wurffbain [1686] 1930–32, vol. 2, p. 136.

31. From an anonymous account of the first trading expedition by the British East India Company in 1601 under the command of Sir James Lancaster, in Foster 1940, p. 81.

32. Idleness is a universal trope in European discussions of Africans and Pacific islanders (e.g., Merensky [1886] 1912), and of the Khoikhoi in particular (Coetzee 1988).

33. E.g., Frederick Andersen Bolling (1678), reproduced in Raven-Hart 1971, vol. 1, p. 147.

34. Gilman's (1985, p. 225) reading becomes even less accurate for the later eighteenth and nineteenth centuries. As European attention turned increasingly to skin color, the distance between the "yellow" Khoikhoi and "black" Africans increased. Europeans in this case were not projecting their repressed sexual desires onto the Khoikhoi (Fanon [1952] 1967); instead, the Khoikhoi served as a kind of fetish, in the Freudian sense. Their partial "self-castration" afforded the European male colonizer an opportunity to simultaneously acknowledge the threat of castration and to displace the anxieties associated with this threat onto a distant and exotic other, in an act of disavowal (Freud 1963).

of Khoikhoi sexuality focused on signifiers of perversity. The Englishman Thomas Herbert, who visited the Cape in 1627 before the founding of the Dutch colony, described the Khoikhoi as incestuous "Troglodites," a "whole Tribe commonly keeping together, equally villainous, coupling without distinction." Herbert reported that the Khoikhoi had "unnatural mixtures" with apes.[35] Several writers during the early decades of contact asserted that Khoikhoi men had unusually large penises.[36]

Khoikhoi were also described as the epitome of the impure and the abject. Polluting objects, according to Julia Kristeva, "always relate to bodily orifices," and these fall mainly "into two types: excremental and menstrual."[37] Of all Khoikhoi deviations, early European observers were perhaps most distressed by their uses of cow intestines. Numerous writers claimed that the Khoikhoi consumed the cattle's intestines raw, or nearly raw, along with the excrement inside.[38] As illustrated by figures 2.1–2.3, entrails loomed large in early visualizations of Khoikhoi. Another example of abjection is related to male initiation and marriage ceremonies, which involved urination by a priest onto the initiate or married couple (fig. 2.5).[39] The most infamous aspect of abjection was contained in the literature on the "Hottentot apron" (defined as "a hypertrophy of the labia and nymphae") and Khoikhoi "steatopygia," or protruding buttocks.[40] Throughout the eighteenth and nineteenth centuries, Khoikhoi women in the Cape and Greater Namqualand were inspected and measured by hordes of European travelers and scientists, including Francis Galton.[41] As Sander Gilman

35. Herbert (1638), reprinted in Raven-Hart 1967, p. 123 n. 30, 120.

36. See Georg Meister 1692, translated in Raven-Hart 1971, vol. 1, p. 204; and Langhansz 1705, pp. 401ff., translated in Raven-Hart 1971, vol. 2, p. 406.

37. Kristeva 1982, p. 71. Kristeva continues: "Excrement and its equivalents . . . stand for the danger to identity that comes from without."

38. See, for example, Wurffbain [1686] 1930–32, vol. 2, p. 136. See also *Ostindische Reise*, by Christopher Fryke (Frick), originally published at Ulm in 1692 (in Raven-Hart 1971, vol. 2, p. 233–34; Fryke [1700] 1929), and Johann Wilhelm Vogel's *Ost-Indianische Reise-Beschreibung*, from 1716 (Raven-Hart 1971, vol. 1, p. 218). Peter Kolb's revisionist ethnography from 1719, discussed below, denied accusations of Khoikhoi coprophagy (Kolb 1979, pp. 39–40).

39. See the comments of Wikar von Gotheberg (1778–79, translated in Moritz 1918, p. 74) and Tindall (1959, p. 28). Ritual urination was located closer to the abject than to genital sexuality in the European subjectivity of the era.

40. Gilman 1985, p. 232. On visual discourses of steatopygia in twentieth-century South Africa, see Rassool and Hayes 2001.

41. Galton (1835, pp. 87–88) provided a particularly repellent example of this gentlemanly voyeurism. He claimed to have worked out the dimensions of a particular "Venus among the Hottentots" from a distance, using sextant, trigonometry, and logarithms (see also Alexander

notes, female Khoikhoi sexual characteristics were mobilized in arguments for the "primitive nature of the Hottentot's anatomical structure."[42] Indeed, the German anatomist Gustav Fritsch insisted that the uncivilized character of the "Hottentots" was revealed by the very form of their skeletons.[43]

There were techniques for visually arranging comparisons between Khoikhoi and Europeans to encourage the desired interpretation. The simplest way to call attention to Khoikhoi deviations was to include Europeans in the picture, as in figure 2.1, from Willem Lodewycksz's account of the first voyage of the Dutch East Indies Company, under Cornelius de Houtman, in 1595–97. In this image the fully clothed Dutchmen are juxtaposed to the Khoikhoi, who are nearly naked and shown devouring entrails. A more complex visual format, in which Khoikhoi personages amalgamate features and poses familiar from Classical European art with specific dissonant elements, was also used. An example of this is a drawing of the Cape of Good Hope that accompanied Albrecht Herport's 1669 *Description of a Voyage to East India* (*Ost-Indianische Reisebeschreibung;* fig. 2.2). The image is structured by the rules of linear perspective that were codified in the Italian Renaissance, and the horizon and vanishing points are high, putting the viewer in a slightly elevated position. The details of skin, light, shadow, and meaningful gesture are rendered according to classical conventions traceable to antique statuary. The use of such conventions would have allowed the European viewer to make sense of the basic layout of the scene, and by extension to recognize the crucial deviations from the European standard.[44] One might attribute this reliance on traditional pictorial conventions and

---

1838 [1967], vol. 1, p. 231). John Barrow, who believed the Bushmen shared "a common origin with the Hottentots," claimed to have examined the "interior labia" of an entire "horde" of Bosjesmans, and insisted that "without the least offense to modesty, there was no difficulty in satisfying curiosity" (Barrow 1801–4, vol. 1, pp. 277–79). Anthropologist Gustav Fritsch, the leading German expert on South Africans during the last third of the nineteenth century, investigated a "freshly prepared Labia Minora/Hottentot apron" in Berlin (1872, p. 282). Berlin University anthropologist Felix von Luschan (1906) examined "a series of pure Bushmen and Hottentots" with his wife while in South Africa. See also Somerville 1979, app. 2, "On the Structure of Hottentot Women"; Kretzschmar 1853, pp. 205–6; Merensky 1875a, p. 18; and "Messungen von Buschmännern und Hottentotten," *Verhandlungen der Berliner Gesellschaft für Anthropologie, Ethnologie und Urgeschichte* 17 (1885): 59–62.

42. Gilman 1985, p. 238.

43. Fritsch 1872, p. 291.

44. The rhinoceros and ostrich in fig. 2.2 suggest a non-European locale, but the ethnic identity of the human figures is not obviously non-European. One person is smoking a pipe—a practice that the Dutch introduced into Khoikhoi culture. In contrast to fig. 2.3, the women's breasts are revealed only discreetly here.

FIGURE 2.1 Cape Khoikhoi. From the Willem Lodewijcksz account of Cornelius de Houtman's expedition to the East Indies in 1595–97, in De Bry 1599, plate 7.

FIGURE 2.2 *Cape of Good Hope.* From Herport [1669] 1930, p. 20.

Europeanized physiognomies to the fact that the artists who executed the final etchings for early modern travel publications had rarely traveled outside Europe. But when Europeanization was combined with specific markers of savagery, it could encourage a condemning judgment of the depicted "savages." Cow intestines are the key signifier of abjection in figure 2.2. Placed in the center of the image, with the marks on the face of Table Mountain directing the viewer's eye toward them, the entrails being passed from the standing male figure to the sitting figure are the focal point for the viewer's attention. Entrails are also wrapped around the figures' calves and are being eaten or cooked over a fire by the sitting female.

An etching accompanying Thomas Herbert's 1627 travel account (fig. 2.3) provides a cruder example of the same idea. A Khoikhoi woman is shown brandishing a dripping length of cow intestines. In another standard symbol of Khoikhoi debasement, the woman's distended right breast is slung over her shoulder to feed her child. Markings on the figures' skin suggests cicatrization, another Khoikhoi practice that horrified Europeans. Like figure 2.4, an illustration from Olfert Dapper's book on Africa (1660), Herbert's illustration uses a low horizon line. This calls attention to the intestines coiled around the Khoikhoi figures' ankles by placing them directly in the viewer's line of sight. The low horizon also causes the figures to loom monstrously over the civilized spectator.

The pictures accompanying the narratives of European visitors and pioneer ethnographers shaped the "scientific" race theories that emerged during the eighteenth century. For example, the *System of Nature* by Linnaeus (Carl von Linné) in 1753 placed the "Hottentots" in the human category of *"Homo monstrous,"* who were described telegraphically with the words "head conic."[45]

THE INTERACTION BETWEEN EUROPEAN ETHNOGRAPHIC REPRESENTATIONS AND COLONIALISM

The tropes of lack, perversity, and abjection were not confined to travelers and armchair theorists but also permeated the official discourse of the administration of the Cape Colony. In the early decades of Dutch colonialism, the discourse of Khoikhoi lack took precedence. The colony's first commander, Van Riebeeck, described the Cape's natives as a "dull, stupid, lazy, and stinking people" and contrasted them unfavorably with the "more intelligent Japanese or Tonquinese." Similar views were expressed at all levels of

45. Reproduced in Eze 1997, p. 13.

FIGURE 2.3 *A Man and Woman at the Cape of Good Hope.* From Herbert 1627, p. 18.

FIGURE 2.4 *Clothing and Weapons of the Hottentots.* From Dapper 1660, p. 618.

the colonial administration, down to the local Landdrost, or chief magistrate in rural districts. Even in the nineteenth century, after control of the Cape Colony had passed into British hands, the same images continued to circulate within the colonial state. In 1884, the British resident magistrate of Walwich (Walvis) Bay, which was primarily inhabited by Khoikhoi, reiterated a centuries-old slogan in his contribution to the official *Blue-Book on Native Affairs,* stating that "the Hottentot is proverbially a lazy indolent fellow."[46]

Ethnographic perceptions emerged from ongoing colonial interactions with the Khoikhoi and reshaped them in turn. These descriptions usually included practical recommendations for actively dominating the indigenes. From the beginning of his tenure Van Riebeeck contemplated enslaving or exterminating the Khoikhoi and expropriating their cattle. Three centuries after Van Riebeeck, a British official in the northern border region marveled that the "farmers have not taken law in their own hands and shot down these cumberers of the ground." The best solution, according to this administrator, would be to "scatter the heads of families, thus leaving children destitute to be apprenticed."[47] Eduard Kretzschmar's mid-nineteenth-century book concluded a discussion of Khoikhoi character with nuggets of practical wisdom: "Every colonist knows that a few hefty blows are better than words when dealing with natives." "The Hottentot," Kretzschmar added, "has to remember that he has a *Baas.*"[48]

The conflict between European and Khoikhoi settlers at the Kat River in the middle decades of the nineteenth century illustrates the interplay between ethnographic descriptions and historical-political processes. In 1829 the "liberal" British government at the Cape had settled Khoikhoi and Baster families on land taken from the Xhosa with the goal of providing a "breastwork against an exasperated, powerful enemy" in "the most vulnerable and dangerous" section of the frontier.[49] In 1846 the white Kat River settler J. M. Bowker gave a notorious speech in which he compared "the natives to the springboks which had vanished before the face of the white man, to the country's great benefit."[50] This speech blended a central

46. J. Simpson, "Walwich Bay," in Cape of Good Hope, *Blue-Book on Native Affairs* (1884), sec. 8, p. 191. See also Coetzee's *Waiting for the Barbarians* (1980) for a brilliant allegorical evocation of this colonial contact zone.

47. John H. Scott, "Report of the Northern Border District," in Cape of Good Hope, *Blue-Book on Native Affairs* (1883), no. 38, p. 123.

48. Kretzschmar 1853, p. 211.

49. Sir Andries Stockenstrom (1854), the commissioner general of the eastern districts who suggested the creation of the Kat River settlement, quoted in Kirk 1973, p. 412.

50. Quoted in Marais [1939] 1957, p. 238 n. 7.

image of lack, in which Khoikhoi were equated with wild animals, with the emerging proto-Darwinian discussion of the "necessary extinction of the primitive peoples."[51] After a half century in which alternative views of the Khoikhoi had been circulating (see below), Bowker's speech epitomized resurgent white resentment against the Cape's original inhabitants.

Ethnographic representations were shaped by practical interactions with the observed, even though they were rarely empirically accurate in their general themes or specific details. Thus, the Ovaherero, by refusing to convert to Christianity or to divulge their own religious beliefs, encouraged a hostile discussion among the missionaries of "Herero secretiveness." European insistence on the deviousness of the "lazy Hottentot" did not index any natural trait, but it *was* related to the frustrating indifference of the Khoikhoi to European goods in the early years, and to their pastoral mode of living.[52] The natural tendency of the Khoikhoi to move from place to place, traceable to South Africa's arid environment, nourished European perceptions of them as lacking the wherewithal to put down roots and build lasting settlements. As in nineteenth-century Namibia, the limited native interest in selling livestock or land to Europeans was a source of incessant ill-will.[53]

DISSENTING VIEWS OF THE EARLY CAPE KHOIKHOI

Social historians who are interested in plumbing European travel literature for evidence about historical Cape Khoikhoi culture sometimes express concern about the unremitting reciprocal plagiarism in early accounts. Most of these texts relentlessly repeat familiar formulas and the names of the same small group of authorities. Seen from a different angle, however, this reiteration of standard phrases and ideas reveals the hegemony of a specific European view of the Khoikhoi.

Nonetheless, European discourse on the Khoikhoi before the end of the eighteenth century was not entirely homogeneous. Countervailing tropes

---

51. For the nineteenth-century discourse of extinction see Quatrefages de Bréau 1864; and Gerland 1868. Elbourne 2000, p. 26, discusses the "frontier conservatives" in the nineteenth-century Cape who claimed that "Africans would melt away like Native Americans."

52. The Dutch never enslaved the Khoikhoi, but many were forced into serflike service until 1828, when ordinance 50 made them equal to Europeans before the law (Boonzaier, Malherbe, Smith, and Berens 1996, p. 109).

53. See *The Last East-India Voyage* (London, 1606), reprinted in Foster 1943, for an early example of conflict between the English and the Khoikhoi around the latter's unwillingness to part with their herds.

occasionally disturbed texts or images that were governed by the code of abjection. Khoikhoi voices were sometimes interpolated into travel narratives in ways that called into question the author's explicit message.[54] In other cases European writers set out to refute "white writing" directly. For example, in the relatively simple rhetorical strategy of "revindication," discussed by Mary Louise Pratt, authors retained their Eurocentric criteria of "civilization" but insisted that the Khoikhoi (or some other non-European community) in fact possessed these traits.

Three major alternative codes appeared in the early modern literature on the Khoikhoi. In one, Khoikhoi were described as noble savages. Rousseau had characterized the "Hottentots" as presocial primitives who had not yet advanced to his preferred "third stage" of human development, which was "precisely the stage most of the savage peoples known to us have reached."[55] But some of Rousseau's followers, including Le Vaillant, valorized the Khoikhoi as noble savages. This Rousseau-influenced code is evolutionist in figuring the savage as an ancestor of the observer's own culture, affectionate in its emotional stance toward the Other, and often tragic in anticipating the extinction of savage cultures. Contemporary "savages" in the eighteenth and nineteenth centuries were often compared to ancient Greeks, Romans, and (in German writing) to the pagan Germanic tribes.

Noble savagery was in many ways a simple inversion of social-evolutionary theory. The latter approach represents "savages" as civilized man *in nuce*. Social evolutionism saw savages as being capable of developing to higher stages of civilization or *Kultur* if exposed to the proper conditions.[56] Depending on the social evolutionist in question, the savages' advancement might require a benevolent colonizing power or precisely the opposite, freedom from colonization (the latter view was advanced by Georg Forster, discussed in chap. 4). Like noble savagery, this approach broke with biological racism and the polygenetic theories that described cultures like the Khoikhoi as being condemned to permanent inferiority.

We can occasionally catch a glimpse of a third, *relativizing* vision of the Khoikhoi in European texts and pictures from this period. The Khoikhoi appear here as simply *different* from Europeans, but this difference is not fitted into any comparative developmental scheme. Some Europeans noted that Khoikhoi were swift runners, skillful throwers of the *assagai*, or

---

54. See Pratt 1992 for an analysis of this sort of disturbance in colonial texts; and Jan-Mohamed 1985 on the nondialogic character of most colonialist literature.

55. Rousseau [1755] 1988, p. 39. See Lovejoy 1955.

56. Stocking 1987.

talented singers and dancers, without turning these traits into markers of primitivism or of an earlier, more "noble," stage. In his essay "On Cannibals" (1580) Michel de Montaigne laid the groundwork for both the noble savage frame and cultural relativism. On the one hand, he wrote, "these nations . . . are still governed by natural laws and very little corrupted by our own"; "They are in . . . a state of purity." On the other hand, he relativized: "I do not believe . . . that there is anything barbarous or savage about them, except that we call barbarous anything that is contrary to our own habits."[57]

A RELATIVIZING TREATMENT OF THE KHOIKHOI: PETER KOLB

Most discussions of the Khoikhoi before the mid-nineteenth century were structured by the codes of abject savagery, even if they were punctuated by one or the other of the additional approaches.[58] The most famous relativizing treatment of the Khoikhoi was Peter Kolb's narrative, first published in German in 1719 and subsequently translated into French, English, and Dutch.[59] Kolb's discussion opens with the statement that "few histories have been handed into the world with so much falsehood and imperfection as the accounts we have hitherto had of the people about the Cape of Good Hope."[60] Much of Kolb's text is structured as a series of corrections to this literature.[61] In addition to a revindicating assimilation of Khoi cultural paradigms to European ones, Kolb uses their customs to criticize European cultural mores, arguing for instance that they take better care of their children than the Germans.[62] The most interesting sections of

57. Montaigne [1580] 1958b, pp. 108–9.

58. The relativistic view of the Khoikhoi received its first significant expression in a long essay by the Cape settler Grevenbroek from 1695, who wrote (1933, pp. 239, 195) that the Khoikhoi were "miles ahead of many Europeans" in terms of hospitality, adding, "I only wish our citizens would learn from them."

59. Kolb studied Oriental languages in Halle before going to the Cape in 1705 to conduct astronomical and meteorological studies for a Prussian nobleman. Kolb was employed by the Dutch East Indies Company between 1707 and 1712 and returned to Germany in 1713 (W. Jopp, introduction to Kolb 1979, pp. 17–18).

60. Kolb 1731, p. 25.

61. Pratt 1992. Against dominant views, Kolb insisted that the Khoikhoi have government and religion, that they do not "cohabit promiscuously with their Women," and that they are not afraid of water.

62. Kolb 1731, pp. 160, 254, 39. Kolb also countered a central negative stereotype about Khoikhoi idleness but in doing so embraced another structure of domination, arguing that they "make excellent servants."

Kolb's text, however, are culturally relativist. Kolb notes of a certain Khoikhoi woman that "the Hottentots look'd upon [her] as a very great Beauty," suggesting a plurality of aesthetic standards. He alludes to alternative approaches to medicine, writing that "in every Kraal there is a Physician well skilled in Botany, Surgery and Medicine of the Hottentots." Kolb observes that while Khoikhoi food may appear "nauseous and uncleanly" to Europeans, it "agrees very well with their Constitutions."[63] Elsewhere Kolb writes that Africans reject butter as "inedible," which raises the question "Who are the barbarians and who the civilized?"[64] The most strongly formulated relativizing passage appears in a discussion of a practice that many contemporary Europeans saw as epitomizing Khoikhoi barbarism: the abandonment of the aged to their fate in the wild. Kolb counters the conventional view by interpolating into his text a Khoikhoi voice, which asks a European whether it is not equally cruel "to suffer either Man or Woman to languish any considerable Time under a heavy motionless Old Age?"[65] This passage is interesting both for its formal "dialogical" technique of granting equal status to an aboriginal speaker and for its substance. Even if the Khoikhoi speaker is a complete fabrication, it matters that Kolb is breaking with the convention of only allowing Europeans to be heard.[66]

The engravings in Kolb's book that depict groups of Khoikhoi engaged in various daily activities come closest to a visual expression of cultural relativism in this period. Rather than being structured around contrasts between Khoikhoi and European attributes, these images focus on the seriousness, strangeness, and self-evident normalness of Khoikhoi practices. There is less insistence on activities that Europeans would have construed as grotesque. The composition of Kolb's picture of the Khoikhoi male initiation ceremony (fig. 2.5), for example, draws attention to its collective and ritual aspects—a group of males sitting in a circle—rather than emphasizing the figure on the right side of the picture. Indeed, without the accompanying text the viewer might not even realize that this represents a Khoikhoi priest urinating on the initiate.[67] Kolb's portrait of a "Hottentot woman" (fig. 2.6) emphasizes

63. Kolb 1731, pp. 87, 39–40, 48.

64. Pratt 1992, p. 43.

65. Kolb 1731, p. 320.

66. Kolb also suggested that various features of Khoikhoi culture stemmed from contact with Europeans, using the rhetorical figure of "historicization," discussed below. Of course, Kolb did not break entirely with the conventions of his era, including slavery (Pratt 1992), and some of his specific claims about Khoikhoi culture have been questioned.

67. Figure 2.5 is taken from the 1731 English edition, in which the engravings were copied from the 1719 German original but were much smaller. In the original version (Kolb 1719, p. 426, plate XI) the image is reversed, which means that the urinating priest is the first image

FIGURE 2.5 (above) *The Young
Males receiv'd into the Society of Men.*
From Kolb 1731, p. 120, fig. 1.

FIGURE 2.6 (right) *The Apparel
of the Hottentot Woomen.* From Kolb
1731, p. 190.

stark difference without posting a European figure in the picture to generate an explicit comparison. The African-style houses and the coils around the wrists and ankles are presented matter-of-factly, as is the presence of a bare-breasted, pipe-smoking woman. In contrast to figure 2.2, there is no attempt to emphasize that the bracelets are made of cow guts, and the breasts are de-emphasized rather than distended. The perspective is not strictly linear; the village scene in the background is tipped forward. The effect, whether intentional or not, is to render the composition more stylistically African, at least insofar as linear perspective was established and perceived by this time as modern and European.

LE VAILLANT: THE KHOIKHOI AS NOBLE SAVAGE

I made a country real, a normal place,
Romantic, I agree, and odd but
Savage the right way at last. I showed
There were no Giants, club-footed or one-eyed . . .

PATRICK CULLINAN, "1818. M. François le Vaillant Recalls his Travels to the Interior Parts of Africa 1780–1785"

Kolb pioneered a relativizing treatment of the Khoikhoi that was widely read but rarely emulated. A more common dissenting approach to the Khoikhoi in the eighteenth century depicted them as noble savages.[68] In his *Essai sur les moeurs et l'esprit des nations*, Voltaire described Khoikhoi "mores" as "soft and innocent."[69] Diderot insisted that the "Hottentots" were "not at all stupid as was believed," and he praised them for dwelling "in the happiness, innocence and tranquility of a patriarchal life." Expanding on the distinctive gender roles within the noble savage perspective, Diderot quoted from "two Hottentot songs" given to him by the Cape traveler Robert Gordon: "'Run to me, my women; sing, I return from far away. Your song will delight me.' Here is their war chant: 'To war, to war; to arms, to arms; let us go, let us go to war. Courage, my friends, if we have courage we shall defeat our enemies.'"[70] This vision of Khoikhoi women as delightful sensu-

---

for the eye accustomed to reading from left to right, and the act of urination is more explicitly rendered. See R. Kennedy 1975, vol. 1, caption for images K27–K128, for a comparison of the images in the various editions of Kolb.

68. A recent example of this is J. M. Coetzee's boyhood memoir, which describes a "Hottentot" boy as having "kept all his life to the path of nature and innocence" (1997, p. 61).

69. Voltaire 1963, vol. 2, p. 308. Voltaire began work on the 1769 *Essai* as early as 1741. See Pomeau 1963 for the complex publishing history.

70. Diderot [1819] 1876, p. 445, in the translation by Cullinan (1992, p. 23).

alists and Khoikhoi men as courageous warriors received its most extensive elaboration in the travel narratives of Le Vaillant, who visited the Cape's northern regions during the 1780s. Le Vaillant claimed to be drawing directly on Rousseau for inspiration, and he named his son Jean Jacques.[71] He referred repeatedly to the Khoikhoi as "men of nature" whose very life philosophy was derived directly from nature. The Khoikhoi were associated with friendliness and generosity, courage, love of freedom and equality, and innocence. They were, he wrote, "essentially good."[72]

Le Vaillant's writings resembled the literature on Khoikhoi abject savagery insofar as he defined "savagery" by juxtaposing it against European civilization—the only difference was that the valence was reversed. The preference of the "Hottentots" for a simple, natural life was contrasted with the indolence of the rich in the great European cities. This theme was connected to a polemic against colonialism. Repeating Voltaire's formula, Le Vaillant argued that "primitive" people were "mild and amiable" as long as they were left in their "natural" state, that is, when they were "not irritated and treated with injustice." The culmination of this critique was a passage in which Le Vaillant asked how Europeans would respond if they were colonized by the "savages of Africa and America." He suggested that the killing of Captain Cook in Hawai'i a decade earlier had been a justifiable act of revenge for outrages committed.[73]

The central place of gender in the discourse of noble savagery emerged clearly in Le Vaillant's writing. For Le Vaillant, Khoikhoi women were simultaneously sensual and innocent. The "naturalness" of Khoikhoi and other "savage" women rendered them both attractive and available to the Western male observer.[74] Indeed, Le Vaillant included a chapter on his flirtation with a Khoikhoi woman, Narina, whose sentiments of love for the Frenchman suggested "how strong the first impressions of *nature* are."[75] Khoikhoi men were depicted as dignified, primitive warriors, anticipating

71. Bokhorst 1973a, p. 11.

72. Le Vaillant 1790, vol. 2, p. 35; 1796, vol. 1, p. 150; 1796, vol. 2, p. 362; 1796, vol. 2, p. 176; 1790, vol. 3, p. 335; 1790, vol. 2, pp. 14-15; 1790, vol. 2, pp. 67, 136-37; 1790, vol. 2, p. 149.

73. Le Vaillant 1790, vol. 1, p. 306; 1796, vol. 1, pp. 150-52.

74. On the centrality of plots of cross-cultural, interracial colonial "love" in precolonial literature on the Americas during the second half of the eighteenth century, see Zantop (1997). The eighteenth-century depiction of indigenous men as noble savages differs from earlier treatments of native American men as feminized and sexually decadent. Zantop's book ignores the strand of the noble savage discourse that glorifies the dignified primitive warrior, and it also ignores James Fenimore Cooper, despite his enormous popularity in Germany and elsewhere.

75. Le Vaillant 1790, vol. 1, p. 429 (my emphasis). Narina was a member of the Gonaqua (or Hoengiqua), a Khoikhoi or mixed Khoikhoi-Xhosa tribe in the Eastern Cape.

Chateaubriand's portrayal of a Natchez Indian in *Atala* (1801) and James Fenimore Cooper's portrayal of the young Mohican Uncas in *The Last of the Mohicans* (1826).[76]

As in Kolb's text there is a proliferation of disparate codes in Le Vaillant. In a relativist vein he noted that Europeans could smell offensive to Khoikhoi.[77] Discussing the shape of the nose among the Houswaana Khoi he observed that "mine being the only [nose] formed after the European manner, I appeared in their eyes as a being disfigured by nature."[78] Other passages activated the older code of abject savagery, rehearsing the theme of laziness or granting the Khoikhoi only a "slight portion of intelligence."[79] Following in the "ignoble" footsteps of European sailors and gentlemen scientists, Le Vaillant pressured Khoikhoi women to allow him to examine them, and executed four paintings of the so-called Hottentot apron.[80] And despite his critique of colonialism Le Vaillant boasted about his personal techniques for managing the "natives"—a standard feature in the exotic travel literature and pioneer ethnology of this period.[81]

Le Vaillant's travel accounts were discussed in revolutionary France and were translated into English, German, and at least five other languages.[82] Numerous nineteenth-century African travelers claimed to have been inspired by Le Vaillant.[83] But the case of Le Vaillant also illustrates the disputational politics of reputation. Ethnographic discourse was as much a "field" in Bourdieu's sense as was the colonial state. The British travel

76. Uncas is described as an "upright, flexible figure," "graceful and unrestrained in the attitudes and movements of nature," revealing "all the finest proportions of a noble head"; his facial expression is "proud and determined, though wild" (Cooper [1826] 1986, pp. 52–53). The "young warrior," an "unblemished specimen of the noblest proportions of man," is compared to a "precious relic of the Grecian chisel."

77. Le Vaillant 1790, vol. 2, p. 51.

78. Le Vaillant 1796, vol. 3, p. 165. The Houswaana are sometimes characterized as Bushmen rather than Khoikhoi in current historiography (Shaw 1973, p. 144; but compare Elphick [1975] 1985, p. 28).

79. Le Vaillant 1790, vol. 1, p. 98; 1796, vol. 2, pp. 290, 298, 348-49.

80. Le Vaillant 1796, vol. 2, p. 182; Shaw 1973, p. 132.

81. In one passage Le Vaillant shoots some birds and then offers a Khoikhoi man the opportunity to test his gun. Le Vaillant loads the weapon with powder but no shot in order to "persuade [the native] by his own experience, that there was an enormous difference between European and *Hottentot*" (1790, vol. 2, p. 9).

82. According to Bokhorst "there was no writer on the Cape while it was still under Dutch rule whose works were more widely read than those of François Le Vaillant" (1973a, p. 12).

83. See Burchell 1822-24, p. 50; G. Thompson [1827] 1968, vol. 1, p. 2. Le Vaillant's books were familiar enough in Europe to play a central role in Wilhelm Raabe's popular 1881 novel *Stopfkuchen* (*Tubby Schaumann*); see Hell 1992.

writer, colonial official, and navy secretary John Barrow insinuated that Le Vaillant may never even have existed.[84] For Barrow, Le Vaillant was at best "a French traveller in Southern Africa, the veracity of whose writings have been called into question."[85]

Le Vaillant's drawings and paintings of Khoikhoi life provided a visual transcoding of noble savagery. In one sense his pictures are merely naive, revealing his weakness as a draftsman.[86] But this very naïveté releases his pictures from the oppressive *comparative* impetus that dominated the first set of images examined above. At the same time, Le Vaillant's pictures do not produce the same effect as some of Kolb's engravings of peering into a radically incommensurable world. His childlike painting of Narina's village (plate 1), for example, emphasizes its quaint, pastoral, and verdant aspects rather than the almost otherworldly practices communicated by Kolb. Only the corpselike figure lying on the ground in the lower left corner adds a hint of the uncanny atmosphere that permeates many of Kolb's engravings. Khoikhoi figures assume "classical" poses, and the landscapes suggest an Edenic past. The portraits of Narina (fig. 2.7) and of an unnamed Namaqua woman (fig. 2.8) call attention to *natural* beauty and grace; an engraving of an unnamed "Hottentot woman" (fig. 2.9) emphasizes voluptuousness rather than grotesqueness. The portraits of Khoikhoi men emphasize amiability (fig. 2.10), dignity (fig. 2.11), and grace (fig. 2.12), qualities thought to characterize "natural man." It is significant that some of the Khoikhoi in Le Vaillant's illustrations are not mere "types" but are given individual names, which serves to rehumanize them. After all, at least one distinguished nineteenth-century British traveler insisted that the Khoikhoi, as ignorant as "the beasts which perish," lacked even personal names.[87]

84. See Barrow 1801-4, vol. 1, p. 360; also "Query," *Cape Monthly Magazine,* July-December 1857, p. 59. A German specialist called Le Vaillant "unreliable" (Fritsch 1872, p. 272). Barrow was the main founder of the Royal Geographical Society, and he served as second secretary to the British navy for forty years. Before that he had served as treasurer on Lord Macartney's embassy to China in 1793 (see chap. 6) and accompanied Macartney to the Cape Colony in 1797. Barrow held various posts in the first British government at the Cape and returned to England in 1803 when the colony reverted temporarily to Dutch control (C. Lloyd 1970). His account of the embassy to China was written and published *after* the book on South Africa.

85. Barrow 1801-4, vol. 1, p. 359; see also pp. 279-80, 382.

86. These etchings were based either on Le Vaillant's original sketches or on an intermediate series of watercolors completed by Le Vaillant or his collaborators (Bokhorst 1973a, p. 7; 1973b, p. 99). Unlike the watercolor landscape scenes, none of the watercolor portraits were executed by Le Vaillant himself.

87. Alexander [1838] 1967, vol. 1, p. 165.

FIGURE 2.7 (lower left)
Narina, a young Gonaquais. From
Le Vaillant 1790, vol. 1, facing
p. 428.

FIGURE 2.8 (left) *Head of a
Housouana woman.* From Cape
Town Library of Parliament
1973, vol. 1, plate 63.

FIGURE 2.9 (lower right)
Female Hottentot. From Le Vaillant 1790, vol. 2, facing p. 50.

FIGURE 2.10 (right) *A Hotten-tot captain, in his ceremonial dress.* From Le Vaillant 1973, vol. 1, plate 34.

FIGURE 2.11 (lower right) *Klaas, The Author's favorite Hottentot.* From Le Vaillant 1790, vol. 1, facing p. 252.

FIGURE 2.12 (lower left) *A Gonaquais Hottentot.* From Le

EARLY BRITISH RULE, THE LONDON MISSIONARY
SOCIETY, AND THE HISTORICIZING APPROACH
TO THE KHOIKHOI

An alternative ethnographic perspective began to emerge in the half century between the end of Dutch rule in the Cape Colony and the Kat River
rebellion. This approach, which temporarily dominated official British
representations of the Khoikhoi, was more realistic, humane, and historical. The historicizing perspective avoided the comparative structure that
organized most of the earlier discourse on the Khoikhoi. Like the noble
savage view, it was concerned with change over time, but it eschewed linear
developmental models with fixed starting points, intermediate stages, and
endings. In contrast to early modern relativists like Kolb, the historicizing perspective made no assumptions about the static, timeless character of
cultures and nations.

This approach was so novel and so strongly associated with a minority of
British officials and LMS missionaries in the nineteenth-century Cape Colony that it was incapable of structuring any author's entire text. Instead, the
historicizing approach jostled for position with other codes. In this respect,
historicization was similar to the other alternative frames—relativism,
revindication, and noble savagery—none of which was able to hold its own
uninterruptedly through an entire essay or book. Any attempt to deviate
from the dominant paradigm was subjected to the pressure of European assumptions about race, religion, and evolution. In the writing of missionaries like John Philip and James Read Jr. of the LMS, and RMG missionaries
like Johannes Olpp, the historicizing treatment of the Khoikhoi was overcoded by the Christian and Protestant framework, which was historicist-
evolutionary and plotted according to a narrative of conversion or awakening.
While tracing in some historical detail the destructive impact of European
colonialism on indigenous culture, these critics offered seemingly contradictory accounts of Khoikhoi as progressing toward "civilization" or as being condemned to damnation by their biblical stigma as sons of Ham.

One example of a partially historicizing approach to the Khoikhoi was
contained in John Barrow's two-volume *Account of Travels into the Interior of
South Africa* (1801-4). Barrow's discussion of the Khoikhoi began on a properly historical note, emphasizing that "the ancient manners and primitive
character of this extraordinary race of men are, no doubt, much changed
since their connection with the colonists." Barrow criticized the Dutch for
having failed to "encourage the Hottentots in useful labour, by giving them
an interest in the produce of that labour" and for neglecting to make them

"feel they have a place and a value in society." This critical-historical mode was abandoned in the rest of Barrow's text, however, although it reappeared in his narration of a raid on a Bushman camp.[88] Barrow's text turned next to a language of revindication, acknowledging that "low as they are sunk in the scale of humanity," the character of the Khoikhoi had been "very much traduced and misrepresented." They were less hideous than had often been claimed and were in fact a "mild, quiet, and timid people; perfectly harmless, honest, faithful; and, though extremely phlegmatic, . . . kind and affectionate to each other, and not incapable of strong attachments." In a significant breach with the discourse of "Hottentot" mimicry that was also emerging at this time, Barrow insisted that the Khoikhoi "have little of that kind of *art of cunning* that savages generally possess," and that "if accused of crimes of which they have been guilty, they generally divulge the truth." Barrow explained the rationale behind various Khoikhoi customs, noting that "there are always two ways of representing things, and unfortunately for the poor Hottentot his character has been painted in the worst light." And in a comparison that was intended as praise but that later nourished perceptions of their racial ambiguity, Barrow compared the Khoikhoi to the Chinese, whom he called "the most civilized and ingenious *species*."[89]

The historicizing code was even more central to *Researches in South Africa* (1828) by the Reverend John Philip, longtime superintendent of the London Missionary Society at the Cape. Unlike most of his contemporaries Philip did not attribute a static, timeless character to the Khoikhoi, although he clearly held up Christianity and European civilization as a higher plane to which all Africans could and should aspire. Yet Philip also argued that colonialism necessarily resulted in a "*reciprocity* of injuries," traced the "degradation of the Hottentot character" to European abuse, and questioned the superiority of some versions of European "civilization."[90] Other South

88. Pratt (1992) argues that Barrow's description of the raid breaks with the ostensible timelessness of the "ethnographic present" and reveals the historicity of Bushman culture. But at the beginning of Barrow's chapter on the raid the Bushmen are introduced as "justly entitled to the name of savage" and as infamous for the "concealed manner in which they make their approaches to kill and to plunder" (Barrow 1801-4, vol. I, p. 234). Barrow's treatment of the Bushmen is thus multivocal, like most ethnographic writing concerning the Khoikhoi. The difference is that the representation of the Khoikhoi *begins* on a historicizing platform and moves to the ethnographic present, while the chapter on the Bushmen begins in the ethnographic present and culminates in a historical event.

89. Quotes from Barrow (1801-4), vol. I. pp. 150, 46, 151, 156, 157, 282 (my emphasis). Barrow was not as positive about the Chinese in his (later) book on China.

90. Philip [1828] 1969, vol. I, pp. 2, 57, xxxii (my emphasis). See also Comaroff and Comaroff 1992; and Elbourne 2003, pp. 390-92.

African missionaries in this period, including James Read, Jr., echoed this historicizing approach. But it remained a minority view, and Philip and Read were treated harshly by officials and settlers at the Cape.[91]

FROM IGNOBLE SAVAGERY TO MIMICRY

The clearest indication of the ways in which European views of the Khoikhoi were shaped, at least indirectly, by ongoing interactions between colonizer and colonized and by historical changes in Khoikhoi culture is the shift from themes of lack, perversity, and ignoble abjection to the nineteenth-century emphasis on *mimicry*. For an anthropologist like Friedrich Müller, writing in 1873, the "talent for mimicry" was the defining feature of the "Hottentot."[92]

As I suggested in the preceding chapter, we need to distinguish between two different conditions, both of which could be characterized as variants of mimicry. The first resulted from the context of cultural "bilingualism" that confronted modern colonizers. Government policies aimed at stabilization were motivated by this form of mimicry, this condition of cultural in-betweenness that was perceived as empowering the native to evade colonial control. This condition was less an effect of colonialism than of precoloniality.[93] The second form of mimicry was related to intentional colonial projects that attempted to solidify a constant cultural position located between full assimilation and radical difference. This is closer to Bhabha's definition of mimicry, which he says originates in a colonial regime's need for a "system of subject formation." This leads to deliberate efforts to "construct a particularly appropriate form of colonial subjectivity"—a form that is almost the same as the European, but with a crucial difference.[94] Of course, such projects can never really succeed. Stabilization is the goal of native policy, giving it direction, but not its actual effect, even if some interventions can take hold temporarily if the colonized are willing to play along. I am more concerned in this chapter with the first, precolonial type of mimicry.

The shift in dominant European descriptions of the Khoikhoi, from abject savagery to unsettling mimicry, lagged behind actual changes in Khoikhoi culture. Khoikhoi had already started to trade with Europeans

---

91. Read 1852; see Elbourne 2000, p. 38, on the negative views of Read and his missionary father.

92. Friedrich Müller 1873, p. 79.

93. On the notion of "precoloniality" see Steinmetz 2002.

94. Bhabha 1994c, p. 87.

even before the founding of the Dutch East Indies Company garrison under the slopes of Table Mountain in 1652. Many of these Khoikhoi learned English or Dutch and began using European goods like tobacco. During the seventeenth century, individual Khoikhoi traveled to England and the East Indies and returned to the Cape. News of these distant places spread among the native inhabitants of the Cape, sometimes sparking resistance to the Dutch.[95] Sweeping changes in Khoikhoi culture were unleashed by the expansion of internal markets in labor and commodities and by the expropriation of their land and livestock. Khoikhoi culture was also reshaped by Christianity and the lifestyle associated with mission stations, beginning with the founding of the Herrnhut Moravian mission by Georg Schmidt in the 1730s. Schmidt's indigenous clients were baptized, given new names, and instructed in the foreign, European language, inaugurating an approach that would be emulated by the LMS and RMG.[96]

After the British gained firm control of the Cape in 1806, they supported government and missionary efforts to Europeanize the Khoikhoi. A mainstay of the regime's system of subject formation during the early decades of the nineteenth century was sedentarizing the Cape natives by requiring them to have a "fixed place of abode."[97] The Khoikhoi who were granted plots of land (erven) at the Kat River in 1829 were expected to plant trees, enclose their grounds, and build brick or stone houses with glass windows and more than one room.[98] Initially the British tried to gain control over Khoikhoi polities by appointing their captains, but most of the captains' powers were subsequently abolished by the 1809 "Hottentot Proclamation" by Governor Caledon (Du Prc Alexander, second Earl of Caledon).[99] The colonial governments inducted Khoikhoi into military formations, beginning with the Dutch in 1793. The Cape Corps, or Cape Regiment, formed

95. A Cape Khoikhoi named Coree (Cory) was abducted to England in 1613 (Terry 1655, pp. 20–22). Another Khoikhoi called Doman traveled to Batavia in a DEIC ship and returned to tell his compatriots about Dutch atrocities there (Moodie [1838] 1960, p. 164). Other cases of Khoikhoi cultural intermediaries in the early decades of contact and colonialism include Autshumato ("Herry"), Van Riebeeck's first interpreter (1611–63), who also traveled to the East Indies and back, and Korotoa ("Eve"), an interpreter and the first Khoikhoi Christian convert.

96. Georg Schmidt, the first full-time Christian missionary to the Khoikhoi, between 1737 and 1744, argued against Dutch officials who believed that the Khoikhoi were "the worst of all nations" and "too savage to be helped." The Dutch tried unsuccessfully to prevent Schmidt from baptizing his Khoikhoi clients (Georg Schmidt 1981, pp. 338, 340, 392, 484).

97. Marais [1939] 1957, p. 152.

98. Elbourne 2000, p. 39.

99. Boonzaier, Malherbe, Smith, and Berens 1996, p. 101.

during the first British occupation, had 250–800 Khoikhoi troops.[100] More Khoikhoi were incorporated into the colonial army after they proved their value in fighting against the Zulu *Mfecane* uprising during the 1820s, filling a gap in military manpower while giving the British an opportunity to work on them culturally. Another dimension of this integration policy was a system of treaties with independent Khoikhoi communities.

Missions like the LMS were in the forefront of Europeanization.[101] Residence at a mission station provided individual Africans with some protection against settler exploitation and colonial state violence. Many switched from herding to sedentary horticulture, abandoned their traditional portable mat huts in favor of cottages, and began wearing European clothes and speaking Cape Dutch. The cultural revolution linked to Christianity was not limited to changes in religious beliefs but encompassed an entire world of social practices, as Jean and John Comaroff have shown for the South African Twsana during the same period.[102]

The widespread impression that Khoikhoi were becoming partially "civilized" during the first half of the nineteenth century was related to these ongoing processes. But partial assimilation did not lead most colonizers to see the Khoikhoi as becoming genuinely and fully Europeanized. Instead, a more hostile view of the Khoikhoi as mercurial mimic men, seesawing uncontrollably between their abject origins and modern assimilated lifestyles, came into focus. This framework was strengthened by the collapse of collaboration between the British government and the Khoikhoi during the Kat River rebellion.[103] Now the Khoikhoi stopped being perceived as "useful agents of rule." The government's "reliance on the Khoikhoi as soldiers was radically scaled back," and racial hatred was now more openly expressed.[104] Khoikhoi continued to be used in private "commando raids" by Boer settlers against Bushmen, but they became increasingly marginal to the official system of rule. The colonial governor at midcentury, Harry Smith, described the Khoikhoi as sliding backward into "barbarism."[105]

These shifts in dominant colonial perceptions of the Khoikhoi resulted from the end of the collaborative relationship, from ongoing changes in their culture, and from open resistance. Developments far removed from

---

100. The regiment was downsized after 1827 and renamed the Cape Mounted Rifles (Marais [1939] 1957, pp. 132–33).

101. Du Plessis 1911, pp. 91–119; see also Campbell 1814; Moffat 1842; and Merensky 1875b.

102. See Beidelman 1982; Keane 1998; and Comaroff and Comaroff 1991–97.

103. Ross 1999; Bradlow 1989.

104. Elbourne 2000, pp. 40, 27; 2002.

105. In Kirk 1973, p. 411.

the immediate colonial stage also played a role. The most important of these was European science, with its increasing emphasis on clear-cut differences between natural categories, including the human "races." Crucial developments included the abandonment of the sharp distinction between man and the rest of natural creation in the systems of Linnaeus, Georges-Louis Leclerc Buffon, Georges Cuvier, and others; the extension of the word *race* from animals to humans; and new human "racial" typologies.[106] These intellectual developments influenced views of the Khoikhoi, who were neither black nor white, nor easily categorized as a "mixed race."

According to the prevailing formula in nineteenth-century European discussions, the "Hottentot" embodied a series of contradictions between "primitive" and "civilized" traits. Anders Sparrman, a Swedish student of Linnaeus, concluded his *Voyage to the Cape of Good Hope* (1785) by summarizing Cape society as "a world composed almost entirely of contradictions."[107] Volatility came to be seen as the very essence of the Khoikhoi. Gustav Fritsch summarized the Khoikhoi as having a pronounced "unpredictability of character" (Unberechenbarkeit des Charakters).[108] Fritsch acknowledged their considerable intelligence but insisted that this was offset by an "abysmal witlessness" (bodenloser Leichtsinn). The suggestion was not that the Khoikhoi lacked self-control and veered *unwittingly* between traditional and modern behaviors but rather that these wild fluctuations were motivated by a certain devious cleverness. A Cape Colony newspaper article published at the beginning of the twentieth century crystallized this revised viewpoint, arguing that the Khoikhoi were "neither negroes nor uncivilized savages . . . but through their Hottentot ancestry and later intercourse with Dutch colonists, they are that repulsive compost, a yellow mongrel horde in a land of blacks and whites. . . . [they are] *cultivated in deceit*. . . . and their vaunts are of successful duplicity."[109] Where the Khoikhoi had earlier been described as "idle and dull," a Rhenish Missionary Society publica-

---

106. See Linné [1735] 1806; and Buffon 1749. These race-theoretic systems depended on the older paradigm of the "great chain of being," according to which natural objects were divided into discrete classes rather than being seen as "members of a qualitative continuum" (Lovejoy [1936] 1964, p. 228). According to Mungello (1999, p. 93) "the division of mankind into four or five races began with the Frenchman François Bernier, who published the *New Division of the Earth* (*Nouvelle division de la terre*) in 1684." Netanyahu (1995) pushes this back even further, arguing that European race thinking began with the Iberian *Reconquista*, with its focus on purity of blood. But the elision of the man-animal distinction (as opposed to the demonizing of certain classes of people) was a legacy of eighteenth- and nineteenth-century science.

107. Sparrman [1785] 1975, vol. 2, p. 256.

108. Fritsch 1872, pp. 305-7.

109. "German South-West Africa," *Owl*, November 18, 1904, p. 11.

tion in 1852 claimed they had become "more enterprising than all of their neighbors." Even though the leading goal of almost every missionary in Africa was to stimulate "industriousness," in this case the idea of "enterprise" prompted an anxious warning. The report worried that the newly energized Khoikhoi, with their "fondness for migration and travel," were "striving to penetrate the black population of South Africa and to combine with them" in disruptive ways.[110]

Anders Sparrman (1748–1820)

Anders Sparrman was a Swedish medical doctor, a student of Linnaeus, and a traveler who spent twenty-one months at the Cape of Good Hope during the 1770s. He also accompanied Captain Cook on his second voyage in the *Resolution* in the role of a naturalist.[111] Sparrman's Cape narrative is symptomatic of the transition at the end of the eighteenth century from Enlightenment-inspired perceptions of the Khoikhoi to the nineteenth-century concern with mimicry. Le Vaillant disrupted the discourse of Khoikhoi ignoble abjection. Writing at the same time as Le Vaillant, Sparrman explicitly called attention to ongoing revisions of the traditional perspective, but his text failed to reach any final conclusions concerning Khoikhoi nature. The text initially relies on the code of revindication.[112] Recalling Le Vaillant and his more famous Enlightenment predecessor Georg Forster, Sparrman mobilizes the Khoikhoi for an oblique criticism of European class society, insisting that the "equality of fortune and happiness . . . enjoyed by these people, cannot but have a singular effect in preventing their breasts from being disturbed by this baneful passion" (i.e., envy).[113] The next time the Khoikhoi appear in his text, however, Sparrman reverts to the older paradigm, describing the "leading characteristic of their minds" as a "dull, inactive, and I had almost said, entirely listless disposition."[114] Only the odd interpolation ("I had almost said") suggests some discomfort with this backward slippage. The next passage narrates an encounter in which the author tries unsuccessfully to induce a young Khoikhoi man to join his exploring party. He initially perceives the man through the conventional filter, focusing on his "extreme indolence," which "excited in [Sparrman] . . . the greatest indignation, as well as the

110. "Die Haukoïn oder Bergdamra," *Berichte der RMG* 9 (14, 1852): 215.
111. See foreword to Sparrman ([1785] 1975), vol. I, by V. S. Forbes.
112. Sparrman [1785] 1975, vol. I, pp. 189, 200.
113. Ibid., p. 192.
114. Ibid., p. 209.

utmost contempt for the Hottentot nation." Later, however, after the author has had sufficient time to "consider the matter more impartially," he revises his initial opinion and concludes that "the lad, from his habits as well as nature, could very easily make shift with a moderate quantity of food, and with this could and actually did enjoy what to him was a real substantial pleasure, viz., his ease and tobacco."[115] This passage narrates the attainment of a more rational ethnographic vision by Sparrman and points to the specific, alternative rationality of the Khoikhoi. At the end of part I, the Khoikhoi and the "civilized nations" are described as being equally unsuccessful and criminal.[116] Finally there is a historicizing moment, with Sparrman diagnosing Khoikhoi customs as corrupted by slavery.[117]

John Philip's historicizing social evolutionism was atypical among Cape missionaries, many of whom accepted the emerging view of the Khoikhoi as unstable mimics. Alexander Merensky, a missionary in South Africa during the mid-nineteenth century, combined the revindicating and historicizing approaches with the more recent tropes of trickery. Merensky remarked that the Khoikhoi, like all other "natural peoples," interacted quite differently with whites than with their own kind. While whites "usually try to exploit the colored, and quickly become their enemy," the colored are "polite and loving" with one another.[118] Yet Merensky also insisted that "the Hottentot has a mobile [*bewegliche*] nature. . . . his emotions are easily excited," and that he "easily becomes obstinate, stubborn, and disobedient." According to Merensky the Khoikhoi were highly intelligent and skilled at learning languages, but also lazy and prone to nomadism. The Khoikhoi were "receptive to the impressions of the Gospel, sensitive, and inclined to sob, weep, and pray," but these impressions "often vanish as quickly as they have appeared."[119] Merensky offered a portrait of the Khoikhoi as

---

115. Ibid., p. 210.
116. Ibid., p. 325.
117. Ibid., p. 322.
118. Merensky 1875b, p. 82. A similar description can be found in the Rhenish Mission's official history; see Rohden 1888, p. 104.
119. To illustrate this capriciousness Merensky recounted an anecdote about a young female Koranna (a Khoikhoi branch). While nearly fainting from emotion during his sermon, this woman was also busy at the same time "seducing one of our young men, and had to be expelled from the station" (Merensky 1875b, p. 82; [1899] 1996, p. 528 n. 125). This anecdote appears in a passage contrasting "Hottentot character" unfavorably with the Basuto (Sotho) and the so-called Kaffers, or Xhosa. After returning to Germany Merensky became a colonial propagandist; see Merensky [1886] 1912; and van der Heyden's introduction to Merensky [1899] 1996, pp. 6–20.

unreliable, shrewd mimics, even as he appeared to blame this condition partly on colonial exploitation.

For Europeans imbued with the categories of race science the most obvious site of Khoikhoi shiftiness was "race" itself. Part of the ambiguity had to do with skin color. The earliest European visitors to the Cape had assimilated the Khoikhoi to a general category of "blacks" or "Ethiopians" and called them "progeny of Ham."[120] But the notion that "the Hottentot" was "the essential black" for nineteenth-century Europeans is deeply misleading.[121] Soon after the founding of the Dutch colony Europeans began describing Khoikhoi as "yellowish," "swarthy," "tawny," "chestnut-colored," or "olevaster," defined as "that sort of black we see [among] the *Americans* that live under the Aequator."[122] In the nineteenth-century Khoikhoi were usually called "yellowmen" or "redmen." Europeans did not see the Khoikhoi as mixed-race or half-castes.[123]

Another aspect of Khoikhoi racial identity that served further to unsettle them in European eyes concerned their "mysterious" origins. There was less interest in this topic during the seventeenth and eighteenth centuries. The focus on origins became more intense as the Khoikhoi became more similar to the Europeans. The uncertainty surrounding Khoikhoi origins was associated with a negative affect that recalled the mistrust of arrivés in European upper-class ideology. One apartheid-era South African historian described the Khoikhoi as "a sort of poor relation" to the Europeans.[124] They were argued variously to have descended from the Phoenicians, Chinese, Jews, and even Fijians.[125]

120. Raven-Hart 1967, pp. 119, 130.

121. Gilman 1985, p. 231. Gilman also seems unaware in this essay of the availability of a nonderogatory term for "Hottentots," that is, Khoikhoi.

122. Raven-Hart 1967, pp. 45, 175; Purchas [1625] 2004, p. 150; Wurffbain [1686] 1930–32, vol. 2, p. 136; and Herbert 1677, p. 16. See also Kolb (1731), who insisted that "Negroes" are "a People very different from Hottentots."

123. Dutch settlers used the term "Baster-Hottentots" to describe people descended from Xhosa and Khoikhoi, suggesting that the "Hottentot" was not itself already considered a mixed or "bastard" category. For Herder ([1784] 1985, p. 165) and German anthropologist Georg Ludwig Kriegk (1854, p. 4), the Khoikhoi were a "transitional" race.

124. Marais [1939] 1957, p. 275.

125. See Schapera 1933, p. v. Kolb (1979) writes that the Hottentots "have much in common with Jews and old Troglodytes" (pp. 26–28, also pp. 76, 152–53, 265); see also T. Hahn 1870, p. 15; and Moritz 1916, pp. 146, 150. For the thesis of Chinese origins, see "Das Land und Volk der Damra," *Berichte der RMG* 6 (21, 1849): 321; Krönlein 1852, p. 315; Galton 1853, p. 124; Alexander [1838] 1967, p. 56; Andersson 1856, p. 24; Mossop 1935, p. 161; Sparrmann [1785] 1975, vol. 1, p. 219; Le Vaillant 1790, vol. 2, p. 141; Rudolf Virchow's comments on the "Bushmen currently in Berlin," in Berliner Gesellschaft für Anthropologie, Ethologie und

Another discussion that called into question the reliability of the Khoi-khoi revolved around their relationship to the Bushmen.[126] Europeans had initially seen the Bushmen as impoverished or outcast Khoi-khoi.[127] James Prichard, author of the influential *Researches into the Physical History of Man* (1813), applied the language of "degeneration" to the Bushmen, describing them as offshoots of the Khoikhoi.[128] Other writers reversed this theory, speculating that Khoikhoi derived from Bushmen.[129] A new theory in the nineteenth century posited that the two groups had distinct origins but had intermingled subsequently.[130] Given that the earliest interpretation of the Bushmen saw them as impoverished Khoikhoi, it was ironic that a zoologist could describe the Bushmen of coastal Namibia in the early twentieth century as being "*bastardized* with Hottentots."[131] By this time Bushmen were starting to be seen as preferable to the Khoikhoi, as more natural and unspoiled. Prior to the late nineteenth century, however, any affiliation with Bushmen had negative connotations.[132]

The colonial project of rendering the colonized familiar but not

---

Urgeschichte, "Verhandlungen," *Zeitschrift für Ethnologie* 18 (1886): 221–37; and Fritsch, "Verwertung von Rassenmerkmalen für allgemeine Vergleichungen," *Zeitschrift für Ethnologie* 43 (1911): 272–79. On the theory of the Phoenician origins of the Khoikhoi, see Chapman [1868] 1971, vol. I, p. 191; and "Diskussion über den Vortrag des Hrn. v. Luschan," *Zeitschrift für Ethnologie* 38 (1906): 904. For speculation about a Khoikhoi connection to Pacific islanders (especially Fijians), see Hoffmeister 1882, p. 214.

126. According to historian Robert Gordon (1992, p. 6), "Bushman" was a "Lumpen" category designating indigenes who "failed to conform." Despite its originally pejorative connotations Gordon prefers the term "Bushmen" to partial or inaccurate alternatives like "San" and "!Kung." The first use of the term *Bosjesman* in a colonial document is reported for 1685, more than half a century after the first use of "Hottentot" (Elphick [1975] 1985, p. 24).

127. The British missionary Joseph Tindall repeated the theory that the Bushmen had "sprung from poor Hottentots" (Tindall 1856, p. 25); see also Philip ([1828] 1869, vol. 2, p. 2).

128. Stocking 1973, p. lxxxviii.

129. Somerville [1799–1802] 1979, p. 28.

130. On a fundamental difference between "Hottentot" and "Bushman" see Lichtenstein [1811–12] 1967, vol. I, p. 188; Holub 1881, vol. 2, p. 438; and John H. Scott, "Northern Border," in Cape of Good Hope, *Blue-Book on Native Affairs*, no. 43 (1885), p. 43. The label "coloured" sometimes lumped the two groups together again (Marais [1939] 1957), but in the nineteenth century it referred mainly to descendants of slaves whose ancestors had been brought from Madagascar and elsewhere outside the Cape (Bradlow 1989, p. 411). The boundaries between "Hottentot" and "Bushman" remained porous well into the nineteenth century, and the text by C. Rose (1829, p. 111) slips continuously from one to the other.

131. Schultze 1907, p. 98 (my emphasis).

132. Nowadays the Bushmen still figure as the ultimate noble savages in some anthropological discourse. For an early version of this see Bayer 1909, p. 185; and Passarge 1997. On scientific racism and images of the Bushmen in twentieth-century white South Africa, see Rassool and Hayes 2001; and Skotnes 1996.

identical to the colonizer seemed to have failed in the case of the Cape Khoikhoi. As a result of their seemingly anarchic oscillation between "nature" and "culture," the Khoikhoi were increasingly *hors catégorie,* or unclassifiable. Their aggravating "hybridity" accounts for the paradox that Europeans experienced the Khoikhoi as increasingly "mysterious" as cultural contact stretched into the centuries, rather than becoming more familiar.[133]

EUROPEANS AND THE NAMIBIAN
KHOIKHOI BEFORE COLONIALISM

The older Khoi communities of Namibia struck some Europeans as the "Last of the Mohicans," the "only true Hottentots" left.[134] The more Europeanized Khoi communities, by contrast, "call themselves *Orlams,* in distinction from the aborigines, the Namaquas, and by this they mean to say that they are no longer uncivilized."[135] Nineteenth-century Europeans also often referred to groups like the Witbooi simply as "Nama," and this usage is widespread in contemporary Namibia as a term for all Khoikhoi. But most historians distinguish the Orlams from the Nama based on their origins in the Cape, their relatively recent migration (in the eighteenth and nineteenth centuries) to Greater Namaqualand, and their cultural intermediacy. Most Namibian Orlams were organized as "commando groups" led by *kapteins,* a structure that was patterned partly on the commando raids in which many Cape Khoikhoi had participated.[136] Orlams rode horses and used rifles. Many were Christians, often former "national assistants" of the missionaries, and many had Western names in addition to their traditional Khoisan names. The two most prominent leaders in nineteenth-century Namibia, Jonker Afrikaner (c. 1790–1861) and Hendrik Witbooi (c. 1838–1905), were Orlams, according to this description.[137]

The Afrikaner or //Aixa//ain Orlam community had emerged as a raiding party along the banks of the Orange River after 1823. They were

133. Dove 1896b, p. 79.

134. Quotes from T. Hahn 1869b, p. 13; 1870, p. 4; 1867, p. 238.

135. T. Hahn 1881, p. 153 n. 10. According to Theo Hahn the name Orlam signified "a shrewd, smart fellow" in Cape Dutch. Others claimed it was a contraction of "oor landers" or "o'erlands"—people "from other lands" or "overland"; see Wilmsen 1989, p. 92; and Kienetz 1977, p. 554 n. 5.

136. On the Cape "commando system" and Southwest African Orlams see T. Hahn 1868; and Lau 1987a, 1987b.

137. Dedering 1993a, p. 56.

then called into the northern territory by the Red Nation (Kai//khuan), who had genealogical seniority and ultimate sovereignty over all other Nama, and who were looking for help in their struggle with the Ovaherero.[138] By 1840 Jonker had settled with his people in Windhoek, the future capital of the German colony. During the middle decades of the nineteenth century the Afrikaners survived mainly by cattle raiding, pastoralism, and a semifeudal subordination of the Berg Damara and some Ovaherero.[139] Under Jonker's leadership the Afrikaners had replaced the Red Nation as the dominant political force in central Namibia by the middle of the nineteenth century.[140] The Rhenish missionaries who arrived in Windhoek in 1842 were compelled to rely on Jonker for protection.[141] Jonker's death in 1861 marked the beginning of the decline of Afrikaner power in central Namibia. Several European adventurers and copper miners, assisted by Rhenish missionaries, armed the Ovaherero for a "war of liberation" against Orlam domination in 1863.[142] The Afrikaner tribe continued to exist until 1897, when it staged an uprising against the Germans. Colonial troops commanded by the district commissioner of Keetmanshoop, Dr. Golinelli, hunted down the rebels and put them on trial "before a war tribunal." The entire Afrikaner community was put before a firing squad.[143] The colonial governor Theodor Leutwein was perfectly willing to seal the fate of certain "natural peoples" while trying to rescue others.

As the influence of the Afrikaner Orlams declined, the Witbooi emerged

138. Vedder [1938] 1966, p. 180.

139. On the Berg Damara see Lau 1979; Carl Hugo Hahn, "Damaraland and the Berg Damaras," *Cape Monthly Magazine*, April 1877, pp. 218ff.; "Wie man mit Miss. Hugo Hahn zu den armen Kindern von N.-Barmen reist," *Berichte der RMG* 9 (1, 1852): 9; "Die Haukoïn oder Bergdamra," *Berichte der RMG* 9 (14, 1852): 209–23; "Die Bergdamra," *Berichte der RMG* 23 (5, 1867): 131–34; "Otjozandjupa oder Waterberg," *Berichte der RMG* 31 (9, 1875): 76; and Carl Gotthilf Büttner, "Die Bergdamra," *Berichte der RMG* 34 (1–2, 1878): 29–42.

140. According to Loth (1963), the Afrikaner Orlams were beginning to create a territorial state in central Namibia during this period. Jonker Afrikaner had indeed consolidated control over the means of coercion within this territory, particularly with respect to the Ovaherero, and had started to improve roads and to engage in the "predatory" activities that are characteristic of states in general (Levi 1981).

141. See Carl Hugo Hahn's 1844 diary entry (1984, pt. I, p. 202), according to which the missionaries' reliance on Jonker was their only protection against the allegedly murderous Ovaherero. Hahn's enthusiasm cooled when Jonker prevented him from traveling to a conference in 1847 ("Groß-Namaqua-Mission," *Monats-Berichte der Rheinischen Missionsgesellschaft* 4 [2, 1847]: 11).

142. See Andersson 1989, vol. 2, pp. 236–48; and Hahn, "Meine Heimreise" (1873), VEM, RMG I.577b, p. 7.

143. T. Leutwein 1907a, p. 143; Kurd Schwabe 1910, p. 235.

as the leading political force in the region.[144] The Witbooi were a loosely structured "tribe," or *!haos*, composed of "various family groups" (for example, Keister, Jod, and Rooman), some of which made up a clan. These clans "stood in a fixed relationship to each other with the chief's clan ranking at the top of the socio-political hierarchy."[145] During the eighteenth century the Witbooi had "roamed the Cape as wealthy herders," and by the beginning of the nineteenth century they were "regarded as the most powerful group between Steinkopf and the Orange River."[146] They migrated across the Orange in the 1840s and 1850s and eventually settled in Gibeon (Kachatsus) in 1863, which was "given as a fief to the Witboois by the 'traditional' overlord of Great Namaqualand, the Red Nation." Their economy continued to be pastoralist and communalist, with no conceptions of private property in land or fixed territorial boundaries. For example, when "a trader paid his license, for traveling through Witbooi territory, in the form of gunpowder, the chief distributed it among the whole tribe to enable his men to engage in hunting expeditions."[147] The elderly chief Kido (David Moses) Witbooi died in 1875 after leading his people for almost seventy years, and his son, Little Kido (Moses) Witbooi, who was already sixty-eight years old, assumed the chieftaincy in 1876. The most important figure in the community at this time, however, was Moses Witbooi's son Hendrik. After being trained by the Rhenish missionary Johannes Olpp and becoming a church elder in the 1870s, Hendrik Witbooi led a commando group of about three hundred Witbooi on a sweep through Hereroland, beginning in May 1884. Over the next three years Hendrik continued his cattle rustling and fighting with Ovaherero and other groups while attracting many new followers and eliminating rivals among the Witbooi and other Nama and Orlam groups. In 1888 Hendrik settled his followers at Hornkrans, which they fortified and organized as a Christian community. I will return to the story of the Witbooi under German colonialism in the next chapter.

The Rehoboth Basters were the third Khoikhoi-related group destined to become a central target of German colonial policy. In the first half of the 1860s a Baster community was founded at De Tuin under the leadership of

144. Jonker Afrikaner's son Jan Jonker was killed in a battle with the Witbooi in 1889 (Goldblatt 1971, p. 112; Vedder [1938] 1966, p. 500), signaling the shift in power. The best recent treatment of the Witbooi is Kössler 2005.

145. Bochert 1980, p. 13. I use the word *tribe* with the proviso that collectivities in precolonial Namibia tended to be fluid and ethnically open. Budack 1972 provides a detailed discussion of the Witbooi political structure.

146. Dedering 1997, p. 62; also J. Olpp, "Beitrag zur Missionsgeschichte des Witbooistammes," VEM, RMG 1.404.

147. Bochert 1980, pp. 15, 17–18.

Rhenish missionary Peter Sterrenberg. After failing to secure legal rights to landed property, this community migrated north across the Orange with their new missionary, Johann Heidmann, in 1868.[148] After several years of negotiations with the established leaders in the region, the De Tuin Basters gained permission to settle at Rehoboth.[149] The Basters were more Europeanized than most Orlams. They were also determined to remain at Rehoboth, and began immediately to make improvements, blasting the rocks to obtain water and building Cape-style frontier housing (fig. 3.18). And their nascent government possessed two key elements considered by Europeans to be markers of modernity—a legal code, which was initially drafted during their northward trek and which continued to evolve, and a national flag.[150] The Rehobothers generally regarded themselves as superior to the Nama and Ovaherero.[151]

GERMAN PERCEPTIONS OF THE NAMIBIAN KHOIKHOI

The Southwest African precolony inherited from the Cape a multilayered storehouse of ethnographic representations of the Khoikhoi, and this became the most important source of precolonial perceptions of the Khoikhoi north of the Orange. Nonetheless, European representations of the Namibian Khoikhoi had a distinctive history and configuration. Europeans from the Cape Colony first crossed the Orange River in the 1760s, and various explorers such as Hendrik Jacob Wikar, Robert Gordon, and Willem van Reenen traveled in the region in the next few decades.[152] White colonists began settling beyond the northwestern frontier, and the first mission stations were created in 1806 at Warmbad and Heirachabis.[153] Between 1806 and the German annexation, most of the Europeans in Namibia were missionaries, and after 1842 most of these missionaries were associated with the RMG. Other Europeans in Namibia were involved in hunting, trading, and cop-

148. On Sterrenberg see "Und führe uns nicht in Versuchung," *Missionsblatt* (Barmen), 67 (September 1892): 67–70; Heidmann, "Gemeindechronik der Bastardgemeinde Rehoboth," VEM, RMG 3.538b, pp. 15, 43v; and Union of South Africa 1927, pp. 28–29.

149. Rehoboth's previous occupants were the Swaartbooi (//Khau-/goan) Nama.

150. For a brief history of the legal code and its revisions between 1868 and 1919 see Britz, Lang, and Limpricht 1999, pp. 61–82.

151. See the comments by missionary Heidman in VEM, RMG 3.538b, p. 59r (letter to Barmen, Warmbad, April 5, 1869, comments on the Basters' legal code), p. 192r (letter to Barmen, Rehoboth, October 14, 1884, comment on the Basters' flag), and p. 119r (letter to Barmen, Rehoboth, December 27, 1877, on Basters' feelings of superiority to other indigenes).

152. Mossop 1935, 1947.

153. Legassick 1979; Penn 1999.

per mining, and some got mixed up in indigenous politics. The last group of Europeans to arrive before 1884 was a handful of British officials from the Cape Colony.[154] These were the main sources of descriptions of the Namibian Orlams, Nama, Basters, Berg Damara, and Ovaherero before the 1880s.

The first graduates of the Rhenish Mission school in Barmen who were sent to South Africa voyaged with John Philip and worked under the guidance of London missionaries. The Rhenish missionaries soon founded a series of mission stations in the colony's northwestern frontier regions, and in 1842 they started working in Namibia. Their stations became the original building blocks of the future colonial state. Rhenish missionaries circulated between the Cape and Southwest Africa, producing a continuous intermingling of ethnographic ideas. All of the RMG missionaries were required to keep a diary and to report regularly to the mission's German headquarters, and lengthy excerpts from these letters were published in the mission society's reports. Thousands of readers in Germany were thus exposed to the missionaries' vision of the indigenous residents of the pre-colony.[155] The character of the various Namibian populations was vigorously discussed by the inner circle of the RMG, some of whose leaders would become architects of the colonial state in the 1880s.

THE NAMA

The prevailing construction of the Southwest African Nama as "traditional Hottentots" was sometimes intended as praise, but it also remobilized the web of older significations centered on abject and ignoble savagery. As the Barmen mission's annual report put it in 1847, the Nama were "even worse barbarians" than the Orlams.[156] Another report alerted its readers that the Red Nation Namaqua were even more "wild and raw than the Orlams" because "the old Namaqua paganism . . . has best survived here."[157] "The authentic Hottentot," according to one Namibian missionary, had a "leg-

154. Precolonial European travels in Namibia are collected and summarized in Moritz 1912, 1916, and 1918. On the earliest missionaries in the region see Tindall 1959; Rohden 1888, pp. 173–216; and Dedering 1997.

155. The RMG's *Missionsblatt* began publication in 1826, with a circulation that rose from twelve thousand to twenty-one thousand later in the century (Rohden 1888, p. 10). Like the weekly and annual reports, it often printed long diary entries from the missionaries.

156. "Neu-Barmen; Missionar Hugo Hahn mit Gattin; Missionar Rath," *Jahresbericht der Rheinischen Missions-Gesellschaft* 18 (1846–47): 37.

157. "Das rothe Volk," *Berichte der RMG* 11 (17, 1854): 258. On the Red Nation in relation to other Nama, see Budack 1986.

endary" pleasure in "laziness and filthiness."[158] This legend convinced missionary Hugo Hahn that "the Hottentot tribes are nomads and hunters and are so fiercely attached to this lifestyle that civilization seems to have no attraction at all for them.[159]

Others echoed these missionary sentiments. For Charles Andersson, who spent a great deal of time with Rhenish missionaries, the Namaqua were an "excessively idle race" and "sunk in barbarism."[160] James Chapman, who lived in Namibia from 1849 to 1863, saw the Nama as "men of impulse" with "idle and dissolute habits" who were prone to "jabbering with their hideous clicks." Southwest African Namaqua were thus assimilated to the traditional images of the Cape Khoikhoi. Chapman proposed that "a white man could control the Damaras [i.e., the Ovaherero] as their chief" and lead them in an "expulsion of the whole Hottentot race over the Auass mountains."[161] As we will see, however, European opinion later swung against the Ovaherero as well.

The tropes of capricious mimicry were also applied to the Namaqua over the course of the nineteenth century. The older Nama communities were quick to adopt certain aspects of European culture from the Orlams and, somewhat later, from Europeans.[162] Pioneer anthropologist Hans Schinz claimed that there was no longer any difference at all between Orlam and

158. Büttner 1884, p. 24.

159. See C. H. Hahn 1984–85, vol. 3, p. 661; see also vol. 4, pp. 1103–5. Even in his brutal judgments of the Nama Hahn was inconsistent, insisting that they had declined from their earlier state of "half civilization" (1984–85, vol. 4, p. 1108). Hahn speculated frequently about the Nama's inevitable extinction, writing in his diary, "I shudder to think of the future of the Namaqua. . . . I fear the Namaqua are *past recovery*'" (in English in the original; 1984–85, vol. 4, p. 1117 [my emphasis]). Hahn was considered to be an extreme "pessimist" by the heads of the Rhenish Missionary Society during the 1860s, but he ran the Augustinum at Otijimbingwe until 1872 and was then appointed superintendent of the entire "Hottentot and Nama mission" in Southwest Africa (Menzel 1992, pp. 16–17). Missionary Johann Heidmann also saw the Nama as "indolent," "weak," "extraordinarily reckless," and "easily excited" (VEM, RMG 3.538b, pp. 118v, 155v, 172r).

160. Andersson 1856, pp. 335, 329. In his 1864 journal (1987–89, p. 122) Andersson referred to the "Hottentots" as "baboon-faced scoundrels."

161. Chapman [1968] 1971, vol. 1, pp. 168, 228; vol. 2, p. 188. This suggestion was made in the context of the Ovaherero "war of liberation" against Jonker Afrikaner and was stimulated by Charles Andersson's unsuccessful bid to become Ovaherero chief (Andersson 1987–89, vol. 2, pp. 110–11 and app. 3). For another nonmissionary view of the Nama see Alexander [1838] 1967, vol. 1, pp. 161, 165, 190; vol. 2, p. 208.

162. Lau (1987b, p. 148) therefore argued that the Orlams were themselves the original "colonizers" of Namaland.

Nama at the dawn of the German colonial era.[163] German missionary reports often emphasized the cultural vacillation of the Nama. One article offered the following summary: "The Hottentots are . . . nomads, but they are not even competent herdsmen. . . . Their *instability* [*Unbeständigkeit*] . . . [is due especially to the fact that] the Namaquas don't know how to make anything orderly out of their country. But they are always quick to develop European needs."[164] Another mission article referred to the "volatile, tiny Nama nation with its wolflike nature."[165]

A few Rhenish missionaries and other Europeans in Southwest Africa were more sympathetic to the Nama, and some married Nama women. One of the most vigorous defenders of the Nama was Theophilus (Theo) Hahn, the son of a Nama missionary who had grown up among Khoikhoi children and earned a Ph.D. in philology at Halle University. During his German sojourn Theo Hahn spent his holidays at Poschwitz, the castle of Georg von der Gabelentz, a famed linguist and Sinologist, where he "had free access" to the professor's "excellent African library."[166] After his studies Hahn returned to Southwest Africa, where he lived as a trader and published a book and a dozen articles on the territory's native inhabitants.

Theo Hahn's texts, like those of Kolb and Le Vaillant, were unusually sympathetic to the Khoikhoi but also multivocal. He relied on the frameworks of noble savagery, revindication, and relativism to defend the Khoikhoi. Hahn observed that Nama manners were "still very simple and natural," not dictated by "absurd" fashion.[167] In the revindication mode, he compared Khoikhoi traditions to German ones and insisted that "it is also a prominent feature in the character of the Khoikhoi that they are *not* inclined to steal."[168] Discussing the decimal system of the "Redman" (Kai//Khuan), Hahn proclaimed that "these numerals . . . rank their inventors with the ancestors of our own Aryan race as far *as mental power is concerned*."[169] Hahn's most systematic efforts at revindication were focused on Nama religion, which

163. Schinz 1891, p. 104; also Kienetz 1977, p. 565.

164. "Unsere Namaqua- oder Hottentotten-Mission," *Berichte der RMG* 36 (5, 1880): 142 (my emphasis).

165. "Unsere Namaqua- und Herero-Mission," *Berichte der RMG* 11 (10, 1854–55): 152.

166. T. Hahn 1881, p. xi. According to Gordon 1992, p. 45, Hahn was the first South African to earn a doctorate in philology. He was not related to Hugo Hahn.

167. T. Hahn 1881, p. 54.

168. Ibid., p. 32; Hahn 1878, p. 264. Elsewhere Theo Hahn compared the condition of the Khoikhoi to that of the Germans "at the time of Caesar" (1881, p. 151) and likened the story of the Afrikaner Orlams to "deeds of which our medieval knights need not be ashamed" (1881, p. 98).

169. T. Hahn 1881, p. 16.

he compared favorably to the religions of "civilized and civilizing antique nations."[170] The most important fact was that "the Hottentots also worship a god."[171] A moment of relativism also crept into Hahn's writing when he quoted a Nama, "the famous !Nanib," who, when "called upon to turn a Christian . . . answered 'Never; my Tsūi//goab is as good as your Christ.'"[172] Hahn's discussion of the "refined taste of the ancient Khoikhoi" also comes close to relativism, since it was clear to readers that traditional Khoikhoi "tastes" were markedly different from European preferences.[173] Hahn relativized European notions of private property and theft at a time when the establishment of such rules was a top priority among settlers.[174] According to Hahn the missionaries and "so-called civilization" were ruthlessly extirpating the Nama. Soon, he said, all that would remain of the Nama would be "mutilated geographic names, as the ruined linguistic monuments to a people vanished without a trace."[175]

Theo Hahn was widely respected as the "best authority on Great Namaland" by early colonial-era officials. He consulted with Heinrich Vogelsang, the agent for Adolf Lüderitz who negotiated the first treaties with Namibians.[176] Hahn was highly regarded by the first imperial commissary, Heinrich Ernst Goering, by Goering's successor, Curt von François, and by leading scientific students of the colony, including Hans Schinz.[177] Like most of the missionaries in the precolony during the 1870s and early 1880s Hahn supported a program of "civilizing" the Nama, and he explicitly rejected the "Exeter Hall philanthropy" that advocated the rights of indigenous peoples.[178] He personally delivered his precolonial ethnographic representations to the nascent colony.

170. Ibid., pp. 150–51. Theo Hahn differentiated between "superstition" and "true religion," defining the latter as focused on "the purest conceptions of the Invisible." Even "the most cultivated mind" was prone to superstition, however, proving that "we are linked in an unbroken chain to primaeval men" (ibid., p. 75).

171. T. Hahn 1878, p. 262.

172. T. Hahn 1881, pp. 63–64.

173. Ibid., p. 22.

174. T. Hahn 1867, p. 306.

175. Ibid., p. 336.

176. Esterhuyse 1968, p. 39.

177. On von François's and Goering's respect for Hahn see Voeltz 1988, p. 34; also Schinz 1891, p. 75.

178. T. Hahn 1881, p. 76. Exeter Hall in London was the site of meetings and lectures by evangelical, philanthropic, missionary, and scientific associations during the nineteenth century.

THE ORLAMS

The Orlams' mix of independent-mindedness and acculturation made them more useful than the Nama but also less trustworthy in European eyes. Missionaries were troubled by their opacity and *"inconstancy."* Missionary Johann Heidmann compared them to Jews, writing that the eyes of one Orlam leader had a "Jewish and lurking [*lauerndes*]" quality.[179] The Cape government's special commissioner to the region, W. Coates Palgrave, described the Orlams as "sullenly hostile." The commissioner sketched an evolutionary curve running from "savagedom" to "rude civilization," and characterized the Orlams as occupying not an intermediate position along this curve but an *"indefinable"* one.[180]

The Orlams were the most assertive Namibian community during the nineteenth century, with strong leadership and modern weapons. During the middle decades Jonker Afrikaner succeeded in limiting the influence of the Rhenish missionaries and continued to harass white traders and adventurers in his territories. This encouraged the Europeans to arm and train the Ovaherero for war against the Afrikaners. The supervisor of the Rhenish Mission in Southwest Africa, Hugo Hahn, arrived at Windhoek in 1842 and was positively inclined toward Jonker at first, but soon became bitterly opposed to him. Hugo Hahn charged Jonker with "disgusting hypocrisy" and "inner and exterior decay."[181] Hahn wrote that Jonker's son Jan, who became *kaptein* of the Afrikaners in 1863, combined "cleverness, forked-tonguedness [*Doppelzüngigkeit*] and insincerity" with "noble and knightly traits."[182] As we will see in the next chapter, Orlam leader Hendrik Witbooi was described with the same seemingly in-compatible mix of tropes.

One of the most explicit elaborations of the theme of Orlam mimicry

179. Heidmann in VEM, RMG 3.538b, p. 70r–70v. Heidmann also referred to Kamaherero as "a certain Jewish type, with respect to his emotions" (ibid., p. 72r). In the printed version of this communiqué in the RMG's monthly report this passage was edited to read: "his face has a certain pagan character"; see Missionar Heidmann, "Conferenzreise nach Otjimbingué," *Berichte der RMG* 27 (4, 1871): 110.

180. "Special Commissioner to the Tribes North of the Orange River," in Cape of Good Hope, *Blue-Book on Native Affairs* (1879), pp. 135, 146 (my emphasis). Palgrave referred in general terms to the "Namaquas," but it is clear from the context that he meant Orlams in particular.

181. C. H. Hahn 1984–85, vol. 4, p. 1131 (diary entry from January 13, 1859). See also the negative portrayal of the Orlams in Hugo Hahn's wife's letters (E. Hahn 1992, pp. 67–68).

182. C. H. Hahn, "Mein Heimreise" (1873), VEM, RMG 1.577b, p. 28.

came from missionary Johann Georg Krönlein, who worked among the /Hai-/khauan Orlam people at Berseba. In an annual report from 1852 Krönlein started out by remarking that his students were often as good as European ones, but he went on to claim that "these people *want* to appear stupid to us Europeans because they know that *we* think they are stupid, and because they can conceal behind this supposed stupidity their *sophisticated intrigues* [*geschliffene Ränke*], which are not so different from those of the Chinese."[183] A sign of this shiftiness was that the Orlams spoke "extraordinarily rapidly in their own language, faster than the French." This was a picture of all-around deviousness.

The third major Orlam group in Southwest Africa was the Witbooi, who consolidated their presence at Gibeon after 1863. This community seemed to have ended its peregrinations during the 1860s and 1870s, and as a result the missionaries did not describe them as mimic men. Many Witbooi converted to Christianity in these decades. The Rhenish missionary to the Witbooi at Gibeon between 1868 and 1879 was Johannes Olpp.[184] Olpp's paternalistic description of Hendrik Witbooi as a "well-behaved Namab" (ein braver Namab) suggests that he believed that this mercurial group had finally calmed down.[185] In a lengthy treatment of the Witbooi Olpp argued that they were essentially identical to Europeans, and he used them to develop a mild critique of European class society and colonialism. Olpp noted that the label "Hottentot" was "in their eyes a horrific injustice."[186] The missionaries' influence during the 1870s was limited to the thousand or so Witbooi living at or near the station and was particularly strong among the wealthier and more powerful parts of the community, especially the Witbooi family itself.[187]

Conditions changed dramatically for the Witbooi during the five years between Olpp's departure from Gibeon and the declaration of the German protectorate. The August 1880 massacre at Okahandja that was ordered by Ovaherero chief Kamaherero (Maherero Tjamuaha) against all Khoikhoi living in his lands sparked a full-scale war between Ovaherero and a tem-

183. Krönlein 1852, p. 315 (my emphasis). Krönlein worked in Namibia from 1851 to 1877.

184. See Denzler 1991; VEM, RMG 2.580a, p. 59. The earlier missionary to the Witbooi, from April 1863 to 1887, was Jacob Knauer.

185. Olpp 1881. This text was published in 1881 during the turning point in Hendrik's career, but Olpp was no longer in Southwest Africa at that time and was unaware of Hendrik's evolution. On the mission's emphasis on sedentarizing Namibians see Panzergrau 1998, p. 137.

186. "Zur Charakteristik der Namas (Namaquas)," *Berichte der RMG* 32 (3, 1876): 78.

187. Bochert 1980, pp. 54–55.

porarily united front of Nama, Orlams, and Basters under the leadership of Hendrik Witbooi's father Moses.[188] Building on this new constellation of forces, Hendrik proceeded during the second half of the 1880s to subordinate the colony's Khoikhoi groups, including the Red Nation. In 1884 Hendrik began the first of his treks, striking out with his followers and raiding Ovaherero cattle posts. One motive was to resettle his people farther to the north, at Hornkrans. According to Hendrik, Gibeon had always been intended as a "temporary abode only."[189] Hendrik began to reject the advice of the Rhenish missionaries and to develop his own personal brand of Christianity. His campaign was inspired partly by a religious revelation following his close escape from the 1880 massacre. Hendrik began to style himself as a prophet or biblical king and to frame his actions in the language of the Old Testament.[190] He also developed an explicit anticolonial program, and unlike most of the other Namibian leaders, refused to sign protection treaties with the Germans in the early 1880s.[191]

The missionaries' views of Hendrik also began to change during this period. The new missionary at Gibeon, Friedrich Rust, claimed at the beginning of the 1880s that his regard for Hendrik was almost as favorable as Olpp's. But he saw Hendrik as the "great exception to the rule here." According to Rust, "one almost wants to ask oneself whether [Hendrik] really is a Hottentot, since he seems to have so few of the typical shortcomings of his race."[192] Rust's admiration for Hendrik also diminished, however, and by 1884 he was describing him as completely opaque. In 1891, missionary Heidmann deplored "Hendrik Witbooi's ever greater regression into Jewishness, superstition, delusion, fanaticism, and reverie."[193] This emphasis on a kind of mad millenarianism introduced new elements into the discourse on mimicry, but the core structure remained the same. On the one hand, Hendrik Witbooi's actions were associated with Judaism, which was stigmatized in German Protestant eyes; on the other hand, Hendrik's neonomadism represented a reversion to "Hottentot" ways. This mélange made

188. Missionary Heidmann, letter of January 4, 1882, to Barmen, VEM, RMG 3.538b, p. 160v. On the 1880 massacre, see Menzel 2000, p. 8; and Pool 1991, pp. 50–58.

189. See Brigitte Lau in Witbooi 1996, p. xi.

190. Panzergrau 1998, pp. 136–53. On the "Ethiopian movement" in Africa at this time see Merensky 1906.

191. Menzel 2000, p. 140, citing a report by missionary Friedrich Judt of !Hoaxanas (Hoachanas) from September 1889 (VEM, RMG 1.616, pp. 116b–119b); see also Witbooi 1996.

192. Menzel 2000, p. 41, quoting from Rust's 1880 report. Rust worked among the Witbooi from June 1880 to the end of 1887 (Bochert 1980, p. 45).

193. Menzel 2000, p. 145.

Hendrik and his followers difficult to pin down. As missionary Friedrich Judt put it in 1889, the Witbooi "want to live like before. The way they understand this word, 'before,' it is a very elastic notion. To all appearances, the idea is to force the entire development of the country backward one hundred years into the past."[194]

For most Europeans, this slippery combination of Europeanized modernity and African archaism was more disturbing than any simple "paganism" or "savagery."[195] The fact that Hendrik Witbooi claimed to have received inspiration for his rebellious campaign from a Christian God underscored the dangers of transculturation. As the official Cape Colony *Blue-Book on Native Affairs* put it in 1886, Witbooi "had behaved in a way which with any other human being but a Hottentot would be a manifestation of complete insanity."[196] This was the prevailing German view of the Witbooi at the onset of the colonial era.

The Rehoboth Basters: Pure Intermediacy

Like the Orlams and Nama, the Namibian Basters were viewed through colonial lenses that had been forged at the Cape. Like the Khoikhoi they were subject to suspicion as elusive cultural mimics. Yet their intermediateness was constructed somewhat differently. Before the end of the nineteenth-century, whites tended to describe the Basters as superior to pure Khoikhoi, due to their admixture of "white blood." According to one German Cape settler, writing in 1853, "authorities claim they can make out veritable portraits of the Dutch-African aristocracy wandering around in the border region, without putting undue stress on their imaginations."[197] A letter in the *Cape Monthly Magazine* reasoned that the Basters "from having a mixture of European blood in them, are generally more intelligent than the unmixed breed." For pioneer ethnographer Karl Dove the Basters "inherit the

194. Friedrich Judt, quoted in Menzel 2000, p. 141 (from VEM, RMG 1.616a, pp. 116b–119b).

195. See, for instance, missionary Heidmann's comment: "According to many whites it is much easier to interact with a pagan who has had no contact, or very little, with the mission than with the baptized ones. . . . In many cases this is sadly often true" (VEM, RMG 3.538b, p. 108v).

196. John H. Scott, special commissioner, Northern Border, January 15, 1886, in Cape of Good Hope, *Blue-Book on Native Affairs* (1886), p. 41.

197. Kretzschmar (1853, p. 214). This author described the Basters as a "refinement" of the Hottentot, "at least in terms of their names," which stemmed from "the oldest, most respected Dutch families of the colony" (ibid.).

unreliability, laziness and begging from the Hottentot, but from whites they inherit greater intelligence, independence, and some industriousness."[198]

To be sure, other whites saw the "Baster race" as "a bad one" that combined "all the vices of whites and Hottentots."[199] Le Vaillant wrote that the Basters had "more courage and energy" than the Khoikhoi and were also more "mischievous," and he asserted that "it is not uncommon to see them assassinate the masters to whom they have sold their services." In this respect the Basters were "even worse than the negroes."[200] And while the Basters heartily embraced their national-ethnic label, for Europeans the word *bastard* was highly resistant to resignification. In many other colonial settings "half-castes" aroused greater European suspicion than natives of unmixed ancestry.[201] In general, however, the Basters' European blood was understood as tempering the negative impact of their Khoikhoi inheritance.[202]

Europeans saw the Rehobothers as privileged interlocutors and collaborators. When Hugo Hahn invited the Cape Basters to resettle in Greater Namaqualand at the end of the 1860s he predicted they would be a "neutral power" and a "guarantee for security" in the war-torn region.[203] Coming in the wake of the founding of the mission colony at Otjimbingwe and the missionaries' successful mediation of the 1870 peace conference between Jan Jonker Afrikaner and Kamaherero, this stance also demonstrates that Hugo Hahn had a *protocolonial* orientation toward devising a regime of native policy that would make it possible for "any European hunter, trader or missionary to do as he pleased" in the region.[204] The Rhenish Mission reported in 1880 that the Basters were "obviously . . . much more promising than the Namaqua," having "become sedentary and pursued gardening or properly raising cattle" in the Cape Colony while "under the influence of

198. Dove 1896b, p. 82; *Cape Monthly Magazine,* July–December 1857, p. 123.

199. McKiernan 1954, p. 89. McKiernan was an American trader who lived in Southwest Africa from 1874 to 1879.

200. Le Vaillant 1790, vol. 2, p. 164.

201. See Salesa 1997 on this phenomenon in nineteenth-century Samoa.

202. While this view gained ground with the rise of social Darwinism, some eugenicists hypothesized that race mixing would lead to the inheritance of the *worst* characteristics of the parent races. Eugen Fischer's research on the Rehobothers was designed to test this theory (see chap. 3).

203. Hahn quoted by Heidmann, in his report from Warmbad on April 5, 1869, to the RMG, VEM, RMG 3.538b, p. 63r.

204. See Lau (1987b, p. 141), who argues that the end of Afrikaner Orlam sovereignty in central Namibia between 1863 and 1870 "clearly marks the beginning of the colonial epoch for Namibia" (ibid., p. 142). I would argue this was the beginning of a *protocolonial* situation, since sovereignty was still in aboriginal hands.

the whites." In Southwest Africa, the report continued, one "immediately gains the impression that these people are advancing while the Namaquas are regressing almost everywhere."[205]

This positive inclination notwithstanding, the Basters were clearly categorized as *natives* in precolonial and colonial-era legal arrangements.[206] Missionary Hahn visited Rehoboth in 1873 and described the inhabitants as being "in a certain sense half-civilized." Hahn contined in an ambivalent vein: "They can barely make any progress. They are remarkable people. In their external appearance some resemble the Hottentot type, others the Dutch.... With respect to their character, they are completely lacking in energy [*ohne alle Energie*]."[207] Hahn went on to articulate the central problem presented by the Basters' version of intermediacy. Missionaries and colonial rulers were eager to identify and reinforce clear and stable definitions of racial, ethnic, or national character. But missionary work among the Basters was vexing, according to Hahn, since they were "not a people [*Volk*] at all but rather a randomly assembled heap of families who have elected a chief and who only obey him as long as they care to."[208] Missionary Heidmann attacked Hahn for being "filled with all sorts of negative prejudices against the Basters," but Heidmann might have been describing himself.[209] Heidmann also believed that the Basters' main problem stemmed from their imbalanced mix of Khoikhoi and European traits. In his 1871 annual report on Rehoboth, he wrote that the Basters "are after all only that—bastards. They have no national feeling or ties that bind them. Their blood is a motley mixture; most are the offspring of the transgression of the Sixth Commandment. They have no home, no fatherland. They are thrown together from the most varied parts of southern Africa."[210] Elsewhere Heidmann noted that it was "sadly often true"— as "many whites" had already asserted—that it was "much easier to interact with a pagan than with a baptized native." As intermediate beings the Basters were "compelled to struggle constantly against the old ways within themselves." He described these venerable "Hottentot" traits in "classical" terms as stupidity, carefreeness, superficiality, inability to clearly express

---

205. "Unsere Namaqua- oder Hottentotten-Mission," *Berichte der RMG* 36 (5, 1880): 143.

206. Even in the absence of a colonial state, traders and Cape Colonial officials implemented a rough legal system in Southwest Africa. See the discussion of juries for court cases involving white merchants and for cases of Basters against whites, Heidman's report from Rehoboth, February 21, 1876, VEM, RMG 3.538b, p. 101r.

207. C. H. Hahn, "Meine Heimreise" (1873), VEM, RMG 1.577b, p. 32.

208. Ibid.

209. Letter by Heidmann, Chamis, November 16, 1870, VEM, RMG 2.589, p. 83.

210. Heidmann's "Jahresbericht über Rehoboth, 1871," VEM, RMG 3.538b, p. 85r.

interior events, and nomadic tendencies (*Unseßhaftigkeit*).[211] Even among the "best" Basters these older tendencies constantly threatened to burst forth. Heidmann speculated that pagans had "lost all awareness of their own humanity" and therefore "feel the great superiority" of the white man, becoming "shy and obsequious" in his presence. Converts like the Basters, by contrast, had become conscious of their humanity, leading them to "demand to be treated as humans." If they were not treated humanely, however, "their *natural* lack of restraint [*Ungezügeltheit*], which before was repressed to some extent by fear and timidity, would burst through directly."[212] In 1884 Heidmann discussed the case of another Baster community, the Kalkfonteiners, who had allegedly slipped backward to an earlier stage, becoming "half Namaqua in their customs and lifestyle," by living among Khoikhoi.[213]

Despite their "partial civilization" and "white blood," the Basters' cultural heterogeneity and instability suggested that they would not necessarily be easy to govern. But the missionaries' understanding of "semicivilization" differed in one important respect from the views of the secular colonizers. Missionaries were motivated to eradicate all traces of pre-Christian culture.[214] Colonial rulers, by contrast, were perfectly happy to have the Basters remain in a "halfway" condition, as long as they hewed to it consistently. What the missionaries and colonizers shared was their desire to eliminate any *unstable* forms of hybridity.

The Ovaherero: A Radically Simplified Ethnographic Discourse

European perceptions of the Ovaherero at the beginning of the German annexation of Namibia were more monolithic than the discourses exam-

211. VEM, RMG 3.538b, pp. 108v (Heidmann report, February 21, 1876), 42r (report, June 10, 1867), 62v (report, April 5, 1869), 87r–87v ("Jahresbericht über Rehoboth, 1871"), 99v (report, January 6, 1875), and 92r (report, April 21, 1874)

212. Heidmann to mission headquarters in Barmen, February 21, 1876, VEM, RMG 3.538b, p. 109r (my emphasis).

213. Heidmann to Schreiber, March 21, 1884, VEM, RMG 3.538b, p. 181r.

214. Todorov (1984) argues that missionaries were indifferent to extant native culture. This was less true of some LMS missionaries in nineteenth-century Samoa and of Jesuits in late Ming and early Qing China, who found these cultures so attractive that they struck compromises with them, tolerating syncretic versions of Christianity. Richard Wilhelm and the Weimar Mission, discussed in chap. 7, went even further and tried to engage Chinese culture and religion on its own terms. But only the most open minded and observant missionaries to the Ovaherero, such as Gottlieb Viehe (see below), showed any interest in traditional culture, and this curiosity emerged in response to resistance to Christian conversion.

ined thus far. Representations of the Ovaherero were overwhelmingly hateful, even exterminationist. The uniformity of this discursive formation had grave implications for the course of German native policy directed at the Ovaherero. What were the sources of this ethnoideology?

The earliest written references to Ovaherero are from a Portuguese conquistador, Cerveira Pereira, who founded the presidio of Benguela in 1617 on the southern Angolan coast.[215] Pereira and other European travelers based in Angola described a nation that may have been the ancestors of the branch of Ovaherero now known as the Himba, who live in northwestern Namibia.[216] Europeans coming northward from the Cape described Ovaherero in vague terms during the eighteenth century. The first missionary to reach the Ovaherero was Heinrich Schmelen of the London Missionary Society, who visited Okahandja in 1814.[217] Prolonged contact began in 1844 when the Rhenish missionaries Hugo Hahn and Franz Kleinschmidt established a mission station at Otijikango (Gross Barmen) near Windhoek.[218] As noted above, a small number of traders, copper miners, and adventurers lived and traveled in the precolony, and one of them, Charles Andersson, published three widely circulated books on Namibia between 1856 and 1875. The British Cape government established a desultory presence in Hereroland after 1875, resulting in a small amount of official ethnographic attention. In 1876 and 1877 the Cape government named W. Coates Palgrave

215. Estermann 1981, pp. 8–9.

216. According to one theory, Ovaherero had originally migrated into Namibia from Botswana (Vedder [1938] 1966, pp. 131–51). Oral tradition collected since Hugo Hahn's time suggests that Otjiherero speakers arrived in what is now Namibia "between the sixteenth and the eighteenth centuries" from the area around Lake Victoria in East Africa, "settling over much of north-central Namibia and also in the far north-western [Kaokoveld] area." Many Ovaherero then "drifted south, looking for better cattle pasture" (Wallace 2003, p. 356; Grothpeter 1994, pp. 193–94), where they encountered Khoi-speaking peoples, who called the Ovaherero Damara. Other historians believe that the pastoralist societies of central Namibia were ethnically undefined until the mid-nineteenth century, and that the Ovaherero "developed out of people, cultures and economies already existent within Namibia prior to . . . the 16th century" (Gewald 2000, p. 188). "Ovaherero" is the nation's self-designation. It is the plural of "Umherero." I will refer to "the Ovaherero" even though this formula, taken literally, repeats the definite article. On the Himba see Bollig and Mbunguha 1997.

217. Schmelen, a German born near Bremen, arrived in South Africa in 1811 as an employee of the LMS. He did not stay among the Ovaherero but worked among the Nama to the south (Grothpeter 1994, p. 454).

218. In 1760, Jakob Coetzee led the first scientific expedition to Southwest Africa and reported on the "Damara" by hearsay but did not encounter them (Moritz 1912, p. 163). Willem van Reenen traveled to Damaraland in 1791–92 and encountered Ovaherero (ibid., pp. 190–94).

"special commissioner to the tribes north of the Orange River" and charged him with pacifying, and, in the future, possibly annexing the territory. The Cape also appointed Major B. D. Musgrave as Resident at Okahandja and charged him with the exercise of "moral" influence, which encompassed "diplomatic" but not judicial functions.[219] In 1878 Britain annexed Walvis Bay on the Namibian coast and posted an official there.[220]

One of the most striking features of this ethnographic formation is the absence of any hint of anxiousness about Ovaherero cultural schizophrenia. This difference is due partly to the shorter period of sustained contact with the Ovaherero, who had comparatively little time to familiarize themselves with their European intruders. Even in 1884, numerous local Ovaherero groupings remained completely untouched by missionaries. Very few Ovaherero converted to Christianity until their defeat in the 1904 war, and European customs such as wearing cloth clothing were widespread only near the mission stations.[221] Ovaherero were involved in dense and dynamic trading networks with the Cape, in which cattle were exchanged for guns and horses, but their cultural connections with Europeans were sparse and indirect. For the Ovaherero, relations of circulation were more developed than relations of connectivity.[222]

Although most Europeans agreed that "Herero and Namaqua are two of the most different peoples [*Völker*] . . . one could find," the two groups were compared incessantly.[223] The Rhenish missionaries acknowledged that the "Namaqua are in one sense more advanced than the Damra [Ovaherero], insofar as more European culture is implanted in them," but they were "ruined" by centuries of abuse and acculturation and slippery in ways that always threatened to escape the missionaries' grasp. The missionar-

219. See "Memorandum of the Honourable the Secretary for Native Affairs," in Cape of Good Hope, *Blue-Book on Native Affairs* (1875), p. 105; and Davies 1942; see also Palgrave's reports in Cape of Good Hope, *Blue-Book on Native Affairs* (1878), pp. 138-44, and (1879), pp. 127ff.

220. Cape of Good Hope, *Blue-Book on Native Affairs* (1883), pp. 126ff., and (1887), p. 101.

221. Henrichsen 2000, p. 184.

222. See Lau 1987b, chap. 5; and Henrichsen 1997, 2000. On the difference between "circulation" and "connectivity" see LiPuma and Lee 2005. Although the Ovaherero were deeply involved in Cape trading networks in the 1860s and 1870s, the items that were exported—mainly cattle but also tusks and ostrich feathers—tended to flow through the hands of European middlemen. A few indigenous traders made independent journeys to the trading centers, but the "cost and effort in traveling to these trade centers on a regular basis was clearly too high" (Lau 1987b, p. 103). Lau (1987b, p. 87) noted that there is very little economic or ethnographic information on these circuits, since "traders rarely kept diaries or wrote letters."

223. "Neu-Barmen im Ovahererolande," *Berichte der RMG* 5 (10, 1848): 80.

ies were initially more confident that they could control the trajectory of cultural revolution among the unspoiled Ovaherero.[224] The RMG tried to minimize Ovaherero contact with the white copper miners and traders who were swarming into the territory. Hugo Hahn's explicit aim in creating a European "mission colony" at Otjimbingwe in 1864 was to provide Ovaherero with positive behavioral models in what the RMG called a "civilizatory workshop."[225] This "colony" included European farmers, blacksmiths, wheelwrights, and shopkeepers, all direct employees of the mission. The missionaries hoped that Ovaherero could be inducted into capitalism and Christianity while remaining rural and nonindustrial. The RMG also created a Mission Trade Society (Missions-Handelsgesellschaft) that sold European commodities to Ovaherero with the goal of animating them to become wage laborers. The mission encouraged the Ovaherero to become sedentary, plant gardens, wear cloth garments, exchange their traditional beehive-shaped shelters for European-style housing, and stop coating their bodies with ocher and grease. Indeed, the missionaries approved of almost any movement toward Europeanization among the Ovaherero, even though it was acknowledged that this would produce cultural "freaks [*Missgestalten*]" and "crippled figures."[226] The missionaries accepted that this cultural transformation of the Ovaherero was a project for the very long term. As one report noted in 1866, "It will take generations before these people begin to understand Christianity and appropriate it for themselves, even after they have been baptized."[227] The "pagan" Ovaherero type was likely to keep reappearing, in pure or diluted form, for many years.

224. The mission believed that individuals could slip backward culturally, as in the case of Kamahero, who had fallen into the hands of "witch doctors" after his tentative movement toward Christianity ("Kamahero," *Berichte der RMG* 33 [4, 1877]: 97–100; "Ein Besuch im Hereroland," *Berichte der RMG* 36 [10, 1880]: 302). In contrast to Jan Afrikaner, who was described as "devious, untruthful through and through, and energetic besides," Kamahero was seen as lazy and somewhat ridiculous ("Friedens-Congreß in Damaraland," *Berichte der RMG* 27 [4, 1871]: 100).

225. Ritter 1868, p. 337. On the mission colony see "Otjimbingué," *Berichte der RMG* 21 (8, 1865): 244; Büttner 1885a; and Sundermeier 1968. The Rhenish Mission in Hereroland was comparable in this respect to the project of the Methodist missionaries to the Tswana, analyzed in Comaroff and Comaroff 1991–97.

226. Letter from Friedrich Fabri to Hahn, November 5, 1869, VEM, RMG 1.577a, pp. 31, 33. Here Fabri argues against Hahn's project of training Ovaherero ministers and teachers: "It is a risky and irresponsible business to remove these youths from their uncultivated and raw community and to transfer them suddenly and completely into a European-oriented educational sphere" (ibid., p. 33).

227. "Ein Conferenz-Protokoll aus Heredland (vom 4. Dezember 1865)," *Berichte der RMG* 22 (8, 1866): 227.

The Rhenish missionaries believed that they could locate every individual on a scale running from pagan savagery to complete assimilation. Hugo Hahn illustrated this by showing how a single signifier—in this case, the European horse-drawn carriage—could take on entirely different meanings in traditional and assimilated contexts: "It is entirely absurd and ridiculous, for example, when you encounter a carriage and are greeted by twenty or more black beauties dripping with butter and red dye. Among the . . . Christianized natives, however, carriages and many other things which are a caricature among the others are perfectly justified. These [natives] are clean, wear European clothing, pursue orderly lives, cultivate the earth . . . and do not ramble on foot through the countryside." Hahn then described a carriage driven by an Ovaherero chief, Solomon Aponda, as an object belonging to both of these civilizational stages. Aponda was seated in the front of the carriage "wearing European clothing" and representing "modernity," but from the "thoroughly filthy" rear part of the carriage Hahn was able to detect "the grinning faces" of a couple of "greasy, naked youths," representing "the old times."[228]

The founder and leader of the Ovaherero mission, along with his co-founder, Kleinschmidt, had an enormous influence on the way other Europeans viewed this particular people. Praise for Ovaherero bodies and facial features was a constant theme from the start. Missionaries reported that the Ovaherero were "handsome," with "almost European facial features"—"stronger and more beautiful than the Namaquas."[229] After his initially positive impressions of the Ovaherero, however, Hugo Hahn quickly became quite negative, repeating the theme of moral decline. The mission's annual report for 1846–47, which was based almost entirely on Hahn's dispatches, summarized the Ovaherero as "handsome and strong . . . but more deeply submerged in pagan horror than just about any other southern people." For Hahn, their "entire character" consisted of "robbery and murder, theft and whoring, hypocrisy and lies."[230] Echoing discussions of the "natural extinction of the lower races," Hahn suggested that the Ovaherero were

228. C. H. Hahn, "Meine Heimreise" (1873), VEM, RMG 1.577b, p. 17.

229. "Aus Kleinschmidt's Tagebuch," *Berichte der RMG* 3 (6, 1846): 44. See also the comments by Kleinschmidt in *Auszüge aus den Berichten und Briefe der Sendboten der Rheinischen Missionsgesellschaft* (1840–41), 2nd supp., pp. 17–18; "Zwei verschlagene engl. Seeleute besuchen Scheppmannsdorf, Rehoboth und Bethanien," *Berichte der RMG* 6 (20, 1849): 309; C. H. Hahn, "Dammaraland" [*sic*], *Monats-Berichte der Rheinischen Missionsgesellschaft* 1 (2, 1844): 16; and Irle 1906, pp. 53–54.

230. *Jahresbericht der Rheinischen Missions-Gesellschaft* 18 (1846–47): 31.

innately less "capable" and likely to die out.[231] He insisted that they were little more than the "scattered remains of a cowardly, no longer existing nation, located almost at the lowest stage of civilization."[232] It is difficult to avoid reading Hahn's insistence on this inevitable extinction as a wishful fantasy prefiguring the genocide of 1904–7. In his diary Hahn described the skulls of his Ovaherero charges in amateur craniometrical style, positing a correlation between their supposedly small "brain pan" (Hirnschale) and a limited capacity for ratiocination.[233] There was an eerie echo of this race-scientific passage during the war of 1904–7, when German soldiers sent heads and body parts of Ovaherero and Khoikhoi to German universities for anatomical study (fig. 3.13). Although the missionaries still officially hoped for complete assimilation of the Ovaherero, a precedent was being created for characterizing them as barely human.

The aggressiveness that filled the reports by Hahn and his coworkers stemmed in part from their failure to convert or even to understand the Ovaherero, that is, from antimissionary resistance. The first baptism took place in 1858 after Hahn had worked for seventeen years among the Ovaherero. Baptism rates remained low: only 69 adults had been baptized by mid-1871; less than 1 percent of all Ovaherero by 1874; and just 6 percent by 1904.[234] A new phase in relations between the Ovaherero and the German missionaries announced itself in the 1860s. Rhenish Mission Society publications celebrated the handful of newly converted and partly assimilated Ovaherero.[235] In 1864 Hahn inaugurated a training institute at Otjimbingwe, the Augustinum, whose purpose was to educate indigenous teachers and ministers, called "national assistants."[236] A broad neotraditionalist movement against the missionaries arose at the end of the 1860s, after it was noticed that some Ovaherero children were refusing to participate in "the rituals of ancestor worship and magic with which the entire life of the Ovaherero and all of their ideas are interwoven."[237] The vacillation of chief Kamaherero, who had shown some interest in Christianity, symbolized this struggle.

231. C. H. Hahn 1984–85, vol. 4, p. 930, journal entry for August 10, 1856.

232. Ibid., p. 922, entry for May 12, 1856.

233. C. H. Hahn 1984–85, vol. 2, pp. 324–25, entry for May 10, 1846.

234. Lau 1987b, p. 144; Irle 1906, p. 345.

235. See the RMG pamphlets Die Hereró-Mission (Barmen: Verlag des Missionshauses, 1867), p. 32; and, for example, Frau Missionar Eich, Elia Kandirikirira: Lebensbild eines Herero-Evangelisten (Barmen: Verlag des Missionshauses, 1901).

236. The institute was referred to as the Augustineum after 1885 (Menzel 1992, p. 36).

237. See Hahn's comments in 1859: "Aus dem Damaralande," Berichte der RMG 15 (7–8, 1859): 108. On the "pagan countermovement" against the mission see "Aus Hereró-Land,"

In 1869 a traditionalist leader, Kambezembi, allegedly forced Kamaherero to leave Otjimbingwe, with its dense concentration of missionaries and Christian converts, for Okahandja, where Kamaherero's father was buried. Kamaherero's move sparked a sudden migration of twenty to thirty thousand Ovaherero to Okahandja.[238] Missionary Gottlieb Viehe, one of the most observant of the nineteenth-century missionaries in Namibia, noticed in 1876 that anti-Christian "paganism" had become much more "tangible" among Ovaherero at his station in Okozondye.[239] The local Ovaherero chief, Tjaherani, forbade his people to become Christians.[240] Three years later Viehe documented a powerful form of ostracism directed against Christian converts, who were excluded from access to the *okuruuo*, or sacred fire. The same sanction was applied to "paramount chief" Samuel Maherero when he was helped into power by the Germans in 1890.[241]

This traditionalist movement provoked varying responses from the missionaries. Some perceived the emergence of "a certain national consciousness."[242] Most began to regard the Ovaherero as secretive, cold, and arrogant. Unlike the more Christianized Khoikhoi, who were usually described as overly emotional, the Ovaherero were stereotyped as "hard-hearted."[243] Hugo Hahn revealed his own hermeneutic difficulties by insisting that the Ovaherero had no inner life at all: "It is nearly impossible to force oneself into their narrow mentality. There is thus almost no point of contact [*Anknüpfungspunkt*] there, externally or internally. Their conscience

---

Berichte der RMG 24 (12, 1868): 353; Beiderbecke 1875, p. 264; and "Aus Briefen und Berichten des Miss. H. Hahn," *Berichte der RMG* 25 (9, 1869): 258.

238. "Aus Briefen und Berichten des Miss. H. Hahn," *Berichte der RMG* 25 (9, 1869): 261. On Kambezembi see Beiderbecke 1924, pt. 3.

239. Viehe 1876, p. 109.

240. "Entwickelungen und Verwickelungen im Herero-Lande," *Berichte der RMG* 36 (3, 1880): 76.

241. Viehe 1879, p. 378. On the Ovaherero *okuruuo* see Viehe 1876, pp. 85–86; and Beiderbecke 1924, p. 28. As Wallace summarizes, the *okuruuo* was "the stage for all important Herero observances, including those for birth, coming-of-age, marriage and death" (2003, p. 359).

242. Ritter 1868, p. 338; "Die Lage der Dinge im Hererolande," *Berichte der RMG* 24 (11, 1868): 322.

243. Missionary Brincker discussed Ovaherero *Hartherzigkeit* in "Neu-Barmen," *Berichte der RMG* 26 (10, 1870): 304. Hugo Hahn's diary contained an entire passage subtitled "Lack of Feelings among the Herero," where he asserted that "a Herero has . . . no feelings of love or hate, compassion, pity, or revenge" (C. H. Hahn 1984–85, vol. 3, p. 592, entry for April 11, 1852). Missionary Carl Gotthilf Büttner (1884, p. 58) linked the Ovaherero trait of "hard-heartedness" (*Herzenshärtigkeit* or *Hartherzigkeit*) to their antagonism to Christianity.

is sleeping the sleep of the dead, their rationality and understanding nearly the same."[244] Missionary Heinrich Schöneberg at Otjikango seemed to despise his own parishioners, writing that "a human emotion is still unknown to them" and concluding that "God is exterminating the Herero because of their doglike nature, their sharing of wives, their sodomy, their incest and sins with animals. . . . The Hottentots are the stick with which God is striking them."[245] The counterpart to secrecy and lack of empathy, according to various missionary reports, was an "insolent" haughtiness.[246]

The 1860s and 1870s also saw an upsurge of European anger against the Ovaherero due to their reluctance to sell livestock, which they were said to worship like gods. Here the religious critique of idolatry combined seamlessly with the economic critique of "irrational" market behavior. At the same time Ovaherero were faulted for "stinginess," for their quasi-Calvinist drive to *accumulate* cattle. This was ironic given that Europeans had criticized the Khoikhoi for the opposite sin, namely, indulgent excess and a lack of foresight. Ovaherero avarice became the official legitimation during the middle decade of German rule for depriving them of land and livestock by force.[247]

A third development during this protocolonial period that was refracted in ethnographic perceptions began with the 1863 battle of Otijimbingwe, during which Kamaherero's supporters defeated the Afrikaner Orlams in what Europeans called a "war of liberation." This conflict marked the beginning of six years of bloody conflict that drew in nearly all of the indigenous Namibian communities.[248] A peace treaty was finally brokered by missionaries Hahn and Krönlein in 1870. In 1880 Kamaherero responded to Orlam raids on his cattle by ordering the execution of all Khoikhoi present in Hereroland, reigniting armed conflict with the Nama.

This newfound Ovaherero assertiveness reverberated in European eth-

244. Hahn entry for August 10, 1856, *Tagebuch*, pt. 16, May 25, 1856–December 7, 1856, VEM, RMG 1.575, p. 249v. This passage was underlined in red, suggesting that someone in the Barmen mission headquarters paid special attention to it.

245. "Otjikango," *Berichte der RMG* 10 (16, 1853): 241; "Neun Jahre im Hererolande," *Berichte der RMG* 11 (15, 1854): 228.

246. Quote from Beiderbecke 1875, p. 264; see also Büttner's letter of May 22, 1878, in Menzel 1992, p. 73, condemning Ovaherero "Hochmuth" (pride) and "Übermut" (insolence).

247. Missionary Beiderbecke (1875, pp. 268–69) recognized that their arrogance could also be be seen as "a feeling of honor" and "their stinginess" as "thriftiness." The Ovaherero, he concluded, "are not emotional people like the Nama, but rational people."

248. The most complete record of Namibian history during these decades is still, unfortunately, the work of the racist missionary and historian Heinrich Vedder ([1938] 1966).

nographic representations. During the 1850s and 1860s most whites had derided the Ovaherero for their passivity and cowardice.[249] After the collapse of the Afrikaner polity, the Ovaherero started to be described as demonically cruel.[250] This was an amplification of Hugo Hahn's earlier descriptions of Ovaherero as addicted to murder.[251] Missionary Beiderbecke insisted in 1875 that paganism still exercised *"demonic* power" among the "majority of the Herero" at his station at Otjozondjupa (Waterberg). According to Beiderbecke, the first potential candidate for baptism at the station had been poisoned by an Ovaherero "magician" (*Zauberer*).[252] Five years later he wrote again about the "inhumane" behavior of the Ovaherero, who had "tortured to death" the weak and defenseless when they attacked settlements of Bushmen and Berg Damara.[253] Although missionaries assumed that the devil was active among all "pagans," the insistence on the satanic essence of the Ovaherero was especially strong.

My aim in reconstructing these ethnographic representations is to set the stage for the analysis of colonial native policy in the next chapter. As we have seen, however, some European practices before 1884 already prefigured formal colonialism. There are also a number of bridging figures like Theo Hahn who imported pre-1884 ethnographic imagery directly into the bosom of the nascent colonial regime. One missionary who personally delivered ethnographic ideologies to the German colony and who was present at the primal scene of colonizing the Ovaherero was Carl Gotthilf Büttner. Büttner was dispatched to Otjimbingwe by the RMG in 1872 to replace Hugo Hahn as director of the Augustinum. After resigning from the RMG and returning to Germany in 1880, Büttner became an outspoken advocate of German colonialism.[254] In 1885 he accompanied the new German "imperial commissary" (*Kaiserlicher Kommissar*), Heinrich Goering, to Southwest Africa in the role of "authorized representative of the kaiser."

249. See the comments of the American Charles Green, who assisted Charles Andersson in leading the Ovaherero assault on Jonker Afrikaner in 1864, in Andersson 1987–89, vol. 2, pp. 241, 246.

250. See missionary Heidmann's letters of February 1880 and September 14, 1880, to VEM, RMG 3.538b, pp. 130v and 132v.

251. Hahn's diary entry from December 25, 1884 (C. H. Hahn 1984–85, vol. 1, p. 202).

252. Beiderbecke 1875, p. 273 (my emphasis).

253. "Entwickelungen und Verwickelungen im Hererolande (Schluß)," *Berichte der RMG* 36 (4, 1880: 103).

254. See Büttner 1885a, p. 39; and Menzel 1992. Büttner returned to Germany again in 1885. In 1886 he became the inspector for the newly founded German-East African Protestant Missionary Society, and in 1887 he was appointed to teach Swahili at the newly founded Seminar for Oriental Languages at the University of Berlin. He also edited the *Zeitschrift für afrikanische Sprachen* from 1887 to 1890 (Menzel 1992; Legère 1988).

Büttner's familiarity with Ovaherero leaders helped convince Kamaherero to sign a "protection treaty" with the German government on October 21, 1885.[255] Büttner's initial impressions of the Ovaherero after his arrival in Otjimbingwe in 1873, like those of many other Rhenish missionaries, were dominated by outward appearances: "They are powerful and handsome people."[256] Büttner's first report began with the remark "I find the character of this people actually to be quite different from the way that Negroes are depicted in books."[257] In fact, Büttner was as much a captive of prevailing conceptions as other Europeans, as revealed by the nasty turn in his ethnographic rhetoric. After a few years he was calling the Ovaherero "riff-raff" (*Lumpengesindel*) and "an entire nation of whore-mongers, thieves, liars, and misers who . . . deserve to be put into prison every weekend."[258] Büttner published an article about the Ovaherero in 1876 which concluded ominously that "nothing at all can be done with these people, petrified and ossified as they are in earthly things, before God's hand has again struck them down and smashed them to pieces."[259] In another article Büttner suggested that Ovaherero culture was "the program of the Commune": "Here among the Herero, immovable property is possessed by all alike, and movable property is essentially unprotected; theft is almost exempt from punishment; begging and vagabondage are honorable . . . women are shared, and there are no taxes, no police, no oaths, no loyalty, and no God."[260] These were the views of the "expert informant" who accompanied the first German ruler to meet the Ovaherero in 1885.

Toward Colonialism

The most authoritative "scientific" discussion of the Ovaherero before the colonial era, Gustav Fritsch's *Natives of South Africa*, divided European views of the Ovaherero into two camps, the naive "panegyrists" and "admirers of

255. Hugo Hahn wrote to Kamaherero to convince him to sign the treaty. The difference between a protection treaty (*Schutzvertrag*) and the private contracts signed by Lüderitz's agents is that the indigenous signatories legally retained ownership of the land in the former case but not in the latter (Külz 1909, p. 12).

256. Büttner to RMG Deputation, April 13, 1873, in Menzel 1992, p. 24.

257. Ibid. Büttner had studied for several years at the University of Königsberg before his missionary service.

258. Letters from August 29, 1875, and November 21, 1876, quoted in Menzel 1992, p. 26.

259. "Eine Untersuchungsreise im Hereróland," *Berichte der RMG* 32 (5, 1876): 130.

260. Büttner, "Sociale Verhältnisse im Hereróland," *Berichte der RMG* 32 (12, 1876): 377. After returning to Germany Büttner elaborated on this comparison, suggesting that Hereroland would be an appropriate place to which the German Social Democrats could be exiled. See Büttner's letter to RMG headquarters, September 9, 1879, quoted in Menzel 1992, p. 35.

the Herero," who would soon be disabused of their enthusiasms, and the more realistic critics like Fritsch himself.[261] Yet in the recorded discourse on the Ovaherero before 1884 there is barely a trace of the revindicating, relativizing, Rousseauian, or historicizing approaches. It is revealing that Fritsch fails to name a single "panegyrist." German discourse on the Ovaherero on the eve of colonialism was entirely dominated by Fritsch's "realists," those who described unconverted Ovaherero as arrogant, stingy, inhumane, and cruel. This was not a discourse of mimicry, according to which the Other veers between contradictory positions in uncontrollable or strategically manipulative ways. Europeans found the Khoikhoi perpetually puzzling and resistant to categorization, but they were confident in their placement of the Ovaherero. This meant that the Ovaherero did not present the colonizers with an acute dilemma of cultural instability. Instead, Ovaherero tended to be seen as occupying a transparently obvious position near the savagery pole of the spectrum. The next chapter will explore the colonial results of the greater "obviousness" of Ovaherero identity. It is fruitless to argue about which of the two ethnographic formations— Khoikhoi or Ovaherero—was more racist. What is clear is that the inherited representations of the Ovaherero provided the colonizers with a narrower range of possible policy moves. It was the flatness and uniformity of this discourse as much as its substance that shaped the course of German policy toward the Ovaherero.

261. Fritsch 1872, pp. 217, 219.

THREE

From Native Policy to Genocide to Eugenics ⸙ German Southwest Africa

Accessing the Inaccessible

German colonialism in Southwest Africa has proven oddly difficult for historians to interpret, or even to narrate. Only a few writers have taken up the challenge of providing an analytic account of the entire thirty-year course of German colonial rule in Namibia. The two most influential studies, by Horst Drechsler and Helmut Bley, were written more than three decades ago. Both are invaluable and pioneering studies, yet neither offers a convincing and coherent interpretation of the colony's development. Much can be learned by focusing on the lacunae in these texts and the contradictions between their stated theoretical projects and their actual results.

GERMAN SOUTHWEST AFRICA AND CAPITALIST DEVELOPMENT: THE INSIGHTS AND SHORTCOMINGS OF MARXIST COLONIAL HISTORIOGRAPHY

Drechsler's 1966 book *Südwestafrika unter deutscher Kolonialherrschaft* (Southwest Africa under German Colonial Rule) begins with the observation that "South West Africa (Namibia) is one of the most inaccessible regions of Africa."[1] The region's geographic impenetrability seems to be paralleled by a sort of interpretive inaccessibility in the historical literature, as if the forces driving the colony's evolution are continually escaping from the historian's

---

1. Drechsler [1966] 1980, p. 17. In the English edition the title was somewhat misleadingly translated as *Let Us Die Fighting: The Struggle of the Herero and Nama against German Imperialism*. It will become clear below why the original German title more closely matched the author's intentions, if not his actual accomplishments.

field of vision into the Kalahari. Drechsler attempts to bring some order to this vague terrain by ordering German colonialism in Southwest Africa according to the economic logic of the transition from free market capitalism to "imperialism." This framing leads him to focus on the large landowning and mining companies that bought up huge tracts of land in Southwest Africa in the 1880s and 1890s. But as Drechsler admits in the introduction to *Südwestafrika,* the colony was insignificant as a source of raw materials for German industry or as a market for German exports. The biggest and oldest of the land and mining societies, the German Colonial Society for South West Africa (*Kolonialgesellschaft*), was inactive during the colony's first two foundational decades, although it began to make huge profits during the 1904 German-Ovaherero war by "plunging . . . into the trading business." It paid enormous dividends to its shareholders after the discovery of diamonds in 1908.[2] The other leading company, the British-owned South West Africa Company (SWAC), began exploring for minerals in the 1890s, but it only really began to make profits once its sister company, the Otavi Mine and Railway Company, had built a railway line to the copper mines at Tsumeb.[3] But none of the financial investors in Southwest Africa—from the colony's "founder," Adolf Lüderitz, to the *Kolonialgesellschaft,* which bought up the bankrupt Lüderitz's shares in 1885, to the SWAC—made any money at all during the first two decades of German rule.

Drechsler distributes his attention equally across the entire thirty-year history of German colonialism in Namibia, but it proves impossible to reconcile his "economic" focus with this chronological sweep.[4] He acknowledges that the colony's annexation cannot be explained in economic terms. In 1884 there was no evidence at all that valuable minerals would ever be discovered in the colony, and the desultory sums invested by the German Colonial Society for South West Africa reflected the investors' low expectations. Realistic observers recognized that the arid region would never support intensive farming or plantation agriculture. Bismarck justified his

2. Ibid., p. 217; see also Drechsler 1996, p. 276 ff.

3. Gaydish 2001, pp. 57-59. The Otavi Mine and Railway Company, a copper-mining outfit that was capitalized with funds from the SWAC, began operations in 1906 and immediately became very profitable (Drechsler 1996, pp. 193-221).

4. It is obviously entirely possible to write a history of Southwest Africa (or any other colony) focusing exclusively on European investors, as Drechsler demonstrated in his more recent book (1996). But this approach cannot and does not claim to make sense of the main lines of colonial development, including native policy. After the 1904-7 war, native policy did become more closely attuned to the needs of capitalist development, although, as I will show in this chapter, economic motives alone cannot explain these interventions.

unwillingness throughout the 1880s to commit enough funding for even a small colonial security force with reference to the region's lack of economic promise.

Reflecting the economic torpor of the first two decades of German rule in Namibia, almost two-thirds of Drechsler's book is concerned with government efforts to control and regulate indigenous life and with the numerous revolts that disrupted these plans. Drechsler's economic categories are of little use to him in making sense of interactions between colonizer and colonized during this period, and he is too good a historian to force every event into this procrustean bed.[5] The result is that his account of the interplay between German native policies and indigenous responses lacks a theoretical or interpretive framework altogether, aside from an overarching anticolonial affect.[6]

Many German policies during the first two decades of colonial rule in Southwest Africa had economic effects, even if they were not dictated by the land and mining companies. Drechsler's book gestures toward these effects. Specifically, native policy shaped class structures, land ownership, labor markets, modes of production, and the spread of commodity markets. As in late-nineteenth-century metropolitan Germany, colonial political elites with little immediate stake in financial or industrial capital nonetheless oriented their polices in a general way toward the expansion and reproduction of capitalist commodity and labor markets.[7] Indeed, all the governors

5. Lau (1995b, p. 42) also remarks that "Drechsler's account is so well-researched" that his own materials provide evidence to support her alternative interpretation.

6. Drechsler's 1966 book was of course written under the constraints of official East German "Marxist" orthodoxy. One of the reasons East German colonial historiography was often so good despite these constraints is that its authors were largely released from orthodox interpretive baggage—all that was required of them was a display of anticolonial verve. Drechsler's (1984) shorter book on the Ovaherero and Nama uprisings avoided the "imperialism" framework altogether. The shifts in communist views of anticolonial struggles during the twentieth century meant that precolonial and "Oriental" societies were no longer viewed as "undignified, stagnatory, and vegetative," and colonialism was no longer understood as a primarily progressive socioeconomic force, as in Marx's writings on India (Marx and Engels 1972, p. 41). The result was that Loth (1963) could analyze the politics of the Orlams in mid-nineteenth-century Namibia as a progressive instance of "state formation." By contrast, "Western" Marxists have analyzed precolonial Namibia as a case of the penetration of merchant capitalism (Lau 1987a; Reinhard 1988; W. Werner 1998, chap. 1) or of the "articulation of modes of production" (Dedering 1988).

7. In an earlier study of German social policy in the same period (Steinmetz 1993), I found that elites with backgrounds in the traditional aristocracy or the educated noncapitalist middle classes were often driven to tailor their policies to the (perceived) needs of capitalist markets and accumulation almost despite themselves.

of German Southwest Africa shared this overarching orientation, although this was not the case in colonial Qingdao and Samoa. Governor Theodor Leutwein's unremitting campaign to deprive the Ovaherero of their cattle and land was rooted in a general orientation toward a model of colonial economic development dominated by European settlers rather than indigenous producers. Yet by squatting on huge tracts of land through the 1880s and 1890s, the private companies not only infringed on the ability of the Ovaherero and Khoikhoi to use these areas for cattle grazing but also strictly limited the number of German farmers who could settle in the colony.[8] Hence, there were two contradictory models of economic development, one centered on finance capital and oriented toward the eventual discovery of valuable mineral deposits and an extractive mode of production, the other centered on a ranching economy and livestock production for local and European markets. Yet both were models of capitalism controlled by Europeans rather than Africans.

Other official policies ran directly contrary to both of these versions of capitalist development. The massacre of the Ovaherero in 1904 deprived both German farmers and the future mining industry of their primary labor force and necessitated a search for alternatives. Ovaherero survivors who stayed in the colony after 1904 were forced to work, and South African contract workers and Ovambo migrants from the colony's north also entered the labor force.[9] The decision to create a Witbooi reserve in 1898 had a political logic, since the governor at this point considered the Witbooi to be key military collaborators, but it deprived the Germans of a large parcel of land that was ideal for settlement and mining.[10] Moreover, the Witbooi were never considered as potential laborers, even after their uprising was defeated in 1905. Another autochthonous group whose landholdings were protected from European development and exploitation were the Rehoboth

8. The vast majority of this land was in the parts of the country that were the least valuable agriculturally. This was especially significant with respect to the northern border of Hereroland, which was fixed in a secret treaty signed by Governor Leutwein and Samuel Maherero on December 6, 1895. The government's enforcement of the ban on Ovaherero cattle grazing and settlement north of this border was directly influenced by the SWAC, which had purchased the "Damaraland concession" in 1892 (Drechsler 1996, pp. 85–92). The area south of Hereroland, however, was Crown land owned by the Siedlungsgesellschaft (Settlement Society). Enforcement of this border had economic implications but did not directly reflect "capitalist" pressures.

9. Chinese "coolies" were also discussed as potential workers in this period. As Clarence-Smith and Moorsom (1975, p. 378) point out, foreign contract workers "proved expensive both in wages and in transport costs." On the Ovambo migrant laborers in German Southwest Africa, see Nitsche 1913; and Eirola 1992.

10. T. Leutwein 1907a, p. 272.

Basters. The Rehobothers' political value to the colonial state as allies out-weighed economic considerations. Even after 1910, when the colonial econ-omy began to grow rapidly, economic life in Rehoboth was treated by the German Chamber of Commerce in Windhoek as if it were taking place in a separate country.[11] An exclusive focus on the economic aspects of colonial-ism would thus lead the historian to ignore two of the three indigenous groups that most preoccupied the German colonial state. Capitalist develop-ment was not the state's central goal before 1904 and it was just one among several criteria guiding policy thereafter.

Even in the realm of explicitly economic policy, the problem of stabiliz-ing native culture unavoidably imposed itself on the colonial state's calcu-lations. For example, the official campaign to reduce the amount of land available to the central Namibian Ovaherero had as its main purpose the appropriation of land and cattle for European use. This program could not solve the native policy problem that it had generated: how to deal with the Ovaherero who were now confined within a shrunken territory. Another example is the project of transforming the colonized into wage workers. This could be accomplished by migration systems or resettlement, by ap-pealing to a "natural" desire for wages and allowing "free" labor markets to match jobs and people, by depriving the colonized of other opportunities for survival or forcing them to pay taxes, or by directly allocating individu-als to workplaces (forced labor). Each of these options would in turn neces-sitate additional programs of sociocultural regulation. Even a liberal policy of "free labor markets," as in German Kiaochow, required a supplementary layer of native policy to prevent the colonized from acting as if they were equal to European laborers.

COLONIALISM, RAISON D'ÉTAT, AND TOTALITARIANISM

Helmut Bley's book *South-West Africa under German Rule, 1894–1914* is also extremely rich in historical documentation. But Bley is even less able than Drechsler to make theoretical sense of the disorderly dynamics of Ger-man colonial history in Namibia.[12] Writing in West Germany in a period in which the exceptionalist approach to German history was extremely

11. See *Jahresbericht der Windhuker Handelskammer* (1913), p. 36.

12. The original German title of Bley's book is *Kolonialherrschaft und Sozialstruktur in Deutsch-Südwestafrika 1894–1914*. The first conceptual term in this title—*Kolonialherrschaft*, or colonial rule—is the same as Drechsler's. For the second term, Bley substitutes "social structure" for Drechsler's "imperialism." Social structure here seems to refer mainly to the internal dynamics among the German settlers, a topic to which Bley devotes a great deal of attention but which is less central for my own purposes.

influential, Bley framed his study as a contrast between German colonialism and the supposedly more normal British or Western version.[13] As he announced on the first page of his introduction, "We shall be concerned with deviation from the normal, and in particular with the processes which prevented the European community in German South-West Africa from ever reaching political and social normalcy." This helps us to piece together the largely implicit interpretative frame that underpins Bley's narrative.

The full-fledged historical version of the *Sonderweg* (special path) thesis as it emerged in the postwar period argued that the modernization of politics and culture lagged behind the economic sphere in imperial Germany. The tensions and pressures that resulted from this fatal disjuncture eventually led to Nazism. A more specific claim, harking back to arguments made by Karl Marx, Max Weber, and many nineteenth-century liberals and socialists, was that the German bourgeoisie had failed to embrace and defend its "natural" class ideology, liberalism, and had instead emulated the aristocracy and adopted the cultural conservatism and antidemocratic politics associated with that class. Theorists of German exceptionalism were concerned almost entirely with "metropolitan" German history, however, and only rarely addressed the inner workings of the overseas colonies; indeed, they tended to adopt a national container view of European history and a "core-centric" approach to global history, such that the German acquisition of colonies in the 1880s was attributed to "domestic" dynamics.[14] The difference between Bley and other exceptionalists was that he exported the site of German deviation to the colony.[15]

Bley's specific aim was to account for the undeniably peculiar extremism of German Southwest Africa. Toward the end of his book there is a section entitled "Growing Totalitarianism," and in the final pages he turns explicitly to Hannah Arendt's hypothesis that modern fascism was prefig-

13. Bley [1971] 1996, p. xvii. The interpretation of German history within the West German version of the Sonderweg theory appears in retrospect to be identical in its main lines to the Marxist version, presented by writers like Abusch (1946) and Lukács ([1954] 1973). In the context of the cold war, the language of modernization theory was substituted for Marxism, but the deeper structure of the account remained the same (Steinmetz 1997).

14. The most influential proponent of the Sonderweg approach, Hans-Ulrich Wehler (1972, 1984) attributes Bismarck's decision to acquire colonies to the same intra-German dynamics that Eckart Kehr, Max Weber, and others had described as the sources of Germany's political exceptionalism.

15. Bley was satisfied to show that metropolitan dynamics were simply reproduced in the colonies. In contrast to my argument here, he did not theorize the colonial state as a distinct kind of field in which metropolitan politics might resurface in a new guise.

ured, if not produced, in the overseas colonies, especially in sub-Saharan Africa. Bley even hints that Southwest Africa may have evolved into a kind of fascism due to German colonialism's "lateness," an argument that superficially echoes the exceptionalist trope of the disastrous effects of belated modernization.[16] All of the individual components of the exceptionalism narrative are thus present in Bley's account but in a disaggregated and rudimentary form: lateness leads to a deviation from Western normalcy and to extremism, eventually culminating in totalitarianism. The argument follows the rhetorical form of the *enthymeme*, a truncated syllogism in which an implicit premise is left unstated. Considered as an ideological form, the *enthymeme* relies on the reader or audience to supply from its "stock of knowledge and opinions" certain premises that are never set forth explicitly in the argument.[17] In Bley's text, the unstated premise is the German exceptionalism thesis itself. It can be safely assumed that most members of his German audience would have been able to supply the missing premises. But Bley does *not* mobilize the analytic centerpiece of the classic exceptionalism approach, namely, the power of an antidemocratic aristocracy and the fatal emulation of this class by the modern bourgeoisie in a context of rapid socioeconomic growth. Bley's narrative of the intense conflict between Governor Leutwein and General Lothar von Trotha certainly hints at dynamics of intraelite class resentment, and I will focus on this conflict myself. But Bley does not map this conflict onto the disjuncture between tradition and modernity or the broader lines of German colonial development.

Bley also makes the methodological error common to many arguments for national exceptionalism, German or otherwise, by failing to provide explicit comparisons with other national cases. Here the relevant comparison would have been the colonial policies of the other major European powers, including the exceptionalists' paragon of modernity, Britain. The German assault on the Ovaherero may have been the first genocide of the twentieth century, but the last full-blooded Tasmanian had died twenty-eight years earlier in British-governed Van Diemen's Land (Tasmania). The Australian destruction of the Queensland Aborigines between 1840 and 1897 has also been described as genocidal.[18] That said, the massacre of the Ovaherero in 1904 (and the Witbooi and other Khoikhoi between 1904 and 1907) may well have been a unique case of twentieth-century colonial genocide. But the dynamics that led to it seem to be quite different from those mobilized in

16. Bley [1971] 1996, pp. xvii, 223–25, 282.
17. Bordwell 1989, p. 208.
18. Cocker 1998, pt. 2; Palmer 2000.

the exceptionalist explanation of the Nazi genocide against the Jews. Most important, the leading opponent of the extermination of the Ovaherero in 1904 was the middle-class governor Theodor Leutwein, while the main perpetrators were members of the traditional nobility in the military and the metropolitan government. I will analyze this intraelite confrontation in detail below.

Further ambiguity arises from the fact that Bley's account stresses discontinuity while the exceptionalism thesis foregrounds continuity. Bley argues that the "path to extremism" began with the colonial wars of 1904–7, when "pre-war trends and policies *ceased abruptly*." Indeed, Bley does not offer any coherent analytic narrative of events in Namibia between 1894 and 1904, and the decade before Leutwein's arrival in the colony is completely absent from the book. Bley suggests that Leutwein conceived of himself during the 1890s as a medieval emperor and relied on older German views of the state as instantiating the "general good," but he offers no evidence that these ideas actually influenced Leutwein's practical policy-making.[19] The entire pre-1904 period is thus theoretically "inaccessible" and is not connected causally to the road to extremism.

Bley's suggestion that the political configuration before 1904 is less available to analysis is unconvincing, but it does raise several interesting questions. What *were* the determinants of German native policy in Namibia before 1904? Were they more complex, more overdetermined, than after the colonial war? And were there not, in fact, deeper levels of continuity between the prewar and postwar configurations?[20]

A final linked set of problems relates to the concepts of native policy and totalitarianism. Bley's use of the term *native policy* is strictly nominalist.[21] Only *after* 1904 did the colonial government began to use the term *Eingeborenenpolitik;* only after 1904 does Bley speak of "native policy." According to Bley, the post-1904 native regulations "did not restrict themselves to a discussion of the economic and political pressures by which the labour laws could be enforced. Instead, they aimed at totally changing the Africans' personality by recreating their feelings, wiping out their memories, and making their legal status dependent on their political attitudes."[22]

19. Bley [1971] 1996, pp. 43–46 (my emphasis).

20. Interestingly, a recent book by a student of Bley, Gesine Krüger (1999), while excellent, implicitly reproduces Bley's discontinuity thesis in an even more dramatic way by starting its narrative abruptly with the 1904 German-Ovaherero war.

21. Bley [1971] 1996, p. 49. See also Zimmerer 2001 for a nominialist use of the concept "native policy."

22. Bley [1971] 1996, p. 224.

The implication is that polices that do not attempt to "wipe out" indigenous memories, policies that try to change personalities only partially or to insert the colonized into an economic system defined and controlled by Europeans cannot be called "native policies." Yet even the most mild-mannered colonial governments sought to erase *certain* aspects of the extant culture in order to make it more easily governable. Indeed, sociocultural regulation in general, even in democratic metropolitan settings, constantly involves the deliberate "wiping out" of extant ways of life. Yet Bley's book connects the emergence of native policy to the rise of "totalitarianism." German colonial rule in Southwest African after 1903 may well qualify as extreme, but this is not because it engaged in native policy or because it tried to transform the subjectivity of the colonized. In 1952, Franz Fanon described a process of "wiping out memories" and "changing the Africans' personality" in terms almost identical to Bley's (though Fanon is not cited by Bley). For Fanon, cultural annihilation did not define totalitarianism or even a particularly *extreme* version of colonialism but was characteristic of colonialism *tout court*.[23]

Bley's discussion of colonial totalitarianism is still useful.[24] His portrayal of German attempts at a cultural and psychological *Gleichschaltung* (total control) of the Ovaherero bears some resemblance to Arendt's portrait of totalitarianism as a demand for "unlimited power" to dominate all of life and homogenize and atomize the masses.[25] This relates to the idea that colonial policies may seek to partially assimilate the colonized while still insisting on their unrevisable subalternity. Native policy's aim would not be a complete identification of master and subject but rather an insertion of the colonized into a subordinated location within a common space of mutually comprehensible symbols. Creating this sort of asymmetrical relationship to a shared culture was one aim of German native policy vis-à-vis the Ovaherero after 1904. While the colonizers hoped that their subjects

---

23. See Fanon [1952] 1967, pp. 110, 116. Fanon's analysis might itself be faulted for failing to explicitly thematize "preservationist" forms of colonialism, but this reflects the fact that he wrote *Black Skins* after having lived in Martinique and in Algeria, two colonies where "preservationism" was not practiced. In Algeria, the French had engaged in massacre and in "associationist" policies (G. Wright 1991; Le Cour Grandmaison 2005), but by the time Fanon was writing the French rulers had little interest in "cultural difference." It is also interesting that Fanon did not discuss Arendt's totalitarianism book, which was published in English in 1950. (Arendt did read Fanon, but she reduced him to an apologist of "violence for violence's sake"; H. Arendt 1970, p. 65; by contrast see Bhabha 2004.)

24. Bley [1971] 1996, pp. 223–25.

25. H. Arendt [1950] 1958, pp. 438, 456.

would relate to these cultural constructs from an abjectly inferior position, there was no guarantee that the colonized would not recode these signifiers. The fact that anti-colonial struggles were often framed in terms of a Christian discourse that the colonized shared with their colonizers—as in the Witbooi rebellions—cautions us against assuming that colonial signifiers are ever "uniaccentual." Nevertheless, the insertion of the colonized into a shared semiotic system marked a decisive cultural shift, compelling non-Europeans to confront their colonizers on a cultural terrain that was not of their own making.[26]

Bley's *implicitly* comparative approach also underscores the need for more *explicit* and systematic comparisons both among colonies and within them. The apparent contradiction between Bley's insistence on discontinuity and the Sonderweg theory's emphasis on continuity reminds us of the need to make sense of the pre-1904 period in Southwest Africa. His oblique references to German exceptionalism suggest that we need to explore the ways in which the Sonderweg theory's core, and still useful, explanatory structure—the fraught relationship between the German nobility and the middle classes—played itself out in the colonial field. Bley's unsuccessful effort to describe German Southwest Africa as totalitarian, finally, emphasizes the need to differentiate among forms of colonial assimilationism.[27]

PRECOLONIAL ETHNOGRAPHIC DISCOURSE
AND THE COLONIAL STATE

If theoretical frameworks centered on capitalism or German exceptionalism are inadequate, can we make better sense of colonial native policy in

26. For a subtle treatment of the combination of gains and losses that accompany conversion to the culture of the colonizer, see Elbourne 1992.

27. An excellent recent study of German colonialism in Southwest Africa by Jürgen Zimmerer (2001) represents a kind of synthesis of Bley and Drechsler in its basic interpretive strategy, although it goes beyond both in uncovering much original historical material. Unlike the present study, which is concerned with variations in the treatment of different indigenous groups, Zimmerer's work focuses on native policy in general, that is, on policies that were applied to all Africans in the Police Zone (he also examines briefly the Germans' treatment of migrant workers from Ovamboland and from the Cape Colony). Like Bley's, Zimmerer's text is still rooted in a quasi-exceptionalist framework, in which German colonialism is torn between the "premodern goal" of creating a sort of neofeudal order of estates, or *Stände*, and "modern methods" of rule. Like Drechsler, Zimmerer focuses almost exclusively on the connections between native policy and the creation of a capitalist economy. Thus, his analysis of native schools is mainly interested in efforts to "educate the African to work." Religious instruction and other civilizational goals are not relevant in this context, even though the schools in German Southwest Africa were run by missionaries.

Southwest Africa by connecting it to precolonial representations of indigenous cultures? The writings of German colonial officials after 1884 reveal a close familiarity with scientific and missionary writing on Southwest Africans.[28] Indeed, the connections between precolonial ethnographic representations and colonial officials were even more concrete and can be documented through records of specific interactions and encounters. The colony's "founder," Adolf Lüderitz, was accompanied in his travels through the nascent colony by Hans Schinz, who published the first extensive anthropological study of the new colony. Lüderitz's agent Heinrich Vogelsang consulted with Theo Hahn. Heinrich Goering, the colony's first imperial commissary, was accompanied on his first tour of the new protectorate by Carl Büttner, the former missionary to the Ovaherero discussed in chapter 2.

Ethnographic texts continued to be produced during the colonial era, and they often had a direct relationship with the colonial state, but now the causal traffic moved in both directions. Scientific and popular ethnographic discourse about a particular indigenous group tended to correspond closely to the basic thrust of native policy in a given period. This does not mean that native policy continued to evolve in response to changes in the ethnographic imagination. Instead, the impact of the colonial state on the ongoing production of ethnographic discourse was now more powerful than the impact of *new* ethnographic discourse on policymaking. The determinative relations between ethnography and colonialism were reciprocal rather than unidirectional, but the character of the causal influence was different at the two poles. The ethnographic portraits that underwrote native policy predated the colonial regime and continued to constrain its activities, defining an authoritative universe of possible approaches to the native.[29] The colonial state, by contrast, was able to fortify a particular strand of ethnographic discourse within this preestablished archive. This

---

28. Hugo von François, an officer in the colony's first *Schutztruppe* and brother of the colony's second governor, referred repeatedly to earlier experts, including Le Vaillant, Theo Hahn, Fritsch, Schinz, and earlier missionaries such as Heidmann (H. von François 1895, pp. 77–78, 205, 232). Hugo's brother Curt was familiar with the writings of colonial-era writers like Ludloff, Schinz, von Bülow, Pfeil, Dove, and others discussed below (C. von François 1899, pp. 41, 139). Theodor Leutwein referred to Schinz, Irle, Kurd Schwabe, von Deimling, and Georg Hartmann (1904), Franz Joseph von Bülow (1896), and Else von Sonnenberg (1905).

29. This is not to say that new ethnographic visions could not arise within the colonial setting. But the creation of a novel ethnographic framework requires more than a single eccentric or visionary observer.

could involve practical measures such as offering travelers, journalists, and ethnologists protection and privileged access. Less directly, the colonial state, like the state in general, gives structure to discursive fields during periods of relative state legitimacy even if it cannot monopolize cultural production.[30] Simplifying somewhat, we can say that *precolonial* ethnographic discourse shaped colonial native policy, while the colonial state shaped the ongoing production of *new* ethnographic discourse.

The Germans and the Witbooi People

"Hendrik Witbooi . . . actually had traits that Cooper's imagination ascribed to the leaders of the redskins."

KARL DOVE (1896a)

"Surely Herr von Trotha does not derive his colonial policies from [Cooper's] 'Leatherstocking' [tales]."

DR. M. J. BONN, "Die wissenschaftliche Begründung der Trotha'schen Eingeborenenpolitik," *Frankfurter Zeitung*, no. 45, February 14, 1909

"Hurry back to the big ships on which you traveled over the sea, because my father will soon come and chase all of the white men out of the country."

MARGARETE, daughter of Hendrik Witbooi, in the Windhoek prisoner-of-war camp (1893)[31]

THE WITBOOI AND THE DEVIL'S HANDWRITING

German colonial interactions with the Witbooi people can be arranged into three clearly identifiable patterns, each of which lasted almost exactly ten years.[32] During the first (1884–94) and third (1904–15) periods, native policy

30. Bourdieu ([1993] 1999) argues that the state becomes a field of metacapital where the value of the different types of specific capital is set.

31. Quoted in Dove 1896a, p. 187.

32. As a result of the plethora of different languages used in Southwest Africa before and during the German colonial period, and the variability in systems of transcribing indigenous languages, there is little agreement among historians about the appropriate way to write the names of specific people, places, or collectivities. I have generally used today's prevailing forms when referring to collectivities or ethnic groups that still exist (hence "Basters" rather than "Bastards" or "Bastaards," and "Ovaherero" rather than "Damara"). When referring to place names, I have generally tried to give a sense of contemporaries' own usage, particularly since the borders of these places often changed over time. Thus, the vaguely defined precolonial region called "Damaraland" is not precisely the same place as colonial-era "Hereroland," even if both referred to the homeland of the Ovaherero people. Individual names are also

was guided by the goals of subduing the Witbooi militarily and ultimately exterminating the tribe or driving it out of the colony. There was little interest in either of these periods in transforming the Witbooi into a productive labor force. Before 1894 the Germans tended to ally with the Ovaherero against the Witbooi. The middle decade provides a stark contrast. Between 1894 and 1904, the Witbooi were allowed to keep their "tribal" power structure, including the office of *kaptein*. They were also allowed to retain a valuable area of land around Gibeon as a reservation and were integrated into the colonial army under the terms of a "protection and friendship treaty." During these same years the Germans began to systematically strip the Ovaherero of their land and cattle.

It is not difficult to account for the timing of these shifts in native policy. The middle era was demarcated on one end by the military subjection of the Witbooi and on the other by their final stand against the Germans. The larger explanatory problem is to account for the specific contents of native policy in each period. Why were the Witbooi "pardoned," integrated, and allowed to keep their guns in 1894? And why was the German response relentlessly genocidal after 1904? Unlike the case of the Ovaherero, who might be seen as predestined for a sanguinary clash with the Germans due to the Europeans' extraordinarily harsh views of them throughout the nineteenth century, precolonial representations of the Witbooi offered a variety of different perspectives. Clearly, a more complicated explanation than the one offered by the devil's handwriting thesis is needed.

HEINRICH GOERING, THE VON FRANÇOIS BROTHERS, AND HENDRIK WITBOOI, 1884–94

During the first four years of the German "protectorate" the government had no military presence at all, and Southwest Africa was a state in name only.[33] Although most native groups, including the Ovaherero and the Re-

---

complicated because many Southwest Africans had names in both European and African languages. Here I have used the more familiar names but provided the others when they are known. For example, since the leader of the 1904 uprising has gone down in history as "Samuel Maherero" I have used his "Christian" rather than his Otjiherero name, Uereani.

33. The German colony called itself a "protectorate" from the start, even though the protection treaties were broken by both sides. Some contemporaries believed that the term *protectorate* referred to the protection of whites in the colony. Despite the linguistic obfuscation, nearly all Germans regarded Southwest Africa as a colony in the 1880s and 1890s; see Büttner 1885b; and Fabri 1884. Dove (1896a), Rohlfs (1884), and Seidel (1898) all used the phrase "Germany's first colony" in their book titles. The first *Landeshauptmann*, Curt von François, used the term *colonization* in his 1899 book title.

FIGURE 3.1 Hendrik Witbooi. (Courtesy of Stadt- u. Universitätsbibliothek Frankfurt, Bildsammlung der Deutschen Kolonialgesellschaft.)

hoboth Basters, signed protection treaties with the Germans, Hendrik Witbooi (fig. 3.1) and his father Moses refused at least four treaty offers before 1894. Hendrik sold no land to whites and allowed only Englishmen but not Germans to prospect on his land. By 1894 "there was not single white settler residing in Witbooi territory."[34] Ensconced at Hornkrans after 1889, the Witbooi continued raiding and extracting taxes and tribute from other natives and even from white settlers. They controlled much of Namaland and seemed oblivious to the Germans.[35] In one of his letters to Goering, Hendrik admonished him to "stay neutral, dear Sir" with regard to intra-Namibian conflict, adding that the Germans should "give us ammunition so we can have it out."[36] Witbooi lectured Ovaherero chief Kamaherero that "all the different nations have their own leaders," including Hereroland, which "belongs to the Herero nation," and Namaland, which "belongs to all the Red nations," and added that Kamaherero would "eternally regret that [he had] given [his] land and [his] right to rule into the hands of the White man." Paraphrasing a Nama fable, Witbooi warned that "surrendering yourself over to government by another, by White people . . . will become to you like

34. Bochert 1980, pp. 45, III.
35. Dedering 1993a, p. 64.
36. Witbooi to Goering, March 23, 1889, in Witbooi 1996, p. 32.

carrying the sun on your back."[37] Hendrik's prophetic Christianity, which he had first developed in a movement of independence from his missionary teachers, now began to focus on the colonizers and the need for disciplined guerilla action against them.[38]

The first contingent of German troops for the *Schutztruppe* arrived in the colony in 1889.[39] They were led by Captain Curt von François; the other officer was his brother, Lieutenant Hugo von François.[40] In 1891 Captain von François replaced Goering as *Landeshauptmann,* an office that had traditionally referred to the head of a self-administering Prussian province and that combined the roles of military commander and imperial commissary. The Germans were finally making an effort to take control of the "means of violence" within the territory.

Tensions between the Germans and the Witbooi increased steadily. In 1889 Hendrik killed Jan Jonker and defeated the Afrikaner Orlams, his main competitors for hegemony over the diverse groups of Namibian Khoikhoi. He also "inflicted serious defeats on the Red Nation, who were expelled from their territory and became completely impoverished thereafter."[41] Hendrik then sued the Ovaherero for peace. In the same year Samuel Maherero (fig. 3.2) was elevated to the position of "paramount chief" of the Ovaherero, following the death of his father Kamaherero and a bitter and controversial succession struggle. In June 1892 Landeshauptmann von François offered Hendrik Witbooi an annual salary of five thousand marks if he would submit to a protection treaty. But Witbooi remained a "principled opponent of any subjection to German rule," as von François reported.[42] Indeed, Witbooi asked impertinently, "What is 'protection'? What are we being protected against?" and maintained that it was "the German himself is that man who . . . is doing exactly what he said we would be protected from."[43] On June 9, 1892, Witbooi told von François that he could not

37. Witbooi to Maherero, May 30, 1890, in Witbooi 1996, pp. 50–52. According to the editors of Witbooi's papers, in the Nama fable "the jackal accepts the sun as a rider and barely survives with a permanently scorched back" (ibid., p. 52 n. 55).

38. Dedering 1993a, pp. 76–77.

39. The German Colonial Society for South West Africa had created a desultory police force of six German and twenty African soldiers in May 1888, but this force was dissolved one year later (Esterhuyse 1968).

40. Curt von François had been involved in an expedition in Togo and joined his brother and the troops bound for Southwest Africa at Tenerife, where he assumed command.

41. Bochert 1980, p. 35.

42. C. von François 1899, p. 153.

43. Record of a meeting between Witbooi and Curt von François, June 9, 1892; and Witbooi's letter to John Cleverly, British magistrate at Walvis Bay, August 4, 1892 (Witbooi 1996, pp. 85, 98).

FIGURE 3.2 Samuel Maherero with German uniform
in his "Kaiser Wilhelm" pose. (Courtesy of Archiv- und
Museumsstiftung Wuppertal.)

place himself under German protection, and he lectured the German commander on the concept of sovereignty: "An independent and autonomous
chief is chief of his people and land. . . . When one chief stands under the
protection of another, the underling is no longer independent, and is no longer master of himself, or of his people and country. . . . This part of Africa
is the realm of us Red chiefs. . . . 'Come brothers, let us together oppose this
danger which threatens to invade our Africa, for we are one in colour and
custom, and this Africa is ours.'" [44] In the same year, like Goering in 1888,
von François tried unsuccessfully to mobilize the Ovaherero for a joint attack on Witbooi. Instead, Hendrik Witbooi was able to convince Samuel

44. Witbooi 1996, pp. 85–86, record of a meeting between Witbooi and Curt von François,
June 9, 1892.

Maherero to sign a peace treaty, and he then began urging Samuel to unite with him against the Germans.[45]

The initial instructions to the *Schutztruppe* stipulated that they were to retain a strictly neutral stance in the colony's "ancient race war between yellows and blacks."[46] Von François remarked that he was not even sure whether he was permitted to use his weapons *defensively*. By 1892–93, however, a new interpretation of the role of the *Schutztruppe* had emerged. The first small group of German settlers had been sent out by the German Colonial Society for South West Africa, arriving in June of 1892. The Colonial Society pressed the government to take action against Witbooi.[47] A central motive for abandoning the neutral posture was "concern that Hendrik Witbooi's attempts at reconciliation with the Herero would lead to a united native front against the small German troop."[48] Von François obtained military reinforcements from Berlin, and the size of the *Schutztruppe* increased from fifty in 1890 to three hundred in 1893.[49] On April 12, 1893, nearly two hundred troops launched a surprise attack on the central Witbooi compound at Hornkrans. Von François's new orders were to "destroy the tribe."[50] The Witbooi were completely unprepared for the raid, believing that the *Schutztruppe* was still committed to neutrality.[51] As a result, around one hundred people were killed in the early morning massacre, mainly women and children.[52] The ferocity of the attack is suggested by the fact that the German troops, armed with two hundred rifles, used sixteen thousand rounds of ammunition in thirty minutes.[53] Most of the male Witbooi fighters escaped, however, and continued to elude the Germans during the following months. Previously Hendrik had scrupulously avoided harm-

45. C. von François 1889, pp. 160–62.

46. C. von François 1899, p. 37.

47. Heinrich Bokemeyer, "Über Ansiedlungsverhältnisse in Südwestafrika vom Gesichtspunkte der organisierten Kolonisation (Schluß)," *Deutsche Kolonialzeitung*, n.s., 3 (27, December 27, 1890): 323.

48. Kienetz 1976, p. 618.

49. Alverdes 1906, p. 257.

50. F. von Bülow 1896, p. 286; also Olpp in VEM, RMG 1.404, p. 60.

51. Bochert 1980, p. 88.

52. Estimates of the number of Witbooi killed at Hornkrans on April 12 range from 80 to 150. The low estimate is from Lieutenant von François's telegram of April 12 in BA-Berlin, RKA, vol. 1483, p. 9. The high estimate is from Lieutenant Kurd Schwabe (1899, p. 35; 1910, p. 39). Missionary Olpp received a report from a Witbooi that was "so trustworthy that I can give the names of the fallen, wounded, and imprisoned"; the number of dead in this report was 85 women and children and 10 men (VEM, RMG 1.404, p. 61).

53. F. von Bülow 1896, p. 287.

FIGURE 3.3 Theodor Leutwein. (Courtesy of Archiv- und Museumsstiftung Wuppertal.)

ing German soldiers, but now he was compelled to join the colonizers in battle. In a series of running skirmishes that lasted for more than a year the Witbooi had great success, stealing horses and livestock from the headquarters of the *Schutztruppe* in Windhoek. At the end of 1893 the metropolitan government sent Theodor Leutwein (fig. 3.3) to the colony to investigate the reasons for the continuing failure to subdue the Witbooi. Leutwein soon replaced von François as *Landeshauptmann*. Witbooi ran low on ammunition and was refused aid by the English at the Cape and Walvis Bay and by Cecil Rhodes—one of many instances of British cooperation with Germany across the colonial boundary.[54] Leutwein asked for another 250 troops, and they arrived in July 1894. With this enlarged army Leutwein was able to defeat Hendrik Witbooi and force him to sign a protection treaty.[55]

54. Bochert 1980, pp. 118–19.
55. Treaty of September 15, 1894 (T. Leutwein 1907a, pp. 57–58).

Lieutenant Hugo von François claimed in his 1895 book (*Nama and Damara*) that the Germans' decision to take sides against the Witbooi was the deliberate result of "long years of observation." German native policy did flow from long-standing observations, but these were mainly inherited from earlier generations of Europeans in the precolony. Native policy targeting the Witbooi during the first decade was couched in terms of the dominant strand of precolonial discourse according to which Orlam Khoikhoi tended to swing menacingly between the poles of partial Europeanization and "savagery." Not all constructions of mimicry yielded native policies as brutal as those directed at the Witbooi in 1892–93 and after 1904. What distinguished one mimicry paradigm from the next was the substantive content of the "traditional" half of the dualistic structure. Hendrik's Christian rhetoric, modern weapons, and European vestments, his reliance on written correspondence, treaties, and formal declarations of war, were viewed as signs of acculturation. The Germans' interpretation of the older part of the divided "Hottentot" soul was derived from the seventeenth- and eighteenth-century discourse of abject savagery, however, and this framework motivated a murderous approach to the Witbooi, who were seen as fundamentally averse to labor and an orderly lifestyle. In 1895, Lieutenant Hugo von François looked back at the Germans' decision to take sides against Hendrik Witbooi. This decision was not motivated by moral considerations, he claimed, since Hendrik's position had been morally superior to that of the Ovaherero at the beginning of their conflict. The deciding factor for the Germans was the growing conviction that the Ovaherero represented the colony's "future bearers of productive labor" (kulturfähige Arbeits-Production).[56] The lieutenant's brother agreed that Commissary Heinrich Goering sided with the Ovaherero after it became evident that the colony's economic development would depend on cattle farming rather than mining, since the Ovaherero owned the largest herds of cattle and were superior herdsmen.[57] Of course, some Germans expressed support for Hendrik Witbooi precisely because his raids seemed like the best way to strip Ovaherero of their cattle. The ideological figure of Witbooi mimicry did not provide a basis for colonial stabilization. Like British policy toward Khoi-khoi at the Cape after midcentury, the Germans "resigned" themselves to the extinction of the Witbooi.

Lieutenant von François's book is a revealing guide to the interweaving of ethnographic discourse and practical native policy in the 1889–94

56. H. von François 1895, p. 159.
57. C. von François 1899, pp. 72–73.

period.[58] Von François opened his discussion of the "Hottentots' culture and mores" with a section reminiscent of older Cape colonial literature, focusing on their facial structure, hair texture, "unpleasant" skin color, and "pronounced ugliness." He devoted an entire page to female steatopygia, complete with photograph. Reproducing the language of some of the earliest European callers at the Cape, von François referred to the Khoikhoi as "bizarre red people" with an "animal-like" clicking language. His text then shifted from the first half of the binary structure of Khoikhoi mimicry—the tropes of abject savagery—to the later half, which was focused on acculturation. The text's narrative sequence tracked the historical transformation of European perceptions of the Khoikhoi. Von François attributed the dissolution of their earlier, more stable mode of life to economic modernization and incomplete Europeanization. The Khoikhoi had tried to "imitate" the white man, he insisted, and were therefore responsible for their own downfall.[59] During the period that had just ended the Witbooi had been the main target of repression by the *Schutztruppe*. It is thus perhaps understandable that Hendrik Witbooi himself figured as the lieutenant's main example of Khoikhoi mimicry. He described Hendrik as highly intelligent and decisive but also ruthless and trembling with energy and a "fanatical fire." His prognosis was that the Khoikhoi had "outlived their day" and would "decline more and more and eventually be destroyed." This passive formulation was the result of wishful thinking rather than empirical analysis, since the decimation of the Witbooi was hardly the result of natural causes.[60] There was a remarkable unanimity between colonial-era thinking and precolonial discourse.

Another officer active in the colony at this time, First Lieutenant Franz Joseph von Bülow, published a book on German Southwest Africa in 1896 entitled *Three Years in the Land of Hendrik Witbooi*. For von Bülow, Hendrik and his people epitomized Orlam mimicry. He argued that Hendrik had never actually overcome the "animal instincts of this raw people, which had inherited extremely base moral categories from its forebears." Hendrik's success lay rather "in the *appearance* of good morals." The Witbooi gave "*the impression* of being positively civilized," but according to von Bülow they

58. The colony's first commissioner, Heinrich Goering, had little effect on colonial policy, especially with respect to the Witbooi, and was important mainly in generating signatures on protection treaties and stimulating research on the colony.

59. H. von François 1895, pp. 202–4, 77, 224.

60. Ibid., pp. 137, 142, 217, 216. Franz Joseph von Bülow described Hendrik as "the last Hottentot hero," leading the "desperate remains of a dying race" (1896, pp. 346, 339). Theodor Leutwein spoke similarly of Hendrik Witbooi as "the last national hero of a race doomed to ruination" (1907a, p. 306), but this was after the 1904–7 extermination campaign.

were "only interested in eating, drinking, and sleeping," like "any other native." These "primitive" traits were combined with modern ones in a volatile mix. Hendrik was a master of the "art, widespread among natives, of hiding his feelings and controlling his facial muscles." Von Bülow emphasized his "hard, expressionless, and restless slanty little black eyes." Hendrik was a "practical and intelligent man who knew his people very well and used their weaknesses to his own advantage," exploiting their credulous acceptance of his "holy mission." The divergence between *Sein* and *Schein* mapped neatly onto the conventional topos of Khoikhoi shiftiness.[61]

Germans outside the colonial administration added fuel to the fire. Some of the Rhenish missionaries reached the same exterminationist conclusions as von François and von Bülow. Mission inspector Fabri warned in 1884 against the "very volatile character" of the Witbooi and predicted that Hendrik's movement would turn into a maniacal fundamentalism and culminate in a "bloodbath."[62] Five years later, missionary Friedrich Judt suggested that the best solution would be for the German colonizers to "reach for the sword."[63] Most of the missionaries saw Hendrik as the colony's public enemy number 1 during these years, and the mission headquarters in Barmen bombarded the Colonial Department with demands to "put an end to Hendrik Witbooi's business once and for all."[64] The German Colonial Society for South West Africa called repeatedly for decisive action against the "robber chief."[65]

The first "scientific" study of the Witbooi was written by Hans Schinz, whose fieldwork in 1884–87 was sponsored by the colony's "godfather," Adolf Lüderitz.[66] Like many eighteenth- and nineteenth-century travel writers, Schinz was a botanist by training, but unlike Henry David Thoreau, Schinz did more than go "a-botanizing."[67] As a scientist Schinz claimed to have a particularly acute understanding of indigenous cultures, instructing his readers to try to "get inside their heads."[68] Nonetheless, his ethnic portrait

61. F. von Bülow 1896, pp. 156, 150, 152 (my emphasis).

62. Menzel 2000, p. 65, citing Fabri.

63. Ibid., p. 140, citing Judt from September 9, 1889.

64. Missionary August Schreiber to Dr. Kayser in the Colonial Department, April 6, 1893, BA-Berlin, RKA, vol. 2131, p. 47.

65. See C. von François 1899, p. 140, for a report on the meeting of the German Colonial Society on June 29–30, 1891.

66. Gordon 1992, p. 236 n. 3; C. A. Lüderitz 1945, pp. 165–66.

67. Thoreau's journal entry of September 7, 1856, in Thoreau 1949, p. 66.

68. Schinz 1891, p. 83. Schinz was Swiss, not German. His view of the Khoikhoi cannot be understood as an effect of the state's harsher policies toward the Witbooi, since these policies were only beginning when Schinz published his text in 1891. This is an example of a

was identical to that of the military writers and missionaries. Along the lines of the ancient Cape discourse he insisted that the smell of the "Hottentots" was ineradicable, persisting even after they were taught the rules of hygiene. Schinz described a group of Khoikhoi men as crouching "monkey-like" on the ground. Yet he went on to detail the ways in which the Khoikhoi had moved beyond ignoble savagery. In contrast to missionary writing, however, he roundly condemned incomplete forms of civilization. Schinz argued that the Khoikhoi had gained nothing by forsaking their traditional gods; their conversion to Christianity had left "nothing but a gaping void." According to Schinz, the earlier distinctions among Orlams and Nama had disappeared; all three groups were now little more than "Hottentots." Schinz tapped into European fears of dissimulation, writing that the "Hottentot" face instinctively "awakens feelings of discomfort and suspicion in us" because it "strongly recalls the Chinese race." Echoing many others, Schinz concluded that "the Hottentot is on the road to extinction."[69]

The repetition of brutal formulas in nearly all German discussions of the Khoikhoi during this period is striking. A travel narrative by Dr. R. F. Ludloff concluded that "contact with civilization seems to make the savage more savage." Hendrik Witbooi was a "clever, diplomatically cunning fox," and one of his sons recalled Richard III, "Gloster, the bloodiest figure in the Shakespearian royal dramas." Ludloff suggested that it would be best "if our security force were quickly strengthened to the point that they could be directed to make Hornkrans and Witbooi disappear from the colony without a trace." He predicted that the Witbooi would vanish "like snow melting in the flames."[70]

A form of mimicry containing such an unattractive version of "tradition" did not recommend native policies of "salvage" or retraditionalization. The centrality of idleness and nomadism in the older discourse also meant that the Witbooi were not seen as candidates for proletarianization. The only remaining option, apparently, was extermination. The year after the Hornkrans raid, however, a shift in the colony's leadership led to a change in strategy based on an alternative ethnographic precedent.

---

colonial-era text which may have influenced colonial policy rather than the other way around, but only because the colonial state barely existed in the 1880s. In a sense then, Schinz's text was still a precolonial one.

69. Schinz 1891, pp. 81, 31, 100, 104, 79, and 517. See also "Vortrag des Herrn Dr. Hans Schinz über die Bedeutung von Südwestafrika als Kolonie," *Deutsche Kolonialzeitung*, n.s., 4 (8, July 1891): 105.

70. Ludloff 1891, pp. 45, 91–92, 98, 46.

THE WITBOOI AS NOBLE SAVAGES, 1894–1904

By the time Lieutenant von François had returned to Germany and written his treatise, Theodor Leutwein had been appointed *Landeshauptmann* and subdued Hendrik Witbooi. Rather than completing von François's extermination plan, however, Leutwein embarked immediately on a strategy of cooptation and ethnic "salvage." The Witbooi were neither executed nor imprisoned, but were resettled at their former base in Gibeon, where a new German garrison was installed.[71] Their territory was reduced in size but still measured twenty thousand square kilometers, and it included "one of the best farming areas of Great Namaqualand."[72] The defeated Witbooi were permitted to keep their guns and horses and were enlisted as military allies. In 1895 they were integrated into the *Schutztruppe*.[73] Between 1894 and 1904 Witbooi fighters helped the Germans repress numerous insurgencies.[74] Since the *Schutztruppe* remained "a relatively small force" of 780 German soldiers as late as 1903, this "Witbooi auxiliary of 750 men" made a significant difference.[75] The Witbooi fought alongside Germans against the Ovaherero during the first nine months of the 1904 war. Hendrik remained "captain" of the Witbooi after 1894 and was paid an annual salary of two thousand marks, and he participated in the annual celebrations of the kaiser's birthday.[76] He was allowed to adjudicate all legal disputes inside the Witbooi territory involving natives.[77] Cases involving a white and a Witbooi were decided in a

71. T. Leutwein 1912, p. 22. See also "Die Kämpfe gegen H. Witboi," *Deutsche Kolonialzeitung*, n.s., 7 (13, December 1894): 164.

72. Bochert 1980, p. 135. The 1894 treaty with the Witbooi resembled those from the mid-1880s insofar as it used the word *protection* (*Schutzherrschaft*) rather than *suzerainty* (*Oberherrschaft*; Drechsler [1966] 1980, p. 77). The latter had been used since the early 1890s and suggested a more explicit foreign domination, even if *protection* had also been euphemistic. What matters most in the present context is that the Witbooi were being given preferential treatment.

73. The integration was accomplished through an addition to the 1894 treaty, signed on November 16, 1895. See "Deutsch-Südwestafrika: Zum Schutzvertrag zwischen Major Leutwein und Hendrik Witbooi," *Deutsches Kolonialblatt* 17 (1906): 104.

74. "Ueber die Niederwerfung des Aufstandes der Khauas-Hottentotten," *Beilage zum "Deutschen Kolonialblatt"* 7 (1896): 2. See Burgsdorff-Garath 1982 for an account of these campaigns; also Drechsler [1966] 1980, pp. 82, 100; and Bochert 1980, pp. 156–57.

75. Dedering 1993a, p. 65.

76. "Ueber die Feier des Geburtstages Seiner Majestät des Kaisers," *Deutsches Kolonialblatt* 6 (1895): 212. See also "Deutsch-Südwestafrika: Bericht des Gouverneurs Leutwein über seinen Zug nach dem Süden des Schutzgebietes," *Deutsches Kolonialblatt* 10 (1, January 1899): 17ff.

77. Külz 1909, p. 17.

German court, but the Witbooi chief could appoint one of his councilors to the trial.[78] An addendum in 1896 specified that leading Witbooi families were "excluded from flogging as punishment"—a special dispensation granted to Samoans and to a few other select groups in the German colonial empire.[79]

As in German Samoa, the colonial state did not simply preserve Witbooi culture but transformed it in ways that tended to concentrate power in the colonizer's hands. But this did not preclude policies that were also acceptable to the colonized. For example, in 1898 a reservation was created for the Witbooi at Rietmond and Kalkfontein. This was the colony's only functioning reservation prior to the 1904-7 war, although the first Ovaherero reservation was on the verge of being created when fighting broke out.[80] Reservations represented islands of "traditionalism" insofar as they were self-governing and whites were prohibited from settling or buying land inside their borders.

Native policy during this middle decade was organized around representations of Witbooi men as noble warrior-savages. The portrait of the scheming, unreliable mimic man receded into the background.[81] The noble savagery frame provided a basis for a positive policy of stabilization. Witbooi soldiers were constructed as courageous and loyal warriors, gifted with extraordinarily keen vision and skilled in tracking enemies across the colony's illegible landscape.[82] German officials sang the praise of Witbooi bravery and intelligence.[83] Witbooi women were not sensualized, as in Le Vaillant and in the discourse of Polynesian noble savagery (see chap. 4), but neither were they abjectified.

78. Bochert 1980, p. 130.

79. Ibid., p. 140. See chap. 5 for the history of flogging legislation involving Chinese workers in the German Pacific and chap. 7 on flogging in German Kiaochow.

80. T. Leutwein 1907a, p. 272; Sudholt 1975, p. 151.

81. Dedering (1993a, p. 66) states misleadingly that "by the end of the nineteenth century the European image of the Witbooi Orlams increasingly centered on Social-Darwinist notions of a 'primitive' African society." He cites only two publications to support this claim, and only one of them dates from this period: Hugo von François's *Nama und Damara*. But Hugo von François and his brother were both vehemently opposed to Leutwein's new course with the Witbooi. Their views of the Witbooi cannot be taken as representative of the 1894-1904 decade. The other publication cited here is Theodor Leutwein's *Elf Jahre Gouverneur in Deutsch-Südwestafrika*, which was published in 1907, *after* the second Witbooi uprising. Dedering's other quotes are from missionaries, who were understandably bitter about losing spiritual control over the Witbooi to Hendrik. But because they had terminated their relations with the Witbooi, they had little influence on German discussions of Hendrik and his community during the 1894-1904 period.

82. C. von François 1899, p. 204.

83. Kurd Schwabe 1899, pp. 33, 35.

Theodor Leutwein set the tone for this resignification of the Witbooi people. In a report to Berlin several months after Hendrik's surrender Leutwein wrote that while Hendrik would certainly "think back longingly on the days when he was an independent captain," he was also "the kind of man who . . . has a certain pride in keeping his word."[84] In a lecture to the German Colonial Society in 1898, Leutwein described Hendrik as an "imposing" figure who radiated "unbending willpower, grounded tranquility, and confidence." According to Leutwein, "his speech is deliberate but certain," and "his tightly drawn lips communicate energy and an unmistakable air of acerbity."[85] Leutwein repeatedly described the Witbooi as "natural soldier material" and as the best "among our native tribes."[86] They were the exception to the rule: other "Nama tribes" were less noble and would probably have engaged in "sneaky, deceptive attacks" rather than playing the role of the "honest enemy," as Hendrik did in 1893-94.[87]

The question is what motivated Theodor Leutwein to forge his own band of noble Witbooi warriors after 1894 and to describe them with such pathos. Why did he break with his predecessor's homicidal approach? The previous chapter established that alternative readings of the Khoikhoi were available in the ethnographic archive.[88] But the mere existence of these alternatives cannot explain the governor's embrace of the noble savagery paradigm. His effort to enlist the Witbooi as collaborators might seem like an obviously rational strategy, but this would overlook the fact that repression was often the preferred response to colonial uprisings, and that many Germans

84. "Hendrik Witbooi," *Deutsches Kolonialblatt* 7 (1895): 274.

85. T. Leutwein 1898, p. 8.

86. See extracts from Leutwein's May 3, 1895, report in "Deutsch-Südwestafrika," *Deutsches Kolonialblatt* 7 (1895): 547; also Leutwein 1898-99, p. 2. Leutwein wrote, "A white can always live next to Hottentots, but living with Herero is difficult" (Leutwein to chancellor, February 3, 1895, BA-Berlin, RKA, vol. 2100, p. 131r; crossed out in original).

87. Leutwein as overheard by missionary Johannes Olpp: "Beitrag zur Missionsgeschichte des Witbooistammes," VEM, RMG 1.404, p. 64. Leutwein's son Paul published a doggerel poem called "Hoornkrans" four years after his father's return to Germany, which begins with a description of "the noble Hendrik Witboy." Hendrik was "our hero," Paul Leutwein wrote, "the last great Hottentot prince," and his people were "created by God as a knightly people." While there is little mystery about the motives that led Paul Leutwein to defend his father's legacy, his formulations are of some interest. Hendrik's daughter Margarete is described as looking "scornfully" at "the lieutenants" (i.e., the von François brothers) and crying out: "You whites are jackals, but one day my father will destroy you like a lion!" (P. Leutwein 1909, pp. 15-17). Other writers described Margarete's defiance; see the epigraph to this section from a book by Karl Dove, who was present at the Hornkrans massacre.

88. Although there is no direct evidence that Leutwein had read these earlier writers, he often referred to contemporary works on Southwest Africa which themselves cited "deviant" classics like Peter Kolb and Le Vaillant.

were calling for the Witbooi people's annihilation after their defeat in 1894. Nor was Leutwein averse to violence: he had executed the captain of the Khauas Orlams, Andries Lambert, earlier in 1894, for the murder of a German trader, even though he admitted that Lambert had neither committed the murder nor even directly ordered it.[89] After his 1896 campaign against the Khauas and Ovambanderu Leutwein placed all of the survivors in a prison for exploitation as forced labor.[90]

Leutwein's approach to the Witbooi was motivated not just by a divide-and-rule logic but also by his class-based quest for symbolic distinction. Leutwein's competition with aristocratic members of the German officer corps is a leitmotif throughout his entire career, and it was ultimately the main cause of his ignominious dismissal from the governorship in 1905.[91] Leutwein had initially been dispatched to the colony because of criticism of von François's inability to subdue Hendrik Witbooi. Leutwein's relationship with the former *Landeshauptmann* was therefore destined to be antagonistic. This transition in the colony's leadership mirrored the overarching struggle between the nobility and the middle class that was taking place in the Wilhelmine army and the schismatic German elite. The transposition of this intraelite class struggle onto the colonial stage had powerful effects on native policy during the coming years.

To clarify this we need to focus on the class backgrounds and aspirations of these officials. Theodor Leutwein, born in 1849, was the son of a Lutheran minister. He had enjoyed a classical gymnasium education and attended a university. Leutwein broke off his law studies and entered the military. At the time of his appointment as *Landeshauptmann* he was a lecturer in military tactics at the military academy at Bad Hersfeld, which is to say that he was a pedagogue rather than a fighting officer.[92] The von François brothers, by contrast, were members of the Prussian nobility whose

89. "Deutsch-Südwestafrika," *Deutsches Kolonialblatt* 5 (1894): 321. In this report Leutwein equates Lambert with Hendrik Witbooi. This suggests that he did not *already* harbor a favorable view of the Witbooi when he arrived in Southwest Africa but elaborated this in response to local experiences.

90. Bochert 1980, p. 144.

91. As discussed below, Leutwein's conflict with Lothar von Trotha was much more bitter than his interactions with the von François brothers. Although one might attribute his fall from grace to the 1904 uprising, it is notable that Count Adolf von Götzen, governor of German East Africa in the same era as the Ovaherero rebellion, was confronted by the equally disruptive and bloody Maji-Maji uprising but was not forced out of power. Instead, Governor von Götzen was put in charge of a commission to investigate the causes of the 1905 rebellion. Although von Götzen was replaced in 1906, there was none of the bitterness associated with Leutwein's marginalization. See Gründer 2004, pp. 159–64.

92. Esterhuyse 1968, p. 202.

FIGURE 3.4 Lothar von Trotha. (Courtesy of Stadt- u. Universitätsbibliothek Frankfurt, Bildsammlung der Deutschen Kolonialgesellschaft.)

ancestor August von François had received the title "deutsche Reichsadel" in 1774, and whose father, General Bruno von François, was a hero of the Franco-Prussian War.[93] Leutwein's struggle with the von François brothers involved not just "classes on paper" (Bourdieu) but social class as it was lived and understood. This class antagonism overcoded the tension that was already built into the relationship between a new *Landeshauptmann* and those whose power he was usurping. Ten years later, an almost identical constellation would find Leutwein confronting General von Trotha, a scion of the "ancient aristocracy of the Saale district" (fig. 3.4). Von Trotha was a veteran of the crushing defeat of the French at the Battle of Sedan and numerous military engagements in German East Africa, where he commanded the *Schutztruppe* between 1894 and 1897. He was also one of many

93. Bruno von François had fallen at Spichern in 1870 as commander of the Twenty-seventh Brigade. See F. von Bülow 1896, p. 330; and *Meyer's Lexikon*, 7th ed. (Leipzig: Bibliographisches Institut, 1926), vol. 4, p. 996.

participants in the 1904 German-Ovaherero war who had taken part just three years earlier in the brutal allied campaign against the Chinese Boxers, where he had commanded the First Infantry Brigade of the German East Asian Expeditionary Corps.[94]

In contrast to his later conflict with von Trotha, Leutwein's relationship with the von François brothers never turned into an open battle for professional survival. But the two parties sparred repeatedly, each insisting on the superiority of their ethnographic and colonial-political judgment. As Leutwein explained in an essay in the official *Militär-Wochenblatt* (Military Weekly) in 1894, his intention had been to prove to the Witbooi that "we will *not* always shoot to kill"—an unmistakable dig at the commanding officer of the Hornkrans massacre.[95] In a lecture to the German Colonial Society in Berlin four years later Leutwein emphasized that he had been determined in 1894 not to undermine the possibility of future friendship with the Witbooi, and commented that "the conditions offered to Witbooi were mild. I had gotten to know him as an honorable opponent, worthy of respect, whose friendship seemed to be worth having. . . . [He has] kept his word since then and . . . is now His Majesty's most loyal subject." Evidence of the ongoing tension in this relationship can be seen in Leutwein's letter to the Colonial Office from August 1904, which attributes rumors of an imminent Witbooi uprising to the "François family."[96]

The von François brothers were not oblivious to Leutwein's needling. By arguing explicitly against policies that every reader associated with Leutwein, they managed to attack him without ever uttering his name, in a strategy of *totschweigen,* or killing with silence. Leutwein's mild treatment of the Witbooi was criticized in "colonial circles inside Germany, who had been influenced by the settlers and by [Curt von] François himself." These critics insisted on a harsher stance, including "the execution of Witbooi and the disarming of the tribe."[97] Indeed, Hugo von François concluded that colonizers were compelled to "instill absolute respect for the superiority of German power and intellectual authority," even at "the risk of causing the extinction of the historical Hottentot."[98] After Leutwein created the Witbooi reservation in 1898, Curt von François wrote that the Germans should

---

94. Pool 1991, pp. 243-44; von Salzmann 1905, 187. On von Trotha in China see *Deutschland in China* 1902, pp. 230ff.

95. T. Leutwein 1894, p. 2576 (my emphasis).

96. T. Leutwein 1898-99, p. 18; Leutwein to Colonial Department, August 24, 1904, BA-Berlin, RKA, vol. 2133, p. 4r.

97. Bley [1971] 1996, p. 33.

98. H. von François 1895, p. 225.

follow the example of "the Cape Colony and the United States" by expelling indigenous people from their land and pushing them into "servile and dependent positions, the only ones for which they are suited."[99] And in a 1905 pamphlet on the "Hottentot uprising," Major Alfred von François, the elder brother of Hugo and Curt, took another jab at Leutwein, insisting that "the character of the Nama" was so corrupt that any expressions of loyalty on their part—the basis of Leutwein's Witbooi strategy—had to be taken with a grain of salt.[100]

The von François brothers were located in the same competitive social field as Leutwein, whether they liked it or not. This is suggested by their insistence on their own ethnographic sagacity. Hugo von François began a long chapter called "Images of Culture and Mores" by emphasizing that every colonizer should familiarize himself with the natives' "universe of representations and forms of practice" (Vorstellungswelt und Handlungsweise). Even as he revealed himself as a consummate racist, von François insisted that the European should evaluate this foreign universe "completely on its own terms," allowing himself to be taken into (sich hineinbegeben) the indigenous culture. According to the lieutenant it was only possible to "get to know these populations by . . . interacting closely with them for years." Sounding like a predecessor of Bronislaw Malinowski, von François counseled that the European should not "be afraid to crawl into [the natives'] evil-smelling smoky houses and pontoks."[101] These sentiments may seem surprising coming from the perpetrator of a colonial massacre, but this discourse can be read as a claim to a certain kind of ethnographic authority, and as a rebuttal to Leutwein's counterclaim to possess a more refined hermeneutic.

One of the signs of status claimed by different groups of colonial Germans was recognition as an "old African" (alter Afrikaner), a phrase referring to Europeans with long years of experience in Africa. When Leutwein first arrived in the colony in 1894 he lacked experience not just on the battlefield but also overseas. Curt von François, by contrast, had participated in Wissmann's Central Africa expedition in 1880–82 and had received the Medal of the Southern Cross from the Belgian king Leopold. In 1887 he had con-

99. C. von François 1899, p. 203.

100. A. von François 1905, p. 87. Alfred von François played a small but significant role in shaping native policy toward the Witbooi simply by virtue of his family ties, without ever being officially posted to Southwest Africa. He visited the colony in 1891, interviewed Hendrik Witbooi, and wrote reports on economic, native, and military policy. See H. von François 1895, pp. 136–42; and C. von François 1899, pp. 193–211.

101. H. von François 1895, pp. 157–58.

ducted an expedition in the Togolese hinterland.[102] As Curt von François boasted, "I was an old soldier and student of Africa. I feel that I can instinctively sense when the natives are up to something."[103] General von Trotha made a similar claim to possess the insight of the "old African" who knows "these African tribes."[104]

Leutwein felt compelled to distinguish himself not only from these military aristocrats but also from the settlers. As he insisted in 1907, the "mass of whites . . . felt superior and paid no attention to the protection treaties" and did not understand that the colonial government "had to rely on the good will of the natives for the sake of their own safety." Leutwein characterized the typical German as "undemocratic" and added that "when he finds someone who is beneath him, he likes to let him feel it." Writing while German troops were still confronting Khoikhoi guerillas on the battlefield, Leutwein blamed the rebellion on the "exacerbation of racial contradictions" resulting from settler exploitation and oppression. Leutwein observed that some settlers "could never understand how an administrative official could shake the hand of a 'greasy' native." He recalled that two settlers had volunteered for a police action against the Bondelswart chief in 1903, because they "expected a merry armed confrontation with the 'inferior and filthy' Hottentots."[105] Governor Solf in Samoa shared this critical view of the German settler.

Leutwein's efforts to distinguish himself from the settlers and the military aristocrats only partly accounts for his conciliatory treatment of Hendrik Witbooi. His gravitation toward the code of noble savagery was also rooted in an imaginary identification with an imago of the Witbooi, particularly with an idealized image of Hendrik himself. Educated middle-class German men like Leutwein in this period often distanced themselves from the cultural signifiers of the traditional upper classes and proudly insisted on their own rational middle-class values. Yet colonizers like Leutwein sometimes sought a kind of *imaginary* ennoblement through their interactions with colonized groups they constructed as noble. In this respect, Leutwein and others like him were engaged in an imaginary form of "upward mobility" in the social class hierarchy. Leutwein clearly enjoyed his position as the "chief" of an honorable group of Witbooi warrior-savages between 1894 and 1904. Even after the beginning of the Witbooi insurrection

102. See C. von François 1972 for his diaries of the Togo expedition.

103. C. von François 1899, p. 161.

104. Von Trotha to von Schlieffen, October 4, 1904, BA-Berlin, RKA, vol. 2089, p. 5r-v; von Trotha to Leutwein, November 5, 1904, BA-Berlin, RKA, vol. 2089, p. 100v.

105. T. Leutwein 1907b, pp. 112, 109.

in 1904, Leutwein still spoke proudly of standing "side by side" with Hendrik Witbooi as they fought against the Bondelswart insurrection the previous year.[106] Just two weeks after the Waterberg battle—and shortly before Hendrik's rebellion—Leutwein requested that the Witbooi leader's annual salary be raised from 3,500 to 5,000 marks.[107] Even when he was confronted with Hendrik's betrayal in October, Leutwein did not back down immediately but suggested that Hendrik's hand might have been forced by public opinion among his people, or that his son might actually be in charge.[108] The nobility of the Witbooi had a specifically martial character, and this was attractive to Leutwein in light of the military prestige of his main social competitors and his own lack of inherited military capital.

Leutwein did not generalize his treatment of the Witbooi to other groups of Khoikhoi, but stressed that Hendrik was unique, "an honest enemy in war who never launched sneaky, deceptive attacks, like the other Nama tribes."[109] Leutwein never romanticized any of the secondary Khoikhoi leaders who joined Hendrik Witbooi in his 1904 rebellion, men like Simon Kopper, captain of the Franzman (!Kharakhoen) Nama, or the legendary Jacob Marengo.[110] But certain aspects of Hendrik Witbooi's behavior made him well suited for the imaginary role of the faithful noble savage. Hendrik's language was permeated with the words and gestures of honor, loyalty, and justice. Even his discourse of "Africa for the Africans" resonated with European notions of national pride.

Leutwein's power as the head of a colonial state allowed him to put his stamp on the ongoing production of ethnographic discourse concerning the Witbooi. More than any explicit recommendations to ethnographic writers, this ideological channeling flowed naturally from the vision of the Witbooi that was embedded within native policy. The "official mind" of the colonial state was replicated in the discourse of lower-level officials. One example of the former was Lieutenant Kurd Schwabe, who came to Southwest Africa in 1893 to participate in the *Schutztruppe* and was later appointed head of the military-administrative headquarters at Swakopmund.[111] Schwabe stayed in

106. Leutwein to von Trotha, October 30, 1904, BA-Berlin, RKA, vol. 2089, p. 30r.

107. Leutwein to Colonial Department, August 26, 1904, BA-Berlin, RKA, vol. 2133, p. 4v.

108. Telegram from Leutwein to Colonial Department, October 7, 1904, BA-Berlin, RKA, vol. 2089, p. 30v; and BA-Berlin, RKA, vol. 2133, p. 10.

109. Leutwein, as overheard by an acquaintance of Johannes Olpp, Jr., quoted in Olpp, "Beitrag z. Missionsgeschichte des Witbooistammes," VEM, RMG 1.404, p. 64.

110. Uwe Timm's novel *Morengo* ([1978] 2003) uses the alternative spelling of Marengo's name that was widespread at the time.

111. Kurd Schwabe 1899, p. 102.

the colony for four years, serving first under von François and then under Leutwein, and returned to Southwest Africa in 1904 to take part in the war. In his memoirs, published in 1899, Schwabe compared the Witbooi to the *Huns*—a symbol with positive connotations in German military circles at the time, as exemplified by the kaiser's *Hunnenrede* (see chap. 1), and also a symbol that suggested the image of a primitive warrior with "strong feelings of independence." Schwabe characterized the Witbooi as "knightly" (ritterlich) and as "superbly disciplined" fighters.[112] Another official who adopted Leutwein's perspective was the district commissioner at Gibeon, Henning von Burgsdorff. Ironically, he was the first German official killed by the Witbooi at the start of their uprising in 1904. Captain von Burgsdorff called the Witbooi "the most vigorous [*lebenskräftigste*] community in Namaland," and he recognized Hendrik as a "powerful personality," even a "great man," who would be "as good as his word."[113]

Even figures associated with the colony's pre-1894 governments now embraced elements of the noble savagery paradigm. Lieutenant von François's book was published in 1895, just after Hendrik's surrender and his integration into the *Schutztruppe,* and was intended as a justification of the policies of his brother's government. Yet at one point the author listed the characteristics of the Khoikhoi as "communicativeness, hospitality, amiability, and obligingness"—exactly as in Le Vaillant, an author to whom von François referred. He praised the "racial characteristics" of the Witbooi soldiers, including their "admirable speed," "great intelligence," "excellent sensory perception," and "marvelous agility" and described Hendrik Witbooi as possessing a powerful "sense of justice."[114] Franz Joseph von Bülow referred to the Witbooi as "yellowskins" (*Gelbhäute*), a term that summoned up the romantic German image of American "redskins," and claimed that they "represented freedom in every respect." The German soldiers were no match, he wrote, for these "agile little Hottentots, who grow up on horseback with a gun in their hands, who know every corner of the country and every track in the sand, and for whom war is a pleasure, and hunger and thirst no cause for alarm."[115]

The fact that the new official position made its way even into the writing of the architects of the earlier regime underscores the power of the co-

---

112. Ibid., pp. 54, 361; 1907, p. 316.
113. Von Burgsdorff, "Hendrik Witbooi: Eine Skizze," *Militär-Wochenblatt* 80 (44, 1895): 1174; Burgsdorff-Garath 1982, pp. 100, 40.
114. H. von François 1895, pp. 94, 232, 205, 225-26. See also Estorff 1911, p. 81.
115. F. von Bülow 1899, pp. 295, 304.

lonial state to dominate ongoing ethnographic perception. This influence radiated beyond the narrow circles of colonial officials and officers. One of the most widely read writers on Southwest Africa in this decade was Karl Dove, who became the "organic intellectual" of the noble savagery approach to colonizing the Witbooi and the leading authority on the colony in this period.[116] Dove had been sent to Africa by the German Colonial Society to conduct economic, meteorological, and cartographic research, and he took charge of the society's initiative to encourage German settlement.[117] Dove referred to Le Vaillant as an authority, but his rendering of the Khoikhoi also relied on the romantic depictions of the American Indian that had appeared in the nineteenth century. Searching for an image powerful enough to wrench the Khoikhoi away from their connotations of abjection and volatility, Dove described Hendrik Witbooi as "actually [having] traits that Cooper's imagination ascribed to the leaders of the redskins," and like von Bülow he called the Witbooi "yellowskins." Dove focused particularly on Witbooi warrior qualities, praising their "experienced, Indian-like eyesight" and their unflappability in battle, which he illustrated with a scene of warriors riding calmly into enemy gunfire. Hendrik Witbooi was said to control his "knightly" soldiers with a "manly, iron discipline." Such courage and self-possession was the direct opposite of the skittish unreliability that was attributed to the Khoikhoi within the mimicry framework. The warriors' self-control was a metonym for the general stability that the colonial state hoped to promote.[118]

Some of the missionaries and settlers also moved toward a less negative view of the Witbooi during the Leutwein years. Missionary Heinrich Brincker compared them favorably to their "brothers in color, the American

116. Although von François was heading the colony during Dove's stay there, his books were written later and resonated more with Leutwein's new approach. Kienetz (1976, p. 841) describes Dove as "*the* leading contemporary authority on this German colony right up to the end of the German period." This is perhaps correct with respect to his *geographic* expertise, but Dove's ethnographic perceptions were strongly associated with the middle decade of German rule and were out of line with dominant views afterward. Even in 1913, for instance, Dove continued to describe the Khoikhoi as skilled warriors and as particularly intelligent, poetic, and musical, and he still referred to them with the romantically tinged label "yellowskins" and compared them to American "Indians" (Dove 1913b, pp. 10, 203, 208). By this time, of course, most of the Witbooi were dead.

117. BA-Berlin, R. 8023, vol. 820; Dove, "Koloniale Aufgaben in Südwestafrika," *Deutsche Kolonialzeitung*, n.s., 8 (33, 1895): 250–53; and Kienetz 1976, p. 839. After returning to Germany Dove became a *Privatdozent* at the Berlin Seminar for Oriental Languages and continued to publish on the German colonies.

118. Dove 1896a, pp. 54, 283, 314, 53, 159, 235.

redskins."[119] In an internal report for the Barmen mission, Johannes Olpp included a section titled "The Witbooi Prove Themselves as Allies." One German settler admitted that while many Germans had condemned Leutwein for failing to annihilate the Witbooi in 1894, Hendrik had proved to be a "loyal subject."[120] A German farmer in the Gibeon district praised Hendrik Witbooi for "standing loyally on our side, even against kindred Hottentot tribes."[121]

Although this construction of the Witbooi had originated in the colonial contact zone, it now began circulating back to Germany, where it was enshrined in the 1896 Colonial Exhibition in Berlin. Following the customary formula for such events, the Germans imported not just colonial artwork but living colonial subjects who were paid to staff "native villages," perform dances, and engage in other picturesque activities. The subjects sent to Berlin in 1896 included some Witbooi, including Hendrik's nephew.[122] The exhibition attracted two million visitors, including the emperor and empress. But while most of the imported colonial subjects were exhibited in exotic settings and attire, the "Hottentot" men were presented in European garments and were mounted on horseback, bearing firearms and wearing feathers in their caps (fig. 3.5). The text in the official catalog explained that the "Hottentots and Herero" at the exhibition were going to reenact a trek. Yet the white feathers in the Witbooi men's hats signified warfare. Hendrik Witbooi and his followers would wrap white cloths around their hats when they went to war against the Germans in 1904. That this militant symbol did not disturb the organizers of the Exhibition demonstrates not just their ignorance but also their conviction that Hendrik's warrior qualities had been successfully harnessed to the colonial project. The essay on Southwest Africa for the official catalog was written by none other than Karl Dove.[123]

119. Brincker 1899, p. 127.

120. Olpp, "Beitrag zur Missionsgeschichte des Witbooistammes," VEM, RMG 1.404; Seidel 1898, p. 17. Seidel was in the colony from 1888 to 1897.

121. In *Tägliche Rundschau* (Berlin), July 13, 1904, quoted in Burgsdorff-Garath 1982, p. 94.

122. Burgsdorff-Garath 1982, p. 100.

123. An incident on the margins of the exhibition underscores the multivocality of German ethnographic discourse, even in a period when the colonial state was endorsing one particular construction. Rhenish missionaries had been put in charge of recruiting Ovaherero and Khoikhoi for the exhibition. After several months in Berlin these representatives asked to return home, complaining that they were being called upon to perform "all manner of pagan activities" for the public. The fact that the same Namibian delegation was asked to perform both a (Europeanized) trek and "pagan activities" suggests that the up-to-date constructions of the Witbooi coexisted with a more generic colonial-racial ideology that encompassed all nonwhites. See Arbeitsausschuss der Deutschen Kolonial-Ausstellung 1896, pp. 31, 37, 40;

FIGURE 3.5 "Hottentots at the pontok": Namibians at the 1896 Berlin Colonial Exhibition, from the official catalog. From Arbeitsausschuss 1897, p. 157.

THE 1904–7 NAMA REBELLION AND THE ATTEMPTED EXTERMINATION OF THE WITBOOI

Leutwein's policy collapsed abruptly on October 4, 1904, when the Witbooi declared war on the Germans and killed forty officials and settlers. Various reasons have been advanced for the timing of this decision. The Witbooi had become quite impoverished. By 1902 Hendrik had sold nearly a third of the Witbooi territory to whites, eliminating access to most of the open water holes. Settler violence against Witbooi was increasing.[124] The Witbooi realized that Leutwein had been replaced by von Trotha, and news of the latter's genocidal program was communicated back to Gibeon from the Witbooi soldiers on the front lines. The Witbooi may have feared that von Trotha, who had no history of cooperation with any colonized group, would turn against the Khoikhoi after he had finished with the Ovaherero. The Witbooi also suspected that the settlers who wanted to disarm them and seize their land would receive more backing from the colony's new leadership. A strategic consideration was that German troops were still occupied with the Ovaherero in the north, and only four German soldiers were present

---

and letter from RMG missionary August Schreiber to Colonial Department, August 12, 1896, BA-Berlin, RKA, vol. 6349, p. 163.

124. Bochert 1980, pp. 167–68, 173.

in the Gibeon district in October.[125] Another factor is the presence of a certain prophet called Klaas Shappart, or Sheperd (aka Sturmann Skipper), from the Cape Colony, who may have been associated with the "Ethiopian church movement," and who emerged as a moral force behind the Nama uprising.[126] A final determinant was the onset of the guerilla war led by the legendary Nama leader Jacob Marengo in southern Namibia in July 1904.[127] These more immediate conditions condensed with longer-term grievances, pushing the well-armed Witbooi into rebellion.

Hendrik's declaration of war catalyzed resistance by most Khoikhoi groups in the colony, with the exception of the peoples of Bethany (the !Aman Orlam) and Berseba, and in Keetmanshoop, a town that served as the base for German military operations in Namaland and was therefore closely patrolled. Hendrik tried to unite with Marengo and scattered Ovaherero leaders who were still active after 1904. The Witbooi guerilla campaign lasted more than a year. In this same period the number of German troops in Namibia rose from seven thousand to fourteen thousand, while "the number of armed Nama certainly never exceeded two thousand."[128] Hendrik died of battle wounds on November 22, 1905, and his son and successor Samuel Isaak Witbooi capitulated soon afterward.[129] The movement of the other Nama ended with the surrender of the Bondelswarts on December 31, 1906, and the war ended officially on March 31, 1907, even though the Germans continued to fight various groups well into 1909.[130]

The colonizers' goal after October 1904 was to annihilate the entire Witbooi people, including women and children. On April 22, 1905, von Trotha issued a proclamation to the "rebellious Hottentots" in which he threatened that "those few who do not surrender will suffer the same fate as the Herero people, who in their blindness also believed that they could defeat the powerful German kaiser and the great German people. I ask you, where are the Herero people today, where are their chiefs? . . . Some died of hunger and thirst in the Sandveld, others were killed by the German troops." Although this was directed at all of the Nama, von Trotha specified that his first target was Hendrik Witbooi, for whom he offered an award of five thousand marks "dead or alive."[131]

125. Ibid., p. 179.

126. Sturmann had already been sighted among the Witbooi in June of 1904 (Bochert 1980, p. 178).

127. Dedering 1993a, pp. 70–72.

128. Hillebrecht 2003, pp. 126–30.

129. Telegram of December 11, 1905, BA-Berlin, RKA, vol. 2137, p. 109.

130. See Alexander 1981.

131. Kriegsgeschichtliche Abteilung I des Grossen Generalstabs 1906–7, vol. 2, p. 186.

The German response to Khoikhoi betrayal was extraordinarily harsh. Some repressive polices were directed at Nama and Ovaherero alike, and at all others legally defined as "natives." This included the "native ordinances" of 1907, which required all indigenes over seven years of age to carry an identification tag, or "pass" (*Paßmarke*), without which they could be arrested by any European. These dog tags were numbered, and the colonial government's totalitarian fantasy was that eventually every native in the colony would be tagged and registered, allowing "a more precise surveillance of their activities," as the acting governor wrote in 1905.[132] If Africans were caught without the required "service book" indicating their place of employment, they could be charged with "vagabondage." Natives also had to be registered with the government and to live in a location, or *werft*, with no more than ten native families or individual native laborers on a single plot. The *werft* was to be supervised and controlled by the employer, by the appointed "native commissioners," or by an indigenous headman assigned by the government.[133] The native commissioners, some of whom were missionaries, were supposed to organize and spy on the colonized and to encourage them to work and to "lose their warlike attributes," but they were also to be advocates for native interests who would defend the colonized against illegal abuses by employers and settlers.[134] With the exception of one or two communities, including the Rehoboth Basters, all natives were prohibited from owning land, breeding cattle, or keeping horses without the governor's permission.[135] Later ordinances in 1911 and 1913 stipulated that natives could not leave their *werfts* at night, and that they had to be registered with the local police office.[136]

132. Acting Governor Tecklenburg to RKA, July 17, 1905, BA-Berlin, RKA, vol. 1212, pp. 31v, 32v.

133. Prein 1994, p. 115.

134. Zimmerer 2001, p. 123; "Keine Reservate!" *Deutsch-Südwestafrikanische Zeitung* 7 (44, November 1, 1905): 1.

135. For the text of the laws, see *Deutsches Kolonialblatt* 18 (1907): 1179–84. The identification marker system had already been proposed in 1900 and introduced in the Swakopmund district in May 1904 (McGregor and Häberling 1991). The text of the detailed discussions of the regulations by the Gouvernementsrat is in BA-Berlin, RKA, vol. 2174, "Verhandlungen des Gouvernementsrats in Windhuk, 1906." Wege 1969, 1971; Prein 1994; and Zimmerer 2001 all emphasize the gap between the laws and their actual enforcement. My focus here, however, is on the administration's strategy and intentions.

136. The exact curfew times varied from place to place; see *Amtsblatt für das Schutzgebiet Deutsch-Südwestafrika* 2 (1911): 14, April 1, 1911, decree on "Aufenthalt der Eingeborenen auf ihren Werften" for Omaruru; and the parallel decree for Gibeon in ibid., p. 86 (May 11, 1911, decree). On registration, see ibid., 3 (1913): 402, decree of November 19, 1913, on "Meldepflicht" (requirement to register) for natives.

The government expropriated all of the land and property and most of the livestock from both the Nama and Ovaherero communities, granting exceptions only to the Bondelswarts and the Berseba Orlams.[137] Neither Khoikhoi nor Ovaherero were allowed to have captains or reservations, and they were broken up into smaller groups or imprisoned and allocated to sites of German labor demand. They were forbidden to own livestock (although some exceptions were granted and some Ovaherero succeeded in replenishing their herds in the following decade). The Germans also attempted to transplant the Khoikhoi to the colony's north, away from their traditional homes. In the early stages of this discussion the Ovaherero were to be moved to the south of the colony, completing the population transfer. This project was based on a view held by Governor Friedrich von Lindequist and other postwar officials that Africans could best be controlled and reeducated by severing their culturally saturated connections with a specific territory.[138]

The Witbooi were encompassed within these general regulations, but the colonial government also meted out particularly severe punishments to them, punishments that amounted to genocide in their deliberate attempt to exterminate the entire population. The government terminated its "Protection and Friendship" treaty with the Witbooi in October 1904. The eighty Witbooi soldiers who were fighting alongside the *Schutztruppe* against the Ovaherero were disarmed before they had even heard about Hendrik's decision to take up arms against the Germans. These men were deported to Togo, where they were forced to fill in swamps and build roads. As missionary Carl Osswald of the North German Mission Society (Norddeutsche Missionsgesellschaft) reported from Lomé in February 1905, "everyone recognizes that it was a mistake to bring these poor people to Togoland." But it was in fact quite deliberate, as demonstrated by the government's response to the missionaries' pleas.[139] According to Osswald the Witbooi prisoners were extremely weak, rapidly losing weight, and dying.[140] Government Councilor (*Regierungsrat*) Hans Tecklenburg, who had been promoted by

137. See Bley [1971] 1996, pp. 171–72; *Deutsches Kolonialblatt* 18 (1907): 981. A "resolution of the Reichstag on May 30, 1906, demanded the return of this land, but it was ignored by the government" (Hillebrecht 2003, p. 131).

138. This theory was somewhat paradoxical, of course, given the constant attacks on the Khoikhoi in earlier decades for their nomadism. The German government may also have moved to southern Namibia some Ovaherero who did not participate in the 1904 war (Silvester 2000, p. 483).

139. Copy of letter from missionary Osswald in Lomé, February 6, 1905, VEM, RMG 2.500a, p. 246r.

140. Ibid., p. 245v.

von Trotha to the highest civilian post in Southwest Africa and was named deputy governor in 1905, vehemently opposed returning the prisoners to the colony, and insisted that "the high mortality does not surprise anyone here, and must be seen as *retribution for the uprising.*"[141] Less than half of the Witbooi prisoners were still alive in September 1905, when they were moved to Cameroon. Conditions there were no healthier for people used to the arid climate of Southwest Africa, and many died from the heavy labor of pulling wagons filled with railway iron.[142] A handful of survivors returned to Southwest Africa in July 1906.[143]

The rest of the Witbooi people numbered around 1,600 in November 1905, when they capitulated and signed a peace treaty with the Germans. At first the Witbooi were allowed to return to Gibeon, but after two months they were shipped to a concentration camp in Windhoek.[144] This deportation entailed a breach in the terms of the peace treaty, which had promised them their freedom.[145] But this was not the most severe violation of that accord. The Witbooi were soon deported to the more notorious concentration camp on Shark Island, which was especially dreaded due to the extraordinary mortality rate there, estimated to exceed 10 percent monthly among Khoikhoi prisoners (fig. 3.6).[146] One historian has described Shark Island as the forerunner of the Nazi *Vernichtungslager,* or extermination camp.[147] A Rhenish missionary reported in 1907 that on an average day eight Khoikhoi perished at Shark Island, but that "on some days 18-20 die." Ninety percent of those deported died eventually, due to a policy of deliberate

141. Tecklenburg to Colonial Department, July 4, 1905, BA-Berlin, RKA, vol. 2090, p. 22 (my emphasis).

142. See comments of a former Witbooi prisoner named Lambert in Union of South Africa 1918, p. 99.

143. Zimmerer 2001, p. 52.

144. Missionary Spellmeyer's report from November 16, 1906, VEM, RMG 2.500a, p. 239r; telegram from Berlin to governor of the colony, December 28, 1905, BA-Berlin, RKA, vol. 2137, p. 150; telegram from von Lindequist to Colonial Office, February 4, 1906, BA-Berlin, RKA, vol. 2138, p. 30.

145. Telegram from von Lindequist to Foreign Office, December 5, 1905, in which the governor acknowledges that Samuel Isaak's capitulation was concluded according to the conditions stipulated by the army rather than the government, meaning that "he was guaranteed freedom" (BA-Berlin, RKA, vol. 2137, p. 93). See Estorff 1968, p. 123, on this German betrayal.

146. Report on mortality in concentration camps, for High Command of the *Schutztruppe,* March 23, 1908, BA-Berlin, RKA, vol. 2140, pp. 161–62; J. Zeller 2003, p. 74. The death rate on Shark Island fell in April 1907 as soon as the newly appointed commander of the *Schutztruppe,* Ludwig von Estorff, moved the camp to the mainland.

147. Erichsen 2003, 2004.

FIGURE 3.6 Shark Island concentration camp (ca. 1904–5). (Courtesy of NAN.)

neglect.[148] The vast majority of the prisoners were women and children.[149] A British military attaché who visited the Shark Island camp during the war wrote at the time that "it is not easy to avoid the impression that the extinction of [the Witbooi] would be welcomed by the authorities."[150] There is copious official correspondence in which the Witbooi are knowingly condemned to deadly conditions, even if the refusal to move the Shark Island prisoners to a healthier location on shore was defended mainly in terms of the danger of prisoners escaping, just as the government's refusal to allow the Witbooi to return from Cameroon was justified by security concerns. There is a systematic pattern of abuse that is suggestive of a desire to kill or cause "serious bodily or mental harm to members of the group"—criteria for genocide, according to the United Nations Convention on the Prevention and Punishment of the Crime of Genocide.

Even after hostilities with other Khoikhoi insurgents had ended, the Germans continued to treat the surviving Witbooi community with exceptional hostility. In July 1906, Governor von Lindequist proposed to the Colonial Department that "the entire tribe of the Witbooi" be deported to Sa-

148. Missionary Hermann Nyhof, letter of January 18, 1907, reproduced in Erichsen 2003, p. 84; Kössler 2003, p. 182.

149. According to a British diamond prospector who visited the concentration camp, the bodies of dead prisoners were fed to the sharks (Cornell [1920] 1986, p. 42).

150. Quoted by Silvester and Gewald 2003, p. xxvi.

moa. This led to a serious discussion in the Colonial Department, in which Dr. Albert Hahl, governor of German New Guinea, suggested that the Witbooi be deported to the Mariana Islands.[151] In the end this proved unworkable, and the authorities in Berlin decided to deport only the "big men" and troublemakers. On September 11, 1907, a special government proclamation seized all "tribal property" belonging to the Witbooi.[152] By 1910, there were only about ninety-six Witbooi left. This tiny group, which included the Protestant minister "little Hendrik Witbooi," son of the former *kaptein* and a longtime protégé of the Rhenish Missionary Society, was deported to Cameroon, following in the footsteps of the earlier contingent. The death rate from tropical illnesses and from "living together in the close quarters of the prison" was appallingly high. One visitor described these Witbooi as "walking corpses." By 1912 only thirty-eight of them were left.[153] The RMG and the German officers guarding these prisoners protested, but the Windhoek government insisted that the Witbooi were still "criminals endangering the state" whose well-being was less important than the "security of the German population in Southwest Africa."[154] After the Reichstag passed a resolution on March 8, 1913, the Colonial Office claimed to have "heard the voice of humanity" and allowed the handful of survivors to return to Southwest Africa in October.[155] Astonishingly, these Witbooi continued to be prisoners of war until the South African expeditionary force occupied the country in 1915.[156]

In sum, the Germans' treatment of the Witbooi starting in 1904 was as ferocious as their assault on the Ovaherero. Already in 1905 the discourse of

151. Telegram from von Lindequist to Ausw. Amt., July 10, 1906, BA-Berlin, RKA, vol. 2090, p. 62; Colonial Department meeting of August 23, 1906, ibid., pp. 78–79.

152. *Deutsches Kolonialblatt* 18 (1907): 981.

153. Kaiserliches Gouvernement von Kamerun (Imperial Government of Cameroon), Buea, October 22, 1911, BA-Berlin, RKA, vol. 2090, p. 144; Berner, July 5, 1912, describing a report by missionary Anna Wuhrmann (in the *Mitteilungen aus der Basler Frauenmission*, 12 [2, March 1912]: 24–25), on her visit to the fortified German station Dschang, where the Witbooi were being held, in BA-Berlin, RKA, vol. 2090, p. 147v; missionary Vielhauer in Cameroon, July 26, 1912, to RMG headquarters in Barmen, VEM, RMG 2.597, pp. 28–30; and remarks by Social Democrat Reichstag representative Gustav Noske, in Reichstag, *Stenographische Berichte*, vol. 288, 128th session, March 7, 1913, p. 4348.

154. Oberverwaltungsgerichtsrat Berner to missionary director Spiecker, November 13, 1912, VEM, RMG vol. 2.597, pp. 45–46.

155. Mumm, RKA, to missionary director Spiecker, November 20, 1913, VEM, RMG 2.597, p. 56; Conze, RKA, to Gouv. Windhuk, March 18, 1913, BA-Berlin, RKA, vol. 2090, pp. 178–79; Reichstag, 13. Legislative Period, I. Session, 1912/13, Resolution No. 139.

156. Hillebrecht 2003, p. 132; Kössler 2005, p. 182. On the recovery of the Witbooi people after their return to Gibeon in 1915 see Kössler 2005, pp. 184–254.

revenge against the Ovaherero started to give way to an interest in exploiting them as laborers, and after 1908 the restrictions on changing employers and holding cattle were unofficially loosened in response to Ovaherero pressure.[157] By contrast, even in 1913, when panic around labor shortages in the colony had grown acute, the governor once again raised the possibility of banning "the Hottentots" to some South Sea island, arguing that their indolent "love for living in the bush can never be stamped out."[158]

It is also revealing to briefly contrast the fate of the Witbooi with that of another group of Khoikhoi rebels, the Bondelswarts. The Bondelswart uprising in 1903 had initiated the entire period of warfare and had drawn the governor and his *Schutztruppe* into the southern part of the colony, creating the power vacuum in the north that allowed the Ovaherero initially to overpower the Germans. Although the Bondelswarts were subdued by Leutwein and Hendrik Witbooi's troops in 1904, they rose again the next year and fought the Germans until the end of December 1906. Nonetheless, the terms of the Ukamas peace treaty allowed the Bondelswarts to remain in their homeland as a coherent "tribe" with a "captain" and to continue raising livestock. Governor von Lindequist protested heatedly against these conditions, insisting that the "native's pride can only be broken by a more or less lengthy term in prison" and that "every Hottentot must . . . be banished from his home territory."[159] The "main goal of the military campaign," he insisted, had been the "destruction of the tribal organizations and the elimination of the chiefdomship," but this goal had been "abandoned" by the terms of the Ukamas treaty.[160] Yet von Lindequist was overruled in this instance by the chancellor himself.[161] The Bondelswarts were allocated a "native commissioner" who was responsible for *all* members of the "tribe" regardless of where they lived. The implication was that the Bondelswarts would continue to be recognized as a coherent ethnic entity. In August 1914, after the outbreak of World War I, the Bondelswarts were finally deported to the north in trains and forced to work on the construction of the Ambo railway.[162]

157. See Prein 1994; Gewald 1998a; and Krüger 1998, 1999, on the resurgence of the Ovaherero after the 1904 war.

158. Governor Seitz to RKA, August 12, 1913, BA-Berlin, RKA, vol. 2091, p. 11.

159. Governor von Lindequist, minute, February 1, 1907, BA-Berlin, RKA, vol. 2140, p. 32; Deimling 1930, p. 120.

160. BA-Berlin, RKA, vol. 2140, p. 31.

161. Chancellor von Bülow to Acting Director of Colonial Department of Foreign Office Dernburg, February 15, 1907, BA-Berlin, RKA, vol. 2140, p. 39.

162. Zimmerer 2001, pp. 123, 175 n. 240.

Why was the German response to the Witbooi so violent? One obvious motive was revenge. Hendrik's betrayal was considered especially egregious because of his people's special treatment between 1894 and 1904. For some colonial officials and army officers this campaign was also a form of revenge against Theodor Leutwein. General von Trotha helped set the new tone. The intense struggle between von Trotha and Leutwein that culminated in Leutwein's demission was gathering steam. The ire of the new regime was increased by its perception of the Witbooi as Leutwein's personal favorites. When Governor von Lindequist visited the imprisoned Witbooi at Shark Island in March 1906, he explained to them that they were "the guiltiest of all of the colony's natives who had raised their weapons against the German government, since the Germans had treated them so well" and that the "appropriate punishment," given this betrayal, "would have been death."[163]

The murderous direction of German policy against the Witbooi was accompanied by a resurgence of the older discourse of Khoikhoi mimicry. The continuing grip of the alternative discourse of savage nobility at the very beginning of the uprising is revealed by the fact that District Commissioner Henning von Burgsdorff believed that Hendrik could be talked out of his plan, and that he rode out from Gibeon alone to meet him on October 4.[164] Leutwein seemed genuinely shocked at Hendrik's betrayal, and initially defended his earlier views. In a report to the Colonial Department in November 1904, Leutwein wrote that Hendrik had "changed completely": "The loyal servant of the German government and personal friend of the governor has turned into a sinister fanatic."[165] This formulation placed equal emphasis on the genuineness of Hendrik's earlier loyalty and his subsequent lapse. Indeed, Leutwein was convinced at this time that an outside agitator from the Cape Colony, the "Ethiopian" prophet Sturmann, was responsible for Hendrik's "relapse." Three years later, however, Leutwein characterized Hendrik Witbooi as a split personality with "two souls in his breast": "The soul he showed during the ten-year period of peace under our domination was Christian and decent. The other was the cruel, fanatic Hottentot soul, which evidently had simply been dormant."[166] Just as others had adjusted their views of the Witbooi in Leutwein's direction a decade earlier, Leutwein's views now moved into line with the revived orthodoxy.

163. Kurd Schwabe 1907, p. 412.

164. Burgsdorff-Garath 1982, p. 107.

165. Leutwein to Ausw. Amt, Colonial Department, November 11, 1904, BA-Berlin, RKA, vol. 2134, p. 32.

166. T. Leutwein 1907a, p. 305.

The sea change in ethnographic perception was almost as striking as the turn in policy. The *Tageblatt für Nordchina* (North China Daily) published a doggerel poem called "Hendrik Witbooi, the Blackest of the Blacks," which ended with line "one can never trust blacks, here or in Africa," and equated the formerly "yellow" or "red" Orlams with their "tribally related" comrades, the Ovaherero.[167] Alfred von François perceived in the very abruptness of Witbooi's decision to break ties with the Germans a sign of the essential unsteadiness of "Nama character."[168] The suggestion of a kind of cultural schizophrenia was made explicit by Kurd Schwabe, who reversed his earlier views and concluded in 1905 that the "Hottentots'" character "borders on insanity."[169] In a widely read 1906 memoir of his participation in the Nama war, Hermann Alverdes wrote that the "Hottentot" was a jumbled and contradictory character, "led by his emotions" (ein Gefühlsmensch), but also a fatalist and a crafty liar, "wily and shifty like the jackal." Hendrik was "the jackal of the jackals."[170]

This shift was also felt in the more "scientific" literature. The best example of the return to a discourse of Khoikhoi mimicry is a monograph by Leonhard Schultze of Jena University entitled *Aus Namaland und Kalahari* (From Namaland and the Kalahari), which was written for the Prussian Academy of Sciences in 1907.[171] The visage of the "Hottentot," Schultze wrote, was a "strange mirror" (ein fremdartiger Spiegel)—and not, as in the discourse of noble savagery, an uncannily familiar one that provided the European with a glimpse of his own past. The Khoikhoi had not yet lost bad traits like the "old nomadic drive," which could only be broken by "generations of education." Indeed, they would prefer "the hardships of migration and the privations of spending many months in the wilderness" to being forced to work "day in and day out." Like his scientific forerunner Schinz, Schultze criticized the Khoikhoi for relinquishing their "traditional customs," which had contained many "good principles and maxims." The final

167. "Hendrik Witbooi, der Schwärzeste der Schwarzen," newspaper clipping, VEM, RMG 2.604e, p. 117, February 13, 1905. A similar view is presented in C. Falkenhorst, "Die Witboois," *General-Anzeiger* (Frankfurt am Main), no. 256 (October 30, 1904).

168. A. von François 1905, pp. 86–87.

169. Kurd Schwabe 1905, p. 222. Schwabe's later books returned to his original mode of describing the Khoikhoi (Kurd Schwabe 1907, pp. 316–17; 1910, p. 34), but they were written after the military destruction of the Witbooi.

170. Alverdes 1906, pp. 260, 276, 273, 275, 277, 250. See below on the figure of the jackal in Khoikhoi storytelling.

171. Like many other eighteenth- and nineteenth-century portraitists of exotic cultures, Schultze was a professor of zoology, not an anthropologist. He later conducted research on New Guinea, Macedonia, and Guatemala and translated the Mayan Popol Vuh.

result of combining the remnants of "Hottentot" tradition with scraps of civilization was that they had been "morally degenerating" (sittlich verwahrlosen) in ways that made them not only useless but even menacing: "We have to admit openly by now that *the Hottentot knows us better than we know him.* . . . He never loses interest in studying the white invader. Schooled for generations and from childhood on to be cunning, he allows the white a glimpse of his own human observations only in the rarest instances."[172] In a discussion of "Hottentot fables" Schultze criticized the Khoikhoi for identifying with the figure of the jackal. The jackal, characterized in Khoikhoi stories as triumphing through "guile and cheating," was representative of their social condition.[173] Schultze argued that Hendrik was the "idol" of the Nama and that he epitomized their worst aspects.[174] He concluded with a drastic formulation that recalled Bowker's 1846 "springbok" speech: the Nama insist desperately that "this land was once ours and we want to be its masters again." But here too "another race will disappear from the face of the earth."[175] At a time when the government was considering plans to educate the Bushmen for work as livestock herders, the Witbooi and other "warlike Hottentots" were being written off completely as "the least useful workers."[176] Captain Maximilian Bayer wrote in 1906 that "due to their absolute uselessness as productive workers we don't even need to exterminate them; nature will take care of that for us."[177] In fact, the Germans gave "nature" more than a helping hand.

"Rivers of Blood and Rivers of Money": Germans and Ovaherero

I, the great General of the German soldiers, send this letter to the Herero people. The Herero are no longer German subjects. . . . The Herero nation must . . . leave the country. If they do not leave, I will force them out with the *Groot Rohr* [big gun]. All Herero, armed or unarmed . . . will be shot dead within the Ger-

172. Quotes, in sequence, from Schultze 1907, pp. 174, 549, 332, 335 (my emphasis).

173. Schultze criticized the "primitive comparison" that Khoikhoi fables drew between their own racial "decline" and "animals' struggle for existence in the wild"—a strange complaint for a student of the social Darwinist Ernst Haeckel (Schultze 1910, p. 212). On Haeckel, see Mosse 1985, pp. 86–88.

174. Schultze 1910, p. 212.

175. Schultze 1907, p. 549.

176. In the words of settler Carl Schlettwein 1907, p. 176.

177. Bayer 1906a, p. 11. Bayer included the Ovaherero in this sweeping judgment. *Both* the Khoikhoi and the Ovaherero, he claimed, were "fundamentally different from us" and impossible to work with, "their pride and sense of independence are too strongly developed, their resistance to any cultural labor too great" (ibid., p. 6).

man borders. I will no longer accept women and children, but will force them back to their people or shoot at them.These are my words to the Herero people. (signed) *The great General of the powerful German emperor*

Proclamation by GENERAL LOTHAR VON TROTHA to the Herero people, October 2, 1904[178]

I know enough tribes in Africa. They are all alike insofar as they only yield to violence. My policy was, and is, to exercise this violence with blatant terrorism [*mit krassem Terrorismus*] and even cruelty. I finish off the rebellious tribes with *rivers of blood and rivers of money*. Only from these seeds will something new and permanent be able to grow.

GENERAL LOTHAR VON TROTHA to Governor Theodor Leutwein, November 5, 1904[179]

The Ovaherero were immortalized as the ambiguous, shifting figures in Thomas Pynchon's *Gravity's Rainbow*. In recent years anthropologists and the Ovaherero themselves have debated the meaning of their troop ceremonies, which involve a sort of military play-acting in which Ovaherero wear European, partly German costumes to commemorate their dead leaders. In 2001, the Ovaherero sued the Deutsche Bank and two other German companies for reparations for the extermination campaign and the massive use of forced labor from the concentration camps between 1904 and 1907 leaders. In 2002 a conflict erupted around the demand made by a member of the Namibian Parliament from the SWAPO party that the military uniforms worn by Ovaherero during their annual commemoration ceremony be banned.[180] And in the summer of 2004 the German government apologized for the 1904 massacre and the use of forced labor, and followed this with an aid package targeting the Nama, Ovaherero, and Damara people, descendants of the victims from the 1904–7 war.

Despite the relative abundance of literature on the Ovaherero, however, no one has explained exactly how and why German policy evolved into genocide between August and October 1904. Historian Helmut Bley depicts the 1904 massacre and the policies of the postwar period as a sharp break with the pre-1904 era. More recent studies of the Ovaherero have tended to accept Bley's judgment, if only by focusing on the war and the postwar

178. BA-Berlin, RKA, vol. 2089, p. 7r.

179. In BA-Berlin, RKA, vol. 2089, p. 100v.

180. See "Request for German Military Uniforms to be Banned," at http://www.grnnet .gov.na/News/Archive/2002/February/Week3/military.htm.

period.[181] German policies before 1904 were less homogeneous than afterward, but a similar logic underpinned both.

ETHNOGRAPHIC DISCOURSE AND GERMAN-OVAHERERO RELATIONS, 1884–94

The goal of transferring land and cattle to the Germans dominated discussions of the Ovaherero during the first two decades of German rule in Southwest Africa. There had been some copper mining in Namibia since the 1850s,[182] and the anticipated discovery of diamonds was one of the lures for German investors in the new colony. During the first years of German suzerainty some colonizers actively opposed plans to base the colonial economy on stock farming.[183] But copper mining had already been abandoned as unprofitable in the 1860s and was not taken up on a significant scale in Southwest Africa until 1906, when the railway to Tsumeb was completed.[184] Diamonds were not discovered until 1908. The result was that already in 1886, Imperial Commissary Heinrich Goering's plans for the colonial economy emphasized agricultural exports, especially livestock.

The unavoidable implication of these plans, even if it was not always acknowledged, was that land and cattle would pass from Ovaherero into German hands. There was a mounting chorus in Germany, already audible in 1883–85 and growing gradually louder over the next few years, which insisted that Southwest Africa should become a settlement colony. As one historian writes, "It had become widely recognized by the early 1890s that a German colonization of SWA would have to start with agricultural settlement rather than with mining."[185] Concerned to legitimate their presence and to justify the costs of holding on to the colony, officials began to embrace the agrarian-settler framework. These plans mainly implicated the Ovaherero, who occupied the prime grazing land in the middle of the colony and owned the largest livestock herds. Most Germans agreed the colony's south was "unsuited for all smallholder German settlements and more generally

---

181. This is true of the excellent studies by Gesine Krüger and Jürgen Zimmerer. The major exception is Gewald 1998a.

182. See especially Charles Andersson's correspondence (1987–89) concerning his years as manager of the Matchless copper mine (1855–59). Esterhuyse 1968, pp. 10–11, lists some of the copper-mining companies operating in Southwest Africa during the 1850s and 1860s.

183. E.g., Büttner 1885c, pp. 56–57.

184. Silvester, Wallace, and Hayes 1998, p. 28.

185. Kienetz 1976, p. 610; see also W. Smith 1978.

for any real colonization."[186] Ovamboland, in the far north, was fertile but malarial and was still completely beyond the reach of German power.[187]

The result was a concentration of colonial interest on Hereroland, that is, the territory claimed by Kamaherero in 1884 in a formal declaration.[188] The German colonial government initially established its headquarters not in Namaqualand but at Otjimbingwe, the "capital" of Hereroland. In 1890, while still under instructions to avoid hostilities with the locals, Curt von François called attention to the existence of a supposedly depopulated buffer zone between the territories of the Khoikhoi and Ovaherero.[189] The general secretary of the German Colonial Society advocated a wedgelike "neutral zone" of colonists between Nama and Herero."[190] Most of these early plans envisioned German communities engaging in farming. By 1892, however, the tide of colonial opinion had shifted to models of extensive stock breeding. This change was due in part to the writings of Count Joachim Pfeil, who tried unsuccessfully to recruit a pioneering group of settlers from the Cape Colony in 1892. Karl Dove, the other influential student of this topic in the mid-1890s, also supported large-scale stock farming. This bias toward extensive cattle ranching meant that the existing "buffer zone" was too small for more than a handful of settlers. Furthermore, once the Witbooi had been subdued in 1894, Ovaherero and Khoikhoi both began grazing their cattle in the areas that the Germans had previously declared "empty." This underscored the need for an increase in privately owned German property or "Crown" land. The most significant stumbling block was the unwillingness of most Ovaherero to sell their cattle. As the German chief of the Swakopmund district, Dr. Fuchs, wrote, "For the Herero, everything, really everything, revolves around livestock. . . . He lives and dies for his cattle."[191]

---

186. Ludloff 1891, p. 121.

187. Hugo Hahn wrote in 1887 that "the real fever region begins in Ovamboland." See C. H. Hahn, "Unsere südafrikanischen Kolonien und Schutzgebiete," *Das Ausland* 60 (43, 1887): 844.

188. For the narrowing of economic focus see Eduard Pechuel-Loesche, "Zur Bewirtschaftung Südwest-Afrikas," *Deutsche Kolonialzeitung*, n.s., 1 (32–34, 1888): 252–55, 260–63, 270–71. Maherero's 1884 proclamation is reprinted in Krüger 2003, p. 24.

189. C. von François 1899, pp. 64, 131–32.

190. Heinrich Bokemeyer, "Über Ansiedlungsverhältnisse in Südwestafrika vom Gesichtspunkte der organisierten Kolonisation (Schluß)," *Deutsche Kolonialzeitung*, n.s., 3 (27, December 27, 1890): 309.

191. Report of Dr. Fuchs in "Der Herero-Aufstand in Deutsch-Südwestafrika," *Deutsches Kolonialblatt* 15 (1904): 221. See also "Bericht des Dr. Hindorf," in "Denkschrift, betreffend das südwestafrikanische Schutzgebiet" 1895, p. 446.

How was precolonial ethnographic discourse related to the development of policy toward the Ovaherero? One common feature of policy before and after 1904 is an almost complete lack of interest in preserving any aspect of Ovaherero culture. This corresponded to the inherited, homogeneous, and overwhelmingly hostile European view of Ovaherero. Missionary and non-missionary discourse pointed toward policies of assimilation, even if the missionaries were seeking to acculturate the Ovaherero into a somewhat more equal status. The depiction of traditional Ovaherero was so unappealing that Europeans saw no reason to oppose the assault on the material foundations of their culture.[192]

In the initial years of the German protectorate there was little indication of open hostility to the Ovaherero. In his 1886 report to the *Deutsche Kolonialzeitung*, Heinrich Goering contrasted the "thrifty and diligent" Ovaherero with the "lazy" Khoikhoi and did not even mention German agricultural settlement, although he did discuss the possibility of bringing in Boer settlers.[193] The 1885 protection treaty[194] was voided in 1888, when the Ovaherero forced Goering to leave their territory. For the next two years there was not even the pretense of a colonial relationship between the two sides. In 1890 the Ovaherero signed a new protection treaty, and the Germans turned their attention to the problem of subduing Hendrik Witbooi.

This does not mean that German representations of the Ovaherero during this first decade of colonialism were benign. The most important ethnographic voices before 1894 were again the von François brothers. Hugo von François emphasized Ovaherero *cruelty*, including their mutilation of the corpses of enemies in wartime. Lieutenant von François even hinted at cannibalism—something none of the precolonial literature had ever suggested—informing his readers that the Ovaherero had mutilated one of Hendrik Witbooi's sons' corpses, "cutting out the inner side of his thighs, together with the testicles, probably to make a challenging meal [*Kraftspeise*] of it." Continuing in this vein, von François compared the long fingers of the Ovaherero to "reptilian tentacles." The Ovaherero, he said, were "black devils." Sometimes their faces were "coarse and hulking," other times "crafty and cunning" like "furiously bartering Jews." The lieutenant summarized

192. Scheulen (1998, p. 76) asserts misleadingly that the early image of the Ovaherero during the German colonial period was "positive." What is true is that the colonial goverment was initially more favorable to the Ovaherero that to the Witbooi.

193. Kienetz 1976, pp. 431–41.

194. See BA-Berlin, RKA, vol. 2025, for the protection treaty signed with the Ovaherero at Omaruru; and Wallenkampf 1969, p. 390, for an English translation of the treaty.

Ovaherero character as "greed, brutality, arrogance toward the weak, and as a pendant to these traits, obsequiousness, cowardice, and docility when confronted with a firm will." This horrid portrait was coupled somewhat paradoxically with the insistence that the Ovaherero were destined to become the colony's future working class. Since the Ovaherero seemed unwilling to hire themselves out, the implication was that their culture would have to change.[195]

Curt von François's book illustrates the way inherited ethnographic representations could be reproduced despite massive counterevidence and despite a proclaimed intention to avoid stereotyping. The former *Landeshauptmann* began his narrative with the swirling "rumors about the natives" to which he was exposed immediately after setting foot in Walvis Bay: "My head was reeling from this nasty colonial gossip, which was not at all confirmed by my later experiences." Just two sentences later, however, the author quoted a memorandum by missionary Brincker according to which Ovaherero could only be subdued by the application of brute force. His narrative then proceeded to reintroduce almost all of the preexisting stereotypes. Striking the pose of the "old African," von François wrote that "I had encountered many Negro tribes, but never one that looked down their noses at whites with such unconcealed disdain" as the Ovaherero. He concluded that the natives' "right to the land . . . could only be contested . . . with the barrel of a gun."[196]

Lieutenants von Bülow and Schwabe, two of the key ethnographic portraitists of the Ovaherero during the 1890s, agreed with the von François brothers. According to von Bülow, the Ovaherero were "indolent" and "taciturn," resembling the "proud children of rich parents." Given these characteristics, they were bound to respond to "European invasion" with "guerilla warfare, betrayal, cowardly murder, and bestial crimes against our women and children."[197] A Rhenish missionary at Otjimbingwe reported that it was "high time that the Damara [Ovaherero] receive a blow to the neck [*eine Faust aufs Genick*] . . . The younger generation is so insolent and supercilious that we cannot bear it much longer. I believe that the Damara will become really nice fellows once they are finally given a proper beating [*mal ordentlich unter die Knute kommen*]."[198] Kurd Schwabe, who had such positive things

195. H. von François 1895, pp. 96, 161, 108, 159, 190, 159, 180.

196. C. von François 1899, pp. 45, 47, 49.

197. F. von Bülow 1896, pp. 63, 221, 223. Von Bülow and the von François brothers belong to the pre-Leutwein era politically and in terms of their ethnographic descriptions, even if their most important books were written between 1895 and 1899.

198. This report was sent to missionary Brincker in Stellenbosch, who forwarded it to the German consulate in Cape Town, which in turn sent a copy to the Colonial Department in

to say about the Witbooi in his 1899 book, summarized the Ovaherero as "mistrustful, conceited, proud, and at the same time beggarly and cringing, deceitful and disloyal, thieving and—when they are in the majority— violent and cruel." In a claim to ethnographic authority Schwabe claimed that his portrait was the fruit of living among the Ovaherero "for many years."[199]

The period 1884-94 was thus one in which precolonial views of the Ovaherero were reproduced and the project of stripping them of their resources and turning them into an abject proletariat was openly discussed.

"A PEACEFUL BLEEDING": PASSIVE NATIVE POLICY AND THE OVAHERERO DURING THE LEUTWEIN ERA

If the Germans had seemed to take sides with the Ovaherero in the early 1890s, this was simply because the Witbooi posed the more urgent security problem. Almost immediately after the Witbooi defeat the colonial government's designs for the Ovaherero became more aggressive. The Germans began to work systematically to shift cattle and land from Ovaherero to the state, private investors, and settlers. Governor Leutwein stated that "the entire future of the colony lies in the gradual transfer of land from the hands of the work-shy natives to the Europeans." Leutwein simply wanted this to happen "in the most peaceful way" possible.[200] The centerpiece of this effort was the "Treaty on Borders" from July 1, 1895, which allowed the government to confiscate 5 percent of any herd of Ovaherero cattle that was found grazing on Crown land or on privately owned (that is, European) property. This law was applied energetically.[201] Leutwein acknowledged that the goal was "to hem in the Ovaherero from both sides," and the colonial judge and future governor Friedrich von Lindequist explained that the policy was aimed at an "ongoing peaceful bleeding [of the Ovaherero] by German traders, the same thing that Hendrik Witbooi had accomplished through

---

Berlin. Gewald (1998a, p. 37) mistakenly attributes these comments to Brincker himself. See the copy of the unsigned letter, dated September 17, 1889, and addressed to Brincker, in BA-Berlin, RKA, vol. 2107, pp. 40-44 (quote from p. 44r-v). Brincker had retired to Stellenbosch in 1884; see VEM, RMG 1.594a.

199. Kurd Schwabe 1899, p. 156. Schwabe was so sure of his judgment that in his 1910 book he summarized Ovaherero by simply quoting this passage verbatim from his 1899 book (Kurd Schwabe 1910, p. 112).

200. Leutwein to chancellor, December 13 1894, BA-Berlin, RKA, vol. 2100, p. 101v.

201. For the initial 1894 treaty on the southern border of Hereroland see BA-Berlin, RKA, vol. 2100, p. 103; also Bley [1971] 1996, pp. 58-59; and Pool 1991, chaps. 9-10.

violent means up until three years ago."[202] Leutwein announced that any Ovaherero who resisted the seizure of their errant livestock would be shot. In official correspondence Leutwein speculated that a war against the Ovaherero "could be worthwhile, given the number of oxen they have."[203] A year later, the German government confiscated as many as twelve thousand cattle from the rebellious Eastern Ovaherero (Ovambanderu).[204]

The results of this "economic" policy clashed with the government's goal of *stabilizing* the colonized. Hereroland was inhabited by "what was observed to be a relatively large (80,000–100,000) and virile population" of stockmen, passionately committed to their calling, "who could not easily be dislodged."[205] Since Ovaherero traditions were thoroughly entwined with the cattle that the Germans sought to attain, any program of stabilization based on codified tradition was ruled out from the start.

The colonial government did make tentative moves after the turn of the century toward a compromise solution in which the Ovaherero would be granted protected land on reservations. The earliest official discussion of the idea of native reserves in 1893–94 had already argued that the Ovaherero would "decline as a people" and "no longer stand in our way" once they were confined to reserves.[206] Theodor Leutwein announced that "we will have a freer hand once the natives are contained within reservations, creating a spatial separation between the white and black races."[207]

The reservations as they were envisioned were small and located in unattractive parts of the colony. Some historians have therefore concluded that the reservations were little more than a smoke screen for ongoing expropriation. This overlooks the government's structurally induced compulsion to stabilize its aboriginal subjects. The Ovaherero had become impoverished after the 1897 rinderpest epidemic, which had decimated their herds. As a result Samuel Maherero had accelerated land sales to Europeans.[208] If the

202. Von Lindequist in *Deutsches Kolonialblatt* 6 (1895): 165.

203. Leutwein's report on conditions in Hereroland and on strengthening the *Schutztruppe*, October 31, 1895, BA-Berlin, RKA, vol. 2100, p. 165r.

204. Pool 1991, p. 153.

205. Kienetz 1976, p. 383.

206. See "Bericht des Dr. Hindorf," in "Denkschrift, betreffend das südwestafrikanische Schutzgebiet" 1895: 447. Heinrich Bokemeyer's settlement plan of 1892 had already included land for reservations, as had plans by the von François brothers during the 1890s (Kienetz 1976, pp. 747, 814–16; C. von François 1899, map after p. 132).

207. *Denkschrift über Eingeborenen-Politik und Herero-Aufstand in Deutsch-Südwestafrika* 1904, p. 80.

208. Some Ovaherero leaders supported the reservation policy, while Samuel Maherero wanted to keep the reservations as small as possible so he could continue to sell land. See Förster 1905, p. 525; *Denkschrift über Eingeborenen-Politik und Herero-Aufstand in Deutsch-*

government had been interested *only* in expropriation it would not have sought to limit Samuel's ability to sell all of his land. Colonial rule was oriented toward multiple aims, whose requirements were not necessarily identical and were sometimes even contradictory. The policy of reservations for the Ovaherero was a compromise between two distinct goals.

In November 1901, following extensive lobbying by the Rhenish Missionary Society and with the support of civil servants in the colony, Leutwein was given a green light by the authorities in Berlin to select areas for reserves of unalienable Ovaherero land.[209] The Ovaherero would be prohibited from selling land inside reservation boundaries, but they would not be required to live on the reservations and could continue to dispose of tribal land outside the reservations as they saw fit. In 1902 Leutwein announced the imminent creation of the first Ovaherero reservation at Otjimbingwe, and in May 1903 he issued a circular that sought a balance between the imperatives of stabilization and expropriation. District officials were instructed to generate plans for additional reservations whose borders would be drawn so as not "to lay claim to overly extensive tracts of land."[210] But the war with the Ovaherero broke out just a month after the Otjimbingwe reservation was created.

With the exception of these limited moves toward the creation of Ovaherero reservations, the colonial government showed less interest in preserving Ovaherero society than in disrupting its customary arrangements. The German government's "liberation" of the Berg Damara from their Ovaherero overlords in 1894 exemplified this.[211] Rhenish missionaries had long decried the "serfdom" of the Berg Damara, and the government was interested in making them available as a labor force.[212] The Germans also interfered with internal Ovaherero leadership structures. During the struggle over Ovaherero succession to the title of chief of Okahandja after Kamaherero's death in 1890 the government and the missionaries

---

Südwestafrika 1904, p. 81; and Leutwein to Colonial Department, June 2, 1904, BA-Berlin, RKA, vol. 2115, p. 108.

209. Pool 1991, p. 179; a map of the projected Otjimbingwe reservation is in Leutwein's report of December 8, 1903, in BA-Berlin, RKA, vol. 1219, p. 15.

210. Leutwein's report to Colonial Department, September 28, 1904, BA-Berlin, RKA, vol. 2116, p. 129v; *Denkschrift über Eingeborenen-Politik und Herero-Aufstand in Deutsch-Südwestafrika* 1904, pp. 78–79.

211. On the cession of the Ovaherero location Okombahe to the Berg Damara as a quasi reservation, see Leutwein's report of December 11, 1894, in BA-Berlin, RKA, vol. 2169, p. 4.

212. *Denkschrift über Eingeborenen-Politik und Herero-Aufstand in Deutsch-Südwestafrika* 1904, p. 1; and Bley [1971] 1996, p. 23–25. Palgrave's 1877 report had already called for removing the Berg Damara from Ovaherero control and transferring them to "locations" where they could serve as a labor force (Palgrave [1877] 1969, pp. 52, 89).

supported Samuel Maherero, weakening the hand of more legitimate claimants to the title. Samuel was proclaimed "paramount chief" of all Ovaherero, a position that had not existed before.[213] According to Ovaherero custom Samuel's claims to the chieftaincy were more tenuous than those of his rivals. Because he was a Christian, he was not permitted to carry out the cultic aspects of the chieftaincy, such as tending the *okuruuo*. After he was forced out of Okahandja by his opponents in 1894, the Germans reinstalled Samuel as chief and began paying him a salary.[214] Leutwein argued that the Germans should support Samuel precisely because of the opposition from the other Ovaherero contenders to the throne, concluding that a "politically divided Herero nation is easier to deal with than a united and coherent one."[215]

The post-1904 effort to promote a subaltern form of assimilation among the Ovaherero began to emerge in rough outlines during this period. Where the Witbooi were constructed as noble savages, Leutwein insisted in 1895 that the Ovaherero would need to move "closer to our own notions."[216] He warned that "a peaceful coexistence with the Hereros was impossible in the long run unless they *completely change their customs and views*." They would have to "accustom themselves to a way of life appropriate to a well-to-do people"—that is, a "wage-earning people." The alternative, should the Ovaherero refuse to "adopt this more rational way of life," would be a "war of annihilation" (Vernichtungskampf).[217] It is noteworthy that Leutwein at this time was already using the term *Vernichtung*, which has historically been associated with von Trotha's 1904 "extermination order." In both cases this language could not possibly have had the traditional German mil-

---

213. On the traditional Ovaherero organization of chiefly succession see Lehmann 1951. Some have argued that the Germans and Samuel Maherero both tried to use one another against their opponents in this series of events (Gewald 1998a, chap. 2; 2000, pp. 190–91; Pool 1991, pp. 77–84). Samuel seemed like the better candidate to the Germans because he was contributing to the breakup of tradition and the insertion of Ovaherero into commodity capitalism. Samuel supported a group of young Ovaherero "soldiers" who rebelled against the traditional elite (Henrichsen 1997, pp. 431-32), and his land sales contributed to ongoing proletarianization.

214. Pool 1991, p. 84, 115; Gewald 2000, pp. 192–93.

215. Leutwein to Caprivi, June 17, 1894, BA-Berlin, RKA, vol. 1486, pp. 85–86, quoted in Drechsler [1966] 1980, p. 84. Even the 1895 treaty on the frontiers of Hereroland had been designed to divide the Ovaherero, insofar as Samuel Maherero was to personally receive half the proceeds from the cattle that wandered across the border and were seized and sold (Pool 1991, p. 131).

216. Leutwein to missionary Viehe, October 22, 1895, BA-Berlin, RKA, vol. 2100, p. 167v.

217. Ibid., pp. 166r, 166v, 167r (my emphasis).

itary meaning of inflicting a crushing defeat in battle. Leutwein's behavior during the 1896 rebellion of the Khauas Orlams and Ovambanderu is also revealing. Just two years after defeating and pardoning Hendrik Witbooi he insisted on his right *not* to extend "the Geneva Convention to colonial wars," writing to the German chancellor, "As yet, I have only been accused of excessively humane treatment of the natives, which gives me even more right to oppose such views. Peaceful natives must be treated humanely at all events. But to adopt the same approach toward rebellious natives is to neglect humanity toward our own countrymen. . . . Given that, a consistent colonial policy would undoubtedly require that all prisoners capable of bearing arms be executed, although I myself would not like to take this step."[218] The difference between Leutwein's views in the 1890s and von Trotha's approach in 1904 was that the former excluded women, children, and non-arms-bearing subjects from his sanguinary calculations. An immediate beneficiary of Leutwein's execution of the rebellious Ovambanderu chiefs Kahimemua Nguvauva and Nikodemus Kavikunua in 1896 was Samuel Maherero. The Germans forced chieftains "to submit to him in the face of German firepower."[219] On the other hand the events of 1896 foreshadowed the German assault on Maherero himself in the not-so-distant future.

Unofficial representations of the Ovaherero during the Leutwein era continued in the same vein as in previous decades, except that the discourse of Witbooi savage nobility tended to shed an even more negative comparative light on the Ovaherero. According to the great champion of the Witbooi, Karl Dove, the Ovaherero would "someday be a dangerous enemy, once they realize without a doubt that their independence is at stake, along with the unchallenged ownership of their land. . . . The Herero are not likely to declare war openly on the German troops; instead, one morning the farmers will be found murdered on their farms, along with their wives and children. The Kaffir's hatred of the enemy turns him into a wild beast."[220]

218. Leutwein to Chancellor Hohenlohe-Schillingfurst, July 4, 1896, BA-Berlin, RKA, vol. 1489, pp. 35v–36r. The first Geneva Convention, "For the Amelioration of the Wounded in Time of War," passed in 1864, was designed to save lives during warfare and to provide for the removal and care of the wounded. Leutwein was thus alluding to a "take no prisoners" approach. International conventions on warfare in this period were always "implicitly limited to the so-called 'civilized' peoples" (C. Marx 1999, p. 255). The British demonstrated time and again that they did not feel it necessary to apply regular international conventions to colonial wars in their treatment of German border infractions in Southwest Africa (e.g., Drechsler [1966] 1980, p. 109).

219. Gewald 2000, p. 195; Drechsler [1966] 1980, p. 93; Pool 1991, pp. 150–53.

220. Dove 1896a, p. 43.

Echoing Leutwein, Dove insisted that "leniency vis-à-vis the colored is the equivalent of cruelty toward the whites."[221]

The difference in the treatment of Ovambanderu and Witbooi rebels during the 1890s reveals the interweaving of inherited ethnographic perceptions, social dynamics among the colonizers, and psychic processes of identification. European representations of the Ovaherero were so negative that the only policy options available were annihilation or abject semi-assimilation. For Europeans, there was simply nothing worth preserving. The narrowness of ethnographic options also limited the space for symbolic competition over ethnographic capital. And as seen through European eyes the Ovaherero offered no attractive images for positive cross-identification (although a sadistic imaginary identification with a demonic imago appealed to von Trotha).

FROM RACIST ETHNOGRAPHY TO A COLONIAL THEATER OF CRUELTY: THE GERMAN-OVAHERERO WAR AS AN INTERRUPTION OF NATIVE POLICY

"Who owns Hereroland? We own Hereroland!"
Chant of Ovaherero women during the 1904 war[222]

Then came the news that the enemy, after overcoming and passing the great stretch of waterless country, where thousands of them had perished, were situated far to the east on the further side of the sand field by some miserable water-holes. The general decided to follow them thither, to attack them and force them to go northward into thirst and death, so that the colony would be left in peace and quiet for all time.

GUSTAV FRENSSEN, *Peter Moor's Journey to Southwest Africa*[223]

The Hereros' cattle . . . lay in the bush with the mass of their people, dead of thirst, strewn along the path of their death march. . . . Carrion vultures and jackals gorged themselves for days but could not finish these provisions. . . . When we unsaddled in the bush, our feet bumped up against corpses. A young woman with a shriveled breast, her paralyzed face covered with flies, a shrunken miscarriage pressed to her hip. An old woman who could no longer run: eight

---

221. Dove makes this statement immediately after discussing the Ovaherero in both his more "scientific" study (1896b, p. 75) and in the more popular narrative (1896a, p. 45). For similar views from this period see Kurd Schwabe 1899, pp. 148–54, 361; and Seidel 1898, p. 9.

222. Rohrbach 1907, p. 332.

223. Frenssen [1905] 1908, pp. 198–99.

or ten leg-rings of heavy iron-pearls, the symbol of her status and wealth, had bitten into her flesh all the way to the bone. . . . There a boy, still alive, staring into space . . . an idiot grin on his face.

ADOLF FISCHER, *Menschen und Tiere in Deutsch-Südwest*[224]

The death rattle of the dying and the furious screams of madness. . . . faded away in the sublime silence of infinitude.

CONCLUSION OF OFFICIAL REPORT OF THE GERMAN GENERAL STAFF ON THE OVAHERERO-GERMAN WAR[225]

Historians have debated whether there was a premeditated Ovaherero revolt in 1904 or whether their uprising was a response to an unprovoked German assault. At this time the majority of German settlers and members of the *Schutztruppe* were opposed to the government's plan to create reservations, since this would limit their ability to acquire land in the future. The Germans projected their own aggressiveness onto the Ovaherero, and rumors of an imminent uprising began to circulate at the end of 1903. According to a reconstruction of the events of January 1904 by historian Jan Bart Gewald, the war started when German troops opened fire on Ovaherero at Okahandja on January 12, 1904. Settlers and soldiers also launched an attack in Otjimbingwe, ignoring Ovaherero protestations of loyalty. In the aftermath of the war, missionaries and military figures contributed to the myth of a long-planned revolt, according to Gewald.[226] Other historians have drawn their conclusions from Samuel Maherero's order to rebel, which fell into the missionaries' hands on February 19 and was dated January 11.[227] Whether or not this order was actually given on January 11, it is clear that the Ovaherero did not pursue a fully coordinated attack but entered the fray at differing times in each location. The Ovaherero had numerous grievances in addition to the expropriation of land and cattle: the accumulation of debt with German traders, the anger of the Ovaherero "conservative party" about the way in which the borders of the Otijimbingwe reservation were being drawn, and the domineering stance of the settlers.[228] During the first

224. A. Fischer 1914, pp. 94-95.

225. Kriegsgeschichtliche Abteilung I des Grossen Generalstabs 1906-7, vol. I, p. 214.

226. See Gewald 1998a, pp. 154-91.

227. See Pool 1991, p. 202. Indeed, Gewald is the first historian to question the validity of the dating of this letter, but his research suggests that the dating is a forgery.

228. The phrase "altkonservative Partei" was used by Leutwein to refer to Ovaherero elites such as Assa Riarua who opposed Samuel Maherero's course before 1904. Leutwein referred to this group as a cause of the uprising, in his report "The Historical Development of the

days of the uprising, 126 Europeans were killed.[229] With a few exceptions, German women, children, and missionaries were spared, as were non-German Europeans, following Samuel Maherero's orders.[230]

I am not interested in reconstructing the outbreak of the war or the numerous battles, but rather in the evolution of the German stance toward the Ovaherero.[231] The war effort was initially conducted by Leutwein, whose position as governor made him commander of the *Schutztruppe*. But he became entangled in disagreements with the Colonial Department because of his "moderate" stance. Leutwein wrote in February: "I cannot agree with those imprudent voices which would now like to see the Herero completely destroyed (*vernichtet*). Aside from the fact that a people with sixty to seventy thousand souls is not so easy to annihilate, I would consider such a measure a grave mistake from an economic point of view. We still need the Hereros as breeders of small livestock and especially as workers. We only have to kill them politically. If possible, they should no longer be allowed to have a tribal government and should be confined to reservations that are just big enough to meet their needs."[232] Suspicions that Leutwein was "too soft" were fueled by settlers, who claimed that the Ovaherero had become Leutwein's "favorite tribe."[233] Ultimate responsibility for the conduct of the war had already been transferred from the colonial governor to the General Staff of the German army in Berlin.[234] The decision to dismiss Leutwein altogether was made after he withdrew from a battle with the massed Ovaherero warriors at Oviumbo on April 13 to await reinforcements from Germany. In May the emperor appointed General Lothar von Trotha as supreme commander of

Protectorate and Its Connection to the Herero Uprising" (September, 1904), BA-Berlin, RKA, vol. 2116, p. 147v. Leutwein referred to Samuel Maherero's letter of January 11, 1904, which explained that "he and his people could no longer stand the whites' bearing [*das Auftreten*]."

229. Kurd Schwabe 1910 p. 249.

230. On this question see Leutwein to Colonial Department, May 17, 1904, BA-Berlin, RKA, vol. 2115, p. 64v; also "Verzeichnis der während des Herero-Aufstandes ermordeteten und im Gefecht gefallenen Personen," BA-Berlin, RKA, vol. 2114, pp. 227-31.

231. There are several histories of the German and Ovaherero war; see Drechsler [1966] 1980, chap. 4; and 1984; Bridgman 1981; Nuhn 1989; Krüger 1999; and Dedering 1993b; also Kriegsgeschichtliche Abteilung I des Grossen Generalstabs 1906-7; and Kurd Schwabe 1907.

232. Leutwein to Colonial Department, February 23, 1904, BA-Berlin, RKA, vol. 2113, p. 89v.

233. According to a settler's article published in *Deutsche Warthe*, June 13, 1904, no. 161, extract in BA-Berlin, RKA, vol. 2116, pp. 160-61; quote from p. 161r. Leutwein may also have hesitated because of the possibility of mutiny by the soldiers.

234. Spraul 1988, p. 721.

the war effort, although he gave von Trotha no specific instructions.[235] Von Trotha declared martial law in the colony on June 11, 1904, and he was effectively in charge of the colony until August 1905, when a new governor was appointed. Von Trotha was relieved as commander of the *Schutztruppe* by Berthold von Deimling on November 2, 1905.

Pursuing his plan to crush Ovaherero military resistance in a single blow, von Trotha waited until he had received massive reinforcements from Germany and then encircled the Ovaherero at the Waterberg plateau, where tens of thousands of Ovaherero were gathered, including men, women, and children, along with all of their livestock.[236] Von Trotha launched his attack on August 11, 1904, with as many as two thousand troops, including three machine-gun batteries (against an estimated five to six thousand Ovaherero warriors).[237] Most of the Ovaherero escaped through a gap in the German encirclement that channeled them into the parched Omaheke Desert.[238] There they were pursued by German patrols for almost two months, which drove them deeper and deeper into the sand plains. An unknown number, but probably tens of thousands, perished. The decision to create a fanlike troop formation to cut off Ovaherero lines of escape and to continue pushing them farther into the Omaheke marked a shift toward an explicitly genocidal strategy, since "death from thirst did not distinguish between men, women, and children" (all Ovaherero warriors were men).[239] One German lieutenant involved in the pursuit wrote that "occasionally we found spots where the Herero had burrowed desperately for water; there was not

---

235. *Deutsch-Südwestafrikanische Zeitung*, May 4, 1904, special edition ("Extra-Blatt"); von Trotha to Leutwein, November 5, 1904, BA-Berlin, RKA, vol. 2089, pp. 100-102.

236. Some historians have suggested that these numbers may be exaggerated, for example, Sudholt 1975, pp. 185-86; and Lau 1995b. This question of numbers is irrelevant for the question of genocidal intent. The German military at the time assumed that most of the Ovaherero nation was at Waterberg in August, and their policies targeted all Ovaherero.

237. Lau 1995b, p. 43; Kurd Schwabe 1907, p. 268. Lieutenant Schwabe reported on the decisive effect of the machine guns in overpowering the Ovaherero (Kurd Schwabe 1907, p. 284; Nuhn 1989, p. 225).

238. Nuhn 1989, p. 261; on the smaller groups of fleeing Ovaherero see ibid., pp. 290ff., with a map of their paths on pp. 296-97. The Germans managed to capture thousands of cattle abandoned by the Ovaherero at the battle of Waterberg and afterward, but most of them were "already half dead" and subsequently perished (Rohrbach 1909b, p. 170) or were eaten by the troops.

239. Lundtofte 2003, p. 37. If the interpretation of the double meaning of the term *Vernichten* is not enough, it is worth noting that the widely circulated and respectable *Schulthess's europäischer Geschichtskalender* for the year 1904 (p. 166, quoted in Sproul 1988, p. 720) referred to the "Ausrottung" (extermination) of the Ovaherero as an unambiguous historical fact.

a single drop of liquid in these sand holes."[240] They were compelled to slit the throats of their cattle and drink their blood or to squeeze the fluid from the animals' stomachs.[241]

General von Trotha has gone down in history as the author of the *Vernichtungsbefehl*, or "order of annihilation," against the Ovaherero, which he issued on October 2, 1904 (see epigraph to this section). Rather than heeding the words of Leutwein and the Rhenish missionaries and entering into peace negotiations with the Ovaherero, von Trotha stated his goal bluntly in a letter to the chief of the Great General Staff, Count von Schlieffen: "to annihilate the nation as such, or when this proves impossible through tactical blows, to expel it from the country." If there was any ambiguity at all, he added, "I think it is better if the nation as such perishes."[242] Rather than continuing to press the Ovaherero further into the desert, von Trotha used the dry season, which he knew would last until January, to do the killing for him. He ordered his troops to seal off the western edge of the Sandveld along a cordon stretching about 250 kilometers and to occupy the water holes.[243] Major (later First Lieutenant) Ludwig von Estorff, commander of the Eastern Division (*Ostabteilung*) during the Waterberg campaign, was one of the men who conducted numerous patrols into the Omaheke that were intended to continue pushing the Ovaherero farther in and to block their return:

> I followed their tracks. . . . The Herero fled from us farther into the Sandveld. Again and again the same terrible scene was repeated: with feverish speed the men had worked at opening a well, but the water and the wells became ever more scarce. They fled from one well to the next and lost almost all of their livestock and a large number of people. The nation dwindled down to meager remnants which gradually fell into our hands. . . . The policy of thus decimating the people was as foolish as it was cruel; we could have saved many of the people and their herds of cattle if we had spared them and allowed them to return; their punishment had already been sufficient. I suggested this to General von Trotha, but he desired their complete annihilation.[244]

Ovaherero men who tried to surrender were killed; women and children were driven back into the Sandveld.[245] According to the Rhenish missionary

240. Bayer 1909, p. 195.

241. Pool 1991, pp. 251, 264; Lau 1995b, p. 51.

242. Von Trotha to von Schlieffen, October 4, 1904, BA-Berlin, RKA, vol. 2089, pp. 5r, 6r–v.

243. Kriegsgeschichtliche Abteilung I des Grossen Generalstabs 1906–7, vol. I, p. 208.

244. Estorff 1968, p. 117.

245. Nuhn 1989, pp. 281–83.

Johann Irle, the war "turned Hereroland into a desert, full of human corpses and the cadavers of livestock. Everywhere we encounter the bleaching bones of the Herero and the graves of brave German soldiers. The country has become a giant cemetery in which whites and blacks rest facing one another [entgegenruhen]."[246] The official General Staff report summarized this strategy bluntly: "The waterless Omaheke was supposed to complete the job that the German weapons had started: the annihilation of the Herero people."[247]

Although von Trotha arrived at this exterminationist policy independently after the Waterberg battle, it was approved at the highest levels. In a letter to the chancellor on November 23, Count von Schlieffen wrote that "one can concur with [General von Trotha] that the entire nation should be exterminated or driven from the country." Von Schlieffen offered as a possible alternative for the Ovaherero a "permanent state of forced labor, that is, a form of slavery," adding that "the race war, once it has broken out, can only be ended by the extermination [Vernichtung] or the complete subjugation of one of the parties."[248] At the urging of missionaries, the chancellor, and finally the kaiser, von Schlieffen finally telegrammed von Trotha on December 9, ordering him to pardon all Ovaherero except those who were "directly guilty" or leaders.[249] But by that time it was too late. When the rainy season started in March, First Lieutenant Count von Schweinitz followed a broad trail through the Omaheke that had "obviously" been used by "great bands of fleeing Hereros in August or September of the previous

246. Irle 1906, p. 344. For explicit contemporary accounts, see also the diary of Captain Viktor Franke, BA-Koblenz, Nachlass 30/1. The oral testimony collected for the 1918 British Blue Book (Union of South Africa 1918, chap. 15) is harrowing, but pace Silvester and Gewald (2003, pp. xxi ff.), historians cannot take this publication at face value since it was a document of ideological imperial competition intended to bolster Britain's effort to help South Africa assume "mandate" power over Namibia. The firsthand sworn testimony in the Blue Book was presented as evidence against the Germans' fitness to colonize. This is not to say that the testimony given in the Blue Book is false, but that without alternative corroborating sources we can grant it only secondary status as a historical document. British reports generated for internal, official consumption or written at the time of the war are less likely to be fabricated or distorted. The diaries of von Estorff and Franke, which are damning enough, were not written for publication.

247. Kriegsgeschichtliche Abteilung I des Grossen Generalstabs 1906–7, vol. 1, p. 207.

248. Von Schlieffen to chancellor, November 23, 1904, BA-Berlin, RKA, vol. 2089, pp. 4r–v. The English translation of this passage in Bley [1971] 1996, p. 165, is problematic, since it translates Vernichtung as "destruction." Since von Schlieffen's letter has just written that the Ovaherero "have forfeited their lives" (ihr Leben verwirkt; p. 4r), the nonmilitary meaning of Vernichtung as "extermination" seems incontestable.

249. Telegram from von Schlieffen to von Trotha, December 9, 1904, BA-Berlin, RKA, vol. 2089, p. 52.

year." Along the path von Schweinitz saw hundreds of skeletons of humans and horses lying side by side and piled on top of each other.[250]

An unknown number of Ovaherero had perished in what this officer called their "death march [*Todeszug*] through the Sandveld." Although there are no reliable figures, their numbers may have declined by as much as 70 or 80 percent from prewar levels.[251] The largest estimates of the number of Ovaherero survivors of the war and prison camps range from sixteen to twenty thousand.[252] The scattered survivors, as von Trotha wrote to Ber-

250. Quotes from a report on Graf von Schweinitz's reconnaissance mission in *Militär-wochenblatt*, no. 96 (1905): 2215; see also Kriegsgeschichtliche Abteilung I des Grossen Generalstabs 1906–7, vol. I, p. 214, for a slightly different and even grislier rendition of the same report; also see *Meine Kriegs-Erlebnisse in Deutsch-Süd-West-Afrika* 1907, p. 83, with a crude drawing of vultures circling over an African corpse in the Sandveld.

251. Bley 1995, p. 152.

252. The highest survivor figure is from Lau 1995b, p. 44; see also Pool 1976, pp. 403–26; and Nuhn 1989, p. 315. The total number of Ovaherero and Ovambanderu in Namibia was estimated by missionary Brincker at 50,000 in 1873 ("Reise und Arbeit im Hererólande," *Berichte der RMG* 29 [8, 1873]: 232); just a year later, however, the mission's annual report raised the estimate to 100,000 (*Jahresbericht der Rheinischen Missionsgesellschaft* 46 [1874]: 18); and in 1887 missionary Viehe put the number at 80,000 ("Jahresfest der Rheinischen Missionsgesellschaft," *Berichte der RMG* 43 [9, 1887]: 275). Settler Margarete von Eckenbrecher agreed with the prewar figure of 100,000 Ovaherero (1907, p. 77), while Adolf Fischer put the number at 200,000 (A. Fischer 1914, p. 92). Governor Leutwein cited a figure of 60,000–70,000 in February 1904 (Leutwein to Colonial Department, February 23, 1904, BA-Berlin, RKA, vol. 2113, p. 89v). Even if we accept Leutwein's low estimate—65,000 Ovaherero before the genocide—this would indicate a loss of 74 percent of the Ovaherero population between February 1904 and the first census after the war, on January 1, 1908, which found 16,303 Ovaherero in the colony. Of course, some Ovaherero were still in the bush or in foreign territory at this time. Between 600 and 1,000 had managed to escape westward across the colony to the British zone at Walvis Bay (Nuhn 1989, p. 314). British authorities believed that another 1,000 Ovaherero had settled in what was then the British Bechuanaland protectorate. By 1911 the number of Ovaherero counted in the colony had risen to 18,387. Even if we assume that *all* of these additional Ovaherero between 1908 and 1911 were adults returning or turning themselves in to the authorities, and disregard births, and even if we add the 2,000 Ovaherero in British territory (giving a total of 20,387), this would still mean that in 1911 some 69 percent of the prewar Ovaherero population was missing or dead. It is impossible to know how many Ovaherero were still in hiding at this time. See *Taschenbuch für Südwestafrika* (Berlin: Wilhelm Weicher, 1911), pt. I, p. 226, for Ovaherero population figures; also Lau 1995b and Dedering 1993b for discussion of Ovaherero deaths. A recent demographic article has suggested that the number of Ovaherero refugees to the British Bechuanaland protectorate might have been as high as 6,000–9,000, but this cannot be reconciled with earlier British or German estimates (Pennington and Harpenning 1991; see Durham 1993, vol. I, pp. 67–68). Moreover, this demographic research is based on pure speculation about the levels of migration between Botswana and Namibia during the twentieth century and on highly problematic assumptions about the relationship between the researchers' sampling techniques and the

lin, were "the last ruins of a nation that has stopped hoping for rescue or restoration."[253] The Ovaherero people, according to Lieutenant Schwabe, had "met its terrible but well-deserved destiny."[254] Colonel Berthold von "Deimling, who led the pursuit of the Ovaherero into the desert, paraphrased the General Staff's report in 1929 in his personal memoirs, writing that the conclusion of the campaign was that "the Herero ended their existence as an autonomous people."[255] Of course, such statements were as much wishful fantasies as accurate historical statements. The Ovaherero were not entirely exterminated. They continued to be exploited severely in slavelike forced labor after 1904, and as "free" laborers after 1907. The fact remains that von Trotha sought deliberately to wipe out the Ovaherero in 1904, and that he was supported in this by his officers and soldiers and by many of the highest authorities in Berlin. This concerted movement beyond native policy into an unambiguous policy of genocide calls for an explanation. It cannot be dismissed as a historical aberration. Nor can General von Trotha's behavior be reduced to an example of *Tropenkoller* (tropical madness) or to an eerie precursor of Nazism, as suggested by Thomas Pynchon in *V* and *Gravity's Rainbow*.[256] The threat from an African rebellion to German prestige abroad was certainly a factor, but this did not dictate a specifically genocidal course of action.

To account for the genocide we need to return to the triple analytic focus on ethnographic discourse, symbolic competition, and imaginary identification with the colonized as determinants of native policy. With respect to

actual size of the current Otjiherero-speaking population in Botswana. The "history" in the article's title is a pure statistical fabrication.

253. Quoted in Kurd Schwabe 1907, p. 300.

254. Ibid., p. 305.

255. "Lebenserinnerungen," BA-MA-Freiburg, Nachlass Deimling (N 559), vol. 2, p. 20.

256. The colonial novelist Frieda von Bülow made the concept of *Tropenkoller* famous with her 1896 novel of the same title; see Wildenthal 2001. Pynchon's *V* has an entire chapter focused obliquely on the massacre of the Ovaherero (chap. 9, "Mondaugen's Story"), in which a sadistic Lieutenant Weissmann ("white man") in the Union mandate colony of Southwest Africa in 1922 suggests a link between the Ovaherero massacre and Hitler. Weissmann tortures Africans and pronounces the name Hitler as if it were "the name of an avant-garde play" (Pynchon 1963, p. 224). The Weissmann figure reappears as Blicero in *Gravity's Rainbow*, whose setting is the Nazi "Oven State" and its postwar aftermath, the "Zone." The Ovaherero appear here as part of the Nazi war machine—the "Schwarzkommando," who are dressed in "pieces here and there of old Wehrmacht and SS uniforms" and worship and work on a rocket program. The topos of the Schwarzkommando reinforces Pynchon's suggestion of a linkage between Nazism and the "scrupulous butcher named von Trotha," who is responsible for the Ovaherero dedication to suicide and for their deculturation ("eanda and oruzo have lost their force out here"; Pynchon 1973, pp. 367–69, 420–21). For analyses of von Trotha and the Ovaherero in Pynchon's fiction, see Seed 1982; Selmeci and Henrichsen 1995; and Ivison 1997.

the first, the Ovaherero had been demonized for decades, and fantasies of extermination had been rife. If the massacre was a caesura in terms of actual policy, the destruction had deep roots in German ethnographic visions. Von Trotha was no more disparaging of Ovaherero culture than earlier German officials or precolonial missionaries. If von Trotha's language sometimes bordered on the delirious, we need only refer back to Hugo Hahn's railing against the Ovaherero a half century earlier to see the continuity with a long tradition. The massacre of the Ovaherero in 1904 was not so much an aberration as an extreme expression of the German "devil's handwriting."

The demonization of black Africans in general and the Ovaherero in particular was a necessary but not a sufficient condition for the shift to genocide. After all, Leutwein had not attempted to massacre even a fraction of the rebellious Ovaherero in 1896. The specific constellation of the colonial state field was a second necessary factor. The extreme polarization between Leutwein and von Trotha crystallized in highly exaggerated form the class hostility that arose "naturally" in Wilhelmine Germany between a military aristocrat and a pastor's son who flaunted his classical education.[257] This tension was heightened by the way in which von Trotha entered the colonial arena as a usurper of the governor's power. Leutwein tried to salvage his authority through a frantic correspondence with Berlin, in which he attacked von Trotha and the officers allied with him. According to Leutwein, von Trotha had "the standpoint of a plucky lieutenant [*eines tapferen Leutnants*], not a colonizer."[258] When von Trotha transferred command for the campaign against the Khoikhoi rebellion from Leutwein to Colonel von Deimling in October 1904, Leutwein maligned the latter as possessed of a nervous temperament that was "particularly inappropriate for [a posting] in Africa."[259]

Viewed as a symbolic class conflict, Leutwein's struggle with von Trotha and von Deimling recalls his earlier battles with the von François brothers. Leutwein's argument against the extermination of the Ovaherero in the second half of 1904 was driven above all by these situational dynamics within the colonial state field.[260] In 1904, as in 1894, Leutwein tried to ex-

---

257. Pool 1991, pp. 243–44.

258. Leutwein to Colonial Department, November 12, 1904, BA-Berlin, RKA, vol. 2089, p. 98v.

259. Leutwein to von Trotha, November 5, 1904, BA-Berlin, RKA, vol. 2089, p. 43v.

260. Another alternative, of course, is that Leutwein had undergone a "learning process" between 1894 to 1904. His defense of the Ovaherero reservations in 1902 and 1903 would seem to support this. But the archival documentation suggests that he still had nothing positive to say about Ovaherero culture during this period.

emplify a more refined, educated sensibility than his aristocratic opponents. But in the earlier conflict Leutwein was the agent of official metropolitan criticism of the existing governor rather than the source of Berlin's dissatisfaction. The other difference has to do with the constraining effect of precolonial representations. In the dispute about the Witbooi Leutwein was able to cull a rich array of positive images from the ethnographic archive. But it was impossible for him to come up with a rhetorically powerful defense of the Ovaherero, no matter how much the situation called for it. Flailing about for an alternative framing of the Ovaherero, Leutwein compared their uprising to the Vespers revolt of the Sicilians against their Angevin rulers in 1282.[261] While this served to display Leutwein's cultural refinement and to distinguish it from von Trotha's crassness ("rivers of blood"), the comparison was hardly compelling, since most Europeans refused to grant the Ovaherero membership in their own family tree.[262] Precolonial discourse constrained and limited colonial practice in addition to providing its contents.

Leutwein also became increasingly vehement in his attacks on the settlers, whose most vociferous representatives approved of von Trotha's approach. In a long report to the Colonial Department in May 1904 Leutwein argued that "the bitterness of the Hereros against the whites, especially against the Germans," was a "natural" response. He wrote that "one can no longer say that the whites have shown themselves to be the morally superior race," and went on to criticize the "destructive practice of expelling inappropriate elements from Germany into the colony." The "ultimate expression of [the settler's] attitudes was the demand by the German Colonial Society that every white should be regarded as a 'higher being' by the natives." Leutwein summarized his view: "The lower the cultural level of a particular white, the greater the appeal of this demand."[263] Governor Solf was fighting a very similar battle in Samoa during this same period, and used an almost identical formula in attacking opponents of his "liberal" course, but he was much more successful. One reason for Solf's greater success was the richness of the available materials in the ethnographic repertoire, which resonated with his policies.

261. Leutwein to Colonial Department, May 17, 1904, BA-Berlin, RKA, vol. 2115, p. 66r.

262. But see Rohrbach 1909b, p. 160, which calls the Ovaherero uprising a "war of liberation against us" and compares their savage practices in warfare to those of the ancient Cherusci, "our ancestors, after all," whose leader, Arminius, was called "Germany's liberator" by Tacitus. Rohrbach's sociological position within the colonial state field was, after all, even more "dominated" than Leutwein's.

263. Leutwein to Colonial Department, May 17, 1904, BA-Berlin, RKA, vol. 2115, p. 65v.

Von Trotha's hostility to Leutwein led him to adopt an ever harsher "ethnographic" approach, and this spiraling clash had dire consequences for the Ovaherero. Von Trotha relished the dual resonance of the term *Vernichtung*. In conventional German military language, *vernichten* meant "to deal a devastating blow" to the enemy, breaking his resistance. Von Trotha's language in the second half of 1904 increasingly evoked the connotations of that term that were tied specifically to the colonial context. For centuries, Europeans (including Germans) had discussed and sometimes deplored the extermination of non-Western peoples due to colonial conquest.[264] The traditional European military concept of the *Vernichtungskrieg* would never have been associated with images of "rivers of blood" or "blatant terrorism and cruelty"—these were colonial amendments.[265] Von Trotha was reasserting the specific cultural capital of the Prussian and German nobility, its specialization in the arts of domination and violence, under conditions that a European imagination perceived as lying outside the borders of civilization. Given the mounting criticism of his actions after October 1904 inside the Colonial Department, the Chancellery, the Reichstag, and among some Social Democrats and representatives of the Catholic Center Party, von Trotha's defense of his genocidal approach has an air of Bismarckian obstinacy and bravado. These metropolitan "democratic" opinions, represented in situ by the middle-class upstart Theodor Leutwein, were as much the target of von Trotha's wrath as the Ovaherero themselves. This partly explains the ratcheting up of his aims from military defeat to ethnic annihilation after the battle of Waterberg.[266]

The model of the effects of the demonization of the Ovaherero on the 1904 massacre differs in several respects from Daniel Goldhagen's account of the Nazi Holocaust, to which it bears a superficial resemblance. A set of precolonial ethnographic images could not normally predict later policy because such discourses were usually multivocal. Even when they were

264. As Zantop (1997) demonstrates, the early modern German literature on colonialism emphasized the inhumanity of the Spanish conquest of America and suggested that Germans would be less brutal colonizers.

265. This argument is directed against those like Poewe (1985, p. 65), Sudholt (1975), Lundtofte (2003, p. 31), and Lau (1995b), who read von Trotha's language of *Vernichtung* in strictly military terms, ignoring the fact that the conventional military meaning had already been extended to encompass physical extermination in the official correspondence by Leutwein. For a parallel discussion of whether the language of "destruction" on the North American frontier was military or genocidal, see M. Freeman 1995.

266. Lundtofte 2003, pp. 34ff., focuses on this escalation, but his explanation emphasizes material problems of provisioning the troops.

unusually uniform, as with representations of the Ovaherero, they would not necessarily be turned into practice because of the social dynamics of the state field. If Leutwein had been backed by the German government against von Trotha rather than being pushed out of power, he might have acted to halt the genocide by switching from an ethnographic to an economic logic. Forced to play on a field dominated by von Trotha, Leutwein was helpless to argue the intrinsic merits of the Ovaherero. Novel ethnographic representations cannot be created on command, from scratch.

A third source of von Trotha's genocidal policy was his sadistic imaginary identification with an imago of the colonized. Such cross-cultural identification was a ubiquitous feature of colonial settings, but in von Trotha's case it is perhaps counterintuitive. It is important to recall here that the imagos employed in imaginary identification need not be culturally valued or heroic in any conventional sense. The image of the viciously cruel Ovaherero, already widespread after 1870, became almost universal among colonial Germans in 1904. Ovahereros physically beat to death German settlers and soldiers and mutilated some of their bodies.[267] Lieutenant von Erffa, an officer killed in the first major engagement with the Ovaherero, wrote of the horrors committed by these "black devils": "Mutilated remnants of corpses everywhere! The beasts had raped the women after murdering the men and then slaughtered them like sheep. . . . Patrols found the body parts hanging on trees like meat to be cured: excised breasts, arms, legs. And over there, the Herero women had mutilated half-grown boys with knives and then left them lying there to bleed to death!" The result of these incidents, according to von Erffa, was that "an evil hatred" (ein böser Haß) welled up against these "beasts."[268] But are hatred and revenge sufficient to explain the lynchings, the removal of body parts and skulls for scientific study, and the attempt to exterminate an entire people? It is difficult to understand von Trotha's "irrational" course without attending to his self-image as the "great general of the German soldiers" exercising "terrorism," shedding "rivers of blood," and driving women and children to their death. This self-perception suggests an identification with a European imago of the "cruel Herero," recalling Kaiser Wilhelm's eagerness to identify himself and his soldiers with the "Huns." Challenged by men like Leutwein

267. Pool 1991, p. 226.
268. Erffa 1905, pp. 70, 56, 71. These quotes are from letters written by von Erffa between September 2, 1903, and March 26, 1904. Rhenish missionary J. Irle (1906, p. 198) offered a more relativistic interpretation of this mutilation of enemies' bodies: "The Herero believes that the dead also continue to live. . . . Therefore he takes revenge on the dead as on the living."

who seemed to embody the inexorable demise of noble privilege, von Trotha cross-identified with a caricatured image of the enemy and redirected his savage "Herero" wrath against both the soft opinions of German liberals and the African military opponent.

At another level, von Trotha's aggressiveness indexed a colonial state field in disarray, a field that he himself had unsettled. Von Trotha did not simply come into the colony as an outside military operator but seized control of colonial policy in its entirety. By casting the Ovaherero out of the colony he was challenging the prevailing definition of the colonial state as being organized around native policy. Von Trotha and Leutwein were no longer granting one another recognition of their differing cultural positions. The disappearance of the dialectics of reciprocal recognition that govern even the most stratified social fields generated aggressiveness, just as the disjuncture between image and self-image—the failure of recognition—leads to aggressiveness in the mirror stage.[269] Recognition is replaced by misrecognition, and all of the actors located inside the field in dissolution descend into a morass of agressivity, or simply exit.

Von Trotha's genocidal turn was multiply overdetermined. The first moving force was the weight of ethnographic discourse. Second was his paradoxical identification with an imago of extreme cruelty. This was powered by von Trotha's positioning in a competitive field facing an embodiment of the educated, liberal middle class that threatened Germany's old noble elite. Von Trotha exploded this field, producing a situation of mutual nonrecognition and heightening the aggressive energy of the situation. The result for the Ovaherero was a policy of "colonialism without the colonized."

NATIVE POLICY AFTER 1904: THE SCATTERING TIME

"They [the Ovaherero] were ranchmen and proprietors, and we were there to make them landless workingmen."

GUSTAV FRENSSEN, *Peter Moor's Journey to Southwest Africa*[270]

269. Indeed, Homi Bhabha has argued that the colonizer-colonized relationship *tout court* produces aggressiveness due to the breakdown of recognition. Hegel ([1807] 1910) analyzed the master-slave relation as a dialectic of recognition and saw it as a successor stage to the aggressive Hobbesian war of all against all. For Bhabha hierarchical relations like colonialism give rise to a *new* form of aggressiveness that is not connected to some mythical "state of nature." It is patterned on Lacan's ([1949] 1977, p. 7) account of the *aggressivity* that accompanies the mirror stage. The construction of the colonized Other as "almost the same, but not quite" undercuts his value in granting recognition to the colonizer, just as the mirror image is devalued as misrecognition (due to its reversal of the image or other imperfections).

270. Frenssen [1905] 1908, p. 77.

"'That's when we were scattered' was a frequent remark made about the aftermath of the battle of Hamakari (Waterberg)."

KIRSTEN ALNAES [271]

Von Trotha did not accomplish his goal of exterminating the entire Ovaherero population or driving them out of the colony. With the appointment of von Lindequist as governor in August 1905 the colony began to move slowly back toward a focus on Ovaherero native policy, although this was combined with ongoing deadly negligence in the concentration camps that quietly continued the genocide through 1907. Outside the camps the rulers moved from genocide to ethnocide, that is, toward the destruction of the indigenous group's culture and identity.[272] The Germans were determined not just to punish the Ovaherero but to transform them in ways that made them docile and economically productive. What had been missing from the prewar program, focused as it was on seizing land and livestock from the Ovaherero, was an emphasis on actively reconstituting them as a deracinated, atomized proletariat. Postwar policies were assimilationist insofar as they sought to turn the colonized into something familiar enough to be easily manageable. Rather than a full-scale cultural conversion, however, the goal was to Europeanize Ovaherero in ways that would not violate the rule of difference.[273]

Von Trotha lifted his annihilation order at the beginning of 1905, but he insisted that the Ovaherero should be "shackled and put to work" indefinitely.[274] German soldiers were no longer under orders to kill or repulse any Ovaherero they encountered but were instructed to arrest them (figs. 3.7–3.8). Leutwein's insistence on the economic irrationality of

271. Alnaes 1989, p. 292.

272. See Lemkin 1944, which included under the rubric of genocide the planned destruction of the "essential foundations of the life of national groups," including cultural, religious, and moral forms. I am defining genocide more narrowly as killing; "ethnocide" is defined in Corry 1975, for example, as encompassing "enforced acculturation."

273. Von Trotha's diaries suggest that he too perceived a continuum running from his own policies of extermination to those of the postwar government, writing that "the natives have to give way, see America. *Either* by the bullet or via mission through brandy" (cited in Pool 1991, p. 248 [my emphasis]). The idea of "mission" is associated here with a Christian version of assimilation, while "brandy" is meant to suggest the techniques used by colonizers to reduce indigenous peoples to a degraded condition.

274. Von Trotha to chancellor, January 1, 1905, BA-Berlin, RKA, vol. 2089, p. 138v; von Trotha's letter to missionary Kuhlmann, in Bley [1971] 1996, p. 168. See also von Trotha to von Schlieffen, BA-Berlin, RKA, vol. 2089, p. 52r, where the general insists that these are to be "concentration camps for the . . . remnants of the Herero people and not reservations." A camp already existed in Okahandja as early as May 1904 (Nuhn 1989, p. 306).

FIGURE 3.7 Starving Ovaherero returning from the desert and surrendering to Germans to be registered as prisoners on the Otavi railroad construction site (1904–5). (Courtesy of NAN.)

FIGURE 3.8 Ovaherero prisoners in chains (1904–5). (Courtesy of NAN.)

destroying the Ovaherero began to dominate official discussions (although Leutwein himself was not rehabilitated). Chancellor von Bülow had agreed with Leutwein in 1904 that the colony's "economic future would be completely destroyed by the extermination of the indispensable labor power" of the Ovaherero.[275] By the middle of 1905 Deputy Governor Tecklenburg began to distance himself from von Trotha's exterminationist line, arguing that the death of the Ovaherero would be an economic loss for the colony. But he still insisted that they should also undergo a "period of suffering" (Leidenszeit) in the concentration camps, which would guarantee that they would not "be tempted for generations to repeat the uprising."[276] Like the Witbooi, all Ovaherero who surrendered or were captured were held in camps. Given the deadly conditions in the camps and the mandatory hard labor, the line between extermination and punishment was a blurry one. During 1905 most Ovaherero prisoners were sent to the concentration camp at Swakopmund, where the death rates were astronomical due to exhausting labor, inadequate food, disease, and a cold, wet climate to which they were not accustomed. According to the Rhenish missionary who was attached to the prisoners at Swakopmund, Heinrich Vedder, "thirty people died every day in the worst period" and "their bodies were loaded onto carts and buried in mass graves in the sand."[277]

This formula of "suffering plus proletarianization" characterized the treatment of Ovaherero during the next three years. By the end of 1905 "an estimated 8,800 Herero" had been confined in camps and "put to work as forced labourers."[278] Because most were unwilling to surrender voluntarily under these conditions, the government created a network of *Sammelstellen* (collection stations).[279] The new governor, von Lindequist, issued a proclamation to the Ovaherero on December 1, 1905, assuring them that these stations would be less coercive than the concentration camps and that "no white soldiers [would] be stationed" there.[280] Indeed, the stations were supervised by missionaries, who organized armed patrols of Ovaherero that were sent out into the bush to convince their compatriots to turn themselves

275. "Auszug aus einem Schreiben des Reichskanzlers an Seine Majestät vom 30 Nov. 1904," November 30, 1904, BA-Berlin, RKA, vol. 2089, p. 15r.

276. Tecklenburg to the Colonial Department, July 3, 1905, BA-Berlin, RKA, vol. 2118, p. 154v.

277. Vedder 1955, p. 138; J. Zeller 2003.

278. Gewald 1998a, p. 195.

279. See the reports in *Deutsches Kolonialblatt* 17 (1906): 194–95, 241.

280. See "Omatjivisiro/Bekanntmachung" of governor, December 1, 1905, BA-Berlin, RKA, vol. 2119, p. 14v.

in.[281] Although it was easy for Ovaherero to escape from the *Sammelstellen*, few actually left. The result was that by the end of March 1907 some 12,500 Ovaherero had been rounded up at these stations.

As soon as the collection of Ovaherero was complete, the governor broke his word and transferred them in open-bed railway cars to regular concentration camps (fig. 3.9). When the governor had visited the prisoners at Swakopmund in November 1905, he had announced that "I cannot lighten your destiny until your compatriots who still find themselves in the field end their resistance."[282] But there was no "lightening of destiny" until the end of 1907. The new prisoners were deployed as forced laborers. Some worked for the army, others on the construction of the Otavi railroad (figs. 3.10-3.11) or on maintenance of the Swakopmund-Windhoek line. Many were picked up daily by large civilian companies and by smaller employers to be used as forced laborers. Large firms set up special *werfts* on their own premises where entire groups of imprisoned Ovaherero lived permanently.[283] Death from overwork was widespread among these forced laborers, so much so that at least one firm created a special stamp to print the words "dead due to exhaustion" in its employee registers.[284]

Just as the state's main goal of expropriating Ovaherero resources before the war had been tempered by the policy on reservations, the goal of proletarianization was now combined with a desire to inflict suffering. Some Ovaherero were imprisoned on Shark Island. Those who were believed to be "ringleaders" of the uprising or murderers of German civilians were executed, usually by hanging. Ovaherero victims of lynching were sometimes stripped of their clothing (fig. 3.12).[285] Ovaherero skulls, brains, and heads were sent to German universities for scientific investigation. One anatomist

281. See von Lindquist's report of April 17, 1906, in *Deutsches Kolonialblatt* 17 (1906): 402 (original in BA-Berlin, RKA, vol. 2119, pp. 42-43). See also von Lindequist's report on the new collection station at Otjosongobe from September 1, 1906, according to which the Germans needed to engage in "artful convincing or threats of violence" to collect the Ovaherero who were still at large (*Deutsches Kolonialblatt* 17 [1906]: 712).

282. "Der Besuch der Hererowerft," *Dritte Beilage zur "Deutsch-Südwestafrikanischen Zeitung"* 7 (48, November 29, 1905): 1.

283. Nuhn 1989, p. 308; Zimmerer 1999, pp. 290-91; Gewald 2000, p. 209.

284. See *Genocide and the Second Reich*, directed by David Adetayo Olusoga (Olusoga 2004); and Nuhn 1989, pp. 306-7.

285. Fig. 3.12 was originally printed in the war memoirs of the settler Conrad Rust (1905, p. 196). For other photos reminiscent of the postbellum U.S. South, see Auer 1911, p. 113; *Meine Kriegs-Erlebnisse in Deutsch-Süd-West-Afrika* 1907, p. 145; Vigne 1973, p. 25; and Union of South Africa 1918, frontispiece, plate 1. A representative lynching postcard from the period is reprinted in Nachtwei 1976, p. 37.

FIGURE 3.9 (top left) Prisoners being transported in an open-bed railway car. From Kurd Schwabe 1907, p. 306.

FIGURES 3.10 (bottom) AND 3.11 (top right) Ovaherero forced labor constructing the Otavi railroad. (Courtesy of Stadt- u. Universitätsbibliothek Frankfurt, Bildsammlung der Deutschen Kolonialgesellschaft.)

reported that the Ovaherero whose brains he had examined had died by hanging, suicide, pneumonia, and typhus (fig. 3.13).[286]

286. Sergi 1909, p. 7. Dr. Sergio Sergi investigated at the Berlin Anatomical Institute fourteen Ovaherero brains which had been procured by Leonhard Schultze in Southwest Africa. Other scientists studied Ovaherero heads preserved in formaldehyde; see Zeidler 1914; and Eggeling 1909. According to Krüger 1999, p. 97, one German officer claimed that

FIGURE 3.12 Ovaherero hanged by Germans. From Union of South Africa 1918, frontispiece, plate 1.

FIGURE 3.13 Soldiers examining a crate full of skulls of Ovaherero who were hanged or killed in the 1904 war, being sent off to the Pathological Institute in Berlin for craniometric study. From *Meine Kriegs-Erlebnisse in Deutsch-Süd-West-Afrika* 1907, p. 114.

The most direct blow to traditional or prewar Ovaherero culture was the expropriation of all movable and fixed property and the ban on ownership of cattle and land (decree of August 8, 1906). The post of Ovaherero captainship or chief was eliminated. Most Ovaherero leaders had been killed in the war or escaped into exile.[287] Communities were radically disrupted. For many years after the war, few Ovaherero were "able to maintain regular and close contacts with their kindred," as one anthropologist found in interviews with elderly Ovahereros during the 1950s. The "complex system of rights and duties which [previously] had linked the individual to both his patrilineal and matrilineal kin . . . was more or less completely suspended" in this period.[288] Individuals and families were resettled in "locations" attached to European workplaces or on the outskirts of larger settlements and towns inhabited by colonizers. Like most other Namibians in this era, Ovaherero were required to live in a location or *werft* with no more than ten native families or individual native laborers on a single plot. Whereas the prewar "reservations" had tended to *remove* their residents, along with their land and livestock, from the capitalist economy, the postwar "locations" inserted the colonized directly into capitalist labor relations. A spatially discontinuous, pointillistic galaxy of *werfts* emerged, scattered across the map largely according to colonizers' needs. This map was completely different from the earlier array of central locations organized around chieftaincies and mission stations.

The Ovaherero were not entirely atomized after 1904. Colonial officials sometimes tried not to break up families.[289] After the lifting of forced labor in 1908 the Ovaherero were able to reconstitute social networks and to create new forms of national community through the Protestant church and inside the *Schutztruppe*. Economic logics were overdetermined by the imperatives of native policy, which sometimes reconsolidated communities. For example, the "native locations" in Windhoek and Lüderitz were divided

---

Ovaherero women prisoners were forced to use shards of glass to scrape the flesh from skulls that were sent to Berlin for scientific study. It is impossible to determine whether this story is part of the gothic imagination of contemporary historians of the Namibian genocide, since no verifiable source is provided.

287. Drießler 1932, p. 207.

288. Wagner 1954, p. 118. Wagner was perhaps personally invested in this outcome, as an adviser on "ethnicity" to the government in Southwest Africa; see his unpublished "Ethnic Survey of South West Africa," pt. 1, "District of Windhoek" (1951), in NAN.

289. As von Lindequist noted in a report on the concentration camp at Otjihaenena, "we have followed the principle in all cases that families are not to be broken up" (report to Colonial Department, April 17, 1906, BA-Berlin, RKA, vol. 2119, p. 43v).

into "tribal" sections.[290] Locations close to the colonizer were preferred because they were more easily supervised and because their proximity would have "educative" effects on Africans.[291] The cultural shock of the 1904 war and the period of suffering in the camps produced massive changes in Ovaherero culture. In many respects they exchanged their traditions and signifiers for those of the colonizers.

The partial assimilation of the Ovaherero was also an emotional project. As an article in the *Windhuker Nachrichten* put it in 1906, "We demand that the Herero adapt to the attitudes prescribed [in Southwest Africa] by German law and *make these the basis of his emotions*" (hieraus sein Empfinden konstruiert).[292] Paul Rohrbach, the Commissary for Settlement (*Ansiedlungskommissar*) in Southwest Africa between 1903 and 1906, summarized this idea: "Our task is to divest this tribe . . . of their specific *völkisch* and national characteristics and to gradually meld them with the other natives into a single colored work force."[293] Although Ovaherero cultural memories were certainly not erased, anthropologists later found evidence of discontinuities and amnesias that are less typical of societies which have not undergone such traumatic events.[294]

After the prisoner-of-war status was lifted in 1908, it was left to the discretion of individual Ovaherero "to decide where [he or she] wishes to

290. See Gaydish 2001, p. 69.

291. Arguments for an "educative effect" can be found in "Keine Reservate!" *Deutsch-Südwestafrikanische Zeitung* 7 (44, November 1, 1905): 1; and in Förster 1905, p. 527.

292. *Windhuker Nachrichten*, April 5, 1906, quoted in Bley 1995, p. 153 (my emphasis).

293. Rohrbach 1907, p. 21. The German adjective *völkisch* combines the cultural emphasis of the adjective *ethnic* with the biological connotations of the word *racial*. Gewald 1998b, p. 137, reports the existence of a file on the Ovaherero in the colonial archives, initiated in 1911 by an official in German Southwest Africa, bearing the title "Dissolved Tribes."

294. In her research among the Ovaherero of Mahalapye in Botswana, Deborah Durham found a general lack of national historical awareness as well as widespread "negative self-representations," including descriptions of the Ovaherero as alcohol abusers (Durham 1993, vol. 2, pp. viii, 2, 59–60). Durham wonders whether she might have "elicited a picture of a past and 'pure' Herero tradition" if she had not been restricted to the women's society (p. xii). Research among the Botswana Ovaherero a decade earlier found that "to the Herero the war against the Germans and the flight across the Kalahari desert was an experience of holocaust-like dimensions," and that this "experience has been perpetuated through subsequent generations; even thinking of it today causes distress in members of the generation born after their arrival in Botswana" (Alnaes 1989, p. 291). The Ovaherero songs analyzed by Alnaes emphasize "death and mortuary rituals" and "disorder and loss of meaning," as well as historical events, heroism, and cattle. But she also finds "an ingredient of revitalization in their performance" (pp. 274, 283, 294). Poewe 1985 makes the strongest case for Ovaherero "cultural disintegration."

work."[295] The term used to designate freedom of movement in Germany, *Freizügigkeit*, was now applied to Ovaherero, as was the idea of the autonomous individual with a "will." Individual Africans who did not have a job were punished as "vagabonds" (*Landstreicher*), just as they were in Germany and Prussia.[296] But the legal and cultural equation of the African and European ended there. The 1907 "native ordinances" required that the colonized subject carry an identification marker at all times. The governor recommended that employers add numbers to the names of workers with the same name.[297] Others called for tattooing workers with numbers or other symbols so they could be identified when they ran away.[298] All of this took place within a bifurcated and racialized legal system in which any "white" was allowed to arrest any "native" for suspected legal infractions, European employers were charged with the surveillance and punishment of their employees, and sentences were much more lenient for crimes committed by whites than for crimes committed by natives.

The Germans' project was to transform the Ovaherero from fundamentally incomprehensible others into a degraded mirror image of themselves. An example of the combination of similarity with degradation concerns the so-called *Bambusen*, young indigenous helpers and mascots, mainly Ovaherero, who were attached to individual Germans in the *Schutztruppe* after 1890 and later also in civilian life (see figs. 3.14, 3.15).[299] Curt von François explained that each of his soldiers had one or two servants and that the "obsequiousness of the natives" allowed them to "play at being masters" and to "flatter their vanity."[300] *Bambusen* were often given German names that

295. Decree by Governor Schuckmann, January 18, 1908, BA-Berlin, R. 1002, vol. 2591, p. 9.

296. "Verordnung des Gouverneurs von Deutsch-Südwestafrika, betr. Maßregeln zur Kontrolle der Eingeborenen" [Decree of the Governor of Southwest Africa on Measures to Control the Natives], par. 4, in *Deutsches Kolonialblatt* 18 (1907): 1181; compare the "Gesetz über die Bestrafung der Landstreicher, Bettler und Arbeitsscheuen" [Law on the Punishment of Vagabonds, Beggars, and Malingerers] of January 6, 1843, in *Gesetz-Sammlung für die königlichen Preußischen Staaten* 1843 (Berlin: im vereinigten Gesetz-Sammlungs-Debits- und Zeitungs-Komptoir, 1844), no. 2320, pp. 19-20. I discuss the discourse of vagabondage and nomadism in nineteenth-century Germany, and the public and private policies that were created to combat it, in Steinmetz 1993, chap. 5.

297. See Gewald 1998a, p. 190; and memo of July 13, 1911, Governor Seitz to Kaiserliche Bezirks- u. Distrikts-Amt, BA-Berlin, R. 1002, vol. 2591, p. 36. In Samoa, Chinese immigrant workers were also identified by numbers; see Tom 1986, pp. 76-80.

298. Spectator Germanicus 1913, p. 251; also Zimmerer 2003, p. 40.

299. Gewald 1998a, pp. 205-6; Henrichsen 2004.

300. C. von François 1899, pp. 80-81.

sounded comical to native speakers—"names like Mumpitz, little Kohn . . .
Bebel, etc." Equally important was the fact that these names would also
"awaken the memory of a small piece of . . . life in Germany."[301] The *Bambusen* may also have had a relationship to their given German names, which
"hailed" them as subjects.[302] Many of the thousands of Ovaherero children
orphaned by the 1904 war became *Bambusen,* and their youth may have
made them more susceptible to the informal program of quotidian indoc-
trination into German colonial worldviews. As historian Dag Henrichsen
remarks in the context of military *Bambusen,* "The German military had
become a projective screen for a proletariat of juvenile war victims." Of
course, we cannot make any assumptions about the success of colonial projects in remaking the subjectivity of the Ovaherero. It is no more certain
(though more flattering to present-day sensibilities) to insist that the dominated subject "sidesteps the identifications given him" and initiates "a disturbance that places the entire symbolic order in question."[303] In the present
context, however, I am more concerned with the formulation of the colonial
project than with its reception by the colonized.

From the standpoint of the colonizers the institution of the *Bambusen*
was a central component of native policy. Their *partial* similarity to the Germans made the *Bambusen* more recognizable. Theodor Leutwein included
in his memoir *Eleven Years as Governor in Southwest Africa* a staged "hu-
morous picture" (*Scherzbild*) of *Bambusen* being served by German soldiers
(fig. 3.14).[304] *Bambusen* also wore bits and pieces of German and European
military uniforms (fig. 3.15). Similarly, in Cameroon and Togo the Germans
distributed Prussian helmets and special military outfits to indigenous
chiefs while mocking these costumes at the same time.[305]

301. Freimut 1909, p. 37.

302. On "hailing" see Althusser 1971b. For another example of the desire for the emotional warmth associated with a partially shared culture combined with efforts to reaffirm
the racist boundary, Paul Rohrbach's comments on his family *Bambuse,* Pensmann. Rohrbach
observed that Pensmann and the other "natives" in the family household "were very attached
to us and definitely wanted to return with us to Germany" and had to be talked out of this
gently by Frau Rohrbach, who explained to them that it was "much too cold for them there"
(in fact, such immigration to Germany was illegal). As Rohrbach boasted, "we had engaged
in educational labor with them," a labor that "could also be called practical native policy"
(1953, pp. 65, 76).

303. Henrichsen 2004, pp. 180–82; de Certeau 1986, p. 70.

304. Although some have interpreted this photograph as an ironic reversal of colonial
power relations, I think it needs to be read against the historically specific institution of the
Bambuse in German Southwest Africa.

305. Trotha 1994, pp. 315ff.

FIGURE 3.14 (above) Staged picture of German officials serving *Bambusen*. From Leutwein 1907a, p. 293.

FIGURE 3.15 (left) Southwest African with German uniform in "Kaiser Wilhelm" pose. (Courtesy of Stadt- u. Universitätsbibliothek Frankfurt, Bildsammlung der deutschen Kolonialgesellschaft.)

Just as the system of native policy that was applied to the Witbooi between 1894 and 1904 depended on the cooperation of the Witbooi, Ovaherero helped make this program of negative assimilation succeed. The integration of Ovaherero men into the army led to a "voluntary" adoption of the colonizers' culture. The earliest signs of the famous *Oturupa,* or troop player (*Truppenspieler*), ceremonies appeared during the period in which many Ovaherero were exchanging their own web of cultural signifiers for those of the enemy, 1905–8.[306] In the decade after World War I the *Oturupa* organized themselves into district regiments, with ranking individuals taking the names and titles of their former German officers.[307] They conducted German-style drills using sticks for rifles and sent one another "handwritten notes in German."[308] The *Oturupa* (like the Protestant church) took on new meanings in subsequent decades, becoming a site of mutual aid and resistance to the South African colonial state. But it is also evident that it emerged from the post-1904, postgenocide context of defeat and identification with the aggressor. Moreover, the *Truppenspieler* took on an *abject* version of the enemy's culture.[309] The timing of the sudden wave of Ovaher-

306. Durham 1993, vol. 2, p. 224. Young Ovaherero men were observed by Curt von François wearing German-style uniforms and drilling "according to the German rule book" as early as 1891 (Henrichsen 2004, p. 166). But the next sightings of Ovaherero drilling are from 1916 (Werner 1990, p. 382).

307. W. Werner 1990, pp. 482, 484.

308. Durham 1993, vol. 2, p. 226; Gewald 2003, p. 172.

309. There is also evidence that Ovaherero women had been shifting from their traditional clothing to long, Victorian-style dresses and other European fashions before the war, though this seems to have intensified afterward (Rust 1905). One anthropologist has insisted quite implausibly that "the reason for wearing the uniforms" was never "in imitation of the European colonialists" (Hendrickson 1992, p. 132). Hendrickson traces the connections between the Ovaherero troop ceremonies and earlier practices of *okuyambere,* visiting the "fathers" at their graves, and celebrations of Ovaherero heroes. But there was no long historical Ovaherero tradition of competitive dancing or parading (Durham 1993, vol. 2, p. 229). Hendrickson accepts at face value the statements of her contemporary Ovaherero informants that they "wore the clothes of their bosses" because "if you wear the clothes of your enemy, the spirit of the enemy is weakened" (Hendrickson 1992, p. 238). Here she misses the important point that Ovaherero did *not* adopt the clothing of their *Khoikhoi* enemies or Orlam overlords in the nineteenth century, which suggests that the cultural developments after 1904 had a fundamentally different quality. Clearly the problem is a theoretical one that cannot be resolved in strictly empirical terms by reference to actors' self-interpretations and one that turns on the conceptualization of subjectivity and culture. The fact that the Ovaherero adopted the signifiers of the Germans but not of their earlier Khoikhoi enemies, and that they did so en masse only after the defeat of 1904, is the crucial point. A more nuanced position is offered by W. Werner (1990), who acknowledges the peculiarity of adopting the customs of the aggressor while also stressing the troop societies' role in mutual aid and resistance during

ero conversion immediately after the war underscores the context of social crisis in which these cultural transformations occurred.[310] It is noteworthy, for example, that the *Truppenspieler* "could easily have turned around, and imitated the South African administration," but that uniforms modeled on the Union defense forces were in fact not introduced for several generations.[311] The "voluntary" changes in Ovaherero culture thus corresponded to the main thrust of postwar colonial native policy, even if the Germans did not directly engineer them (and sometimes even opposed them).[312] This was one instance in which the colonized did contribute to designing, or at least revising, some of their own native policies.

No native policy scheme was ever guaranteed to succeed, or even to survive, as was shown by the breakdown of Leutwein's collaborative system with the Witbooi. The Ovaherero were not transferred to the southern part of the colony en masse, and the Khoikhoi were not moved northward.[313] Ovaherero locations were not supervised as closely as originally intended,

---

the 1920s and 1930s. By contrast, Gewald insists overdramatically that depth-psychological studies "have done what the German colonial state so anxiously hoped for but failed to do: rob the Herero completely of independent action and thought" (1998a, p. 5). This seems to reflect a well-intentioned but theoretically naive desire to ally with the forces of "agency" over "structure," as if wishing for a world in which voluntaristic ontology applies and structural constraints are absent could bring that world into existence.

310. The percentage of Ovaherero who had converted to Christianity before the war was extremely low; see chap. 2, n. 234. The mass baptisms after 1904 probably occurred because the church offered a replacement for national solidarity and the missionaries a substitute for the lost Ovaherero chiefs (Bley [1971] 1996, p. 257). It is a remarkable parallel to the rapid adoption of Christianity by the "battered remnants of Khoikhoi communities of the Eastern and Western Cape in the late eighteenth and early nineteenth centuries," societies that were in a "state of profound crisis" (Elbourne 1992, p. 3). This emphasis on the crisis context in which Christianity is adopted does not make the converts mere victims or dupes; in the case of Hendrik Witbooi, missionary doctrines were reformulated in empowering ways, and this was certainly the case for some of the Ovaherero converts after 1904. As we will see in chap. 5, the Samoans converted to Christianity en masse during a period of much less profound social crisis, but rather than abandoning their existing culture and creating a new one they largely adapted the new religion to it.

311. Durham 1993, vol. 2, pp. 229–30.

312. Lieutenant Streitwolf was appalled to see an Ovaherero refugee in British Bechuanaland wearing the uniform of a fallen German, for example, and he complained to the British district official, who promised to at least remove the insignia from the uniform. See Streitwolf's report on his 1905 trip to the Lake Ngami district, August 24, 1905, BA-Berlin, RKA, vol. 2118, p. 181v; on Streitwolf, see Stals 1979.

313. Dove 1913a, p. 59. See statistics on the distribution of Ovaherero in *Die deutschen Schutzgebiete in Afrika und der Südsee*, 1912/13, Statistischer Teil, p. 46. Only Gibeon and Keetmanshoop in the south had appreciable numbers of Ovaherero at this time.

and the population of many *werfts* grew far beyond the size stipulated by the original ordinance. The population of some of the prewar Ovaherero districts, such as Okahandja and Omaruru, again became predominantly Ovaherero after 1908.[314] Some Ovaherero had already begun to replenish their herds of cattle before 1914 through arrangements with the government and illicit deals with settlers in exchange for services.[315] When the South African troops entered the colony in 1915, Ovaherero moved quickly to "recoup some of the losses suffered under the Germans, both in terms of acquiring means of production and recreating new social and political structures on the shattered foundations."[316] But neither Ovaherero resistance nor the relative weakness of the colonial state were enough to prompt an overall change in the direction of native policy before 1914.

Collaboration and the Rule of Difference: The Rehoboth Basters under German Rule

Above all I want to reject the common view that each Bastard . . . inherits *only* the bad traits of the two mixing races, that every Bastard is worse than *both* parental races. *That is incorrect!* . . . Nonetheless, he is often *truly* worse than both of the parental races, for the following reason: the character of the lower native race often includes more violent, cruel, and cunning traits. Yet the imposed constraints of civilization prevent the Bastard from following these instincts. Along with this heritage, the Bastard also receives a portion of intelligence from the other side, and is thus equipped to find ways to burst the chains and to express his primitive instincts. He becomes much nastier and more bestial than the *pure* savage. Malevolence and meanness require intelligence in order to be cleverly carried out.

EUGEN FISCHER[317]

I attribute the alleged inferiority of the Bastards almost entirely to the social milieu, to their being expelled from the "higher" race, and so on.

EUGEN FISCHER[318]

314. See population statistics for Okahandja and Omaruru in *Deutsches Kolonialblatt* 20 (1909): 62, 404.

315. Hintrager to RKA, August 30, 1912, BA-Berlin, RKA, vol. 2097, p. 5; also Hintrager to RKA, August 26, 1913, ibid., p. 12v. On the methods of gaining livestock illicitly see Gewald 1998a, p. 235; also Krüger 1998, 1999.

316. W. Werner 1990, p. 479.

317. E. Fischer 1909b, p. 1050.

318. E. Fischer 1914, pp. 16–17.

THE DOUBLING OF HYBRIDITY

German colonial officials perceived the Rehoboth Basters as presenting the same basic challenge as the Witbooi. Their goal was to find a way to stabilize a culture that seemed to shift uncontrollably between positions of similarity and difference, a culture in which (in the colonizer's view) "difference" was enhanced and rendered even "nastier and more bestial" by civilized intelligence, as geneticist Eugen Fischer argued.[319] The challenge to any colonial regime was to elaborate a network of signs that promised to put an end to this constant oscillation. In the case of the Basters this problem was further complicated by the fact that the poles of similarity and difference were defined not only in terms of culture but also biological "race." By contrast, "biculturalism" among the Witbooi was attributed to their participation in two separate psychic and cultural worlds. By the late nineteenth century most Europeans defined race in biological or genetic terms. Some scientists argued that "mixed-race" populations might become a genetically stable "new type," while others believed they would remain forever "in flux," expressing a mishmash of traits from both parent races, splitting into two opposing types, or reverting to one of the two ancestral genotypes.[320] The instability of "mixed-race" peoples could thus be a function of race, culture, or both.

Some writers have suggested that "mixed-race" people are *always* unsettling for colonial regimes.[321] But the sweeping denunciations of "mixed marriage" and "half-breeds" in the German colonies after 1900 have obscured, for historians, the *distinguishing* thrust of the racist imagination. A mixed *racial* heritage was not always unsettling to Europeans. Because they drew sharp distinctions among different non-European cultures, representations of partly European communities could vary as a function of the perception of the indigenous ancestry. Indeed, throughout the colonial era most Germans described the Rehoboth Basters as the native group with whom the colonial power could "certainly accomplish the most."[322] The Basters' "admixture of white blood" was often understood as making them more

319. The historiography on the Rehoboth Basters is very thin; see Bayer 1906; E. Fischer 1909a, 1909b, 1913; Oosthuizen 1996; Britz et al. 1990; and the special issue, edited by Dr. K. F. R. Budack, of the journal *Namibiana*, no. 13 (1997). Kjæret and Stokke 2003 deals with the Rehoboth Basters after 1990.

320. E. Fischer 1909b, p. 1050.

321. E.g., Schulte-Althoff 1985.

322. "Entwickelung der Dinge im Namaqua- und Damra-Lande," *Berichte der RMG* 41 (2, February 1885): 36.

reliable and "amenable to civilization" than other groups in the colony. In nineteenth-century Samoa, by contrast, "half-castes" were regularly described as particularly "troublesome."[323] These divergent constructions of half-castes cannot be traced to objective differences in behavior. Just as there were eager "half-caste" collaborators with the Germans in Samoa, some of the Rehoboth Basters took up arms against the Germans in 1904. During the years leading up to the First World War many Germans believed that mingled populations, including the Basters, provided the agitators and leaders for native uprisings because their "in-between position" (*Zwitterstellung*) inevitably turned them into "dissatisfied elements."[324] The figure of the "dangerous half-caste" was present here as well, and it was codified in a legal ban on mixed marriages in 1905.[325]

It is therefore puzzling that German native policy concerning the Rehobothers did *not* change significantly during the three decades of colonial rule, despite the deepening fissures in ethnographic discourse and the supposed panic around intermarriage. German native policy with respect to the Rehobothers was a program of enforced intermediateness. Cultural hybridity should not be confused with mimicry: the former denotes a stabilizing solution that a colonial regime seeks to impose while the latter refers to the "unstable" condition that native policy sets out to remedy. The policies directed at the Rehoboth Basters combined unique privileges with adherence to the rule of colonial difference.

GERMAN NATIVE POLICY AND THE REHOBOTH BASTERS

By the 1880s there were three Baster communities in Southwest Africa, located at Rehoboth, Grootfontein, and Rietfontein.[326] In October 1884 the Rehobothers (whose precolonial history was discussed in the preceding chap-

---

323. Salesa 1997.

324. "Die südafrikanischen Bastards: Betrachtungen zur Rassenfrage," *Kolonie und Heimat* 4 (13, 1910): 3.

325. On the German discussion of *Mischlinge* and *Mischehen* in this period, see Schulte-Althoff 1985; Wildenthal 2001, chap. 3. Good examples of this discourse of fear include P. Acker (Provincial der Väter vom heiligen Geist), "Zur Frage der Rassenmischehe," *Koloniale Rundschau* 3 (1912): 462–68; and Rohrbach 1907, pp. 54–58; see also Hermann 1906; G. Braun 1912; and Grentrup 1914. On the 1905 ban see Schmidt-Lauber 1998, pp. 367–73.

326. BA-Berlin, RKA, vols. 2167, 2170, and 2171. Individual Basters also lived scattered among various *werfts*. This underscores the fact that "tribal" names in Southwest Africa often referred to sociopolitical entities, despite the colonial state's efforts to erect sharp distinctions among "tribes" and "races." For instance, one Baster family was first associated with the Berseba Khoikhoi leader Dietrich Izaak and moved with the latter to Gibeon in 1894, joining the newly pacified and resettled Witbooi (Burgsdorff-Garath 1982, p. 31).

ter) signed a treaty with an agent of Adolf Lüderitz named Hoepfner. On September 15, 1885, they concluded a "Treaty of Protection and Friendship" with the German government.[327] The Rehobothers were the most significant Baster community in Southwest Africa, both politically and numerically—perhaps 2,500 of the colony's 3,500 Basters lived there. In 1896 the Grootfontein Basters, led by Klaas Swartz (or Swart), signed a treaty in which they agreed to provide military assistance to the Germans.[328] When they rebelled in 1901, the male Grootfonteiners became prisoners in Windhoek and their women were integrated into the Rehoboth community.[329] The community of the so-called Philander (Vilander) Basters was located on both sides of the border between the German colony and British Bechuanaland, but most were at Rietfontein.[330]

The Germans treated the Rehobothers as a political and spatial "wedge between the Ovaherero and the Hottentots."[331] Rehoboth was in a useful location for the colonizers, lying directly between the southern homeland of most of the colony's Khoikhoi and the central and northern zones where most Ovaherero lived. In exchange for their cooperation the Basters were granted various privileges. The Germans treated the Rehoboth territory like a native reservation even before that term had entered the colony's lexicon. This meant that the Basters were self-governing to an extent not found in any of the other nominally self-governing indigenous communities. The 1885 protection treaty recognized the "rights and freedoms" of the Rehobothers as an "independent" people. Article 7 referred to "the two governments" as being committed to resolving "any other issues that might arise" through "agreements." This suggested a certain legal equality between Germany and Rehoboth.[332] One critic of the Basters' privileged status

---

327. See the Rehobothers' letter requesting the protection of the German kaiser, October 11, 1884, VEM, RMG 3.538b, p. 188; the first draft of the 1884 treaty in ibid., pp. 195–96; and Esterhuyse 1968, p. 70.

328. See "Abschluß eines Wehrvertrages mit den Bastards," *Deutsches Kolonialblatt* 8 (1897): 168–69; and "Jahresberichte der Station Grootfontein," *Deutsches Kolonialblatt* 8 (1897): 543–44.

329. Heidmann's letter to the RMG deputation, January 15, 1902, VEM, RMG 3.538b, p. 310; Leutnant Gentz, "Die Geschichte des südwestafrikanischen Bastardvolkes," *Globus* 84 (1903): 29.

330. Leutwein to Chancellor Caprivi, October 18, 1897, BA-Berlin, RKA, vol. 2167, p. 4; on the Rietfontein Basters, see Union of South Africa 1927, p. 30.

331. Schinz 1891, p. 516. The idea of creating such a wedge was also developed with respect to German settlers; see "Die Besiedelung des südwestafrikanischen Schutzgebietes mit deutschen Bauern," *Deutsches Kolonialblatt* 1 (1890): 91–93.

332. See the text of the treaty in *Stenographische Berichte über die Verhandlungen des Reichstags*, 6th legislative period, 2nd session, 1885–86, Anlagen, vol. 100, document no. 277,

complained that Rehoboth was a "state within a state."[333] The Rehobother captain continued to collect taxes from his people throughout the colonial period. Whites living in the territory did not benefit from fiscal extraterritoriality, but were required to pay these taxes. In 1885 Germany also "undertook to respect all existing treaties concluded between the Rehoboth Community and other nations."[334] The Rehobothers' Governing Council (*Volksraad*, or *Gemeinderat*) continued to deliberate and to enact new laws throughout the German colonial period.[335] Like the rest of the colony, Rehoboth was slowly integrated into the German administration, which was represented locally by a district officer.[336] When Baster captain Hermanus van Wyk died in 1905, after twenty-nine years in office, the Germans did not permit the Basters to elect a new captain. As in Samoa, the colonial rulers gradually removed certain aspects of indigenous sovereignty. But also as in Samoa, they did not try to transform Rehobother culture, and even protected it from various external threats.

The Basters' special status within the colonial regime is indicated by the legal arrangements that were created by the 1885 treaty. Legal conflicts between Europeans and Africans were the main arena in which the "protection" treaties of the 1880s eroded native sovereignty. Germans were never required to stand before an indigenous judge, but the opposite was not true. The Rehobothers' situation was exceptional. The Rehobothers had already written up a legal code before German annexation, and it remained in effect after 1885.[337] Civil or criminal legal cases that pitted Rehobothers against Europeans were to be judged by a mixed court (*ein gemischtes Gericht*) with a German and a Baster judge appointed by the kaiser and the Rehoboth cap-

---

p. 1388. The signatories were Carl Büttner, as the representative of the German kaiser; missionary Johann Heidmann; Hermanus van Wyk, the captain of the Rehoboth Basters; and six other Baster men.

333. Zwergern 1911.

334. Secretariat of the United Nations 1955, p. 175.

335. Dr. Y. J. D. Peters, "On the Discrimination of the Rehoboth Basters," paper prepared for the eleventh session of the Working Group on Indigenous Populations and the 45th Session of the Subcommission on Prevention of Discrimination and Protection of Minorities of the United Nations Commission on Human Rights, Geneva, July–August 1993.

336. This official was called *Distriktchef* until 1910 and *Bezirksamtmann* thereafter. See "Verfügung des Gouverneurs, betr. die Umwandlung der Distrikämter Rehoboth und Warmbad in Bezirksämter," *Deutsches Kolonialblatt* 21 (1910): 620.

337. The legal code of 1872 and the revisions of 1876 built upon the original communal ordinance (*Gemeente Ordening voor het Institut Komaggas*) dated August 12, 1857. See Union of South Africa 1927, p. 26 and Annexures 3 and 6; ibid., pp. 79–91; also Secretariat of the United Nations 1955, pp. 181–88.

tain.[338] In most of the other protection treaties, adjudication of "legal conflicts between the races" was carried out by the German kaiser via his local representative.[339] In the 1885 treaty with the Ovaherero, for example, the imperial commissary was to judge mixed cases with the "assistance" of an Ovaherero Council member (*unter Zuziehung eines Rathsmitgliedes*), and the latter was accepted only for the time being.[340] This unusual situation was partly "corrected" by a decree in 1889 that transferred the adjudication of ordinary civil "disputes between whites and [Baster] natives (where the Defendant is a native) . . . to the administrative organs of the Protectorate." It was still stipulated that "a native assessor [is] to be called in, in accordance with the Protection Treaties."[341] According to the German public prosecutor who served in Rehoboth between 1907 and 1912, the district official in that period "decided [each] case and passed sentence." The Baster assessors were appointed not by their own captain or council but by the German district official, whom they "did not sit next to . . . on the Bench." They "had no right to ask the witness any questions" and were not consulted before sentence was passed, but were "only allowed to make representations after sentence."[342] Nonetheless, Rehobothers continued to be positioned above other native groups in legal terms, even if they were now clearly subordinated to the Europeans in a "rule of difference."

Another unique aspect of the Rehobothers' situation was the size and integrity of their territory. The 1885 protection treaty gave the Basters the right to determine the conditions under which foreigners could settle in their country. Commissary Goering's first official report on the Basters noted that Rehoboth's earlier inhabitants, the Swartbooi, or //Khau-/goan, whom he called the "wanderlustigste Hottentottenstamm" (the most wanderlusty Hottentot tribe), had relinquished their claims on the territory, and that the Basters were now "rightly laying claim to Rehoboth."[343] Most Ger-

338. See *Stenographische Berichte über die Verhandlungen des Reichstags*, 6th legislative period, 2nd session, 1885–86, Anlagen, vol. 100, document no. 277, p. 1388; and Esterhuyse 1968, p. 103.

339. Sudholt 1975, p. 50.

340. "German-Herero Treaty" of October 23, 1885, in *Stenographische Berichte über die Verhandlungen des Reichstags*, 6th legislative period, 2nd session, 1885–86, Anlagen, vol. 100, document no. 277, p. 1389. This treaty held out the possibility that a different method could be determined by a future "special agreement between His Majesty the German Kaiser's Government and the chiefs in Hereroland."

341. Union of South Africa 1927, p. 61.

342. Lahmeyer, in Union of South Africa 1927, p. 59.

343. Goering to von Bismarck, November 21, 1885, BA-Berlin, RKA, vol. 2124, pp. 2r, 4r.

man commentators considered the Basters' territory to be inviolable in this period.[344] Attempts were made during the next three decades to encroach on the Rehobothers' land, and some officials insisted that it was being held by the Basters only "provisionally."[345] But there was little change. Following the defeat of Hendrik Witbooi in 1894, Leutwein and the Rehobothers drew up a map of Rehoboth. Friedrich von Lindequist, heading a boundary commission to determine the western borders of "Bastardland" in 1898, argued that the area granted to the Basters was much too large for such a small group.[346] But Leutwein insisted on keeping the existing borders, with minor alterations.[347] No other changes were made to Rehoboth's borders during the German colonial period, even if some land was placed under eminent domain by the government for the construction of a railway and other projects.[348]

Although Rehoboth was initially seen as too arid for European settlement, by the 1890s it was being described as perhaps the best real estate in the country.[349] The settlers who began arriving complained about the Basters' unwillingness to sell land or even to lease it for more than five years.[350] In contrast to the situation in the "reservations," there were no legal barriers to selling Rehoboth land to outsiders except for the approval of the community's own Governing Council. Unlike the Ovaherero and Khoikhoi, the Basters divided most of their territory into individual farms, but the land continued to be owned by the community in common. By the 1920s no more than a quarter of Rehoboth had been sold to outsiders.[351] The most

344. Kienetz 1976, p. 715 n. 1.

345. Deputy Governor Tecklenburg to Colonial Department, July 17, 1905, BA-Berlin, RKA, vol. 1212, p. 30v.

346. Deputy Governor von Lindequist to Colonial Department, January 30, 1898, BA-Berlin, RKA, vol. 2124, p. 34.

347. Leutwein to Colonial Department, March 24, 1898, BA-Berlin, RKA, vol. 2124, p. 44; and letter from Acting Governor von Lindequist to Colonial Department, January 30, 1898, ibid., p. 37r.

348. For a sense of Rehoboth's territorial integrity see the map bound between pages 98 and 99 in Union of South Africa 1927; and the memorandum of Mr. Dewdney W. Drew, in ibid., pp. 208–309. On the Rehobothers' complaints about illegal German land seizures, see Secretariat of the United Nations 1955, pp. 178–79.

349. Zwergern 1911. According to Paul Rohrbach (1907, p. 144), "not a few experts declare Bastardland . . . to be the best part of the colony for grazing cattle."

350. See report by Governor von Lindequist, April 13, 1906, BA-Berlin, RKA, vol. 2124, p. 65v.

351. See Heidmann's reports, April 20, 1898, and mid-January 1900, VEM, RMG 3.538b, pp. 290v and 301v. District official Böttlin estimated that the Basters had alienated about one-

serious threat to territorial integrity came from mining companies and set-tlers. In the original 1884 treaty, Lüderitz's agent had gained the right to first options on any mining concessions that the Basters might decide to sell, and these rights were inherited by the German Colonial Society for South West Africa. European companies mounted prospecting expeditions in Rehoboth in 1888, 1899–1900, and 1910, but they were never able to lo-cate enough gold or copper for a profitable mining operation.[352] If they had succeeded, the relative equilibrium in "Bastardland" would probably have been disrupted.

By 1910 colonial officials were beginning to argue that the Basters' grip on their territory would have to be broken. The district official for Rehoboth, First Lieutenant Hölscher, wrote to Berlin that it was "an obvious require-ment of our colonization that most of the Bastards' land, which is the very best land—the very heartland of the colony—will some day become white property; it is only a question of how we will achieve this goal."[353] Yet the Germans made few moves in this direction before 1915. The Rehobothers' ability to hold on to their "tribal" land up to the present day, despite severe restrictions on their self-government by the South Africans after 1925,[354] is the strongest evidence of their favored status within the colonial system, especially when considered against the massive land losses suffered by the Khoikhoi and Ovaherero.

As with the Witbooi, the emergence of a colonial strategy for regulat-ing the Basters was closely tied to the establishment of the *Schutztruppe*. Here again the Basters had a unique status. The first *Schutztruppe* in the colony was organized by the German Colonial Society, and it consisted of

---

sixth of their total possession to white people between 1898 and 1905 (Union of South Africa 1927, p. 186, Böttlin's report of July 15, 1905).

352. On the 1888 exploration see Heidmann, "Stationsbericht über Rehoboth 1888 (Janu-ary 1888)," VEM, RMG 3.538a, p. 215v; on the 1899–1900 and 1910 explorations see Drechsler 1996, chaps. 2.2 and 3.3. Although the colonial government succeeded in 1912 in obtaining a "formal declaration of waiver" of the Basters' rights to control all prospecting or mining within their territory, this was subsequent to the unsuccessful prospecting expedition in 1910 and posed little danger. Nonetheless, even this concession was obtained by the government "with great difficulty, and after exercising pressure" (Goldblatt 1971, p. 153; see also "Exhibit 'V,'" in Union of South Africa 1927, p. 150).

353. Hölscher to State Secretary of the Colonies von Lindequist, "Report on the Mood and Situation in Bastardland," November 30, 1910, BA-Berlin, RKA, vol. 2124, pp. 129r-v. Ironi-cally, Hölscher described himself as a "representative of the Bastard Council" (ibid., p. 129r). But this was in line with the self-understanding of the "native commissioners," whose role was advocacy and protection as well as surveillance and control.

354. See Budack 1974; Secretariat of the United Nations 1955.

two officers, five noncommissioned officers, and twenty Rehobothers.[355] In 1893, Rehoboth *kaptein* Hermanus van Wyk agreed to provide Captain von François with fifty men for the operations against Hendrik Witbooi. This was the first time an indigenous group was enlisted in the government *Schutz-truppe*.[356] In 1894 Theodor Leutwein included a large number of Basters in his campaign against Hendrik Witbooi.[357] In 1895 the Basters were the first indigenous community to sign a treaty committing themselves to supply the *Schutztruppe* with soldiers on a regular basis.[358] Baster soldiers helped suppress uprisings of Khauas and Ovambanderu in 1896, the Swartbooi in 1898, and Bondelswarts in 1903.[359] According to Eugen Fischer, General von Trotha "honored the Basters by allowing them (and the Witboois)," alone among the "helping peoples" (*Hilfsvölker*), to "remain on the front lines" during the "Herero campaign."[360]

This special treatment was counterbalanced by a constant concern with retaining a clear line of demarcation between Basters and "whites." The Basters' name called attention to their second-class status and illegitimacy, at least in European eyes. They were defined as natives (*Eingeborene*) in colonial law and official correspondence.[361] This approach was continuous with the protocolonial interventions by W. Coates Palgrave, for whom the category of native had "expressly included the Basters."[362] When it became clear

355. Sudholt 1975, p. 134.

356. Missionary Heidmann's report on Rehoboth for the period January 1893–May 1893, VEM, RMG 3.538b, p. 259r–v.

357. Missionary Heidmann's report on Rehoboth for the period mid-August 1893 through the end of May 1894, VEM, RMG 3.538b, p. 268r; Heidmann to Schreiber, July 24, 1894, in ibid., p. 269v; Heidmann's report of October 23, 1894, in ibid., p. 273v; T. Leutwein 1907a, p. 41.

358. Reheboth promised to provide each year for military training fifteen to twenty men, who would then serve as reserves. See *Deutsches Kolonialblatt* 6 (1895): 535-36; 8 (1897): 168-69; and T. Leutwein 1907a, pp. 216-18.

359. See Bayer [1906] 1984, pp. 28, 30; missionary Heidmann's report of April 20, 1898, VEM, RMG 3.538b, p. 291r; and Budack 1974, p. 41.

360. E. Fischer 1913, p. 41; see also "Unsere Bastardsoldaten in Südwestafrika," *Militär-Wochenblatt* 90 (III, 1905): 2540-42.

361. See, for example, "Verfügung zur Ausführung der Kaiserlichen Verordnung, betreffend die Eheschließung und die Beurkundung des Personenstandes für das südwestafrikanische Schutzgebiet, vom 8. November 1892," in *Deutsches Kolonialblatt* 5 (1894): 122, which specified that the Basters were to count as "natives" for the purposes of the law. A decision by the Windhoek High Court in 1913 reaffirmed that "everyone whose genealogical tree can be traced back from mother's or father's side to a native, therefore also a *Baster*, must be considered as being a native and be treated accordingly" (Union of South Africa 1927, p. 193).

362. Missionary Heidmann's report from Rehoboth, February 1880, VEM, RMG 3.538b, p. 130r.

that children of Rehobother women and German men were able to become German citizens under existing law, the colonial regime moved to remedy this violation of the rule of difference. The borderline between Baster and white was breached in a handful of widely discussed cases. Basters with German citizenship (or Basters recognized as British subjects) were increasingly visible in white colonial society and some attended schools for European children.[363] Some suggested that the rule of difference could be reasserted if mixed-"race" individuals were permitted to join European society on a case-by-case basis, with the decision contingent on showing evidence of complete cultural assimilation.[364]

The Basters were not unaffected by the colony's overall shift toward more repressive native policies and by the intensification of blood-based racism, but the impact was less dramatic than for the Ovaherero and Khoikhoi. The Rehobothers were not encompassed in the orders expropriating tribal property after the 1904 war, and no limits were placed on their ownership of livestock. The more aggressive members of the colony's advisory Governing Council tried to include the Rehobothers in the ordinance requiring natives to carry identification tags, but the government countered that this would make them "feel like they were being equated with the other natives."[365] Basters residing in the Rehoboth district were exempted from the final version of the pass law, though it was recommended that they carry a pass when leaving their territory.[366] Rehobothers were allowed to keep their guns, although the deputy governor in 1905 indicated that disarmament was a long-term goal.[367] Like other indigenous groups, they were prohibited from appointing a captain after the 1904-7 war, but they were allowed to elect a Foreman (*Gemeindevorsteher*). The Rehobothers continued to refer to their leader as "captain" nevertheless.[368] They retained complete control over "all matters that concern[ed] the internal, private affairs of minor

363. See Gentz 1902-3, p. 91; Wildenthal 2001, pp. 92-93.

364. E.g., Gentz 1902-3, pp. 91-92.

365. Windhoek Governing Council meeting of October 16, 1906, BA-Berlin, RKA, vol. 2174, p. 52r.

366. *Deutsches Kolonialblatt* 18 (1907): 1181-82; also von Lindequist's circular of August 18, 1907, on the "control and identity marker requirement for natives," in Köbner and Gerstmeyer 1908, pp. 352-57; and "Die südafrikanischen Bastards: Betrachtungen zur Rassenfrage," *Kolonie und Heimat* 4 (13, 1910): 3.

367. Deputy Governor Tecklenburg to Colonial Department, July 17, 1905, BA-Berlin, RKA, vol. 1212, p. 31r.

368. Eugen Fischer to RKA, August 28, 1912, reporting that Cornelius von Wyk was still generally referred to as captain in Rehoboth, BA-Berlin, RKA, vol. 2124, p. 168r.

importance," even if the "more important affairs" were now to be resolved through joint discussions between the district official and the Rehoboth *Gemeinderat*.[369] The policy of minimal government interference in Rehobother affairs was reaffirmed in 1906 when the settler Carl Schlettwein insisted at a meeting of the Governing Council that "there are many people in the Rehoboth Bastard area who are more Hottentot than Bastard and do not deserve any special status." The government replied that the Basters' own "council of elders" should be charged with weeding out any inauthentic residents.[370]

One of the most dramatic assertions of the rule of difference involved the instruction to marriage registry officials that "effective 1 January 1906, they were no longer to perform civil marriage ceremonies between 'whites' and 'natives,' including Basters."[371] Nevertheless, religious marriages between Europeans and Bastards continued in some cases.[372] Opponents of race mixing argued that German men were particularly attracted to Baster women, since they were Christian and Europeanized, sedentary, spoke Dutch, and, as one German writer approvingly reported, sometimes had a part in their hair. Rehobothers were also more likely to bring a sizable dowry to a marriage than other indigenous women.[373] There was fear that the German soldiers who remained in the colony after the war would marry Rehobother women, which would add to the population of *Mischlinge* (mulattoes) with

369. Report by Governor von Lindequist, April 13, 1906, BA-Berlin, RKA, vol. 2124, p. 65r. See the article "Über eine Dienstreise im Gebiet der Rehobother Bastards," *Deutsches Kolonialblatt* 17 (1906): 400–401. The Basters' 1874 communal constitution was actually more democratic than the German one at the time, insofar as women had the right to vote (female suffrage was introduced in Germany in the Weimar Republic). The Baster legal code specified that a husband who left his wife "without cause" would have his goods confiscated and "given to the wife" and that "ill treatment" of one's wife was a criminal offense (articles 46 and 52). German commentators failed to notice that the Basters were actually more advanced in this respect than their colonizers. See "Die südafrikanischen Bastards: Betrachtungen zur Rassenfrage," *Kolonie und Heimat* 4 (13, 1910): 3.

370. Windhoek Governing Council meeting of October 16, 1906, BA-Berlin, RKA, vol. 2174, p. 57r. On Schlettwein see Bley [1971] 1996, p. 227 n. 186.

371. Instruction by Tecklenburg and Oskar Hintrager, quoted in Wildenthal 2001, p. 94.

372. See "Eine Kriegserklärung gegen die weisse Rasse?" *Keetmanshooper Zeitung*, May 22, 1912, pp. 2–3, on a Catholic marriage ceremony in Gibeon, performed by the prefect of the southern region of the protectorate, wedding a German man with a "Bastard girl."

373. "Die südwestafrikanischen Bastards," *Kolonie und Heimat* 1 (13, 1908): 6; "Die südafrikanischen Bastards: Betrachtungen zur Rassenfrage," *Kolonie und Heimat* 4 (13, 1910): 3; Schreiber 1909, p. 95. As the authors of the 1925 South African De Villiers commission report pointed out, "in Rietfontein and Rehoboth, according to *Baster* law and custom, a white man marrying a *Baster* woman obtained a farm with his bride" (Union of South Africa 1927, p. 18).

German citizenship who might not remain sequestered in Rehoboth but would instead move into European settler society.[374] Such Germanized "half-castes" were much more threatening than the original Basters, who kept to themselves.

The decree banning mixed marriage did not mark a fundamental shift in the treatment of the Rehobothers but was largely an attempt to *maintain* a colonial status quo in which the Basters were both privileged and dominated.[375] The colonizers' original definition of the Rehobothers was centered on their stabilized mixture of blood rather than any prognosis of a change in the balance of white and Khoikhoi blood.[376] Lieutenant Kurd Schwabe distinguished between Basters and *Mischlinge,* arguing that the former were a stable union (*Verband*) that had inherited the whites' "good characteristics" and that "leaned more toward the whites than toward the natives due to the preponderance of European blood in their veins." This made them "loyal and valuable allies," and indeed, they were "the only tribe we can rely on in the moment of danger."[377]

Nonetheless, the *debate* on mixed marriage did start to unsettle the assumptions that undergirded official policy toward the Rehobothers. If the categories "Baster" and "Mischling" were interchangeable, as contemporary discussions often suggested, that suggested that the Basters were *not* a hermetically sealed community. All of the threats associated with race mixing could then bleed over into discussions of the Rehobothers.

I will return below to the relationship between the older category of "Baster" and the post-1904 discussions of race mixing, but first I want to ask about the forces that animated native policies toward this group before 1904. The crucial determinants of German native policy toward the Basters were ethnographic imagery and patterns of collaboration, or cooperation.

374. T. Leutwein 1909, p. 313. The actual numbers of mixed marriages were very small, however; see Hermann 1906; Schulte-Althoff 1985, p. 54 n. 6.

375. As Wildenthal 2001, pp. 89–90, points out, Curt von François, Theodor Leutwein, and Henning von Burgsdorff had already opposed mixed marriage during the 1890s. Oberregierungsrat Schreiber defended the marriage ban and "keeping the German race pure" while insisting that the Basters "who have arisen now, i.e., under German rule, have German blood in their veins and are not the same as Bastards who arose in earlier periods. They are more intelligent than natives and also have a higher moral standing than the colored." "Zur Frage der Mischehen zwischen Weißen und Eingeborenen im deutschen Schutzgebiete Südwestafrika," *Zeitschrift für Kolonialpolitik, Kolonialrecht und Kolonialwirtschaft* 11 (2, 1909): 88, 96.

376. For contrasting projects of racial whitening as official projects of postcolonial states see Loveman 2001, on Brazil; and Palmer 2000, on Australia.

377. Kurd Schwabe 1910, pp. 41, 238; 1899, p. 39.

Since the Basters did not provide a mirror for imaginary identifications, disagreements among German officials about the proper treatment of the Basters were rare.

THE PRECOLONIAL ETHNOGRAPHIC ARCHIVE AND THE EVOLUTION OF DISCOURSE ON THE BASTERS

As with the other two communities discussed in this chapter, native policy in the case of Rehoboth was haunted by precoloniality. The Basters had already been treated as more reliable than other indigenous groups before 1884. The career of the Rehobothers' long-serving missionary Johann Heidmann spanned both eras. Eugen Fischer, the leading expert on the Basters during the German colonial period, consulted with Heidmann.

The prevailing opinion in Southwest Africa during the first two decades of German rule was that the Basters were a comforting ally, vastly preferable to other groups of natives. In one of the Foreign Office's earliest reports on the colony the Rehobothers were discussed as "powerful, intelligent and especially well suited for induction into European civilization." [378] According to Lieutenant Hugo von François, "the future of the colony clearly belongs to this mixed race"; they were "definitely the best element in the land." [379] Von François described the Basters as "better herdsmen and farmers than the Herero and Berg Damara, useful for all purposes as workers," while Theodor Leutwein considered them to be "good soldier material"—as good as the German recruits. [380] A series of articles published at the end of the 1880s by the plenipotentiary of the German Colonial Society in Southwest Africa agreed that the Basters were a "peaceful, diligent, and orderly people," the "best element in Nama- and Damaland," who "had to be respected in every possible way." [381] The Basters' "white blood" made them more, not less, attractive to most of the colonizers. Captain Maximilian Bayer, the

378. Von Bismarck to kaiser, February 24, 1886, BA-Berlin, RKA, vol. 2124, p. 15v.

379. H. von François 1895, p. 239; "Die Landschaft um Windhoek (Südwest-Afrika) nach einem Bericht des Lieutenants v. François," *Deutsches Kolonialblatt* 2 (1891): 354.

380. "Die Landschaft um Windhoek (Südwest-Afrika) nach einem Bericht des Lieutenants v. François," p. 354; Leutwein's report in "Deutsch-Südwestafrika: Ueber die Frage der Heranziehung der Eingeborenen zum Militärdienst," *Deutsches Kolonialblatt* 7 (1896): 642.

381. E. Hermann, "Groß-Namaland," *Deutsche Kolonialzeitung*, n.s., 3 (13, 1890): 158; E. Hermann, "Aus Südwestafrika," *Deutsche Kolonialzeitung*, n.s., 2 (26, 1889): 204; n.s., 2 (27, 1889): 215. Ernst Hermann, who owned an estate in Pomerania and was a retired first lieutenant of the reserve, was sent to Southwest Africa by the Kolonialgesellschaft as a purchasing representative; see Esterhuyse 1968, pp. 177-78, 199.

only colonizer to write a sustained treatment of the Rehobothers, believed that their European heritage made them "easier for us to understand."[382] A mining company representative and explorer, Georg Hartmann, argued at the German Colonial Congress that the Basters were "a human type that we unquestionably have to rank above the unmixed natives."[383]

As the clamor about "mulattoes" arose, some commentators tried to differentiate between Basters and other "half-castes." An article in the journal *Globus* began by criticizing the colony's "half-castes," claiming that they "frequently inherit only the worst traits from both races" and were "arrogant," "unreliable," and "dishonest." Yet none of this applied to the Basters, who were praised for their sedentary and orderly family lifestyle.[384] For Karl Dove, the older Baster communities were "not to be confused with the *Mischlinge* of the most recent period."[385] Governor Leutwein, who was opposed to mixed marriage and any increase in the population of "half-castes," wrote glowingly about the Basters' contributions to the German regime. The crux of this praise was the belief that Rehoboth was closed to outside influences: the Basters had not taken in any new "white blood" since their "early days" in the Cape Colony, "when white women apparently were still lacking."[386] Nonetheless, the very fact that these writers felt the need to insist on the difference between Rehobothers and other "Mischlinge" suggests that the two categories were in fact being lumped together. As we will see, Eugen Fischer was forced to retreat beyond "race" to "culture" in order to resituate the Rehobothers on solid intermediate ground.

This ethnographic formation was not entirely homogenous. Baron von Üchtritz, who was commissioned by the German Colonial Society in 1892 to study the possibility of sending out European settlers to Southwest Africa, reported that the Basters were "very indolent."[387] The Rehobothers' own

382. Bayer [1906] 1984, p. 43.

383. Hartmann 1910, p. 913.

384. Indeed, the Basters were said to be culturally more advanced than the poorer class of Boers; see Gentz, "Die Mischlinge in Deutsch-Südwestafrika," *Globus* 84 (1903): 337.

385. Dove 1913a, p. 62. See also Dove's entry, "Bastards," in Schnee 1920, vol. I, p. 140.

386. T. Leutwein 1907a, p. 417.

387. Von Üchtritz's report, quoted by Kienetz (1976, p. 714), who notes that the German Colonial Society censored this very part of von Üchtritz's handwritten report in its published version. This suggests that in 1891 this view of the Basters was not considered acceptable. Dr. Bokemeyer, the society's general secretary, also presented an exceptionally harsh picture of the Rehoboth Basters in an internal publication, but he had probably derived this material from von Üchtritz's report (ibid., p. 756).

missionary suggested in 1884 that Basters could devolve into "half Nam-aqua" under certain circumstances.[388] The official *Denkschrift* for Southwest Africa in 1893–94 described the Basters as "inconstant" (*wankelmütig*)—an adjective suggestive of the "mimicry" syndrome. Only the defeat of the Wit-booi at Hornkrans finally convinced the Basters to take the Germans' side, according to this report.[389]

Many of the Basters' critics focused on their mixed "racial" heritage, and this race-based critique took a new twist after 1900.[390] Racist ideology in the nineteenth century had sometimes argued that each additional drop of "white blood" produced a linear improvement in the racial stock. Others saw the beneficial effects of white blood as being offset in the South Afri-can context by the legendary ignobility and volatility of the "Hottentot."[391] Over time, racially mixed natives were increasingly seen as less rather than more reliable. As eugenics became mixed in with new discourses on cultural degeneration, a harsher light was cast on the Rehobothers, even though Eugen Fischer acknowledged that "racially pure groups no longer exist, except perhaps . . . in the most inaccessible parts" of the world.[392] Ac-cording to one interpreter of this fin-de-siècle zeitgeist, "fearful visions of generalized decadence, degeneration, and the biological decay of modern society were amplified into an apocalyptic feeling of decline."[393] Prominent social Darwinists like Otto Ammon and Ludwig Woltmann argued that racially mixed individuals inherited the shortcomings of the two parent races, damaging the "organic stock of the nobler race."[394] The idea that the Basters inherited the worst traits of both parents had occasionally been

388. Heidmann to missionary Schreiber, March 21, 1884, VEM, RMG 3.538b, p. 181r.

389. "Denkschrift, betreffend das südwestafrikanische Schutzgebiet" (1892–93), in *Stenog-raphische Berichte über die Verhandlungen des Reichstages*, 9th legislative period, 11th session, 1893–94, first "Anlageband," vol. 156, document no. 48 (Berlin: Julius Sittenfeld, 1894), p. 358.

390. Scheulen (1998, p. 163) argues that the negative interpretation of Basters' racial hybridity appeared only after 1908. As the examples here show, this is incorrect.

391. See Dove 1896b, p. 82, according to which the Basters inherited intelligence, inde-pendence, and industriousness from their white forebears but combined these traits with "unreliability" and "laziness" from the Khoikhoi side.

392. E. Fischer 1914, p. 3. On the relations between German eugenics and the discourse of degeneracy see Weingart, Kroll, and Bayertz 1988, pp. 73–79; and Steinmetz 1993, pp. 200–201.

393. P. Schott 1992, p. 20.

394. Woltmann 1903, p. 114. On the odious Ludwig Woltmann, see Proctor 1988. In 1909, the influential Berlin University anthropologist Felix von Luschan gently rebuked those who condemned "half-castes" as inevitably weaker, but he also agreed, in his usual opportunist manner, that it was still best to preserve racial barriers; see Luschan [1909] 1911, p. 23.

expressed in precolonial times, but now it became widespread. Anthropologist Leonhard Schultze condemned the Basters for retaining the negative traits of their Khoikhoi and white forebears while renouncing the "good sides in the tradition of their Hottentot ancestors." In an era of *völkisch* nationalism, Schultze considered it a fatal flaw that the Basters had no original, deeply historical source of *Volkstum* (national culture) from which they could "derive power."[395]

The idea of a race-based instability and degeneracy unsettled the reciprocal obligations and comfortable stereotypes that had initially organized German native policy toward the Basters. According to settler Carl Schlettwein the Basters were "very cunning characters" who combined the "craftiness of the Negro with the intelligence of the European."[396] In this formulation, the Basters' "European intelligence" was recoded as a source of risk rather than comfort. In 1911 a former colonial civil servant evoked the threat of mutiny, arguing that the Rehobothers had simply been "clever enough to officially take our side, the side of the stronger ones," in the last war.[397] The difference between Basters and other "dangerous half-castes" was being called into question.

Both the colonial government and the Colonial Office in Berlin were inclined to continue treating the Basters in the accustomed way. The Rehobothers' loyalty—whatever their motives—during the various insurgencies had been invaluable. This was especially important now that the Germans' other main native ally, the Witbooi, had been eliminated. The Rehobothers' extensive territories continued to provoke settler jealousy. Between 1905 and 1908 the settlers temporarily achieved a greater voice in the colony's affairs. But settler agriculture and demands once again became secondary after diamonds were discovered in the Namib Desert (1908) and Theodor Seitz was appointed governor (1910). The government's emphasis on mining was not impeded by Rehoboth's "self-government," since the Basters had always allowed prospectors onto their territory.

The possibility of a Baster rebellion was present even in the minds of officials who continued to defend the conventional approach. They found it increasingly difficult to defend their position against the view of the Basters as *doubly* unstable. Native policy and ethnographic discourse had come out of joint.

395. Schultze 1907, p. 132. As we saw above, Schultze criticized the Khoikhoi for the same thing—giving up their customs.

396. Schlettwein 1907, p. 173.

397. Zwergern 1911.

EUGEN FISCHER: BASTER CULTURE AS A *MITTELDING*

The most significant contribution to the program of restabilizing the Baster mix of blood and culture was made by the infamous eugenicist Eugen Fischer.[398] Even before his study of the Rehobothers Fischer was the leading German expert on the question of race mixing in general and in Southwest Africa.[399] Fischer corresponded with Franz Boas, participated in numerous anthropological conferences starting in 1902, and was *Privatdozent* at Freiburg University's Anatomical Institute between 1900 and 1912.[400] He visited Rehoboth for four months in 1908, where he conducted research financed by the Prussian Academy of Sciences and the German Anthropological Society.[401] When his book on the Rehobothers was published in 1913 Fischer had just been appointed professor at Freiburg University. In 1918 he became *Ordentlicher Professor* and director of the Freiburg Anatomical Institute. He remained at these posts until 1927, when he was named professor of anthropology at the University of Berlin. In 1933 Fischer became the first rector of Berlin University appointed by the Nazis. He directed the Kaiser Wilhelm Institute for Anthropology, Human Genetics, and Eugenics (Kaiser-Wilhelm Institut für Anthropologie, menschliche Erblehre und Eugenik), which was founded in 1927 "as a research facility that would help combat the 'physical and mental degeneration of the German people.'" The institute is notorious for its participation in the Nazi eugenics programs and in the training of SS physicians.[402] Fischer supported the "law for the prevention of bearing hereditarily diseased offspring" of June 28, 1933, which set up courts to judge hereditary health and decreed sterilization in certain cases. He served as a judge in Berlin's Appelate Genetic Health Court and contributed to reports on individuals' "racial purity" and hereditary illnesses. His institute inspired and advised the Gestapo in the sterilization of the so-called Rhineland Bastards, offspring of German women and French

---

398. The word *eugenics* comes from the Greek *eu* (good) and *gen* (to produce). *Eugen* thus means "well born." The usual German translation of eugenics was *Rassenhygiene* (racial hygiene).

399. See Hartmann 1910, which refers to Fischer's 1909 article in the *Korrespondezblatt der Deutschen Anthropolgischen Gesellschaft*.

400. Gessler 2000, p. 16

401. Fischer also received invaluable assistance from the Rhenish missionary at Rehoboth; see E. Fischer 1913, p. iv; and Lösch 1997, p. 62.

402. Proctor 1988, pp. 145, 148, 160. See Lösch 1997, pt. 2, for the most detailed study of Fischer's activities at the Kaiser-Wilhelm Institut and the University of Berlin from 1927 to 1945.

Senegalese soldiers in post–World War I occupied Germany. Fischer made few explicitly anti-Semitic comments before 1933 and was not directly involved in the Final Solution, but as rector of Berlin University he supervised its "Aryanization." Fischer's explicitly anti-Semitic publications date from 1941.[403] His work is thus a good example of the "devil's handwriting."

Fischer's 1913 book is the only sustained study of the Rehobothers. It combines a genetic approach with physical anthropology and ethnology. Although the ethnographic dimension has been ignored by most commentators, it is essential to understanding the book's relationship to the German colonial context. Fischer's project was motivated not just by the "rediscovery of Mendelian genetics in 1900" but by the explosion of interest in "race-mixing" in the colonies and Germany.[404] The book can be read as attempt to recenter the representation of the Basters in the wake of the disruptive discussions of *Mischlinge* and *Mischehen*. Ironically, Fischer accomplished this by *ignoring* the genetic aspects of the problem.

The book begins as an attempt to demonstrate the laws of Mendelian inheritance in humans, asking whether traits are inherited in clusters or individually, whether one of the two parent races expresses itself more strongly in succeeding generations, and whether a coherent "new race" can result from racial mingling. Ludwig Woltmann had argued that race mixing led to biological degeneration and that the "species characteristics of the parents" were likely to simply "stand next to one another in a disorderly fashion" rather than being "unified into an organic whole."[405] Fischer rejected the first of these arguments and partly accepted the second.[406] Measuring the size, facial structure, nose, lips, ears, hair, eyelids, and eye color of 310 Rehobothers, Fischer determined that they had not inherited entire clusters of traits. Instead, Khoikhoi and European features appeared in a myriad of possible combinations. Like Franz Boas, Fischer found that "populations

403. Lösch 1997, pp. 339-55; on the "Rhineland Bastards," see Pommerin 1979. On Fischer, see also Crips 1993. On Fischer and anti-Semitism see Gessler 2000, pp. 90, 170-71. Fischer and Kittel 1943 is a study of ancient Judaism from a "racial" perspective.

404. Proctor 1988, p. 145. On eugenics and the discussion of race mixing in Wilhelmine Germany see Schmuhl 1987; Weindling 1989; Weiss 1990; Labisch 1986; and Weingart, Kroll, and Bayertz 1988. Anti-Semitism was not a driving force behind eugenics in nineteenth-century Germany. Indeed, some of the pioneering German eugenicists were Jewish, and early German racial hygienists denounced anti-Semitism (Proctor 1988, p. 144 n. 2).

405. Woltmann 1903, p. 114.

406. E. Fischer 1909b, p. 1050; 1913, pp. 176-223. I am not concerned here with the methodological shortcomings of Fischer's study from a natural science standpoint; for this, see Gessler 2000, p. 76; Lösch 1997, pp. 65ff.

mix without blending" and that traits persisted because "particular racial alleles had never in fact been lost to the population."[407] The Rehobothers, he concluded, were "ein Rassengemisch . . . keine Mischrasse" (a racial mix, not a mixed race).[408]

By discovering that the Rehobothers did not constitute a stabilized "mixed race," Fischer's Mendelian analysis pointed to the core dilemma of colonial governance. One implication of this genetic "messiness" was that racial half-castes could exhibit "disharmonious" traits.[409] As an ambitious scientist reflecting on a colonial setting and hoping to contribute to policy discussions, Fischer faced the problem of reconciling his scientific finding of a "disharmonious" distribution of traits with the political need to devise a basis for native policy. That he was fully caught up in the colonial problematic is revealed by his inclusion in his book of an appendix entitled "The Political Significance of the Basters for the Colony," which explicitly addressed the problem of native governance.[410] Fischer concluded that the Rehobothers had enormous political value. Although their sense of superiority to other native groups was "exaggerated," it could be "usefully exploited" by deploying them as a "native police force."[411]

This adoption of the colonial state's definition of the situation was not confined to the book's appendix, however, but influenced the arguments throughout. Fischer ignored the seemingly obvious conclusion that the Rehobothers must be as culturally capricious as they were genetically variegated. Instead, he looked for a less centrifugal anchor for identity within the realm of culture. Faced with the Basters' indeterminate genetic foundation, Fischer abandoned his eugenicist program, ignoring biology and remobilizing their mixture of blood almost alchemically as the foundation for a coherent identity. Perhaps it is not surprising that the solution he arrived at was identical to the formula guiding earlier colonial interventions: the Baster was a culturally immobile *"Mittelding"*—literally, an "intermediate thing." Leonhard Schultze had criticized the Basters for lacking a uniform culture, but Fischer countered that they had a stabilized *in-between* culture. Fischer's discourse clarified a formulation that had long been embedded

---

407. Proctor 1988, p. 146.

408. E. Fischer 1913, p. 223.

409. Ibid., p. 298.

410. This appendix is omitted in the 1961 edition of *The Rehoboth Basters* and described by the editors as "irrelevant nowadays" (E. Fischer 1961, p. iv). In fact, the colonial project provides the key to the book's organization.

411. E. Fischer 1913, p. 301.

in government policy.[412] Indeed, Hugo von François had used precisely the same term as Fischer in describing the Basters' political constitution as "a *Mittelding* between a tribal and a municipal constitution."[413]

The long section of Fischer's book that followed the investigation of inherited traits was entitled "Ergology of the Rehoboth Bastards." Since ergology is the study of work's effects on the mind and body, Fischer seemed here to be gesturing toward the power of "nurture" (i.e., Baster culture) over "nature" (i.e., Baster genotypes). His working assumption in this section was that the Rehobothers do in fact form a cultural unity, located halfway between the Khoikhoi and the Boer. He described the typical Baster cane as "a true 'Bastard' product between a European walking stick and an African '*kirri*' (knobkerrie, a killing stick)" (fig. 3.16). Rehobother burial rituals were said to be a settled "mixture" of "Hottentot and Christian customs." The typical headgear of Rehobother women was also doubled and hybrid: "A colorful or white cloth is first wrapped around the head" and worn at all times, Khoikhoi-style. But "when they go out, especially to church, they wear over this cloth a bonnet called a 'Kappie,' which is just like the Dutch version" (fig. 3.17). And a photo of a "Bastard house" was presented in a way that underscored its combination of a settler-style structure—a "typical Dutch 'Stoep'"—with a "Hottentot round hut"—an architectural "Mittelding" (fig. 3.18).[414]

In the end, Fischer reasserted the primacy of blood over culture, turning back to genetic arguments in a gesture of remobilizing racial supremacy. Here he repeated the traditional view of the Basters as having "mental endowments and character" that were "decidedly superior to those of the Hottentots" but insisted that their Khoikhoi heritage condemned them to a position of inferiority vis-à-vis whites.[415] The crux of the matter was "not whether or not half-breeds come into existence, but only that they must under all circumstances continue to be natives."[416]

412. Fischer had read Maximilian Bayer's pamphlet on the Basters several months before leaving for Southwest Africa and had spoken with an old school friend, Max Bartenstein, who had just returned from serving as a captain in the *Schutztruppe* there (E. Fischer 1959, pp. 45–46; Lösch 1997, p. 54).

413. H. von François 1895, p. 243.

414. Fischer's discussion of Bastard vernacular architecture revealed another *Mittelding*— a ventilated hut with a flat roof, used for women's work and cooking (E. Fischer 1913, pp. 249, 282, 257, 245-46).

415. E. Fischer 1909a, p. 76.

416. E. Fischer 1913, p. 303.

FIGURE 3.16 (upper left) An "intermediate object": Rehobother Baster walking stick, or *kirri* (knobkerrie). From E. Fischer 1913, p. 249.

FIGURE 3.17 (upper right) Rehobother woman's "Kappie." From E. Fischer 1913, p. 257.

FIGURE 3.18 Rehobother habitation, showing "typical Dutch 'Stoep'" and "Hottentot round hut." From E. Fischer 1913, p. 245.

Fischer's study illustrates the web of reciprocal reinforcements between native policy and ethnographic representations during the colonial period. Given Fischer's prestige, his research provided a powerful support for the conventional political approach—enough to keep it intact until 1915.

FROM COLLABORATION TO THE 1915 UPRISING

Another reason why German native policy vis-à-vis the Rehobothers remained unchanged until World War I has to do with indigenous collaboration. The reproduction of any framework of native policy required cooperation on the part of the colonized. The Basters largely accepted the role of favored subaltern assigned to them by the colonial state. Indeed, they had requested the "protection" of the German kaiser even before it was offered to them. When von François's troops entered Rehoboth in 1890, they were greeted "in the most festive manner."[417] Not only did the Basters *not* protest the ban on mixed marriages, but when Colonial State Secretary Solf visited Rehoboth in 1912, they agreed with him that mixed marriage was "not good for their tribe."[418] They were a closed, stable community, not one that sought to intermingle with white society. In 1910, when the colonial government decided to include the Basters in a new property tax (*Grundsteuer*) regulation, they protested and petitioned the German emperor, arguing that this was a violation of the 1885 protection treaty and of a 1895 agreement on freedom from taxation.[419] The district commissioner, Captain Böttlin, reported that the Basters would "take up arms if the tax were to be introduced," and rumors of rebellion were rife.[420] Deputy Governor Hintrager agreed with Böttlin that the tax should be lifted to "prevent an increase in bitterness and agitation," and he minuted that "the disadvantages of a possible uprising by the Basters are not worth the price of the political and fiscal advantages" offered by the tax.[421] But this was another false alarm. Two years later the Rehobothers signed a treaty with Governor Seitz

417. "Deutsche Schutztruppe für Südwest-afrika," *Deutsches Kolonialblatt* 1 (1890): 113.

418. "Tagebuch über die Dienstreise Sr. Exzellenz des Herrn Staatssek. Dr. Solf nach Südwest-, Süd-, u. Ostafrika, 27 Mai bis Okt. 1912," BA-Koblenz, Nachlass Solf, vol. 34, p. 7.

419. Petition by Rehoboth Basters to German kaiser, May 19, 1910, BA-Berlin, RKA, vol. 2124, p. 102.

420. Conze to von Lindequist, Berlin, June 22, 1910, BA-Berlin, RKA, vol. 2124, p. 97; see also the report of Bezirksamtmann Brill to governor, Windhoek, April 26, 1910, ibid., pp. 72–73; and Distriktchef von Vietsch, Rehoboth, May 6, 1910, ibid., p. 74.

421. Hintrager to Vietsch, May 12, 1910, BA-Berlin, RKA, vol. 2124, p. 78.

in which they promised to pay six thousand marks annually in property taxes. In return the government agreed that the tax revenues would be used "for public works (road construction, the opening up of water sources, poor relief and care for the sick, etc.) in Bastardland."[422] Each side still seemed to be benefiting from the arrangement.

But there were fractures in this collaborative structure. Individual Rehobothers teamed up with insurgents in the Ovaherero and Nama wars, even though their "tribe" was officially supporting the Germans. Some Rehobothers resisted being treated as inferior to the colonizer in exchange for privileges. Eugen Fischer reported the indignant response of one Rehobother who told him that he should conduct a study of the white missionaries and the German district chief instead of the Basters.[423]

The Rehobothers finally broke with their colonial masters in 1915 when the Germans were facing the troops of the Union of South Africa. A Baster Corps had been mobilized at the start of World War I. The Rehobothers protested, fearing that they would lose their land if they fought against the South Africans and Germany lost the war.[424] Governor Seitz promised them that they would be used only for police duties. When the Baster Corps was put in charge of guarding imprisoned white Union soldiers at the prisoner-of-war camp at Uitdraai, Rehoboth headman Cornelius van Wijk went to meet South African General Botha in Swakopmund and asked the British to pardon his people for this infringement.[425] Ironically, the Basters' withdrawal from the collaborative system was couched in terms of their commitment to the colonial premise of their inferiority to "whites." By putting the Basters in charge of guarding South African prisoners of war the Germans had violated the rules of their own colonial game, and the Basters used these rules to rescue their position in the future colonial system.

When the Germans announced on April 13, 1915, that they were going to transfer the Baster Corps to the colony's north, the Rehoboth Governing Council resisted. After several days of negotiations most of the Baster soldiers deserted, and on April 18 the Germans began to disarm the remaining ones. In the ensuing confusion one disarmed Rehobother was killed while fleeing from German soldiers. The next day the Rehobothers killed a

---

422. Governor Seitz to RKA, February 12, 1912, BA-Berlin, RKA, vol. 2124, p. 163; translation of agreement in Union of South Africa 1927, pp. 149–50.

423. E. Fischer 1913, p. 57.

424. See Budack 1974 on the 1915 Rehobother uprising, and the comments of Cornelius van Wijk and others in Union of South Africa 1918, pp. 126–34. See also Goldblatt 1971, p. 205.

425. This meeting is believed to have taken place on April 1, 1915 (Budack 1974, p. 46).

German police sergeant, and this was followed by a series of shootings of German soldiers and farmers.[426] The Germans terminated the 1885 protection treaty on April 22 and declared war on the Rehobothers. The Baster rebels were eventually cornered by German troops at Tsamkhubis (Sam-Kubis), but they were saved by the arrival of Union forces under General Mackenzie. Thus ended a thirty-year colonial collaboration.

Conclusion

A single colony, Southwest Africa, already presents a sweeping array of native polices, and the rest of this book will broaden this spectrum even further. The colonies of Southwest Africa and Kiaochow illustrate the breaching of the outer boundaries of native policy in two different directions. German policy in Kiaochow partly abandoned the rule of difference. German policy in Southwest Africa adhered tenaciously to that rule but abandoned native policy for native massacre. This colony also demonstrates three distinct forms of native policy. The Rehoboth Basters were treated as racially and culturally intermediate between European and Khoikhoi. The Witbooi after 1894 were described as noble savages and treated in a protective manner that enforced certain "traditional" or "customary" ways of life. The Ovaherero after 1904 were subjected to a program of partial assimilation. This project of turning the colonized into abject partial copies of their colonizers was not pursued in such a relentless manner anywhere else in the German colonial empire.

426. The settler Gustav Voigts later claimed that the Basters murdered "about twelve farmers in the Rehoboth district and plundered the farms" at the beginning of hostilities ("Auszug aus den Äusserungen des Mitgliedes des Landesrats, Farmers und Kaufmanns Gustav Voigts aus Windhuk," April 4, 1918, BA-Berlin, RKA, vol. 2124, p. 175). According to Budack 1974, p. 64, thirteen Germans were murdered by Rehobothers and ten more fell in battle with them.

PART TWO *Samoa*

FOUR

"A Foreign Race That All Travelers Have Agreed to Be the Most Engaging" ❧ The Creation of the Samoan Noble Savage, by Way of Tahiti

B. And I have formed a high opinion of the manners and customs of Tahiti, and of Orou's speeches.

A. Yes, even though they are cast somewhat in a European mold.

DENIS DIDEROT, *Supplement to Bougainville's "Voyage"*[1]

The Idea of Polynesian Noble Savagery

In his surly book about Oceania Paul Theroux observes that "a place that is finely described in a novel by such a person"—he is speaking of Robert Louis Stevenson—"is given a power of bewitchment that it never really loses, no matter how much its reality changes. Not only Samoa, but other islands, and in a sense, the whole of the South Pacific is a clear example of this sort of transformation because it has been used so effectively as a setting by writers. . . . Fiction has that capacity. . . . The simple mention of the name of a place can make that place become singular, never mind what it looks like."[2] Tahiti was at the origin of this mythmaking process, epitomizing Polynesia for European travelers in the late eighteenth and much of the nineteenth century. But even as European contact, settlement, and colonization caused Tahiti to lose many of the charming qualities which had been assembled into the early myth, other Polynesian islands and cultures came to fill Tahiti's role.[3] During the second half of the nineteenth century, Samoa was one of the places that inherited the Tahitian mantle and repre-

1. Diderot [1772] 1958, pp. 216–17.

2. Theroux 1993, p. 322.

3. For example, members of Captain Cook's crew interpreted Maori practices in New Zealand "in relation to what they had already witnessed in Tahiti" (Thomas and Berghof, in G. Forster [1777] 2000, vol. I, p. 441 n. 25).

sented Ur-Polynesia.[4] We thus cannot understand the evolving European picture of Samoa without first briefly examining the construction of Tahiti and its place within the "fifth continent" of Oceania during the late eighteenth and early nineteenth centuries.

As with Southern Africa and China, Europeans were far from unanimous in their descriptions of Pacific cultures. Yet this was a relatively hegemonized discursive formation from the late eighteenth century through to at least 1914. In the eighteenth century, the view of Tahitian and Polynesian culture more generally as a variant of noble savagery predominated.[5] Noble savagery was even powerful enough to take over texts whose authors set out to reject it. For example, the travel narrative of Sydney Parkinson, who accompanied James Cook on his first voyage, begins by criticizing the "celebrated writer" (that is, Rousseau) who argued that civilization renders mankind unhappy, only to state on the very next page that Pacific islanders are "in constitutions, what the ancient Britons were before their civilization" and therefore "happier than Europeans."[6] This image of the foreign culture as an earlier version of the European one, located at a simpler and happier intermediate stage of development, already contains the entire noble savagery paradigm in a nutshell.

The specifically Polynesian variant evolved in a peculiar direction after starting out from precedents that were shared with Le Valliant's Khoikhoi and Cooper's Native Americans. One of the key distinctions between "ignoble" and "noble" savages in Oceania revolved around the axis of pacifism and hospitality versus militarism and hostility. The figure of the noble savage was correspondingly more pacific in the Pacific than in Southern Africa. Such differences in emphasis and expectation partly reflect the differing histories of the initial contact zones. At the early Cape, Khoikhoi were mainly victims and rarely attacked the intrusive Europeans. Either they were culturally defeated or they escaped to the colony's northern frontiers, where they posed more of a threat to one another than to the expanding colonial state. In Transorangia the Khoikhoi armed themselves for

4. The quotation from Robert Louis Stevenson's letter to John Addington Symonds, November 11, 1888, in Stevenson 1985, vol. 6, p. 223, that forms the title of this chapter provides an example. It is from Stevenson's first half year of traveling in the Pacific and refers to Polynesians in general, but it is echoed in his later letters from Samoa (see Stevenson 1895).

5. One exception was the Russian explorer Krusenstern ([1813] 1869, vol. 1, p. 182), who traveled around the world between 1803 and 1806, had nothing good to say about Oceanic peoples, and insisted that the Nuku Hivans were not noble at all, but "savages," pure and simple.

6. Parkinson 1773, pp. 23–24. Parkinson died on the voyage, and his narrative was edited and published by his brother, Stanfield.

internecine struggles long before the threatening Europeans arrived. The earliest Rhenish missionaries in Namibia were completely dependent on armed Khoikhoi for protection. Most Khoikhoi leaders, especially the more powerful Orlams, sought to attract missionaries into their midst. Far from disarming the indigenous population, the Rhenish missionaries fed the nineteenth-century "arms race" between Khoikhoi and Ovaherero by selling them weapons. The early missionaries, who decisively shaped the German ethnographic archive in Namibia, were not especially fixated on the topics of militancy or the unfriendly reception.

Initial contact in Oceania, by contrast, was frequently a much more fraught affair, and the early impressions had perduring effects, if not always direct ones. The story of Cook at Hawai'i—greeted as a god on his first landing and killed the second time around—is emblematic of the extremes of early Oceanic contact, as filtered through European perceptions.[7] The vagaries of late-eighteenth- and early-nineteenth-century Pacific explorations lent a vital intensity to the issue of islanders' reception of Europeans. Pacific explorers were existentially dependent on access to islands for fresh water and food, and commanders like Cook believed they needed to allow their male crews occasional access to women to prevent trouble. Missionaries in nineteenth-century Namibia also depended on Africans for protection, food, and labor, but their proximity to the Cape Colony meant that they were never so dramatically cut off from Europeans and their products. The missionaries who initially entered Namibia had little interest in founding a colonial state, while the modern European penetration of the Pacific took the form of official voyages of naval and scientific exploration with a barely concealed colonizing mission. The difference between these two sorts of contact zone—a colonial frontier and a distant "external area"— had lasting effects on ethnographic perceptions, and ultimately on colonial native polices.

Preexisting European theories of race overdetermined the framing of hospitality and militancy in early representations of Polynesia. Racial perceptions of Oceania had a thoroughly comparative quality. During the "great phase of exploration of the Pacific" that started after the Seven Years' War in 1763, European visitors began almost immediately to divide Pacific islanders into distinct races.[8] One of the most salient categorical impositions was naturalist Johann Forster's "two great varieties of people in the South

---

7. This qualification is necessary because European views are my concern here, and because it avoids the debate over whether Cook really was seen as a god by the Hawai'ians.

8. Clark 2003, p. 155.

Seas," labeled "Melanesians" and "Polynesians" by Jules Dumont d'Urville in 1832 (although these terms had both been used earlier).[9] This French botanist turned explorer, sometimes called "the last great discoverer,"[10] specified that Melanesians were a branch of the "Ethiopian race" and Polynesians a part of the "Asian race." Melanesians were said to be less intelligent, less beautiful, and less civilized than Polynesians, and to have a less centralized and complex political system.[11] Melanesians were also said to be preoccupied with warfare and to be hostile to outsiders. They were "natural enemies of the whites" who had "always shown obstinate defiance and pronounced antipathy to Europeans."[12] The topos of the unfriendly welcome was associated with cannibalism, a practice that was thought to be more common in the "darker-skinned" islands. The Russian explorer Adam Johann von Krusenstern concluded his long discussion of cannibalism with the sentiment "Woe to the navigator whose ship is lost upon this dangerous coast"—cannibalistic New Caledonia.[13] By contrast, Horatio Hale of the United States Exploring Expedition (1838–42) insisted on the association between Polynesia and hospitality: "The difference of character in the . . . Oceanic races is most clearly displayed in the reception which they have given to their earliest civilized visitors. With the black tribes, a strong disposition has generally been evinced to get rid of the strangers as soon as possible. . . . The Polynesian islanders, on the other hand, have almost always received them with a

9. J. Forster [1778] 1996, p. 153; Dumont D'Urville 1832, pp. 5–6, which also distinguished Micronesia and Malaysia as the two other regions or races of the "Great Ocean." See Thomas 1997, 2002, and Clark 2003 on this classificatory system. The question of the impact of the earlier Spanish, Portuguese, and Dutch accounts of Oceania on nineteenth-century European representations awaits its historian. Dalrymple's (1770) collection included descriptions of the voyages of de Quiros, Le Maire, Schouten, Tasman, and Roggewein and was widely read at the time. Yet B. Smith (1985), Edmond (1997), and Thomas (1997) all begin their accounts with Captain Cook, ignoring these earlier explorers; an exception is Tcherkézoff (2003), who briefly discusses Quiros and Dampier and also notes that Dumont d'Urville did not invent the word "Polynesia," which was used as early as 1756 by Charles de Brosses, or even the term "Melanesia," a version of which ("Mélanien") was coined by another French writer, Bory de Saint-Vincent, in 1825.

10. Jacob 1995.

11. See also Dumont d'Urville 1842–54, vol. 2; and contrast Georg Forster ([1777] 2000, vol. 2, pp. 480–81), who agreed that while Melanesians were less handsome, they were "the most intelligent people" encountered on Cook's second voyage. For an example of the petrification of this classificatory scheme see G. Brown 1910.

12. Dumont d'Urville 1832, pp. 11–12.

13. Krusenstern [1813] 1869, vol. 1, p. 184. The ethnographic system was fairly flexible: cultures could be classified as Polynesian even if they evinced cannibalism or human sacrifice, or as Melanesian even if they were perceived as intelligent; see Thomas and Berghof 2000.

clamorous welcome and apparent friendship."[14] Cook's renaming of islands as the "Friendly Islands" and the "Society Islands" emphasizes this core theme.[15]

Europeans on Polynesia in the Wake of Wallis and Bougainville: The Tahitian Metonym

The first European explorer to "discover" Tahiti in the modern era of Pacific exploration was Captain Samuel Wallis, who landed there in June 1767. The reality of cross-cultural encounter and interaction filtered into these early European representations of Tahitians only indirectly. Wallis's arrival was marked by a battle in which one Tahitian was killed; several days later there was another fight between the British interlopers and Tahitians armed with slings and stones. Despite this unpropitious beginning, the official account of Wallis's visit painted an extremely favorable portrait of the locals. Indeed, it was Wallis's successful "pacification" of Tahiti that cleared the way for the depiction of the island as idyllic. Here, as in Samoa, where an extremely violent initial interaction was subsequently erased from the dominant register of ethnographic memory, later reconstructions mattered more than the original events.

Wallis's account was written by John Hawkesworth, who was also responsible for the official publication of the chronicle of Captain Cook's first voyage. The Wallis/Hawkesworth book described Tahiti as "one of the most healthy as well as delightful spots in the world," with the most "romantic appearance that can be imagined." Of special importance for the future elaboration of the European myth of Polynesia was the portrayal of Tahitian women: "all handsome, and some of them extremely beautiful." Most important, it seemed, was that "chastity does not seem to be considered as a virtue among them." This was emphasized by passages describing Tahitian women "stripping themselves naked," making "wanton gestures" at the British sailors, and granting them "personal favours."[16] The specific coding

14. Hale [1846] 1986, pp. 73–74. Of course, these distinctions were not clearly defined. Captain Erskine of the British ship *Havannah* was not alone in equating "Melanesia" with "the Polynesian Negro races" (Erskine 1853), p. 2.

15. Tcherkézoff 2003, p. 193 n. 42, suggests that the Society Islands were thus named in honor of the Royal Society of Astronomy, which had "helped the Admiralty plan Cook's first expedition," but others have attributed the name to the islanders' sociable reception of the explorers.

16. Some historians may be more interested in Wallis's original notebooks, and there have been repeated complaints over the centuries, beginning with Cook himself, about

of sexuality and gender that came to characterize the Polynesian variant of noble savagery was already present in this early account.

Louis-Antoine de Bougainville arrived in Tahiti just ten months after Wallis, but the initial accounts of his voyage, including an English translation of his book-length narrative from 1772, appeared in print before Wallis/Hawkesworth.[17] Upon returning to France in 1769, Bougainville immediately published a pamphlet about the island he called New Cythera, after the Greek island mythically associated with Aphrodite, goddess of love and beauty. His rendering of Tahiti as a living museum of European antiquity became a mainstay of subsequent representations of Polynesia.[18] According to Bougainville, the New Cytherians were living "in peace among themselves, and know neither hatred, quarrels, dissention, nor civil war; they have no offensive or defensive weapons."[19] This was inaccurate, as the incidents around Wallis's landfall had only recently demonstrated, but the misrepresentation was crucial for the elaboration of the idea of Polynesian friendliness. Tahitian culture was located at the ideal intermediate point that Rousseauians preferred to both corrupt civilization and the animal-like state of nature. On the one hand, the Tahitians could be classed with "all the other wise and well-policed nations" (nations sages et policées). On the other hand, they were closer to a natural state, lacking any concept of private property, dancing "*naturally* and without any set order," and being "vivacious and gay by *nature*."[20]

The surgeon-naturalist Philibert Commerson, who accompanied Bougainville, characterized the Tahitians even more explicitly as noble savages in an essay published in the *Mercure de France*.[21] Commerson avoided the word *savage*, which for him suggested the abject and ignoble, but he did use the adjective "noble" and referred directly to Rousseau. Commerson suggested the name Utopia for the island, but also mentioned the local

---

Hawkesworth's editorial decisions and romantic prose. For my purposes, however, the versions that were read by the wider public are of more interest. An undoctored version of Cook's own journals was published by John Barrow in 1860, and historians can also consult the meticulous edition by Beaglehole (1955–67). Quotes from Wallis in Hawkesworth 1775, vol. 1, pp. 218, 175, 211, 178, 194.

17. See Margueron 1989; Dauphiné 1985.

18. E.g., Krämer-Bannow n.d., p. 1, on the "proud people who once wandered in almost Greek beauty" in the South Sea islands. Bernard Smith has carefully traced this classicization for the visual arts; see B. Smith 1985 and 1992, esp. chap. 9, "Greece and the Colonisation of the Pacific"; also Joppien and Smith 1985–88.

19. Bougainville [1769] 1970a, p. 27.

20. Bougainville [1769] 1970b, pp. 3–4 (my emphasis).

21. On Commerson see Taillemitte 1977, vol. 1, pp. 87ff.

name, Taïti, for the first time in print. The Tahitians were "men without vices, without prejudice, without needs, without dissention."[22] They were "governed by family fathers rather than kings"—a crucial distinction for enthusiasts of noble savagery, who did not necessarily oppose political domination but usually preferred the *patriarchal* form of rule, which they understood as softer and more flexible, to the more authoritarian and centralized monarchical forms.[23] Like Hawkesworth, Commerson emphasized that the Tahitians "know no other god than love":

All of their days are devoted to him, the entire island is his temple, and all of the women are his idols and the men his worshippers. And what women! Rivals of the Georgians in beauty, sisters of the Graces without veils. Neither prudery nor modesty exercise their tyranny here. . . . The act of procreation is an act of religion; the vows and songs of all the assembled people encourage its preliminaries, and its conclusion is celebrated with universal applause. . . . [Thus] the good Tahitian [*le bon Taïtien*] enjoys himself/orgasms [*jouit*] unceasingly, either by experiencing his own pleasures, or else by taking in the spectacle of others' pleasures.

Commerson inaugurated a core theme in the ethnographic paradigm concerning Polynesia by linking the amiable welcome to female sexuality. He noted that all foreigners (*tout étranger*) were "invited to participate in these happy mysteries" and that "it is even considered an obligation of hospitality to invite them."[24] Lest his reader equate these sensual pleasures

---

22. Commerson [1769] 1915, pp. 461–62, 466.

23. Ibid., p. 462. Liebersohn (1999) identifies a nineteenth-century discourse of "savage nobility" arising in the context of rejections of the French Revolution, one in which centralized political systems like the nineteenth-century Hawai'i "kingship" were valorized. This is compatible with my argument that formations of ethnographic discourse are generally multivocal, but this was a minor strand in representations of Polynesia. Like Cannadine (2001), Liebersohn suggests that Europeans were looking for a *mirror* of European monarchy after the Napoleonic wars. But this was clearly not the dominant approach, since a centralized and authoritarian model of politics often made European colonial entrée into the Pacific more difficult. As we will see below, Europeans dropped the demand for a Samoan kingship as soon as they began planning for a colonial takeover. It is also important to attend to the social class position of precolonial European observers. Some of the most influential European commentators on Polynesia, including both of the Forsters and Adalbert von Chamisso, and nearly all of the LMS missionaries in Samoa, were not monarchists but preferred more egalitarian and decentralized forms of government. They were decidedly cool toward Oceanic cultures that reminded them of European feudalism or monarchy.

24. Commerson [1769] 1915, p. 462.

with the corrupt decadence of civilized countries, Commerson insisted that the Tahitian represented "natural man, born essentially good, free from all prejudices, and following, without suspicion and without remorse, the gentle impulses of an instinct that is always sure because it has not yet *degenerated* into reason."[25]

The transformation of Tahiti into an island of love was just one aspect of a sweeping *feminization* of Polynesia that was eventually linked to strategies of colonial domination. A related aspect was the emphasis in modern European discussions on the way different societies treated their women as indicating comparative levels of civilization.[26] Johann Forster claimed that "the more debased the situation of a nation is, and of course the more remote from civilization, the more harshly we found the women treated."[27] Nineteenth-century European writings on China or Africa usually devoted more space to men, with women's degraded condition being addressed as a sort of supplemental commentary on, or confirmation of, the overall cultural level.[28] Colonial regimes often tried to feminize their male subjects, but with respect to Polynesia there was a tendency to marginalize men or ignore them altogether.

Bougainville's definitive account of his voyage, published two years after his New Cythera pamphlet, dealt with a number of different islands and topics, including the debate over the height of the natives of Tierra del Fuego. But it was his discussion of Tahiti that attracted the most attention. Bougainville's emphasis on hospitality is especially significant in light of the militant atmosphere that had been occasioned by Wallis's visit. According to Bougainville, the French were greeted by "an immense crowd of men and women [who] . . . could not be tired with looking at us; the boldest among them came to touch us; . . . none of them wore any arms, not so much as a stick. They sufficiently expressed their joy at our arrival." Bougainville enthused: "I thought I was transported into the Garden of Eden."[29] The most notorious passage in Bougainville's account returned to the nexus of sex

25. Commerson [1769] 1915, p. 462. Commerson's equation of Tahitian culture with the state of nature was somewhat atypical; most Europeans who praised the same aspects of Tahitian life followed Johann Forster ([1778] 1996, p. 260) in locating them "one remove above barbarians."

26. Thomas 1994, pp. 102–3.

27. J. Forster [1778] 1996, p. 258.

28. See, for example, Ko 2002, p. 149, on footbinding as a "paramount symbol of Confucian misogyny."

29. Bougainville [1772] 1967, pp. 220, 228. Bougainville landed not at Matavai Bay, like Wallis, but on the far side of Tahiti.

and hospitality. He began his discussion of Tahitian women by emphasizing their amicability: "As we came nearer the shore, the number of islanders surrounding our ships increased. . . . All these people were crying out *tayo*, which means friend, and gave a thousand signs of friendship. . . . Their periaguas were full of females; who, for agreeable features, are not inferior to most European women; and who in point of beauty of the body might, with much reason, vie with them all." The passage culminated in an episode from a sexual Arcadia, an early version of sex tourism: "Most of these fair females were naked. . . . The [Tahitian] men . . . pressed us to choose a woman, and to come on shore with her; and their gestures, which were nothing less than equivocal, denoted in what manner we should form an acquaintance with her. . . . A young girl came on board, and . . . carelessly dropt a cloth, which covered her, and appeared to the eyes of all beholders, such as Venus shewed herself to the Phrygian shepherd, having, indeed, the celestial form of that goddess."[30] At this point, however, Bougainville introduced a key distinction. Wallis had described Tahitian women as prostitutes. Bougainville resisted this construction, insisting that the women's "glances" "seemed to [reveal] some degree of uneasiness, notwithstanding the *innocent* manner in which they were given; perhaps, because nature has every where embellished their sex with a *natural* timidity."[31] This specific articulation of *innocence* and *voluptuousness* constituted the essence of the female noble savage role—not just in Polynesia but also in South Africa (as in the discussion of the Narina figure in Le Vaillant's *Voyages*) and America (as with the "mestiza" girl Toni in Kleist's "Betrothal in Santo Domingo").[32] This particular mixture differentiated the female noble savage from other images of non-Western women, including those in the Oriental harem as portrayed by painter Jean-Léon Gérôme or in the colonial postcards analyzed by Malek Alloula.[33]

A number of literary and philosophical works published in the late eighteenth century drew on Bougainville and Commerson to criticize European society and to celebrate its Tahitian counterpart.[34] The most famous of these,

30. Ibid., pp. 217-19.
31. Ibid., p. 218 (my emphasis).
32. In Kleist's story, Toni is a half-white girl who betrays her mother's vengeful hatred of whites by falling in love with Gustav, a Swiss officer in the French army in Santo Domingo. Her assignment is to seduce Gustav and to lure him to his death at the hands of the "terrible old negro" Congo Hoango. Toni is innocent, but also sensual, with "something extraordinarily graceful about her limbs and about the long lashes that drooped over her lowered eyes" (Kleist [1811] 1978, pp. 231, 243).
33. See Ackerman 1986 on Gérôme; Alloula 1986.
34. See Gray 1970; Poulton 1988, chap. 1.

Diderot's *Supplement to Bougainville's "Voyage"*, was a transparent critique of French and European society, but it also entered the library of received ideas about Tahiti and Polynesia.[35] As the subtitle explains, the *Supplement* is a "dialogue between A and B on the undesirability of attaching moral values to certain physical acts which carry no such implications." Interlocutor B, the more self-confident and articulate of the two, argues that Tahitian customs do not "stigmatize as evil something that is not by its nature evil." Tahitians eschew private property, and are characterized by "innocence, repose and felicity." Most important for B, the Tahitians do not condemn sexuality, as illustrated by the farewell speech of an old Tahitian man: "A little while ago, [a] young Tahitian girl blissfully abandoned herself to the embraces of a Tahitian youth. . . . She was proud of her ability to excite men's desires. . . . In our presence, without shame, in the center of a throng of innocent Tahitians . . . she accepted the caresses of the young man." Diderot adheres to the conventional story of social evolution, according to which "the Tahitian is close to the origin of the world, while the European is close to its old age," and there is no ambiguity about which condition he considers superior. As B concludes, "you won't find the human condition perfectly happy anywhere but in Tahiti."[36] The third voice in the text is that of the old Tahitian man, who condemns the Europeans for bringing corruption to the island. The *Supplement* epitomizes the early framework of Polynesian noble savagery by focusing on Tahiti, ranking its culture above Europe's, rejecting colonialism as destructive, and foregrounding innocent sensuality.

The next European caller at Tahiti, and the most renowned in the English-speaking world, was Captain James Cook, who visited "New Cythera" on all three of his voyages. Cook's travels are almost as famous for the conflicts around their publication as for their actual discoveries. Although Cook was upset that the Admiralty would not let him write the official account of his first voyage and although he "did not think highly of the volumes on any score," Hawkesworth's text became a best seller in England and was quickly translated into German and other languages.[37] Hawkesworth's discussion of Tahiti relied on the codes of noble savagery, and to a lesser extent, relativism. In the long, static ethnographic portrait that was appended, in standard eighteenth-century style, to the chronological

35. Diderot's *Supplement* was written in 1772 but not published until 1796; see Diderot [1796] 1956; Papin 1984.

36. Diderot [1796] 1956, pp. 217, 190, 186, 226.

37. Beaglehole, "Textual Introduction," in Cook 1955–67, vol. 1, p. ccxlvi, on the Cook-Hawkesworth relation; and Moorhead [1966] 2000, p. 48.

narrative, Hawkesworth described Tahitians as welcoming, "brave, open, and candid, without either suspicion or treachery, cruelty or revenge."[38] In conformity with the idea that noble savages live closer to a "state of nature," he attributed the Tahitians' strong sense of "right and wrong" to a *natural conscience.*"[39] Alongside stereotypical descriptions of Tahitian men as brave and "noble," Hawkesworth alluded to the Bougainvillean combination of sensuality and innocence, describing the women's eyes as "sometimes sparkling with fire, and sometimes melting with softness."[40] In neutral terms he described the Tahitians' sexual practices, including an event that caught the attention of other diarists on the *Endeavour* in which a man performed the "rites of Venus with a little girl about eleven or twelve years of age before several of our people" while "several women of superior rank," including the woman they called the queen, "gave instructions to the girl how to perform her part." Rather than passing judgment Hawkesworth turned immediately to a dissertation on the topic of shame, asking whether it is occasioned by nature or custom. He supported the latter, relativist position.[41] In the manner of Montaigne and Voltaire, Hawkesworth insisted that "we must indeed estimate the virtue of these people, by the only standard of morality, the conformity of their conduct to what *in their opinion* is right."[42]

The only disturbance in this harmonious portrait came from the *arioi*, a quasi-secret society with ritual functions whose members traveled from place to place putting on "dramatic dances" and inducting new members into "the mysteries of the God Oro," a symbol of male strength and aggression who was associated in precontact times with procreation and fertility, the underworld, war and peace, and fallen warriors.[43] Missionaries like William Ellis of the LMS harshly condemned the *arioi* as "privileged libertines" who engaged in "abominable, unutterable," and "obscene exhibitions."[44]

38. Hawkesworth 1775, vol. 2, p. 39. The Tahitian's hospitality is clear from the opening section, in which they arrive at Cook's ship in canoes bearing gifts (ibid., vol. 1, p. 431).

39. Ibid., vol. 1, p. 448 (my emphasis).

40. Ibid., vol. 2, p. 38.

41. Ibid., vol. 1, p. 469; see also vol. 1, p. 452.

42. Ibid., vol. 1, p. 448 (my emphasis). Hawkesworth similarly comments on the equivalent "absurdities" of all religions (ibid., vol. 1, p. 4).

43. J. Forster [1778] 1996, p. 255; Moerenhout 1837, vol. 1, p. 484; Mühlmann 1955, pp. 155, 161, 166. Similar institutions existed throughout the Society Islands and in the Carolines (Ellis 1853, vol. 1, p. 230). Fictional treatments of the *arioi* include Segalen's *Les Immémoriaux* (1907) and Jean Dorsenne's "C'était le soir des dieux" [1926] 1996.

44. Ellis 1853, vol. 1, pp. 234, 237. See also Moerenhout 1837, vol. 1, pp. 484-503, and vol. 2, pp. 129-36. As Mühlmann notes, there is actually very little specific evidence about the exact contents of the "obscene" *arioi heiva*. Moerenhout observed that "prostitution, dance,

Most infamously, the *arioi* were bound to childlessness and practiced infanticide.[45] All European observers were taken aback by the *arioi*, including Cook, who found it difficult to assess them dispassionately or to recognize their religious significance.[46] Hawkesworth abandoned his framework of noble savagery and relativism when it came to the *arioi*, speaking of their "diabolical prostitution."[47] But the *arioi* did not figure centrally in the travel accounts, and writers like Johann Forster insisted on their atypical status "within a nation, which upon the whole, is not destitute of humanity, but rather inclined to practice kindness and goodnature, in a manner which would do honour to a more enlightened and civilized race of men."[48] One of the obvious problems with the *arioi* was their emphasis on *masculine* sex and violence, whereas the male European visitor in Polynesia wanted to domesticate the men and emphasize the women.

The artists who accompanied Cook produced images of Tahiti that were even more idealized than the textual accounts. The engravings were sold separately or printed with the published versions of Cook's voyages. As Bernard Smith has shown, these artists engaged in various types of generalization, idealization, romanticization, and classicization. William Hodges in particular, the painter who accompanied Cook on his second voyage, was influenced by the "grand style of history painting" and the continuing "Italianate domination of English taste" in painting during the eighteenth century. According to the prevailing view, defended by Sir Joshua Reynolds, first president of the Royal Academy of Arts, art was *compelled* to deviate from strict empirical evidence or historical facts in order to reach a higher poetic truth.[49] As a result, nearly all the depictions of Tahitians and Polynesian figures from this period drew on poses and gestures "whose ultimate

---

and indecent representations were only for the lowest class of the *arioi*" (1837, vol. 1, p. 495). Henry (1928) and Mühlmann (1955, p. 79) interpret the dances of the *arioi* as fertility or procreation rituals. Gell (1993), though more recent, adds little to Mühlmann's exhaustive treatment of the subject.

45. Ellis 1853, vol. 1, pp. 248–58; Mühlmann 1955, pp. 113–38.

46. Beaglehole, "Textual Introduction," in Cook 1955–67, vol. 1, p. clxxxviii.

47. Hawkesworth 1775, vol. 2, p. 55.

48. J. Forster [1778] 1996, p. 256. The fact that as much as a fifth of the entire population belonged to the *arioi* society was overlooked by early European observers, probably because it did not fit with their image of Tahiti. The missionaries, by contrast, embarked immediately on a campaign to eradicate the *arioi*, and by the 1820s it had been banned in Tahiti by the "missionary theocracy" headed by Pomare II (Mühlmann 1955, pp. 194–212; Laux 2000).

49. B. Smith 1992, pp. 176, 178; on Hodges see also Guest 1992; Quilley and Bonehill 2004.

origin lies in classical statuary."[50] Most of the engravers who transformed drawings and paintings for reproduction followed these conventions.[51] The engraving of Hodges's painting of Cook's landing at Middleburgh ('Eua) in the Friendly Islands is a case in point (fig. 4.1). Georg Forster criticized the engraving that accompanied the official account of the voyage for exhibiting "to our eyes the pleasing forms of antique figures and draperies" and "Greek contours and features . . . which have never existed in the South Sea."[52] Independently existing artistic conventions *ennobled* the artists' subject matter and in so doing reinforced the framework of noble savagery.[53]

As Smith notes, these works also contain ethnographic, artistic, and historical details that exceed the bounds of stereotype. Some of the artists created irreducibly individualizing portraits of specific Polynesians, for instance. Emerging directions in nineteenth-century art, especially the "academic" emphasis on empirical naturalism, worked at cross-purposes to noble savagery in the field of ethnographic painting.[54] Other trends in the arts, especially romanticism at the beginning and neoromanticism at the end of the century, worked hand in hand with the noble savagery framework. Images and concepts that did not fit the view of Polynesia as a tropical paradise were also often marginalized in the engraving, reproduction, distribution, and reception of the original images. The official publication of the description of Cook's third voyage, for example, omitted the image of Cook's death.[55]

50. Joppien and Smith 1985–88, vol. 2, p. 92, here discussing Hodges. The same can be said of most of the artists in this period involved in the representation of non-Western peoples who had already been described as noble. See, for example, the engraving from Herport's *Neue Ost-Indianische Reisebeschreibung* (fig. 2.2), which classicizes even as it differentiates the Khoikhoi via individual signs of abjection.

51. As Joppien and Smith demonstrate (1985–88, vol. 1, pp. 10-19), the inhabitants of Tierra del Fuego were transformed into noble and classical figures by the engraver for Hawkesworth's book, Bartolozzi, even though these same people were rendered as abject and animal-like in the original image by Alexander Buchan and in Cook's journal.

52. G. Forster [1777] 2000, vol. 1, p. 232; similarly, J. Forster [1778] 1996, p. 249n.

53. Bernard Smith also argues that John Webber's neomannerism led him to elongate human figures, including Polynesian ones, and to depict them with exaggeratedly small heads—proportions that were understood then as ennobling. Artists who wanted to depict natives as animal-like savages typically gave them exaggeratedly *large* heads.

54. Smith emphasizes ascendant aesthetic naturalism and theories of race as working against the visual codes of noble savagery in the nineteenth century. At the same time, he shows again and again how specific influential European artists and writers were in fact committed to this discourse, including Hawkesworth, Joseph Banks, and Georg Forster.

55. This volume did include an engraving based on Webber's portrayal of the incident of human sacrifice that he and Cook witnessed at Tahiti. Yet while the image scandalized

FIGURE 4.1 J. K. Shirwin [Sherwin], *The Landing at Middleburgh, One of the Friendly Isles*, detail. Engraving after a painting by William Hodges. From Cook 1777, vol. 1, plate 54, following p. 192.

Smith writes that Hodges "aspired to the production of an alternative dream—of Tahiti as a tropical paradise of sunshine and sensuous, liberated women—even more beautiful, more tempting than Italy."[56] He traces Hodges's move away from "the picturesque classicism" that he had learned in the studio of his instructor, Richard Wilson, to a point of view that is certainly romantic.[57] Although romanticism was still emerging in this period,

the missionaries, it did not pose a fundamental challenge to the discourse of noble savagery. Webber depicts Cook as an interested, not appalled, onlooker. In his journals Cook called the custom "extraordinary and Barbarous" but reported dispassionately on it. Captain Clerke, who took over the command of the *Resolution* after Cook's death, described the same event as an ethnological curiosity. The paragraph in Clerke's journal that discusses the sacrifice concludes with the remark that "we fared most sumptuously and spent our time exceedingly agreeably with these hospitable, benevolent People." Quotes from Beaglehole 1955-67, vol. 3, pt. 1, p. 199, and vol. 3, pt. 2, p. 1316. In one of the most romantic depictions of Tahiti, Jean Dorsenne's "C'était le soir des dieux" ([1926] 1996), the central character, Nohoraï, offers herself as a human sacrifice out of love for the chief priest.

56. B. Smith 1992, p. 132.

57. Joppien and Smith 1985-88, vol. 2, p. 24.

Hodges's work reveals a protoromantic emotionalism and sensualism, and a juxtaposition of extremes of light and dark and of signs of the ancient and the modern. In the first version of Hodges's *View of Matavai Bay* (fig. 4.2), the scene is dominated by the powerful figures of Tahitian men and their warships, but in a later version of the same scene (fig. 4.3), English ships also appear in the picture. Whereas Joppien and Smith argue that the theme of this second version is Cook's "control of the critical moments of contact and the establishment of a market,"[58] the juxtaposition of signs of the ancient and the modern also produces a protoromantic shock effect similar to Caspar David Friedrich's romantic ruins paintings, where an archaic past coexists with the modern present. This can be read as still privileging the "savage" figures in the foreground as against the smaller European ships in the bay. Hodges's romanticism is especially evident in one of his most famous paintings, *A View Taken in the Bay of Otaheite Peha* (Vaitepiha) (plate 2), which depicts two women bathing peacefully beside the statue of a pagan god.

The images by John Webber, who accompanied Cook on his Third Voyage, are generally less romantic, evincing an attentiveness to naturalistic detail not found in Hodges.[59] Nonetheless, Webber contributed to the visual discourse of Polynesian noble savagery by filtering most of the negative elements out of his drawings and paintings, rendering the South Pacific as "an alternative, happy and carefree, utopian world."[60] Webber's portrait of Poedua, the daughter of the chief of Raiatea (an island in the "Society" group close to Tahiti geographically and culturally), builds on the image of Polynesia as "young, feminine, desirable and vulnerable, an ocean of desire" (fig. 4.4).[61]

Actual Polynesian men continued to present counterevidence that was too powerful to overlook and that seemed to call for an adjustment of reality to the European ideal (or vice versa). The idea of male noble savages as brave warriors, which worked so well for Theodor Leutwein in Southwest Africa and for James Fenimore Cooper in the United States, was more problematic in Polynesia. The noblest of Polynesian warriors, most observers agreed, were the Maori of New Zealand. But Maori had defied the crew of Cook's *Endeavour* in 1770 and had killed and cannibalized twenty-six members of a French commercial exploring voyage commanded by Marion du Fresne two

58. Ibid., p. 63.
59. B. Smith 1992, p. 76. Webber was the son of a Swiss sculptor who had received his formative training in Bern.
60. Joppien and Smith 1985–88, vol. 3, pt. I, p. 193.
61. B. Smith 1992, p. 210.

FIGURE 4.2 (top) William Hodges, *A View of Matavai Bay, Otaheite* (ca. 1775–76).

FIGURE 4.3 (bottom) William Hodges, *A View of Maitavie Bay, Otaheite* (1776).

FIGURE 4.4 John Webber, *A Portrait of Poedua* (1777).

years later.[62] Most of the images of New Zealanders by Sydney Parkinson, who accompanied Cook on his first voyage, and most of those in Hawkesworth's book on that voyage, depicted men in war canoes, dressed for battle. In 1787 John Webber painted *A Chief of the Sandwich Islands Leading His Party to Battle* (fig. 4.5), an image that led Captain James King to comment on the "Nobleness of Countenance & manliness of figure" of its subjects.[63] Yet few

62. See reports by Jean Roux and Paul Chevallard de Montesson on the cannibalism incident in June 1772, in Ollivier 1985, pp. 204–5, 243. On Maori defiance of Cook's crew see Stanley Parkinson's 1770 image *New Zealand War Canoe Bidding Defiance to the Ship,* in Joppien and Smith 1985–88, vol. I, p. 198. Liebersohn 1999, p. 58, misses the fact that populations who were seen as "tough combative warriors," like the Maori, were *not* usually Europeans' preferred natives in the Pacific.

63. King's journal, in Beaglehole 1955–67, vol. 3, pt. I, p. 612.

FIGURE 4.5 John Webber, *A Chief of the Sandwich Islands Leading His Party to Battle* (1787).

contemporaries would have been able to dissociate these fierce Hawaiʻian warriors from the men who had killed Captain Cook. Indeed, the murderer in Webber's famous painting of Cook's death strongly resembles the chief in this later painting. Male noble savages were more problematic than female ones in a labile contact zone that had not yet stabilized in colonial or quasi-colonial ways, and in which armed conflict between Europeans and locals was an ever-present possibility.[64]

In sum, these early voyages produced a romantic and classicizing vision of Polynesia, concretized as Tahiti, whose inhabitants were nobler and closer to nature than Europeans. By the time the neoclassical revival

64. Zantop (1997) agrees, arguing that the positive German image of the male American noble savage arose in periods of colonial stability. Berkhofer (1978, p. 88) observes that "American authors and artists of the Eastern United States only conceived of the Indian as noble after that section of the country had eliminated its Indian problem."

and romanticism had given way to naturalism, these earlier images of Polynesia were already in wide circulation.[65] At the center of this paradigm were the ideas of hospitality, feminized sensuality, and relative social equality. The problem of the militant Polynesian man remained but would be partly "solved" by ongoing transformations over the course of the nineteenth century. Before discussing these developments, however, we need to ask how the early images of Tahiti were received and elaborated in German writing.

Polynesia and Tahiti in German Eyes, 1770s–1850

The influence of these early Pacific reports was as powerful in German-speaking Europe as elsewhere. The most influential German contributors to the early elaboration of the picture of Polynesia were Georg Forster and his father, naturalist Johann Reinhold Forster. Other important figures included the playwright August von Kotzebue, Adelbert von Chamisso (a literary and scientific world traveler like Georg Forster), and Friedrich Gerstäcker, the best-selling German travel and adventure novelist. During the second half of the nineteenth century, specialized literatures emerged in German on the various parts of Oceania, including a literature focused specifically on Samoa starting in the 1860s.[66] But German discussions of Polynesia initially centered on Tahiti.

GEORG AND JOHANN REINHOLD FORSTER

The descriptions of Tahiti by Georg and Johann Forster are not only the most detailed sections of their travel narratives but also the most arresting published accounts of any of Cook's voyages. The Forsters were also the first writers to give the discourse on Oceania a "German" accent. In addition to their eyewitness accounts, both men translated numerous travel narratives

65. Bernard Smith (1992, p. 188) refers to a bifurcation of representations of Oceania into the images of an Arcadia, on the one hand, and an abode of ghastly, pagan monsters, on the other. But the latter set of images referred mainly to Melanesians or partly acculturated Polynesians. None of the artists on Cook's voyages, to my knowledge, produced a single ghastly image of Tahiti or Polynesia.

66. Many other Germans commented briefly on Tahiti or Polynesia. Volk (1934) discusses the literary aspects of this material. Polynesia also figured increasingly in systematic race theories. According to Blumenbach's ([1865] 1978) influential schema there were five races—the Caucasian, Mongolian, Ethiopian, American, and Malay, and this was modified by geographer Freidrich Ratzel (1882–91, vol. 2, p. 580) to include a sixth, Melanesian, race.

from English and French into German and both helped to raise the level of Central European interest in Polynesia.[67]

Georg Forster was born in Prussia and moved to England in 1766 at the age of twelve with his father. Both men accompanied Cook on the *Resolution* in 1772. The first published account of Cook's second voyage was published under Georg's name in English in 1777 as *A Voyage Round the World*. Georg quickly translated his own book into German, and it went through numerous editions. Georg moved back to Germany in 1778, where he held several academic positions and published and translated widely until 1783, when he was stranded in Paris as a delegate of the Mainz Republic at the height of the Terror, and died.[68] Georg is also known for his writings on literature, politics, and the natural sciences, but it is fair to say that "the entirety of his main work rests on the scientific and artistic reworking of experiences during travel and expeditions."[69] Johann Forster's *Observations Made During a Voyage round the World* was also written and published in English (in 1778) before being translated by his son into German. The elder Forster returned to Germany in 1780, taking up an academic appointment at Halle University, where he lectured on a wide range of scientific topics and "lived to become a legend."[70]

The Forsters mediated an essentially pan-European vision of Oceania to a German audience while making few substantive changes. Georg Forster himself observed that "the faithful descriptions of Schouten, Le Maire, and Tasman . . . corresponded in every material particular with our own observations"—and he might have added Hawkesworth and Bougainville to this list.[71] The Forsters did not reject the figure of noble savagery but reworked

67. See, for example, the discussion of Georg Forster's travels through Central Europe with the original copper engravings from the English publication of Cook's third voyage, in the editor's comments, *Georg Forsters Werke*, vol. 5 (Berlin: Akademie Verlag, 1985), pp. 707–50. Blumenbach was inspired by Johann Forster to "revive the tradition of training and sending out explorers from Göttingen" (Hoare 1976, p. 310). Johann Forster edited the *Magazin von merkwürdigen neuen Reisebeschreibungen aus fremden Sprachen übersetzt*.

68. Georg Forster's reputation in Germany suffered somewhat during the reactionary period that followed the Congress of Vienna, but his works were frequently published during the nineteenth century, including a Brockhaus edition of his collected works in 1843. On the dueling East and West German approaches to Georg Forster, see Schneider 1998; on Forster's contribution to German cultural sciences, see M. Braun 1991; for recent discussions, see Agnew 1999a, 1999b.

69. Schneider 1998, p. 684.

70. Hoare 1976, p. 307.

71. G. Forster [1777] 2000, vol. 1, p. 256. Forster also refers at various points to Kolb, Bougainville, Mandeville, and Peter Osbeck—the latter one of the many students of Linnaeus who traveled to China.

and clarified it. Their most original contribution, in my view, was to attack the problem of the Polynesian male warrior head-on.

In their treatment of Pacific cultures, both of the Forsters waver between cultural relativism and confidence in the superiority of modern civilization.[72] Georg's *Voyage* weaves together several distinct registers and tropes, including cultural relativism and revindication; Johann sometimes emphasizes a climatological determinism of culture. The conventional code of noble savagery plays a significant role in both of their accounts, alongside other interpretive devices.[73] Like Bougainville, Georg Forster emphasizes Polynesian hospitality, concluding that the "good and simple Taheitians" lead a happy and wholesome life and are burdened with no "remembrance of injuries" or "spirit of revenge." Their frugal simplicity serves to "soften" class distinctions and "to reduce them to a level"; even the king himself is "not yet depraved by false notions of an empty state," and he "often paddles his own canoe." Although the literal language of nobility is not a necessary component of the discourse of noble savagery—Bougainville spoke of "good" (*bons*) islanders, not "noble" ones—both Forsters refer explicitly to Tahitians as "noble."[74] In Bougainvillean style, the Tahitian landscape itself is described by Georg Forster as "paradise-like."[75]

Analytically we can distinguish three dimensions of the discourse of noble savagery in the Forsters' writing: the explanatory-analytic, the descriptive, and the normative-evaluative. Both of the Forsters assume a universal developmental hierarchy. Johann is more explicit about this, positing a four-stage progression from animality through savagery and barbarism, culminating in civilization. These social conditions parallel the stages in the life of an individual: infancy, childhood, adolescence, and manhood.

72. Schneider (1998) traces the dualisms in Georg Forster's writing. Berman contrasts Georg Forster's interest in "alternative rationalities" with the abstract geometric empiricism and "instrumental rationality" of Cook's journals, but he neglects the Orientalist aspects of Georg Forster's writing (Berman 1998, pp. 40, 48). Berman is, I think, more interested in extracting from Forster's *Voyage* expressions of the second face of the Enlightenment, which he calls "emancipatory reason" (1998, p. 40). While these elements are certainly present, this does not justify the claim that "Forster encounters various societies with little need to lock them into a hierarchy" (1998, p. 55). Moreover, Berman does not relate Forster's differing evaluations of various Oceanic societies to the existing ethnographic conventions, especially the racial hierarchy of Melanesians and Polynesians and the special status of Tahiti.

73. The issue of whether Forster is *original* is a different question; as with Hodges and with all great travel writers and naturalist artists, there is an interweaving of direct observation, original interpretation, and established codes.

74. G. Forster [1777] 2000, pp. 176, 199. For "nobility" see ibid., pp. 219, 226, 380; J. Forster [1778] 1996, pp. 236–37, 244.

75. G. Forster 1985a, p. 49.

Arguing that "men in a similar state of civilization resemble each other," Johann Forster implies that Polynesians can be directly equated with Ancient Greece or Rome. This classicizing gesture suggests that "they" are an earlier stage of "us" and lends a positive emotional valence to the Other, even if it also encourages paternalism.[76]

The Forsters superimpose this civilizational hierarchy on the map of Oceania, placing Tahitians and some other Polynesians at the top, the Maoris of New Zealand in the middle, and the inhabitants of Tierra del Fuego at the bottom. Europeans were ranked above the Tahitians, of course, but this did not necessarily make them *morally* superior.[77] Georg was disturbed by the threat to the Tahitians' "happy equality" from their chiefs' "indolence," and he compared the Tahitian status hierarchy to European feudalism.[78] Once he had read George Keate's 1788 rendition of Captain Henry Wilson's shipwreck on Palau, Georg Forster decided that the Palauers were the best representatives of the happy medium since they had not yet progressed "beyond that stage of education at which a *romantic synergy* of simplicity and virtue is possible."[79] The Maoris were described by Georg as courageous, open, and honest—noble traits, to be sure—but also as brutally adhering to the survival of the fittest.[80] The Tierra del Fuegans had fallen to a crude natural level, or had never risen beyond it, and were deprived of human reason. Johann attributed their degeneration to the frigid climate and their isolation from more educated societies. Georg described these people as "fully submerged in indolence and stupid numbness."[81] It is at this point in his narrative that Georg suddenly insists on the "superior happiness" of a

76. G. Forster [1777] 2000, vol. 1, pp. 377-78; J. Forster [1778] 1996, p. 227. The earliest Greek comparison is in Johann Forster's journal from the *Resolution;* see J. Forster 1982, vol. 3, pp. 512-13.

77. This hierarchy is more explicit in Johann's *Observations.* Georg complicates the hierarchy of Melanesians and Polynesians. His discussion of the Malakulans compares them to monkeys but also calls them "the most intelligent people we had ever met with in the South Seas" (G. Forster [1777] 2000, vol. 2, p. 481). Berman (1998) and Thomas and Berghof (2000) point out that Georg Forster is an unusually open-minded observer for his time. One might add that this open-mindedness is expressed symptomatically in Forster's texts (as in the writings of Kolb and Le Vaillant) in the multiplication of disparate codes and tropes that we nowadays tend to read as mutually exclusive.

78. G. Forster [1777] 2000, vol. 1, p. 199.

79. G. Forster 1985d, p. 327 (my emphasis).

80. G. Forster [1777] 2000, vol. 1, pp. 102-3; see also the editors' comments in ibid., vol. 1, p. xxxiii.

81. G. Forster 1985c, p. 267. For Bougainville's description of the Tierra del Fuegans, see Taillemite 1977, vol. 1, pp. 284-85.

"civilized life over that of a savage," after having praised Polynesian life at the "romantic" intermediate stage as superior.[82]

Both of the Forsters give preference to a condition located between the "state of nature" and civilized European corruption like Rousseau, whose ideal was the "happy medium" in which "man is no longer an animal and is not yet the miserable creature he is to become."[83] For Johann, the ideal is that the savage be "brought nearer to a more improved, more civilized" state but "without the addition of these evils, which abuses, luxury and vice have introduced among our societies."[84] Georg notes of the Tahitians that they are not satisfied "simply to still their pressing needs but also *press a step forward culturally* in order to enjoy the little comforts of life."[85] Johann insists again and again that "our own civilized countries . . . [are] far outdone in real goodness and benevolence by a set of innocent people."[86] Here he drops his evolutionary hierarchy altogether and gives Tahiti the preference to "our mixed and degenerating societies."[87] Georg insists that the Tahitians are in fact "not more savage" than the Britons. The compassionate behavior of a Tahitian is described at one point as putting "those civilized Europeans

82. G. Forster [1777] 2000, vol. 2, p. 631. Thomas and Berghof insist, oddly, that there were no "stereotypic characterizations of noble and ignoble savages" in Georg Forster's account (2000, pp. xxxiii; also p. 451 n. 18). In part this is the same argument that has been going on since Lovejoy's famous essay (1955), which rigidly equated "noble savagery" with the "state of nature" and was then able to demonstrate that noble savagery thus defined was not Rousseau's desideratum. The fact that Forster interweaves Oceanic figures of noble and ignoble savagery with passages that are less encumbered by stereotypic figures, or that he sometimes uses alternative codes such as "revindication" in discussing Pacific islanders, does not mean that he is free of "stereotypes." As with all of the writers discussed in this book, familiar codes ("stereotypes") are used to structure unique observations and formulations in his writing. Thomas and Berghof also seem to assume that an image of noble savagery has to be pacific, whereas the Native American and Khoikhoi versions of this discourse emphasized men's warrior status. These authors rightly emphasize that both Forsters deviated from the standard approach of their era in downplaying the racial determination of cultural difference (Thomas and Berghof 2000, p. 450 n. 37; see G. Forster [1786] 1974).

83. Todorov 1993, p. 280. Neither of the Forsters is fully consistent in his use of these categories; on the page before his four-stage scheme, Johann seems to equate "savage" and "barbarian" ([1778] 1996, p. 199).

84. J. Forster [1778] 1996, p. 199. Nicholas Thomas relates Johann Forster's ambivalence about progress to the Scottish Enlightenment. The elder Forster also clearly has Rousseau in mind—the popular, misunderstood Rousseau—when referring to the insistence on the "happiness of the savage" by "some philosophers" (ibid.).

85. G. Forster 1985a, p. 51 (my emphasis).

86. J. Forster ([1778] 1996), p. 223.

87. J. Forster [1778] 1996, pp. 222.

to the blush, who have humanity so often on their lips, and so seldom in their hearts!"[88] Georg repeatedly alludes to the superiority of Polynesian over British life, observing that the sailors might well prefer to stay in Tahiti—a speculation that was borne out in 1789 when the mutineers of the *Bounty* demonstrated that they preferred life in Tahiti to working under Captain William Bligh. (Bligh acknowledged that the mutineers "assured themselves of a more happy life among the Otaheitians than they could possibly have in England.")[89] European civilization is comparatively more corrupt: "For one villain in these isles, we can shew at least fifty in England." This taste for an intermediate, *partially* civilized position is characteristic of the noble savagery perspective in general.[90]

It has been argued that the discourse of noble savagery disappeared after the shock of the Terror in the French Revolution and the violence of the Haitian revolution, a reaction led by "evangelical Christians," or even that it was a figment of intellectual historians' imaginations.[91] But it is child's play to follow the ongoing elaboration of the figures of noble savagery in European and German culture with respect to Polynesia over the course of the nineteenth century. The centerpiece of the further development of this set of tropes was the theme of gender and sexuality. Oceania was increasingly divided between, on the one hand, Melanesia and the more "primitive" parts of Polynesia, which figured as "male," and, on the other hand, the more "feminine" Tahiti and Polynesia.[92] Although many sailors may have been perfectly happy with an image of Polynesian women as prostitutes, the Forsters understood that it was necessary to emphasize the Bougainvillean formula (sensuality + innocence) if Polynesia were to gain wide acceptance in Europe.[93] In his discussion of Tahiti Georg Forster went to some lengths to insist on this point: "A great number of women of the lowest class . . . remained on board at sun-set . . . to pass a night on board. . . . This evening was . . . completely dedicated to mirth and pleasure. . . . The variety of dances . . . did not exactly correspond with our ideas of decency.

88. G. Forster [1777] 2000, vol. 1, pp. 177, 330.

89. G. Forster [1777] 2000, vol. 1, pp. 199, 379; Bligh quoted in Dening 1992, p. 8.

90. G. Forster [1777] 2000, vol. 1, p. 210. The difference between this stereotype and the perception of the Rehoboth Basters, who were also classed as occupying an intermediate location between savagery and civilization, is that the Basters' intermediacy was defined in biological, racial terms. As a result the Rehobothers did not provide an imaginary surface for European cross-identification.

91. Linnekin 1991a.

92. On the Western image of Polynesian women, see Sturma 2002.

93. Bougainville's *Voyage* had been translated into English by Johann Forster.

However, if we consider that the simplicity of their education and of their dress, makes many actions perfectly innocent here, which according to our customs, would be blameable, we cannot impute that degree of unbounded licentiousness to them, with which the prostitutes of civilized Europe are unhappily reproached." Georg remarked later that "instead of finding the inhabitants of these isles wholly plunged in sensuality, as former voyagers have falsely represented them, we have met with the most generous and exalted sentiments among them, that do honour to the human race in general."[94] Johann offered a similar portrait of Tahitian women as combining "modesty" with obliviousness to any "notion of turpitude."[95]

This effort to dissociate Polynesian women from European prostitutes was relevant to projects of future colonization, even if it was not undertaken with that in mind. Colonial conquest was not an official goal of Cook's voyages, but the entire choreography of this era in which Europeans stepped onto beaches and planted their national flags, naming and claiming islands, classifying new species of plants and animals, and subjecting cultures and cartographies to a standardizing grid, has a strikingly protocolonial flavor.[96] By introducing new objects and animals and setting in motion cultural revolutions, scientific explorers were sowing the seeds for a more formal annexation sometime in the future. Johann Forster seemed to endorse the idea of a scientific colonialism, an educational developmental state led by men "capable of enlarging their minds with new ideas relative to science, arts and manufactures, of instilling the principles of true morality and virtue into their breasts, or of communicating to them notions of a well regulated government."[97] But Georg recognized that European impact was primarily destructive.[98] Like Herman Melville in his second novel, *Omoo*, the younger Forster singled out the missionaries' "voluptuous priest-craft"

---

94. G. Forster [1777] 2000, vol. I, pp. 184–85, 210. Forster's text also presents a modernist relativism that describes radical difference without judging it or arraying it on a developmental scale. See his discussions of sex and cannibalism (ibid., pp. 250, 280–81); for an alternative reading see Agnew 1999b.

95. J. Forster [1778] 1996, p. 244. See also ibid., pp. 289–90, for Forster's portrait of a Raiatean girl who combined promiscuousness with "modesty of repentance," "bashful behaviour," and tears signifying condemnation of her own "immorality"; also ibid., p. 260, where J. Forster summarizes the women of "O-Taheitee, and its neighborhood" with a similar combination of traits.

96. Not just in Oceania and among the other *Naturvölker*, but also among *Kulturvölker*: Macartney's mission to China, like Cook's voyages, included a full range of artists and scientists along with diplomats (see chap. 6; and Dabringhaus 1996).

97. J. Forster [1778] 1996, p. 201; see also p. 238.

98. G. Forster 1985b.

for special criticism. And in one of the most explicitly anticolonial European comments since Bartolomé de Las Casas, Georg suggested that "it were indeed sincerely to be wished, that the intercourse which has lately subsisted between Europeans and the natives of the South Sea islands may be broken off in time, before the corruption of manners which unhappily characterizes civilized regions, may reach that innocent race of men, who live here fortunate in their ignorance and simplicity."[99]

In light of these comments about the "fatal impact" of Europeans it is ironic that the Fosters' comments on gender and aggression implicitly laid the groundwork for a model of "soft" colonialism that would be implemented much later in German Samoa. As we have seen, modern colonialism always entailed projects of cultural regulation, and these required at least minimal cooperation on the part of the colonized. Georg Forster interpreted the fact that Tahitian men offered their wives and daughters to the European visitors as a form of hospitality, and this provided a powerfully insinuating image of future colonial native policy.[100] Reading this as prostitution would not only have degraded it, but in European eyes it would also have turned the Polynesians into equal trading partners. Georg Forster preferred to understand this as a gift economy: Mauss rather than Marx. By the same token, Polynesian men's admirable warrior characteristics had to be dissociated from any threat of unpredictable violence. Georg Forster remarked that war was able to shake "these people, whose culture has such simplicity, completely out of their usual self-control and cast them backward a stage into barbarism."[101] The "taming" of Oceanic men by their own women, who were described as partners in colonization, was one way to prevent such cultural backsliding.[102] The Forsters almost hoped to demilitarize Oceanic men magically by describing them as less militant than they actually were. In explaining incidents of violence or theft against Europeans, Georg referred to Polynesians' anomalous cultural understandings and expectations. The hostilities that periodically erupted between Europeans and Pacific islanders were provoked by the interlopers.[103] He described Tahitian warships as "one of the most magnificent sights which it is possible to be entertained with in the South Sea,"

99. G. Forster [1777] 2000, vol. 1, p. 168; William Wales's 1778 polemic against Forster is reprinted in ibid., vol. 2, pp. 699–753.

100. G. Forster 1985a, p. 66.

101. G. Forster 1985c, p. 90.

102. According to Harriet Guest, Johann Forster described Tahitian women as indigenous protocolonizers, seducing their own men "by virtue of their sexualized art of pleasing into civilizing softness" (in J. Forster [1778] 1996, p. liv).

103. Thomas and Berghof, in G. Forster [1777] 2000, vol. 2, p. 822 n. 67.

recalling Hodges's paintings of the same ships. This aestheticization stripped the ships of their militant connotations.[104] Forster was fully aware that Tahitians had welcomed Cook only because they had already been cowed into submission by Wallis's guns, but he seemed to assume that Tahitians would never endanger Europeans.[105] The redescription of Polynesian men as harmless was itself an act of symbolic violence premised on acts of physical violence. This redescription adumbrated a colonial policy that would "feminize" indigenous men and in certain respects favor indigenous women.

TAHITI AS A ROMANTIC PARADISE IN GERMAN LITERATURE AT THE TURN OF THE EIGHTEENTH CENTURY

Georg Forster's *Voyage Round the World* had an immediate impact in Germany. In 1777, the year it was published, a group of German writers associated with the Pietistic *Empfindsamkeit* (sentimentality) movement came up with a utopian plan for emigration to Tahiti. One of them described Tahiti as "Eden, God's pleasure garden, where one can drink the creator's goodness from an unmuddied source, and where one can find his image again in man, an image that Adam may have lost for himself, but that he could not lose for an entire species." The long-term goal was a population of racially mixed descendants who would combine "the insights of cultivated humanity" with the natives' "innocence and goodness of heart."[106] The same year, Friedrich Wilhelm Zachariä published a poem called "Tahiti or the Happy Island," inspired by Bougainville's voyage and Zachariä's self-described "irresistible partiality for travel literature." All of the tropes of Polynesian noble savagery were combined with an anticolonialism even more pronounced than Georg Forster's:

O Muse, tear me away from the tumult
The burden of this European world,
Where war, and hunger, and the spirit of persecution,
Rage constantly! Let us flee
To the tranquil meadows in the island's bosom,
Where love, repose, and peace and innocence rule.

104. G. Forster [1777] 2000, vol. I, p. 355.
105. G. Forster 1985b, p. 265.
106. Letter from Adolf Overbeck to Johann Heinrich Voss, November 17, 1777, quoted in Herbst 1872, vol. I, pp. 199–200.

Later Zachariä describes Bougainville's landing on Tahiti:

> Six of the most beautiful girls approached, so beautiful that
> A European's fantasy could barely imagine them.
> They were naked, other than a light gown
> Flowing around hips painted with dark blue patterns.
> Their roguish eyes, filled with golden arrows,
> With unfeigned love, smiled at the white men, sure of victory.
> . . . .
> In the shadow of every coconut tree,
> At every silver fountain, sat, mixed,
> The white with the savage . . .

The poem concludes with a critique of imperialist aggression:

> But you, bloodthirsty spawn of murderous Europe,
> Could not obey the law of holy hospitality (unknown to you!)
> Even for a few days! Your thundering powder,
> Your polished steel, flew ferociously
> Through the naked breasts of your new friends!
> . . . .
> O once so peaceful people! Hidden
> From the European mania for conquest
> And from the ravagers' feverish thirst for gold
> By motherly nature!
> . . . .
> Unhappy land! Soon the sailing ships
> Of the Europeans will return! Deceit and murder
> Will rage more openly!
> Innocents' freedom will flee weeping, and with it
> The customs of equality and the
> Refreshing community of property! Tyranny
> Will rule over you! [107]

A secret society was formed some years later among Tübingen University students with the goal of emigrating to Polynesia and creating a colony without money where freedom would be "guaranteed to us for centuries." These Swabians, whose conspiracy was broken up by the police, had been inspired by reading Georg Forster.[108]

---

107. Zachariä 1778, pp. 142, 153, 162, 165–66, 171–72.
108. Volk 1934, p. 61.

An anonymous book called *Otaheitische Gemälde* (Tahitian Paintings), published in Bremen in 1803, combines a fictional narrative with a twenty-seven-page "introduction" that is a strange mixture of poetic invocation and ethnographic description of Tahiti. Undistinguished as prose and unoriginal as ethnography, *Otaheitische Gemälde* demonstrates that the image of uncorrupted Polynesian noble savages had survived the rise of a harsher science of race in Germany at the turn of the century, codified by the likes of Samuel Thomas von Soemmering and Christoph Meiners and fueled by reaction to the Haitian revolution.[109] Yet the antirevolutionary, reactionary political turn in Germany did not have uniform effects on literary and scientific culture. For some people, the impetus to seek utopia, or at least improvement, outside Europe was correlatively enhanced as democratic possibilities and social utopianism withered at home (as in the paean to equality and communal property in Zachariä's poem). This tendency to flee from the realities of the time and the narrowing compass of domestic democratic possibilities into "utopias of escape" (*Fluchtutopien*) is related not just to utopian socialism but also to the proliferation in German literature before 1848 of idyllic images of Tahiti and Polynesia as well as India and other parts of the "Orient."[110] The cultural context for these utopias was the emergence of German romanticism. This explains why the discourse of noble savagery was not limited to the eighteenth century but continued to develop and adopt new accents after 1800.

Otaheitische Gemälde again describes Tahiti as a Garden of Eden. Its inhabitants are models of "virtue, innocence, and naturalness," whose skin is "so white that any embarrassing thought causes them to blush visibly": "Growing up innocently in the bosom of beautiful nature, soft and mild, they are contented and wealthy without gold; courteous, sincere, and noble in their conduct. . . . O, this is the Golden Age, a place even more delightful than Arcadia, where we imagine everything that would turn the earth into Eden. . . . The most charming island in the world."[111] In terms of genre, the text is situated between the exaggerated pathos of the literature of *Empfindsamkeit*, melodrama, and "scientific" travel narrative. The text is strewn with Tahitian words, historical names, and footnotes that reveal the author's familiarity with the contemporary travel literature. The story involves a love affair between two Tahitians, Mahána and Aurea,

109. Soemmering 1785; Meiners 1811. On the correlation between the rise of a more racist theory in Germany and the impact of the Haitian and French revolutions, see Zantop 1997, chap. 5, pp. 154ff.; Buck-Morss 2000.

110. Brunner 1967, p. 133.

111. *Otaheitische Gemälde* 1803, pp. 18, 12, 23-24.

nineteen years after Wallis's visit. Following established conventions, Aurea is described lewdly, producing an awkward form of pornography: she has "golden tresses," "rosy lips" that give "fiery kisses," and breasts that are often bared and repeatedly described as "heaving."[112] As a noble savage, however, Aurea is entirely innocent. The "heavenly lust" of her relationship with Mahána is contrasted with the "basest lust" of the Tahitian *arioi* and the European sailors. An even nobler figure is Mahána's father, Manurái, who sagely weighs the advantages and disadvantages of contact with Europeans. Manurái concludes that the Tahitians are happier than the British, though less "educated" and at a "very low stage" of development, and that it would have been preferable if the Europeans "had never visited this happy island."[113] He is the direct, plagiarized heir of the "old man" in Diderot's *Supplement,* translated into German.

AUGUST VON KOTZEBUE AND POLYNESIA

The first artistic presentation of Polynesia in German literature was August von Kotzebue's play *La Peyrouse.* Kotzebue was a popular and prolific playwright whose work was widely performed in Germany, England, and France during the late eighteenth and early nineteenth centuries.[114] He was born in Weimar and wrote in German but spent over half of his life in Russia. Many of his plays, especially those written in the decade after the French Revolution, deal with colonialism, slavery, and cultural contact between Europeans and non-Europeans.[115] In several of these plays, as Susanne Zantop has shown, Kotzebue relies on a plot structure that was fairly conventional at the time, in which the contradictions of racism are magically resolved through intermarriage.[116] Equally important for the present discussion of German representations of Polynesia is Kotzebue's "Rousseauian"

112. *Otaheitische Gemälde* 1803, pp. 39, 143, 33. Aurea's breasts are described as "hoch sich erhebend, um schmachend zu sinken," "sich hebend," "sanft sich wölbend," "wallend," "bebend," and so on (ibid., pp. 33, 39, 44, 143, 55).

113. Ibid., pp. 63, 91, 89, 92.

114. On performances of Kotzebue in England, see Sellier 1901; for France, see Denis 1976; for Germany, see Zantop 1997, chap. 7.

115. The most notable of these are *The Virgin of the Sun* (*Die Sonnen-Jungfrau*), *The East Indian* (*Die Indianer in England*), *Pizarro* (*Die Spanier in Peru*), *The Negro Slaves* (*Die Negersklaven*), and *La Peyrouse.*

116. As Hulme (1986) shows, this model was already well established in the fictional literature on encounters in the New World, in the stories of John Smith and Pocahontas or Inkle and Yarico.

preference in his early plays for the partially civilized cultures of *outre-mer*, as against ruined and corrupt Europe. In the play *Brother Moritz, the Eccentric; or the Colony for the Palau Islands* (1791), the main figure describes the inhabitants of Palau, who were "discovered by an Englishman, Wilson," as "good, unspoiled creatures."[117] In *The Negro Slaves* (1796), the noble slave Lilli reminisces about her African homeland: "In Congo and Loango, we are always happy; we live for today und relish today and never speak: tomorrow is another day. That's why hospitality is alive in our huts, and we disdain greed. That's why we call the Europeans '*clenched hands*.' We do not think about the past; we count our years no more than we count the drops of water that the great Volta River washes under our feet." Lest one read this Africa as brutish rather than noble, Lilli adds that "we believe in the highest God, Numbo, although he is much too distinguished to busy himself with our affairs."[118] For most Europeans, lack of religion was a serious deficit that could call into question the merits of an otherwise admirable culture, and monotheism ("the highest God") was especially praiseworthy. Kotzebue's play *The East Indian* (1789) centers on the "Nabob of Mysore," who has been forced by internal politics to go into exile in an English seaport town. The narrative culminates in the marriages of the Nabob's son and daughter to the children of an English colonial merchant, in a neat resolution of colonial contradictions. More interesting in the present context is the fact that the Indian girl (called "Gurli") is described by her father as a "child of nature." Kotzebue's suggestions for staging characterize "Gurli" and her brother as exhibiting the "joy of an uncorrupted nature."[119] In Kotzebue's fiercest critique of colonialism, *The Virgin of the Sun* (1789), the central figure is a Spanish nobleman, Don Alonzo, who throws in his lot with the Incas to help them resist Pizarro.[120] In the sequel, *Pizarro* (1794–95), European corruption and barbarism are condensed in the figure of the eponymous conquistador. Pizarro is a "pirate, treating men as brutes" and "the world as booty." Las Casas, who appears in the play as a moral authority, describes the Peruvians as "children of innocence" who received the Spanish "as cherish'd guests with eager hospitality."[121] Even Pizarro is finally forced to

---

117. Kotzebue [1791] 1840, p. 184.

118. Kotzebue [1796] 1840, p. 180.

119. Kotzebue [1789] 1800a, pp. 73, 82; the same staging comments are given in the German original.

120. Kotzebue [1789] 1800b. Kotzebue's play was one of many reworkings of the novel *Les Incas* by Jean-François Marmontel (1777), which is discussed by Zantop (1997, pp. 123–26).

121. Kotzebue [1795] 1800, pp. 1, 6.

acknowledge the "rude honor of a savage foe—before whose native dignity of soul I have sunk confounded and subdued."[122]

One explicitly "Rousseauian" feature of Kotzebue's plays from this period is their valorization of a civilizational stage located between corrupt Europe and the base state of nature. This preference emerges most clearly in the final scene of *The Virgin of the Sun*, which depicts the Inca polity as advancing civilizationally from a primitive authoritarianism to a system that is moderate and humane but still more natural and uncorrupted than Europe. The Inca king renounces the harsh, ancient traditions that would have condemned the Virgin of the Sun to death. The high priest explains that the vow of chastity for consecrated virgins was instituted during "rude times" when "reason was so much in its infancy," but observes that "a long series of years has changed a forced obedience to the laws of order, into an inward feeling of their beauty, and where this rules, compulsive institutions are no longer necessary."[123] Similarly, in *The Negro Slaves*, the emphasis on hospitality and monotheism in Lilli's homeland elevates Africa above any suspicions of lowly primitivism. Another African, Zameo, is driven by noble familial love to take his father's place on the slave ship headed to Jamaica, and the same lofty familial sentiments motivate Zameo's father to make his way to Jamaica in turn and to substitute himself for his son. The most admirable figure in *The East Indian* is the Mysorean Nabob, whose discrete modesty about his aristocratic background is contrasted favorably with the pretentious behavior of the English merchant's German wife, who is forever boasting about her "ancient and honorable blood" from the venerable family of the "Quirliquitsch."[124]

La Peyrouse is Kotzebue's only play set in the Pacific. It concerns the fate of the French explorer Lapérouse, whose voyage played a central but

---

122. Ibid., p. 48.

123. Kotzebue [1789] 1800b, pp. 95-96. The decisive interventions in *The Virgin of the Sun* are not accomplished by the Spaniards, pace Zantop (1997, p. 130), but by the Incas, and Don Alonzo is *not* the only character who is "given more complexity." The king's revoking of tradition at the urging of the high priest and Rolla's decision to take up arms against his own king are depicted as difficult choices reached after extensive deliberation. One of the Spanish characters, Don Juan Velasquez, clings to the rule of the (Inca) law in a rigid and authoritarian manner that mirrors the behavior of the traditionalist Inca priest Xaria, insisting that he "will not commit a crime" against the Inca laws "even to save [Don Alonzo]." In another passage, Don Alonzo compares his Spanish companions to "the brute, who looks to sense alone for his enjoyments" (Kotzebue [1789] 1800b, pp. 71, 29). The Incas' civilizational advance is indeed attributed partly to the influence of Europeans, but these are Europeans who reject the dominant European colonial model.

124. Kotzebue ([1789] 1800a), pp. 10, 32.

peculiar role in European views of Samoa (see below).[125] *La Peyrouse* is a melodramatic Robinsonade, the story of a man stranded on an (almost) deserted island. At the beginning of the play it is revealed that Lapérouse actually survived his famous shipwreck, having been rescued by a native woman, Malvina, who was visiting the uninhabited island with her family when he washed up on shore. The figure of a European man being rescued by a native women was ubiquitous in the literature of the time, gesturing toward the European colonizers' dependence on the people they set out to conquer.

At the beginning of the play, Lapérouse and Malvina are in love and have a son. Lapérouse has taught Malvina his language and religion, reversing the terms of his initial dependence: She now prays to a European god in French. The plot is set in motion by the sudden arrival on the island of Lapérouse's wife, Adelaide, who has been searching for her lost husband throughout the Pacific. She is accompanied by her husband's other son, who was born after Lapérouse set sail from France eight years earlier. Adelaide quickly realizes that Malvina has risked her own life to save Lapérouse and abandoned her own culture and family to be with him. Malvina, in her "natural innocence," suggests that Lapérouse return to France with both wives, but she is told that this would be culturally impossible. Her next proposal is that all three remain together on the island, since "nature here is the lawgiver." Again she is rebuffed.[126]

The entire fin-de-siècle ideological formation of Polynesian noble savagery is present in Kotzebue's drama. Like the Inca, East Indian, and African figures in his earlier plays, Malvina is portrayed as being superior to the simple savagery of her ancestors *and* to the corrupt Europeans. When Malvina warns Adelaide against eating a lethal fruit, Adelaide takes this as evidence of the native woman's "noble mind," and contrasts this natural, innocent goodness with the "detestable, artful passions" to which Europeans are prone. Adelaide and Lapérouse both exemplify the decadence of Europe by attempting the "unnatural" act of suicide.[127] Adelaide's brother, Clairville, then arrives on the scene. He reports that France is undergoing revolutionary turmoil and that it would be senseless to return to that

---

125. Even today France continues to search for Lapérouse's lost vessels; see Zecchini 2005.

126. Kotzebue [1789] 1800b, p. 26. Kotzebue eliminated the line about nature as "lawgiver" from the second, revised version of the play which he wrote around 1818. I will discuss this second version below.

127. Ibid., p. 32. Malvina also prays for the "courage to die," but unlike the two Europeans, she does not reach for a weapon (ibid., p. 37). Again, hers is an intermediate position.

"degenerated country." Clairville proposes that the entire group remain in this "verdant grove for pure love" to "lay the foundation of a colony." Like Alonzo in *Virgin of the Sun* and the mutineers on Captain Bligh's *Bounty,* these refugees from a morally bankrupt civilization seek refuge in a "paradise of innocence."[128]

This is not the first time that Germans envisioned a colonial settlement in Polynesia, but it is probably the first German text that begins to imagine the details of a properly colonial mode of regulation of Polynesian culture.[129] Native policy is reduced here to the problem of managing a single "native." In a premonition of the colonial rule of difference the European characters seem to sense that Malvina's polygamous suggestion would entail too great a rapprochement between European and Polynesian culture. The alternative is for Adelaide and Malvina to become "sisters" and relate to Lapérouse as a brother, with all three constituting a "joyful family" together with their children. The men and women retire to separate huts at night. This infusion of native practices with European meanings—the invention of a sort of polygamy without sex—anticipates the later German colonial strategy of regulated preservation of native culture in Samoa. Malvina is "salvaged" in her noble difference and the Europeans are protected from going native.[130] Cultural difference is maintained even within the intimate sphere of the intercultural family—"sisters" need not be identical to one another, but a fully sexual union between Malvina and Lapérouse would erode the boundaries between the two subjects, yielding a third, métis term. The contradictions of colonialism receive a sort of imaginary resolution through the stabilized ménage.

Like the Tahitian women discussed by Johann Forster, Malvina is also depicted as having "tamed" her savage brother and father. They had threatened to kill Lapérouse, but "the tears of Malvina only saved him." Indeed, there are no native men at all in Kotzebue's Pacific paradise. Similarly in *Virgin of the Sun,* the volatile Inca warrior Rolla first loses his beloved Cora to the Spaniard Don Alonzo in a romantic competition, and in the later play Rolla dies saving the child of Don Alonzo and Cora. The longing for a native population without indigenous men reaches its apotheosis in European

128. Ibid., pp. 38–40.

129. The island colony in Schnabel's earlier *Insel Felsenburg* (1731–43; see Schnabel 1902) is located somewhere in the "East Indies"; more important, there are no natives on that island.

130. Similarly in *The Virgin of the Sun,* Don Alonzo agrees to pray to the sun god with Cora, but he remains a Christian, proclaiming, "'Tis true that this is but an idol's Temple, yet God is every where, even in this place, where he is adored in the image of what he himself created" (Kotzebue [1789] 1800b, p. 82).

thinking about the South Sea. In Pierre Loti's *Marriage of Loti,* which takes place in Tahiti, and in Paul Gauguin's Polynesian images, young indigenous men recede almost entirely into the background.

The relations between noble savagery, Polynesian women, and colonization that were adumbrated in Bougainville and Georg Forster thus receive a surprisingly complete integration in Kotzebue's play. It is worth noting, however, that Kotzebue became dissatisfied with the ending to *La Peyrouse* and rewrote it more than two decades later. In the later version, Adelaide proposes the same familial ménage à trois, but Malvina kills herself, declaring that "we three can never be happy together—neither here nor in your fatherland."[131] Kotzebue claimed that he had changed the ending because "it was not satisfying," yet the original version of the play was widely reedited, translated, and performed.[132] His decision may have been related to the fact that English and French audiences found even the desexualized ménage too shocking and directors were already beginning to change the ending on their own. In the English adaptation of the play (1801), Lapérouse was rescued by a chimpanzee instead of a woman, and in the French adaptation that opened in 1810, the "Europeans and the savages go their separate ways after a peaceful reconciliation, each living in their own country," with Lapérouse being allowed to keep one of the children by his native wife.[133] Kotzebue himself may have found the idea of a peaceful colonialism based on intercultural "families in difference" increasingly implausible.

What disappeared in the nineteenth century was not the trope of the noble savage but the fantasy of a colonialism based on intimate relations between Europeans and "savages." It is significant that Kotzebue did not rewrite the character of Malvina, or any of his other noble non-Western characters. Instead, what he changed was the intimate relationship between colonizer and colonized, which was no longer allowed to function as the protocolony's stable foundation. In German exotic fiction between the 1820s and midcentury, such intercultural intimacies were generally doomed to failure, as Zantop shows. The result in Kotzebue's second version of *La Peyrouse* was a colonialism without the colonized, or rather the termination of a colony

131. Kotzebue 1841, p. 60.

132. Sellier 1901, p. 76.

133. Ibid., p. 74; Denis 1976, vol. 3, p. 1223. By killing off Malvina, Kotzebue was also following the example of Goethe, who had revised his controversial play *Stella* (1776, second version written in 1805 and published in 1816), also a love triangle with two women and one man, along similar lines.

before it ever started. This makes some sense when we consider that this was a historical period in which practical colonialism was not a possibility for Germany. And this shift in patterns of exotic fiction was common throughout Europe. It cannot be explained solely in terms of a panic around the Haitian revolution but has to be connected to a more sweeping change: the slowing pace of European annexation of colonies in an era of anticolonial revolutions in the Americas and the subsequent British hegemonization of the world system.[134] Gerstäcker's novel *Tahiti* carries to an extreme this skepticism about resolving colonial tension through intercultural love. But this novel was published in 1852, when European colonial annexation was beginning to move back onto the global agenda. I will return to this novel below.

ADELBERT VON CHAMISSO, LOUIS CHORIS, AND POLYNESIAN NOBLE SAVAGERY

Adelbert von Chamisso was the scion of an old French noble family that had emigrated to Prussia during the French Revolution.[135] In addition to his renown as a poet, naturalist, and author of the fantasy story *Peter Schlemihl,* Chamisso is notable for having been the first person to undertake a voyage around the world starting from Berlin.[136] Between 1815 and 1818 Chamisso sailed with an exploring expedition financed by Nikolai Petrovich Rumiantsev (Romanzov) and commanded by Otto von Kotzebue, son of the German playwright and a captain in the Russian navy. Their ship, the *Rurik,* visited South America, California, Alaska, and the Cape of Good Hope, but Chamisso was most intrigued by Oceania. The bulk of his long essay "Notes and Opinions" (published as volume three of Otto von Kotzebue's official account of the voyage) and most of his full-length travel narrative were devoted to Hawai'i, the Carolines, and the Marshall Islands. Chamisso also wrote essays about the Hawai'ian language (1836) and the Hawai'ian king's visit to London (1824). As a result, Chamisso briefly became the Forsters' successor as the German expert on matters Polynesian.

Although Chamisso explicitly lodged "a solemn protest against the designation 'savages' in its application to the South Sea islanders," his description

---

134. Despite some major exceptions, like British government control of India after the Mutiny or the French annexations of Algeria and Tahiti, the pace of colonial annexation slowed after 1820 and picked up again only in the last two decades of the century (Bergesen and Schoenberg 1980).

135. Liebersohn 2003.

136. Chamisso [1821] 1986, p. 8.

of these cultures hews closely to the contemporary tropes of Polynesian noble savagery. This is most evident in his discussion of the people of Ratak (the eastern part of the Marshall Islands), a passage in his book that was familiar to Germans even at the beginning of the twentieth century.[137] The Ratakians' culture was neither "estranged from nature" nor mired in a raw state of nature, but located blessedly in between these poles, and in the process of "developing." The character of this "clean, attractive people" included "great honesty" and "pure, uncorrupted customs, charm, grace, and the gracious bloom of modesty." In line with the conventional emphasis on hospitality, Chamisso stressed that the Ratakians were "generous" and "not concerned with profit." The ceremony in which Ratakians exchanged names with the Europeans impressed everyone who reported on the voyage. The landscape of Ratak was idyllic, the forests "a flowing, luxurious green," and "nowhere is the sky fairer, the temperature more uniform."[138]

Ratak and the Carolines were set off against Europe ("we barbarians") and Hawai'i. Chamisso likened the Hawai'ian social system to European feudalism and monarchy. Like Georg Forster, Chamisso found the highly stratified Oceanic societies less attractive than places like Ratak, where he claimed to discern an "equality in the concourse between chief and vassals." In Ratak there was "no humbling of one's self before more powerful men." The Hawai'ians, by contrast, Chamisso found to be "self-serving, graceless, and unclean. In their relations with strangers . . . they have forgotten their natural hospitality. . . . The women are beautiful but without charm." Repeating a leitmotif that ran through most German writing on Polynesia, Chamisso blamed Hawai'i's lack of charm on the missionaries: "It is already becoming too late. In Tahiti and O-Waihi the missionary shirts already veil the beautiful bodies, all artistic activity is becoming mute, and the taboo of the Sabbath is sinking quietly and sadly upon the children of joy."[139]

Chamisso also contributed to the ongoing European elaboration of Polynesian gender roles. He praised Ratakian "women's comportment" for being "shy and reserved."[140] With his portrait of Kadu, a native of Woleai in the western Carolines, Chamisso continued the demilitarization of the image of the Polynesian male. One of the "chief features of Kadu's character" was

---

137. See Krämer 1906, p. 69. Ratak was written "Radak" in the nineteenth century. The island chain had been visited by Spaniards in the early sixteenth century and was named after the British explorer who landed there in 1788. See Krämer and Nevermann 1938.

138. Chamisso [1821] 1986, pp. 268, 277, 130, 129, 134, 136, 139.

139. Ibid., pp. 277, 313, 125.

140. Ibid., p. 277.

"his deeply rooted repugnance toward war, the murder of human beings."
Chamisso called Kadu "one of finest characters I have met in my life," and
the two men "became friends without reservation."[141] Kadu was Chamisso's
privileged native informant on Ratak and the Carolines, exemplifying the
"creative contribution of indigenous people to their ethnography."[142]

Louis Choris, the artist on board the *Rurik*, was a Russian painter of
Ukrainian German parentage. Choris included an image of Ratakians in his
own published travel narrative that underscored their intermediate status,
their combined proximity to and distance from nature (plate 3).[143] The figures' partial nudity and the simplicity of their shelters suggest "savagery,"
while the staged elegance of their gestures and poses and the overall arrangement of the figures communicate grace and taste. And while the women
figures correspond to the established stereotypes of noble savagery, the man
in the right foreground is made to appear harmless, in keeping with the
desire for a demilitarized Polynesian masculinity. His hands are folded de-
murely in his lap, and he is wearing various accoutrements that would have
appeared feminine to European eyes—earrings, grass skirt, and an elaborate vertical coiffure.

Nineteenth-Century Social Change in Polynesia and the Increasing Attractiveness of Samoa

The European longing to be welcomed by the very people they would subsequently dispossess began to seem like a somewhat more realistic goal during the first half of the nineteenth century. Missionaries played an especially important role in the pacification of Polynesian-European relations.
The modern missionary penetration of Polynesia began with the voyage
of the *Duff,* a ship financed by the London Missionary Society and commanded by James Wilson, which set sail in 1796.[144] The *Duff*'s main cargo
was missionaries bound for Tahiti, Tongatapu, and the Marquesas. Missionaries moved into Polynesia in ever greater numbers in the following
decades, converting Tahitians, Hawai'ians, and Samoans in large num-

141. Ibid., pp. 267, 129.

142. R. Firth 2001.

143. In addition to his own publications (especially Choris 1822) and recently published
journals (Choris 1999), see Charlot 1958; Forbes 1992, p. 56; and Liebersohn 1999.

144. Of course, Jesuit missionaries arrived in the Mariana Islands in 1668 after they
were claimed by the Spanish Crown (in 1565). I am ignoring early modern colonization in the
region later known as Micronesia.

bers.[145] Somewhat later, European powers began to assume formal colonial control over certain key Pacific islands. Britain declared its sovereignty over New Zealand in 1840 and Fiji in 1874; France claimed Tahiti and the Marquesas as protectorates in the 1840s and New Caledonia in 1853. Violence was not eliminated from European-Oceanic relations, but it was increasingly monopolized by the outsiders. Colonial aggression took various forms, ranging from the repression of "pagan" traditions to interventions by naval gunboats. Polynesians resisted these incursions, but full-scale uprisings were perhaps less frequent than in colonial Africa. The ideological correlation between Polynesians and peacefulness was strengthened as a result.

Accompanying these changes was a metamorphosis in the image of Tahiti. During the early decades of the century Tahiti became the European metropolis of the South Pacific islands, flooded with industrially produced commodities and with the largest contingent of missionaries, traders, European sailing crews. Consuls from France and England struggled for influence.[146] The culture that had so captivated Bougainville, Commerson, and the Forsters dissolved under the impact of these novelties or was actively repressed by missionaries allied with the Tahitian king and Christian convert Pomare II. The result was a "missionary theocracy" on the island prior to French colonial rule.[147] Gauguin's Tahitian paintings and prints are usually read as expressions of the Arcadian imagery of noble savagery, but many of them focus instead on the *tristesse tropicale,* the melancholy gulf between desolate colonial modernity and lost traditions.[148] Victor Segalen's 1907 novel *Les Immémoriaux* (translated as *A Lapse of Memory*) thematizes this Tahitian cultural amnesia.

Missionaries also generated a formidable counterdiscourse to noble savagery. James Wilson, captain of the ship that brought the first group of LMS missionaries to the Pacific, concluded his account of that voyage with a comparison of the various islands. In terms of "manners," he pronounced, Tahiti was "the most dissolute." Where Georg Forster had seen class despotism as a *potential* threat to equality in Tahiti, Wilson insisted that "the despotic rule at Otaheite . . . and the insolent demands of the arreoy [*arioi*] society, tend to destroy all industry." The women of Tahiti, far from being

145. See Wilson [1799] 1966; Laux 2000.

146. Gilson 1970, p. 67.

147. See Mühlmann 1955; Laux 2000; and Oliver 1974, vol. 3, chap. 30.

148. See Gauguin's book *Noa Noa* (1919) and paintings by Gauguin such as *Ancestors of Tehamana* (1893).

the sirens of Commerson and Diderot, were physically unattractive and often "very disgusting."[149] An antimissionary position consolidated itself in response, focusing on the cultural dereliction caused by missionary and European interventions in the Pacific, but it could not reinstall the obsolete portrait.[150]

The ongoing changes in Tahiti and the missionaries' assault on its traditions meant that the ideological space formerly occupied by Tahiti was increasingly available for occupation by some other New Cythera. Hawai'i was a plausible candidate,[151] but Cook's infamous murder continued to cast a shadow over those islands for Europeans. An extensive comparative study of Oceania published in 1873 by two German ethnologists introduced its discussion of Hawai'i with an image of Cook's grave, and the next image was of Cook's death.[152] The erosion of tradition in Hawai'i was at least as dramatic as in Tahiti, beginning with the formal abrogation of the entire tabu system in 1819.[153] German ethnologist Arthur Baessler wrote in 1895 that he had "seldom been . . . so disappointed" as in his approach to "the coast of Oahu": "Before my eyes lay . . . an American city that could just as well have arisen in the gold fields of California or anywhere else in the world."[154] For Jack London, writing at the beginning of the twentieth century, Hawai'i was a symbol of colonial decay, leprosy, madness, and exploitation by missionaries and planters.[155] Only with the rise of mass tourism and advertising campaigns in the twentieth century was the Bougainvillean image of Tahiti forcibly reassociated with Hawai'i. Another candidate for the newer Cythera was Nuku Hiva in the Marquesas, which was praised by some early

149. Wilson [1799] 1966, pp. 407–8.

150. Once Tahiti came under official French colonial control it was subject to the usual pressure to seek a stabilizing native policy. It was in this context that the discourse of noble savagery reemerged as a foundation for colonial governance. Loti's novel *The Marriage of Loti*, written under conditions of full-blown colonialism, is an ideological throwback to Bougainville, its island populated by innocent and sensuous Tahitians. By contrast, one of Gauguin's best paintings of Tahitian nontraditionalism, *Ta matete* (*The Market*, 1892), is an image of Tahitian prostitutes on a park bench smoking cigarettes and grasping public health inspection certificates (Eisenman 1997, p. 155).

151. See, for example, Webber's painting *Poedua* (fig. 4.4). There was a tendency throughout the nineteenth century to depict Hawai'i and its women as sensuous and dignified, as in Theodore Wores's painting *The Lei Maker* (1901).

152. Christmann and Oberländer 1873, vol. 2, p. 319.

153. Sahlins 1981, p. 56.

154. Baessler 1895, p. 341.

155. See especially London's "leprosy trilogy." For Robert Louis Stevenson Hawai'ians retained a degree of eccentric autonomy but their actions were shaped as much by the omnipresent agents of imperialism as by their own traditions and folkloric "imps."

explorers. In 1813, however, Krusenstern declared the Nuku Hivans to be notorious cannibals and liars, and Melville seemed to reach the same conclusion in his novel *Typee*.[156] Other islands in Micronesia were described as spoiled. A German visitor to Ratak, Elisabeth Krämer-Bannow, wrote in 1913 that it was possible to find "only a few houses built in the traditional style, in the most remote areas." Reflecting on the charm that Ratak had once exerted over Chamisso, she asked, "Where have they gone . . . the lovely female figures in their becoming costumes made of mats?" and bemoaned the fact that the "strong, copiously tattooed men in grass skirts" in Choris's paintings were now clad in "shirts, trousers, jackets, and European-style hats, which after a short period of use lends them a shabby, beggarly appearance."[157] The traditional housing and colorful mat clothing in Kusae (now called Kosrae) had been abandoned or suppressed by American missionaries, and in Ponape (Pohnpei) the people had been taught to disdain their ancient customs. Palau was described in idyllic "Tahitian" terms, but it was too small and unfamiliar to take the place of Tahiti.[158]

Instead, it was Samoa that emerged to epitomize the Polynesian Eden between 1850 and the 1920s. By the end of the nineteenth century the American artist John La Farge was painting Samoa to make it look like Hodges's Tahiti. In the 1920s, Margaret Mead opened her panegyric to Samoan sexual freedom with a tableau entitled "A Day in Samoa," which described "half-clad, unhurried women" and girls stopping "to giggle over some young ne'er-do-well who escaped during the night from an angry father's pursuit." Mead's chapter ended with "a group of merry youths [who] dance for the pleasure of some visiting maiden" and, finally, with "the whisper of lovers."[159] From Commerson to Mead, an unbroken thread of discourse.

156. See Krusenstern [1813] 1869, pp. 151–84. *Typee* concerns an American sailor, Tom (or Tommo), who is stranded in Nuku Hiva. Toward the beginning of the novel the first-person narrator compares the island's women to "so many mermaids" and worries about the "contaminating contact with the white man." The narrator criticizes the use of the word *savages* and concludes that the islanders may be happier than civilized man. The Typee chief Mehevi is explicitly called a "noble savage," and Rousseau is mentioned. The middle section of the novel concerns Tommo's romance with the scantily clad and "beauteous nymph Fayaway" (Melville [1846] 1996, pp. 14, 90, 85). Yet it eventually becomes clear that the "Typees" are, in fact, cannibals and that they are holding Tommo hostage. Like Fontane's *Effi Briest*, whose shifting depiction of the "Chinaman" figure recapitulates the evolution of European views of China (see chap. 6), *Typee*'s narrative arc from noble to abject savagery tracks the trajectory of nineteenth-century Western representations of Nuku Hiva.

157. Krämer-Bannow n.d., p. 4.

158. See Keate 1788.

159. Mead [1928] 1973, pp. 15, 19. The cover illustrations on the various editions of *Coming of Age in Samoa* reinforce this message.

Before turning to Samoa, however, let us briefly examine the only nineteenth-century German novel on Tahiti, which was written in the transitional period before full-scale colonialism in those islands. Given Gerstäcker's enormous popularity in Germany, it is plausible that this novel influenced later German thinking about Samoa.

GERSTÄCKER'S *TAHITI*:
COLONIAL EXPULSION FROM PARADISE

Friedrich Gerstäcker was the most widely read German adventure novelist and travel writer of the middle decades of the nineteenth century. His novels were often reworkings of his extensive travels, which included a trip to the Pacific in 1850 and 1851. The novels borrow unabashedly from Cooper, Chateaubriand, Defoe, and Melville.[160] Gerstäcker's Tahitians are exemplary Polynesian noble savages, but his novel also registers ongoing shifts in that set of conventions and in the image of Tahiti. The island's women are innocent and sensuous; the men are honorable warriors who become aggressive only when unjustly provoked. A leitmotif in all of Gerstäcker's novels is the animosity between sailors and missionaries, and he clearly sides with the former. The main character in *Tahiti* is a completely unreligious Frenchman, René, whose main nemesis is a missionary, Mr. Rowe.[161]

Published in 1852, a decade after the French annexation of the island, *Tahiti* presents a highly ambivalent view of colonialism. At the level of social commentary this is an explicitly anticolonial novel, detailing the brutality of the French campaign to eliminate British competition and crush indigenous resistance and the racism that seems to increase steadily as a function of colonization.[162] Yet the novel's *plot* is a melodramatic love affair, a "dramaturgy of excess and overstatement."[163] As with Kotzebue, we can anticipate that the author's treatment of a romance across the colonial cul-

160. Gerstäcker's narrative of his own travels makes up 1,176 pages of his *Gesammelte Schriften*. See Ostwald 1976, pp. 108–11, 119. The main character in one of Gerstäcker's best-known stories, "Der Schiffszimmermann" (The Ship's Carpenter), a Scottish escapee from a whaling ship living on a Polynesian island, is based on one of the author's encounters during his Oceanic voyages.

161. Gerstäcker's later novel *Die Missionäre* is an even more direct attack on the missionaries.

162. As the Russian formalists explained, a narrative contains both a "story" and a "plot." The story is "the series of causal events as they occur in chronological order and presumed duration and frequency." In most narratives, however, the "events are not presented in exact chronological order; the order in which they occur in the actual [text] is their *plot* order" (Bordwell and Thompson 1979, p. 52; Steinmetz 1992).

163. Brooks [1976] 1995, p. ix.

tural divide will be diagnostic of his views of empire and race more generally. At this level Gerstäcker's anticolonialism is no longer a foregone conclusion. If we follow Fredric Jameson in reading a novel's plot as an attempted
ideological solution to real social contradictions, a *successful* romance might
be read as signifying that colonialism is possible after all. But it does not
follow that an *unsuccessful* romance can be read straightforwardly as a crisis
of colonial confidence. Instead, Gerstäcker's novel suggests both an alternative, milder form of colonialism and the impossibility of any colonialism
based on cross-cultural intimacy.

The main character, René, is an escapee from an oppressive American
whaling ship. As in Jack London's *Sea-Wolf* and Georg Forster's *Voyage*, the
white denizens of the ship are brutalized characters, clearly morally inferior to Polynesians. René deserts at the small island of Atiu in the Cook
Islands between Tahiti and Samoa. Like Lapérouse in Kotzebue's play and
Chactas in Chateaubriand's *Atala and René*, René is rescued from certain
death at the hands of the natives by a local woman, Sadie.[164] She is initially described as an ideal female noble savage: "She was a young woman of
breathtaking beauty, perhaps sixteen years old, slender like the palm trees
in her forests. . . . [with] jet-black locks, anointed in fragrant coconut oil
and fluttering wildly around her brown forehead, and . . . large, pretty, dark
eyes. . . . a forest nymph." Sadie has been raised by a missionary, and she
displays a natural innocence mixed with a naive Christianity that prevents
the reader from confounding her with the Tahitian prostitutes who appear
later in the story. When René first spots Sadie, she averts her gaze shame-
fully, and René perceives the "dark blushing that colored her temples and
cheeks"—by now, a familiar trope in Polynesian literature.[165]

Sadie and René fall in love and marry. Their wedlock is vehemently opposed by the chief LMS missionary in the region, Mr. Rowe. Sadie and René
leave Atiu for Tahiti, where their lives become fatefully interwoven with
the machinations of the fanatic London missionary and the French colonial
regime. Unlike Atiu, Tahiti has been "spoiled and destroyed" by European
"ambition and fanaticism, sensualism, greed and careless negligence."[166]

Initially all goes well for the couple, but Sadie soon realizes that she
will never be accepted by the European settlers as an equal, and she be-

164. The relationship of Gerstäcker's novel to Chateaubriand's *Atala and René* ([1802] 1961)
is already signaled by the name of the central character, but Gerstäcker scrambles the materials. A nearly identical plot, complete with a white man rescued from certain death at the
hands of natives by a beautiful local woman, is recycled in Terrence Malick's ponderous film
The New World (2005).

165. Gerstäcker [1852] 1885, pp. 35–36.

166. Ibid., p. 145.

comes increasingly unhappy. René is drawn back into European society, where he becomes attracted to an American woman, Susanne. This domestic drama is superimposed on a backdrop of historical events.[167] In 1843 the French declare themselves the sole "protectors" of Tahiti and deport the British consul; the Tahitians resist the French and receive arms from British settlers and LMS missionaries. As the political troubles intensify, Sadie returns to Atiu and René promises to join her there quickly. Initially he refuses to side with his compatriots, declaring himself neutral and arguing that the Tahitians are simply "defending their fatherland."[168] The French governor, Bruat, talks René into acting as a liaison between the government and the Tahitians and agrees with René that the colonizers should govern by respecting local customs—a remarkable anticipation by Gerstäcker of the model of salvage colonialism implemented later in Samoa. The Tahitian chiefs refuse to surrender and mount an attack on Pape'ete, the colonial capital. At this point René joins his countrymen in the battle, not because he has changed his mind but simply for reasons of self-defense. Nonetheless, René is now "objectively" on the side of the colonizer. Indeed, he distinguishes himself in combat, leads the French to victory, and is badly wounded. René is nursed back to health by Susanne, and his ties to the American become stronger. After René has recovered enough to travel, the French admiral Dupetit-Thouars proposes that he return to France to present the metropolitan government with a report on the military campaign. René is the ideal candidate for justifying the massacre to skeptical French officials, as a "man who is . . . familiar with the conditions here and who was also . . . independent and uninvolved until forced by necessity and self-preservation to take up arms." The decisive factor in René's decision to accept the offer is the fact that Susanne will also be present on the ship that will return him to France. René plans to visit Sadie on the way home but a storm prevents the ship from stopping at Atiu. The narrative then shifts forward eleven years. René returns to Atiu. He has aged so quickly that he is almost unrecognizable to the people who had known him earlier. He learns that Mr. Rowe had prevented his letters from reaching Sadie during his absence. Sadie died of grief, believing that René had married Susanne.[169]

At one level *Tahiti* is an anticolonial novel. The destructive effects of colonialism and missionaries are presented in detail. The failure of the in-

---

167. Gerstäcker's novel closely follows the actual course of political events in Tahiti during the mid-nineteenth century; see Newbury 1980, chap. 4.

168. Gerstäcker [1852] 1885, p. 498.

169. Ibid., p. 632.

terracial marriage that stood for the possibility of a more egalitarian relationship between Polynesia and Europe is traced to the fanatic missionary and the racist European settlers. At one point René feels compelled to duel a French officer who has addressed his wife as a prostitute, but most of the settlers insist that a duel is inappropriate because civilized notions of honor do not apply to Polynesians. The marriage is also undermined by the increasingly colonial orientation of the French and the resulting polarization, which forces René to face Memmi's paradox of the "colonizer who refuses."[170] The novel also alludes to an internalized racism on René's part. After his duel it appears for a short time that René will be able to sustain the tension of living as a European with a "native," without himself "going native." René's attraction to the white American woman is portrayed by many of the Europeans around him as a natural development. The fact that Susanne insults Sadie in racist language does not prevent René from falling in love with the American, although he objects weakly that she is "importing prejudices from a distant world."[171] The question that the novel leaves open is whether the force pulling him irresistibly toward Susanne is race or *racism*.

The novel does seem finally to suggest that radically differing cultural backgrounds make intimacy impossible, even though the third-person omniscient narrator never uses the word "race." Sadie's intense discomfort around Europeans is more than a response to racism: She exhibits an almost corporeal shrinking from Europeans before she has even interacted with them. Similarly, René has trouble adjusting to the "indolent" lifestyle on Atiu. Sadie and René are so fundamentally different—whether due to nature or culture—that their marriage seems doomed from the start.

Gerstäcker's *Tahiti* reinforces the gendered images of Polynesian noble savagery and gestures toward a colonial methodology suited to such honorable counterparts. Colonial takeover is unavoidable given the imbalance of power: "What can the unarmed masses possibly do against the firearms of the soldiers and the cannons of the warships?" asks René.[172] But even if colonialism is a foregone conclusion, the question remains: What sort of colonialism? The preservationist model of colonial rule, associated with René, is "obviously" best suited to the uncorrupted Polynesians. The impossibility of intercultural intimacy resonates with a colonialism that recognizes, accepts, and even reinforces the intrinsic otherness of the colonized. A politics

170. Memmi [1965] 1991.
171. Gerstäcker [1852] 1885, p. 280.
172. Ibid., p. 383.

of regulated traditionalism in German Samoa was not at all incompatible with illiberal laws banning marriages like the one in Gerstäcker's novel.

Nineteenth-Century Samoa: From Lapérouse to the Germans

The correlation between a friendly initial encounter and the subsequent depiction of a culture as "noble" and "Polynesian" was not a perfect one, and Samoa is a case in point. The first European to report on Samoa was the Dutch commander Jacob Roggeveen in 1722, who was impressed by the people of T'au village in Manu'a as a "harmless good sort of people" with "nothing in their behavior that was wild or savage." But the Samoans' more famous encounter with Lapérouse led Europeans to malign them for some time as highly dangerous.[173] Yet here again, subsequent ethnographic representations proved to be perfectly capable of ignoring the historical and contemporary realities of the contact zone.

Lapérouse claimed that two races had originally inhabited the Samoan islands: the earliest inhabitants, who were similar to the New Guineans, and a conquering Malayan race. The end result of the mixing of these two components was, in his words, a "very black" race.[174] This already marked a deviation from the Tahitian template, according to which the natives' complexion had been described in the official account of Cook's first voyage as a "kind of clear olive, or Brunette" and their skin as "most delicately smooth and soft."[175] Unlike the "classic" Tahitian, Lapérouse's Samoans were not "magnanimous" but interested only in trade. Nor were they overly impressed by European guns. Twelve of Lapérouse's men were killed, in an encounter that seemed more "Melanesian" than "Polynesian." Lapérouse characterized Samoan government as "feudal," a political form that was anathema to enthusiasts of noble savagery. He blamed this for the Samoans' "perfidiousness," "ferocity of mores," and "treasons."[176]

173. Roggeveen, quoted in J. Holmes 1967, p. 4; Linnekin 1991a.

174. Lapérouse 1799, p. 154. I am drawing here on the original official account of Lapérouse's voyage, edited by Milet-Mureau and published in French in 1799, rather than the more recent editions of his original notebooks or the English translations. The spelling Lapérouse is preferred in current French scholarship, rather than La Pérouse (as he sometimes signed his name), La Peyrouse (the eighteenth-century Anglicized and Germanized spelling), or Lapeyrouse, which is found in nineteenth-century French writing (e.g., Lafond de Lurcy 1845). See La Pérouse 1994–95, vol. 1, pp. xi–xiv.

175. Hawkesworth 1775, vol. 2, p. 38.

176. Lapérouse 1799, p. 154.

Lapérouse's disastrous encounter at Samoa (which he called "the Navigator Islands") caused most European and American ships to avoid the archipelago during the following three decades.[177] Yet the mounting evidence of similarities between Samoa and the familiar parts of Polynesia made it difficult to stick to the original story. Lapérouse had noticed that Samoans spoke a "dialect" of the language of the "peoples of the Society and Friendly Islands." It was also believed that Tahitians traced their spiritual ancestry to the western Samoan island of Savai'i.[178]

MISSIONARIES AND NOBLE SAVAGERY IN SAMOA

The most important precondition for the recategorization of Samoans as noble savages was the demilitarization of their male warriors. This pacification was the work, above all, of the missionaries. In 1830, John Williams and Charles Barff from the London Missionary Society deposited in Samoa a group of indigenous missionaries from Aitutaki in the Cook Islands and from the Leeward chain in the Society Islands.[179] This marked the origin of the *lotu taiti*, or "Tahitian church," as the LMS was called in Samoa. Six years later a group of English missionaries arrived in Samoa, which subsequently became the central node for the LMS in the region.[180] The London missionaries proceeded to convert the Samoans with great alacrity. Three decades after Williams's arrival, missionary Archibald Murray reported confidently that "heathenism no longer exists in Samoa." Murray asserted that "among the thirty-four thousand who people the group, there remain perhaps not ten heathen; and with the disappearance of heathenism heathen practices have also largely disappeared."[181] Murray's distinction between *heathenism* and *heathen practices* pointed to a deeper underlying problem. The version of Christianity that came to predominate in Samoa was a mixture of European and Samoan customs. The islanders' rapid conversion has been attributed to the fact that Samoan converts did not "receive the gospel in exactly the

177. Gilson 1970, pp. 66–67.

178. The navigational chart drawn for Johann Forster by a Tahitian listed an island called O-Heavài as the "father of all islands." Some later interpreters, including Greg Dening, proposed that "O-Heavài" was actually Savai'i in Samoa (Thomas, Guest, and Dettelbach, in J. Forster [1778] 1996, p. 429 n. 20). In the map that Johann Forster published in the 1778 edition of *Observations*, however, the "Navigators" are shown as a different group from "Oheavai" (J. Forster [1778] 1996, pp. 304–5).

179. Gilson 1970, p. 69; Lovett 1899, vol. 1, chap. 3.

180. Phillips 1890, pp. 21–23.

181. Murray 1863, p. 456.

same way in which European missionaries intended." As historian Malama Meleisea notes, Samoans believe that "it was not foreigners who inspired their religious transformation but Samoa's own gods, who decreed that this must happen, and who had undoubtedly inspired the events in England that led to the rise of missionary evangelism, as well as the prior history of the Christian church, and had ultimately guided John Williams to Samoa to fulfill their purpose."[182] What mattered most to the LMS, however, was the extraordinary rate of nominal conversion. One missionary claimed that 90 percent of the native population was attending church services every Sunday by the end of the century.[183] Catholic missionaries were also active in Samoa after 1845, attracting a smaller group of adherents to the *lotu Pope* (the Pope's church). The Wesleyan mission, or *lotu toga* (Tongan church), was initially quite successful but dwindled in importance after midcentury.[184]

In their official publications the missionaries vehemently opposed the image of Polynesians as "happy innocent children of nature." As Murray wrote: "Among these islands the writer has been dwelling and voyaging for a period approaching forty years, and, with every disposition to judge favourably of the natives, he has never had the good fortune to fall in with any of these happy children of nature. So far as he knows, Samoa was about the most likely place to find them; but we have only to look beneath the surface to be satisfied that even in Samoa the vaunted innocence and happiness are all a delusion,—that they have no existence except in the fancy of superficial observers."[185] John Williams did not even bother to address the "romantic" theory in his *Narrative of Missionary Enterprises in the South Sea Islands* (1837). For Williams, "civilization" and increased commerce represented incontrovertible improvements in the lives of Samoans. Charles Phillips, head of the LMS Samoan mission in the late nineteenth century, pointed to the spread of telephones as an indicator of the "wonderful change which [had] been brought about" by the Protestant missions.[186]

These comments would seem to point to an ideological convergence, even an alliance, between missionaries and traders or settlers. Both groups opposed the fanciful theories of voyagers and ethnologists. Indeed, John

182. First quote from Elbourne 1992, p. 9, discussing a similar self-interpretation of Khoisan conversion in South Africa; second quote from Meleisea 1999, p. 59.

183. Phillips 1890, p. 5. Church membership was lower than rates of conversion (Gilson 1970, pp. 133–37).

184. Phillips 1890, pp. 23–24; Gilson 1970, pp. 81–88, 125–27; Meleisea 1987b, chap. 4; Garrett 1973; and Hamilton 1998.

185. Murray 1876, pp. 39–40.

186. Phillips 1890, p. 80.

Williams's 1837 book explicitly tried to encourage an alliance of interests between British capitalists and missionaries.[187] But the evolving field of representations of Samoa did not settle into any simple binary structure. Instead, nineteenth-century missionaries gained the reputation of supporting Samoans in their conflicts with European settlers.[188] If the missionaries emphasized "education for labor" and other cultural changes that pointed generally in the direction of capitalist modernization, their activities were not always compatible with settler dreams of Samoan proletarianization. For example, the LMS emphasized literacy as a condition for membership in the church. Captain Charles Wilkes of the United States Exploring Expedition (1838–42) noted that everywhere he went in Samoa he saw people reading.[189] Missionary and capitalist perspectives also diverged with respect to questions of inequality. Many of the LMS missionaries came from modest social backgrounds and were pleased that Samoa showed no extreme differences of individual wealth.[190]

Missionaries also bolstered the plausibility of the noble savagery framework unwittingly—for example, by describing Samoans as being already "almost civilized" at the moment of first European contact.[191] As we have seen, adherents of the noble savagery approach preferred this intermediate, "semicivilized" condition to the two extremes. If the Samoans were savages, they were at least "savages of the best type," according to missionary Murray.[192] John Williams argued in 1832 that the Samoans had never practiced cannibalism or human sacrifice (although this claim was refuted by ethnologists at the end of the nineteenth century). Even in the realm of religion the missionaries portrayed traditional Samoa as having been more civilized than certain other "heathen" societies. The mission recognized that the Samoans were polytheistic, but it also believed that they had at least a "vague idea of a Supreme being" and were not idolatrous.[193] The LMS compiled a publication on the ancient Samoan lineages long before German ethnologist Augustin Krämer, assisting in "the preservation of a traditional element in Samoan political life in times of change."[194]

Missionaries' ethnographic descriptions and practices also partly con-

187. J. Williams 1837, chap. 32.
188. Gilson 1970, p. 108.
189. Ibid., p. 95; Wilkes 1845, vol. 2, p. 79.
190. Phillips 1890, p. 10.
191. Ibid., p. 15.
192. Murray 1876, p. 398; see also Phillips 1890, p. 15.
193. J. Williams 1837, p. 489; Murray 1876, p. 171.
194. J. Davidson 1967, p. 70.

verged with the noble savagery paradigm, even if the mission never deliberately tried to preserve or reconstitute "pagan" customs. Missionaries
showed more appreciation for the diffused rather than the centralizing aspects of the Samoan system and encouraged a practical deconcentration of
power. In part, this simply took the form of describing Samoan society as
inherently decentralized and insisting that the kingship that emerged in the
nineteenth century was not a traditional institution.[195] The LMS urged the
early rehabilitation and return from exile of the Vaivai, the disgraced losing
party in Samoan warfare, which weakened the ability of the Mālō, or win-
ning party, to consolidate itself as an autocracy.[196] This resonated with the
antimonarchical sentiments of European liberals and radicals like Georg
Forster, but it clashed with the interests of the merchants, who generally
believed that a centralized political structure was a precondition for inte-
grating Samoa into the circuits of international trade. European politicians
and merchants floated various plans, including a kingship along the lines
of Tonga or Hawai'i or a subsumption of Samoa under one of these other
Polynesian monarchies.[197] Traditionally, the holder of all four royal Samoan
titles (ao) became the supreme chief, or Tafa'ifā (literally, the "holder of
four"), even if local politics remained relatively autonomous. A legitimate
Samoan king (O le Tupu, or tupu O Samoa; literally, "highest in the land")
could exist only when the four sacrosanct titles were bestowed on a single
individual.[198] The tupu position was thus continuous with the Tafa'ifā; experts spoke of the "tafa'ifa kings" of Samoa and the "tupu tafa'ifa.[199] Starting in the 1870s European consuls pressured the Samoans to place a king or
a duumvirate of two kings at the head of the governing oligarchy of chiefs
(Ta'imua). The Ta'imua had been created under the influence of the Ameri-

195. J. Williams 1837, p. 474.

196. On the meanings of Mālō and Vaivai see Gilson 1970, pp. 62, 189; and Mageo 1988,
p. 26.

197. Decentralization has been a criterion of political backwardness for theorists of "political development" like Huntington and Dominguez (1975). For a critique of this model as
applied to Samoa see Meleisea (1987b) and Hjarnø (1979-80, p. 87), who argue that Samoa's
unified system of titles conferring power over land and service obligations was capable of
producing national-level rulers under specific conditions.

198. See Schoeffel 1987 on these ancient titles.

199. Krämer 1899, p. 188; Schultz-Ewerth 1911, p. 48. The first Tafa'ifā was Salamāsina
(Krämer 1923; Meleisea 1987a). Captain Wilkes (1845, vol. 2, pp. 152-53) noted that Tamafago,
a chief who had recently died, had taken the title "O le Tupu o Savaii"—but not Tupu of Samoa. See also Krämer (1994-95, vol. 1, p. 11), who specified that the "king" of Samoa did not
exercise the power associated with that title except during war.

can "special agent" Albert Steinberger, who played an important role in Samoan politics during the mid-1870s. Steinberger proposed a system in which the two most powerful traditional royal title lineages, Mālietoa and Tupua, would hold the kingship in alternating four-year terms. In the following two decades the intrigues that resulted from competition among various foreign and Samoan parties led to a tangled confusion of rapidly changing governments.[200]

The missionaries' desire for political decentralization was related to their campaign to pacify Samoan male warrior culture, a campaign that went beyond rhetorical insistence on Samoan hospitality.[201] The LMS missionaries disrupted the Lapérousian view of the Samoans as ignoble savages simply by remaining in the islands in the early decades. The missionaries made it seem safe for Europeans to live in an area torn by internecine warfare, since Samoans rarely harmed Europeans: only a single European was killed intentionally by a Samoan between 1841 and 1876.[202] The mission took the position that war was "contrary to the will of God," "except in the strictest self-defense," and one of its main goals was the abolition of intra-Samoan warfare.[203] Samoan warfare was endemic after the death in 1841 of Mālietoa Vainu'upō, who had been made *Tafa'ifā* in 1829.[204] Fighting broke out among Samoan camps in 1848, 1868, 1876, 1888, and 1898, but the missionaries were sometimes able to deflect or prevent hostilities.[205] The LMS missionaries also made warfare less ferocious, according to Charles Phillips, by preaching against the taking of heads as "trophies of war," the destruction of the property of the defeated party, and other "diabolic cruelties."[206] One of the stumbling blocks to the plausibility of the noble savagery discourse, which envisioned Samoan men as hospitable, was thus partly overcome by missionaries who ostensibly opposed that discourse.

200. Gilson 1970, pp. 185, 195, 311, 383ff.

201. See the comments by missionary George Turner (1861, pp. 198–201; 1884, pp. 114–15); for Ellis (1853, vol. 1, p. 95), a colleague of Williams and Barff, the Pacific islanders' hospitality was "proverbial." Captain Wilkes (1845, vol. 2, pp. 144, 148–49) described the traveling "parties of pleasure" (*malaga*) as hospitality taken to an extreme.

202. Gilson 1970, p. 213.

203. Ibid., pp. 116, 96.

204. The prolonged period of struggle over the royal titles after 1829 may also have been an unintentional effect of the arrival of the LMS, for reasons discussed by Meleisea (1987a, p. 74).

205. For reports on missionaries preventing or deescalating Samoan warfare, see Wilkes 1845, vol. 2, p. 65; and Murray 1876, pp. 137–39.

206. Phillips 1890, pp. 85–86.

The Tahitian ethnographic formula was applied to Samoans repeatedly after 1830. The French explorer Gabriel Lafond de Lurcy landed at Samoa in 1831 and described a musician as a "bon sauvage."[207] At the end of that decade Dumont d'Urville wrote that the Samoan men "must have been a dangerous race in their initial, savage state" but that their faces now had "kindly expressions."[208] Captain Wilkes agreed that "the natives, as far as our experience goes, are not the blood-thirsty race they have been reported to be."[209] Captain John Erskine, who landed at Samoa in 1849, reported that the missionaries had made "considerable progress among the people . . . and for several years, in spite of occasional vexatious wars among the tribes, a stranger may consider his life and property as safe in Samoa . . . as in any other part of the world."[210] Erskine began his Samoan narrative by describing how his group was led to a "fala-tele . . . the house for the reception of strangers, who may remain as long as they please."[211] Even in 1925, New Zealand's official *Handbook of Western Samoa* described "the Samoan" as being "in his native state, mild, friendly and hospitable."[212]

The London missionaries' other main concern was to ban the "brutal licentiousness and moral degradation," the "shameful rites and orgies" that they found in Samoa and elsewhere in Polynesia.[213] They were concerned to stamp out dancing, especially the more "obscene" *pōula,* or "night dance" variety, and also targeted adultery and polygamy, premarital sex, and public defloration ceremonies.[214] They tried to impose "new standards of dress, including 'full coverage' for women." They urged hair styles " 'appropriate' to the individual's sex"—long for men and short for young women—which turned out to be the opposite of the traditional style. They encouraged Samoans to install external blinds and internal partitioning in their houses.[215] The missionaries took heart from the fact that a ban on premarital sex was enforced at least with respect to the village princess or *taupou.*[216]

207. Lafond de Lurcy 1845, p. 16.
208. Dumont d'Urville 1842–54, vol. 4, p. 123.
209. Wilkes 1845, vol. 2, p. 73.
210. Erskine 1853, p. 9.
211. Ibid., p. 36.
212. Administration of Western Samoa 1925, p. 41; for a similar statement see Baessler 1895, p. 15.
213. Ellis 1853, vol. 1, pp. 97–98.
214. See Meleisea 1980, p. 27; Mageo 1998; and Stair [1897] 1983, p. 134.
215. Gilson 1970, p. 96.
216. The debate over the differing interpretations by Margaret Mead and Derek Freeman revolves centrally around Mead's emphasis on unencumbered premarital sexuality among young non-*taupou* Samoans. But the existence of the *taupou* hardly settles the question, for

The missionaries were not entirely successful in stamping out Samoan "sensualism." Their interventions were more likely to give rise to mixed and neotraditional forms, just as their religious practices were melded with Samoan ritual elements. Missionary pressures led to structural transformations of the *pōula*. Traditionally girls danced naked at the end of the *pōula* in the so-called spirit frenzy (*'ale'aleaitu*), when only the younger people remained in the audience and sometimes "eloped" with one another.[217] Anthropologist Jeannette Mageo argues that the comic and sexual aspects of the *pōula* continue to exist even today but that they were separated off from the synchronized dances and were performed on the outskirts of the village and later in the bush rather than at the center as before. But as late as 1895 Arthur Baessler attended a night dance that included *siva* dancing (traditionally performed sitting) and a performance by a "prima ballerina" whom he called a "downright dazzling beauty": "She wore nothing but a very small . . . *titi*, or waistcloth for dancing, and a thin *ula*, or flower chain, around her neck. . . . The less ambiguous her movements became, the greater was the spectators' joy."[218] The songs at this performance mingled European and Samoan styles. Baessler was not the only visitor to remark on the persistence of a supposed custom according to which "every distinguished guest was given a pretty young companion by a chief when he stayed the night."[219] Yet women had never been offered (or offered themselves) so aggressively to visitors in Samoa as elsewhere in Polynesia.

The noble savagery perspective emphasized the treatment of women as a marker of a society's goodness, and here Samoa was seen as fairly advanced. The missionaries often remarked on the relative equality of Samoan men and women. For the most part this was not a result of missionary interventions, although they did raise women's status somewhat by teaching them to read.[220] Captain Wilkes noted in 1839 that Samoan girls had "what

---

several reasons, as noted by Schwartz (1983, pp. 925–26): (a) the same society could easily "both stress virginity and encourage premarital sexual experimentation"; (b) the virgin could have been "an object of eroticism rather than one whose sexuality was either denied or concealed" and was selected above all for her beauty; and (c) the very institution of virginity "incites a great deal of sexual activity that eludes Christian rules of proper sex," as male Samoan life becomes a competitive quest to end virginity.

217. Mageo 1998, pp. 121, 196.

218. Baessler 1895, pp. 38–39.

219. B. von Werner (1889, pp. 259–60) concurred with Baessler that this custom had been preserved only on Savai'i. According to Baessler, even in Savai'i things had changed; the mother of the "pretty young companion" now accompanied her as a duenna (1895, p. 19).

220. Phillips 1890, p. 15; also H. Cooper 1880, vol. 2, p. 4.

is rare in Polynesia," namely, "some degree of bashfulness," and that "there is no indiscriminate intercourse, the marriage tie is respected."[221] The earliest known *Tafa'ifā*, Salamāsina, was a woman.[222] Women could also hold *matai* (chief) titles, although this was rare. Historical anthropologists have concluded that age, not gender, was the primary axis of social stratification in old Samoa, and that "the *tapu* imposed upon women as described in eastern Polynesia was not observed in Samoa by outsiders in the early 19th century."[223] The arrival of missionaries and other Europeans in Samoa changed the overall configuration of ethnographic discourse, but the noble savagery trope did not disappear or even recede. Instead, it continued to evolve, with new points of emphasis and revised images of men and women. Before examining this evolution we should first review the German economic and political influx into Samoa during the second half of the nineteenth century.

THE GERMANS IN PRECOLONIAL SAMOA

Samoa was the target of the earliest German efforts at colonial annexation and the site of a plantation economy created by the Godeffroy firm, which began its operations there in 1857.[224] After 1864 Godeffroy's agent in Samoa, Theodor Weber, began drying coconut meat (copra) in Samoa before shipping it to Europe for the extraction of the oil.[225] Godeffroy's other products were coffee, cocoa, and, during the American Civil War, cotton. Samoa experienced a small "land rush" in 1870–72. Europeans made property claims that were eventually calculated to equal two and a half times the islands' total land mass. Theodor Weber bought up 25,000 acres of Samoan land for Godeffroy's operation. The Pacific regional branch of the Godeffroy company was reorganized in 1880 under the name Deutsche Handels- und Plantagen-Gesellschaft der Südsee-Inseln zu Hamburg (German Trade and Plantation Society for the South Sea Islands in Hamburg, or DHPG). By this time Germans were the largest investors in Samoa, controlling 4,500 of the 5,000 acres under regular cultivation and employing nearly all

221. Wilkes 1845, vol. 2, pp. 125, 73.
222. Krämer 1923; Schoeffel 1987; Meleisea 1999.
223. Schoeffel 1987, p. 176.
224. Schultz-Ewerth 1924; P. Kennedy 1974, pp. 6, 101; Obermüller 1989. The early attempts at colonial annexation of Samoa came to naught because they were generated in situ without the backing of Bismarck and the Foreign Office.
225. P. Kennedy 1974, p. 101.

of the indentured agricultural laborers, or "blackbirds," who were brought in from other parts of the Pacific.[226] When an international commission was created in the 1890s to resolve Samoan land claims, German landholders came away with the largest area of confirmed claims.[227]

Germany's unification in 1870–71 increased its political influence over Samoa. A Hamburg consulate had already been installed at Apia in 1861, but the Hanseatic city-state was unable to provide naval support. This began to change once the new "imperial navy" assumed responsibility for protecting German merchants overseas. A German warship destroyed Samoan villages in a campaign to force recognition of some of Godeffroy's land claims in 1874.[228] Backed by the German navy, German consuls made a series of interventions, including the imposition of a German-Samoan "friendship treaty" in 1879–80, the banishment to another island of the main contender to the Samoan crown (Laupepa) in 1887, and the installation in 1887–88 of a short-lived German-Samoan government that was soon toppled by the joint efforts of the other Samoan party together with the United States and Britain. A three-power conference held in Berlin in April 1889 devised a political system for the administration of Samoa. During the next decade the islands were governed by foreign consuls from Germany, Britain, and the United States, a "chief justice" nominated by the three Western powers, and the Samoans themselves. Apia was administered by a European or American "president" appointed by the town council.[229] The chief justice and Apia's president acted as "advisers" to the Samoan king.

The Germans emerged as the most influential players in this tug-of-war over Samoa. When the country was partitioned at the end of the century, Germany received the western islands of 'Upolu and Savai'i, where the plantation economy and Samoan politics were concentrated. The United States was more interested in keeping the protected harbor at Pago Pago as a naval base and was therefore satisfied with the smaller eastern island of Tutuila. The United States also received the Manu'a group, where Margaret Mead did her fieldwork in the 1920s.[230]

226. Marin 1888, p. 149.

227. Figures in Gilson 1970, p. 411.

228. Ibid., pp. 250, 308.

229. Since 1879 Apia had been a self-governing and quasi-colonial enclave in which Samoans charged with crimes were tried by a mixed court consisting of a European and a Samoan magistrate (ibid., p. 361). The 1889 Berlin act preserved Apia's municipal magistrate.

230. Germany also received the smaller but traditionally important islands of Apolima and Manono.

The Evolution of European and German
Representations of Samoa

We can now return to the evolution of European and German views of Samoa in the nineteenth century. The discourse of noble savagery reemerged in new forms after midcentury and flourished in the context of fin-de-siècle *Kulturkritik,* the criticism of decadent Western civilization associated with Nietzsche, symbolism, and neoromanticism, and culminating in Oswald Spengler's *The Decline of the West* (published just after World War I). Similarly, Americans began to accept the description of the Indian offered by Chateaubriand and Fenimore Cooper and to transform him from "a bloodthirsty demon into a noble savage."[231] Le Vaillant's depiction of the Khoikhoi as noble savages had little resonance during the nineteenth century until it was revived in the 1890s. The discourse of Polynesian noble savagery waxed and waned, but it reemerged in full force toward the end the century, with Samoa as a major point of reference.

The reason for focusing on the ethnographic productions of academics, novelists, artists, and politicians rather than missionaries, traders, or settlers is that German colonial rulers in Samoa after 1899 were particularly attentive to the former. This reflected the academic background and the personal predilections of the two men chosen to govern the colony, Wilhelm Solf and Erich Schultz, and the fact that German missionaries had not been active in precolonial Samoa. By contrast, the first German attempt to take control of Samoa through a policy of indirect rule—the government headed by Eugen Brandeis—revealed that Germans were not necessarily opposed to the more brutal approach backed by settlers, planters, and merchants. The regime of Brandeis and the Samoan king Tamasese was dominated by planter interests. A head tax for Samoans was implemented and the money was spent on building roads to the large plantations. Samoans who protested against the tax were deported. The most dramatic difference between this regime and the colonial government after 1899 was that Brandeis distributed ammunition to the supporters of Tamasese and trained a Samoan force to oppose the backers of Mālietoa, whereas Solf began disarming the Samoans immediately after taking office.[232]

If Europeans had expressed a desire for a demilitarization of Polynesian men throughout the century, Samoan men had not been domesticated. This

---

231. Berkhofer 1978, p. 88.

232. P. Kennedy 1974, pp. 74–75. Brandeis and Tamasese were defeated by the forces of Mālietoa, which put an abrupt end to the early German experiment in indirect rule in Samoa.

was demonstrated in 1888 and throughout the 1890s. In the battles of 1888, Samoan men killed German sailors, decapitating some of the corpses.[233] Yet most Europeans seemed to avert their gaze from these discrepant realities. Thus, for example, when the journal of popular naval propaganda, *Überall*, reported on earlier "diplomatic negotiations with the chiefs of Samoa" at the time of colonial annexation, the text was accompanied by photographs of topless Samoan "beauties." The same volume of *Überall* included a photo of Boxer leaders being executed by German soldiers.[234] The image of the Polynesian male had been so effectively linked in the European mind to pacifism that it seemed unperturbed by actual militancy.[235]

Arguments originally associated with missionaries were recapitulated by nonmissionary Samoan specialists. Some praised the country's "patriarchal-democratic" government and the fact that Samoan chiefs shared "mundane daily tasks with the average man," just as LMS missionaries seemed unperturbed by Samoa's "communistic" egalitarianism.[236] The missionaries' vision of Samoa as less barbarous than the rest of Oceania was echoed in the widespread suggestion of a fictive kinship between ancient Europeans and Samoans. Just as Forster and the artists on Cook's voyages had compared Tahiti to classical Greece and Rome, the American artist John La Farge, who lived in Samoa in 1890 and 1891, represented its inhabitants as figures from classical antiquity.[237] Robert Louis Stevenson's study of the struggle of the great powers for control of Samoa, *A Footnote to History* (1892), likened the Samoans to Stevenson's own Scottish ancestors, "who drove their chariots on the wrong side of the Roman wall," suggesting a kinship of barbarism and conquest by "an alien authority."[238]

Travelers, scientists, artists, and novelists refined these ideas during the last three decades of the century. Sometimes this involved little more than transferring elements of the earlier "Tahitian" idyll to Samoa. German

233. On the 1888 battle between the German and Tamasese forces and those of Mata'afa, see Marques 1889, p. 139; P. Kennedy 1974, p. 77.

234. Compare "Diplomatische Verhandlung mit Häuptlingen Samoas vor 27 Jahren," *Überall* 3, pt. 1 (1900-1901): 665-66; and "Das Strafgericht in Paotingfu," *Überall* 3, pt. 1 (1900-1901): 603.

235. For similary views of Samoans see Böhr 1876, p. 427; Meinecke 1875-76, vol. 2, p. 111; H. Cooper 1880, vol. 2, pp. 16-17; Churchward 1887, pp. 390-91; Christmann and Oberländer 1873, vol. 2, p. 212; B. von Werner 1889, p. 249; and Marques 1889, p. 72.

236. Christmann and Oberländer 1873, p. 220; Marques 1889, pp. 62, 71; Phillips 1890, p. 10.

237. Yarnall 1998, p. 83.

238. Stevenson 1996, p. 1; [1890] 1998, p. 12.

ethnologist Georg Hartwig argued in 1861 that Samoa was "more entic-
ing, more delightful" than Tahiti and its people more beautiful and "nobler" than Tahitians.[239] Samoa was described by the French naval captain
Édouard Petit in 1888 as an "Eden of demigods and their beautiful companions," a "radiant place" where "it seems that man could not be unhappy."[240]
Otto Ehlers, author of *Samoa, Pearl of the South Seas* (1895), called Samoa "a
fairytale land" whose inhabitants were "the most beautiful people I have
ever encountered."[241]

The formulas that had originally been proposed in discussions of Tahitian women were transferred to Samoans. Early Europeans had contrasted
Samoan women unfavorably with Tahitians, calling them "far from good-
looking," "rather ill-formed and stout," and "almost masculine in their appearance."[242] Over time, however, Samoan women came to resemble the
earlier, more feminine image of Tahitians, whereas Tahitian women were
now often described as prostitutes. Petit contrasted the "wild maidens of
New Cythera" to the Samoans, who presented a "Britannic prudery" while
simultaneously remaining "naive in their superb nudity, like Eve before
the temptation."[243] The German navy surgeon Ernst Böhr rhapsodized
in 1876: "Our painters, our poets . . . should come and see these Samoan
girls . . . how their large, pretty eyes sparkle, and their black tresses fly; how
their slender brown limbs express passion and elegance with every movement! . . . A happy people . . . living a life of cheerful sensual enjoyment."[244]
Rear Admiral von Werner, in his 1889 book about the Pacific, described the
women of Samoa as "differing from their sisters on the Polynesian islands
I have hitherto visited": "gentle, ingratiating, and capable of devotion" and
"domestically inclined, as a rule."[245]

Samoa was not one of those islands where initial contact had been marked
by local women offering themselves to European sailors. Such images
seemed to derive from age-old understandings of Polynesian women in general as "sexually available."[246] Prostitution may have been common in Apia
by the latter decades of the nineteenth century, but many of the prostitutes
were "half-caste" women.[247] Samoan women, who never appeared fully na-

239. Hartwig [1861] 1871, pp. 345, 354.
240. Marin 1888, pp. 140–41.
241. Ehlers 1895, p. 81.
242. Wilkes 1845, vol. 2, pp. 73, 125; Dumont d'Urville 1842–54, vol. 4, p. 124.
243. Marin 1888, p. 142.
244. Böhr 1876, p. 426.
245. B. von Werner 1889, p. 249.
246. Harms 1991, p. 167.
247. Gilson 1970, p. 180; Salesa 1997, chap. 5, p. 9.

ked indoors or in broad daylight, had been convinced by decades of missionary pressure not to appear unclothed in public even during the *pōula*. Sex in Samoa took place in the dark, at night, and away from the public eye.[248] But Augustin Krämer's *Samoa Islands*, the first self-consciously scientific ethnology of Samoa, included photographs of nude Samoan women in various poses—"lying down, seen sideways from behind," "half recumbent," and so on (see fig. 4.6).[249] Krämer's images of women therefore disrupt the sober empiricism that governs the rest of his text and represent links in an unbroken tradition of erotic Polynesian imagery reaching back to Commerson.[250] Along similar lines, the published journal of a British lieutenant who had served in the South Pacific during the 1860s, Herbert Meade, included an etching of naked women swimming in an idyllic landscape in New Zealand as its frontispiece (fig. 4.7). The American writer Charles Warren Stoddard included in his collection *Summer Cruising in the South Sea* (1874) an image of nude Polynesians surfing (fig. 4.8).[251]

One might simply interpret Krämer's inclusion of these images in his book as prurient. But they also seem to be a shot across the bow of the missionaries' repressive refashioning of Samoan tradition. This relates to Krämer's goal of reversing the tide of history through a kind of salvage colonialism modeled on the salvage anthropology that he helped to pioneer in Oceania. The latter involved frantically recording memories and traditions from elders before they disappeared with their cultures. French zoologist and anthropologist Armand de Quatrefages had speculated in 1864 that "inferior races" were dying out due to the pressures of imported disease, commercial civilization, and a "discouragement or a sort of spleen inspired by the invasion of their homeland" that "eliminates the desire to bring into the world children who would inherit a profound feeling of decline." A London missionary in Samoa in 1887 commented that "though the gospels of Jesus

248. See Tcherkézoff 2001, especially pp. 36–37, for a compelling account that steers clear of both Mead and Freeman.

249. See photos 11 and 19–22 in Krämer 1994–95, vol. 2. Krämer also included a detailed discussion of the various shapes and sizes of Samoan women's breasts (ibid., p. 50).

250. Krämer's book also includes profile shots in the standard anthropometric style, in an attempt to distinguish Samoans "racially" from Melanesians (1902–3, vol. 2, plates 13–15). The anthropometric style was already familiar to Krämer, who had been in contact in 1900 with Felix von Luschan, author of "Instructions for Scientific Observations." In Krämer's Samoan nudes, however, the women are set against backdrops of picturesque tapa cloth, palm fronds, or generic landscape, rather than the plain backdrops preferred in anthropometric portraiture.

251. Stoddard is distinctive for treating Polynesian men and women identically; see Roger Austen (1991) on Stoddard's "double life." James Michener's novel *Hawaii* includes a scene of provocatively naked Hawai'ian women surfing alongside a ship carrying missionaries.

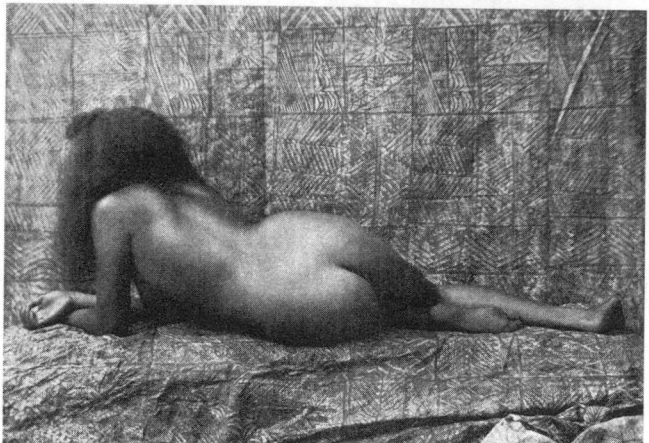

FIGURE 4.6 *Figure of a Samoan Woman Lying Down, Seen Sideways from Behind.* From Krämer 1902-3, vol. 2, plate 21.

Christ may help to alleviate the miseries of [Samoan] extinction I cannot hope that it will prevent it."[252] Although social Darwinists could rationalize away the "inexorable extinction of the natural peoples" as an inevitable result of natural selection, the response among romantics and professional ethnologists was anxious regret, and a sense that "Anthropology had to be done *now,*" in the words of Margaret Mead.[253] Krämer sought out the oldest individuals with the greatest knowledge of tradition to help preserve "the cultual heritage of the slowly dying-out peoples of the Pacific."[254] This preservationist approach to ethnology also exemplifies the way precolonial representations contained implicit guidelines for native policy.

One of the most absurd aspects of European discussions of "race" during the nineteenth century is the way in which certain populations "changed color" as their relative standing within comparative ethnographic discourse shifted. Thus, the Witbooi changed from black to yellow after 1894 (chap. 3) and the Chinese changed from white to yellow over the course of the nineteenth century (chap. 6). Samoans underwent a process of racial lightening, becoming more like the early image of Tahitians—who themselves began to seem swarthier to Europeans as they lost their charm. Although Lapérouse

252. First quote from Quatrefages de Bréau 1864, p. 75; second from Salesa 1997, chap. 5, p. 13.

253. Mead 1972, p. 114.

254. Krämer's (1994-95, vol. I, p. vii) preface to *The Samoa Islands* spells out this salvage ethos. Krämer also collected boatloads of physical artifacts, which were brought back to Europe and sold to museums (Schleip 1989).

FIGURE 4.7 (left) *Ohinemutu Geyser, Mokaia Island and Lake Rotorua*. Frontispiece from Meade and Meade 1871.

FIGURE 4.8 (below) Frontispiece from Stoddard, *Summer Cruising in the South Seas* (1874).

had described the Samoans as "very black," voyagers by the 1860s were describing them as "copperish-tawny" (*kupferbräunlich*).[255] Two German specialists in Pacific affairs insisted in 1872 that the Samoans were "the lightest-skinned Oceanians,"[256] and a British traveler described them in 1880 as having "a light brown colour, many of them not being so dark as some Italians or Spaniards."[257] William Churchward, the British consul at Samoa from 1881 to 1885, described Samoans as "true Polynesians, of the lightest colour of the race." Underscoring the ways in which perceptions of race were linked to other criteria of ethnic valuation, Churchward's text veered immediately from skin color to a comment on the Samoans' "mental and social disposition," with respect to which they were said to "hold the highest position in the Pacific."[258] French traveler Joseph Hübner described the Samoans as having "little color" at all, except perhaps a light olive tint, adding that "if the Olympian deities were Greeks . . . it is hardly probably that they had a lighter complexion."[259] Where Lapérouse had speculated about the Samoan's dusky Melanesian ancestors, the common lore by the end of the nineteenth century was that they had "kept themselves pure," by preventing "any influx of black [Melanesian] blood."[260] The culmination of this bleaching process was the comment by the most powerful figure in early German ethnology, Adolf Bastian, that these "children of nature" could be seen as "cousins" of the "Caucasian" race.[261] And when a branch of the Nazi Party was formed among German settlers in Apia in 1934, they "presented their evidence to Berlin" that Polynesians were, indeed, "Aryans."[262]

Samoa was increasingly seen as embodying Ur-Polynesia, both as the original source of Polynesian culture and the place where it was best maintained. Horatio Hale, the philologist on Captain Wilkes's United States Exploring Expedition, agreed that all Polynesians could trace their ancestry to Savai'i. Hale's thesis was that Samoa was not only the "source of population to the other groups of Polynesia," including New Zealand, but also the

255. Dr. Fr. Spiegel, "Die ethnographische Ausbeute der Novara-Reise," *Das Ausland* 41 (1868): 1114. On changing perceptions of skin color among Tongans and other South Pacific islanders see Gailey 1994.

256. Christmann and Oberländer 1873, vol. 2, p. 213.

257. H. Cooper 1880, vol. 2, p. 14.

258. Churchward 1887, p. 390.

259. Hübner 1886, vol. 2, p. 409.

260. Baguet 1891, p. 25; see also Krämer 1994–95, vol. 2, p. 40.

261. Bastian (1889, pp. 55, 76) seemed, however, more interested in discovering intellectual than racial kinship with this "philosophically inclined little people [*Völkchen*]."

262. Field 1991, p. 218.

birthplace of their traditions and language.[263] Quatrefages argued that "it is from the Samoan archipelago, and from Savaï in particular, that all the great expeditions appear to have started."[264] Some later writers rejected Hale's model on evidentiary grounds, but Erich Schultz, the second governor of German Samoa and an expert in Samoan customary law, believed that Samoa had been a "point of departure for Polynesian colonization crusades."[265] Augustin Krämer decided to study Samoa because it was "considered by most people who know the South Seas to be the central island from which the other Polynesian islands were populated."[266] Samoa had moved from the margins to the very center of the European fantasy of Polynesia.

This privileged status was connected to the idea that the Samoans had conserved their traditions despite Christianization. To some extent this indexed real differences in the postcontact history of Samoa and Tahiti. Samoa's dangerous reputation delayed the influx of Europeans. The addition of Germany and the United States to the field of competition for influence made it difficult for any single power to claim preeminence in Samoa, and this delayed colonial annexation. Neither Catholicism nor even a specific variant of Protestantism monopolized the religious field in Samoa, which increased Samoans' cultural leverage.[267] Christian conversion was not as destructive of Samoan tradition as it might have been. Samoans who continued to practice tattooing, ceremonial exchange, and other old customs were not excluded from the Catholic church. Under pressure from its religious competitors and from rank-and-file native Samoan teachers, the LMS relaxed its efforts to ban "pagan" traditions.[268] As a result, Samoan Christianity came to incorporate precontact customs such as the kava ceremony, the idea of tabu, and belief in various *aitu*, or traditional spirits.[269]

263. Hale [1846] 1946, pp. 119–20; also pp. 124–25, 130–31, 138, 146–47, 170; chart of migrations, pp. xiv–xv.

264. Quatrefages de Bréau 1879, p. 191; also 1864. Professor Alfred Kirchhoff (1880, p. 251) at Halle University described Samoa as the place from which "Malayans" had radiated out into the Pacific.

265. Schultz-Ewerth 1924, p. 89. For the rejection of this thesis see Lesson 1880–84, vol. 2, pp. 491–523.

266. Krämer 1994–95, vol. 1, p. 2.

267. Despite the LMS's head start in Samoa the Catholic mission gained a significant presence. Mata'afa, the Samoan *ali'i sili* after 1900, was a Catholic convert, for example.

268. On Samoan mission teachers' struggles with LMS authorities in the mid-nineteenth century see Gilson 1970, pp. 127, 135–37.

269. On "arrangements" between Fa'a Samoa and European Christian ways, see Schneider-Christians 1992, pp. 216–38, 425–73; and Bargatzky 1997; on *aitu*, see G. Turner 1884, chap. 3–5; Stuebel 1896; and Bastian 1883, pp. 42–58; 1894. Indigenous Christian move-

As noted above, some Samoans apparently believed that Christianization itself was an endogenous affair, predestined by the war goddess Nafanua.[270] And if the LMS missionaries were dedicated to the transformation of indigenous culture, many were also devoted portraitists of Samoans' lives and chroniclers of their history. In this respect, missionaries like John Williams, George Turner, and Archibald Murray were the earliest practitioners of a quasi-salvage anthropology in Samoa.[271]

Some of the protocolonial policies that were put into place before 1900 also pointed in the direction of salvage colonialism. The land commission created by the Berlin Act of 1889 invalidated many more claims than it recognized and put an end to all further land sales. The DHPG did not try to force Samoans to work on their plantations, but turned to indentured migrant laborers from other parts of the Pacific.[272] The Godeffroy firm employed naturalists, sponsored an ethnological and naturalist journal starting in 1873, and created the first and at the time the finest museum of Oceanic artifacts in Europe.[273] The DHPG helped protect Samoans from the sorts of wrenching changes that were imposed on the Ovaherero starting in the 1890s.

Samoan culture was of course deeply affected by the influx of European settlers, missionaries, and commodities and by the growing presence of non-Samoan laborers and Euro-Samoans. One response was Samoan neotraditionalism. The Samoan kingship was largely a product of European pressure, but a centralized institution was also better suited for resisting European encroachments and was embraced by most Samoan elites. The influx of Melanesian laborers provoked a reaffirmation of Samoan distinctiveness that sometimes seemed racist and that undermined the traditional Samoan openness to outsiders.[274]

The peculiarities of Samoa's insertion into global capitalism, colonialism, and missionary Christianity meant that it maintained or even accentu-

---

ments like the Sio Vili cult, which preexisted the LMS in Samoa, gave the Samoans additional leverage in the struggle to inject Christianity with Samoan meaning.

270. Meleisea 1999.

271. J. Williams 1837; G. Turner 1861, 1884; Murray 1863, 1876.

272. On foreign labor recruitment to Samoa, see Moses 1977; S. Firth 1973; Munro and Firth 1990; and Tom 1986.

273. See *Journal des Museums Godeffroy* for 1873 through 1910; Spoehr 1963; and Penny 2002, p. 54.

274. Churchward (1887, p. 210) reported on a Samoan who murdered a Melanesian laborer in 1883 and then "strolled quietly back to his village, shouting out that he had killed a 'black pig.'"

ated tradition to an extent probably not found in other major Pacific islands. Rear Admiral von Werner observed in 1889 that the Samoans were "clinging pretty fiercely to their old folkways and especially to their old style of dress," and Otto Ehlers expressed surprise that the Samoans "could retain so many attractive characteristics after sixty years of contact with Europeans."[275]

Precolonial Guidelines for a Future Native Policy

Europeans who were entranced by images of Samoan nobility tried to find ways to rescue this culture despite, or with the help of, the seemingly inevitable colonial annexation. One option was suggested by René in Gerstäcker's Tahitian novel, who argued for a gentle and protective colonial policy. Robert Louis Stevenson, who lived in Samoa from 1890 until his death in 1894, came closest to working out the details of this approach.

ROBERT LOUIS STEVENSON IN SAMOA: PATERNALISTIC PRESERVATIONISM

Although Robert Louis Stevenson supported the Samoans' struggle to avoid colonial takeover and had no official political functions, his Samoan writings and activities are suggestive of the sorts of native policy that were already being elaborated in the protocolony. Stevenson's everyday relations with Samoans at his estate in Vailima were strikingly similar to the later native policies of the German government.[276] Stevenson addressed Samoans as children and presented himself as a benevolent but pedantic father, adumbrating a program that Governor Solf developed to a fine art.[277] After mobilizing a group of Samoans to build a road to his estate at Vailima (without payment), Stevenson gave an address of thanks to the assembled chiefs that began, "you have worked for Tusitala." (Tusitala, "the Writer," was the name given to Stevenson by the Samoans.) His speech reiterated the familiar European notion that Polynesian men should be peaceful citizens rather than warriors. As a model of rule that combined love with hierarchy, paternalism seemed ideally suited to these conditions. Stevenson described civilized warfare as "fully uglier" than "barbarous war" and while

275. B. von Werner 1889, p. 250; Ehlers 1895, p. 82.
276. Stevenson 1895, vol. 2, pp. 270, 272.
277. See ibid., vol. 1, p. 59; vol. 2, pp. 156–57; and Stevenson [1982] 1996, pp. 5, 14, 23. Stevenson reports giving one of his Samoan workers the "heavy end of my whip over the buttocks" (1895, vol. 1, p. 201).

observing Samoan internal fighting was led to exclaim "Lord! what fun!"[278] This suggested that Samoan warriors were actually playing a game, which served to demasculinize them.

Stevenson also began to cross-identify with Samoans, like some of the later German colonizers. He was clearly pleased to find that his Samoan workers "really and fairly accept[ed him] as a *chief*," as he reported to his publisher and correspondent Sidney Colvin, and he was thrilled when a chief called out his special name—possibly a "kava name"—during a kava-drinking ceremony.[279] At a celebration following Samoan war dances, Stevenson heard "the description of my gift and myself as the *alii Tusitala, O le alii O malo tetele*"—the great teller of tales and "chief of the great governments." He furnished part of his house in Samoan style and wore a lavalava (wraparound) at home when he was not expecting visitors.[280] As a Scots nationalist, Stevenson identified with the Samoans as victims of colonialism. He called on them "to occupy and use [their] country," adding, "If you do not . . . others will," and "it will not continue to be yours or your children's": "You and your children will in that case be cast out into outer darkness. . . . I who speak to you have seen these things. . . . I have seen them in Ireland, and I have seen them in the mountains of my own country—Scotland—and my heart was sad. They were a fine people in the past—brave, gay, faithful, and very much like the Samoans."[281] Stevenson's identification with the Samoans did not clash with any colonial rule of difference, since the land was still ostensibly self-governed and the Europeans pretended to address the king as an equal, state to state. And Stevenson was running a (small) estate, not a colonial state. The well-wrought image of the Samoans as noble savages seems to have made them ideal mirrors for imaginary identification across cultural boundaries, and this in turn reinforced Europeans' desire to salvage Samoa as they imagined it.

COLONIAL AIKIDO: DOMINATION THROUGH CUSTOM

Stevenson seemed to have understood that the best way to manage Samoans was through their own customs, using their own force against them in a

278. Stevenson 1895, vol. 2, pp. 274, 171.

279. Ibid., pp. 196, 13. Keesing (1956, p. 73) notes that "titled individuals have special *kava* names" which must be called out during the distribution of kava at the beginning of every meeting of chiefs; see also Schultz-Ewerth 1911, p. 48.

280. Stevenson 1895, vol. 2, p. 13; Deeken 1901, p. 31.

281. Stevenson 1895, vol. 2, p. 271.

kind of cultural aikido. Two years before he mobilized the road builders Stevenson had discussed the Samoan custom of "malanga" (i.e., *malaga*), the visiting parties in which people "go from village to village, junketing and gossiping" and receiving the kava, food, entertainment, and other forms of hospitality required by the society's unwritten rules. He had commented on Samoan "communism" and the "conduct prescribed for a Samoan"—"to give and to continue giving," until reaching the point of utter destitution.[282] It was also widely known that high chiefs were "entitled to the free work of the people" in building houses, for example.[283] The parsimonious Stevenson used this culture of gift giving to his own advantage and acted as if he were accepting the chiefs' offer of free labor only because he thought it might provide a valuable "lesson," "might be more useful to Samoa than a thousand breadfruit trees." Profiting from the Samoans' "communist" gift culture while admonishing them to become industrious workers may seem scandalously hypocritical, but it was not unusual. Many years later Somerset Maugham wrote a story about a cunning colonial official in the mandate colony who got Samoans "to do the work he wanted for wages that were almost nominal."[284] When the Samoans tried to resist, the official vanquished them through their own commitment to the obligations of hospitality.

Even Europeans who were less enamored of the Samoans tended to believe that they could be best governed through tradition. A case in point is William T. Pritchard, acting British consul at Samoa from 1856 to 1858.[285] Pritchard had come to the islands with his father, who had been expelled from Tahiti by the French and was appointed British consul to Samoa in 1847. Pritchard fils set a benchmark, developing an explicit strategy for regulating Samoans. In order "to gain my ends," he wrote, the "application of [the natives'] old traditions is almost always more effective than volumes of the most eloquent exhortations." Pritchard used Samoan idioms and folk tales in a technique perfected by Solf.[286]

The writings of Augustin Krämer, which were published during the transition to German colonial rule, provided a veritable blueprint for the nascent regime. Krämer was the leading foreign authority on Samoa before

282. Stevenson [1892] 1996, pp. 6–7.

283. Churchward 1887, p. 167.

284. Maugham 1977, p. 155.

285. Pritchard was later appointed British consul to Fiji. See "W. J. Pritchards Beobachtungen und Erlebnisse unter den Südsee-Insulanern," *Das Ausland* 40 (13): 289–94.

286. W. Pritchard 1866, pp. 90, 68, 96–97, 103.

Margaret Mead. He entered the navy in 1889 after studying medicine at the universities of Tübingen and Berlin and began his career as a naval doctor in 1893 with a three-year cruise in the Pacific. In terms of his class background he was the Stephen Maturin of the German navy, not the Jack Aubrey (to draw on the novels of Patrick O'Brian), resembling Solf and Schultz and many other educated, liberal, middle-class colonizers. Krämer's first major work, *Die Samoa-Inseln (The Samoa Islands)* was a two-volume, thousand-page "ethnological" monograph that is still in print in English translation. It is an encyclopedic compendium of Samoan lineages or "pedigrees" in the form of *fa'alupega* (ceremonial greetings) for each village and district. It also includes transcriptions of historical stories and traditions, photographs of people, places, and practices (dances, production processes, etc.), and descriptions of ceremonial meetings (*fono*), historical customs, and geographic names. Krämer spent a year in Samoa during his 1893-95 cruise, laying the foundation for these studies, and another year and a half during a voyage to the Pacific that lasted from 1897 to 1899. Krämer also visited Hawai'i and eastern Micronesia during that second voyage and later conducted research in German Micronesia (1906-7, 1909-10) and New Mecklenburg (New Ireland; 1908-9). In 1909 he left the German navy to become the director of the Linden Museum for Ethnology in Stuttgart, a job that lasted from 1911 to 1914. He received a teaching post in anthropology at Tübingen University in 1919 and remained there until his retirement in 1933.[287]

Like most anthropological field-workers and collectors in this era before the creation of university anthropology departments, Krämer was an autodidact in his chosen field. During his 1897-99 cruise Krämer was able to live "totally according to his own inclinations." He engaged in intensive discussions with Samoans about the fine points of their culture, and by the end of this period he felt that he "understood Samoan fairly well." Although he conducted many interviews in his house in Apia he also spent extended periods of time in the villages, living with locals in their homes. He speculated that "seldom has any white made such frequent and thoroughgoing claims [on Samoan hospitality]." Krämer drank kava with his informants and watched the dances and entertainments. He offered medical care in exchange for ethnographic information.[288] At the same time, Krämer described his most important Samoan informant, a *tulāfale* (orator) named Sauni, as his "best teacher" and an "unshakable friend." Sauni was born before the start of the Christian era in 1830 and was "generally looked upon

---

287. Harms 1991, p. 165; 1992.
288. Krämer 1906, pp. 156, 468-69; 1994-95, vol. 1, pp. 5-6.

by the other Samoans as one of the wisest men among them." Sauni "devoted himself completely to [Krämer's] studies, almost even more unselfishly than [his] earlier informants," sitting with him "day and night, indefatigably." Krämer also worked with a local, Fred Pace or Feleki (Feleti), whom he called his "Mädchen für alles" ("girl Friday"), for all of his written translations. He concluded that if his undertaking was successful it was "due only to the endurance and dedication of my Samoan friends whose names I have listed above and to whom I am indebted." He mastered the technique of bringing Samoans into his personal debt as a means of pumping them for information, and at the same time he became almost entirely dependent on them.[289]

In addition to the empirical richness of his work, Krämer's interpretive stance was of a piece with the discourse of Polynesian noble savagery. On the one hand, he was not afraid to acknowledge the "savage" sides of Samoan life. He included in his book a photograph of a Samoan man dressed for war and holding a "beheading knife." Although the missionaries had insisted for decades that the Samoans had never practiced cannibalism, Krämer refuted this in a section called "The Edible Animals and Their Preparation," which dispassionately discussed the old methods of cooking human beings in the oven. He elaborated on historic Samoan cannibalism in an essay published several years later.[290] Discussing the traditional ceremony of the public defloration of the *taupou*, or village maiden, Krämer turned the missionary evaluation on its head, writing, "It is frightening to think of the level of morality to which such a people can sink through the *removal* of such a custom." Listing traditional forms of dance, he was careful to include one style called the *sā'ē*, a "nude dance by women at the poula."[291] Krämer emphasized the beauty and naturalness of practices that the missionaries reviled or regarded suspiciously. He characterized the entrenched culture of sharing (Samoan "communism") as a "noble custom" (edle Angewohnheit).[292] He attacked the myth of the "lazy native" that was widespread among settlers, planters, and, he said, lazy politicians in Berlin. While acknowledging that the Samoans did not "work themselves to death," Krämer

289. Krämer 1906, pp. 513, 477; 1994–95, vol. 1, pp. 4, 6.

290. Krämer 1994–95, vol. 2, pp. 185–86; Krämer 1909b, p. 137. In the latter essay colonial power is described as putting an end to "old Samoa" rather than conserving it (ibid., p. 138).

291. Krämer 1994–95, vol. 1, p. 47 n. 87 (my emphasis); vol. 2, p. 367. For a summary of historical information on the *sā'ē* and interpretation, see Mageo 1998, pp. 194–98.

292. Krämer 1906, p. 165. The second governor of German Samoa, Erich Schultz (Schultz-Ewerth 1924, p. 126), described Samoa as a "familial" version of communism (*Sippenkommunismus*).

included detailed and lengthy chapters on traditional forms of work and lauded Samoan building techniques and vernacular architecture.[293]

Several historians have portrayed Krämer as solipsistically building his future career by collecting artifacts and engaging in intrigues against competitors from other ethnographic museums.[294] But he also pursued projects that were more public. Krämer's desire to defend Samoan traditional culture against missionaries and Westernization was coupled with a resigned conviction that only European annexation could accomplish this goal. On the eve of the partition he suggested that the best the Germans could do was to "help the Samoan electorate, the Tumua, exercise its rights guaranteed by the Berlin treaty [of 1889] and to elect a king according to its own customs and traditions."[295] In the context of the events of 1898–99, Krämer's argument for respecting the Tumua flew in the face of the decision by the American chief justice of Samoa, William Chambers, who had ruled in favor of the claim of another Samoan, Mālietoa Tanumafili, to the four traditional titles and the kingship. Tanumafili was supported by the Mālietoa royal line, while the Tumua and Pule and the majority of Samoans were supporting Mata'afa's claim to the titles.[296] Krämer's argument played into

293. Krämer 1994–95, vol. 2, p. 96; 1906, p. 475: "There is no equal in the architecture of the *Naturvölker* for the beauty and regularity of the straight and curved lines in the Samoan house."

294. Harms (1991), Schleip (1989), and Zimmerman (2001, pp. 235–36) all depict Krämer as a quarrelsome, authoritarian, and simple-minded pillager. Krämer collected mainly for the Linden Museum in Stuttgart, although some of the objects he acquired in the Pacific ended up in the Hamburg and Tübingen museums. Schleip's article uses the phrase "colonial praxis" in its title but does not actually deal with colonialism, although it depicts Krämer's collecting itself as a sort of colonialism. Zimmerman (2001) ignores Krämer's work in the precolonial Samoan context, on which his reputation was originally based, focusing entirely on his later work in Micronesia and New Mecklenburg. Zimmerman suggests (2001, p. 237) that Krämer did not attain "a level of immediacy, almost intimacy, with his subjects," but this seems to be based on a somewhat stereotypical image of modern-day fieldwork (compare Keane 2005). Krämer (1994–95, vol. 1, p. 2) described his research as being concerned with the "spiritual property" of the Samoans, and his work is replete with discussions of prolonged, semi-intimate encounters with his informants. For a more nuanced discussion of Krämer see D. Freeman 1964, p. 555; and Harms 2004.

295. Krämer 1899, p. 188. The *Tumua* was a confederation of *tulāfale* (orators, or "talking chiefs") from the districts of A'ana and Atua in 'Upolu which conferred the most important of the honorific titles and the members of which therefore considered themselves the traditional kingmakers, along with their counterparts on the island of Savai'i, called the *Pule* (Keesing 1934, chap. 2; 1956, p. 23; Gilson 1970, p. 56).

296. See also W. E. Williamson, "Men Who Made Trouble in Samoa," *San Francisco Call*, July 2, 1899; and *Samoa Weekly Herald*, July 8, 1899, pp. 2–3. Mālietoa Tanumafili was the father of Mālietoa Tanumafili II, who died in 2007 after serving as Samoan head of state for forty-five years.

the hands of the German forces in Samoa, who were supporting Mata'afa against the U.S.- and British-backed Tanumafili. The political crisis that resulted from the chief justice's decision led to the partition of the islands a year later, after the Germans took advantage of the ongoing Boer War to force Britain to sign the agreement.[297] Krämer's defense of tradition thus drew him into the coalition supporting a German colony. Nonetheless, his insistence on following Samoan tradition was consistent with arguments in his other ethnographic publications and does not seem to have been motivated simply by nationalist opposition to the Americans, much less by a one-dimensional pillaging approach. Krämer had also been happy to advise the American chief justice in 1899 about "Samoan customs and the Samoan constitution" before it had become evident that Samoa would be subjected to colonial annexation.[298] Furthermore, the Germans had opposed Mata'afa's accession to the Samoan crown earlier in the decade, so it was clear that they were following rules of political expediency rather than adhering to Samoan customary law. Krämer's role was comparable to that of figures like Carl Gotthilf Büttner and Theophilus Hahn in Southwest Africa: he transported precolonial ethnographic representations directly to the nascent colonial state. His work was read and cited by both of the German governors.[299]

Krämer's argument for colonialism as a salvage operation became more explicit after 1900. In the introduction to *The Samoa Islands*, published in 1902, Krämer wrote: "I especially hope that the new governments [Germany and the United States] will be able to profit from this book. . . . May these studies above all be a stimulus to compile similar material for other islands before it is too late. Now is the best time for Polynesia and Melanesia; for the fruits fall from the tree if the roots are attacked, the moth lays its eggs before it must die. . . . Fruit must be picked when it is ripe. Although green fruit often ripens later, once decayed it is irretrievably lost."[300] A colonial government should protect the "roots" of Samoan culture and might even be able to rescue the "fruit" and allow it to "ripen." A more detailed discussion of this project appeared in Krämer's account of his second Pacific voyage (1897–99), which was published in 1906. Here he wrote that "there is nothing for Europeans to govern in a new native colony. . . . The colored . . . have been governing themselves since ancient times all by themselves, and

297. See P. Kennedy 1974, chap. 5, on the events of 1899.
298. Krämer 1906, p. 534.
299. See NZNA AGCA XVII.A.1, pt. 5, between pp. 72 and 73, Solf to Foreign Office, July 6, 1909, referring to Krämer's *Samoa-Inseln;* Schultz-Ewerth 1926, p. 21.
300. Krämer 1994–95, vol. 1, p. 7 (translation altered according to German original).

have usually done quite a good job of it. And when whites start intruding in their government, the native state is destroyed, and with it the organic components."[301] Krämer went on to imagine a "genuine colonization" (eine wahre Kolonisierung) that would benefit the colonized rather than effecting "depopulation" and cultural destruction, as in Hawai'i. This was also a core theme in public statements by the first German governor of Samoa. Krämer called for a "wise" colonial government that would work against missionaries and settlers in a "mitigating" way. This was plausible in Samoa, he argued, given the "strong national character" of the Samoans, who had not yet "had the *tastelessness* to put on trousers."[302] His wife, Elisabeth Krämer-Bannow, called on the colonizers to protect and strengthen the "original people who until now have resisted with tenacious stubbornness the so-called culture offered by the whites."[303]

One historian has claimed that the Germans turned Samoa into a sort of anthropological nature reserve.[304] As I will show in the next chapter, this formulation overlooks the ways in which colonialism necessarily redefines indigenous culture in the very act of traditionalizing it. To describe German policy as simple preservationism is as much a euphemism as the term Germany used for its colonies, *protectorate*. Of course, Krämer actually did suggest that the Germans turn another of their Polynesian colonies, Palau, "including its indigenous population," into a nature park (*Naturschutzpark*): "The old chiefs will gladly come . . . and tell stories, with sparkling eyes. . . . How seductive it is when the stately women and girls bring the food offerings, clad only in grass skirts. . . . Ban the settlement of whites . . . ban corrugated metal and trousers!"[305] The German colonial government did, in fact, try to prevent the use of corrugated metal roofing material, if not trousers, and suppressed the more obnoxious settlers. Elisabeth Krämer-Bannow accompanied her husband on two trips to the Pacific and created countless sketches, watercolors, photographs, and sound recordings throughout the Pacific. She also wrote a popular ethnography of the island of New Mecklenburg in which she suggested that the German colonial regimes and missionaries should require "that the natives replace any ethnographic objects they sold [to collectors] with copies of equal quality, thereby retaining the

301. Krämer 1906, p. 224.
302. Ibid., pp. 226, 244 (my emphasis).
303. Krämer-Bannow n.d., pp. 6–7.
304. Hiery 1995.
305. Krämer 1914, pp. 160–61.

art of their homeland."[306] Of course, anthropologists like Krämer-Bannow were not colonial officials and could therefore ignore the imperatives of security and economic profitability.

But in an already protocolonial situation, they did not ignore the rule of difference. Despite his relativism, sympathy for Polynesians, and orientation toward salvaging dying traditions, Augustin Krämer presented himself to Samoans as a cultural superior. He was vitally dependent on his informants' hospitality, but he always paid or gave gifts to his hosts so that they would not ask to stay with him in Apia. Although he insisted that Europeans should always drink kava, sit cross-legged on the floor, and follow other Samoan customs when in the countryside, Krämer was adamant about defining his own house in Apia as a European enclave. His relationship with his translator and housekeeper was clearly hierarchical. Krämer noted in one travel narrative that "success in a scientific voyage is often utterly dependent on a servant," and in this he was indistinguishable from more obvious racist travelers like Baron Ferdinand von Richthofen, discussed in chapter 6.[307] The techniques for using indigenous customs to dominate Samoans on a daily basis were not antithetical to the "salvage" approach to colonialism but were integral to its native policies.

Augustin Kramer wrote that he was "ensnared by the magic of Samoa," and he provided Samoa with an invaluable written record of its ancient customs and title lineages. Robert Louis Stevenson was "thrilled" by Samoa and, in Theroux's words, he communicated its "power of bewitchment." Yet these men felt superior to the culture that had enchanted them and developed mechanisms for manipulating and exploiting it. The next chapter explores the vicissitudes of this dual process of ensnaring and being ensnared within the more explicitly colonial context after 1900.

306. Krämer-Bannow and Krämer 1916. She also called for "human protection" of Germany's colonial subjects in their "natural innocence," insisting that "our European trousers are in any case the last thing we should give to the natives," who were more attractive and comfortable in their traditional clothing (Krämer-Bannow 1913, pp. 356, 359). On Krämer-Bannow see Pytlik 1997.

307. Krämer 1906, pp. 83, 157.

FIVE

"The Spirit of the German Nation at Work in the Antipodes" ⁊ German Colonialism in Samoa, 1900–1914

A retired *matai* [chief]. . . . ends his days in peace and quietness, treated with that peculiar delicacy and consideration of which Samoan custom can be so pleasantly capable *when the circumstances are favourable.*

F. J. H. GRATTAN, Secretary of Samoan Affairs, Western Samoa, during New Zealand rule[1]

Salvage Colonialism

German colonialism in Samoa contrasts starkly with the dismal story of German Southwest Africa. The Samoan administration took its ethnographic cues mainly from nonmissionary elements, whereas the views of the Southwest African government was powerfully shaped by the Rhenish missionary accounts. The government in Samoa was willing to oppose the missions on important matters like the creation of a secular school for assimilated Samoans in 1908–9.[2] There was even more tension between the government and the planters. Governor Wilhelm Solf (fig. 5.1) saw white settlers as the greatest threat to Samoa and to overseas colonies in general. In contrast to pre-1904 Namibia, there was no talk of creating native reservations or scattering settlers throughout the islands.[3] Instead, most Europeans clustered

1. Grattan 1948, p. 15 (my emphasis). Grattan had an anthropology degree from the University of Cambridge.

2. On the "Kulturkampf" in 1908 and 1909 between Solf and the Catholic mission and the German Center Party over the creation of a secular school for forty Samoan students that was intended to qualify them for governmental administrative duties, see "Zentrumspolitik und persönliche Politik auf Samoa," *Tägliche Rundschau*, April 8, 1909; and BA-Berlin, RKA, vol. 2760, including Solf to RKA, August 31, 1909, p. 46.

3. See letter from Solf to Koenig, April 30, 1904, BA-Koblenz, Nachlass Solf, vol. 25, pp. 58–62; Gilson 1970, p. 404.

FIGURE 5.1 Wilhelm Solf. (Courtesy of Stadt- u.
Universitätsbibliothek Frankfurt, Bildsammlung
der Deutschen Kolonialgesellschaft.)

in Apia, as if in a "reservation" for *papalagi*. In 1900 the colonial government reaffirmed the existing ban on alienating any Samoan land that had
not been confirmed as foreign property by the Land Commission (1891–94).[4]
Solf was careful not to offend the DHPG, but that company had already
stopped expanding in the 1880s and was able to organize its own supply of
foreign labor, much of it from Melanesia. Because Samoans cultivated copra
on their own and sold it directly to the Europeans, Solf's protective policies
did not threaten his modus vivendi with the DHPG.[5]

The colonial government presented itself as a protector of Samoan rights
and traditions. In statements to the foreign press and to Samoans Solf
announced proudly that he had no intention of changing local customs,
arguing that this was one reason the Samoans were not dying out like
other native peoples.[6] This approach resonated strongly with Augustin

4. Solf, King George II of Tonga, and Hunter [1907] 1983, p. 57.
5. Firth and Munro 1990.
6. See Solf's comments in "Samoan Affairs," *Samoanische Zeitung*, August 25, 1906; and
also Solf's interview with the *Sydney Evening News*, April 8, 1901.

Krämer's idea of colonialism as a salvage operation. Rather than forcing the indigenous people to relate to their colonizers within a foreign idiom and suppressing their native terminology, as in Southwest Africa, the German administrators governed Samoa within a revised and codified version of their own culture.[7] Erich Schultz (or Schultz-Ewerth, as he called himself later; fig. 5.2), Solf's successor as governor and his protégé, became fluent enough in Samoan to compose his own communications with indigenous officials, although Solf continued to rely on his "half-caste" translator Charles Taylor. As Solf explained to one group of Samoans in 1901, "I have often told natives that the German government wishes them to be ruled, not according to white mans ideas [sic], but according to the Faa Samoa [Samoan custom]. . . . For this reason I do not wish to interfere in your Samoan titles and such things."[8] Schultz described the Germans' project as the "preservation of the Samoans' customs and mores and their peculiar character [ihre Eigenart] per se."[9] The Samoan ali'i sili, or paramount chief, Mata'afa Iosefa (fig. 5.3), seemed to accept this description of the German program, at least in his public communications, stating that "the governor's resolve . . . shows certainly that he wishes to see the Samoan customs preserved."[10] Mata'afa's statement should not be taken at face value, of course. He was deeply committed to certain institutions and customs that the Germans had in fact abolished, above all the position of tupu. But the Germans had helped lift Mata'afa into the national "throne" against his contender. On the one hand, Mata'afa's endorsement of Solf signaled his willingness to play along with the government during the next twelve years and even to accept the role of the noble savage. On the other hand, Mata'afa's insistence on "the governor's resolve" to preserve Samoan "customs" indicated that he would try to push Solf to revoke the ban on the kingship and hold him to his promises more generally. Within the confines of German sovereignty Mata'afa frequently pressed for more Samoan autonomy. It seems presumptuous to label his actions "collaboration" in light of that word's connotations of Vichy France and others who helped the Nazis; "cooperator" seems like a preferable alternative. There was a more direct oppositional tendency against the Germans by people like Lauaki (Namulau'ulu Lauaki Mamoe; fig. 5.4).

7. Joseph Hübner (1886, vol. 2, p. 393) described the colony as "the spirit of the German nation at work in the antipodes."

8. "Savai'i Fono, Minutes of Fono Held in Savai'i during Malaga in July, 1901," BA-Berlin, RKA, vol. 3061, p. 57 (in English).

9. Schulz to Osbahr, March 8, 1914, NZNA AGCA VI 28, pt. 1, p. 61.

10. Letter from Mata'afa to all Samoan officials, October 10, 1900, BA-Koblenz, Nachlass Solf, vol. 20, p. 291.

FIGURE 5.2 (top left) Erich Schultz, or Schultz-Ewerth. (Courtesy of Stadt- u. Universitätsbibliothek Frankfurt, Bildsammlung der Deutschen Kolonialgesellschaft.)

FIGURE 5.3 (top right) Mata'afa Iosefa, Samoan *ali'i sili* (paramount chief) (1900–1912), holding *fue.* (Courtesy of Stadt- u. Universitätsbibliothek Frankfurt, Bildsammlung der Deutschen Kolonialgesellschaft.)

FIGURE 5.4 (left) Lauaki (Namulau'ulu Lauaki Mamoe) with *fue* and orator's staff. (Courtesy of Stadt- u. Universitätsbibliothek Frankfurt, Bildsammlung der Deutschen Kolonialgesellschaft.)

But these opponents were less centrally placed within the colonial system of rule and therefore less able to extract advantages not only for themselves but also for their allies or Samoans in general.

Despite the government's pronouncements it did interfere in Samoan custom, most importantly in the traditional power structure. The colonial state tried to reorganize the internal administration of Samoan affairs from the national level down to the villages, through the creation of an array of salaried and handpicked indigenous officials. The Germans inserted themselves into the very center of Samoan life by creating a new court, the Land and Titles Commission, to settle disputes over the allocation of chiefly *matai* titles and related land claims. A Samoan *matai* bears the title of his *'āiga*, an extended kinship or descent group. Titles were the main markers of power and prestige. The transmission of a *matai* title from one holder to the next was often a conflictual and unpredictable process whose result could not be deduced from biological lines of descent. Indeed, titles were as much *earned* as inherited, and genealogies were rewritten by the victors.[11] One result of this system was that struggles over title inheritance often escalated into war, as in 1898–99. The colonizers had numerous reasons for attempting to understand, rationalize, and channel this central and volatile aspect of Samoan society. The chief justice and head of the Land and Titles Commission during the German colonial era was Erich Schultz, who wrote several studies of Samoan customary law.[12]

Despite these sweeping interventions in Samoan custom, the state's commitment to a cultural salvage operation was not insignificant. The very fact that the Germans worked within the title system rather than ignoring it or trying to abolish it made an enormous difference for the texture of colonial rule (and for the postcolonial aftermath). By creating the Land and Titles Commission the Germans accepted that the elaborate titles system would remain the central medium of Samoan politics. More generally the Germans agreed to move within a world that was draped with Samoan webs of meaning. For example, when the governor created a native school in 1908–9 he designated a *matai* as headmaster.[13] The fact that the Germans

---

11. See Schultz-Ewerth 1924, p. 114, on the *matai*'s *pule* (power). On the Land and Title Commission, see Marsack (1958) and Meleisea (1987a), who argues that the court was established "with the objective, not so much of preserving Samoan institutions . . . but more to manipulate and control the decision making process by which the legitimacy of chiefly titles and authority over land was recognised" (p. xii). While these were indeed the general goals, the *form* was radically distinct from native policy in most other German colonies.

12. E.g., Schultz-Ewerth 1911.

13. Schultz, memo, March 28, 1908, BA-Berlin, RKA, vol. 2760, p. 15r.

incorporated a Samoan category of rank into a government institution stood in stark contrast to Southwest Africa, where they outlawed the positions of chief and *kaptein*. Even in secret official correspondence designated for the Colonial Department the officials referred to the school's *matai*, rather than using German or English terms to designate the position, indicating the degree to which Samoan concepts had permeated the colonial administration.[14] Indeed, the Germans came to depend upon the system of chiefly power to such an extent that they sometimes defended it against "modernizing" Samoans. Governor Schultz was extremely upset to discover in 1914 that some *matai* were giving away their chiefly authority (*pule*) to untitled men (*taulele'a*). These *taulele'a* were said to be neglecting their traditional service requirements (*tautua*) to the *matai*. Such developments would not only dilute the title system but would make it more difficult for the colonial state to identify the actual power holders at the local level. It also threatened to fragment land ownership in the villages; land was owned in common and allocated to individuals and groups for their use by the *matai*. In Samoan custom a *matai* could be replaced if he began to treat land as his personal property. Schultz was mistrustful of the growing influence of the *taulele'a*, many of whom were working for wages at the docks.[15] The embrace of the title system was tied to a more general program of slowing down the "modernization" of Samoan life.

In the next two sections I will first present the practices of "regulated traditionalism" and then turn to the repressive dimensions of policy. I will then ask about the sources of this Janus-faced approach.

REGULATED CUSTOM

The Germans agreed to continue tailoring many of their legal determinations to Samoan understandings, even where these violated "Western" understandings, missionary sensibilities, or settler interests. For example, Chief Justice Schultz agreed to imprison Samoans who insulted chiefs, admitting that the crime might "not be punishable *faapapalagi*" (according to foreign or the white man's law) but that it was "extremely insulting" according to "*faa-Samoa*."[16] This resonated with the German effort to bolster and regulate the system of chiefly titles. German officials were instructed

14. Schultz, memo, April 15, 1908, BA-Berlin, RKA, vol. 2760, p. 15v.

15. Haupt-Agentur der deutschen Handels- und Plantagen-Gesellschaft der Südsee-Inseln zu Hamburg, Apia, May 22, 1914, to Schultz, NZNA AGCA XVII.A.1, vol. 6, p. 150; Schultz, "O le pule Foa'i" [On the Giving Away of Pule], *O le Savali*, April 1914.

16. Schultz, minute of March 31, 1904, NZNA ACGA XVII.B.5 (Aana and Manono), vol. 2.

to treat the Samoan custom of *avaga*—elopement without the consent of the girl's parents—as a form of marriage even if the legal form of the marriage had not been fulfilled, "as long as both parties [were] of a reasonable age and the parents, particularly those of the girl, were in agreement."[17] The colonial state was willing to punish male abductors for reasons that had no equivalent in German law, for example, "if the abductor is of such a common family and the girl of such a noble one, according to Samoan conception, that it is an insult to the girl's family."[18] That this was not a simple case of delegated or indirect rule but rather an attempt to regulate indigenous life through a preferred version of local culture is indicated by the fact that Samoans could be convicted for engaging in an illegal act of *avaga* only by a German official, and not by one of the local Samoan district judges.[19] That this was an active shaping and steering of indigenous practices rather than a passive acceptance of extant custom is also indicated by the fact that the Germans deemed *avaga* to be punishable if violence (*Körperverletzung*) was used, whereas force had been part of the traditional practice of *avaga*.[20]

German meetings with Samoan leaders adhered to the traditional format of the *fono,* or council meeting, with German and Samoan parties typically sitting opposite one another in the meeting house in the positions conventionally reserved for respected outside visitors and local elites (see fig. 5.5).[21] Solf opened and closed all meetings with Samoan leaders with the traditional kava-drinking ritual.[22] This marked a small but symbolically significant break with the style of the American chief justice from

17. NZNA AGCA XVII.A.1, vol. 6, p. 147 (no date; May 1914). A related concept was *taligafafine,* or "abduction of a girl by one or more men, with her connivance and intention to elope with one of them." German officials did punish Samoan men for *avaga* when it was against the wishes of the girl's father; see the case in Schubert to Schultz, September 6, 1913, NZNA AGCA XVII.B.1, vol. 9.

18. Schultz to Amtmann, December 23, 1910, NZNA AGCA XVII.AI., vol. 5, p. 182.

19. "Faatonuga mo Faamasino" [New Instructions for *Fa'amasino*], notes, NZNA AGCA XVII.AI., vol. 5, pp. 203-4.

20. Schultz to Osbahr and Williams, May 13, 1914, NZNA AGCA XVII.AI, vol. 6, pp. 147-48. Judges were also instructed to compel women to return to the husbands they had abandoned. My sense is that this was not an entirely un-Samoan intervention but that it sided with one party in what had previously been a somewhat more equal contest between men and women. See Schoeffel (1987), Mageo (1998), and Mead ([1928] 1973) on "traditional" Samoan gender relations.

21. Krämer 1994-95, vol. 2, p. 278. The only other obvious concession to the Germans visible in fig. 5.5 is that at least one European is sitting with legs outstretched, in a breach of Samoan etiquette.

22. See *Samoanische Zeitung,* August 19, 1905, pp. 7-8; report on *fono* of July 16, 1901, BA-Berlin, RKA, vol. 3061, p. 64; see photo of Solf watching traditional preparation of kava in Hiery 2005, p. 258, plate 525.

FIGURE 5.5 Erich Schultz leading a *fono* with Samoans. (Courtesy of Stadt- u. Universitätsbibliothek Frankfurt, Bildsammlung der Deutschen Kolonialgesellschaft.)

the protocolonial period, William Chambers, who had refused to drink kava with Samoan chiefs. It was also a rapprochement with the approach of Samoan enthusiasts like Stevenson and the German consul from the early 1890s, Oskar Stuebel, none of whom ever refused kava, and Augustin Krämer, who had dissertated lengthily on the customs associated with the root.[23] As shown in figure 5.5, the colonizers sometimes sat in chairs during the *fono*. This seemed to represent a break with tradition, since there were normally no chairs in a Samoan house. It allowed the colonizers to be physically and socially elevated above the Samoans they were addressing. But even this use of chairs could be fitted into existing systems of meaning. In the traditional Samoan *fono* the *tulāfale*—orating or speaking chiefs—stood while presenting their opening orations, and the highest Samoan chiefs were carried in litters and "greeted with elaborate prostration postures."[24]

The colonial government used indigenous terms in addressing the colonized and coined Samoan neologisms to designate new institutions. The German emperor was called the *tupu sili* (paramount king), which usurped the abolished title of the Samoan *tupu* and located him above the *ali'i sili*. The governor's handpicked advisory body of Samoans, created in 1905, was misleadingly called the Mālō Kaisalika, or imperial government, building on the Samoan word *mālō,* which had traditionally referred to the dominant party or faction that was victorious in war but which had been used to designate the indigenous Samoan government in the later nineteenth

23. Krämer 1906, p. 539; Stuebel 1896, p. 156.
24. Sahlins 1958, p. 37.

PLATE 1 The village of Narina, a young Gonaqua woman. From Le Vaillant 1973, vol. 1, plate 12.

PLATE 2 William Hodges, *A View Taken in the Bay of Otaheite Peha* (1775–76).

PLATE 3 Louis Choris, *View in the Radak Islands*. From Choris 1822, plate 19. (Courtesy of Special Collections Library, University of Michigan.)

PLATE 4 The Chinese House in Sanssouci Park, Potsdam. Photo by the author, 2003.

PLATE 5 Johann Gottleib Heymüller, *Bell Player*, at the Chinese House in Sanssouci Park, Potsdam. Photo by the author, 2003.

PLATE 6 Christian Bernhardt Rode, *The Chinese Emperor behind the Plow* (1770).

PLATE 7 Model of the old Imperial Garden (Yuanming Yuan), Beijing. Photo by the author, 2005.

PLATE 8 Ruins of the old Imperial Garden (Yuanming Yuan), Beijing. Photo by the author, 2005.

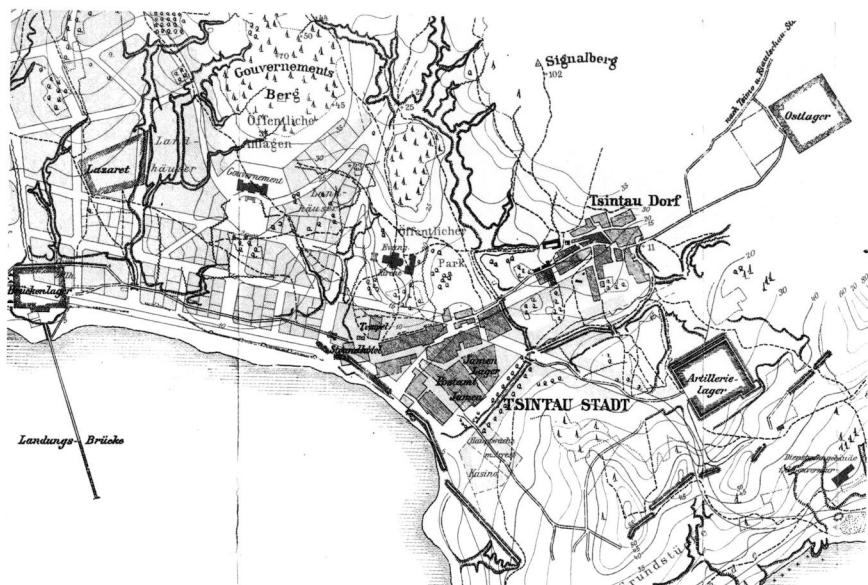

PLATE 9 Excerpt from first city plan for Qingdao, 1898, showing the superimposition of the German street plan and buildings (in red) over the existing Chinese streets and structures (in black). Some details of this plan were subsequently changed, including the layout of streets and the placement of certain buildings. The temple shown in the middle, Tianhougong, was preserved as a Chinese theater.

PLATE 10 Pseudo-spirit-wall in the Tsingtau-Klub, Qingdao. Photo by the author, 2005.

PLATE 11 *Field Marshall Count Waldersee at His Desk in the Beijing Winter Palace.* From *Deutschland in China* 1902, facing p. 164.

PLATE 12 Equestrian statue, Windhoek, with the old German colonial army fortress in the background. Photo by the author, 2004.

century.[25] Solf styled himself the representative of the kaiser's *pule*, using the Samoan term that had originally referred to the orator groups from six towns on the island of Savai'i with traditional privileges, but that had more recently acquired the extended meanings of "authority" or "power." On a tour of Savai'i Solf described his visit to the villages as a *malaga*. *Malaga*, or *tafatafao*, were "customary visits to relatives and villages" in which people traveled "from village to village, junketing and gossiping" and receiving kava, food, entertainment, and other gifts and gestures of hospitality that were required by universally acknowledged rules.[26] *Malaga* were also associated with important political events. Solf's use of this term was meant to suggest that Samoans would be obligated by their own traditions to cooperate with him and to offer him hospitality. When the village of Fagamalo failed to welcome Solf with the proper pomp and ceremony, sending out just "one dirty boat" to greet him, the governor did not punish the locals in "European" fashion with monetary fines or physical violence but demanded that the chiefs make a formal *ifoga*, or ceremonial request for forgiveness.[27] Mata'afa and the members of the Mālō also performed *ifoga* for Solf in April 1905 after the failed 'Oloa movement, discussed below, "sitting for hours in the solemn posture of performing the *Ifo*," before Solf's house.[28]

Solf's communications with the Samoans were framed within Samoan fables and figures of speech. This marked another stylistic departure from the former chief justice, who had called the Samoan chiefs together and read to them "a four-page juridical epistle that was difficult to follow."[29] Speaking to Samoan leaders after their rebellious attempt to set up an independent copra trading company in 1905, Solf described his judgment as being "like a knife which cuts away the rotten part of the breadfruit, and leaves only the healthy part."[30] Solf traveled to the traditional power center of Lufilufi in the district of Atua on 'Upolu and reprimanded the Samoans for their ungratefulness to the colonial government. His speech on this

---

25. J. Davidson 1967, pp. 78, 433; *Samoanische Zeitung,* August 19, 1905, pp. 7–8. Also see Solf to Mata'afa, June 26, 1900, BA-Koblenz, Nachlass Solf, vol. 20, pp. 262ff.

26. Quotes from Salesa 2003, p. 174; and Stevenson [1892] 1996, p. 6.

27. "Fono at Fagamalo, Matautu, July 12, 1901, 8 P.M. People of Matautu, Saleaula, and Le Ala Tele," BA-Berlin, RKA, vol. 3061, pp. 51 and 55, Solf's handwritten note at bottom.

28. Solf to Colonial Department, August 4, 1905, BA-Koblenz, Nachlass Solf, vol. 26, p. 28.

29. Krämer 1906, p. 535.

30. "Speech by the Governor on the August 14th, 1905," BA-Koblenz, Nachlass Solf, vol. 25, p. 203 (in English). The speech was given at Mulinu'u, site of the Samoan Mālō.

occasion took the form of a Samoan fable involving a crab, a rat, a squid, and a plover.[31]

Of course, much of what was regarded as "custom" by 1900 was a version of Samoan practice that had already been reinvented and recoded in response to European incursions in the preceding seven decades. It was this already "neotraditional" version of custom and not some notional pre-contact culture that formed the point of departure for most of the colonial state's interventions.[32] Most important, perhaps, the German government did not bemoan the Samoans' conversion to Christianity or attempt to "repaganize" them. Although the state staked out a position distinct from the missionaries on many questions, it was largely in agreement with them on issues of sex and gender. Thus, Governor Schultz banned an old custom according to which the *manaia*, or chiefly son, was "not required to observe the normal restrictions on relations with women, but [was given] freedom with any of his close female relatives, including mother, daughters and sisters."[33] Schultz took over the administration of divorces from the *fa'amasino* (Samoan district judges, discussed below) in 1904, and he was able to boast to the head of the Catholic mission in Samoa, Bishop Broyer, that "all officials involved in the adjudication of Samoan divorces are instructed to work in each case for a reconciliation of the spouses and to approach the matter more generally in the role of a *protector matrimonii*."[34] Nor did the colonizers try to reintroduce the traditional clothing styles from the pre-Christian era. Instead, lavalavas were manufactured in Germany and sold to Samoans. The lavalava was a nineteenth-century response to European sexual mores, a compromise between the more revealing clothing worn in precontact times and the unhealthy, all-enveloping vestments that missionaries had convinced people to wear in other parts of the Pacific.[35]

The government's neotraditionalist program often entailed a level of hostility to the "modernization" of Samoa that is surprising to theorists of

31. Solf to Colonial Department, August 4, 1905, BA-Koblenz, Nachlass Solf, vol. 26, pp. 29–30.

32. As J. Davidson (1967, p. 46) points out, for instance, the "traditional" Samoan repugnance to the idea of alienating land took root only after the massive sales to Europeans in the 1860s and 1870s. Similarly, many argue that the title of *tupu*, though apparently ancient, was first defined as meaning "king of Samoa" by the missionaries.

33. Schultz, "Ua fai ma Tulafono," *O le Savali*, June 1914, translation in NZNA ACGA, microfilm roll 128, "Samoan administration," p. 112.

34. Schultz to Broyer, August 16, 1913, NZNA AGCA XVII A.1, vol. 6, p. 143; also Wareham 2002, p. 43.

35. Krämer-Bannow 1913, p. 359; and Krämer-Bannow n.d.

colonialism as cultural revolution. The Germans sometimes tried to guide Samoans back to customs that they were abandoning. One case that came before the Land and Titles Commission involved an old and respected chief, Su'atele, who was Samoan chief justice or *fa'amasino sili samoa* on the commission. Su'atele had tried to replace the traditional *mavaega*—"a chief's dying wish concerning the inheritance of his title"—with a written will, which was a foreign and more individualistic concept. Su'atele was trying to bequeath his property to his wife and children. He defended this in terms of the Christian Bible and the "great powers," who "have adopted a method of recording everything," as opposed to the "merely verbal" customs of the Samoans. Chief Justice Schultz, who was superordinate to Su'atele on the Land and Titles Commission, opposed the use of the written will. The *mavaega* was also supported by other members of Su'atele's *'āiga*, who stood to lose out if a written will were used.[36] By rejecting the "modern" institution, Schultz reinforced a more "sociocentric" concept of the self as against a more European or "egocentric" one.[37] In other examples of enforced traditionalism, the government prohibited individual Samoans from selling land to foreigners and urged them to use traditional roofing materials rather than corrugated metal on their houses.[38] The use of manufactured materials in construction was one step toward limiting the traditional migratory mobility not just of individual Samoans but also of the entire *'āiga*, since *papalagi*-style (Western-style) homes involved greater investments and sunk costs than an old-fashioned Samoan *fale*.[39]

Organized resistance in 1904–5 (the 'Oloa movement) and 1908–9 (the Mau a pule) prompted settlers on the islands to call on the government for increased security.[40] The 'Oloa ("commercial or imported goods" or "trade") movement was an attempt to set up a Samoan-controlled copra-producing

36. Meleisea 1987a, p. 55; see also "Suatele's Mavaega," November 28, 1900, NZNA AGCA XVIIb, vol. 1; and Te'o Tuvale and So'oale Tolo to Solf, March 25, 1903, NZNA AGCA XVIIb, vol. 3.

37. See Mageo 1998.

38. On the government's efforts to prevent the use of tin in roofing and promote traditional materials, see Schultz's memo of May 14, 1914, NZNA AGCA XVII.A.1, vol. 6, p. 145; his article "O le Lau e ato a'i Fale Samoa," *O le Savali*, June 1914; and Osbahr to Schultz, May 6, 1914, Schultz to Faatili (*pulenu'u* of Lotofafa in Faleaili District), May 19, 1914, NZNA AGCA XVII.B.2, vol. 2. On British attempts to retraditionalize Fijian culture after annexation in 1874 see Cohn 1981, p. 238.

39. Mageo (1988, p. 45) draws out this comparison in an analysis of Mead's defense of the mobility of children to other members of their *'āiga* as attenuating parental pressure.

40. See, for instance, Deutsche Samoa Gesellschaft, August 11, 1909, BA-Berlin, RKA, vol. 3069, p. 261, calling for a *Schutztruppe* and the permanent stationing of a warship in Samoa.

and copra-trading company.[41] The second movement was aimed at forcing the Germans to restore the political structure that had existed before the 'Oloa. The Mau a pule also argued that Samoan elites should participate in naming the next *ali'i sili* (it was already rumored that Solf would abolish the position after Mata'afa's death).[42] Even though "the Governor and his European aide were convinced that they stood on the knife-edge of a rebellion similar to that of the South-West African Herero in 1904," they refused to attack the rebels, to militarize the colony, or to contemplate creating prison camps.[43] Indeed, the formula "This is not Southwest Africa" was voiced repeatedly in official German circles in Samoa.[44] German Samoa had just a handful of native policemen (*fitafitas*) and no permanently stationed German troops or police (although Imperial Navy warships were invoked as a warning and called occasionally at the islands). The jailhouse in Apia was less than awe inspiring, and prisoners escaped from it with seeming ease.[45] The European advisory council to the governor also opposed the idea of creating a *Schutztruppe* in Samoa, arguing that it would be a source of "permanent uneasiness" for the Samoans.[46] (No German colonist in Southwest Africa ever worried publicly about creating "unease" among Ovaherero.) Flogging was legal as punishment for Chinese immigrant workers in Samoa and in the rest of the German Pacific until 1912, but it was illegal for Samoans.[47] When a gun was fired in one village, Solf tried to enforce order by invoking his accustomed mildness and threatening local officials that he would have to become more violent if they failed to find and punish the culprit, admonishing the local authority, "You are aware that there is a party among the papalagi who grumble that I treat the Samoans with too much kindness. If such things happen, these people are right and I shall change my

41. Schultz to Colonial Department, February 18, 1905, BA-Berlin, RKA, vol. 3063, pp. 129–40; Solf to Colonial Department, August 4, 1905, BA-Koblenz, Nachlass Solf, vol. 26, pp. 19–33.

42. See the deposition by missionary James Edward Nevell in the trial of the settler Moors, who was charged with inciting the 1908–9 events, in BA-Berlin, RKA, vol. 3070, p. 38; also Hempenstall 1978, chap. 2.

43. Hempenstall 1978, p. 60.

44. See "Panem et circenses!" *Samoanische Zeitung,* April 15, 1905.

45. For one of the many jailbreaks see Schulz's report to the Foreign Office from July 6, 1906, on the criminal Sitiviti, NZNA ACGA XVII.B.I, vol. 3.

46. *Samoanische Zeitung,* March 11, 1905, p. 2.

47. See the report on native law in Samoa by District Judge Imhoff, NZNA ACGA XVII.A.I, vol. 4, pp. 156–59. On the flogging of Chinese immigrants, see *Samoanisches Gouvernements-Blatt* 4 (21, January 6, 1911): 71; and Solf's memorandum on the Chinese consul in Apia, January 28, 1911, BA-Berlin, RKA, vol. 5588, p. 4v. On flogging in German colonies see Fritz Müller 1962. On the evolving status of China and colonial flogging policy see chap. 7.

policy, and will show you that I know how to be faasaua [*fa'asāuā*, 'cruel'], if necessary."[48] Solf's relatively mild treatment of the leaders of the 'Oloa and Mau a pule uprisings was worlds away from von Trotha's "extermination order." Solf stated that if Lauaki, the leader of the Mau a pule, had "presented his ideas in the form of desiderata without the accoutrements of warfare," he would have listened to him or at least not regarded him as a rebel.[49] Instead, the ringleaders were exiled to Saipan in the German Marianas. The government-appointed village mayors from the rebellious districts were fired, and their *matai* were forced to pay monetary fines.[50]

Here again it is significant that the colonial regime proceeded decisively but nonviolently and that it selectively emphasized some aspects of tradition while avoiding or suppressing others.[51] Missionaries had tried to suppress the Samoan death penalty, which in this case "appeared repugnant to European views," and to replace it with "fines of valuable property such as fine mats and pigs" during the nineteenth century.[52] By refusing to punish even the most serious crimes by death Solf was acting against older Samoan traditions as well as German practice in Qingdao and Southwest Africa while reinforcing the Christianized version of local custom prevailing at the end of the nineteenth century. Solf acknowledged that banishment could constitute a sort of social death in Samoan eyes, noting that "if these chiefs are taken away and die in foreign lands, this is considered *faa-Samoa*

48. Solf to Faolotoi, *pulenu'u* of Lepa, August 4, 1903, NZNA ACGA XVII.B.I, vol. I, translation from NZNA ACGA, microfilm roll 129, "District Administration: Atua."

49. Bishop Broyer to Solf, February 21, 1909, BA-Berlin, RKA, vol. 2760, p. 19v.

50. Report to German kaiser, by the commander of the SMS *Condor*, June 1, 1909, BA-Berlin, RKA, vol. 3070, pp. 32-33. On the eleven exiled chiefs and their families in Saipan, see the report of the German station at Saipan to RKA, October 10, 1909, ibid., pp. 41-45. Wareham (2002, p. 58) suggests that the Germans failed to respond militarily to the Mau because they had "no hope of victory in guerilla warfare in the Samoan rainforest," but this is contradicted by the fact that the rebels, faced with the "largest German naval detachment Samoa had seen since the civil war of 1898-99" (Hempenstall 1978, p. 62), surrendered without firing a shot. Furthermore, the report of the SMS *Condor* cited above discusses not only the difficulties of a Samoan bush war but also specific measures such as the creation of a "trained reconnaissance line from our Melanesian colonies," since "our European soldiers cannot see the native in the bush" (BA-Berlin, RKA, vol. 3070, p. 30). This is not to deny that the Germans may have become more wary of colonial warfare because of their difficulties in Southwest Africa, but there is no actual evidence that this affected the response to the Mau a pule. Even the commander of the *Condor* predicted that "the extraordinary skill of the governor with natives" would be enough to resolve the crisis (ibid., p. 28).

51. On the banning of so-called bad customs, see BA-Koblenz, Nachlass Solf, vol. 20, p. 45; NZNA AGCA, title XVII.A.I, vol. 5, p. 13; and Solf's report of July 28, 1901, BA-Berlin, RKA, vol. 3061, p. 55.

52. Grattan [1948] 1985, p. 136.

a reproach and dying the death of a dog."[53] At the same time, exile was an eminently Samoan form of punishment—individuals or entire *'āiga* groups could be banished from a village or region.[54] Samoans were also aware that the Germans had deported Samoans in the past and then repatriated them when they were needed again—Mataʻafa was a prominent example—and this may have diminished the horror of banishment.[55] The exiled leaders of the Mau a pule reported to their Samoan relatives that they were quite happy and were convinced that that they would be returned to Samoa after two years, even though Solf insisted that they be given no information at all concerning the length of their punishment.[56]

One precondition for this relatively demilitarized form of colonialism was the looming threat of the German navy's warships. But Solf relied on naval support only in extremis. The absence of a telegraph connection between Samoa and the outside world before 1914 meant that the colonial government could not depend on warships to arrive when they were needed. In 1913 Governor Schultz complained to the Colonial Office that the Samoans had been told years earlier that German warships would be appearing imminently and that the ships had still not appeared, resulting in "all sorts of rumors" and a negative impact on "Germany's reputation."[57]

A COLONIAL SYSTEM NEVERTHELESS

However distant Samoa was from the Southwest African model, it was still a colonial regime. When the flag was raised at Mulinuʻu on March 1, 1900, Germany officially became the internationally recognized ruler of

53. Solf's memorandum of March 31, 1905, signed "C. Taylor," BA-Koblenz, Nachlass Solf, vol. 26, p. 50.

54. In June 1914 Governor Schultz banished to New Guinea the leader of a secret *fono* of fourteen educated Samoan personnel working for the German government (Schultz to RKA, June 6, 1914, NZNA AGCA VII.A.1, vol. 6, pp. 155–58). Interestingly, the government tried to ban banishment when it was implemented by Samoans against other Samoans (see *Samoanische Zeitung*, September 14, 1901). On a recent case of banishment in Samoa see Shore 1982.

55. Mālietoa Laupepa had been deported in 1887 on a German warship, but he was brought back two years later and appointed *tupu* by the three powers. Mataʻafa himself had been exiled by the Germans in 1893 only to be repatriated by them in 1898.

56. In reality Lauaki never saw Samoa again but died on his return voyage in 1915. On Lauaki's exile see Krenzbühler, SMS *Condor*, to kaiser, December 30, 1909, BA-Berlin, RKA, vol. 3070, p. 58; report of Kaiserlichen Station Saipan to RKA, October 10, 1909, ibid., p. 44; and Solf to Saipan station head, February 28, 1910, ibid., p. 63.

57. Schultz to Colonial Office, July 10, 1913, NZNA AGCA XVII.A.2, vol. 5, p. 71.

the Samoan islands of 'Upolu, Savai'i, Apolima, and Manono.[58] The flag-raising ceremony marked a more abrupt and all-encompassing transition to colonialism than in Southwest Africa, where the treaty-signing ceremonies with various indigenous groups had stretched out over more than a decade. Not only did the German colonial era begin more punctually in Samoa, but the exact geographic extension of German rule was clearly defined from the outset. Unlike the pre-1900 regimes in Samoa, the Germans claimed sovereignty over the entire territory, not just Apia.

One way to approach the disagreement between those historians who read German colonialism in Samoa as preservationist and others who describe it as ethnocidal is to distinguish between the colonizers' treatment of specific indigenous *practices* and their approach to the overarching legal, political, or social *institutions* within which those practices were located.[59] German Samoa sought to preserve "customary" social practices like the titles system, the distribution of fine mats, and the cricket matches (which had become wildly popular before 1900), while controlling these practices by inserting German officials and regulations into them. Thus, the Land and Titles Office tried to discipline the titles system; an office was created to classify fine mats, and Solf directed their distribution; cricket was permitted, even though colonial officials saw it as a disruptive waste of time, but matches could be played only on certain days of the week and their duration was limited. Preserving custom and controlling it were *both* salient motives

58. "Hoisting of the Flag," *Samoa Weekly Herald*, March 3, 1900.

59. Hiery (1995) interprets native policy as simple preservationism, ignoring the banning of some practices and the more subtle transformations induced by colonial codification. Other writers on Samoa (e.g., Meleisca 1987a) make the opposite mistake, underestimating the colonizers' desire to reinforce a culture they understood through the discourse of noble savagery. Hiery's book recalls an older style of colonialist historiography that credulously accepts colonizers' statements at face value and eschews any political or psychological analysis of motives. One marvels at his conclusion that "it is a commandment [*Gebot*] of historical honesty to recall that German colonialism saved many more lives than it took" (ibid., p. 249). This recalls the perhaps mythical U.S. army colonel during the Vietnam war who argued that "we had to burn the village to save it." In light of German activities in Southwest Africa (not to mention East Africa, the Marshall Islands, etc.), Hiery's statement is scandalous. Even in the case of Samoa it is far from obvious that German colonialism "saved many more lives than it took." If Hiery has medical interventions in mind (see his comments in Hiery 2001, p. 674), one wonders why his counterfactual imagination does not range far enough to conceive of a *noncolonial* form of Western medical assistance and modernization, as in China at the same time (Lei 1999). Hiery's "handbook" on the German Pacific (2001) is reminiscent of nineteenth-century books in discussing plants and animals (chaps. 2 and 3) before turning to people (chap. 4).

here. In other areas, however, especially with respect to the arrangements of internal Samoan politics, the colonizers were more straightforwardly repressive.

Another approach to this analytic problem was suggested by the second German governor, who admitted that the colonial state was trying to preserve the Samoans' *social* structure while destroying their *political* system.[60] The Germans created an array of posts for Samoan "cooperators" at the local, regional, and national levels. Europeans had tried for decades to fortify a central Samoan authority—a king—whom they could address and hold accountable; the Germans now tried to break the back of the central government and to shift the focus of indigenous politics back to the villages and regions. The title of *tupu* had already been abolished in mid-1899 by the tripartite commission that visited Samoa to settle the dispute between the great powers and the contending cartels of Samoan chiefs.[61] The German member of that commission, Baron Speck von Sternburg, summarized the great powers' view of Samoan politics by writing that "it is precisely the existence of the institution of the kingship which makes orderly administration impossible."[62] The commission introduced a form of government based on the model practiced in British Fiji, under which the only form of native representation at the national level was an annual meeting of district chiefs. The commission had also concluded, however, that "the only natural and normal plan of government for these islands, and the only system which can assure permanent prosperity and tranquility, is a government by one [European] power."[63] While this meant that the 1899 system had almost no time to develop, the "Fijian" model still became the starting point for the Germans' further interventions in the Samoan political system. The Germans recognized Mata'afa as *ali'i sili* but not as *tupu*. Although many Samoans continued to regard Mata'afa as king, Solf's 1900 "Samoan self-government constitution" described the *ali'i sili* not as the country's leader but as "the mediating instance through which the wishes and orders of the governor

60. Schultz's comments to Gouvernementsrat, July 10, 1913, NZNA AGCA XVII.A.2, vol. 5, p. 89.

61. "Proclamation" of June 15, 1899, BA-Berlin, RKA, vol. 3053, p. 152 (internal).

62. Report by Baron Speck von Sternburg, "Entgültige Abschaffung des Königthums in Samoa" [Final Elimination of the Kingship in Samoa], BA-Berlin, RKA, vol. 3053, p. 165. On Speck von Sternburg and Samoa see Rinke 1992, pp. 43–48.

63. "Chiefs to Rule Samoa," *San Francisco Call,* July 31, 1899; and *Samoa Weekly Herald,* July 8, 1899, pp. 2–3. The district boundaries that were set up in 1899 were retained by the Germans.

are communicated to the Samoans."[64] After Mata'afa's death in 1912 the Germans abolished the *ali'i sili* position altogether and replaced it with two advisers to the governor called *fautua,* who represented the leading Samoan families and were "required to swear an oath of allegiance to the German emperor." The Germans also changed the Samoan "national *fa'alupega* (ceremonial address) which had previously honored Tūmua and Pule, the districts, and the paramount families of Sāmoa." The *fautua* ceremonially pledged their allegiance to the German kaiser.[65]

The colonial government appointed an array of salaried indigenous authorities at the local levels. The most important new political positions were the "Taitai Itu" (*ta'ita'i itū*), or district chiefs, and the *pulenu'u,* who were village "mayors" and police authorities. The network of indigenous district judges (*fa'amasino*) was retained from the pre-1900 period, but the Germans removed from their jurisdiction a growing list of crimes that were deemed sensitive or that Samoans supposedly could not treat with objectivity. Above all, the *fa'amasino* were prohibited from hearing cases involving any whites or "half-castes," which would have violated the colonial rule of difference.[66] Samoan officials were given special badges and buttons, cockades, flags, portraits of the kaiser, and other accoutrements signifying that they served at the pleasure of the Germans.[67] This elaborate local-level political structure was intended to limit the influence of the traditional *fonos,* in which the *tulāfale* exercised pervasive control.

Weakening the *tulāfale* was as important to the Germans as curtailing the influence of the paramount chief and the Mālō, but they had more success in the latter endeavor. The core of national Samoan "self-government" in 1900, alongside the *ali'i sili,* was a parliament of district representatives, the *faipule,* and an advisory group consisting of representatives of the leading titles, the *ta'imua.* Together with Mata'afa these two groups constituted

64. Solf to RKA, October 22, 1909, BA-Berlin, RKA, vol. 2760, p. 52.

65. Minutes of the Governing Council, July 10, 1913, NZNA AGCA VI.4, vol. 4, p. 329; Meleisea 1987b, pp. 114–15; Schultz to RKA, July 10, 1913, NZNZ AGCA XVII.A.2, vol. 5, pp. 68–71. As Krämer (1994–95, vol. 1, p. 660) noted, the *fa'alupega* was the oratory that welcomed the important people present at a *fono* and enumerated "all honours (*ao*), the honorary names of the individual village communities, their orator association (*faleupolu*) and the outstanding chiefs."

66. W. von Bülow 1903; *Samoanische Zeitung* August 25, 1905, p. 1; typed instructions for the *ta'ita'i itū, fa'amasino, pulenu'u,* and several other lower positions by R. Williams, Amtmann of Savai'i, April 24, 1903, NZNA AGCA XVII.A.1, vol. 3, pp. 95–103; J. Davidson 1967, p. 80; and Schultz, memo, March 23, 1904, NZNA AGCA XVII.A.1, vol. 3, pp. 293–96.

67. Schultz, minute, July 31, 1911, NZNA AGCA XVII.A.1, vol. 5, p. 192.

the post-1900 Mālō.[68] But Solf was determined from the start to send these chiefs, whom he had not selected, back to their districts.[69] When the Mālō supported the Lafoga 'Oloa in 1904, Solf disbanded it and replaced it with a body that was initially called the Mālō Kaisalika (kaiser's *mālō*) and later Fono a Faipule. He abolished the council of *ta'imua* altogether and began to eliminate the *ta'ita'i itū*, who had grown too powerful, by appointing them as new *faipule kaisalika* (deputies of the kaiser) to the Mālō Kaisalika. The Samoan's national representatives were thus handpicked by the governor rather than being selected by traditional Samoan powerbrokers.[70]

The post-1899 government was also colonial insofar as it systematically separated Samoans and Europeans. Solf argued that colonial governance was "missionary work, in the broadest sense of cultural education," but Schultz admitted that the program of preserving Samoan custom introduced a "fundamental difference between the aims of the government and those of the missions, insofar as the latter preach the equality of all men, while the former recognizes existing gradations of power."[71] Although both governors insisted that they wanted to bring the Samoans up to a higher cultural level through slow and gradual change, Solf specified that they were never supposed to be assimilated to "European culture" but instead elevated to a level that "corresponds to their mental and spiritual character [*Zuschnitt*]."[72] This insistence on the fundamental difference and inequality of Samoans and Europeans helped the Germans justify their presence to themselves and others.

Apia was already a European zone in which Samoans were unwelcome, a condition Solf defended as being "in the interest of the natives" themselves.[73] Internal Samoan legal affairs were handled according to Samoan custom by the *fa'amasino, pulenu'u,* and the Land and Titles Court. In their legal dealings with "foreigners"—a category that included Germans and other "whites," Japanese, and some "half-castes" and Samoan women who had married foreigners—Samoans were treated not simply as different but as inferior. For example, all Samoans who wished to travel to the neighboring islands of Tonga and Fiji were expected to apply for a special travel permit

68. J. Davidson 1967, p. 80.

69. Solf, note of January 22, 1903, NZNA AGCA XVII.B., vol. 3.

70. Solf to Schultz, July 21, 1905, NZNA AGCA XVII.A.2, vol. 2, pp. 121-25; and Solf's "Further Instructions for the Faipule" (n.d.), in ibid., pp. 206-11.

71. Solf, "Entwickelung des Schutzgebiets: Programm" (1906), pt. 6, BA-Koblenz, Nachlass Solf, vol. 27, p. 96; Schulz to Osbahr, March 8, 1914, NZNA AGCA VI 28, pt. 1, p. 66.

72. Quoted in Gründer 2004, p. 182.

73. Solf, "Entwickelung des Schutzgebiets: Programm" (1906), pt. 6, BA-Koblenz, Nachlass Solf, vol. 27, p. 102.

and to pay a fee, and the governor arrogated to himself the power to determine who would be allowed to leave the islands, but this did not apply to "foreigners" who wanted to depart.[74] Even Mataʻafa, the *aliʻi sili*, was supposed to notify the governor before traveling or going on a *malaga*, although he did not necessarily comply.[75] As in other German colonies, the colonized had only limited means of legal redress against "whites" or "foreigners," and almost none against the colonial government.

The treatment of so-called half-castes and the restrictions on mixed marriage illustrate some of the ambiguities that were involved in drawing a clear line between colonizer and colonized.[76] As in Southwest Africa there was a sizable mixed-heritage population in Samoa. Indeed, by 1908 there were more than twice as many "half-castes" as "whites" on the islands. There were more mixed marriages in Samoa involving "white" men and indigenous or "half-caste" women in the years before 1914 than in any of the other German colonies.[77] A significant number of the German colonial officials in Samoa—between 22 and 37 percent, according to different estimates—were married to "half-caste" women.[78]

The citizenship status was clearly defined for indigenous women who married German men or for people born of legitimate mixed marriages. According to the German legal code of 1900, the *Bürgerliches Gesetzbuch*, a wife received the citizenship status of her husband, and legitimate or legally recognized children had the same citizenship as their father.[79] As Solf observed, "The law of the colony recognized only two categories of residents, namely, natives and foreigners or nonnatives. Mixed people (half-bloods, half-whites, half-castes) born of a legal marriage with a foreigner (nonnative) took the legal status of the father and they were whites, despite their dark skin color."[80] The phrase "they were whites, despite their dark skin color" underscores the fact that drawing a distinction between

74. Extract from Reichstag printed materials, 72nd session, March 7, 1913 (discussion of the petition of Dr. William Grevel, planter in Samoa, demanding legitimation of his marriage to a Samoan), BA-Berlin, RKA, vol. 5432, pp. 176–77.

75. Schultz to Mataʻafa, November 14, 1910, NZNA AGCA XVII.A.2, vol. 4, p. 60.

76. See G. Braun 1912; Grentrup 1914; Schulte-Althoff 1985; Salesa 1997; Wareham 2002, chap. 5; and Wildenthal 2001 on mixed marriage in German colonies and the treatment of "half-castes" in German Samoa.

77. Ahlert to kaiser, report on visit of SMS *Condor* in Samoa and Fiji, August 24 1908, BA-Berlin, RKA, vol. 5432, p. 36; Grentrup 1914, pp. 32–34, 88–89.

78. "Zur Mischlingsfrage in Samoa," *Hamburger Nachrichten*, no. 217 (March 9, 1912); see also BA-Berlin, RKA, vol. 5432, p. 105.

79. "Bekanntmachung," July 1, 1900, *Samoanisches Gouvernements-Blatt* 3 (3, August 9, 1900): 13.

80. Minutes of the Governing Council from February 15, 1907.

colonizer and colonized was more important than whether that boundary was defined by "race" or by some other criterion. As long as the citizenship of the father or husband was clearly identifiable, this arrangement did not endanger the rule of difference. But there was a "larger group of half-castes born in unofficial relationships or in uncertain marriages carried out in the period before 1900," and these cases *did* pose a problem for the state.[81] Their legal status had to be determined on a case-by-case basis by the governor or the chief justice, and later by the German district judges. The official criterion for reclassifying these half-castes as "foreigners" was initially their adherence to a "Western" lifestyle (*Lebensführung*); somewhat later the government began to demand evidence of Western "education" and the ability to speak German.[82] Starting in 1903 the official *Samoanisches Gouvernements-Blatt* began publishing a list of "half-castes classified as equal to foreigners," indicating that the system was operating as announced. After an initial burst of recategorizations, however, these numbers began to dwindle.[83] The immediate reason for this was official criticism from the Colonial Department of Solf's "civilizational" answer to the colonial boundary problem. Already in 1903 Colonial Department officials began to insist on a freeze on the reclassification of illegitimate Samoan half-castes.[84] German settlers in the colony claimed that some acculturated half-castes were still more Samoan than European. The general triggering factors for this shift were the same ones discussed in chapter 3: the 1904 genocidal war and the ban on mixed marriages in Southwest Africa, the increased influence of eugenics, and discourses of race hygiene and cultural degeneration. These developments began to influence policy in Samoa, leading first to restrictions on the reclassification of half-castes and eventually to an outright ban on mixed marriage in 1912. Solf implemented this ban immediately after he became state secretary for the colonies. In 1906 he already claimed to have been an "instinctive" opponent of mixed marriage since his first overseas posting to Calcutta (see below), although there is no evidence of this in his correspondence from that period. It is

81. Wareham 2002, p. 127.

82. "Bekanntmachung," July 1, 1900, *Samoanisches Gouvernements-Blatt* 3 (3, August 9, 1900): 13; "Bekanntmachung betreffend die Rechtsverhältnisse der unehelichen Mischlinge," March 3, 1903, in *Samoanisches Gouvernements-Blatt* 3 (19, 1903): 66.

83. "Protokoll über die Sitzung des Gouvernements vom 18. Januar 1913: Stellungnahme zu der Entschliessung des Reichstags vom 8. Mai 1912 betreffend die Mischehen- und Mischlingsfrage," *Samoanisches Gouvernements-Blatt* 4 (41, February 1, 1913): 171.

84. Colonial Department to Solf, November 16, 1903, NZNA AGCA VI.13, vol. I, pp. 164–66; Wareham 2002, pp. 130–31.

more likely that Solf saw this as a way to promote his antisettler campaign against the "little man in the colonies" by framing it in terms of racial danger. The settlers, he argued, were themselves "degenerating" and suffering from "tropical madness" (*Tropenkoller*), "going native" (*Verkanackern*) and descending into the primitive lifestyle of the "beachcomber."[85] Nonetheless, Solf's 1912 ban on mixed marriage continued to allow Samoans and half-castes to apply for legal status as "foreigners" if they "spoke German fluently and could demonstrate a European education."[86] Policing the boundary between colonizer and colonized remained the crucial goal for Solf, though he still allowed that the border could be cultural rather than "racial."

Another leitmotif of German colonial rule in Samoa was its explicit paternalism. The governor styled himself as the "father" of all Samoans. Solf's official residence was Robert Louis Stevenson's former house, renovated and expanded, and he resembled Stevenson in other respects. On more than one occasion Solf opined that "one should never forget that the Samoans are really nothing but big children." He and Schultz both claimed to govern the Samoans "as a father leads his children."[87] Of course, this discourse of colonial paternity was potentially disruptive of the rule of difference, since family members are related to one another in intimate, not just hierarchical terms. Indeed, this contradiction lurked at the heart of all systems structured around the idea of noble savagery, since "noble savages" were potential relatives, if distant ones. This may partly explain why the discourse of paternity was taken up by many Samoans as well. A letter inviting Solf to attend a session of the Mālō proclaimed that "our real and true purpose is to recognize you as our Father, and ourselves as your children."[88]

85. Solf, "Entwickelung des Schutzgebiets: Programm" (1906), pt. 4, BA-Koblenz, Nachlass Solf, vol. 27, pp. 78, 79, 83, and 88; Solf to kaiser, October 3, 1911, BA-Berlin, RKA, vol. 5432, p. 75r.

86. Solf to kaiser, October 3, 1911, BA-Berlin, RKA, vol. 5432, p. 76v; Schultz, "Bekanntmachung," August 2, 1912, in ibid., p. 161.

87. *Samoanische Zeitung*, January 13, 1906, p. 1. This formula is repeated in Solf to Colonial Department, August 4, 1905, BA-Koblenz, Nachlass Solf, vol. 26, p. 26; "Entwickelung des Schutzgebiets: Programm" (1906), pt. 4, BA-Koblenz, Nachlass Solf, vol. 27, p. 65; and Schultz, "Poloa'iga" [Order], *O le Savali*, August 1913.

88. Memo, June 8, 1904, BA-Koblenz, Nachlass Solf, vol. 25, p. 138. See also the account of the journal of Dr. Solf and Captain Grapow of the SMS *Cormoran* on their visit to districts in Savai'i and 'Upolu, in which Solf is greeted by the Pulenu'u of Faasaleleaga as "our father, the deliverer of Samoa" (NZNA AGCA XVII.B., vol. 3). There are countless other examples of this in the archives. Some Samoan leaders called on Solf to return in the 1920s, after New Zealand had taken over control of the islands, although this is open to differing interpretations.

Solf claimed that this discourse was not foreign to them, given the paternalistic structure of the 'āiga. Whether Samoans actually saw Solf as their father was less important for the regime's functioning than the fact that a sizable number of Samoans played their assigned parts in this "familial" drama.

The colonial state was also involved in economic policy, of course, but this did not contradict the central thrust of native policy. The continuous influx of Melanesian and, later, Chinese laborers provoked social tensions and reactive nationalism on the part of some Samoans. But this response was perfectly compatible with the government's native policies. Samoans continued to dominate the production of copra, the colony's most important crop. By 1910 Samoans produced 70 percent of all copra while the DHPG produced 25 percent; the remainder came from small European planters.[89] There was little interest on the part of the colonial state in transforming the indigenous mode of production. Solf did require every Samoan to plant fifty palm trees annually and to pay a head tax, but in reality these activities were organized at the level of the 'āiga or village, not the individual.[90] Indeed, Governor Schultz insisted in 1913 that it would be disastrous to propel Samoans too quickly into an "individualistic" way of life and that they would actually be *less* productive as individuals than in their conventional "communistic" family system.[91]

EARLY NATIVE POLICY: DISARMAMENT AND THE DISTRIBUTION OF FINE MATS

The inseparability of the preservationist and colonial motives in native policy is revealed by two of Solf's early interventions. These policies also reveal the importance of the inherited ethnographic perspective in suggesting the direction of native policy. Solf's first major intervention after becoming governor was to try to disarm the Samoans. He offered to buy guns owned by individuals, and he banned gun ownership (exceptions were later made for hunting). Solf even forbade the use of the hooked knives or hatchets called *nifo'oti* in the traditional Samoan knife dance.[92] The contrast to Leutwein

89. Extract of a petition by the Handelsverein (n.d., 1910), NZNA ACGA XVII.A.1, vol. 5, pp. 174–75.

90. *Samoanische Zeitung* August 19, 1905, pp. 7–8; September 9, 1905, p. 9; April 7, 1906, p. 2; and January 5, 1907, p. 2.

91. Schultz's presentation to the Gouvernementsrat, July 10, 1913, NZNZ AGCA XVII. A.2, vol. 5, p. 89.

92. See Solf's memo, October 18, 1901, on his general plan to buy back the guns, BA-Koblenz, Nachlass Solf, vol. 23, pp. 95–98. On the general ban on gun ownership see Schultz

in Southwest Africa during the 1894–1904 period is striking. Samoans were organized into a native police force, but they were not allowed to keep their own weapons. This was due in part to the much smaller size of the German official contingent in Samoa. Even in 1894 Leutwein had a comparatively large *Schutztruppe* and was able to assign some of his own troops to supervise the Witbooi and coordinate their military engagements. But this was not the main reason for the difference between the two colonies. Solf began the disarmament program as soon as he assumed power. He could have asked Berlin for money for a *Schutztruppe* at this point. After all, the internecine turbulence in Samoa in the two preceding years was on the same scale as the fighting between Ovaherero and Khoikhoi just before the Germans annexed Southwest Africa. But in 1900 Solf was already eschewing the path of militarization.

Disarmament of the Samoans did not reflect an unambiguous preference for "traditional" ways of life. Although firearms were a relatively recent addition, the *nifo'oti* was not. An equally important reason for Solf's emphasis on "gun control" lies in the inherited construction of Samoan savage nobility, which insisted on viewing native warrior violence as an obsolete relic, that is, as one of the "bad" customs that were to be selectively repressed. In the differentiation of types of savage nobility during the nineteenth century, the Witbooi were regarded through a screen devised partly in North America, one in which martial virtues were ascribed to indigenous men. But Polynesians had been defined *against* the warlike and inhospitable Melanesians. Rather than mobilizing armed Samoan men as seconds in a colonial army, Solf preferred to align them with this pacific image.

Almost immediately after assuming office Solf was also forced to deal with the issue of the ceremonial distribution of fine woven mats (*'ie toga*). Fine mats were distributed on the occasion of marriages, formal apologies (*ifoga*), and fines and punishments and when important titles were awarded, and they were also used as currency to pay for things like the construction of houses and canoes.[93] The awarding of the title of *ali'i sili* to Mata'afa in 1900 was one occasion on which convention called for a major distribution of fine mats. Distributions of *'ie toga* had also provoked intra-Samoan

to Talaifana, October 17, 1908, NZNA AGCA XVII.B.1, vol. 5. On the ban on knife dancing see Schultz's memo of July 22, 1905, NZNA AGCA XVII.A.2, vol. 2, p. 130.

93. See Keesing 1937, p. 4; Grattan [1948] 1985, pp. 15, 168. Mats were distributed by *ali'i* to *tulāfale* on other occasions, such as the ceremony at which an *ali'i* received approval for his nomination of a girl as village princess (*taupou*). By the late nineteenth century, at least, mats had also become a generalized form of currency.

warfare in the past, something Solf wanted to avoid at all costs. An even more serious danger stemmed from the conventional meaning of the ceremony in Samoan eyes. In nineteenth-century Samoa fine mats were "passed around among Samoa's nobility, affirming its exclusive identity and divine ancestry."[94] The circulation of mats began in the districts with the local elites, and moved from there to the *tupu*, who then redistributed the mats back to the districts. The direction of this flow signaled to the Samoans that the *tupu* owed his position to the regional *ali'i* and *tulāfale* and to the leading lineage groups, the two high families of Samoa. The Germans, however, wanted to insist that Mata'afa had been crowned *ali'i sili* by the German kaiser and his local representative, the governor.

Solf decided not to ban the mat distribution outright, revealing his determination to retain and defend as many elements of Samoan custom as possible without endangering German domination or the rule of difference. Instead, he attempted to choreograph the ceremony in ways that underscored his own importance. Solf designated the day on which the distribution would be carried out and the order in which different districts would receive their mats. On June 8, 1901, more than two thousand fine mats were brought to a special platform at Mulinu'u, where the governor was waiting with his administrative staff and Mata'afa. According to the reporter for the *New York Tribune*, "all day long these fine mats were paraded before Mata'afa and Governor Solf and the imperial officers. . . . From that time to this the adherents of Mata'afa have been quarrelling over the distribution of these mats."[95] Solf intervened to soothe the feelings of two districts that felt they had been shortchanged, by reallocating mats after Mata'afa's initial distribution. This put Solf, or more precisely, the German emperor, symbolically in the role of paramount chief and undercut Mata'afa's ability to calibrate the number and quality of mats according to his perception of the importance of the various chiefs and districts.[96]

94. Schoeffel 1999, p. 122.

95. "Mataafa's Mat Feast: An Odd Samoan Ceremony Which Generally Causes Trouble," *New York Tribune* [n.d., June 1901], in BA-Koblenz, Nachlass Solf, vol. 21, p. 143.

96. See reports on Solf's activities in July 1901, BA-Berlin, RKA, vol. 3061, pp. 71–81; "Report on . . . the Governor's Journey to Palauli and Satupaitea," *Samoanische Zeitung*, June 22, 1901, and September 14 and 28, 1901; and *Samoanisches Gouvernements-Blatt* 3 (2, September 14, 1901). Krämer (1906, p. 532) discusses an earlier distribution of fine mats when Mata'afa was named *tupu* in 1899, before the American chief justice invalidated the election. Other fine mat distributions were prohibited, however. Mata'afa was refused permission to have a mat distribution to honor his dead father in 1901; see Heinrich Schnee, minute, January 14, 1901, NZNA AGCA XVII.B., vol. 3. Solf banned in advance the distribution of mats as payment for

A related problem concerned the colonizers' inability to distinguish between fine or heirloom-quality mats—'ie toga and 'ie o le mālō ("official" mats with special historical status)—and lagaga or common mats, or even to understand how Samoans assigned monetary values to mats.[97] The government tried to resolve these problems by creating an office staffed by Europeans and Samoans with the task of determining the exact value of each mat and providing it with a government stamp.[98] The impulse was not just to define and stabilize an ambiguous practice but also to prevent Samoans from mingling monetary and sacred value systems in ways that made no sense from a European perspective. From the early nineteenth century on, fine mats had been drifting "in and out of commodity status." Like some of Solf's other interventions, this one shielded certain aspects of Samoan life from the encroachments of capitalism. The policy was partly traditionalist, insofar as 'ie toga were *singularised objects*, "conceptualized as being something other than 'property'" or material wealth and as being given and received only by, or on behalf of, the aristocracy.[99] At the same time this intervention defended the integrity of the capitalist value form.

The Sources of Native Policy in Samoa

German Samoa does not fit with theories of colonialism as being shaped primarily by economic or international security interests. This was already obvious to those involved in Germany's decision to press for the annexation of Samoa during the negotiations in 1899 between Britain, Germany, and the United States. Some of the territories that Britain offered Germany in exchange for 'Upolu had much greater economic and naval strategic value,

the reappointment of the four *pāpā* (high titles) that would become vacant at Mataʻafa's death; see Solf to RKA, September 4, 1910, NZNA AGCA XVII.A.2, vol. 4, pp. 29–32.

97. On the use of mats as currency and the assessment of their value, see Buck 1930, p. 88; Hjarnø 1979–80, pp. 84–85, 97, 102–9; and Linnekin 1990. Hjarnø concludes that the finer mats were those with imported red parakeet feathers from Fiji, finer fibers, famous old names, and other aspects of historical patina. Other literature on Samoan fine mats includes W. von Bülow 1899, pp. 136–42; Schoeffel 1999; and Henniger 1971 (Henniger was involved with the valuation of mats in the German colony). Samoan fine mats were also discussed by Marcel Mauss at the beginning of *The Gift* (1967).

98. Memos on "ie toga" by C. Taylor, February 1, 1908, and by Schultz, February 13, 1908, NZNA AGCA XVII.A.1, vol. 5, pp. 6, 12–14.

99. Quotes from Schoeffel 1999, pp. 130, 124. The notion of "singularised objects" is discussed by Kopytoff (1986). Wareham (2002) interprets the placing of a cash value on mats as forcing Samoans' integration into a cash economy, ignoring its complementary decommodifying, or "singularizing," impetus, with respect to the fine mats.

including the Volta River Delta in West Africa and the neighboring Polynesian island of Tonga, whose harbor was considered superior to those in both 'Upolu and Savai'i. These alternatives were rejected by most members of the Colonial Council (*Kolonialrat*) in Berlin, which advised the German government on colonial policy and was supposedly aligned with elite economic interests; the German navy also rejected the island with the better harbor. But the German public and the kaiser himself were believed to be extremely fond of Samoa, while the navy had "sentimental" attachments to 'Upolu because of the German marines killed there during the fighting of December 1888 and memorialized at Mulinu'u Peninsula.[100]

Nor were the settlers in Samoa able to make native policy conform to their interests. In addition to the state's refusal to meet their demands to force the Samoans to work for them, to create a market in Samoan-owned land, or to install a permanent white police force on the islands, many settlers were involved in mixed marriages and opposed Solf on this issue.[101] Nor did the government accede to German settlers' demands to ban the playing of cricket, although they did limit cricket matches to certain days of the week.[102]

If native policy was not guided by economic or geopolitical military considerations, or by the interests of the settler community, what was its foundation? Samoa resembled German Southwest Africa in terms of the concentration of power in the hands of the governor (except during the period of von Trotha's martial law). Oversight from the metropolitan government

100. P. Kennedy 1974, pp. 219–24. As Kennedy points out, gaining Samoa may have been important propagandistically for the navy's arguments for increasing its fleet, but from a strategic point of view it was doubly suboptimal. Not only was Apia dangerous as a harbor, but German naval policy was oriented toward achieving superiority to Britain in the North Sea, not in the Pacific.

101. See *Samoanische Zeitung*, February 23, 1907, p. 1, discussion in the Government Council of mixed marriage and legal status of "Mischlinge." In one case when Solf advised an individual settler against marrying a Samoan he received "a series of anonymous threatening letters" (Solf, minute, August 16, 1906, BA-Berlin, RKA, vol. 5432, p. 23).

102. Brandeis had banned cricket matches in Samoa in April 1888 during his brief reign (P. Kennedy 1974, p. 74), and Solf was not eager to repeat the mistakes of that earlier German regime. But in 1904 large townships were reported to be carrying cricket "to the extreme," playing uninterruptedly for weeks and even months on end. The government initially declined to limit the game; see C. Taylor, memo, June 16, 1904, NZNA AGCA XVII.A.1, vol. 4, p. 88. In 1906 and again in 1909 restrictions were implemented. According to the 1906 law cricket could be played only in the afternoons; in 1909 this was limited to Wednesday and Saturday afternoons. See Solf's draft of "Law concerning Cricket," February 11, 1906; also the "New Law on Cricket" [Tulafono Fou mo le Kilikiti] of September 17, 1909, NZNA AGCA XVII.A.1, vol. 5, pp. 80, 81–85.

in Berlin was sporadic, loose, and infrequent. Whenever local opposition to Solf's interventions became severe enough to make itself felt in Berlin, the governor received strong support from the Colonial Department and the kaiser. Solf's standing was revealed in his struggle with a group of troublesome settlers, discussed below. The strength of Solf's position was also underscored by his appointment as colonial secretary after leaving Samoa. In a letter to one of the Samoa experts in the Colonial Department Solf wrote in 1903 that "the focal point of administration must be in the colony and the laws have to be made in the colony. If the individual governors are not trusted, one would be best advised to keep sending in new ones until a qualified one is found."[103] Solf was able to pass regulations on the most sweeping issues concerning the colony single-handedly, without interference from Berlin, and he could choose to ignore opposition within the generally compliant consultative body of European councilors (the Governing Council, or *Gouvernementsrat*) when it suited him. The extensive documentation generated by the colonial government suggests a high level of agreement with Solf's overall program by lower-level and district officials. Erich Schultz defended a policy line that was almost identical to that of his predecessor and mentor. The nondemocratic structure of colonial government, the sociological homogeneity of local officialdom, and Solf's personal authority all justify a focus on the governor's activities in characterizing native policy.

THE PROBLEM WITH MIMICRY

Before turning to Solf's native policies, however, we need to specify an important dimension of the situation he inherited. Although the discourse of noble savagery dominated perceptions of Samoans, there was also a mounting sense of menacing cultural mimicry on the eve of colonization, as in other late nineteenth-century precolonies. The "half-caste" population presented only one form of perceived in-betweenness. The religious conversion of most Samoans did not eliminate Europeans' sense of their cultural ambiguity, since Samoan Christianity incorporated precontact customs. The costumes of Samoan Christian missionaries and church officials ranged from the fully traditional, to a mix of suit and tie with lavalava, to a fully "Western" outfit.[104] Events in the period leading up to 1900 had convinced many Germans that Samoans were neither reliably Europeanized, despite

---

103. Solf to von Koenig, May 10, 1903, BA-Koblenz, Nachlass Solf, vol. 20, p. 59r.

104. Barradale 1907, pp. 83–84.

their high level of Christian conversion, nor stably "savage." Nor did the Samoans occupy a completely steady intermediate position; instead they seemed prone to lurching unpredictably between extremes.

This labile condition resulted in part from the often fragmented and centripetal nature of Samoan politics. The many intra-Samoan wars during the nineteenth century rarely endangered white settlers (although they were often provoked by European machinations), but they were nonetheless troubling to Europeans. In the fighting of April 1899, Europeans reported seeing supporters of Tanumafili "carrying three heads of Mataafa men," while the Mata'afans killed American and British officers.[105] As in the case of the Namibian Witbooi it was difficult for Europeans to see any non-European culture as stable as long as it was engaging in *autonomous* warfare, even against other "natives." The differing approaches to Samoan politics by Germany, Britain, and the United States and the changing balance of influence of those powers on Samoa exacerbated the turbulence of domestic affairs. Over and above these unsettling political factors, the very presence of a European community and the interpenetration of Samoan and European economies and legal systems resulted in a permanent cultural churning that could not be contained by the forces of Samoan neotraditionalism.

The Samoan kingship was itself a hybrid institution that blended European ideas of monarchy with local political practices. Given the fragmentary nature of Samoan political life that resulted from the coexistence of multiple traditional titles linked to differing groups and regions, most kings were condemned to weakness. After the death of the *tupu* Mālietoa Vainu'upō in 1841, the rest of the century became "largely the story of the struggle for the kingship, by the chiefs of three of the great families of Samoa."[106]

A condition of precolonial mimicry was also encouraged by interventions that suggested to Samoans that the Europeans were more concerned with superficial adherence to their norms than with substantive conformity. This was shown first in the LMS missionaries' eagerness to accept converts. A revealing incident involved the German consul's pressure on the Samoan chiefs to sentence to death a Samoan who had killed a Melanesian plantation worker in 1882. According to William Churchward, "if they found the prisoner guilty, their countrymen in general would condemn them for punishing an act which they looked upon as of no more importance than crushing a cockroach; whilst if they found him innocent,

---

105. Moors 1986, p. 152. The victor in Samoan civil wars was traditionally the side with largest collection of heads (Schultz-Ewerth 1924, p. 103).

106. D. Freeman 1964, p. 560.

they knew they would have to deal with the Germans, and not only that, but be accused of being unfit for self-government." The Samoans were finally worn down by the German consul's demands. But on the day of the execution the consul reversed course and asked the king to "pardon the culprit." Churchward noted that the murderer's sentence "was commuted to ten year's hard labour, of which he did not serve ten minutes," with the end result that "this man became the leader in his town."[107] This kind of European inconsistency may have encouraged wavering among the Samoans as well.

The dualism that the Europeans themselves had helped to conjure into existence came to be seen as an eternal Samoan trait. The German navy surgeon Böhr, after enthusing about the Samoans, added that the "men in general, including the chiefs, have something mendacious about them."[108] Even less sympathetically, two German specialists in Oceania castigated the Samoans for their "inconstancy" (*Veränderlichkeit*) and "propensity to cheating."[109] Europeans thematized a putative difference between Samoans' professed views and their actual underlying character. Robert Louis Stevenson wrote that the Samoans had accepted European ideas of crime and punishment and the like only "in appearance."[110] The French visitor Joseph Hübner attended a *pōula* (night dance) in 1884 and wrote disapprovingly of the hypocrisy of the "women who go to their church on Sunday, clothed in the regulation chemise," and then "surrender themselves, half-naked to these sorts of amusements."[111] Werner von Bülow, the longtime Samoan resident and pioneer ethnologist, argued that telling the truth was considered by the natives themselves to be "un-Samoan."[112] What all of these suspicions and condemnations had in common was a perceived disjuncture between indigenous essences and appearances.

Thus, many of even those who admired Samoans as noble savages believed that their culture was being steadily eroded and replaced by "semi-civilization." Many agreed with Augustin Krämer that traditional ways of life could be rescued only if some European power took political responsibility. The constructions of noble savagery provided a very specific sense of the social condition that native policy should seek to reconstitute. But this

107. Churchward 1887, pp. 210, 214–15.
108. Böhr 1876, p. 427.
109. Christmann and Oberländer 1873, p. 213.
110. Stevenson [1892] 1996, p. 21.
111. Hübner 1886, vol. 2, p. 407.
112. W. von Bülow 1903, p. 374.

does not yet explain why Solf adopted or accepted this ethnographic vision. To understand this we need to reconstruct Solf's own perspective and his social position.

SOLF'S ETHNOGRAPHIC VISION

Solf's private correspondence and published writings reveal two recurrent themes: the Samoans' radical alterity and their relative superiority to other colonized peoples. Solf believed that the Samoans "don't think like us, have different emotions, and therefore have to be handled differently."[113] In a dispute with the author of a study of the Kalahari Bushman, Siegfried Passarge, Solf insisted that the "Samoans were better than the Herero and Hottentots in every respect"—echoing Augustin Krämer.[114] Solf was adamant that the colonial office should not assimilate the Samoans to other *Naturvölker,* and he argued that "each individual colony has to develop on its own with no analogy to the other protectorates and should be given specific laws corresponding to its conditions.[115] His opposition to a unitary legal system for the colonies emphasized the "racial specificity and the cultural level of the Polynesian population of Samoa."[116] Similarly, Erich Schultz insisted that the Samoans were the "noblest" of Polynesians, with the greatest mental capacities.[117]

Many of the policies already discussed can be interpreted in light of this desire to align Samoan practices with a familiar image of the Polynesian noble savage. These policies include the retention of the system of titles and *matai;* the use of forms such as *ifoga, malaga, mavaega, avaga,* kava drinking, and *fono;* the distribution of fine mats and the emphasis on traditional building materials; support for Samoan land ownership and for communal rather than individual forms of labor; and the overall demilitarization of colonial relations. Solf's opposition to the mingling and marriage of Samoans with Chinese or Europeans was motivated in part by his commitment to the survival of the Samoan "race" and culture. Although he claimed in 1911 that his opposition to mixed marriage had already been

113. Solf, "Entwickelung des Schutzgebiets: Programm" (1906), BA-Koblenz, Nachlass Solf, vol. 27, p. 68.

114. Solf to Passarge, October 29, 1906, BA-Koblenz, Nachlass Solf, vol. 28, p. 2.

115. Solf to von Koenig, Colonial Department, May 10, 1903, BA-Koblenz, Nachlass Solf, vol. 24, p. 59.

116. "Codification of Native Law," Solf to Colonial Department, January 15, 1905, NZNA AGCA XVII A.I, vol. 4, p. 160.

117. Schultz-Ewerth 1924, p. 86.

"instinctive" in 1889, Solf framed the problem in terms of cultural rather than "racial" incommensurability, arguing that "our form of marriage should only be applied to nonnatives."[118] Nor can white suprematism explain why the colonial government tried to separate Samoans from Chinese.[119] Here Solf appears to have been responding in part to Samoan leaders, who themselves insisted on a "strict ban" on Chinese-Samoan marriages and on severe punishment and separation of Chinese-Samoan couples.[120] The later regulation that classified *all* Chinese in the colony as "foreigners" (that is, as legally equal to Europeans) solidified this distinction.[121]

Solf's images of the Samoans emerged as much from interactions with European discourses about the colonized as from interactions with the colonized themselves. It is notable that Solf embarked on his program of salvaging and enforcing Samoan savage nobility almost immediately after he assumed office. Solf had served briefly as a foreign service translator in Calcutta and as a judge in German East Africa before arriving in Apia, but he had no prior experience in Polynesia.

How did Solf assimilate this discourse? It is likely that he had been exposed to some of the literature on Polynesia before arriving in Samoa. Solf was highly educated and ethnographically curious. He immersed himself in the existing literature on Samoan custom soon after arriving on the islands.[122] He also quickly became part of the community of "old Samoa hands" in Apia. One of Solf's translators, Thomas Trood, had arrived on

118. Solf to kaiser, October 3, 1911, BA-Berlin, RKA, vol. 5432, pp. 75r-v.

119. As we will see in the following chapters, liberals in Germany and Kiaochow were typically Sinophiles. I have found no evidence of Sinophobia in Solf's writings or speeches, although Krämer's Sinophobia in his 1902 article seems to reflect his exposure to the discourse on the Chinese in the Pacific and his lack of experience in East Asia and of exposure to China specialists.

120. Transcript of secret *fono* of February 5, 1914, in the government hospital in Motootua, BA-Berlin, RKA, vol. 2760, p. 184. See the article in *O le Sulu Samoa*, June 1914, on LMS opposition to Chinese-Samoan mixing, referring to an earlier resolution calling on indigenous pastors and churchgoers to "do everything in their power to prevent a mixing of the two races . . . in the interest of keeping the Samoan people pure" (NZNA AGCA VI 13, vol. 3, p. 134). Although there is no evidence that the colonial state actually prohibited "Chinese labourers from setting foot in Samoan houses" or forbade "Samoan women from entering Chinese quarters" (Shankman 2001, p. 129), there was strong sentiment in support of these policies among some colonizers, for example, Wegener 1904, p. 54.

121. "Verordnung des Gouverneurs von Samoa, betreffend die rechtliche Gleichstellung der Chinesen mit den Nichteingeborenen," *Samoanisches Gouvernements-Blatt* 4 (21, January 6, 1912): 71.

122. Solf's speech to the people of Alataua, Satupaʻitea, July 18, 1901, NZNA AGCA XVII B 2.

the islands in 1857 and had served for many years as British vice-consul.[123] Specialists in the German Foreign Office, most of whom embraced the noble savage perspective on the Samoans, were another source of ethnographic cues. Ernst Schmidt-Dargitz, who had been posted to Samoa for six years during the 1890s, described the "highly attractive traits of this clever Kanaka people" in a letter to Solf in 1899.[124] Solf's preferred interlocutor and informant inside the Colonial Department was Oskar Stuebel, a former German consul at Samoa who had published an important study of Samoan culture, *Samoanische Texte* (Samoan Texts) in 1896. Solf and Schultz both referred to the writings of Robert Louis Stevenson and Augustin Krämer, and Solf referred dismissively to Pierre Loti, whose Tahitian novel (*The Marriage of Loti*) failed to register the Tahitians' depravation, degeneration, and debauchment, which resulted from the "application of incorrect principles of colonization."[125] There was an important European model for Solf, but it was British, not French, and even here Solf was discriminating, rejecting the British approach in New Zealand.[126]

THE MULTIVOCALITY OF ETHNOGRAPHIC DISCOURSE AND STRATEGIES OF SYMBOLIC CLASS DISTINCTION

Solf's policy of enforced radical alterity might then seem to flow directly from the dominance of the Samoan noble savagery perspective. To understand the adoption of this discourse by Solf and most of the other German officials in Samoa, however, we have to consider the entire force field of intra-European class relations in the colony. Their embrace of this particular vision was hardly a foregone conclusion, since dissonant counterperspectives on the Samoans were circulating in the colony. The most widespread alternative emanated from a group of German settlers led by Richard Deeken. One of the settlers complained in a letter to the governor that Solf was encouraging Samoans to see themselves as "better than any of us whites who is not a government official."[127] This settler perspective described Sa-

123. Watson 1918.

124. Schmidt-Dargitz to Solf, May 31, 1899, BA-Koblenz, Nachlass Solf, vol. 18, pp. 115–16.

125. Solf, King George II of Tonga, and Hunter [1907] 1983, pp. 48–55; Schultz-Ewerth 1926, pp. 21, 153; Solf, "Report on Mixed Marriage," September 15, 1907, BA-Berlin, RKA, vol. 5432, pp. 28–29.

126. See Solf's comments to the Samoa Governing Council on July 10, 1913, NZNA, ACGA, VI.4, vol. 4, pp. 330–31.

127. Von Tyszka to Solf, July 1, 1904, BA-Koblenz, Nachlass Solf, vol. 25, p. 239; also von Tyszka 1904.

moans as lazy (*arbeitsscheu*), complained about their unwillingness to work on foreign plantations, and emphasized their inveterate militarism.[128] Deeken's slogan was "colonies are a business venture or they are nothing," and he insisted that native land be made available for sale to the government, which could then lease it to planters. He suggested that Samoans should be put to work building roads.[129] The settlers received backing from a colonial "expert," professor, and *Geheimer Regierungsrat*, Dr. Ferdinand Wohltmann, who was dispatched to Samoa by the Colonial-Economic Committee of the German Colonial Society in 1902 to investigate the possibilities of increasing cocoa production there. Wohltmann argued that Samoans were actually far behind the "Negro tribes" of the Sudan, Togo, and Cameroon with respect to their "craft and intelligence." He suggested that the Samoans were dying out and that "this depressing natural solution to the native question is for us a happy one nevertheless," since they could then be replaced by a superior labor force.[130] Although Wohltmann's official reports and public lectures, like Deeken's 1901 book, praised Governor Solf's "calm, firm hand," his barely veiled threat concerning the Samoans' extinction stood in direct opposition to the governor's protective strategy.[131] In a letter to another official about the settlers' demands Solf remarked that "it is as though I am expected to sign [the Samoans'] death warrant."[132] Rather than adopting the settlers' perspective, Solf became involved in a drawn-out struggle with Deeken.[133] Solf eventually threw Deeken in jail for abusing workers on his plantation and having him extradited from the colony.[134]

Several conclusions can be drawn from the so-called Deeken affair. First, formations of ethnographic discourse are never completely "mono-

128. Deeken 1901, p. 71.

129. Ibid., pp. 164, 168, 181.

130. Dr. F. Wohltmann, "Reisebericht über Samoa," pt. 2, *Tropenpflanzer: Zeitschrift für tropische Landwirtschaft* 7 (7, 1903): 303-4.

131. Wohltmann, "Pflanzung und Siedlung auf Samoa: Erkundungsbericht," bound with *Tropenpflanzer* 8 (1904): 110; Wohltmann 1903, text to image 11 ("Der Gouverneur Dr. Solf"); Deeken 1901, p. 64.

132. Solf to Schnee, translated in Moses 1977, p. 260 n. 61. Heinrich Schnee held various official posts in the German Pacific and became governor of German East Africa in 1912.

133. Moses 1977.

134. For Solf's complaints about Deeken see telegram to Foreign Office, May 1, 1904, BA-Koblenz, Nachlass Solf, vol. 25, p. 63. On Deeken's jail term and extradition, see Solf's telegram of June 6, 1904, ibid., p. 101; Stuebel (Foreign Office) to Solf, January 7, 1904, ibid., pp. 6-7; and Solf to Foreign Office, September 28, 1903, ibid., vol. 24, pp. 97-98.

accentual." Second, the German colonial state was independent enough from the locally dominant social classes to ignore their interests and demands. In a metropolitan setting, by contrast, social groups in positions analogous to these settlers typically have more power to censure policies that run against their interests. The settler opposition in Samoa had no representative at all inside the colonial state apparatus—although it did have allies in the German Reichstag—and was unable to influence official native policy. Third, the settlers failed to elaborate a full-fledged alternative ethnographic perspective, even as they expressed a diffuse hostility to Samoans. Some of them, including Deeken himself, even echoed Solf's argument that Samoan culture needed special protection, apparently failing to recognize that this contradicted his demands for native proletarianization and land sales.[135] Dr. Wohltmann called the Samoans "noble" and "unusually beautiful and strong" and contradicted his own dire predictions of national extinction by noting that the Samoan people were "truly brimming with health."[136] Deeken's 1901 book *Manuia Samoa!* (To Your Health, Samoa!), which was meant to lure settlers to the islands, was replete with language such as "South Sea idyll" and "paradise" and stories of warm hospitality, combined with images of scantily clad Samoan women caressing visitors and seducing them with the "savage passion" of their dances. Reprising a trope introduced by Bougainville, Deeken characterized Samoan women as combining voluptuousness with natural innocence, describing their dance as "the eruption of a natural fire . . . and not the refined monstrosity of sensual lust."[137] Polynesian noble savagery was so powerful that it permeated even the discourse of its would-be opponents.

Class Distinction and Class Exaltation

For Solf, the colony was simultaneously a mundane social setting, a site for demonstrating his exquisite taste and judgment in matters concerning exotic cultures, and a stage for ideological cross-cultural identifications. Solf's affinity for the dominant ethnographic approach was guided by his symbolic shadowboxing with the dominant fractions of the German elite and his imaginary self-exaltation. Although this is also true of Schultz, we

135. Deeken 1901, p. 197; von Tyszka 1904, p. 28.

136. Wohltmann, "Pflanzung und Siedlung auf Samoa: Erkundungsbericht," bound with *Tropenpflanzer* 8 (1904): 105.

137. Deeken 1901, pp. 142–43. See Deeken 1901, pp. 35, 86, 125, 131–42, 202, 143.

can observe these dynamics most clearly in the case of his predecessor in office.

With respect to the first dimension of intraelite class struggle, Solf used the Samoan setting to distinguish himself from the older aristocratic ruling class and capitalistic settlers. Born in 1862 as the son of a Berlin capitalist, Solf had written a Sanskritist doctoral dissertation and studied law.[138] His flaunting of a "hermeneutic" approach to non-European cultures called attention to the sorts of ethnographic perceptions that his individual holdings of symbolic capital made possible. To Solf and others in similar positions (that is, those with a similar composition of capital), deployment of a scholarly, hermeneutic approach promised to confer cultural leverage against the feudal and bourgeois elites. Solf insinuated that members of the traditional nobility were too enmeshed in brutal, militaristic ways and settlers too crassly materialist to appreciate the nuances of Samoan culture. The language in which Solf attacked Deeken and his cohorts suggests that he wanted to avoid being lumped in with the boorish and avaricious settlers. Offering an explanation for the settlers' racism, Solf speculated that most of them had "too little education to find their way in the complicated mental processes of a Samoan brain," and that they therefore fell back on stock phrases like "bloody Kanaka, this damned nigger!"[139] Solf's battle with Deeken involved an ongoing series of personal insults dealt out over the years.[140]

The problem for Solf with his ban on mixed marriage, even though he was perhaps motivated by a desire to protect Samoan "purity," was that it threatened to make him look like a simple-minded racist himself. Indeed, the German settlers in Samoa tended to be more "liberal" on this question than Solf. He tried to defend himself against this sudden reversal of roles by insisting that he did not hew to a narrow definition of whiteness or Germanness. Solf refused to relabel the legal category of "foreigner" as "white," arguing that it was "*tasteless* and lacking in racial *tact* to use skin color as the criterion for making legal distinctions."[141] He also tried to

138. Moses 1972, p. 44; Solf 1886; and "Lebenslauf," BA-Koblenz, Nachlass Solf, Findbuch, p. 3.

139. "Bloody" and "nigger" are in English in the text (Solf, "Entwickelung des Schutzgebiets: Programm" [1906], BA-Koblenz, Nachlass Solf, vol. 27, pp. 86, 66).

140. Solf also accused many settlers in the Deeken faction of having succumbed to "tropical madness" (*Tropenkoller*) or degeneration due to the climate and alcohol (quoted in Wareham 2002, p. 84).

141. Solf to Colonial Office, June 16, 1906, BA-Berlin, RKA, vol. 2759, p. 155v (my emphasis).

distance himself from those who opposed mixed marriage from a narrowly nationalist perspective. This was connected to his deeply felt Anglophilism and his identification with the category of the English gentleman, including English-style clothing and dinner-party manners.[142] His ban on mixed marriage thus also emulated what he identified as the British policy of separating colonizer and colonized, as against a putatively "Dutch" system of liberal racial mixing.[143] In a brochure entitled *Natives and Settlers in Samoa* Solf approvingly quoted an "unfriendly saying" he attributed to the English that "neatly summarizes the experience of the most important colonizing people on earth: 'Lord made the Whites and Lord made the Blacks, but the Devil made the Halfcastes.'"[144] Solf visited British colonies like Fiji and Australia and invoked them in defense of his own polices. When Solf was attacked by German nationalists for conducting government business in English and for allowing schools to carry out instruction in English and Samoan, he replied quite reasonably that the colony was surrounded by English-speaking and British islands. One of Solf's most trusted officials was an Irishman, Richard Williams, district commissioner (*Bezirksamtmann*) for the island of Savai'i. Solf conducted much of the government's internal correspondence in English and used English phrases in his speeches and written reports.

Solf's tense relations with representatives of the traditional German upper class can be traced back to his earliest career posting with the German consulate in Calcutta in 1889, where he had worked under Baron Edmund von Heyking. The relationship between the aristocratic von Heyking and the bourgeois Solf was extremely antagonistic from the start, and it came

142. See O. Franke 1954, p. 32, on Solf's Anglophilism while at the university in Göttingen.

143. "Nochmals 'Mischlingssorgen in Samoa,'" *Koloniale Zeitschrift* 13 (37, September 13, 1912): 599. The Dutch colonial approach was actually changing at the time, becoming more like what the Germans saw as the English system of preventing mixed marriage (Stoler 2002).

144. Solf's brochure "Eingeborene und Ansiedler auf Samoa," BA-Koblenz, Nachlass Solf, vol. 6, p. 136 (brochure p. 31). Against the "nationalist" position, Schultz argued that knowledge of German awakened "unfulfillable wishes" among the Samoans and that "knowledge of the language of the ruling nation is precisely the door through which darkness enters" (Schultz to RKA, June 7, 1914, BA-Berlin, RKA, vol. 2760, p. 176). Schultz was eight years younger than Solf and also a native of Berlin with a background in law and political economy, and like Solf's, his first posting was as judge in Dar-es-Salaam, in 1899 (Solf, King George II of Tonga, and Hunter [1907] 1983, p. 60). Schultz also resembled Solf in his intense curiosity about languages and indigenous culture and his liberal self-presentation. He condemned African officials like Tecklenburg, whom we encountered in chap. 3, for their authoritarianism (Tecklenburg was appointed chief justice for Samoa in 1914; see Hiery 1995, p. 297).

to a crisis, tellingly, over von Heyking's disapproval of Solf's participation in the venerable Asiatic Society of Bengal—a favorite haunt of British Sanskritists and philologists that had been founded by the famed Orientalist Sir William Jones in 1784.[145] Solf's emphatic self-presentation as an Anglicized student of exotic cultures was a bid for distinction in an occupational milieu—the diplomatic service—that was still dominated by aristocrats like von Heyking. Von Heyking was openly disdainful of the ethnographically curious ranks of the Foreign Office translating staff and tried to ruin Solf's career. Later von Heyking was appointed German consul to China, where he was characterized by one translator as viewing any interest in Chinese culture as a sign of a "subaltern mentality."[146] Solf's allergic reaction to noblemen like von Heyking transferred to officers in the military, who still tended to be aristocrats. In the first year of his governorship in Samoa Solf had a very prickly relationship with a navy captain, Emsmann, who overstayed his welcome in Apia harbor. Emsmann pursued a course of action with the Samoans that was reminiscent of the era of "gunboat diplomacy" but that clashed with Solf's ideas for native policy and infringed on his authority. Solf described Emsmann, a personal friend of the kaiser, as "a nice enough guy, but stupid and vain."[147]

THE IMAGINARY RESOLUTION OF REAL CONTRADICTIONS

The second dimension of Solf's personal class project was closer to the psychic than to the social register or, more precisely, located in the realm of imaginary rather than symbolic identifications. Although there is no evidence that Solf ever wore a lavalava, he often grasped the emblems of the *tulāfale,* the large staff and the *fue,* or fly whisk, when addressing groups of Samoans.[148] In a photograph from a *siva* dance performed in honor of Kaiser Wilhelm's birthday in 1901 Solf appears to be wearing a Samoan necklace.[149] Solf styled himself as a Samoan chief, proclaiming to one group

145. Solf to von Heyking, September 4, 1890, BA-Koblenz, Nachlass Solf, vol. 16, pp. 71–72. On the hostility between the two, see von Heyking to Solf, January 15, 1891, p. 275, in ibid. On Jones and the Asiatic Society of Bengal, see Trautmann 1997.

146. O. Franke 1954, p. 98.

147. Solf to Dr. Siegfried Genthe, February 22, 1900, BA-Koblenz, Nachlass Solf, vol. 20, p. 134.

148. See L. Holmes 1969, pp. 348–49, for an excellent discussion of Samoan oratory and the use of the *fue* and orator's staff.

149. Photo entitled "Junge Frauen aus Samoa tanzen zur Feier des Geburtstages von Kaiser Wilhelm II. vor Dr. Solf, Gouverneur von Samoa," January 27, 1901. In Bildarchiv preußischer Kulturbesitz (Berlin), photo no. 300018098.

"I do not come here as the Governor, but . . . as a Chief amongst Chiefs" and claiming to speak "in the place of . . . our friend Mataafa, the Chief of Samoa."[150] One might interpret these practices as little more than a strategic bid to appropriate indigenous symbols of power, similar to the British use of the durbar in India and Nigeria.[151] But it is difficult to discern a strategic rationality behind the Solfs' giving their daughter a Samoan name, Lagi ("heaven") and their son a Samoan middle name, Tupua. Visiting Hawai'i in 1922, after Germany had lost its colonies, Solf declared, "I am a Polynesian."[152] Nor is it likely that Solf expected Samoans to respect him if he inserted himself into their categories of authority, since his government was loudly declaring those categories to be inferior. Solf seems to have formed an imaginary identification with an imago of Samoan notables, of the highest chiefs and the holders of the most distinguished titles, such as Mata'afa and Lauaki.[153]

This identification provided an attractive imaginary resolution to Solf's own class dilemma, since the titles that are so crucial to Samoan political life are acquired more through strategy, struggle, skill, and deliberate selection than through simple inheritance. Samoa was known as a sort of meritocracy of nobles, a place where struggles for power took the form of seeking achieved status in the guise of ascriptive status. The distinction between ascriptive and acquired status was elided here, as acquisitiveness became inheritance, and the victors of conquests rewrote genealogies such that "the inhabitants of the occupied territories appeared as subordinates in the genealogies of the victors."[154] German social life also continued to be

150. "Report of the Failautusi Sili Auelua on His Excellency the Governor's Journey to Palauli and Satupaitea," *Samoanische Zeitung*, September 28, 1901.

151. See Cohn 1983; Apter 1999.

152. The Solfs' son's full name was Hans-Heinrich Otto Georg Tupua Solf (Hempenstall and Mochida 2005, p. 87). Tupua was the name of one of the two paramount lineage groups of Samoa. Solf's 1922 interview in Hawai'i is from *Honolulu Advertiser*, June 20 1922, in BA-Koblenz, Nachlass Solf, vol. 68.

153. There is a great deal of discussion in the literature on Samoa about the *tulāfale* usurping power in the nineteenth century from the *ali'i*, who had been viewed as quasi-divine. This suggests that by 1900 the imago of the *tulāfale* might have become as attractive as that of the *ali'i* for Europeans seeking imaginary exaltation. For men like Solf, there was the additional attraction connected to the fact that *tulāfale* were rhetoricians.

154. Hjarnø 1979–80, p. 110. According to one Samoan expert, quoted by Meleisea (1999, p. 55), "Samoan traditions were subject to a large amount of local colouring and genealogies were even revised to fit in with the ascendancy and decline of leading families." Even the names and borders of territorial divisions were subject to changing definition, because they were part of this competition for power. Meleisea therefore suggests that "Samoans were postmodernists before they became modern" insofar as "the postmodernist position is one that accepts the notion of multiple 'truths.'"

partly structured around titles, at least in fields like the diplomatic corps or the military, and the most valuable ones were the inherited titles of the older branches of the aristocracy. The Samoan system therefore represented an imaginary solution to the real class dilemma facing upwardly mobile middle-class Germans inside the state field and the field of power more generally. The fact that Samoan status competition rewarded oratory and etiquette could appeal to a *Bildungsbürger* equipped with cultural but little noble capital.

The attractions of identification across the colonial boundary were even stronger with respect to the image of the Chinese mandarin, as we will see in the next two chapters. But the imago of the Samoan notable proved attractive as well. This is perhaps surprising given the Samoans' categorization as *Naturvölker* in German racial theories of the period. The specific contents of the imagery and their relation to particular social-psychic needs mattered more than these abstract classifications.

Conclusion: Resistance and the Limits on Colonial Native Policy

We can now make sense of Solf's strong adherence to the Samoan noble savage perspective and to the associated native policies, and of his equally impassioned rejection of the settlers' alternative. His imaginary identification across the colonial boundary was based on a view of the Samoans as noble savages, and it further reinforced that view, since this identification was psychically "profitable," or pleasurable, for him. This means that his imaginary identifications reinforced the same image of the colonized as his symbolic identifications. Both forms of identification pointed toward the same sorts of native policy, convincing Solf that the formula of regulated tradition he had chosen was the best course of action. This political program allowed him to accomplish three tasks simultaneously: to systematically generate policies that promised to *stabilize indigenous culture;* to accumulate a form of cultural capital, ethnographic capital, specific to the field of the colonial state; and to achieve a kind of imaginary status exaltation through *identification* across the colonial boundary. Only by claiming to appreciate the intricate nuances of a radically incommensurable society was Solf able to assert cultural superiority over the Deekens and von Heykings. Only if Samoan chiefs were constructed as noble, cultivated, and to a certain extent self-made would it make psychic sense for Solf to identify with them. His pursuit of these imaginary roles had implications for the colonized, since it required the fortification of the traditional ways of life that were celebrated in the relevant ethnographic framework.

There was a potential drawback to this for Solf himself, however. His imaginary identification threatened to undermine his symbolic domination of the field of the colonial state. Critics of Solf tried to use his self-styling as a pseudo-Samoan chief to embarrass him.[155]

The Samoan case also reveals two sorts of limits on what colonizers can try to accomplish with the colonized. One constraint involves the preexisting formations of ethnographic representations. Given the weight of earlier descriptions, it would have been nearly impossible for Solf to have single-handedly reconceptualized the Samoans—as a *Kulturvolk,* for example—even if he had wanted to. Such a rearticulation would have been implausible without a broader representational campaign, probably including a cultural struggle by the Samoans themselves, similar to the battles conducted by the provincial governors and other Chinese in Shandong in response to German colonialism in Kiaochow (see chap. 7).

This points to the second limit on Solf's activities, which was the willingness of many Samoans, including the *ali'i sili* himself, to play their parts, much of the time, in his colonial theater. But the colonizers' effort to preserve Samoan social forms while breaking up established political power structures provoked intense resistance. I have already mentioned the two open rebellions against German rule, but as Peter Hempenstall noted, "The most successful instances of opposition occurred where Islanders were able to move between collaboration and resistance, adapting their policies according to the needs of the occasion and never totally rejecting German rule."[156] One example of this is the leader of the Mau a pule of 1908-9, the influential *tulāfale* from Savai'i, Lauaki.[157] In the years before this uprising Lauaki used "rebellious language" against Solf, accusing him of cutting up traditional political districts and weakening Samoan authorities.[158] Although Solf ultimately brought Lauaki under control, he was unable to limit the power of the *tulāfale* more generally. In 1900 Solf struggled against the *tulāfale* of Leulumoega, who tried to depose the *ta'ita'i itū* he had appointed, Alipia. He warned them that they were "wrong now when they call themselves the chiefs and rulers of Leulumoega."[159] Although Solf succeeded in bringing about a reconciliation between Leulumoega and

155. See von Tyszka 1904.

156. Hempenstall 1973, pp. iv-v.

157. "Unruhen in Samoa 1909," BA-Berlin, RKA, vol. 3069-70; Meleisea 1987b, p. 117.

158. Charles Taylor, memos of December 4, 1903, NZNA AGCA XVII.A.2, vol. I, p. 98; and of November 27, 1903, ibid., pp. 110-13.

159. Solf to the *tulāfale* of Leulumoega, November 28, 1900, draft in English, NZNA AGCA XII.B.5 (Aana and Manono), vol. I.

his appointed official, the conflict revealed the entrenched presence of the *tulāfale*.

Labor organization and unrest were also not unknown. Lauaki led a movement by Samoan workers demanding higher pay in 1902.[160] As noted above, the *taulele'a* working at the docks began to insist on wage increases in 1914.[161] The interests of the indentured Chinese workers in Samoa were being defended by the Chinese legation in Berlin and the Chinese government representative in Apia, and in 1912 Governor Schultz gave in to Chinese demands for "higher wages, more food, and the waiving of court costs in individual cases."[162]

Samoans also tried to refunction colonial institutions. German officials complained in 1904 that the *pulenu'u* and the district judges were being disregarded by Samoans, who continued to handle internal disputes internally in the traditional *fono*.[163] One *pulenu'u* went on a *malaga* in order to avoid meeting Erich Schultz when the latter visited his village.[164] Samoans continued to refer to Mata'afa as *tupu* even though that position had been formerly abolished. After 1912 the demand was raised that the *fautua* be not just the voice of the colonial government but also "a conduit by which the Samoans' demands can be sent to the governor."[165] A more immediately political form of resistance was revealed in 1913, when the government discovered that nonofficial village *matai* were calling themselves "pulemau," conducting themselves as officials, and infringing on the authority of the officials appointed by the Germans.[166] One German district official had to formally abolish a number of laws that had been issued by these self-appointed "pulemau."

Although the main lines of native policy were defined by inherited discourses whose existence was not dependent on the Samoans, the colonized could secure the success or failure of a policy once it was implemented.

160. Stünzer to Schnee, June 19, 1902, NZNA AGCA XVII.B., vol. 3.

161. Haupt-Agentur der deutschen Handels- und Plantagen-Gesellschaft der Südsee-Inseln zu Hamburg, Apia, May 22, 1914, to Schultz, NZNA AGCA XVII.A.1, vol. 6, p. 150; Schultz, "O le pule Foa'i," *O le Savali*, April 1914.

162. Moses 1977, pp. 252–53.

163. Von Bülow to Solf, June 18, 1904, NZNA AGCA XVII.A.1, vol. 4, p. 55. On the traditional method of dispute resolution see Meleisea 1987a, p. 56.

164. Schultz to Solf, April 22, 1905, NZNA AGCA XVII.B.1 (Atua), vol. 3. The *pulenu'u* in question was Lesa; the village was Satitoa.

165. "Report on the *fono* on Thursday, February 5, 1914, by Taio Tolo," BA-Berlin, RKA, vol. 2760, p. 183.

166. Schultz to Peters, October 15, 1913, and Peters to Schultz February 17, 1914, NZNA AGCA XVII.A.2, vol. 5, p. 112.

If the Samoans had been unwilling to sell the Germans their firearms in 1900 it is unlikely that Solf would have been able to pursue his other programs. Without a large corps of Samoans willing to discuss the fine points of Samoan law or the valuation of fine mats, the Germans' efforts to regulate these practices would have been for naught. In some cases the colonized became coauthors, or at least copy editors, of their own native policies.

PART THREE *China*

SIX

The Foreign Devil's Handwriting *&*
German Views of China before "Kiautschou"

China borders on the end of Almanye.

GASPAR DA CRUZ (1569)[1]

We need missionaries from the Chinese.

LEIBNIZ (1697)[2]

In the view of the Chinese we are barbarians, and the popular name *Fankwei* [fan gui], "foreign devils," precisely captures the stance we assume toward them.

REINHOLD WERNER, German navy captain (1873)[3]

Whatever the Chinese might have been in the past, today they are nothing but dirty barbarians who need a European master and not a European ambassador—the sooner the better!

ELISABETH VON HEYKING, wife of the German Envoy to China (Beijing, February 1897)[4]

The story of European views of China from Marco Polo through the end of the "long nineteenth century" is usually told in three stages. During the Middle Ages China was only vaguely described, mislocated on maps, and not even consistently named.[5] Yet it was considered to be a wonder-

---

1. Gaspar da Cruz [1569] 1953, p. 72.
2. Leibniz 1994, p. 51.
3. R. Werner 1873, p. 231.
4. Heyking 1926, p. 205.
5. Well into the seventeenth century Europeans still called the parts of China north of the Yellow River "Cathay," while the southern parts were called "Mangi," "Manzi," or even "Upper India."

ful and rich utopia. Marco Polo and his brother visited Kublai Khan, who had extended his hegemony over "Cambulac" (Beijing) and established a summer residence at "Xanadu" (Shangdu) in 1264. In the next century the Franciscan friar Odoric of Pordenone described a country with the greatest cities and rivers in the world, and incredible wealth.[6] Between the sixteenth century and 1750, this medieval discourse of wonder gradually evolved into a more detailed formation that historians have called Sinophilia. Created above all by the Jesuit missionaries to China and their counterparts who stayed in Europe, this was still a predominantly positive representation. China appeared now as an advanced civilization, on a par with or even superior to Europe. From the mid-eighteenth century onward, increasingly negative views of China began to prevail in Europe.[7] Europeans now described China, like India during the same period, as stagnant or in terminal decline, its elites as corrupt, and its culture as less than fully civilized, even barbaric or savage. Slowly, the Chinese were assimilated to the "natives" who populated the European imagination. Sinophobia, as this discourse is conventionally labeled, was partly a response to changes inside Europe and China and the shifting relations between the two. But it was also initially an explicit refutation of Sinophilia, that is, a reversal of fortunes within the field of European proto-Sinology. Increasingly, Sinophobia also encompassed specific technologies for governing China in an anticipated colonial future.

Although this is not my main purpose here, it is worth noting several of the reasons for these broad tendencies in European perceptions of China. European Sinophilia emerged in the context of blossoming European trade in the sixteenth and seventeenth centuries and of perceptions of China as a huge and untapped market. The relative equality between China and Europe was shifting in this same period toward a European lead, but China continued to surpass European states in terms of its sheer territorial expanse and population size.[8] Another source of Sinophilia was the Chinese themselves, who resisted attempts by Europeans to classify them as barbarians, sometimes turning this language back on the Europeans. Matteo Ricci told of one missionary staying in the home of a learned Chinese Christian, who said to him, "I really should feel ashamed in your presence . . . because it seems to me that you put all the Chinese, and particularly myself, in the

6. Odoric arrived in China in 1322 and returned to Italy in 1330, where he dictated a narrative of his journey (Odorico n.d. [1933]; Lach 1965–93, vol. 1, bk. 1, pp. 40–41; Hartig 1913).

7. See Appelton 1951; Lach and Kley 1965–93; Kley 1971; Étiemble 1988; Berger 1990; Jandesek 1992; and Spence 1998.

8. Pomeranz 2000.

same class, into which we Chinese formerly put the unbelieving Tartars and barbarians."[9] This resistance persisted into the nineteenth century and beyond, but with a decreasing ability to influence European ideology.

The Jesuit China mission was responsible for many of the substantive details of Sinophilia. This mission was not separate from the expansion of European capitalism, of course, and certainly was not opposed to it. Missionaries traveled to and from China in the ships of the East Asian trading companies, and until 1596 the Jesuit Chinese mission was based in Macao under the protection of the Portuguese, who operated the first and longest-lived European trading enclave in China.[10] None of this explains the Jesuits' relative success in penetrating the Chinese imperial court or their celebrated "accommodation" to Confucianism. The Jesuit missionaries were renowned for learning local languages, and in China they dressed and coiffed themselves in the style of the mandarins and adopted a nondogmatic approach to what they understood to be the dominant "religion" of the Chinese elite, namely Confucianism.[11] Their goal was to transform China gradually by influencing key members of its official class rather than seeking rapid, wide-scale conversions. Indeed, the number of Chinese converts remained small, due not only to the mission's targeted focus on the mandarin class but also to recalcitrance and resistance. The Jesuit depiction of China remained extremely positive nonetheless, and European images of China were heavily mediated by these productions from the mid-sixteenth until the mid-eighteenth century. Even the literature on China written by Protestants in England, Germany, and the United Provinces drew mainly on Jesuit writings. A new set of motives for endorsing the Jesuit-based view of China appeared during the Enlightenment, as Voltaire and the Protestant philosopher Christian Wolff used China to conjure up the possibility of a rational, enlightened monarchy.[12]

The subsequent Sinophobia in Europe also had numerous sources. The mid-eighteenth century saw a marked increase in aggressiveness toward China by European merchants, who complained bitterly about barriers thrown up against them by local officials. Traders had lamented their treatment by the Chinese in earlier centuries, but little of this reached the ears of broader European publics. All of this changed with the publication of George Anson's *Voyage round the World* (1748), a best-selling account of the

9. Trigault and Ricci [1615] 1953, p. 327; also p. 201. See L. Liu 2004, chap. 2, on this political-semiotic struggle between China and Britain in the nineteenth century.

10. Pons [1999] 2002.

11. Trigault and Ricci [1615] 1953, p. 154.

12. Gerlach and Wollgast 1979.

British commodore's five-month stay in Macao and Canton (Guangzhou) that was translated into German in 1795. Anson's book was structured as a point-by-point refutation of what he called "jesuitical fictions."[13] These ideas were reinforced and elaborated in the accounts written by participants in George Macartney's embassy to China in 1793, most influentially by John Barrow (the same John Barrow we encountered in South Africa), but also Johann Hüttner, the only German accompanying that mission.[14] Britain's nineteenth-century shift toward an energetic enforcement of "open markets," during the period known as "free-trade imperialism," thus accounts partly for the shift in tone. But the two high points of vigorous Sinophobia were actually located in periods without an uncontested hegemon, namely, the decades between the end of Dutch hegemony (roughly 1730) and the rise of British hegemony after 1815, and during the late nineteenth century, when uncontested British global power began to recede.[15] This is not to say that Europeans returned to Sinophilia between 1815 and the 1880s, however. Such a complete reversal was foreclosed by other developments: the rise of "scientific" race theories and of more explicitly Eurocentric philosophies of history, the widening of the technological gap between China and Europe, and the disappearance of the Jesuit mission after 1773. The Protestant overseas missionary societies that began to emerge at the end of the eighteenth century were less appreciative of China than the Jesuits and less interested in striking accommodating compromises with extant Chinese practice.[16] The Protestants were more oriented than the Jesuits had been toward lower Chinese social strata, in an effort to bypass resistance by

13. Anson [1748] 1974, p. 368.

14. Macartney 1962; Barrow [1804] 1806; Marshall 1993; Dabringhaus 1996; Hevia 1995b.

15. During these nonhegemonic periods Europeans struggled for overseas trading advantages against one another and against China, and there was no recognized hegemon to mediate disputes and press China for "open door" access. The mid-nineteenth century, by contrast, was one of unparalleled British economic and naval superiority, and one result of the Opium Wars was greater access to Chinese markets and Chinese souls for *all* European traders and missionaries, not just for the British. For an example of the connections between these polices and descriptions of the Chinese character, see "Free Trade with China," *Chinese Repository* 2 (1833-34): 355-74. On the periodization of the Dutch and British hegemonies see Arrighi 1994.

16. For representative Protestant views of China in this period see Gützlaff 1834, 1838. As we saw in earlier chapters, there were also significant differences in the orientations of the Rhenish Mission in Southwest Africa and the London Missionary Society in Samoa. The former abandoned the idea of working through indigenous elites and tended to collect lower-status people from disparate ethnic groups, while the latter were successful in converting the majority of the population and did not limit their efforts to one class or the other.

the mandarins. They also hoped to convert larger numbers and to forge an indigenous ministry. The growth of democratic sentiment in Europe fed the distaste for China and other traditional hierarchical polities. Karl Marx's revulsion against "ancient despotism" in India and China, for example, nearly canceled out his loathing for European imperial interventions in the same places.

German visions of China have to be placed in a wider European context, as in the earlier chapters. I will first discuss the most influential representations in the pan-European discussion before turning to specifically German ones. Indeed, German images of China in both the Sinophilic and Sinophobic periods corresponded closely to general European trends. All of the influential treatises on China were translated into German, and some of the most important Sinophobic texts were written by Germans, including Hegel, Herder, Marx, and Gützlaff. Max Weber's *Religion of China* can also be considered in this context as a classic example of Sinophobia.[17] Two German specialists on China were directly connected to the occupation of Qingdao: Ferdinand von Richthofen, a geographer who first called German authorities' attention to Jiaozhou, and Elisabeth von Heyking, wife of the German minister to China during Qingdao's annexation and the author of exotic romance novels set in overseas colonies. In the late nineteenth century, Karl May, the prominent German author of adventure tales, wrote three novels set in China, and Theodor Fontane's *Effi Briest* contained the most famous Chinese figure in nineteenth-century German literature. By closely examining a specific national literature I will be able to show that Sinophobia did not completely displace Sinophilia in the nineteenth century but was superimposed upon and interwoven with it. This persistent multivocality of German views of China was of critical importance for native policy in "Kiaochow."

Europe's Cathay

In Xanadu did Kubla Khan
A stately pleasure-dome decree

SAMUEL TAYLOR COLERIDGE, "Kubla Khan"

The most influential medieval European book on the Far East that included a treatment of China was John Mandeville's *Travels*, which "began to cir-

---

17. There is a sizable literature on the older German discourse on China. See Aurich 1935; Debon and Hsia 1985; Fang 1992; Gollwitzer 1962; Hsia 1985; Jacobs 1995; Li 1992; Loh-Loh 1982; Pigulla 1996; E. Rose 1981; Schuster 1988; Selden 1942; and Tscharner 1939. On Weber, see Steinmetz 2006a.

culate in Europe between 1356 and 1366" and was widely reproduced even before the invention of the printing press.[18] Although Mandeville's text has long been decried as a fabrication and a plagiarism, it was immensely popular, surpassing Marco Polo's authentic account in circulation.[19] Indeed, sixty-five of the three hundred extant copies of Mandeville from the era before the invention of the printing press are in German, suggesting that he was probably "more popular in Germany than elsewhere."[20] Mandeville's book was a magical fable that reinforced the general sense of the Far East as "the supreme source of riches and marvels."[21] Mandeville described the "land of Cathay" as "a great country, beautiful, rich, fertile, full of good merchandise," whose people were "marvelously clever in anything they want to do, more than any other people in the world." Of the great khan of Tartary, emperor of Cathay, Mandeville wrote that he was "the greatest King, passing all other Kings, and the richest in gold, all kinds of treasure, and of greatest royalty." Centrally important for future European uses of China was Mandeville's image of the emperor surrounded at his table by "many philosophers and men learned in different branches of knowledge."[22]

Marco Polo's narrative was "the first such work by a Westerner to claim to look at China from the inside," and his "most famous early reader" was Christopher Columbus.[23] Polo's text was also a romance of the court of Kublai Khan that presented China as an enormous, glamorous, and benevolent dictatorship.[24] Versions of Polo's *Travels* appeared in German as early as 1477, and new translations were published in the seventeenth, eighteenth, and nineteenth centuries.

The next stage in the elaboration of Western representations of China resulted from early Portuguese and Spanish mercantile expansion and the establishment of the Jesuit mission. By 1557 the Portuguese had taken control of Macao and started trading in Canton. Several decades later Spaniards were trading illegally along the Chinese coast. In 1624 the Dutch occupied the island they called Formosa; the English arrived in Canton in 1637. By

18. Moseley, introduction to Mandeville 1983, p. 9.

19. Appleton 1951, pp. 5–6. Mandeville's book was translated into German around 1400 and was republished another nine times in German between 1481 and 1507 and again in 1580 and 1600 (Lach 1965–93, vol. 2, pt. 2, pp. 330–31).

20. Lach 1965–93, vol. 2, pt. 2, p. 330.

21. Ibid., p. 325.

22. This places the text historically before or during the conquest of the Southern Song dynasty by Kublai Khan. Quotes from Mandeville 1983, pp. 141, 143, 149, and 151.

23. Spence 1998, pp. 1, 17.

24. Appleton 1951, p. 6; Polo 1993, vol. 1, pp. 266–69.

the early seventeenth century, China had become "a prime object of commercial interest."[25] As a result there were over fifty independent accounts of China published in Europe during the seventeenth century, plus a large number of novels, plays, and historical or comparative treatments.[26] The seventeenth century also saw the beginnings of European chinoiserie, that is, the selective integration of romantic Chinese images into European objets d'art, gardens, and textiles, as well as isolated examples of more serious artistic interaction.[27]

Sinomania

European accounts of China before the mid-eighteenth century echoed Polo and Mandeville in focusing on the country's sheer wealth and grandiosity and its well-ordered state, its excellent form of government.[28] The 1585 book by the Augustine monk Juan González de Mendoza became "the point of departure . . . for all subsequent European works on China written before the eighteenth century."[29] Mendoza's title, in the English translation, summarized his argument: *The Historie of the Great and Mightie Kingdome of China, and the Situation Thereof: Togither with the great riches, huge citties, politike gouernement, and rare inuentions in the same.* He emphasized the "huge bignesse" of the king's "mightie and sumptuous pallace" and concluded "that they liue with so great abundance, that all things do flow so that they lacke nothing necessarie for their bodies," although their souls did of course lack Christianity.[30] Giovanni Botero, in his widely read *Ragion di Stato* (Reason of State, published in 1589), wrote that "there is not in all the world a kingdom . . . that is either greater, more populous, or more rich, or more abounding in all good things, or that hath more ages lasted and endured than that famous and renowned kingdom of China." China was "an extremely well-administered country."[31] In 1583 Matteo Ricci opened the first Catholic mission in China since the departure of the Franciscans two and a half centuries earlier. Ricci's books were extremely favorable to

25. Lach 1965-93, vol. 1, pt. 2, p. 816.

26. Lach 1965-93, vol. 3, pt. 4, p. 1743.

27. Jarry 1981; Gruber 1984; Sullivan 1997.

28. Guy (1963) used the term "Sinomania" in describing this intellectual formation.

29. Lach 1965-93, vol. 1, pt. 2, p. 744.

30. Mendoza 1853, vol. 1, p. 77; vol. 2, p. 287.

31. Botero [1589] 1956, pp. 264-65, 150. For similar praise see Montaigne [1580] 1958, p. 352; Temple 1814, vol. 3, pp. 39, 342; William Whiston (1696; see Appleton 1951, p. 33); and Careri [1704] 1752, p. 327.

China, "offering a picture of a vast, unified, well-ordered country" run by a "professional bureaucracy selected" on the basis of merit, and "held together by a central controlling orthodoxy, that of Confucianism."[32]

Europeans, especially Jesuits, singled out the role of the Chinese scholar-official for special praise. Father Nicolas Trigault, a Jesuit who published the "most influential description of China to appear during the first half of the seventeenth century," based on Ricci's journals, wrote that "the entire Kingdom is administered by the Order of the Learned, commonly known as The Philosophers," who surpassed others in courage, adding that perhaps this "has its origin in the fact that the mind of man is ennobled by the study of letters."[33] The Portuguese Jesuit Gabriel de Magalhães (a distant relative of the explorer and navigator known as Magellan), who lived in Beijing during the reign of the second Qing emperor, wrote that the chief end of "the Law of the *Learned,* as they call it" in China, is "the good Government of the Kingdom."[34] Olfert Dapper, compiler of a text on the second and third Dutch embassies to the Chinese emperor in 1666–68, agreed: "It is remarkable that the entire empire ... is governed by philosophers, who have a pure and undiluted [*unvermengte*] rule."[35]

Europeans in this period often suggested that the Chinese monarchy was controlled by a system of checks and balances. According to Dapper any abuse of power by the emperor had traditionally been prevented by the mandarins, who used their "undaunted freedom and confidence in the admonishing of their Kings and Emperors, when they saw them wander from the way of Vertue." Even now, Dapper wrote, it is "customary that the Governors throw down their badges before the Emperor if he asks them to do something they fear may prove prejudicial to the Realm or if he ignores their admonishment."[36] By the same token, abuses directed against the common people by the provincial mandarin rulers were watched over by a board of investigating censors. Trigault approvingly told the story of one mandarin, "delinquent in the performance of his duty," who was "put out of the way

32. Spence 1998, p. 31. Ricci concluded that the Chinese needed Western logic and Christianity in order to advance (ibid., p. 31–35).

33. Trigault and Ricci [1615] 1953, pp. 55–56; on Trigault, see Lach 1965–93, vol. 3, pt. 1, pp. 512–13.

34. Magalhaes 1688, p. 193.

35. Dapper, "Dritte gesandtschaft an den Kayser von Sina oder Taising," in Dapper 1675, p. 41.

36. This translation is from Montanus 1671, p. 403, a direct translation of Dapper's original Dutch text from 1670, which was itself based on Trigault and Ricci [1615] 1953, p. 50.

with considerable torture."[37] Sir William Temple emphasized that in China "all orders and commands of the King . . . are made upon the recommendation or petition of the council proper and appointed for that affair," and that "all great offices of state are likewise conferred by the King, upon the same recommendations . . . so that none are preferred by the humour of the Prince himself, nor by favour of any Minister, by flattery or corruption, but by force or appearance of merit, of learning, and of virtue."[38]

The theme of the philosophers' role in government was linked to the idea of meritocracy. In 1589 Giovanni Maffei praised the exam system and absence of a hereditary nobility in a country where every man is the "founder of his own fortune."[39] The report on the Dutch embassy of 1666 observed that the "ascent to the greatest place of dignity" in the Chinese government was not "lockt up from any sort of People . . . but opened to every one at the Emperor's pleasure."[40] China's meritocracy was especially attractive to educated Europeans who lacked economic wealth and hereditary cultural capital. The career of Father Johann Adam Schall von Bell, the German Jesuit who worked at the Chinese court and was eventually promoted to the rank of first-class mandarin (see fig. 6.1), enthralled generations of European (and Chinese) intellectuals.

This was related to the theme of education and literacy. Mendoza noted that the Chinese had printed books long before Europe, and Magalhães wrote, "I do not believe there is any Kingdom where there are so many Scholars as there are Bachellors of Art in *China* . . . nor that there is any other Country where the knowledge of letters is so universal and so common."[41]

---

37. Trigault and Ricci [1615] 1953, p. 50; see Hucker 1966 on the Chinese Censorate.

38. Temple 1814, vol. 3, p. 337.

39. Giovanni Pietro Maffei, *Historiarum indicarum libri XVI* (Venice: D. Zenarium, 1589), translated in Lach 1965–93, vol. 1, pt. 2, p. 804. For an almost identical statement see Careri 1704, p. 348.

40. Montanus 1671, pp. 392–93. William Temple wrote, "As other nations are usually distinguished into Noble and Plebian, so that of China may be distinguished into Learned and Illiterate" (1814, vol. 3, p. 330). Many Europeans in the seventeenth century commented on the lack of a hereditary aristocracy in China and found it shocking that schools were open to all based on merit (Lach 1965–93, vol. 3, pt. 4, p. 1627; vol. 1, pt. 2, p. 781).

41. Mendoza 1853, vol. 1, p. 131; Magalhaes 1688, p. 88. Navarrete ([1676] 1962, vol. 1, p. 151) described the Chinese as "much addicted to Learning and inclin'd to Reading." Careri ([1704] 1752, p. 340) asked, "What kingdom is there in the world so full of universities as China?" Even in the middle of the nineteenth century the Catholic missionary Evariste Régis Huc ([1855] 1970, vol. 2, p. 56) described China as a "philosophical oligarchy."

FIGURE 6.1 Johann Adam Schall von Bell. From Athanasius Kircher, *China illustrata* (1667). (Courtesy of Special
Collections Library, University of Michigan.)

China's sheer antiquity and tradition-based stability exercised a powerful grip on European minds in this period, in contrast to the condemnation
of traditionalism by Sinophobes. The Jesuits repeated the Chinese neo-
Confucians' representation of their mother country as ancient, well documented, and unchanging.[42] For Trigault the Chinese were superior to Europeans in disdaining conquest and thus successfully preserving "what
their ancestors have bequeathed them . . . through a period of some thousands of years."[43] This fascination with tranquil stability is understandable
in the context of the religious and political warfare in Europe at the time

42. Osterhammel 1998, p. 391. Osterhammel's magnificent book has not yet been translated into English.

43. Trigault and Ricci [1615] 1953, p. 55.

(especially the Thirty Years' War). The apparently peaceful assimilation of the Manchu conquerors to Chinese ways presented Europeans with a stark contrast to their own factiousness during the Counter-Reformation.

Alongside these central topoi were a variety of other themes that showed China to be equal civilizationally to Europe and even superior in some respects. Again, most of these claims would be disputed or their meanings inverted in the subsequent period:

- The Chinese language was a subject of endless European fascination and, in this period, of praise. Giovanni Careri extolled the language for containing "at least 54,409 letters," which he said were able to express their meaning "with such a grace, vivacity and force, that they seem not to be characters, but voices and tongues that speak, or rather figures and images, which represent every thing to the life."[44] The Berlin proto-Sinologists Andreas Müller and Christian Mentzel, philosopher Gottfried Wilhelm Leibniz, and a number of English scholars were so intrigued with Chinese that they believed it might provide the key to the rediscovery of the primitive universal language of the Bible or the construction of a new one.[45]
- Chinese medicine was widely praised.[46] Careri cited the Jesuit Daniel Bartoli to the effect that Chinese doctors "far outdo our physicians of Europe."[47] Sir William Temple observed that the Chinese physicians were "admirable in the knowledge of the pulse, and by that, in discovering the causes of all inward diseases."[48]
- Chinese politeness was widely admired. Careri contended that "the most courteous and mannerly people among us, in *China* would seem rude and savage."[49] Sinophobes later would reframe this as wasteful pretention.
- Europeans at this time were much more tolerant of the treatment of Chinese women than in a later period. A Scotsman in the employ of the Russian court who took part in an official embassy to China in

44. Careri [1704] 1752, p. 339.

45. Mungello 1985; Appleton 1951, pp. 22–36. John Webb (1669) argued that the Chinese descended from Noah through Shem and that their land had "been peopled while the earth still spoke one language" (Appleton 1951, p. 28).

46. Mungello 1985, p. 39.

47. Careri [1704] 1752, p. 341.

48. Temple 1814, vol. 3, p. 297. Temple was probably drawing on the account of Johann Grueber, discussed below.

49. Careri [1704] 1752, p. 352.

1719–22, John Bell, even praised the Chinese *"above all"* for their "decent treatment of their women of all ranks."[50] Discussing the practice of drowning female infants, Trigault suggested that "this barbarism is probably rendered less atrocious by their belief in metempsychosis, or the transmigration of souls."[51]

• Even in the area of religion there was a surprising level of appreciativeness. In 1659 Rome instructed Jesuit missionaries "that they should adapt Christianity to the indigenous cultures of foreign people rather than imposing European manners and customs." Non-Western cultures "were to be changed only where they contradicted the Christian religion and morality," and there was an emphasis on developing an indigenous clergy.[52] This reinforced the "accomodationist" strategy that had already become standard practice among Jesuits in China. Similarities and points of communication were sought between Christianity and the "religion" of the educated upper classes, Confucianism. Magalhães composed a treatise arguing that "both the Chinese and Europeans were descended from a common Biblical source and that the similarity of the morality of the ancient Chinese to Christianity was due to the Chinese receiving their Old Testament morality directly rather than indirectly through natural theology."[53] Non-Jesuit writers like William Temple, Christian Wolff, and Voltaire were effusive in their praise of Confucian practical ethics. For most of the seventeenth century and well into the eighteenth European readers were provided with a growing literature on Confucianism and translations of many Chinese classics.

One of the most interesting formal aspects of this Sinophilic literature is its high level of dialogism and syncretism as compared to the early literatures on Africans and Polynesians, or to the later Sinophobic literature. Although this seems to reflect the fact that China was indeed a literate culture with a large publishing industry, the "barbarization" of China in the nineteenth century belies the argument that European representations were necessarily tied to observed realities. Many Chinese spent time in Europe, especially in Rome. One eighteenth-century volume included a ten-year correspondence between a Frenchman and two Chinese Jesuits who had studied theology in France and Rome.[54] Another genre was the Chinese

---

50. Bell [1763] 1966, p. 182.
51. Trigault and Ricci [1615] 1953, p. 86.
52. Mungello 1985, p. 24.
53. Ibid., p. 74.
54. Meiners 1778.

response to critical European accounts. A fairly negative depiction of China by Evert Ysbrants Ides from 1706 was published together with a Chinese rejoinder. Voltaire's "Entretiens chinois" (1758–59) is a (fictional) discussion between a Jesuit in China and a Chinese mandarin who has studied in Europe, and his "Catéchisme chinois" (1764) presents a dialogue between a Chinese prince and a scholar. A number of European writers used the device of the "wise and tolerant mandarin" visiting London or Paris and commenting on the inadequacy of European sexual and political behavior."[55] A 1664 religious treatise called *Summary of the Spread of Heavenly Teaching/Tien xue chuan kai* was a "collaborative effort involving several Jesuits and a Chinese convert," and the book's main author was Chinese.[56] Chinese voices were of course frequently filtered through European ones, and even when they were reported directly, the interlocutors were partly Europeanized Christians.[57] The level of syncretism, dialogism, and exchange was still far greater in the case of China than in other parts of the colonized or precolonial world.[58] The inclusion of Chinese characters or formal devices from Chinese-style landscape painting allowed Europeans a glimpse of a radically different culture and aesthetic (see fig. 6.2).[59] Some Chinese texts were also translated into European languages. One that became especially popular in Europe in the eighteenth century was *The Little Orphan of the Family of Tschao* (*Zhao Shi Gu Er*), a fourteenth-century play, which told the story of an abusive mandarin whose career (and life) was ended by the combined efforts of other mandarins and the emperor himself. The play thus ratified

55. Jones 2001, p. 24; see also Blue 1999.

56. Mungello 1985, pp. 92–93; 1982.

57. Only at the end of the nineteenth century did writings by contemporary non-Christian Chinese comparing Western and Chinese culture begin to appear in Europe, for example, Gu Hongming (Ku Hung-Ming; see Ku 1898, 1911) and Chen Jitong (1890, 1892). By that time, however, Sinophobia was in full bloom, and the very presence of Marquis Chen, the Chinese ambassador to Paris, seemed to fan the flames of the "yellow peril" discourse among Europeans (Gollwitzer 1962, p. 31).

58. China was also open to European culture in the Kangxi and Qianlong Emperor periods. The Old Imperial Garden (Yuanming Yuan), originally outside Beijing, was designed by Jesuits and Chinese artists at the command of the Qianlong Emperor between 1737 and 1759 and included baroque-rococo elements alongside traditional Chinese ones (Wong 2001; see plates 7, 8). Europe's openness is also suggested by chinoiserie, however simplified its images. There was almost no comparable stylistic syncretism involving Oceanic or African art until twentieth-century cubism and expressionism (see J. Lloyd 1991; Einstein 1915; and Harrison, Frascina, and Perry 1993). But while Gauguin is often dismissed for imposing contemporary European pictorial conventions on Polynesian subject matter, some of his graphic work does integrate Polynesian formal elements.

59. As in *Regni Chineses descripto* (1639; title page reproduced in Lach 1965–93, vol. 3, pt. 1, plate 72) or the illustrations in Dapper 1675; and Kircher 1670.

FIGURE 6.2 Two Chinese ladies, from Athanasius Kircher, *China illustrata* (1667). (Courtesy of Special Collections Library, University of Michigan.)

the view of the Chinese state as balanced and just. *The Little Orphan* was adapted and translated several times in the next century, most famously by Voltaire as *The Orphan of China* (*L'orphelin de la Chine* [1755]).[60] Voltaire's play was performed almost two hundred times at the Comédie française before 1833 and was translated into other languages, including German.[61] It differed in several significant ways from the Chinese original, including a less tragic ending that allowed Voltaire to produce the synthesis of nature and reason that he saw embodied in Confucian China.[62]

Voltaire was the last prominent European writer before the twentieth century to present an almost uniformly commendatory picture of China in all his works, "even up to the last, when the [China] cult showed signs of

60. Voltaire [1755] 1877, p. 296; Appleton 1951, pp. 82–89. Voltaire wrote the play after reading missionary Joseph Henri Marie de Prémare's translation of the Chinese original, which was published as "Tchao Chi Cou Ell; or, The Little Orphan of the Family of *Tchao*: A Chinese Tragedy," in Du Halde 1741, vol. 3, pp. 193–237.

61. Park 1974, p. 112.

62. Voltaire's play has not been analyzed or even much performed since the eighteenth century (but see Park 1974 on two twentieth-century productions). Formally *L'orphelin* is a mix of classical tragedy and melodrama.

disappearing in France."[63] China, he insisted, was superior to Europe with regard to ethics and government. It was a "vast empire, powerful and wise," even if it was inferior to Europe in scientific and artistic terms.[64] Like the Jesuits, he applauded the combination of a powerful central authority, advised and checked by scholar-officials selected on the basis of merit. Voltaire argued that Chinese tribunals showed Europe "how to manage the blood of man": "for more than four thousand years they have not executed a villager at the outskirts of the empire without sending his case to the emperor, who has it examined three times by his tribunals" before reaching a decision.[65] He vehemently attacked Montesquieu's despotism thesis as well as the more derivative but influential Sinophobe, Cornelius de Pauw.[66] Voltaire's "most extravagant praise" was reserved for Confucius, whose portrait faced him in his study as he worked.[67] Along with his immediate contemporary François Quesnay, Voltaire accomplished the secularization of Jesuit Sinophilia.[68] He applauded China for its strictly empirical historiography, which eschewed creation myths, and for creating a well-regulated (policé) society without relying on superstitions like the idea of hell as a means of controlling the masses.[69] He praised Confucianism as the only religion in the world that had never been "soiled by fanaticism" or sparked civil war.[70] Voltaire even seemed to condone the Yongzheng Emperor, a practicing Buddhist, for driving most of the Christian missionaries out of China, repeating the emperor's question "What would you say if I sent a troop of bonzes or lamas to preach their laws in your country?"[71] Jonathan Spence notes that Voltaire "gave a new twist to Western historiography" by *beginning* his universal

63. Rowbotham 1932, p. 1050.

64. Voltaire 1963, vol. 1, p. 67.

65. Voltaire [1766] 1879, pp. 556–57.

66. Voltaire 1963, vol. 1, p. 216; [1776] 1879b. Voltaire also criticized Commodore Anson for basing his account of China on the "little people of Canton" and conflating them with Chinese officialdom (1963, vol. 1, p. 217).

67. Rowbotham 1932, p. 1057; Voltaire [1776] 1879b, pp. 469–70.

68. Quesnay, economist, leader of the physiocrats, author of the *Tableau économique*, and adviser to Louis XV, was born in 1694, like Voltaire. According to Rowbotham 1932, p. 1051, one of Voltaire's favorite professors was the Jesuit René-Joseph de Tournemine, who corresponded with Father Joachim Bouvet at the Chinese Court in Beijing. Like Leibniz, Voltaire sought interlocutors from the Jesuit China mission.

69. Voltaire 1963, vol. 1, pp. 66–67, 71.

70. Voltaire 1879b, p. 81; 1963, vol. 1, p. 222.

71. Voltaire [1764] 1879, pp. 153–54. The Yongzheng Emperor (ruled 1723–35) curtailed the involvement of the Jesuits at the court and cowed them into being "extraordinarily circumspect in their behavior," but without actually banning or expelling them (Spence 1990, p. 84).

history in *Essai sur les moeurs et l'esprit des nations* with a discussion of China. Hegel would soon begin his lectures in the philosophy of history with China as well, but to radically different effect.[72]

Voltaire's Sinophilia was interwoven with hints of the imperialist approach to China that would wreak so much havoc during the next century. His dedication of *L'orphelin* to Richelieu already gives a hint of the looming protocolonialist attitude toward China that was being articulated by Commodore Anson during the same decade. The Chinese, Voltaire submitted here, "don't yet realize how superior we are to them."[73] Unlike the Jesuits, Voltaire was not referring to spiritual superiority; instead, this represents an early application to China of social-evolutionary theory. Voltaire was closer to Montesquieu in this sense than his more explicit critiques of that writer would indicate. In this respect, he represents a transitional figure, embodying both the apotheosis of Sinophilia and its supercession.

German Views of China in the Era of Sinomania

Some [of the Chinese are] more yealow, *like vnto the Almans,* yellow and red colour.

JUAN GONZÁLEZ DE MENDOZA[74]

To what extent did Germans contribute to Sinophilia's arc? The German-speaking lands were cut off from the beginnings of European overseas expansion due to their political fragmentation and, after the Reformation, because of initial "Protestant hostility to Catholic pilgrimages and victories overseas."[75] Nonetheless, many Germans participated in the pan-European wave of overseas expansion and information gathering. Already during the sixteenth century, "thousands of Germans were involved in the spice trade as merchants and investors, and in the overseas voyages as sailors, gunners, and pilots."[76] In the following century many more traveled to southern Africa and the Far East in the employ of the Dutch East Indies Company (founded in 1602), and smaller numbers in the service of the Russian tsar, or the Jesuit order. China began to play a central role in the systems of German philosophers and social theorists starting with

---

72. Spence 1998, p. 97; Hegel 1956.
73. Voltaire [1755] 1877, p. 298.
74. Mendoza 1853, vol. I, p. 11 (my emphasis).
75. Lach 1965–93, vol. 2, pt. 2, p. 342.
76. Ibid., p. 329.

Herder in the eighteenth century. China figured centrally in Hegel's lectures on the philosophy of history and in Max Weber's sociology of world religions. Little of what these writers said about China was uniquely German, however, but was part of conversations that spanned Europe and its East Asian contact zones. Nonetheless, German imperialists in the nineteenth century sometimes paid special attention to German Sinological legacies.

The ranks of the Jesuits in China began to include Germans after 1611, when Spain and Portugal first allowed missionaries from other countries to work overseas. The Jesuits disseminated information about China in the German-speaking parts of Europe.[77] The most renowned of the German Jesuits in China was Johann Adam Schall von Bell (known in China as Tang Ruowang), who became president of the Astronomical Board (see fig. 6.3) at the emperor's court in Beijing.[78] Continuing a practice introduced by Matteo Ricci and perpetuated by generations of Catholic missionaries, he dressed like a Chinese mandarin. After the Manchu conquest in 1644 he began shaving himself closely in the style of the new ruling elite.[79] The emperor eventually promoted Bell to the rank of first-class mandarin. Bell wrote a history of the Chinese mission, published in Latin in 1665 and translated into German the following year.[80] Another German Jesuit, Johann Schreck, known also as Terrentius or Terrenz (Chinese Teng [Deng] Yü-han), was Bell's predecessor and an acquaintance of Galileo and Kepler, and had also worked at the Beijing Astronomical Board. He reformed the Chinese calendar and translated astronomical and anatomical works into Chinese.[81] According to Athanasius Kircher, who had taught in Würzburg, Schreck was "famous all over Germany, and much liked by princes."[82] Schreck accompanied Nicolas Trigault on his European "propaganda tour" for the China mission in 1616,

77. The names of German Jesuits in China are listed in *Zeitung auss der newen Welt oder Chinesischen Königreichen* (Martini 1654b); for the seventeenth and eighteenth centuries see Hunder 1899, pp. 183–97. On Jesuit education in Germany see Krammer 1988; and Hengst 1981.

78. Bell died in Beijing in 1666 at the age of seventy-four. On Bell, see Duhr 1936; Allan 1975, chap. 8; Malek 1998; and Väth 1991.

79. On Bell's close-shaven look we have the testimony of the Dutch embassy (Montanus 1671, p. 4; also Nieuhof [1669] 1972, p. 117).

80. Schall von Bell 1834.

81. Allan 1975, pp. 118–19; Huard 1953, pp. 269–71; Collani 1998, pp. 85–87. Schreck was born in Konstanz in 1576 and arrived in China in 1621, where he died in 1630 (Reil 1978, p. 64; Iannaccone 1998). Another German Jesuit in seventeenth-century China was Andreas Wolfgang Koffler, who converted a number of high-ranking members of the court of the last Ming dynasty pretender, the Yung-li Emperor, after the Manchu conquest (Collani 1992).

82. Kircher 1670, p. 149.

visiting German cities and courts and speaking to enthusiastic bishops and students, raising money and recruiting new missionaries. One stop was the university in Würzburg, which was staffed by Jesuits.[83] Kilian Stumpf (Chinese Ji Li'an), a young Jesuit from Würzburg, was beguiled by the prospects of a missionary career in a country that seemed much more prosperous and peaceful than Central Europe. Stumpf spent twenty-five years in Beijing, from 1695 until his death in 1720, and was deeply involved in the rites controversy. He served as rector of the Jesuit College and in 1714 as visitator for Japan and China, the highest Jesuit office in East Asia. He also directed the Beijing Astronomical Board and created the first glass factory in China.[84] Stumpf's activities inspired others from Würzburg to seek employment in the China mission. Bavarian Ignaz Kögler (Chinese Dai Jinxian) succeeded Stumpf as director of the Astronomical Board in 1717 during the final years of the Kangxi Emperor's reign.[85] Most German Jesuits in China defended Stumpf's position in the rites controversy, arguing that veneration of ancestors and of Confucious had a "civil" character and could therefore be reconciled with Christianity.[86]

Johannes Grueber (Chinese Bai Naixin) was an Austrian Jesuit known as one of the first Europeans to traverse eastern Tibet. In February 1656 Grueber received official instructions from the Jesuit order in Rome to seek "an overland route to China."[87] The goal was to free the Jesuits of their dependence on the sea route, with its attendant dangers of the conflicts between the Dutch and Portuguese trading companies and the constant threat of pirates, and to begin missionary work among the people living along the

83. Willeke 1974, p. 418. Jesuits frequently returned to Europe from China to recruit new personnel and seek financial support for their mission (Collani 1989, p. 549).

84. Lange [1722] 1968; Reil 1978, pp. 59, 62, 73, 39; Naundorf 1975, 1975–76; Willeke 1974; Bernard 1940. Stumpf translated Newton's *Tabulae mathematicae* into Chinese.

85. See Naundorf 1975–76, p. 270; and Streit 1931, pp. 215–16, listing some of Kögler's publications; also Kögler [1717] 1726. Kögler's successor after his early death in 1720 was August von Hallerstein, an astronomer from Ljubljana (Allan 1975, p. 214). Two Germans from Bohemia, Johann Walter (Chinese Lu Zhongxian) and Ignatz Sichelbarth (or Sickelpart), worked at the imperial court in Beijing as a musician and a painter, respectively. Walter was born in 1708 and died in 1759, and should not be confused with the earlier German composer. Sichelbarth was born in 1708 in Neudek (Nejdek) in the Sudetenland and died in 1780 (Huonder 1899, p. 194).

86. Willeke 1974, p. 423.

87. Wessels 1940, p. 283; and Tronnier 1904, p. 329. Although Grueber was unable to take the land route to China, he did return to Europe via Lhasa and eastern Tibet, Kathmandu, Agra, Lahore, and Isfahan.

FIGURE 6.3 Astronomical instruments created by Stumpf and other Jesuits between 1673 and 1715, on the roof of the Ancient Observatory (*Gu Guanxiangtai*) in Beijing. The azimuth on the right was created according to Stumpf's instructions in 1715 by melting down the old Chinese instruments (Collani 1989, p. 562). Some of the instruments were seized as booty by the Europeans after the Boxer Rebellion and given back to China after World War I (Amelung 1998, p. 172). Photo by the author, 2005.

caravan route.[88] When he arrived back in Rome in February 1664 Grueber was interviewed by Jesuit authorities and corresponded with German notables who were curious about China. Although Grueber never published his own travel account, a long interview with him appeared in print.[89] Although his view of China was similar to that of the other Jesuits, Grueber made a unique contribution to this discourse in his account of being treated by a Chinese doctor. According to Grueber, "their doctors . . . are so excellent that they can tell from your pulse the source and special circumstances of your sickness." His doctor was able to determine "how long I had been sick and all of the attendant symptoms, including their exact duration, and

88. Grueber traveled with a German Jesuit he met while studying theology at the University of Graz, Bernard Diestel, and continued his travels once he reached China, first with a Belgian Jesuit, Albert d'Orville, and then with a Bavarian, P. Heinrich Roth, stationed at Agra (Braumann 1985, pp. 30–41; Kaufmann 1968).

89. This interview was compiled by Count Lorenzo Magalotti and published by the French royal librarian Melchisidec Thévenot; the English translation is Thévenot 1676.

all of the other peculiarities of my suffering, with such precision that I was completely surprised."[90]

An earlier record of Grueber's experiences appeared in the French edition of *China illustrata* (1667) by the Jesuit polyhistor Athanasius Kircher.[91] This was one of the most widely circulated and quoted books on China published in the seventeenth century in any language, including German, and it is still widely available.[92] Never having traveled to China, Kircher conformed to dominant Jesuit opinion in viewing it as "the richest and most powerful empire on earth," and also the "most celebrated or estimable" monarchy. Following in the tradition laid down by Trigault, Kircher wrote that "this state is governed by learned men in the manner of the Platonists, and according to the wishes of the divine philosopher; in which I consider this kingdom happy. . . . This state is well governed."[93] Kircher combined his praise of China "with some very severe criticism," especially concerning the "abominable falsehoods" in Chinese religion and the supposed shortcomings of the language, which he traced to Egyptian hieroglyphics.[94]

Kircher's book is also an early example of the elevation of chinoiserie to a more sophisticated level. It included reproductions of Chinese religious imagery. One is a careful copy of a drawing by Grueber of a wood engraving of the Daoist pantheon. The landscape scroll on the table in figure 6.2 is probably the "earliest representation of a Chinese landscape painting in European art."[95] Kircher created original syntheses of Chinese and European aesthetic forms, as in figure 6.2. He remarked that "the ladies' costume is very modest and gracious, as you can see," and added that the women of Europe wouldn't be able to carry this off so successfully.[96] Comments like this, combined with the cultural syncretism exemplified by some of the illustrations, suggested a relative equality between the two cultures, counter-

90. Translation from the German version in Braumann 1985, pp. 111–12.

91. Kircher's book was translated into French as *La Chine* in 1670; this is the edition I am using here. Mungello 1985, chap. 5, details Kircher's life and work.

92. An Amsterdam publisher first brought out Kircher's book in Latin and, three years later, in French (1670); another Latin edition was edited in Berlin by Andreas Müller in 1672 (Reichwein 1925, p. 19).

93. Kircher 1670, pp. 223, 226.

94. Mungello 1985, pp. 135–36.

95. Sullivan 1997, p. 94.

96. Kircher 1670, p. 155. Sullivan (1997, p. 96) oddly claims that Kircher "makes no mention of this engraving in the text."

balancing the disparagement of Chinese religion and language elsewhere in Kircher's book.

Leibniz was the most influential non-Jesuit champion of China in late-seventeenth- and early-eighteenth-century Germany, and indeed in Europe as a whole. His pamphlet *Latest News from China* (*Novissima Sinica;* 1697) was one of the few texts he wrote for publication. Like Voltaire, he argued that "human cultivation and refinement [is] concentrated . . . in Europe *and* in China." Leibniz believed that Europe was superior in *theoretical* or scientific knowledge, while China surpassed Europe with regard to social and political arrangements.[97] He noted that "it would be highly foolish and presumptuous on our part, having newly arrived compared with them, and scarcely out of barbarism, to want to condemn such an ancient doctrine [Confucianism] simply because it does not appear to agree at first glance with our ordinary scholastic notions." In a celebrated burst of cultural relativism, Leibniz called for "missionaries from the Chinese who might teach us the use and practice of natural religion." The exchange of knowledge between Europe and China, he insisted, "must be reciprocal."[98]

The German Enlightenment thinker Christian Wolff pursued Leibniz's suggestion that the Chinese had succeeded in developing a practical religion based in everyday rationality despite their ignorance of Christianity. Wolff made "allusions to aspects of Chinese thought and history" in most of his works, and discussed Confucian philosophy in some detail.[99] King Frederick William I of Prussia dismissed Wolff from his teaching post at the University of Halle and banished him from the state in 1723. The precipitating cause was a public lecture two years earlier on Chinese practical philosophy in which Wolff had outraged his Pietist enemies by praising the "atheist" Chinese.[100] Wolff's *Oratio de Sinarum philosophia practica* ar-

97. Leibniz 1994, p. 45 (my emphasis). Leibniz looked for correspondences between his binary mathematics and the hexagrams of the *Yijing* (Book of Changes); see his "Discourse on the Natural Theology of the Chinese," in Leibniz 1994, pp. 75–138; also Mungello 1985.

98. Leibniz 1994, pp. 78, 51; 1990, p. 64.

99. Lach 1953, p. 568. Wolff was "associated with Leibniz in a number of ways," though not actually his student, as is sometimes claimed (Corr 1975, p. 249).

100. Wolff's dismissal inspired two hundred polemical tracts, statements of support from several foreign academies, and an honorary professorship from the University of St. Petersburg (Lach 1953, pp. 565–67). In 1736 a commission summoned by Frederick William I determined that there was "nothing dangerous" about Wolff, and in 1740 Wolff was invited back to Prussia by Frederick the Great; a year later he returned to Halle (Lach 1953, p. 571; see also Voltaire [1764] 1879, p. 156; and E. Zeller 1862).

gued that the Chinese had succeeded in their ethical projects by trying to accomplish only "that which is founded in nature." The ethical success of the Chinese resulted also from their leadership by worldly philosophers (*Weltweise*), "following Plato's" recommendation ("nach dem Ausspruch, welchen Plato gethan hat").[101] In a lecture delivered at Marburg in 1750 entitled "The Real Happiness of a People under a Philosophical King," Wolff repeated his view that among the Chinese, "Kings were Philosophers, and Philosophers Kings."[102] Even if the Chinese had only attained the lowest of the three stages of virtue, one that relied "solely on natural powers, and not on true religion or revelation," this was more than could be said for most Christians.[103] Pietists were especially upset by Wolff's comparisons of Confucius with Moses, Mohammed, and Christ.[104] Also important in terms of Sinophilia was Wolff's view of the Chinese as superior to other "pagans" for having maintained their naturally derived powers "undamaged" for millennia, which demonstrated that "natural law was accessible to and attainable by all people," Christian or otherwise.[105] According to Wolff, the Chinese "were able to differentiate perfectly between good and bad practices and between true virtue and its external appearance," even though "they knew nothing of God."[106]

As in France, German Sinophilia did not disappear suddenly but tapered off and became increasingly defensive. The leading German cameralist philosopher of the eighteenth century, Johann von Justi, composed his *Comparisons of European with Asian and Other Supposedly Barbaric Governments* (1762) as a rejoinder to Montesquieu's influential thesis of Chinese despotism. In the first paragraph von Justi struck a chord of relativist tolerance, noting

101. Wolff [1726] 1740, pp. 104, 31. Published by Wolff in Latin 1726 and in German in 1740.

102. Quoted in Lach 1953, p. 569.

103. Wolff [1726] 1740, pp. 120–23. Wolff's argument that "Christian virtue could only be achieved as the final stage in a progression that began with natural experience" and not with revelation was a "fundamental challenge to the theological ethics of the Pietists" (Larrimore 2000, p. 199).

104. Wolff [1726] 1740, pp. 67–77. The Pietists, especially Wolff's chief opponent, Joachim Lange, were also enraged by his claim that Christianity only "provided new significance for ethical acts, customs, and dispositions that were already valuable in their own right," and by the correlative refusal of the Pietist claim that "the only starting point for true ethics was fear of God" (Larrimore 2000, p. 200). Wolff's Leibnizian insistence on a "preestablished harmony," his antivoluntarism, and his precocious defense of a liberal state also did little to endear him to these enemies.

105. Larrimore 2000, pp. 203–4.

106. Wolff [1745] 1995, pars. 507, 540 (pp. 172, 203).

that every nation considers itself superior to the others. He concluded that the Chinese were in fact "much more civilized and enlightened [*gesitteten, erleuchteten*] than we Europeans." Reiterating a familiar theme from the Jesuit literature, von Justi contrasted the wasteful luxury of European monarchs with the more frugal court of the Chinese emperors. Whereas Montesquieu had given more credence to the China-bashing accounts of European merchants in the south, von Justi praised the Chinese government for controlling the foreign merchants strictly such that they could "only show themselves as merchants, and not as conquistadors."[107]

Straightforward Sinophilia became increasingly rare, however, by the end of the eighteenth century and would resurface in new forms only after 1900. Frederick the Great was willing to listen to both sides of the debate, represented for him by Voltaire and de Pauw (although he finally said to Voltaire "I leave the Chinese to you").[108] As in England and France, positive presentations of China were increasingly restricted to the realm of decoration. Frederick the Great built his famous "Chinese House" at Sanssouci Park in Potsdam in 1754–64, combining Chinese and European elements in its decoration and in the life-size gilded figures surrounding the house (plates 4, 5); he also built a Chinese bridge and Chinese-style "Dragon House" in the gardens, and at Lietzenburg (Charlottenburg Palace), Frederick had the Great Gallery and another room decorated in Chinese fashion.[109]

The last and most striking examples of German Sinophilia in the eighteenth century were two allegorical paintings depicting "the Chinese emperor plowing the first furrow of the year in honor of agriculture" (plate 6) and "the Chinese empress plucking the first mulberry leaves in honor of silkweaving," both created in 1771 for the Britz country home of Count Ewald Friedrich von Hertzberg by Christian Bernhardt Rode, future director of the Prussian Academy of Arts.[110] Count von Hertzberg was a Prussian statesman and foreign minister and close adviser of Frederick the Great. His commissioned painting of the Chinese emperor was an almost literal illustration of the physiocratic theory of land as the source of all wealth and

107. Justi [1762] 1978, pp. 35, 70–72, preface p. 8.

108. According to Reichwein 1925, p. 93.

109. The Sanssouci Chinese House was designed by Johann Gottfied Büring and was based on a sketch by the king himself. See Hassels 1993, pp. 116–19, 144–47; Laske 1909; and Komander 1994, pp. 1–7. The Chinese House has now been restored to its approximate original state. On Lietzenburg see Verwaltung der Staatlichen Schlösser und Gärten 1973, pp. 57–58.

110. See Michaelis 1999, pp. 12, 41 n. 46.

of the need for enlightened monarchichal leadership to create the conditions for economic growth. By placing the Chinese rather than the Prussian or French monarch behind the plow, Rode's painting referred more specifically to the interpretation of China offered by the leading physiocrat, François Quesnay. In his *Despotism in China* (1767) Quesnay had disagreed sharply with Montesquieu's interpretation of the emperor as a tyrant, arguing that the "tribunals and the great mandarins" had "the custom of remonstrating with the emperor" and that his decisions did "not violate usages or the public welfare." For Quesnay, the Chinese government was "the oldest, largest, most humane and most flourishing which has ever existed," a model for European states.[111] The greatest praise a physiocrat could offer was to depict the sovereign as being actively involved in cultivating the soil. Indeed, Count von Hertzberg created a "model economy" in the fields around his Britz manor house.[112] The emperor behind the plow had been described in Jean-Baptiste Du Halde's *Description de la Chine* and artists depicting French kings and Austro-Hungarian emperors imitated this image.[113]

The Rise of Sinophobia

The conquest of the country of an inferior race by a superior race that establishes itself there in order to rule is not shocking at all. . . . Unleash this devouring activity on countries like China which are crying aloud for foreign conquest!

ERNEST RENAN, La réforme intellectuelle et morale (1874)[114]

David Mungello writes that the Jesuits were so influential during the seventeenth century that "those with conflicting views [of China] were merely able to criticize and lacked the power to fully establish a competing interpretive

---

111. Quesnay [1767] 1946, 2, pp. 214, 247.

112. Von Krosigk 1998, pp. 22–23.

113. *Gemäldegalerie* 1975, p. 364. See also the images from the last third of the eighteenth century of King Louis XVI and Kaiser Joseph II behind the plow in Budde, Müller-Hofstede, and Sievernich 1985, p. 68. The emperor and other figures in Rode's painting have European features and beards. This recalls the figures at the Sanssouci Chinese House (plate 5), the image of Confucius in Du Halde 1741 (vol. 1, frontispiece), and the images of many Pacific islanders in eighteenth-century travel accounts (B. Smith 1992). Rather than simply dismissing such Europeanization as naive we should emphasize that Chinese or Oceanic and European cultures had not yet been driven so far apart by biological racism in the eighteenth century for these images to seem absurd to artists or their publics.

114. Renan [1871] 1874, pp. 92–93.

framework of their own."[115] By the end of the eighteenth century, Sinophilia had been largely superseded by Sinophobia.

The more negative views associated with commercial circles and Protestant religious challengers emerged on the European continent in the early eighteenth century. Jansenists like Eusebe Renaudot, in his *Anciennes Relations des Indes et de la Chine* (1718), tried to counter the Jesuit picture of China. Christian Wolff's Pietist nemesis at Halle, Joachim Lange, was another early opponent of the Jesuit-influenced theory. These scattered voices gained momentum after 1750 and gradually came to dominate the field, even if they never fully displaced Sinophilia. In the following pages I will sketch the main elements of Sinophobia before examining several of its influential European and German exemplars.

DYEING THE CHINESE YELLOW

One dimension of Sinophobia was an inexorable *racialization* of the Chinese, accomplished in a series of discursive moves over the course of the eighteenth and nineteenth centuries. The Chinese had been located in the upper links of the Great Chain of Being, which was a European paradigm that preceded and in some ways cleared the ground for modern ideas of race.[116] Europeans had also traditionally described the Chinese as white. Gaspar da Cruz, in the first European book devoted solely to China, published in 1569, described Chinese women as "very white." One of the members of the first Spanish mission to China, Martin de Rada, wrote during the next decade that the "people of Taybin [China] are all . . . white and well-built."[117] Most agreed that the Chinese were "in Colour and Complexion . . . like the people of Europe."[118] Mendoza introduced a difference between the southern Chinese, who were "browne of colour like to the Moores," and those "farther within the countrie," who "be like unto Almaines [Germans], Italians and Spanyades, white and redde, and somewhat swart."[119] This distinction

---

115. Mungello 1985, p. 15. Two exceptions were located at the outer reaches of Europe. England, weaker than some of the continental powers during the seventeenth century and not involved in embassies to the Chinese emperor, had more critics than admirers of China. As Appleton (1951, p. 19) points out, the term *Cataian* (Chinese) in the mouths of Shakespeare's characters was "synonymous with a diverting Munchausen." At the other fringe of Europe, Russian embassies to China favored a dry, factual, and often critical approach.

116. Lovejoy [1936] 1964.

117. Cruz [1569] 1953, p. 149; Rada 1953, p. 282.

118. Montanus 1671, p. 713.

119. Mendoza 1853, vol. 1, p. 30.

between "white" (or "almost white") Chinese in the north and the interior and darker Chinese in the "torrid zone" was repeated by countless writers, few of whom had actually visited China.[120] The contrast corresponded closely to a sociopolitical distinction between the mandarins at the court and the emperor, whom the Jesuits admired and cultivated and with whom they had the most intensive contact, and the officials in Canton, who were despised by both the Jesuits and the European merchants.

The Chinese were discussed as an undifferentiated category, however, by eighteenth- and nineteenth-century biologists and race theorists, craniologists, and physical anthropologists. Linnaeus placed the Chinese in the category *"Homo monstrous"* together with the "Hottentots," who were considered by most Europeans at the time as the epitome of human debasement. In 1764 Johann Winckelmann described the shape of the Chinese nose and the angle of the eyes as a "deviation" from Greek ideals of beauty, "for it mars the unity of the forms."[121] Johann Gottfried von Herder introduced a discussion of China in his unfinished masterwork *Ideas for a Philosophy of the History of Mankind* (1784–91) with the assertion that the "shape of head and brain, of body and nerves" shapes the "entire destiny of man." Herder's discussion was premised on an axiomatic contrast between Asia and the "well-formed nations" (or "beautiful people") of Europe and the Near East.[122] John Barrow's widely read 1804 *Travels in China* presented the Chinese in explicitly racial terms, and German translations of Barrow included an engraving that equated Chinese and Khoikhoi faces (fig. 6.4).

German writers often followed Buffon in classing the Chinese within the "Mongol" race, which was described by the protoanthropologist Johann Blumenbach in 1775 as an "extreme degeneration of the human species."[123] In Blumenbach's original schema, the "Caucasian" was located at the center of the system, with the other races arranged around it at different distances.[124]

120. See Trigault and Ricci [1615] 1953, p. 77; Jürgen Andersen and Volquard Iversen, "Orientalische Reise-Beschreibung," in Olearius 1696, p. 105; Careri [1704] 1752, p. 359; Nieuhof [1669] 1972, p. 208; Dapper 1676, p. 155; and Montanus 1671, p. 321.

121. Winckelmann [1767] 1968, vol. I, p. 197.

122. Herder [1784] 1985, pp. 299, 160–64. Herder actually contrasts the "well-formed" (*schöngebildete* or *wohlgebildete*) peoples of Europe and the Near East not only with Asians but also with Africans, Americans, those "near the North Pole," and those "on the islands of the torrid zone."

123. Blumenbach 1865, p. xi, as summarized by Thomas Bendysche, editor of the 1865 edition of Blumenbach's *Anthropological Treatises*. For other uses of Blumenbach's schema and the term "Mongols" (or "Mongolians"), see Maukisch 1836; Goltz 1858, p. 13; and Hoffmeister 1882.

124. Blumenbach claimed to have coined the term "Caucasian," which he took from the Caucasus Mountains (1865, p. 269).

FIGURE 6.4 *The Chinaman (1) and the Hottentot (2) Who Resembles Him.* Frontispiece from Zimmermann 1810; adapted from Barrow 1805, pp. 52–53.

Native Americans (*Amerikaner*) and Malayans (*Malayen*) were closer to the core, Mongols (*Mongolen*) and Ethiopians (*Äthiopier*, or blacks) more distant, as can be seen in figure 6.5, a visualization of Blumenbach's approach.[125]

Other race theorists reversed this hierarchy, placing the "yellow races" above India and Africa. Some writers later in the nineteenth century introduced additional racial categories, which shifted the location of the Chinese. Ferdinand von Richthofen, for example, equated the "racial" category of the "Mongol" with the older meaning of "Mongolian" as "Tartar" and created a separate racial slot for the Chinese.[126]

With the rising prestige of craniometry and race science, the shapes of Chinese skulls and facial angles and the tonality of Chinese skin were brought into causal correlation with specific moral failings such as the

125. From Ranke 1894–1900, vol. 2, p. 208. Ranke was the president of the German Anthropological Society, an advocate of craniometry, and a critic of "the ridiculous popular opinion that Asian cultural peoples [*Kulturvölker*] belong to a lower race," a prejudice he attributed to the emphasis on skin color in racial schemes (ibid., vol. 2, pp. 203ff., 160; see also Zimmerman 2001, p. 91). The diagram in fig. 6.5 thus actually referred to skull forms, which Ranke wanted to disentangle from any implications about cultural or intellectual variation.

126. Richthofen 1873. Others continued to refer to the Chinese as belonging to the "Mongol race," for example, Spiess 1864, p. 263; and Schweiger-Lerchenfeld 1901, p. 86.

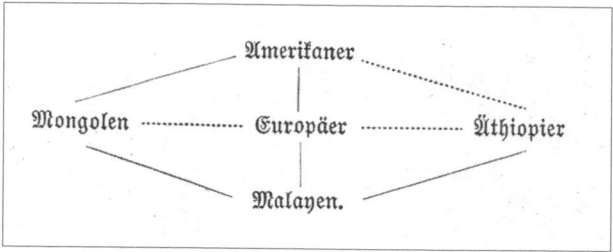

FIGURE 6.5 Johann Friedrich Blumenbach's racial schema as visualized by J. Ranke (1894, 2:208).

legendary "cunningness" of the Canton merchants.[127] Carl Gustav Carus, the German anatomist and psychologist who argued that not just brain size but also the color and inner "constitution" of the skin and the racially distinctive shape of the hand helped to explain differences in intelligence, compared the "Mongols" to a "locustlike" herd with a "certain mediocrity of the soul."[128] Carus drew on Samuel George Morton, the American polygenist who had measured the volume of several Chinese skulls, finding them to be larger than the African and American varieties but smaller than the European.[129] Over the course of the nineteenth century, Chinese skin color changed from "white" to "yellow" in European perceptions.[130] Arthur comte de Gobineau discussed the shape of the Chinese forehead and concluded that the "yellow man has little physical energy," that "his desires are feeble," and that he tends "to mediocrity in everything."[131] After the Sino-Japanese War and the Treaty of Shimonoseki (1895), this chromatic

127. Goltz 1858, pt. 2, pp. 89, 95. An earlier article had already spoken of the "wonderful correspondence between the spirit and bodily form" after listing Chinese physical and moral shortcomings ("Ueber die Natur der Völker im Südlichen Asien, auf den Ostindischen und Südsee-Inseln und in den Südländern," *Göttingisches Historisches Magazin* 7 [1790]: 258–306, esp. p. 303).

128. Carus 1849, pp. 58–60. Carus linked skin color to intelligence via a theory according to which "the finer organization of the skin is crucial for the development of higher mental functions, since the skin is the first and most general sense organ" (ibid., p. 21). Hence, the darker skin of the "night peoples," with its "stronger sedimentation of carbon and its cruder organization," had formidable epistemological implications. The intellectual disadvantaging was diminished among East Asians and the "dusk" (*Dämmerung*) peoples of the New World.

129. Gould 1996, p. 85–87.

130. Demel 1992.

131. Gobineau [1852] 1915, p. 206. Of course, de Gobineau was an equal-opportunity racist and not focused on China (Mosse 1985).

change was linked to the idea of a growing threat to Europe, the "yellow peril."[132]

The raciological vision was crucial in wresting China away from its status as Europe's civilizational equal and realigning it with the catalog of epithets Europeans had long associated with Africans. The conquest of China by the Manchu invaders in the seventeenth century had led Europeans, from Martino Martini through Voltaire, to focus on supposed differences between the "blind and barbarous" Manchus and the "reason and genius" of the Chinese.[133] Lumping the Chinese into the category of "Mongol" together with their Manchu overlords obviously precluded this distinction. The Chinese were never *explicitly* categorized as a *Naturvolk* (natural people) within German discussions, of course.[134] But in the first half of the nineteenth century, Europeans like the pioneering Protestant missionary Karl Gützlaff began calling the Chinese "semi-barbarian" and "half-civilized."[135] This was heightened to "savage" in the writings of John Barrow and to "dirty barbarians" by Elisabeth von Heyking. The transformation of the Chinese into barbarians, savages, and generic "natives" was closely tied to the idea that China was "crying aloud for foreign conquest."

"AN IMITATIVE GENIUS"

Like most of the inhabitants of the global periphery in the nineteenth century, the Chinese were also described as mimic men. Sinophiles had often expressed frustration at the lack of Chinese interest in Europe, but they had never before focused on mimicry. European merchants in Canton, however, thought the Chinese they encountered were exploiting their familiarity with European ways in order to cheat them.

The Chinese variant of mimicry took a specific form that revealed the extent to which Sinophobia was an intradiscursive response to Sinophilia and not just an outgrowth of generic discourses of race or an accurate recording of actual encounters. Chinese mimicry was not blamed, as in the cases of the Khoikhoi or Africans more generally, on the partial adaptation of corrupting Western ways. Gützlaff looked forward to the time when the Chinese would finally begin to "emulate the most civilized nations."[136] The

132. Gollwitzer 1962, pp. 43–44.
133. Voltaire [1755] 1877, p. 296; Martini 1654a.
134. Osterhammel 1998, p. 243.
135. Gützlaff 1838, vol. I, pp. 490–91, 493.
136. Ibid., pp. 507–8.

"manipulative" Chinese merchants in Guangdong were not seen as cultural hermaphrodites. Instead, mimicry was attributed to an intrinsic feature of Chinese culture, that is, to a basic talent for imitation. It was also explained as a response to despotic political conditions, again inverting the Sinophile interpretation of Chinese government. Gützlaff blamed the Chinese educational system, which did nothing but teach students to "copy their ancestors."[137] Herder criticized Chinese education as little more than training in "artificial manners" (Manieren).[138] This interpretation was codified somewhat later in the theory of "face"—the idea that the Chinese "treated all the world as a stage on which appearance was all and reality insignificant."[139] Mimicry was read as the essence of China rather than a sign of deracination. This would make it more difficult for Europeans to imagine how to stabilize Chinese subjects through native policy in a projected colonial future.

As with the Khoikhoi, Europeans linked the "imitative genius" of the Chinese to cunning deceptiveness. According to an article in the *Göttingisches Historisches Magazin* from 1788 entitled "On the Sneakiness of Different Peoples," the Chinese "falsify all of their wares" due to a "lack of any feelings of sympathetic empathy, gratitude, regret, or shame." The author asserted that "if the Chinese have their equals anywhere, or even their superiors, it is among the Negroes of Africa."[140] A German anthropologist heightened this attack, writing in 1858 that he "would rather interact with Negroes, or with an honest poodle or a hound," than with the Chinese, who were known for their "addiction to imitation."[141] Karl Gützlaff claimed that lying was so common among the Chinese as to "incur no odium," since their "strength is in cunning, in litigation."[142] This paradigm received an influential formulation in Commodore Anson's *Voyage round the World*, which painted a portrait of Chinese tricksters manipulating gullible Europeans. According to Anson, "the Chinese are difficult to be paralleled by any other people" in "artifice, falsehood, and an attachment to all kinds of lucre." In a passage widely cited by later writers, he described tricks such as stuffing

137. Ibid., p. 507.

138. Herder [1784] 1985, p. 284.

139. Hevia 1992, p. 316. For an exemplary statement of the "face" theory from the period see A. Brown 1904, pp. 37–38.

140. "Ueber die Verschmitztheit verschiedener Völker," *Göttingisches Historisches Magazin* 3 (1788): 151, 154.

141. Goltz 1858, pt. 2, p. 89.

142. Gützlaff 1838, pp. 505–6.

ducks full of gravel to increase their weight. Anson insisted that Chinese industrial talents were "but of a second rate kind," and that "their principal excellency" lay in copying.[143] Chinese imitation and deceptiveness seemed even more insidious than partial Westernization because it was strategic and intentional.

DESPOTIC STATES OF MIND

From the end of the seventeenth century and all through the eighteenth, a spectre was haunting Europe: the spectre of *despotism*.

ALAIN GROSRICHARD (1998)

The word *despotism* "entered the language fairly late," and from the start it was located specifically in Asia. Like Said's *Orientalism,* however, Alain Grosrichard's book about this category focuses almost entirely on the European fantasy of the near Orient and has little to say about China or the Far East. Yet China played a central role in nineteenth-century discussions of Oriental despotism. Indeed, the transformation of China into a despotism was even more striking than the Orientalist treatment of the Ottoman Empire, which had never been taken as a model for Europe. Grosrichard notes that Europeans "saw the Ottoman regime as having become the overriding image of political monstrosity" during the second half of the seventeenth century—the exact moment when European praise for the Chinese system of government was at its height.[144]

Montesquieu's *Spirit of the Laws* gave despotism its specifically *"Asiatic* features" and became "the obligatory—albeit controversial—reference for the whole of political philosophy in the second half of the eighteenth century."[145] Alongside Anson's *Voyage round the World,* it was also the fount of a literature in which specific aspects of China that had previously been praised were systematically recoded as negative.[146] *Spirit of the Laws* served up China as the epitome of tyranny, a land where life was governed

143. Anson [1748] 1974, pp. 351, 355-56, 367. Anticipating the structure of *colonial* mimicry, Anson mocked the Chinese by quoting one in pidgin English: "Chinese man very great rogue truly, but have fashion, no can help" (ibid., p. 355). See also Timkowski 1827, vol. 2, p. 184.

144. Grosrichard 1998, pp. 3-4, 22.

145. Ibid., p. 30.

146. Anson's narrative was translated into German in 1795; Montesquieu's *Spirit of the Laws* appeared in German just four years after its original French publication in 1748.

exclusively by force and fear, and where power was entirely in the hands of the emperor. Montesquieu endorsed the hostile tone of the merchants' reports, remarking that "our merchants" were preferable to the missionaries as a source of testimony about China—not because they were intrinsically more trustworthy but because they supported the despotism thesis: they alone "show us a settled plan of tyranny, and barbarities committed by rule, that is, in cold blood."[147] Yet the merchants typically had only fleeting contacts with a limited sector of the Chinese population and operated in a context of haggling; the missionaries, by contrast, lived among the Chinese, learned their language, and sometimes entered into more open-ended interactions.[148] Subsequent writers, including missionaries, echoed Montesquieu's language of despotism and his condemnation of the Chinese state.

Karl Gützlaff was one of the first Protestant missionaries in nineteenth-century China, and his prolific writings, especially *China Opened* (1838), advertised that China was now available for a new round of evangelizing by the Protestant denominations that had become dominant in Europe. Gützlaff started his missionary work in China alone, with no formal connections to any mission society or church, and eventually founded a short-lived Protestant society called the Chinese Union.[149] But much of Gützlaff's activity in China took place under the aegis of British imperialism. He undertook his second missionary voyage as translator and doctor for an exploratory expedition of the British East India Company, and his third voyage was with an armed British opium smuggler.[150] He served as "the official interpreter for the British government during the Opium War and helped negotiate the colonizing of Hong Kong and the opening of the five treaty ports" and was employed by the British government as a representative in various Chinese cities and in the colonial government of Hong Kong.[151] In *China Opened* Gützlaff derived Chinese family form and national character

---

147. Montesquieu 1949, p. 123.

148. Montesquieu retracted some of his attack in bk. 19, which suddenly seemed to agree with the Jesuits that the core principle of the Chinese polity was filial submission and love. But as one commentator notes, these chapters "form a sort of cleanly isolated enclave" within *The Spirit of the Laws* and have little impact on the "imperious conclusion" presented in the book's opening sections (Carcassonne 1924, p. 203).

149. This paragraph is based mainly on Schlyter 1946, pp. 12–32, 292–98; 1976. Gützlaff came to China first "under the auspices of the Netherlands Missionary Society, of which he soon declared himself independent" (Hanan 2002, p. 419).

150. Lindsay and Gützlaff 1833.

151. L. Liu 1999b, p. 154.

from the despotic state form itself, in a tone that was indistinguishable from Montesquieu's:

> The government also has imprinted its stamp upon the Chinese character. In every despotic country, the minds of the people are enslaved, they become cringing and adulatory; and being borne down by main force, they are obliged, whilst defending themselves from oppression, to have recourse to deceit, and sundry disingenuous practices. . . . They are a tame, one might say, a pusillanimous nation, filled with trembling and cunning. . . . The constitution of the government, so convenient to those who rule, and so irksome to those who obey, prompts parents to practice tyranny in their domestic circles; thus despotism becomes the order of the day.[152]

Gützlaff's case demonstrates that someone who had studied at the university for just a single semester could become fully conversant with the main lineaments of the Oriental despotism thesis.[153]

STAGNATION AND DECAY:
CHINA AS HIBERNATING *MURMELTIER*

The theme of Chinese stagnation and decay that emerged in the second half of the eighteenth century condemned Chinese civilization as a geriatric ruin, lacking all internal dynamism and capacity for development. The Sinophiles had applauded China for its unchanging culture and political stability. But just as the Ottoman Empire became the "sick man of Europe," China was transformed, in Herder's image, into the "sleeping groundhog" (*Murmeltier*) that could only be shaken from its slumber by the restless European "robbers or merchants" who were circumnavigating the globe.[154] In *The Wealth of Nations* Adam Smith adopted this view of China as "long stationary" and dismissed the reports produced by "weak and wondering travellers" and "frequently by stupid and lying missionaries."[155] Karl Marx's views of China were informed by John Stuart Mill's writings on the "Asiatic form of government."[156] In 1853 Marx enthused about the Taiping rebellion

---

152. Gützlaff 1838, vol. 1, p. 478.

153. Gützlaff enrolled at the University of Berlin in January of 1823 but was already in Holland by June of that year (Schlyter 1946, pp. 292, 21-23).

154. Herder [1784] 1985, p. 298.

155. A. Smith [1776] 1954, vol. 1, p. 63; vol. 2, p. 217.

156. D. Jones 2001, p. 69.

and prophesied that "the next uprising of the people of Europe . . . may depend more probably on what is now passing in the Celestial Empire . . . than on any other political cause that now exists." Yet China seemed to Marx "a living fossil" persisting in "barbarous and hermetic isolation from the civilized world." The empire's dissolution, he wrote, "must follow as surely as that of any mummy carefully preserved in a hermetically sealed coffin, whenever it is brought into contact with the open air." The "Oriental empires," according to Marx, "always show an unchanging social infrastructure coupled with unceasing change in the persons and tribes who manage to ascribe to themselves the political super-structure." Friedrich Engels, even more taken in by fashionable Sinophobia, disparaged China as a "rotting semi-civilisation."[157]

Some Europeans put more emphasis on China's static character, while others preferred the image of obsolescence or decline following earlier eras of grandeur. John Barrow combined the tropes of stasis and decline. The Chinese had already reached "a certain pitch of perfection" when Europe was still barbaric, he wrote, but they had "remained stationary" and even regressed in many respects since then.[158] Joseph Banks, the great promoter of scientific inquiry who accompanied Cook on his first voyage, said in the early 1790s that China had only "the ruins of a state of civilization."[159] For Thomas De Quincey, the opium eater in the years before the Opium Wars, "the vast age of the [Asiatic] race and name overpowers the sense of youth in the individual," such that "a young Chinese seems to me an antediluvian man."[160] According to Alexis de Tocqueville, "when Europeans first arrived in China . . . they found that almost all the arts had reached a certain degree of perfection there, and they were surprised that a people which had attained this point *should not have gone beyond it*. At a later point they discovered traces of some higher branches of science that *had been lost*. . . . This served to explain the *strange immobility* in which they found the minds of this people."[161] By the end of the nineteenth century, one missionary described China as "completely covered with ruins, witnesses of an earlier stage of civilization."[162] But the example he gave was the Old Imperial Gar-

157. Marx 1969b, pp. 67–69; 1969c, p. 442; Engels 1969, p. 184; see also Marx 1977, vol. I, p. 479.

158. Barrow [1804] 1806, p. 238. Barrow's *Travels in China* was based on the British embassy to China of 1793 though not published until 1805.

159. Quoted in Marshall 1993, p. 24.

160. De Quincey [1821] 1950, p. 333.

161. Tocqueville [1835–40] 1945, vol. 2, p. 48 (my emphasis). One could multiply the examples of this trope ad infinitum. See, for example, Maukisch 1836, pp 173–74.

162. Stenz 1899, p. 30.

den, whose ruination was hardly the result of endogenous Chinese decline but of plundering and burning by the Anglo-French troops in 1861 (plates 7, 8).[163] Nothing could better illustrate the confusion of cause and effect in European perceptions of China.

IMPOSTURES INTELLECTUELLES?

Jesuits and Enlightenment philosophers had praised the mandarins for promulgating the "law of the learned." Since Trigault, Jesuits had regarded Confucius as "the equal of the pagan philosophers and superior to most of them"[164] and had praised the Chinese educational system.[165] But Confucius, the mandarins, and Chinese schooling all lost their allure for Europeans after 1750. Rousseau, who had discovered so much to admire among the South African Khoikhoi, turned his attentions to the "immense country where learning is so honored that it takes men to the highest positions in the state": "If the sciences purified morals, taught men to shed their blood for their country, and animated their courage, then the peoples of China ought to be virtuous, free and invincible. But there is no vice that does not dominate them, no crime that is not common among them. . . . Of what use to it were all its scholars?"[166] While Rousseau condemned the Chinese literati for their impotence, others attacked their pretensions of power. Daniel Defoe, in an early novel, *The Consolidator* (1705), mocked Chinese who claimed "many sorts of learning which these parts of the world never heard of," including "such a perfection of knowledge, as to understand one another's thoughts." Defoe told the tale of the "famous Mira-cho-cho-lasmo, vice-admiral of China" about "two thousand years before the deluge," who was in fact "no native of this world, but was born in the moon," and who brought to the Chinese "the most exquisite accomplishments of those lunar regions."[167] In the third part of *Robinson Crusoe* Defoe attacked the Chinese with less humor as a "contemptible Herd or Crowd of ignorant sordid Slaves, subjected to a Government qualified only to rule such a People."[168] The exam system was no longer seen as the centerpiece of a meritocracy but as a sham. Karl May's novel *Der blaurote Methusalem* (1889) contained a vicious satire of the system used to qualify candidates for advancement to mandarin status.

163. On the sacking of the *Yuanming Yuan* see Wong 2001, chap. 7.
164. Trigault and Ricci [1615] 1953, p. 30.
165. Wolff [1726] 1740, p. 185ff.
166. Rousseau [1750] 1975, p. 211.
167. Defoe [1705] 1840, pp. 211, 214, 218.
168. Defoe 1719, p. 298. Marx 1969, p. 68, also attacked China's "pedantic Mandarins."

According to Karl Gützlaff, the Chinese are "early taught that they know everything" and therefore "deem it unnecessary to think for themselves, and so pursue the beaten path."[169]

In his travel narratives, however, Gützlaff frequently acknowledged China's high level of literacy and recognized that this made it an ideal "field for missionary exertion" where "even the smallest tracts will be perused to advantage."[170] And despite their rejection of the Jesuits' accomodationism, many nineteenth-century missionaries, including Gützlaff, were themselves partly engulfed by Chinese culture. Before entering China for the first time in 1830 Gützlaff already claimed to have been "adopted into the Guo clan from Tong'an in Fujian."[171] Gützlaff "adopted a Chinese name and tried . . . in every way to live as a Chinese," dressing at times like a Fujianese fisherman (see fig. 6.6).[172] Even more revealing of his partial identification with a China he claimed to scorn are a series of novels Gützlaff wrote in Chinese, which are set entirely within a Chinese context featuring Chinese Christians. One of these is said to be the "earliest novel in Chinese with a first-person narrator." Significantly, this novel "opens with an 'I' who falls asleep and dreams" and is "both the hero as well as the narrator of the book"; this figure's surname is identical to Gützlaff's adopted Chinese surname, and like Gützlaff's adoptive family he hails from Quanzhou Prefecture.[173] Gützlaff is by no means the only European whose imperial posture was undercut by a strong imaginary identification with a Chinese imago, as we will see in the next chapter.

TURNING LEIBNIZ ON HIS HEAD: JOHN BARROW'S REVERSALS AND RECODINGS

John Barrow's *Travels in China* was the most widely read account from the British embassy to the Chinese emperor led by Lord Macartney in 1793-94.[174] The Macartney mission resembled Captain Cook's voyages and others discussed in chapter 4 in the same period in its emphasis on science and long-range political advantage rather than immediate economic gain (although that consideration was never entirely absent).[175] The embassy included

---

169. Gützlaff 1838, vol. I, p. 507; see also Tocqueville [1835-40] 1945, vol. 2, p. 259.

170. Gützlaff 1834, p. 433.

171. Hanan 2000, p. 420.

172. Schlyter 1946, p. 293.

173. Hanan 2000, pp. 430-31. Unlike other missionaries, Gützlaff probably wrote his Chinese novels without much help from Chinese assistants (ibid., p. 427).

174. See C. Lloyd 1970, for biographical information on Barrow.

175. Dabringhaus 1996, p. 55.

FIGURE 6.6 *Karl Gützlaff from Stettin, English Missionary in China, Wearing the Costume of a Fujian Sailor.* Lithograph by Cäcilie Brand, ca. 1830, based on a painting by George Chinnery. Image from author's collection.

a painter, a draftsman, five German musicians, numerous other experts, and Barrow as treasurer.[176] Unlike earlier Russian and Dutch embassies, the party included no merchants.[177] More than Cook's voyages, the Macartney mission had the central aim of transforming previous ethnographic representations, namely, "finally to overcome the older Jesuit representations of China and to scientifically document the suspected shortcomings of the Chinese mode of government with rich material documentation."[178]

As a result, Barrow's *Travels in China* is structured as a series of explicit refutations of the Sinophile position associated with Jesuits and the European Enlightenment. Whereas the absence of a hereditary nobility and sharp class distinctions and the power of the scholars had pleased the Jesuits, it was repugnant to Barrow. Reversing Justi's earlier juxtaposition

---

176. Some of Alexander's paintings and sketches are reproduced in Susan Legouix-Sloman, "William Alexander," in Budde, Müller-Hofstede, and Sievernich 1985, pp. 173–86.

177. Cranmer-Byng, "Introduction," in Macartney 1962, p. 24.

178. Dabringhaus 1996, p. 55.

of the European and Chinese court societies, Barrow portrayed the Chinese court as materially impoverished rather than thrifty. Whereas the Jesuits had sought to find common ground between Christianity and Confucianism, Barrow insisted that Chinese religious beliefs not only "appear absurd and ridiculous" to us but were also "equally inexplicable by the people themselves who confess them." Where generations of Europeans had praised the Confucian emphasis on filial piety, Barrow attacked the state's enforcement of parental authority. Barrow criticized the Chinese for torpid "mental powers"; for a cruelty "not to be surpassed among the most savage nations"; for tastelessness in architecture, theater, music, and painting; and for a language that was defective and "poor." Ignoring the existence of the stone statues of warriors at the tomb of the Ming Hongwu Emperor in Nanjing and failing to anticipate the discovery in the twentieth century of thousands of life-size figures from the Qin dynasty at Xi'an (Changan), Barrow was quite certain that "in the whole empire there is not a statue . . . that deserves to be mentioned."[179]

Barrow also contributed to racializing the Chinese and downgrading their civilizational status. Exhibiting dubious taste by calling himself a reader of "the ingenious Mr. Pauw," Barrow acknowledged that he had been predisposed to think about the Chinese in racial terms even before his trip.[180] Barrow had spent six years in the harshly racist Cape Colony before writing the account of his earlier trip to China. *Travels in China* repeated his earlier theory about the physical similarities between the Chinese and the Khoikhoi.[181] In the later text he recalled that "a Hottentot, who attended my travelling over Southern Africa, was so very like a Chinese servant I had in Canton, both in person, features, manners, and tone of voice, that I almost always, inadvertently, called him by the name of the latter." For Barrow, all natives looked alike. In earlier centuries it would have seemed implausible to categorize the Chinese as barbarians, much less savages, and even Defoe had forced himself to qualify his judgment by calling them *"little better* than savages." But Barrow noted here that "few *savage tribes* are without the unnatural custom of maiming or lopping off some part of the human body" and added that "among *savage tribes,* the labour and drudgery invariably fall heaviest on the weaker sex."[182] Since "barbarians" were conventionally ranked above "savages" in European ethnodiscourse

179. Barrow [1804] 1806, quotes from pp. 284, 156, 115, 220.
180. Ibid., p. 262.
181. Barrow 1801–4, vol. 1, p. 278; [1804] 1806, p. 33.
182. Barrow [1804] 1806, pp. 33, 50, 93 (my emphasis).

this marked the radical edge of that clash of "barbarisms" characterizing nineteenth-century British-Chinese relations.[183]

Even writers whose explicit aim was to put the Chinese in their savage place sometimes found it difficult to sustain a seamless and systematic argument. Only the most powerful thinkers, such as Hegel and Weber, whose use of China was subordinated to an overarching theoretical argument (and who didn't actually visit China), were able to restrict themselves rigorously to examples from the Sinophobic register. The difficulty in maintaining a consistently Sinophobic line was due in part to the weighty heritage of European Sinophilia, but it also reflected empirical Chinese realities. Most European travelers were able to perceive the difference between pastoralist societies like the Ovaherero and a society organized around a functioning state with a nationwide bureauracy and a partly modernized military that was capable of mounting some successful campaigns (for example, against the Boxer movement in Shandong Province at the end of the century; see chap. 7). Difficulty in hewing to a consistent Sinophobia also stemmed from organized resistance by the Chinese to being treated as barbarians. China was able to successfully resist the flogging of Chinese indentured laborers in German Samoa as "unjust [and] derogatory to the dignity of the Chinese Empire" through its consul in Apia and its envoy in Berlin.[184] Despite resistance from German colonial officials in the Pacific and settlers in Samoa who wanted to see the Chinese categorized along with "Malayans, Chamorros, etc." as "semicultured peoples" (*Halbkulturvölker*) located legally in between "natives" and "whites,"[185] the colonial administration instead reclassified all Chinese in Samoa from "native" into "foreigner" status in 1912 (see chap. 5). The reason for this change, according to the Colonial Office was that "negotiations" in Berlin had made it obvious that "the Chinese government would [never] be satisfied" with being treated like natives.[186]

---

183. L. Liu 2004, chap. 2. Toward the end of his narrative, however, Barrow describes the Chinese as *differing* in their "opinions" from "all the rest of mankind, whether civilized or savage" ([1804] 1806, p. 230).

184. "Memorandum: Treatment of Chinese/Samoan Island," December 23, 1910, Imperial Chinese Embassy, Berlin, BA-Berlin, RKA, vol. 5588, p. 2r.

185. Oßwald, governor of German New Guinea, to RKA, January 22, 1911, BA-Berlin, RKA, vol. 5588, p. 20r.

186. RKA to governor of German Samoa, October 16, 1911, BA-Berlin, RKA, vol. 5588, p. 40r; *Samoanisches Gouvernements-Blatt* 3 (41, April 25, 1905): 133; 4 (21, January 6, 1911): 71. Wilhelm Solf, then still governor of Samoa, agreed that the equation of a "highly developed *Kulturvolk* [the Chinese] with the Samoan natives . . . seems anomalous" (Solf to RKA, Janu-

A brief comparison between Barrow's text and another account of the 1793 British embassy by George Staunton underscores the continuing multivocality of British discourse on China even in this predominantly Sinophobic period. Although Barrow's book achieved "a far wider circulation," Staunton was the embassy's secretary and wrote its official report.[187] Staunton emphasized China's relative superiority to other countries; the "ingenuity," "dexterity," and sustained hard work of the Chinese laborer; the antiquity of useful inventions and "those of decoration and refinement"; and the excellence of plays like *The Orphan of China*. His account highlighted the "maxims of humanity prevalent in the government," the gazettes that published reports of "offenses committed by mandarines," and the meritocratic system of advancement through exams that were "open to all classes of men." Yet these classic Sinophile examples were accompanied by long quotations from Barrow's journals lambasting China.[188] Although Sinomania resurfaced periodically in the eighteenth and nineteenth centuries, writers of Staunton's stature rarely embraced that framework wholeheartedly after 1850. Born thirty-seven years before Barrow and educated while Sinophilia was still dominant, Staunton represents a late excrescence of the receding paradigm. His book is a transcript of what we might call, with Bourdieu, the hysteresis of ideological habitus.[189]

German Sinophobia

Disdain for China in Germany stemmed from sources similar to those elsewhere in Europe. The infamous race theorist Christoph Meiners translated a French Jesuit text on China in 1778 which argued that "this nation, which is in so many respects distant from our own, is just as rich and happy, and perhaps richer and happier, than we are."[190] Meiners noted in his introduction, however, that he favored China's critics. In his next treatment of the Chinese, published in 1795-96, Meiners redeployed evidence

---

ary 28, 1911, BA-Berlin, RKA, vol. 5588, p. 4v). In fact, this had not seemed anomalous to him in 1900.

187. C. Lloyd 1970, p. 28.

188. Staunton 1797, quotes from vol. 3, pp. 100, 105, xii, 111, 317.

189. C. Lloyd 1970, p. 28, claims that Staunton is "pompous" and "almost unreadable." The difference, however, is more ideological than formal. Barrow's ethnographic codes tend to be closer than Staunton's to the neocolonial racism and sweeping cultural generalizations of a writer like Lloyd.

190. Meiners 1778, p. 18.

from the Jesuit literature *against* Sinophilia. The Chinese arts were now said to be nonexistent, not only because the Chinese lacked all natural artistic capacity but also because they were "exclusively oriented toward utilitarian goals"—a quality that writers like Quesnay had singled out for praise. The Chinese, according to Meiners, lacked "acuity and profundity of spirit."[191]

Herder's analyis of China was also largely derivative of the eighteenth-century critics, but he added the accents of the romantic discourse of authenticity.[192] Herder began his discussion of China in *Ideas* with praise for the country's orderliness and lack of a hereditary nobility, but his tone quickly changed. After insisting that a "middle path" had to found between the Jesuits and their critics, Herder's discussion swung toward the latter. He accused the Chinese of bad taste, "semi-Tartarish despotism," an orientation toward imitation and deception, and a mixture of "sensual refinement" with "uninventive ignorance" and argued that they were "like the Jews" in their standoffishness and "vain pride." A people that isolated itself from the rest of the world would automatically degenerate into a "slave culture." In the familiar idioms of German romanticism—which he of course helped to invent—Herder contrasted the "artificial character" of the Chinese with more "natural" cultures. Thus, while biological race science was beginning to assimilate the Chinese to Africans and other "natural peoples," Herder aligned German culture with "nature" and China with the anti-Semitic stereotypes of overcultivated Jews. Chinese men, he wrote, were unnaturally effeminate.[193] And in a critique that inadvertently underscores the imperial dispensation of his thinking (even as he ostensibly rejected colonialism), Herder criticized China's coastline for "almost completely lacking inlets and bays."[194]

191. Meiners 1795-96, vol. 1, pp. 181, 198.

192. Wiethoff 1971.

193. Herder [1784] 1985, pp. 281-85. In an anonymous article in the *Neues Göttingisches Historisches Magazin*, which Meiners coedited, we can read in 1792 that "the Chinese man envies the strong beard of the European, which he sees as a sign of manhood" ("Ueber den Haar- und Baartwuchs der häßlichen und dunkelfarbigen Völker," *Neues Göttingisches Historisches Magazin* 1 [1792]: 502). German criticism of Amerindians also often focused on their underdeveloped beards (Zantop 1997, chap. 3).

194. Herder [1784] 1985, p. 284. Most Europeans before the mid-nineteenth century, including the Sinophobes, were thinking less about colonizing China than about improving it and profiting from it through the extension of trade and property rights. Even in 1872 Walter Bagehot worried that "war with China might precipitate an internal collapse leaving Britain or a western condominium with the baleful consequences of having to 'manage the country'" (Jones 2001, p. 89).

Hegel's Sinophobia was more systematic than Herder's. Like Voltaire, but to very different effect, Hegel placed China at the beginning of his narrative of world history. In *The Philosophy of Right, Philosophy of Religion*, and *Lectures on the Philosophy of History*, China figured as the primitive stage in the historical unfolding of the world spirit toward freedom and self-consciousness. Hegel's analytical narrative was well served by Montesquieu's portrait of despotism. Equating China with the historical moment at which the sole element of subjectivity or individuality was the emperor himself, Hegel argued that in China, and in the "Eastern nations" more generally, only "*one* is free," namely, the emperor, who was "lord over the . . . world of the mandarins." Chinese religion was deficient because it involved the "primitive element of magical influence over nature" and because it remained fused with the state: "The emperor . . . alone approaches heaven." Chinese religion was thus "essentially State-Religion" and "not what *we* call religion," which requires that man withdraws "from his relation to the State" into a "*free*, spiritual, disinterested consciousness." The distinguishing feature of the "character of the Chinese people" was that "everything which belongs to Spirit . . . is alien to it." The emergence of self-consciousness was stunted because Chinese subjectivity was based on *external* rather than internal morality, on mere compulsion rather than the free disposition of the subject. The Chinese sciences were for Hegel "merely empirical" and "absolutely subservient to the Useful on behalf of the State," lacking the "*free* ground of subjectivity, and that properly scientific interest, which make them a truly theoretical occupation of the mind." Hegel repeated the familiar claim that the Chinese were skilled in "imitation" but not in the arts, again tracing this to their childlike heteronomy as despotic subjects.[195] He derided China for the lack of differentiation between the spheres of law and moral sense, religion, and the state, providing twentieth-century modernization theory with its core conceit. The only respect in which Hegel's vision of China disagreed with Anson and de Pauw was his belief that the Middle Kingdom was not "destined to be . . . conquered and subjugated"—in contrast to India, whose "necessary fate" was "to be subjected to Europeans." China had a crucial, if primordial, role to play in the unfolding of the Idea.[196]

195. Quotes from Hegel 1956, pp. 19, 132, 131, 138, 134, 137; 1984–87, vol. 2, p. 555. Africa, for Hegel, had "no movement or development to exhibit" at all, and was therefore completely external to the movement of human history. The discussion of historical differences in the development of the Idea was thus founded on the formation of races, a process that was said to lie beyond history.

196. Hegel 1956, pp. 115, 142.

The thesis of China's primitiveness or decay had specifically German accents even if the basic lines of argument were familiar. For Herder, Hegel, and Friedrich von Schlegel, China had already played its part in world history. Earlier European visitors had described Chinese politeness as a time-consuming but harmless eccentricity, and for some it was a sign of China's excellence. But in 1800, a neo-Herderian text by linguist Johann Christoph Adelung claimed that China, like France, had forfeited its former cultural excellence by *exceeding* optimal levels of cultivation. This argument was redolent of the romantic juxtaposition between French *civilisation* and German *Kultur* and restated Herder's theory about the life cycles of cultures. Where Christian Wolff had seen Chinese culture as corresponding to a rationality founded in nature, romanticism provided a language for rejecting China as a deviation from nature, as artificially theatrical and mendacious, and therefore as antithetical to self-realization and freedom.

En Route to Qingdao: Speaking of the Devil

Sinophobia became all pervasive with the British-led campaigns to force the Qing emperors to open China to trade and missionaries. German Sinophobia prior to the middle of the nineteenth century, by contrast, was mainly a theoretical affair. The disjuncture between the source of raw materials and the location of its theoretical synthesis did not mean that Germans were entirely absent from the eighteenth-century Chinese coastal trade, however. Merchants from Hamburg, Bremen, and Emden, and others sailing under the Prussian flag, landed trading ships in Canton starting in 1747. Prussia and Hamburg operated consulates there during the late eighteenth and early nineteenth centuries (although these consulates were not actually controlled by Germans until later).[197] The Chinese concessions to Britain after the First Opium War led to increased German trading in China and an even larger increase in German shipping companies working the Europe-China routes and the Chinese coast. In 1849 there were only thirty-three German merchants in China, and just four purely German trading companies.[198] By the early 1860s, after the Second Opium War,

---

197. Stoecker 1958, pp. 37–40; Boehm 1859, p. 194. The first Prussian and Saxon consul in Canton was appointed in 1847 (Ratenhof 1985, p. 30). A map of the European settlements in Canton from 1856 shows the extent of the "German zone" ("Briefe eines jungen China-Deutschen aus den Jahren 1855 bis 1859," *Ostasiatischer Rundschau* 12 (6, 1931): 155.

198. Stoecker 1958, p. 45.

as much as two-thirds of Chinese coastal shipping was controlled by German-owned companies, although the German share declined again after the American Civil War.[199] Some of these Germans tried to gain a larger share of the coastal shipping business by treating Chinese merchants and passengers less brutally than the British.[200] This may be one reason that anti-Chinese literature did not emerge directly from the German mercantile contact zone in the 1850s, but had to wait for the Prussian mission of 1860–62.

THE PRUSSIAN EXPEDITION TO CHINA

The 1860 Peking Convention opened new treaty ports to European trade and habitation, permitted foreigners and missionaries to travel in the interior, and created a framework for foreign powers to open legations in Beijing. The first Prussian expedition to East Asia (1860–62) was led by the former consul general to Warsaw and future interior minister, Count Friedrich zu Eulenburg. His main assignment was to negotiate trade advantages for Prussia, although vague colonial plans were also bruited. In 1861 Eulenburg concluded a separate treaty with China that gave Prussia the same rights as Britain and France.

The accounts written by participants in the Prussian expedition followed British precedent in treating the Chinese as an inferior race and the Chinese state as retrogressive.[201] The first chapter of the official report on the Prussian expedition's arrival in China at Shanghai stuck closely to the thesis of Chinese decadence:

> The impression Shanghai makes of a deep decline is also present to a lesser extent in other Chinese cities. It is as if their civilization had exhausted itself [*als hätte ihre Gesittung sich ausgelebt*]. Everywhere the most extreme negligence and decrepitude is found alongside traces of ancient culture, power, and greatness. . . . As for the contemporary Chinese individual, he has a played-out, self-satisfied, even decrepit and undignified character. . . . Their existence has an empty, prosaic, and masklike character. If you ask local Europeans . . . you will hear

199. Ibid., pp. 43–47; Wätjen 1943, p. 237.
200. Stoecker 1958, p. 48; Wätjen 1943, p. 236.
201. Stoecker 1958, p. 63. On the goals and accomplishments of the expedition, see the official report (Berg 1864–73), and, more recently, B. Martin 1988, 1991. Other contemporary accounts include Spiess 1864; R. Werner [1863] 1873; Kreyher 1863; and Maron 1863.

stories of villainousness, treachery, and calculating cruelty. . . . Almost nowhere is human life worth less than in China.[202]

This account elevated local European merchants to the status of privileged informants. A separate treatment of the expedition by Reinhold Werner, at the time a captain-lieutenant in the Prussian navy, reproduced many of the old chestnuts of merchant-class Sinophobia. Werner claimed to have seen children's corpses washing up onto the shore near Canton. According to Werner "there can hardly be a people that is less attached to the truth than the Chinese. To tell a lie is nothing less than honorable."[203] A merchant who accompanied the expedition, Gustav Spiess, described his encounter with a group of Chinese dignitaries and aristocrats as "a shabby comedy" in which "few of us could suppress a smile when a high Chinese bureaucrat, the former viceroy of the province," appeared on the scene. The Chinese official's retinue reminded Spiess of "clowns at the county fair." Recalling De Quincey's picture of "antediluvian" Chinese youth overpowered by the "vast age of the race," Spiess remarked that the women of Beijing were "prematurely wilted," and he echoed contemporary race theory in his observation that they had "an ugly skin color."[204]

FERDINAND VON RICHTHOFEN

One of the most significant German contributions to an explicitly colonial framing of China in the decades leading up to the annexation of Qingdao was made by the pioneer geographer (and unwitting ethnographer) Baron Ferdinand von Richthofen (fig. 6.7).[205] After taking part in the Prussian East Asia expedition, von Richthofen was active for six years as a geographer in the California gold rush. This period was marked by mounting racism against Chinese workers on the west coast of the United States, and von Richthofen's views of the Chinese seem to have been strongly shaped by these experiences. He believed that the Chinese question would soon replace the "Negro question" in importance in the United States. Von Richthofen returned to China in 1868 and traveled for four years through fifteen of the eighteen provinces, scouting out potential ports and mines for future

202. Berg 1864–73, vol. 3, pp. 385–86.
203. R. Werner [1863] 1873, p. 232.
204. Spiess 1864, pp. 226, 255.
205. On von Richthofen, see X. Liu 1986; Osterhammel 1987; and Engelmann 1988.

FIGURE 6.7 Baron Ferdinand von Richthofen.
From Drygalski 1906.

exploitation and gathering material for his multivolume geographic treatise.[206] Between his return to Germany in 1873 and his death in 1905 von
Richthofen was the most influential China expert in the country. In addition to his activity as rector of the University of Berlin von Richthofen was
a member of the national *Kolonialrat*.[207]

From the very beginning von Richthofen's texts constructed the Chinese
as an inferior subject race. In 1861 von Richthofen "communicated that he
found the country unattractive and that he did not think he could warm to

206. Drygalski 1905.

207. Von Richthofen also played a central role in the Berlin Geographical Society for
three decades, founded the Institute for Oceanic Studies at the University of Berlin, participated in international geographic commissions, taught at Bonn, Leipzig, and Berlin universities, and was elected to the Royal Prussian Academy of Sciences in 1899 (Drygalski 1905). His
most famous publication, the five-volume *China* (1877-1912), remained unfinished at his death
and was completed by others. Tiessen 1906 lists all of von Richthofen's publications.

it."[208] His travel diary from 1868 opens with the statement "I was prepared for disappointments all around." Clearly, he had been primed with Sinophobic ideas.[209] In the introduction to his multivolume work he remarked that China "lacks all of the charms that brighten the days of the traveler in Japan."[210] He referred to the Chinese as natives (*Eingeborenen*) throughout his diaries and publications and systematically contrasted them with the category "white."[211] In one diary entry von Richthofen joked with a European missionary that "his angels must belong to the Caucasian race" and received the answer that "there are not yet any slanty-eyed angels."[212] In a 1898 text von Richthofen discussed the "specific odor that is unique to the [Chinese] race and is only noticed by the foreigner."[213] He berated Chinese men for failing to be "masculine and energetic."[214] And while it has still not been established whether there really was a sign at the public garden on the Shanghai Bund reading "No Dogs or Chinese Allowed!" von Richthofen stated unequivocally that a European could never become truly attached to a Chinese "except in the form of the relation between a master and his dog."[215] The category of "Chinese" in von Richthofen's writings was equated with "servant," "worker," and, increasingly over time, "colonial subject." In 1873 he discussed the problem of not being able to tell one "native" from another, along with other urgent matters in native governance: "When we speak of the Chinese here at home, we imagine a certain picture according to the received images in which the slanted position of the eyes and the queue play a central role. If we then travel to China and the fantasy image transforms itself into a real one, all Chinese indeed look alike to us at first. . . . But if we stay long enough in a single place in China we can begin to make out individual differences. We are able to distinguish our servants and other natives with whom we interact . . . from the millions."[216]

---

208. Drygalski 1905, p. 686.

209. Richthofen 1907, vol. 1, p. 23. The discussion in the following paragraph draws on Osterhammel's (1987) important analysis of these diaries.

210. Richthofen 1877–1912, vol. 1, p. xl.

211. Richthofen 1907, vol. 1, pp. 13, 26, 84, 116–17, 119; 1877–1912, vol. 1, p. xii; 1898, p. 137.

212. Richthofen 1907, vol. 1, p. 136.

213. Richthofen 1898, p. 99. For similar remarks, see Kronecker 1913, p. 1.

214. Richthofen 1871, p. 151.

215. Richthofen 1907, vol. 1, p. 144. According to Fairbank (1986, p. 147) the infamous sign was never actually photographed.

216. Richthofen 1873, p. 37.

Von Richthofen's 1898 book *Shandong and Its Port of Entry Jiaozhou,* written to coincide with the colonial takeover, is a crucial source for reconstructing German views of China at the dawn of colonialism in Kiaochow. It is his only book-length treatment of Chinese culture in general and of Shandong in particular, and the only text he wrote before 1900 for a general audience.[217] It is also the only book published during von Richthofen's lifetime that contains selections from his travel diaries. Because it was published in 1898 it cannot be considered entirely "precolonial"—the colony was founded a year earlier—but it provides a sense of influential German views of China at the onset of the occupation. (The book's role is therefore comparable to Augustin Krämer's *Samoan Islands*). Although the problem of running a colony in China is addressed only in the final pages, von Richthofen included passages from his earlier writings that seemed relevant to problems of colonial management. Indeed, the fact that he did not feel a need to distinguish between "the traveler" and "the colonizer" as the addressee for his advice underscores the colonial impetus of his work, which was ostensibly organized around traveling and geography.

Von Richthofen repeated his opinion that "during all of my voyages I have scorned the idea of descending to the level of the Chinese through . . . a simulation" of their appearance and practices.[218] As Osterhammel notes, von Richthofen described himself as imperiously punishing "immediately on the spot," like a colonial ruler.[219] In an astonishing passage in the 1898 book that drew from his diaries, von Richthofen presented a complete scenario to illustrate the method for maintaining a dominant stance while traveling in China. He began with an uncomfortable situation familiar to readers of such stories.[220] First, the European in China hears the cry "Yang Kwéitsze" (*Yang guizi,* that is, "foreign devil"). Next, perhaps, a "little pea or a small object" is thrown; then "more calls are heard"; and then the small

---

217. Von Richthofen's *Chrysanthemum und Drache* was also written in a popular tone and dealt with the period of the Boxer Rebellion. His five-volume *China* was directed toward a "narrower circle" of academic geographers (Richthofen 1877-1912, vol. 1, p. xi).

218. Richthofen 1898, p. 128. In his diaries von Richthofen objected to the adoption of Chinese manners and clothing by European missionaries as a "descent into the customs of a lower race," insisting that missionaries should "assume a higher standpoint than the native in every respect" (1907, vol. 2, p. 140).

219. Osterhammel 1987, p. 179.

220. Similarly, D. F. Rennie, a member of the British occupation forces in Beijing in 1860, kept a daily journal in which he described Chinese throwing worthless iron cash at the British as they passed and calling out "gui zi" (Rennie 1865, vol. 1, p. 72, quoted in L. Liu 2004, p. 102).

projectiles "get bigger, and soon stones are flying." An *"excess"* of this sort would rarely even get started, however, if one followed this sage advice:

> You sit on your horse, displaying yourself openly, and proceed calmly on your way, apparently indifferent, completely ignoring the mob. Because as soon as the crowd's initial state of bewildered curiosity has given way to the second stage of incipient rage you will already have reached a different location with a new crowd that is still at the first stage. If there is the smallest sign of hostility, however, such as the casting of a pea (which always comes at you from behind), you should wheel around with lightning speed; then you will be able to recognize the perpetrator by the anxious collapse of his facial expression. Punishment should then be carried out immediately. . . . [For me] it was usually enough to leap off the horse, grab the perpetrator by the queue, and give him a swift kick.[221]

If this passage illustrates von Richthofen's affinity for colonial practices of everyday domination, another passage spells out the longer-term goals of European presence in China beyond simple motives of economic profit, toward which von Richthofen always had an ambivalent relationship. Discussing missionaries, von Richthofen recommends that they should seek to transmit not just religion but Western culture itself: "Conversion should recast the person and raise him to a higher level in ways that are also visibly recognizable." This was a rejection of the Jesuits' commitment to changing only those aspects of Chinese culture that directly clashed with Christianity. Von Richthofen's comment that these are "the same conclusions Livingstone reached in Africa" underscores his amalgamation of the Chinese into a generic "native" category.[222]

Von Richthofen's description of Chinese culture was as demeaning as his view of the country's inhabitants, whom he already held "in very low esteem" in 1869.[223] Often he simply repeated familiar formulas. In one article he asserted that China would "not take a single step on its own" and that "any initiative will have to come from outside." Von Richthofen claimed that China had moved from "stasis" to "regression."[224] In an essay

---

221. Richthofen 1898, p. 126–27. Elsewhere von Richthofen specifies that "the method of a jovial treatment" of the natives is "often better than a proud dismissal" (1907, vol. 1, p. 110).

222. Richthofen 1898, p. 220.

223. Richthofen 1907, vol. 1, p. 142; 1870, p. 323.

224. Richthofen 1871, p. 151; 1907, vol. 1, p. 142.

published immediately after his return to Germany he specified that the aim of "European-American civilization" must be to "shake the foundations" of "Chinese culture," awakening the country from its "paralysis" and allowing it "to enter the path of progress once again."[225]

Like many other Europeans and Americans at the time, von Richthofen intended to "open China," that is, to make it useful for Euro-American capitalism and missionary work. He wrote two memoranda to Bismarck in 1868 and 1871 while he was still in China that stressed the urgent need for Germany to acquire a permanent spot in East Asia, and he specifically recommended "Tschusan" (Zhoushan) at the entrance to Hangzhou Bay.[226] Von Richthofen also counseled "improving the means of transportation" (especially railways) and laying telegraph lines to promote the "growth of industry and trade."[227] Although the advantages resulting from the construction of a railway between Europe and China would initially accrue to Russia, Germany would probably be "the second to profit from it." In a previous article von Richthofen had discussed ongoing British and French efforts to penetrate Chinese markets.[228]

Despite his class-derived hesitancy about joining the modern bourgeoisie, von Richthofen had the appropriate vision of the laboring masses. In a book on Shandong and Jiaozhou, von Richthofen devoted an entire section to the "diligence and frugality" of the popular classes. The workers of this region were characterized by their "well-built bodies" and "tough muscles." Ever practical, von Richthofen noted that "the common man amazes us with the amount of work he accomplishes and the length of time he labors" as long as he is "provided with a small supply of food [*bei geringer Zuführung von Nahrung*]." And the "Chinaman is also unsurpassed as a servant or boy," von Richthofen added, since he "cares for the welfare of his lord . . . and fulfills his duties silently and with perfect punctuality."[229]

In the second volume of *China*, published in 1882, von Richthofen called Jiaozhou Bay in Shandong Province the "biggest and best ocean harbor in all of northern China" and added that it would be "especially well suited to supply not only all of Shandong but large parts of the great plain with trade goods."[230] His attention was not yet entirely focused on Shandong, however,

225. Richthofen 1873, pp. 47–48; also 1907, vol. 1, p. 28.
226. Richthofen 1898, pp. 71–72; 1907, vol. 1, p. 44; Engelmann 1988, p. 10.
227. Richthofen 1873, p. 48; 1873–74b, p. 125.
228. Richthofen 1873–74a.
229. Richthofen 1898, pp. 114–15.
230. Richthofen 1877–1912, vol. 2, p. 262.

until the annexation of Kiaochow in 1897. As a member of the *Kolonialrat* von Richthofen participated in the discussions of the colonization of Kiaochow, and he explicitly recommended Hong Kong as a model of a "small but distinguished" colonial state.[231]

Despite a seemingly thoroughgoing colonial approach, however, von Richthofen's writings cannot be described as uniformly Sinophobic. This underscores the continuing multivocality of discourse on China even after the Second Opium War and Japan's military defeat of China in 1895. During the 1870s von Richthofen often referred to China as a "cultural people" (*Kulturvolk*) and a "civilization."[232] Von Richthofen asserted that the Chinese were more educated than peasants in some parts of Europe and praised them as being "highly gifted" and oriented toward practical matters.[233] Von Richthofen seemed to become increasingly appreciative of China's cultural conservatism over time, describing it in 1902 as being preferable to "the character of a people that breaks with all traditions from one day to the next and wants to see everything changed." His 1902 book, written in the wake of the hysterical German and European attacks on China around the Boxer Rebellion, distanced itself from "superficial and mocking judgments . . . arising from an overhasty or completely cursory familiarization with [Chinese] customs and mores."[234]

In addition to these amendments and counterweights to Sinophobia, von Richthofen also identified with a positive image of the Chinese mandarin, like the Jesuits since Ricci and contemporary missionaries like Bishop Anzer (discussed below). His self-descriptions during his China travels were patterned on an image of the Chinese mandarin, as Jürgen Osterhammel points out. Already in 1871 von Richthofen mentioned that he was traveling on the Han River in a "mandarin ship outfitted with every comfort."[235] In a later book he suggested various ways in which German officials posted to China could "retain a distinguished standpoint" and their *"authority as high mandarins."*[236] Von Richthofen's discussion of the technique for managing a hostile crowd suggested ironically that he was "objectively playing the

---

231. Richthofen 1898, p. 266. He did express some skepticism about Western intervention in China, however, likening the West's promotion of Chinese modernization to the "suicidal" creation of a "monster" (1897, p. 32; also 1898, p. 306). Already in 1873–74 von Richthofen had raised the specter of a "flood tide" of Chinese workers moving westward (1873–74b, p. 126).

232. Richthofen 1873–74b, p. 126; 1873, p. 46.

233. Richthofen 1907, vol. 1, p. 65; 1873, p. 46.

234. Richthofen 1902, p. 225, 224.

235. Richthofen 1871, p. 153.

236. Richthofen 1898, p. 128 (my emphasis).

ON THE ROAD FROM T'UNG CHAU TO PEKING.

FIGURE 6.8 Self-portrait of Ferdinand von Richthofen sketched during his China travels. From von Richthofen 1907, vol. I, facing p. 18.

role of a member of the indigenous upper class" (see fig. 6.8).[237] Without assuming that von Richthofen's diaries provide an accurate reproduction of events, his self-representation as a Euro-mandarin is indicative of the power of inherited Sinophilia to structure the imagination even of Europeans whose conscious program was colonialist.

By the time he published his diaries von Richthofen was indeed an educated German "mandarin" in historian Fritz Ringer's sense. Like the meritocratically selected mandarins in the Chinese bureaucracy, this Prussian mandarin was a self-made man, at least according to his own account. He frequently reminded his readers of his difficult years in China spent traveling alone, or accompanied only by a servant. Von Richthofen's six-year sojourn in the United States and his references to his excellent American friends contributed to this image of a modern individualist. Yet von Richthofen was also a scion of the Prussian aristocracy, and his career was profoundly shaped by that social class and its proximity to power. His parents were close to the royal family of Württemberg, and his family belonged to the *Alter Briefadel* (old nobility of patent), second in antiquity and prestige only to the *Uradel* (ancient nobility) among the German nobility. Von Richthofen's inclusion in the Prussian expedition to China resulted from family connections: the

237. Osterhammel 1987, p. 179.

original commander of that mission was his uncle, Emil von Richthofen.[238] The fact that von Richthofen reported directly to Bismarck while traveling in China underscores his insider status. His reports were published in the Berlin Geographical Society's journal and in the prestigious geographic journal *Petermanns Mitteilungen*. Von Richthofen became chairman of the Berlin Geographical Society almost immediately after returning to Europe in 1873.[239] All of this, along with his future role as adviser to the government concerning China and the Kiaochow colony,[240] underscore the extent to which von Richthofen participated in all three of the main fractions of the dominant class in imperial Germany: the aristocracy, the academic elite, and the modern bourgeoisie.[241]

Von Richthofen's partial identification with Chinese elites might seem redundant for a member of Prussia's old elite if it were not for the mounting challenges to the nobility's social preeminence, and perhaps to his own insecure professional future during his youthful years in China and California. Imaginary identifications can be organized around fantasies of *defending* one's social standing as well as fantasies of class exaltation, as we saw with Lothar von Trotha in chapter 3. By the time he had become an established academic mandarin, a different set of motives pushed von Richthofen toward Sinophilia, which was still a marker of ethnographic sagacity and cultural refinement in university and Sinological circles. The lack of unity in von Richthofen's views of China, the combination of critical, laudatory, and identificatory approaches, corresponds to his mixed set of class allegiances and interests, his contradictory class location.[242] Von Richthofen's family origins and his connections with Prussia's political elite and with the business world in Germany, California, and Shanghai pushed him toward the Sinophobia typical of those classes. His associations with academia pulled him toward the Sinophilia that was characteristic of practicing Sinologists

---

238. Engelmann 1988, pp. 7–8; Hampe 2001, p. 182.

239. Drygalski 1905, p. 692.

240. See the 1896 report by von Heyking to Chancellor Hohenlohe referring to von Richthofen's work, reprinted in Leutner 1997, pp. 93–95. Navy pastor Hans Weicker (1908, p. 147) also referred to von Richthofen.

241. Von Richthofen's travels in China between 1868 and 1872 were "financed by the Bank of California during the first year and thereafter by the Shanghai Chamber of Commerce," which "represented British and American business interests" (Osterhammel 1987, p. 170).

242. I am adapting E. O. Wright's (1979) suggestive term to the Bourdieuian understanding of class as a subjective and cultural phenomenon based partly on the distribution of material assets but not reducible to the latter.

and that was once again becoming predominant among the intelligentsia in general at the beginning of the twentieth century.

SINOPHILIA IN NINETEENTH-CENTURY GERMAN SINOLOGY, SINOSCOPIA, AND RELATED FIELDS

Between the late eighteenth and the mid-nineteenth centuries most German intellectuals had shifted toward Sinophobia, as exemplified by Hegel. This partly reflected the temporary class alliance between the German *Bildungsbürgertum* and the commercial and industrial bourgeoisie against the aristocracy and monarchy at that time. During the last decades of the nineteenth century, however, the economic bourgeoisie emerged as the dominant fraction of the dominant class in German society. One response among German academics to this altered force field was the emergence of attitudes—including attitudes toward non-Western cultures—that promised to distinguish *Bildungsbürger* from both the older nobility and the modern business elites.

Indeed, professional German Sinology, though a tiny and marginal field, remained committed to Sinophilia throughout the nineteenth century. The pioneering Chinese historian Johann Heinrich Plath contributed an essay entitled "China and the Chinese" to the *Deutsches Staats-Wörterbuch* in 1857 that summarized various Chinese "discoveries in which the Chinese preceded the Europeans." He argued explicitly against the despotism thesis, observing that "if anything, one might speak of a despotism of laws" but not of an unconstrained emperor. And he rejected the "huge prejudice that Chinese history shows no progress or development."[243] In other books and articles Plath relied on Chinese sources to investigate ancient Chinese history.[244] The writings of the Berlin University Orientalist Wilhelm Schott in midcentury showed a great appreciation for Chinese philosophy and literature. One of Schott's stated goals was to correct the "peculiar and absurd opinions about the Chinese" that were common at the time, even if he agreed with the protoimperialists that China could be shaken out of its current paralysis only by Europeans and attributed these shortcomings partly to "race."[245] Schott's successor at the University of Berlin in 1889, Georg

---

243. Plath 1857, pp. 441, 450, 463.

244. E.g., Plath 1864, 1869. On Plath, see the excellent short biography by H. Franke (1960).

245. W. Schott 1826–32, vol. I, p. v, quoted in Leutner 1987, p. 33; See also W. Schott 1830; 1857.

von der Gabelentz, published a translation of a Chinese novel in *Globus* in 1863 and a short book, *Confucius and His Teachings,* in 1888. Von der Gabelentz believed that "the largest cultural people of the Orient is also the most often defamed." Arguing against the idea of "stagnation," he insisted that Europeans should "not apply our own measures were they are least appropriate."[246] Wilhelm Grube, another Berlin professor, argued against the thesis associated with Sinologist Jan Jakob de Groot of Leiden and later Berlin University that "the massacres of Christians in China were due to religious fanaticism." Grube insisted instead on "tolerance" as the defining characteristic of Chinese religious culture and added that "anyone who has firsthand experience in China and has seen the way foreigners behave toward the locals . . . will unfortunately have to admit that the xenophobia found throughout the empire is not completely unfounded and therefore not fully unjustified."[247] Sinologist Otto Franke, who played an important role in German Kiaochow, learned Chinese from Wilhelm Grube, and like his teacher he came to disparage Europeans who believed in the "yellow peril."[248] Many of the instructors and students at Berlin University's Seminar for Oriental Languages, which first offered courses in 1887, stood in this Sinophile tradition (see chap. 7).

Sinoscopic Germans in other fields contributed to the persistence of Sinophilia. Gustav Klemm, director of the Royal Library in Dresden and author of the ten-volume *Cultural History of Mankind,* defended China's "wonderful form of government, wise laws, advanced moral institutions, in sum, its unique culture" in 1847. Klemm concluded his study on an anti-imperialist note, observing that the Chinese were justified in viewing Europeans as barbarians in the wake of the First Opium War (1839–42) and that it was no longer the Manchus who threatened China but "Christian Germanic Europe, namely, England."[249]

MAX WEBER'S EXCEPTIONAL RACISM

There were exceptions to this prevailing academic Sinophila, of course, and one of the most striking examples was sociologist Max Weber. It is well established that Weber's views of Poles were crudely racist.[250] Less obvious is

246. Gabelentz 1888, pp. 2–4. He also rejected the argument that Chinese was a primitive language (Leutner 1987, p. 35).

247. Grube 1910, pp. 11, 5. Ku Hung-Ming (1901, p. 21), discussed in the next chapter, had already polemicized against the European interpretation of the Yihetuan as "fanatics."

248. O. Franke 1911a, p. vi.

249. Klemm 1847, pp. ii, 510.

250. Zimmerman 2006.

his willful and somewhat eccentric Sinophobia. Weber's *Religion of China* was structured around the premise of Chinese economic stagnation, which he explained in terms of shortcomings of Chinese values or national culture. He drew most heavily on the writings of Jan de Groot, who considered the Chinese to be "semi-civilized" and prone to religious "fanaticism."[251] Weber was ignorant of the growth of Chinese capitalism in the late nineteenth century, including in the region around the future German colony in Shandong Province.[252] He also ignored the fettering impact of Western imperialism on Chinese capitalism and of British opium on the Chinese work ethic. Weber accepted de Groot's sweeping assertion that Confucianism was oriented toward "adjustment to the world" rather than "rational transformation of the world" in ways that prevented the emergence of "those great and methodical business conceptions which are rational in nature."[253] Weber's views demonstrate that class position alone did not determine ethnographic postures.

CATHOLIC MISSIONARIES IN SHANDONG IN THE LATE NINETEENTH CENTURY

Another example of unexpected ambivalence and multivocality in the midst of ostensible Sinophobia concerns the German Catholic Steyl Mission (Societas verbum divini, or SVD), which became active in southern Shandong Province during the 1880s. The mission played a central role in ratcheting up tensions between China and Europe and contributed in no small part to sparking the anti-Christian Dadao hui (Big Sword Society) and its successor, the Yihetuan (Boxer) movement.[254] The Bavarian Steyl missionary Johann Baptist Anzer arrived in Shandong in 1880 and was soon joined by missionary Joseph Freinademetz. The Steyl Mission seems at first glance to have been monolithically committed to Sinophobia. Anzer's stated goal was to achieve a "deep humiliation of Chinese pride." The SVD missionaries described China as an "empire of Satan" where "the devil's domain is far greater than in the Christian countries."[255] They summarized the Chinese

---

251. De Groot 1892, p. x.

252. Mühlhahn 2000.

253. M. Weber 1964, pp. 240, 242. Weber's mistake may reveal the dangers to historical sociology of relying too heavily on secondary sources, but even more damaging is the extreme selectivity in his use of sources.

254. Gründer 1982, p. 288; Esherick 1987, pp. 8off.; Schrecker 1971, p. 33; Kuepers 1974. For an overview of missions in Shandong on the eve of German colonization see Richthofen 1898, chap. 6; Stenz 1899 is the best firsthand missionary account.

255. Missionaries Richard Henle and Anton Wewel, quoted by Mühlhahn (2000, p. 331), who gives a number of similar quotes from Steyl missionary reports.

as "yellow slaves of . . . ancient customs" and of a "despotic bureaucracy."[256] After arriving in Shandong, Anzer immediately focused his attention on establishing a mission residence in Yanzhou, the city where Confucius had lived and that was revered by the Chinese. For Anzer Yanzhou was a "bulwark of the devil."[257] Stenz called Yanzhou the "Chinese Mecca, the bulwark of all pagans."[258] According to the German legation secretary, Baron Speck von Sternburg, Yanzhou was the "only place in China aside from Hunan Province where missionaries [had] not yet been able to establish themselves."[259] Chinese resistance to Anzer's provocations was fierce and lasted for years. In 1890 the German *Gesandter,* or envoy, to China, Max von Brandt, succeeded in getting China and France to recognize Germany as the protector of the German missionaries, and in 1891 the Germans used this pretext to stage an aggressive confrontation by the German consul in Tianjin, Baron von Seckendorff, with the Shandong governor in Ji'nan and the Daotai (circuit intendant) of Yanzhou.[260] This was just the first in a series of egregious interventions coordinated by Anzer and his coworkers in the province. Anzer repeatedly urged the German legation in Beijing and the Foreign Office in Berlin to use German navy warships to pressure the Chinese into letting the missionaries into Yanzhou. He finally succeeded in 1896 and set up a seminar for priests there.[261] According to Joseph Esherick, the Steyl missionaries created a parallel political structure in Shandong "which could stand over and against the Chinese polity, as an alternative authority system and indeed a rival for political power."[262] Missionaries intervened before local Chinese magistrates on the side of Chinese Christians in lawsuits. Their actions finally provoked the "Juye incident," the murder of two Steyl missionaries on November 1, 1897, by alleged members of the Dadao hui. This provided Germany

256. *Annalen der Verbreitung des Glaubens* 67 (1899): 30-31.

257. Anzer, quoted in Rivinius 1979, p. 90 n. 8. Yanzhou was the county seat; nearby Qufu was the birthplace of Confucius and the site of the Confucian temple.

258. Stenz 1899, p. 28.

259. Speck von Sternburg 1979, p. 114, report from Puoli, headquarters of the Steyl Mission in Southern Shandong, November 16, 1895.

260. Stoecker 1958, pp. 250-52. The protection of foreign missionaries in China by foreign powers was one dimension of the humiliating policy of extraterritoriality practiced by Europeans until after World War II. The Beijing *Gesandter* was at the top of the German diplomatic hierarchy in China; Germany was also represented by consuls in several cities and had a general consul in Shanghai. Germany first sent an ambassador (*Botschafter*) to China in 1931.

261. Rivinius 1987, pp. 449-456.

262. Esherick 1987, p. 85.

with its excuse for intervening militarily in the province and seizing Qingdao.[263]

Despite this onslaught of epithets and aggression, the Steyl missionaries also "criticized prejudices and discriminations" against the Chinese.[264] Missionary Rudolph Pieper insisted that the Chinese were a "people with an autonomous [selbsteigene] culture" that should not be "underestimated according to European standards."[265] Many of the Steyl missionaries, who tended to come from simple agrarian backgrounds, were attracted to China in ways they did not openly admit. Georg Stenz claimed that wearing Chinese clothing was necessary to avoid being abused by people on the street (though he admitted that the Chinese still "recognized us immediately as Europeans"), and he called this masquerade a "theater."[266] The missionaries always posed in Chinese clothing, even for European portraits.[267] As travelers like von Richthofen noted, Catholic missionaries in Shandong were completely embedded within Chinese material culture (even though some of the Franciscans he met could not speak or read Chinese).[268] The counterexample of the Rhenish missionaries in precolonial Southwest Africa demonstrates that such complete assimilation into local sartorial norms was not an automatic feature of the contact zone (fig. 6.9).

Despite his apparent hostility to the Chinese state, Bishop Anzer wore Chinese clothing from the moment he arrived in China, spoke Chinese, ate Chinese food, and adopted other elements of a Chinese lifestyle. And he strove successfully to move upward within the official Chinese bureaucratic hierarchy. In 1892 Anzer was promoted to the rank of third-class mandarin by the Daotai of Zhou Xian, the birthplace of Mencius. According to von Richthofen, this was the first time in two hundred years that a foreign missionary had been promoted to this rank. Three years later Anzer was promoted to second-class mandarin status.[269] This "brought him numerous privileges," including the title "Excellence" and "the use of the green state

263. On the Juye incident see Stenz 1899, pp. 72–76; Kuepers 1974, pp. 139–40; Schrecker 1971, p. 33; and Esherick 1987, p. 126.

264. Mühlhahn 2000, p. 332.

265. Pieper 1900, p. 9.

266. Stenz 1899, p. 11. The Catholic Church in Shandong "came to adopt more and more of the trappings of the Chinese bureaucratic state in the effort to legitimize its own authority" (Esherick 1987, p. 84). Yet the missionaries' adoption of Chinese accoutrements and honors often seemed to exceed what would have been necessary for legitimation in the eyes of the Chinese.

267. In addition to the numerous photos of Anzer in his mandarin outfit, all of the missionaries depicted in Stenz 1899 are wearing Chinese clothing.

268. Richthofen 1898, pp. 212–20.

269. Richthofen 1898, p. 225; see also Rivinius 1979, pp. 30–33.

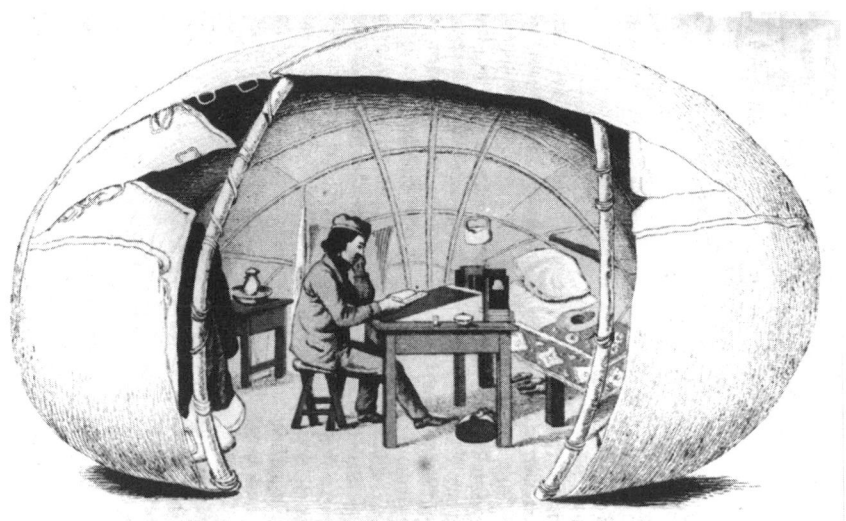

FIGURE 6.9 Rhenish missionary in his Southwest African "mat house," with European furniture and wearing European clothing. From *Berichte der Rheinischen Missionsgesellschaft*, October 1853.

sedan chair with a retinue of ten riders and bearers of his insignia."[270] Finally, in 1902, Anzer ascended to the level of first-class mandarin. He was assisted in his ascent by von Brandt, the long-serving German envoy to Beijing.[271] Anzer wore his mandarin costume for official photographs and crafted a hybrid image with Catholic and Chinese regalia, while Joseph Freinademetz, the cofounder with Anzer of the Steyl mission in Shandong, stuck to a more strictly Chinese image (figs. 6.10, 6.11). Anzer's letters suggest that he was concerned with gaining respectability in the eyes not only of German elites but of Chinese ones as well. In a letter from 1894 to a missionary journal, Anzer announced that he had received "the red button of rank" from the Chinese emperor himself and added that "the announcement of this advancement in status made a very *favorable impression on the mandarins* and *literati*."[272] He described himself proudly, in another European religious publication, as a "mandarin of the second degree."[273] Anzer also followed

270. Gründer 1982, p. 288.

271. Brandt 1901, vol. 3, p. 77. Von Brandt was envoy to China from 1875 to 1893.

272. "Schreiben des Hochwürdigsten Herrn apostolischen Vikars und Bischofs Johann Baptist Anzer von Süd-Schantung an den Geschäftsführer des Ludwig-Mission-Vereines in München," *Annalen der Verbreitung des Glaubens* 33 (1895): 25 (my emphasis).

273. Quoted in Rivinius 1979, p. 92.

FIGURE 6.10 (above) Missionary Johann Baptist Anzer in hybrid Chinese mandarin and European Catholic costume. From Gründer 1982, fig. 33. (Courtesy of Ferdinand Schöningh Verlag.)

FIGURE 6.11 (right) Missionary Joseph Freinademetz. From Stenz 1924, p. 19.

the classic Jesuit strategy of using the texts of Confucius and Mencius with his Chinese students as the basis "for the construction of the Christian religion" and for raising his pupils "according to Chinese customs."[274]

Like von Richthofen, Anzer's discourse on China was far from univocal. His case also illustrates again the ways images of non-European cultures could be used in projects of accumulating symbolic capital and pursuing imaginary identifications. Anzer's specific use of China differed from von Richthofen's, however, due in part to the missionary's humbler social origins and his distinctive social class dilemma. Anzer's father had been an impoverished peasant and butcher.[275] Other missionaries described Anzer as authoritarian and awkward. His heavy drinking was a topic of intrigue among the missionaries he supervised.[276] As an arrivé even within the rela-

274. German envoy to China Speck von Sternburg, report of November 16, 1895, on the Steyl Mission, to chancellor, in Rivinius 1979, pp. 123, 129.

275. Kuepers 1974, p. 21 n. 1.

276. Rivinius 1979 describes the conflicts around Anzer.

tively modest world of the overseas missionaries, Anzer was poorly positioned to assert the distinctive ethnographic virtues of the scholar class. In his search for symbolically recognizable status Anzer therefore gravitated toward the Sinophobic codes that were associated with the German capitalist and aristocratic classes. At the same time, he tried to cultivate an image as a scholar-missionary, as is suggested by his eager accumulation of Chinese honors and titles and his adoption of other signifiers of the Jesuits' "good" China, such as reliance on the Chinese classics.[277] Anzer's Janus-faced relationship to China was only possible due to the multifaceted structure of extant European discourse on Chinese culture.

Multivocality in German Representations of China at the End of the Nineteenth Century

A recent study of colonialism in Kiaochow suggests that precolonial German representations of China were so uniformly "ethnocentric" that they prevented the Germans from "adequately grasping the complex reality of China."[278] But while German views of China were indeed "inadequate," they were far from homogeneous, even in the years immediately preceding the occupation of Jiaozhou and the Boxer uprising. Even von Richthofen and Anzer, men who contributed directly to the conquest of Kiaochow and who could therefore be expected to exhibit a hostile, seamlessly colonialist view of China, revealed a deeper level of respect for China almost despite themselves. If early colonial planners in German Kiaochow drew exclusively from the harshest strands of Sinophobia, this was a selective appropriation and not an inexorable result of the cultural conditions of possibility.

A perusal of the major German encyclopedias, anthropological, geographic, and travel journals, and of certain novels and popular magazines reveals that China continued to be represented as an advanced civilization throughout the nineteenth century, or to be granted a sort of junior status among the civilized nations.[279] The ethnological and anthropological journal *Globus* repeatedly described the Chinese as a *Kulturvolk* that ranked "just behind the Europeans in the scale of intellectual development," in the

277. Anzer also strove to accumulate honors in European fields. He occupied the dual roles of *Provinzial* (administrator) and bishop in China and referred frequently to the "Council of Trent, which had decreed that bishops were *princes* of the church." He also emphasized that he was "highly regarded and befriended in Rome and Berlin" (Rivinius 1979, pp. 41–42; my emphasis).

278. Mühlhahn 2000, p. 180.

279. For a list of the journals examined see the bibliography.

words of its editor.[280] Another *Globus* article argued that there were three races in China—black, brown, and yellow—and that the yellow Chinese in this context civilized their own black and brown "savage" neighbors just like the Europeans civilized their own racial inferiors.[281]

The multivocality of discourse on China allowed writers to reverse their evaluations from one text to the next. One of the most striking examples of a 180-degree turnaround is presented by Karl May. His first two novels on China were permeated by the familiar negative tropes of eighteenth- and nineteenth-century Sinophobia. The second and best-known of these novels, *Der blaurote Methusalem* (1889), is the story of a German university student and fraternity member who travels through China having various adventures. He is promoted to the highest level in the mandarin bureaucracy without even having to study for the examination. While this might be interpreted as little more than the wishful fantasy of a lazy student, the fact that the same narreme also shows up in May's first China novel, *Der Kiang Lu* (1880),[282] and that it is accompanied by criticisms of the Chinese mandarinate, suggests that there is more at stake. The most disturbing passage in *Der blaurote Methusalem* builds a catalog of negative racial and cultural characteristics from an observation of Chinese children: "A nation is easily judged by the activities of its universe of children. Play is the child's work. But how does the Chinese child play? . . . Where can we see the rosy cheeks and the flashing eyes, where can we hear the children's happy high-toned jubilation? Almost nowhere! The Chinese boy steps out of his house slowly and pensively, looks around like an old man, walks without the slightest spring in his step to the playground, and then ruminates on how he is going to occupy himself. . . . *Everything is elderly.*" The author then advances to a general conclusion: "Like the elderly person . . . the Chinaman is not easily moved to adopt the views of others. . . . The changes that have appeared in recent years have either been forced on him or else he has only accepted them for selfish reasons."[283] Just nine years later, however, in the wake of the Boxer Rebellion, May radically altered his view of China. The narrator of *Et*

280. Karl Andree, "Die Veränderung in der gegenseitigen Stellung der Menschenracen und die wirtschaftlichen Verhältnisse," *Globus* 14 (1868): 20.

281. Garnier 1875, pp. 337–38. Gustav Fritsch (1880, p. 293) asked rhetorically "how an anthropological colloquium would react if I suggested calling the Germanic nation the European-Chinese [*Europa-Chinesen*]," and he continued that "the European is closer to the Chinaman than the Bushman is to the Kaffir."

282. *Der Kiang Lu* was first published in 1880 and appeared again in May's collection *Am stillen Ozean* (1894); see May [1894] 1954, chap. 7.

283. May 1889, pp. 194–95.

in terra pax begins his Chinese journey with a self-reflexive passage about prejudices preventing travelers from making anything but the most superficial observations. The racism of two missionaries is portrayed as a form of mental illness.[284]

In other examples from this period representations of China fluctuate within individual texts. Books that set out to criticize or debunk Chinese culture are infused with elements that undercut their intended message. For example, the nineteenth-century German anthropologist Oscar Peschel argued at one point in his *Races of Man* (*Völkerkunde*) that the Chinese had "progressively improved their condition," but he insisted several pages later that "it is everywhere noticeable that the Chinese do not advance beyond a certain grade of intellectual development."[285] Just a few years earlier, Peschel had argued that the Chinese were actually superior to Europeans since they had developed their culture in isolation and despite a poor natural environment.[286] German missionaries and explorers who struck an arrogant colonial stance toward the Chinese unwittingly found that their self-presentation was permeated by gestures and signifiers suggesting admiration and rapprochement. Writings on China were quite distinct in this respect from most texts on Southern Africans or Samoans, which tended to be less ideologically fractured.

EFFI BRIEST: A CHINA CABINET

The most extreme proliferation of disparate interpretations and uses of "China" within a single text comes from one of the most famous German novels of the nineteenth century, *Effi Briest* (1894). Initially, the "Chinaman" in Fontane's novel suggests a generalized object of desire. His first

284. The first edition of *Et in terra pax* appeared in Kürschner's *China* (1901), a glossy three-volume collection.

285. Peschel 1876, pp. 362, 374.

286. Peschel 1867, pp. 916–17. An even more peculiar case is the 1903 novel *Hung Li Tscheng oder der Drache am gelben Meer* by youth writer Friedrich Meister, who had translated James Fenimore Cooper and written a novel about the 1904 war in Southwest Africa (F. Meister 1904). In a preface to *Hung Li Tscheng* dated September 1900—written, that is, in the midst of the European campaign against the Boxers—Meister describes the Chinese as "perhaps the most gifted people on earth." China "possessed a relatively advanced culture five thousand years ago, and has continued to progress from this basis, slowly but surely, ever since," while Europe had developed only during the past 250 years (F. Meister 1903, p. iv). He admits that this image of steady progress flies directly in the face of the fashionable view of China as a "backward, degenerate people, with few positive sides and which must be forcibly taught European culture" (F. Meister 1903, p. iii).

appearance is as an actual historical figure who had previously lived in the provincial German town where young Effi, recently married, has settled with her husband, Baron Geert von Innstetten. The nameless Chinese figure is rumored to have violated a social-sexual taboo by falling in love with the granddaughter of the captain who brought him back from the Far East as a servant. Like the town's historical Chinaman, Effi crosses a "racial" boundary herself by taking up with Crampas, a dark-haired, romantic "ladies' man." According to Innstetten, Crampas is "one of these half Poles, unreliable, and not to be trusted in anything, particularly with women."[287] It may seem paradoxical that China could stand for a sexually charged difference, since sexuality had never been a central aspect of European representations of China. One might conclude that China is being linked through a chain of associations to the rest of the Orient, including the Near East, with its more explicitly sexualized connotations.[288] Samuel Taylor Coleridge's "Xanadu pleasure-dome" illustrates one of the ways China had been brought into this chain. Even more important than such specific connotations, however, is China's role as the inversion or subversion of everything familiar, just as desire is the inversion or subversion of the symbolic order. As Effi remarks at one point, "There's a whole new world to discover," with "all sorts of exotic people," including "perhaps a Negro or a Turk or perhaps even a Chinaman."[289] With its suggestions of radical alterity, China can be linked to sexual desire as a sign of the Lacanian *objet petit a*, the generalized object of desire.

The evolving portrayal of China within European discourse more broadly is echoed in the novel's narrative trajectory. After all, China also stood for radical difference within Sinophobia, but here alterity had a negative valence. By the same token, after figuring first as the "exotic" and erotic, the novel's Chinaman shifts meaning and appears increasingly as a spectral "means of education" (in Crampas' words) mobilized by Innstetten for disciplining his young bride.[290] This pedagogical ghost is introduced into the couple's "haunted house" via a tiny picture stuck to the back of a chair, a picture of a Chinaman. Here the signifier "China" begins to concentrate the punishing, authoritarian patriarchy personified by Effi's husband. Indeed, Instetten is associated with the most stifling aspects of Prussian bureau-

---

287. Fontane [1894] 1967, pp. 137, 138. I developed my analysis of this novel in discussions with Julia Hell. Fontane himself called the Chinaman "a pivot" of the novel (Greenberg 1988: 773).

288. Alloula 1986; Said 1978; Ackerman 1986.

289. Fontane [1894] 1967, p. 48.

290. Ibid., p. 126.

cratic culture, which at the time of Fontane's writing was being dissected by liberals as an expression of semidespotic "eastern" Junkerdom.[291] This evocation of Oriental despotism is heightened by a suggestion of Chinese footbinding. Soon after her wedding Effi begins to take long walks because "her doctor had told her that a lot of exercise in the fresh air was the best thing she could have" in her pregnant condition. Some time later she uses the same excuse to take long walks alone, "undeterred by any unpleasant weather," and especially "in the afternoons, when Innstetten [is] starting to become engrossed in his newspapers," and when her lover Crampas is in town.[292] For centuries European observers had explained footbinding as a strategy used by Chinese men to limit their wives' mobility. As the Jesuit Trigault had written, "probably one of their sages hit upon this idea to keep them in the house."[293] The educating Chinaman is thus not only a Prussian-Oriental despot but one whose energies are aimed specifically at curtailing women's wandering.

At a third level, Fontane taps into a fount of Sinophobia that was omnipresent in his day, specifically the theme of decay. By the late nineteenth century, racial and eugenic sciences had elaborated the topic of degeneracy in ways that linked the "extinction of the primitive peoples" and the ruination of China to the enfeeblement of modern Europeans, psychic disturbances and voluptuousness.[294] In the context of broader discussions of degeneracy, China's status as the leading example of a declining civilization allowed the Chinaman in Fontane's novel to forge a connection between sexual transgression and death. Effi suffers a social death of ostracism, driven out of polite society, when her husband discovers her affair with Crampas. Her fate is the same as the Chinaman's, who "could easily have been buried in the Christian cemetery," according to the local pastor, but who in fact "naturally . . . couldn't be buried in the municipal cemetery" at all, as Innstetten insists. Instead, Effi writes in a letter, the Chinaman "is buried in a lonely spot next to the cemetery."[295] And at the end of the novel, the adultress herself is buried outside the Christian graveyard, in her parents' garden.

The narrative development of *Effi Briest* thus neatly mirrors the evolution of European discourse on China from the Middle Ages to the end of the nineteenth century. Fontane not only draws on the full register of Sino-

---

291. E.g., M. Weber [1895] 1989.
292. Fontane [1894] 1967, pp. 104, 161, 158.
293. Trigault and Ricci [1615] 1953, p. 77.
294. Santner 1996, pp. 6–9.
295. Fontane [1894] 1967, pp. 84, 82, 97.

philic and Sinophobic ideologemes but presents them in the same order as their historical development. The initial fascination with exotic-erotic discovery is overtaken by the frozen stranglehold of despotism, which eventually gives way to stagnation, illness and death.

Toward "German-China"

Despite the perduring multivocality of German discourse about China, colonial and racist representations reached a sort of crescendo in the last years of the century. In 1869 the Prussian navy opened its first East Asian station. Around the same time German politicians, academic specialists, and traders began to press for a territorial base on the Chinese coast. As one colonial propagandist put it in the 1860s, the goal was a "German Macao or Hong Kong."[296] This agitation did not let up until Germany annexed Kiaochow. German envoy Max von Brandt argued in 1872 that Germany should seek a permanent place of its own in China, and that this colony could be acquired "either by purchase or by violence"—both methods were acceptable.[297] German trade with China increased rapidly, and after the Sino-French war (1883–85) Germany became the main exporter of weapons to China.[298] Von Brandt's successor as German envoy, Baron Schenk zu Schweinsberg, advised the Germans to seize Jiaozhou Bay in 1894.[299] China's defeat in the first Sino-Japanese War led the Western powers to see China as even weaker than they had previously believed, and made some Chinese leaders more willing to bend to European demands in exchange for military and economic assistance.

In 1894, the first year of the Sino-Japanese War, Kaiser Wilhelm insisted that if Russia, France, and Great Britain attained "important points in China," "under no circumstances could Germany come up short." During the next three years Germany continually pressured China for a "firm spot" on the coast.[300] In 1895 Wilhelm II produced a crude drawing of a city in flames with clouds of smoke taking the form of an Asiatic dragon and a Buddha, facing off against a group of allegorical female figures

296. Friedel 1867, p. 62. See also Bastian 1871.

297. Brandt 1901, vol. 3, p. 326.

298. Stoecker 1958, p. 211.

299. Schenck to Hohenlohe, November 23, 1894, in Lepsius, Mendelssohn Bartholdy, and Thimme 1922–27, vol. 9, no. 2221, p. 248.

300. Memo from Chancellor Hohenlohe to Foreign Secretary von Marschall of November 11, 1894, in Lepsius, Mendelssohn Bartholdy, and Thimme 1922–27, vol. 9, no. 2219, pp. 245–46.

representing the various European nations (fig. 6.12).[301] The "court" painter Hermann Knackfuß turned Wilhelm's sketch into a lithograph (fig. 6.13) that was officially presented to the Russian tsar in a "special mission" by Generaladjutant and Oberst Helmuth von Moltke.[302] Here the female figure leading the European nations has been turned into a male "war cherub" or St. Michael, the patron saint of the German nation. Although Kaiser Wilhelm did not coin the phrase "yellow peril," as he boasted, his drawing is nonetheless evocative.[303]

Baron Edmund von Heyking arrived in Beijing to replace Schenk zu Schweinsberg as German envoy in 1896. He was accompanied by his wife, Baroness Elisabeth von Heyking. The von Heykings stayed in China until the end of 1899, presiding over the German invasion of Qingdao and experiencing the beginnings of the Boxer uprising. In a memo to the chancellor in August 1896 Edmund argued vigorously for seizing Qingdao and suggested using an incident with German missionaries as a pretext—precisely the scenario that was followed in 1897.[304] He led the negotiations with China over the modalities of the German occupation.

Elisabeth von Heyking's diaries from this period convey a vivid sense of the noxious tone of German anti-Chinese racism in the final years of the century.[305] She approvingly quoted an American official in China who told her that the Chinese are "only fit to be sliced up by the different powers." It did not even occur to the von Heykings to try to learn some of the local language. Instead, Elisbeth's diary criticized the Chinese for being unable to "speak a European language passably." Edmund von Heyking described the Chinese ministers of the Zongli Yamen (Foreign Office) as "all complete

301. Gollwitzer 1962, pp. 42, 206.

302. Ibid., p. 207; Moltke 1922, pp. 190–91. Von Moltke described the leading figure in the version presented to the Russian tsar as a "Cherub des Krieges" (war cherub; Moltke 1922, p. 191).

303. The German anti-Semitic press compared Chinese and Jews starting in 1882 (Gollwitzer 1962, pp. 174ff.).

304. Von Heyking to chancellor, Beijing, August 22, 1896, BA-MA-Freiburg, RMA, vol. 6693, pp. 27–29.

305. In addition to the epigraph to this chapter see also Heyking 1926, pp. 207, 215, for other uses of the word *Barbaren* (barbarians) to describe the Chinese. Elisabeth von Heyking was the granddaughter of Bettina von Arnim, one of the most famous women in German letters and the author of many romantic novels. Von Heyking's epistolary novel *Briefe, die ihn nicht erreichten* (1903) was translated into English and was said to have sold ten million copies before World War I (Ruland 1973, p. 64). Her novel *Tschun: Eine Geschichte aus dem Vorfrühling Chinas* (1914) was based on her Beijing diaries.

FIGURE 6.12 (top) Kaiser Wilhelm II, *People of Europe, Defend Your Most Sacred Treasures:* sketch of Europe defending itself against the "yellow peril" (April 30, 1895). (Courtesy of Stichting Huis Doorn, the Netherlands.)

FIGURE 6.13 (bottom) Hermann Knackfuss, *People of Europe, Defend Your Most Sacred Treasures* (1895). (Courtesy of Stichting Huis Doorn, the Netherlands.)

idiots" and "forbidding, staring masks" (abschreckende stiere Larven).[306] The aristocratic couple was proud of its exalted social status and apparently felt no need to identify across cultural boundaries with an imago of the Chinese mandarin. Nor did they feel obliged to display any specialized knowledge of China or any of the other non-European societies to which the Foreign Office posted them. Indeed, the Sinologist Otto Franke, who acted as interpreter during the Chinese-German negotiations over the annexation of Kiaochow, recalled later that the Baron and the Baroness had adopted an extremely high-handed manner with the Chinese, whom they regarded as "dirty, cowardly, retarded, and disgusting." According to Franke, they saw any interest in Chinese culture as a sign of a "subaltern mentality."[307]

Transition

The broad transition from Sinomania to Sinophobia masks a great deal of continuity and heterogeneity. Only the case of the Khoikhoi, among the other ethnographic formations examined in this book, comes close to the Chinese material in terms of complexity and unsettledness. If the kaiser's "yellow peril" hysteria dominated German discussions of China at the end of the nineteenth century, the formation of discourse on China on the eve of colonial annexation was still extremely multivocal. The layeredness of this discourse had crucial implications for German colonial practice in Qingdao.

Even the condemnatory strands of discourse on China were distinctive in ways that mattered for colonial policy. First, Sinophobia was always haunted by Sinophilia. Sinophile tropes bore the traces of the perspective against which they had originally been directed. Even a negatively coded trope like despotism carried a shadow of the same object, positively cathected—in this case, of the benevolent Chinese state. This is different from dominant perceptions of the Samoans or Ovaherero on the eve of colonization: in the first case the earliest "ignoble savagery" perspective was almost entirely forgotten by the late nineteenth century and the earlier Tahitian precedents had greater influence; within the second discursive formation there was almost no variation in meaning at all.

We have seen in the two earlier discussions that the details of precolonial ethnographic formations shaped the strategies of native policy that were recommended and eventually implemented. The theme of Chinese despotism, intellectual arrogance, and civilizational decline delineated a subject

306. Baron von Heyking quoted in Löbbecke 1982, document 99, p. 234; and in Heyking 1926, pp. 199, 204, 191.

307. O. Franke 1954, p. 98.

population that remained firmly in the grip of a powerful and ancient culture. The country's perceived cultural stability directed colonizers away from projects of fundamentally recasting their subjects or "shaking the foundations" of their culture (despite von Richthofen's recommendations). Europeans recognized that Britain had needed to fight two wars just to get the Chinese to abstain from referring to foreigners with the ideogram they believed signified "barbarian."[308] The combined and mutually reinforcing power of the intact Chinese state, a self-conscious scholarly class, and a relatively homogenous elite culture anchored in canonical texts meant that the German colonizers did not even consider trying to transform their Chinese subjects. The training of Chinese apprentices for work in the German railways, mines, and shipyards was not accompanied by any official suggestion that the goal was to inculcate a modern work ethic, since not even the Sinophobic theorists had accused the Chinese of laziness. After 1905 or so there was a broad German effort to insinuate elements of German culture into China, but this was not conceptualized along the lines of transforming and governing an entire culture. Instead, this was a *noncolonial* (though perhaps imperial) program aimed at China as a whole rather than being concentrated in the Kiaochow colony. The goal was to add a specifically German accent to the process of "modernization/Westernization" that was proceeding apace in China as a whole, and not just in the colonial enclaves. In the eyes of German nationalists, Chinese modernity was being given an overwhelmingly British (and French and American) stamp, threatening to shut Germany out in a much more fundamental way than the earlier lack of colonies. Any project of Germanizing the tiny number of Chinese that lived in Kiaochow seemed to these German nationalists to overlook the more significant cultural battle. The idea of influencing the Chinese did, therefore, gain adherents, but it pointed away from colonialism.

Another aspect of precolonial discourse that constrained future colonial practice was the fact that China was not usually configured as Europe's ancestral cousin. This was one respect in which China was distinguished from the other great and putatively stagnant civilization, India,[309] and also from Polynesia, which was imagined as an ambered version of Europe's own antiquity. No category of "noble barbarian" arose within Sinoscopia in parallel to noble savagery. The fact that the Chinese were difficult for Euro-

---

308. Mistakenly, as it turns out. According to L. Liu (1999b, 2004) the contested Chinese character *yi* did not have a single obvious meaning to Chinese. This did not prevent the British from insisting on the change, however, in the 1858 Treaty of Tianjin (Spence 1990, p. 181).

309. Inden 1986; Pollock 2000.

peans to imagine as part of their own family tree meant that paternalistic strategies of native policy were never formulated.

By acknowledging China's continuing cultural and political power and its radical alterity, European Sinophobia radically reduced the menu of options for colonial native policy. Sinophilia, by contrast, did not construe China as a place that even needed colonization. Although Europeans had discussed China for much longer and in much more detail than Southern Africa and Polynesia, the structure of discourse on China was configured in a way that ultimately left fewer options for colonial governance.[310]

310. The existence of Hong Kong as a model did not alleviate this problem, since the British rulers had entered their Chinese colony with roughly the same set of inherited representations as the Germans and therefore faced the same set of options.

SEVEN

A Pact with the (Foreign) Devil &
Qingdao as a Colony

Now, dear Justinian. . . . Tell us once, where you will begin. . . . In a place
where there are already Christians? or where there are none? Where there
are Christians you come too late. . . . The English, Dutch, Portuguese, and
Spanish control a good part of the farthest seacoast. . . . Where then? . . .
In China only recently the Tartars mercilessly murdered the Christians and
their preachers. Will you go there? Where then, you honest Germans? . . .
Dear Justinian, stop dreaming, lest Satan deceive you in a dream!

Admonition to Justinian von Weltz, Protestant missionary in Latin America,
from JOHANN H. URSINIUS, Lutheran Superintendent at Regensburg (1664)[1]

When China was ruled by the Han and Jin dynasties, the Germans were still
living as savages in the jungles. In the Chinese Six Dynasties period they only
managed to create barbarian tribal states. During the medieval Dark Ages, as
war raged for a thousand years, the [German] people could not even read and
write. . . . Our China, however, that can look back on a unique five-thousand-
year-old culture, is now supposed to take advice [from Germany], contrite and
with its head bowed. . . . What a shame!

KANG YOUWEI, "Research on Germany's Political Development" (1906)[2]

Bumrush the Show: Germans in Colonial
Kiaochow, 1897–1904

During the 1860s the Germans began discussing the possibility of obtaining a coastal entry point from which they could expand inland into China.
After German unification and the emergence of a German navy there was

---

1. Translated from the German text in Grössel 1891 by J. A. Scherer (1969, pp. 100–102).
2. Kang Youwei 1986, pp. 360–62; German translation in Felber 1994, pp. 179–80.

increasing talk of the need for a coaling station for the German East Asia Cruiser Squadron.[3] Following the Treaty of Shimonoseki (1895), German envoys Schenck zu Schweinsburg and von Heyking unsuccessfully petitioned China to provide Germany with a harbor. In 1896 Rear Admiral Alfred Tirpitz (called von Tirpitz starting with his ennoblement in 1900), commander of the East Asia squadron, visited Jiaozhou bay and wrote a memo calling for its occupation.[4] The following year Tirpitz became state secretary for the Imperial Navy Department and began orchestrating the massive buildup of Germany's fleet. At the end of November 1896, Wilhelm II instructed Admiral Eduard von Knorr "to prepare a plan for the occupation of Jiaozhou Bay."[5] It was now just a matter of time before Germany found a pretext to make the first move.

As in Southwest Africa, German missionaries paved the way to colonial conquest. Germany's opportunity arose on November 1, 1897, when two of the Steyl missionaries were killed by supposed Boxers or members of the Dadao hui (Big Sword Society) in Juye County, southwestern Shandong. The Yihetuan, or "Boxers United in Righteousness," were a martial arts group initially concentrated in northwest Shandong and the border regions of Zhili Province who joined the anti-Christian movement in 1899 and spread northward toward Beijing, provoking a response by the first international "coalition of the righteous" in the twentieth century.[6] The Boxers would play an important role in Kiaochow's constitutive period even though most of their activities were conducted far from the colony's borders.

The kaiser learned of the missionaries' murder on November 6. The following day, after receiving assurance that the Russian tsar would not object to a German intervention, Wilhelm II ordered his East Asia squadron, under the command of Admiral Otto von Diederichs, to seize Jiaozhou Bay. The emperor was determined to put an end to what he called Germany's "hypercautious [*hypervorsichtige*] policy in East Asia" and to show the Chinese once and for all, "with the most brutal ruthlessness," that he was "not to be toyed with."[7] German battleships arrived in Jiaozhou Bay on November 13. The next morning about 500 troops landed on the shore, cut the telegraph lines, and occupied Qingdao. The town had been a seaport and fishing vil-

---

3. Schrecker 1971, pp. 5–9.

4. Stichler 1989, pp. 19–20; Hubatsch 1955, p. 33.

5. Lepsius, Mendelssohn Bartholdy, and Thimme 1922–27, vol. 14, pt. 1, p. 47n.

6. Esherick 1987; Cohen 1997.

7. Telegram from kaiser to Foreign Office, November 6, 1897, in Lepsius, Mendelssohn Bartholdy, and Thimme 1922–27, vol. 14, pt. 1, p. 67.

lage since the Ming dynasty and had expanded into a small commercial center with sixty-five shops due to the recent garrisoning of Chinese troops and the completion of the road inland to Jiaozhou.[8] Admiral Diederichs informed General Zhang Gaoyuan, commanding officer at Qingdao, that he had two days to evacuate his 1,600–2,000 troops from the town's four barracks. Under instructions from the central Chinese government, General Zhang capitulated.[9] Diederichs immediately set up a provisional occupational government in the local *yamen* (government building).

The negotiations with officials in Beijing lasted several months and took place under conditions specified by the Germans, led by Baron von Heyking. The Germans were able to insist, in contrast to earlier times, that the negotiations take place in their own legation.[10] An "atonement treaty" was signed on January 15, 1898; in it the Chinese government agreed that Li Bingheng, governor of Shandong at the time of the missionary murders, would never again be employed as a civil servant. China also agreed to contribute money for the construction of cathedrals at several sites in Shandong, including the village where the missionaries had been killed, and to attach banners to the churches proclaiming that they had been built by the Chinese emperor as reparation. The most important result of the negotiations was the "lease treaty" (*Pachtvertrag*) of March 6, 1898, which granted Germany sovereignty over the area it called "Kiautschou" for ninety-nine years.[11] According to boundaries that were worked out by a commission during the coming months, the leasehold was an area of 553 square kilometers encompassing the village of Qingdao, several larger towns (Licun, Cangkou, Shazikou), and 275 tiny villages (see map 5). Qingdao proper had only about seven to eight hundred inhabitants in 1897, not counting the Chinese soldiers stationed there. Another eighty to one hundred thousand lived in the rest of the leasehold.[12] Since most of these people were extremely poor, their ability to choose whether to remain within the German territory or to move was severely curtailed. This is just one of the ways in which the Germans were able to immediately begin treating Kiaochow as a colony in the strict sense. After all, Southwest Africa was based on

8. Zhang Shufeng 1991; also Lu and Lu 2005, p. 11, which reproduces rare photographs of Chinese village life during the first year of the German occupation of Qingdao.

9. Weicker 1908, p. 34; Admiral Otto von Diederichs, "Die Besetzung von Tsingtau am 14.XI.1897," BA-MA-Freiburg, Nachlass Diederichs, vol. 24; Stichler 1989, pp. 23–44.

10. Lindenberg 1900, vol. 2, p. 252; Stichler 1989, pp. 62–63.

11. The treaty is reprinted in Leutner 1997, pp. 164–68; also in Mohr 1911, pp. 1–5. A photograph of the Yanzhou cathedral is reproduced in Stenz 1924, p. 9.

12. Matzat 1998a, p. 106.

protection treaties that were not understood by their African signatories as giving the Germans the right to settle there, but this did not stop the colonizers from treating that "protectorate" as an outpost of German state sovereignty.

The treaty also identified a fifty-kilometer buffer zone surrounding the colony. China retained sovereignty within this zone, but Germany reserved the right to deploy troops there and to participate in the regulation of rivers. More sweepingly, the Chinese agreed to "abstain from taking any measures or issuing any ordinances therein without obtaining the prior consent of the German government" (article 1 of the 1898 treaty). The most contentious sections of the treaty provided for the construction of two railways through Shandong Province by one or more mixed German-Chinese companies. Germany was also granted the right to mine for coal in a zone extending fifteen kilometers inland along each side of the railway line.

Thus arose the first European colony that was located fully on the Chinese mainland.[13] Other European powers seized the opportunity to gain their own mainland concessions or to formalize control over existing spheres of influence. Russia occupied and leased Dalian and Lüshun (Port Arthur) in March 1898, Britain leased Weihaiwei in Shandong in July 1898, and France leased Guangzhouwan in 1899.[14] The Germans also sought to expand more deeply into Shandong Province, taking advantage of divisions within the Chinese governing elite and of the treaty's vague language.

Kiaochow was administered directly by the German navy rather than the Foreign Office, an anomaly within the German colonial empire. The equivalent of the *Schutztruppe* for Qingdao was the Third Naval Infantry Battalion, which was created specifically for Kiaochow. The first Third Battalion troops arrived in Qingdao on January 26, 1898, led by Admiral Oskar Truppel (later von Truppel), who would play a central role as governor of the colony.

13. British Hong Kong, a model for the German planners of Kiaochow, was initially restricted to Hong Kong island: the New Territories that are joined to the Chinese mainland were leased from China to Britain, along with 230 other offshore islands, in 1898, in the wake of Germany's land grab in Qingdao. Macao, across the Pearl River estuary from Hong Kong, had long existed as a Portuguese colony but was also located mainly offshore. A third island, Taiwan, had been ceded to Japan following the first Sino-Japanese War in 1895.

14. Other than Portuguese Macao, British Hong Kong, and Japanese Taiwan, there were no actual colonies in China before Kiaochow (the French Indochinese Union was located in countries that had long been free of Chinese rule), even if there were dozens of treaty ports and foreign settlements with varying degrees of extraterritoriality. On this entire complex of infringements on Chinese sovereignty see Cordier 1901-2, vol. 3, chap. 23; Grünfeld 1913; and Fairbank [1953] 1969.

On April 27, 1898, Kiaochow was declared a German "protectorate" (*Schutzgebiet*), the standard term for a colony in German law.[15] Although this aligned Kiaochow with the general legal framework in force in all of the other overseas colonies, those laws said nothing about the specific regulations, decrees, and policies that would be implemented in any given colony. During the first year of the Kiaochow colony the governor's authority was still limited, insofar as his decisions had to be submitted for approval to the naval authorities in Berlin before they could be published and enforced. Starting in 1899, however, prior approval from Berlin was required only for "the most important and far-reaching regulations." Indeed, no locally adopted regulation was ever overturned by the Berlin authorities, even if Governor Truppel was eventually forced to adopt policies he opposed and was sacked in 1911 for continuing to resist them.[16] This unusual infringement on the governor's authority occurred in the context of a growing sense on the part of metropolitan German authorities that Kiaochow should be released from its colonial status. Colonial governors were always powerless when their colonies were being bargained away by the motherland for some greater diplomatic gain. It was not Kiaochow's leasehold status that differentiated it from the other German colonies but the fact that it was located in China, whose place in German geopolitical calculations began to change in the years leading up to World War I. This change was due to Germany's increasing isolation within Europe and Chinese anticolonial resistance. But in almost all other respects the Germans defined Kiaochow as a colony, just like the colonies in Africa and the Pacific.

Native policy in Kiaochow was hammered out within a context of geopolitical and economic considerations that were complex and changing. Kiaochow continued until 1914 to serve as a coaling, repair, and shipbuilding station for the German navy, but officials did not see this as the colony's main purpose. Admiral von Knorr had already insisted in 1895 that a harbor in China would be worthless to the navy unless it was also an economic entrepôt.[17] Japan's military capacities advanced rapidly in the years immediately following the occupation of Qingdao, and the Germans recognized that Kiaochow could not be defended against Japanese attack.[18] This was

15. See the imperial decrees from 1898 in Mohr 1911, pp. 6–7. The codification of German colonial law started in 1886, culminating in the 1900 "Schutzgebietsgesetz" (Law on German Protectorates); see *Das Schutzgebietsgesetz . . . Textausgabe mit Einleitung, Anmerkungen und Sachregister* (Berlin: Mittler, 1901).

16. Seelemann 1982, p. 87; also p. 106 n. 123; Schrecker 1971, p. 60.

17. Admiral von Knorr, "Denkschrift betr. des Stuetzpunktes in Ostasien," November 8 1895, quoted in Seelemann 1982, p. 131 n. 1.

18. Seelemann 1982, p. 9.

confirmed in 1914, when the colony was overcome by Japanese forces after just two months of fighting. Tirpitz agreed that Kiaochow would never flourish as a mere military base but had to become a trading entrepôt like Hong Kong.[19] He also wanted the colony to become a showcase for the navy's organizational skills as part of his maneuvering vis-à-vis the Reichstag and the kaiser to build up the navy.[20] A memo from Kiaochow's governor to the Naval Office in 1900 emphasized that "the existence of the colony has no justification if it does not become the home base for large German companies trading in the interior."[21] Special emphasis was placed in the colony's first years on building the railway, opening coal mines, improving the harbor, and creating a naval shipyard, activities that were understood as profit-making enterprises servicing international as well as German clients.[22] Qingdao was set up as a "free port," modeled on Hong Kong, although this status was terminated in 1905.[23] Customs duties were charged only for goods that passed through Kiaochow and entered Chinese territory or that were exported abroad.[24]

But if broadly economic goals seemed to have primacy over military ones, the colony still did not correspond to theories of imperialism as being fundamentally driven by capitalist interests. The colonial state ended up running most of the key industries in Kiaochow, since German capitalists like Krupp and Siemens were unwilling to invest there.[25] The urban commercial sector stayed mainly in Chinese (and increasingly, over time, in Japanese) hands. As a result, colonial native policy had to attend to the concerns of Asian businessmen.[26] An exception was the Shandong Railway Company, which became "the only profitable and dividend-paying company that actually penetrated into the interior of Shandong Province." It was in the hands of major German banks.[27] German marines performed much of the original landscaping and early construction work in Qingdao.

19. See Tirpitz 1919, vol. 1, p. 91, for a summary of this view.

20. Berghahn 1971; Witt 1973; Mühlhahn 2000, pp. 114, 201.

21. Jaeschke to RMA, "Ursache des Boxeraufstandes," October 9, 1900, BA-MA-Freiburg, RM 3, vol. 6782, p. 306v.

22. The shipyard built and repaired ships and made everything from boilers to "masts for the telegraph lines between Tibet and Peking" (Seelemann 1982, p. 273).

23. Schrecker 1971, p. 73; Stichler 1989, pp. 238–45.

24. Schrecker 1971, p. 74.

25. Mühlhahn 2000, p. 143.

26. See, for example, the comments in the government's annual *Denkschrift* for 1898–99, p. 27: "Compared to last year, conditions have improved slightly with respect to the small Chinese businessmen. Businessmen from other districts have moved here."

27. Stichler 1989, pp. 93, 126; V. Schmidt 1976.

Native policy in Kiaochow was constrained by the need to attract Chinese inhabitants, business, and workers, since there was never any intention of making Kiaochow into a settlement colony and its German population consisted mainly of navy personnel. Chinese labor was central to the construction of the harbor, government buildings, and railways, and in extracting coal from the German-owned mines.[28] But no Chinese could be compelled to live or work in the colony, since it was surrounded by China, which still claimed the colony's subjects as its own.[29] Of course, it was not feasible for most of the nearly two hundred thousand people who lived within the leasehold at the beginning of the German period to move away, since they had families, temples, ancestral graves, land, and houses in the region. The colony was aided by the fact that it drew trade away from the town of Jiaozhou and the ports on Jiaozhou Bay which had been active trading centers before 1897. Economic activity in Shandong became more oriented toward Qingdao and the leasehold.[30] The city's population reached fifty-five thousand by 1913—an increase of 730 percent in seventeen years.[31]

A more important influence on native policy than the sheer existence of China was the ability of the Chinese state to mount effective challenges to German practice *within* the colony. Germany became increasingly sensitive to Chinese demands after 1904, but even before that time a skillful provincial governor like Yuan Shikai could affect German behavior in the leasehold. Indeed, the entire colonial period was characterized by a struggle between the Germans and the Chinese state over the very definition of the new political entity. The governors in Qingdao and the German navy High Command insisted on referring to Kiaochow as a "protectorate," while Chinese officials in Beijing and Ji'nan insisted on calling Kiaochow a "leasehold." In article 3 of the original 1898 treaty the Germans had conceded that the

28. Falkenberg 1984, 1986.

29. Of course, this does not differentiate Kiaochow fundamentally from colonies in Africa and the Pacific. Colonial armies were generally unable to prevent populations from emigrating to neighboring territories in this period. In 1904 many Ovaherero were able to resettle in Bechuanaland; others slipped past German guards unnoticed and reentered the colony. Samoans traveled to Tonga and Fiji as they pleased, disregarding the German government's requirement that they apply for permission.

30. During Kiaochow's colonial era this part of Shandong became economically more active than the previously dominant areas in the province's southwest around the Imperial Canal, even if modern industry was completely absent in the province (Mühlhahn 2000, p. 40-61).

31. Matzat 1998a, p. 106.

Chinese emperor retained ultimate sovereignty over the Chinese residents of Kiaochow and was granting sovereignty to Germany only temporarily. The Chinese tried repeatedly to undermine the Germans' interpretation of the treaty by suggesting that a Chinese consul and a state official be posted in Qingdao. The Germans countered Chinese efforts to compromise their sovereignty by granting a sort of leasehold citizenship to Chinese who were born in Kiaochow. These Kiaochow citizens were protected from extradition to China and retained a right to residence in the colony while traveling outside it.[32]

Kiaochow had a thoroughly colonial character. The new buildings that were included in the first city plan for German Qingdao in 1898 (plate 9) staked out the rudiments of a new state. These included the government building (completed in 1906), a temporary residence for the governor (replaced in 1907 by the more glorious governor's mansion, which loomed over the European side of town; fig. 7.13), a military hospital, and the railway station (completed in 1901; fig. 7.1).[33] By 1899–1900 the urban master plan included another crucial component of a colonial state—a prison for European prisoners—and this building was quickly completed, along with a second prison for Chinese (in Licun). No new military barracks were included in the original plan because the Germans were able to move their troops immediately into the buildings that had been left behind by the Chinese army, but they soon found these to be inadequate and replaced them.[34]

Although these new buildings laid a symbolic claim to German sovereignty, a peculiar extension of the Chinese state was already present at the heart of the colonial city in the earliest plan—the headquarters of the Chinese customs office. Colonialism as I have defined it involves the transfer of sovereignty from locals to outsiders along with a politics of difference that consigns locals to second-class status. But sovereignty is a continuum, not an either-or affair.[35] In Kiaochow's case the infringement on colonial sovereignty came partly from without, due to the unusual situation of an external state claiming sovereignty over a colony's citizens—not unlike the

32. Crusen 1913.

33. The 1898 city plan also included a slaughterhouse (completed in 1906) and Protestant and Catholic churches, both of which were eventually built in slightly different locations. A provisional Protestant church (*Governementskapelle*) was completed by December 1899, and the Steyl Mission headquarters, which could hold three or four hundred people for services, was completed in 1902; see Lu and Lu 2005, pp. 168–70.

34. New barracks for two divisions of the Third Navy Battalion were already mentioned in the *Denkschrift* for 1898–99, p. 27.

35. Stoler 2006.

FIGURE 7.1 *Top*, Railway station in Qingdao (ca. 1910), the final station of the Shandong railway. From *Ansichten von Tsingtau und dem Hinterlande* (n.p.: n.d., ca. 1910). *Bottom*, Facade of the contemporary Qingdao station (2005). Photo by the author.

West German stance toward the German Democratic Republic before 1990. The infringement in Kiaochow also stemmed from the fact that all colonial states rely on a rudimentary level of toleration and cooperation on the part of the colonized. As a result the colonized are able to gain some control over the ways in which colonial policy is implemented, which is the equivalent of saying that they can take back, or retain, some degree of sovereignty. It would be unrealistic to restrict the definition of colonialism to cases of pure foreign sovereignty. As we will see, Chinese in Kiaochow laid claim to the state in this way to a greater extent than the inhabitants of the other two colonies examined so far, and in doing so they gained incremental control over the state and began to "decolonize" it.

A second defining feature of modern colonialism is the rule of difference, which is linked to native policy in the ways previously discussed. Assumptions of fundamental Chinese inferiority and difference were inscribed into the original urban plan for Qingdao. There was a "villa district" with German street names, restricted to European residents. The governor's provisional residence was located in this neighborhood, next to the home of the "commissary for Chinese affairs," Dr. Wilhelm Schrameier, and the mansion of Captain Freiherr von Liliencron, the governor's adjutant and commander of the Third Naval Infantry Battalion (fig. 7.2).[36] Starting in 1899 the Qingdao master plan also indicated the location of a cemetery restricted to Europeans—as if its authors were reading *Effi Briest*. The 1899 map also recorded the emergence of a new settlement of Chinese laborers at the site that would soon become the workers' district, Taidongzhen ("east of the heights"); a second workers' district known as Taixizhen ("west of the heights") was added somewhat later (map 6). An industrial zone was already emerging along Jiaozhou Bay near the small harbor (map 6).

The neighborhood of Dabaodao (Tapautau) was also sketched into these initial city plans. Its streets' simple grid pattern contrasted with the smoothly curving boulevards of the European district. The Germans called Dabaodao the "Chinesen-Stadt" (Chinese city) and created a cordon sanitaire that divided it from so-called upper Qingdao, although this buffer zone was quickly filled in with new structures. Despite its Chinese name, Dabaodao was designed from the start to become a mixed zone of commercial, industrial, and residential activities in which both Europeans and Chinese could live, work, shop, and own property.[37] It was dominated by simple Chinese and European-style houses, shops, and businesses, along with some larger buildings like the Qingdao branch of the Ruifuxiang store on Kiautschoustrasse (fig. 7.3). Photographs taken in Dabaodao (fig. 7.4) during the German colonial period often show a mix of people wearing

36. On von Liliencron see Hans-Joachim Schmitt, "Die Verteidiger von Tsingtau und ihre Gefangenenschaft in Japan (1914 bis 1920)," "Tsingtau und Japan 1914 bis 1920, Listen, Etatstärke für das Schutzgebiet Kiautschou," at http://www.tsingtau.info/index.html?listen/etat1913.htm; also BA-MA-Freiburg, Nachlass Truppel, vol. 79, p. 9r.

37. Seelemann 1982, p. 70.

FIGURE 7.2 Home of Dr. Wilhelm Schrameier, commissary for Chinese affairs, with the home of Captain Liliencron (adjutant to the governor) in the background, *left* (ca. 1900). From Kiautschou *Denkschrift* for October 1899–October 1900, Anlage 8.

European and Chinese clothing.[38] This district's in-between status was revealed by an ordinance prohibiting "screeching pushcarts" (*kreischende Schiebkarren*) in Qingdao, in order to "spare the European inhabitants of Tsingtao any unpleasant confrontation with Chinese culture." This ordinance was extended to Dabaodao but not to the purely Chinese districts Taidongzhen and Taixizhen.[39] The existence of this zone suggests that the boundaries between colonizer and colonized were already porous in the colony's foundational period. From the very start Kiaochow revealed both the desire to maintain hierarchical difference and countless compromises and infringements on this rule.

My aim in the following section is not to provide a detailed history of every aspect of colonial government in Kiaochow. There are already several solid historical studies of this colony.[40] My focus is instead on native policy.

38. Streets in Dabaodao also combined the names of towns in Shandong Province with the German word *Strasse*, yielding names like Kiautschoustrasse.

39. Mohr 1911, p. 130; Klein 2004, p. 319.

40. Overviews of colonial government in Kiaochow are given in Schrecker 1971; Seelemann 1982; Stichler 1989; F. Huang 1999; and Mühlhahn 2000. Other significant studies are

FIGURE 7.3 Qingdao branch of the Chinese-owned Ruifuxiang store on Kiautschoustrasse in Dabaodao District of Qingdao (ca. 1907). From a postcard.

For that reason I begin with the most striking features of German colonialism in Kiaochow, the strict segregation of urban space and of the legal system, and then turn to other aspects of social apartheid in Kiaochow, as well as the violence directed against the Chinese in the colony and Shandong Province between 1897 and 1905. These policies cohere into a common pattern, guided by an understanding of the Chinese that is strikingly consistent with the Sinophobic discourse discussed in the previous chapter. Like the Ovaherero, the Chinese were treated as radically different and racially inferior. In contrast to the Ovaherero, however, they were not seen as amenable to cultural transformation, given their loyalty to their ancient culture.

Zhang Yufa 1982; Biener 2001; Liu Shanzhang 1991; and Hinz and Lind 1998. Leutner 1997 provides translations into German of historical documents on Kiaochow as well as useful introductions to each of the sections. Berlin China-Studien, edited by Mechthild Leutner, is also important, especially Kuo and Leutner 1986, 1991, and 1994; and Kuo 1986.

FIGURE 7.4 Business premises of Europeans (*top*) and Chinese (*bottom*) in Dabaodao District of Qingdao (ca. 1903). From Kiautschou *Denkschrift* for 1902–3, Anlage 6.

Shaken, Not Stirred: Segregated Colonial Space and Radical Alterity during the First Phase of German Colonialism in Kiaochow, 1897–1904

In the words of a German newspaper published in China at the time of the annexation, the Chinese were "driven out" of old Qingdao.[41] One of the first interventions by Admiral Diederichs was to forbid all land sales in the leasehold without his approval. Proclamations to this effect in Chinese were posted in the villages.[42] Diederichs pressured county officials into giving him copies of the tax books, which he used, along with consulting local experts, to determine who owned each plot of land in the leased territory. Anyone who owned land the Germans thought they would need for their construction plans was forced to sell at prices determined by the Chinese cadastral surveys.[43] The navy administration purchased enough land for the city and harbor, approximately two thousand hectares, or 3.6 percent of the entire area of Kiaochow.[44] After drawing up an initial plan for Qingdao, the government held an auction in October 1898 to sell plots of land in the city that were not going to be used for official construction.[45] According to one German businessman who participated in the public sale of land, it was "full of excitement" and "prices were driven up to three dollars the square meter."[46]

The extant Chinese village was razed and its inhabitants dispossessed, and a new colonial city arose in its place. The Qingdao master plan disregarded the previous location of streets and buildings almost entirely (plate 9). A "tent village" of workers that had sprung up near the site of the future Dabaodao district was dismantled, and even the dirt beneath the settlement was removed, since it was thought to be contaminated.[47] Other

41. "Die bauliche Entwickelung Tsintaus," *Nachrichten aus Kiautschou, Beiblatt zum "Ostasiatischen Lloyd,"* no. 33 (May 20, 1899): 1.

42. Matzat 1985, p. 7; Schrecker 1971, p. 66.

43. Diederichs also convinced thousands of villagers to sign "right of preemption" (*Vorkaufsrecht*) agreements in exchange for payments equal to twice the amount of their annual taxes. This money was then deducted from the sales price if and when the German government decided to buy the land. When some villagers tried to charge "unreasonable" prices for their land, the government issued a decree authorizing expropriation of land through purchase (Schrecker 1971, p. 67; Schrameier 1914, pp. 2–10).

44. Stichler 1989, p. 99; Matzat 1985, p. 13; Schrecker 1971, p. 212.

45. Other land was given to groups such as missions that were "adjudged to serve the public interest" (Schrecker 1971, p. 71).

46. Bigelow 1898, p. 580.

47. There were in fact numerous cases of typhus and intestinal disease among the Germans during the first years of the occupation. See Eckart 1997, pp. 465–66.

nearby neighborhoods and villages that disturbed the planning of colonial urban space were "put to rest" (*niedergelegt*), in the revealing words of one of the navy's surveyors in 1900, describing the village of Yangjiacun (just beyond Taidongzhen) which had grown rapidly as a settlement of people displaced from upper Qingdao.[48]

Strict separation between Europeans and Chinese was the guiding principle of the urban plan. In 1899 one newspaper wrote that "Tsintau today is still Chinese in its external appearance" but "in a few months the impression our Asian colony makes on a stranger will be completely different."[49] According to one of the navy's surveyors the goal was to produce a clear "demarcation of our territory from China." As von Tirpitz noted later, "Thus we avoided being in direct touch with China."[50] The spatial vagueness of these statements is revealing. In reality, only the leasehold could be demarcated from China, since the city of Qingdao did not have a direct border with China, but at the same time, Kiaochow could not avoid "touching" China. The spatial demarcation was thus a doubly internal one, directed against the interior and the exterior Chinese Other. The internal Chinaman was necessary to the colony's livelihood but he was also feared and disdained on "racial" grounds and as a potential agent of the Chinese government. An early German tour book claimed that Qingdao's "greatest advantage compared to other Chinese coastal cities" like Shanghai or Tianjin was "that the Chinese settlement is separated completely from the European one."[51]

The European district, "upper Qingdao," consisted mainly of large villas along the southern bays (Qingdao Bay and Clara Bay, now known as Huiquan Bay, to its east). According to the building code only 55 percent of the land could be built up, and even today this district has large parks. The streets were wide, curving, and wooded and were named after German

48. Deimling 1900, p. 57. Yangjiacun had been described just a year earlier by a German official as "a pretty Chinese village." See Heinrich Mootz, "Die Namen der Orte in Deutsch-Shantung," *Nachrichten aus Kiautschou, Beiblatt zum "Ostasiatischen Lloyd,"* special ed., June 26, 1899, p. 2. Two years after this article appeared, in a book on "place-names in German Shandong" the same author (Mootz 1901, p. 9) referred to Yangjiacun in the past tense.

49. "Ein Bild von Tsintau," *Nachrichten aus Kiautschou, Beiblatt zum "Ostasiatischen Lloyd,"* no. 25 (March 25, 1899): 1.

50. Deimling 1900, p. 50; Tirpitz 1919, vol. 1, p. 103. According to von Tirpitz, the town itself was walled in as "Boxer protection," but he must have been speaking metaphorically. In actuality there were no city walls, since this would have resembled traditional Chinese cities.

51. Behme and Krieger 1906, p. 97. At the same time, according to this guidebook, "the life and activities of the Chinese offer an interesting spectacle" for the European tourist (ibid., p. 99).

rulers.[52] And "millions and millions of trees and bushes were planted" in the colony, since there was "one thing which the German has a very difficult time giving up" when he leaves home—his forests.[53] A green belt of trees was planted around the European zone, although in the spirit of segregation, none were planted in the Chinese section. The government even imported German trees and planted German grapes for wine.[54] According to the boundaries specified in the *Chinesenordnung* (Chinese ordinances) of June 1900 Chinese were not permitted to live in the European neighborhood.[55] It was impossible to exclude Chinese servants from residing there, but they were lodged in small "coolie houses" that were "strictly separated from the Europeans."[56] In addition to the architectural dualism, this absence of Chinese residents in the villa district led German visitors to write things like the following: "When I arrived in Qingdao and . . . looked around the train station a little, I was overcome by the feeling: you're in a completely German territory here [*ganz auf deutschem Boden*]. This feeling accompanied me everywhere during my stay in Qingdao."[57] The German houses, hotels, and official buildings constructed in this period were almost exclusively German or European in style, although some details corresponded to a generic notion of "tropical" architecture.[58] Some of these constructions were shipped to Qingdao from Germany. The governor's first residence, for example, was a prefabricated "tropical house" (*Tropenhaus*). The military hospital was "constructed of pasteboard made in Germany."[59]

Dabaodao was where most of the colony's better-off Chinese lived. The housing was not as luxurious as in the European zone, and the streets and buildings were more densely packed. Houses there often had two stories, in a style that was typical of middle and southern China and that is said to have

52. Godshall 1929, p. 124. Today, these same streets seem narrow and picturesque in comparison to the wide grid pattern typical in most Chinese cities.

53. Weicker 1908, p. 82; also Berensmann 1904, p. 596. Chinese who damaged trees in the colony could be sentenced to forced labor and up to fifty lashes (Mohr 1911, pp. 151–52). For a programmatic argument about this aspect of German colonization, see "Der Nutzen der Aufforstung" in *Der West-östliche Bote*, vol. 1 (6–7, March–April 1914), pp. 184–89.

54. Kiaochow *Denkschrift* for 1900–1901, pp. 39–40.

55. Chinese investors were allowed to buy land and to build in the European zone, and as discussed below, upper-class Chinese were allowed to live there after 1911.

56. Kronecker 1913, p. 8.

57. Schweitzer 1914, p. 136.

58. The first generation of large "villa" houses was built without basements and with other peculiarities that turned out to be disadvantageous in the Qingdao climate (Kronecker 1913, p. 8).

59. Deimling 1900, p. 56; Warner 1994, p. 292; see also Bigelow 1898, p. 580.

FIGURE 7.5 Railway station in Gaomi (ca. 1904). From BA-MA-Freiburg, Nachlass Truppel, vol. 78. (Courtesy of BA-MA-Freiburg.)

reflected the presence of businessmen from the lower Yangzi region and Canton.[60] Some German bureaucrats and employees of the German merchant firms took up residence there as well. If Dabaodao was not as racially restrictive as the other districts, the official *Denkschrift* (Report) showed that the cultural distinction was reproduced internally there, by calling attention to the architectural distinction between European and Chinese "business premises" in the neighborhood (fig. 7.4). In a similar spirit, the railway stations built by the Shantung Eisenbahn Gesellschaft (Shandong Railway Company) were done in German style inside the colony (figs. 7.1, 7.5) and in partly Chinese style outside the colony.

Taidongzhen and Taixizhen were zoned exclusively for Chinese residence. As in Dabaodao, streets in these neighborhoods were laid out in a tight, "very functional and completely regular" grid pattern to facilitate police control (see map 6). The German police station (fig. 7.6) stood in the middle of the district.[61] Streets in Taidongzhen and Taixizhen were given

60. Biener 2001, p. 103.
61. Weicker 1908, p. 67.

FIGURE 7.6 Police station in Taidongzhen District of Qingdao (German colonial period). From Lu and Lu 2005, p. 160.

"typical" Chinese names. As the colony's "Chinese commissary," Wilhelm Schrameier, remarked, the big firms in Qingdao needed large numbers of "cheap coolie houses" for their workers. Although the size of "coolie houses" and rooms in Taidongzhen and Taixizhen was controlled by German regulations, they "ignored the European style of construction and used the typical Chinese one" instead.[62] More substantial houses were also built in these districts, often in the traditional northern Chinese style with enclosed courtyards.[63] The harbor district, finally, had bland industrial buildings and functional housing for the apprentices attending the shipyard's school (see fig. 7.7).

The colony's entire legal and administrative structure was also bifurcated, with separate arrangements for Western civilians (a category that included Japanese) and Chinese.[64] Qingdao had an Imperial Court (*Kaiserliches Gericht*) throughout the colonial period. In 1907 a German Appeals Court was also established in Qingdao. It was independent from the consulate,

62. Schrameier 1914, p. 27.

63. Biener 2001, pp. 103–4.

64. Japanese were treated like Germans and other "nonnative foreigners" in German colonial law in general and in Kiaochow in particular. This was especially important in Qingdao given the large Japanese commercial presence. See Mohr 1911, p. 61 (par. 2 of 1900 decree "Legal Affairs in the German Protectorates").

FIGURE 7.7 Housing for Chinese apprentices in Qingdao (German colonial period). From BA-MA-Freiburg, Nachlass Truppel, vol. 62, p. 11, verso.

which was controlled by the German Foreign Office.[65] European business-men and property owners could elect representatives to a citizens' represen-tative council that advised the governor.[66]

The legal treatment of the Chinese was determined by a mixture of Ger-man and Chinese law, with the latter being filtered through German inter-pretations. This was structurally similar to the approach used in colonies with oral cultures, where indigenous legal understandings were overcoded and mingled with European ones.[67] A "Governor's Order on the Legal Con-ditions of the Chinese" (April 15, 1899) set out the basic guidelines.[68] As in other German colonies, civil or criminal cases pitting Europeans against "natives" were to be tried by Germans—in this case, by the Imperial Court. Any civil case involving only Chinese and in which the stakes were not sufficiently serious was to be judged by the German district commissioner according to his interpretation of Chinese law.[69] The district commissioners

65. Seelemann 1982, p. 94.
66. Schrecker 1971, p. 61; Stichler 1989, pp. 93–94.
67. Mann and Roberts 1991; Mommsen and Moor 1992.
68. Reprinted in Mohr 1911, pp. 72–77.
69. Hoffmann 1907, p. 76. In principle the district commissioners initiated all cases in-volving only Chinese, but they were supposed to forward to the Imperial Court any case that reached a certain level of seriousness. The Kiaochow colony as a whole was divided into

were former translator trainees (*Dolmetschereleven*) and therefore did not need translators.[70] They were instructed to conduct research on Chinese legal views by talking to village elders and local mandarins. They began translating German law into Chinese and the Qing legal code and Chinese imperial decrees into German, a project that was continued by the legal faculty in the Qingdao German-Chinese college in the following years.[71] But while some elements of German law were introduced into the evolving system of jurisprudence, they were "explicitly subordinated to the law of the Chinese empire," at least as that law was interpreted by the colonizers.[72]

The result of this merging of two legal systems was that Chinese residents were placed in double legal jeopardy and could be punished for a wide array of offenses, while Europeans were not subject to punishment for Chinese crimes that had no equivalent in German law. Offenses for which Chinese could be punished included any activities the governor declared illegal (par. 5.1) or any that were illegal according to German law (par. 5.2)—with the exception of practices related to religion, ethics, and so on—as well as anything that violated public order (par. 5.3) or that was publishable according to *Chinese* law (par. 5.4).[73] In civil suits involving only Chinese litigants, the governor could determine which German laws, if any, were applicable (par. 17). Legal proceedings and punishments were also adapted to local conditions as they were perceived by the district officials, producing a mixture of practices that did not fully correspond to either the German or the Chinese system. Thus, in a trial the accused was required to wear chains and to kneel before the judge with his head bowed, in an "analogy to Chinese legal hearings." This procedure was retained in Kiaochow even after it had been abolished in China. The district commissioner was not required to keep a written protocol of the hearings or to explain his legal reasoning, but only to record his final verdict.[74] The list of permissible punishments included flogging of male convicts with government-approved instruments (pars. 8 and 9), fines, forced labor, temporary or lifelong imprisonment,

two large districts, one urban and one rural, each of which had its own district commissioner (Weicker 1908, p. 111).

70. Leupold 1998, p. 144.

71. District commissioner Heinrich Mootz completed a translation of the German penal code into Chinese in 1908; see "Denkschrift über Einrichtung chinesischer Schulen im Schutzgebiet," BA-Berlin, DBC, vol. 1258, p. 46v. See also Kiaochow *Denkschrift* for 1899–1900, p. 26.

72. Crusen 1914, p. 137.

73. Ibid., p. 137.

74. Hövermann 1914, p. 64; Klein 2004, p. 323.

and execution, although the latter had to be approved by the governor (pars. 6, 10, and 14).[75] Torture was forbidden, although Chinese prisoners reported that it was widely used, and decapitation was substituted for the Chinese punishment of dismemberment.[76] But the Germans frequently employed variants of the *cangue* (wooden collar) even after the reform movement eliminated its use in China (fig. 7.8).[77] The selective application of Chinese legal procedures is illustrated by the chief justice's argument that parents, elder brothers, and guardians could all be punished for crimes committed by youths under the age of eighteen. The Germans amended this to specify that no relative could be punished for crimes committed by children younger than twelve.[78]

The relationship between the colonial government and its Chinese subjects was specified in some detail by the Chinese ordinances (*Chinesenordnung*) promulgated on June 14, 1900. The philologist and translator Wilhelm Schrameier was appointed as the first Chinese commissary (*Chinesenkommissar*), heading a "Chinese Bureau" (later called the Chinese Chancery).[79] Qingdao was divided into nine urban districts, each of which had a Chinese district head and several Chinese inspectors. All of these Chinese subofficials were under Schrameier's supervision.

The segregation of everyday life that was embedded in the city's spatial layout and its legal system was enhanced by additional regulations. Europeans and Chinese in Qingdao were found in separate hospitals, schools, prisons, bordellos, graveyards, and chambers of commerce.[80] The Chinese were allowed to visit Qingdao's famous beaches, but they had to use separate toilets there. Although Europeans could travel anywhere in the colony (and indeed, anywhere in China, as a result of the treaties concluded after the Opium Wars), Chinese were required to carry a lantern when they went out on the streets between 9:00 p.m. and sunrise and had to provide a "definite reason for being outside" if they were questioned.[81] Although the Germans

75. This stipulation was similar to the one governing criminal jurisdiction in German East Africa, Togo, Cameroon, and Southwest Africa, where the district commissioner could independently order flogging, fines, and imprisonment with forced labor but required the governor's order for the death penalty.

76. Leupold 1998, p. 144. For Chinese reports on torture in German prisons from 1906 see Shandongsheng lishi xuehui 1961, pp. 148–50.

77. Mühlhahn 2000, p. 264.

78. Crusen 1914, p. 138.

79. See Schrameier's numerous publications, listed in Matzat 1985, 1986, 1998b.

80. Kronecker 1913, pp. 17–81; Mühlhahn 2000, p. 259.

81. Mohr 1911, p. 23; Seelemann 1982, p. 71.

FIGURE 7.8 Punishment of Chinese in Qingdao (German
colonial period). From M. and D. Lu 2005, p. 162.

eventually agreed to let Chinese financiers participate in the mining and
railway companies, there were no Chinese members on these companies'
boards of directors.[82] Chinese were not permitted to join the elite Tsingtau
Club or any of the other German social clubs. Children of mixed heritage
were prohibited from attending the German schools.[83]

Another important aspect of German activity during this period with implications for native policy was the aggressive campaign to extend German
sovereignty beyond the colony's borders. Although the ostensible motives
behind this expansionism were to protect European missionaries and to defeat the Yihetuan and other forms of anti-Western militancy, the Germans

82. Stichler 1989, p. 149. Chinese railway and mine workers were also separated from
non-Chinese workers (ibid., p. 150).

83. Seelemann 1982, p. 422; Reinbothe 1992, p. 11; Zhang Yufa 1999.

seized any pretext to extend their military presence during the first seven years of the leasehold, as described by John Schrecker in his pioneering work on Chinese nationalism and German colonialism. More interesting in the present context is the fact that these military campaigns were conducted in a way that expressed aggressive disdain for the Chinese, especially for Chinese literati, antiforeigner secret societies, and symbols of Chinese tradition and religion. Early in 1898 German soldiers sacked the Confucius temple in Jimo and "damaged a statue of the great wise one," bringing down upon themselves the "fury of the Chinese intellectuals," including the leading reformer Kang Youwei.[84] The next conflict exploded in November 1898 following an attack on missionary Stenz in the village of Jietou near Rizhao.[85] This area lay outside the fifty-kilometer buffer zone. Nonetheless, the colonial governor, Captain Paul Jaeschke, sent Lieutenant Hannemann and translator Heinrich Mootz to investigate the incident. These two were allegedly attacked by a crowd in the village of Hanjiacun in Yizhoufu Prefecture on March 29, 1899.[86] They opened fire and killed several Chinese. Jaeschke then sent an expedition of 160 men to the prefecture, where they destroyed Hanjiacun and another village, Baitianju. The German troops then proceeded to the larger neighboring town, Rizhao, where they occupied the *yamen* and demanded food and money from the local inhabitants. When the Germans left Rizhao five days later they kidnapped five mandarins as hostages and demanded the arrest of Stenz's attackers and other concessions in exchange for the local officials' release.[87] The *Ostasiatischer Lloyd*, a German newspaper covering all of China, wrote after the completion of this campaign that "the Chinese offices are apparently already starting to understand that the German Government in Kiaochow cannot be toyed with."[88] The "scorched

84. Felber 1994, p. 166.

85. See telegrams from German legation in China (von Heyking) to Foreign Office, January 16 and February 23, 1899, PA-AA, R 18239 (no pagination). Stenz had been with missionaries Nies and Henle when they were murdered in 1897.

86. Chinese officials first argued that the crowd consisted simply of curious onlookers and later claimed that it was a voluntary militia created to fight banditry in the region.

87. Tirpitz to Foreign Secretary von Bülow, March 28, 1899; his telegram to von Bülow of April 4, 1899; telegram from Tsungli (Zongli) Yamen Beijing, April 8, 1900; protest letter from Chinese Envoy to von Bülow, April 20 1899; Tirpitz to von Bülow, April 20, 1899 (specifying that Hanjiacun was "completely destroyed" but that the smaller village of Baitianju was only "half destroyed"); all in PA-AA, R 18240-18241. See also the report by Lieutenant Hannemann from April 7, 1899, on the destruction of Hanjiacun, BA-MA-Freiburg, RM 3, vol. 6778. pp. 211-12; and Stichler 1989, 128-32; Mühlhahn 2000, 307-13.

88. "Die Strafexpedition ins Innere," *Nachrichten aus Kiautschou, Beiblatt zum "Ostasiatischen Lloyd,"* no. 28 (April 15, 1899): 1.

earth" strategy and vituperative comments directed specifically against "literati" in Shandong are suggestive of the Sinophobia in European and German circles in the years surrounding the Boxer uprising.[89]

The next series of German military interventions in Shandong Province was sparked by protests against the construction of the railway from Qingdao to Ji'nan (the *Jiaoji* railroad).[90] Early in 1899 the Germans began buying land and laying down rails. In the process they destroyed farmers' irrigation systems, divided their fields, violated ancestral burial sites, and generally infuriated villagers, who responded by sabotaging the railway tracks and destroying offices of the Shantung Eisenbahn Gesellschaft.[91] Germans killed three Chinese in a village that refused to pay a fine for stealing markers and beacons posted along the railway bed.[92] German soldiers were stationed in Gaomi, the center of the unrest, and an expedition was conducted against Jiaozhou city.[93] During the summer of 1899 various towns in the region began to arm and barricade themselves with help from Yihetuan and related groups.[94] The Germans responded with a full-scale military campaign, under the leadership of Hauptmann Mauve, in which about fifteen Chinese were killed. The *Ostasiatischer Lloyd* reported proudly on the "furor teutonicus" of the German "brave knights" in Gaomi, boasting that "our firearms have so much power that the human head explodes completely when it is hit at less than four hundred meters."[95]

During the height of the Boxer Rebellion large expeditions were sent out into the province from Qingdao. Early in 1900 one hundred villages south of the Shandong railway line banded together to resist the Germans under the leadership of the Dadao hui and Yihetuan. Protective walls were built around villages, German railway workers were taken hostage, and engi-

---

89. See Tirpitz's comments on the "oppositionally oriented literati [*Litteraten*]" in his telegram to the kaiser, April 7, 1899, PA-AA, R 18241.

90. On the German depredations in the towns and countryside around Qingdao see Admiral von Diederichs, "Die Besetzung von Tsingtau am 14.XI.1897," BA-MA-Freiburg, Nachlass Diederichs, vol. 24, p. 49; Schrecker 1971; Zhu 1994, pp. 314ff.; *Dongfang Zazhi*, vol. 1, no. 4, pp. 8–9; and Shandongsheng lishi xuehui 1961, vol. 3, pp. 91–95.

91. On the destruction of Chinese graves see Yuan Rongsu [1928] 1969, vol. 1, pt. 2, sec. 18; also Stichler 1988, p. 112; 1989, p. 138.

92. "Renitenz chinesischer Lokalbeamten," *Nachrichten aus Kiautschou, Beiblatt zum "Ostasiatischen Lloyd,"* special ed., May 1, 1899, pp. 1–2.

93. Stichler 1989, p. 148.

94. Mühlhahn 2000, pp. 113–14.

95. "Die Vorgaenge in Kaumi," *Nachrichten aus Kiautschou, Beiblatt zum "Ostasiatischen Lloyd,"* no. 40 (July 8, 1899): 1–2.

neers were attacked.[96] In October the Germans struck the villages of Kelan and Lijiaying, which were supposedly harboring Boxers, and over two hundred Chinese were killed.[97] In November German troops killed as many as five hundred villagers in Shawo (nowadays called Dujia) and burned the village.[98] Permanent barracks, each large enough for two hundred soldiers, were built in Gaomi and Jiaozhou. The troops stayed in these towns until 1905. The stationing of troops "far beyond the 'leasehold' boundaries contradicted all of the contractual agreements that had previously been forced on China."[99]

Accompanying this ongoing assault on Chinese sovereignty in the province was a fierce denigration of the Chinese. When the German soldiers occupied Gaomi in 1899, for instance, they moved into the academy (*shuyuan*) and burned valuable books from its library.[100] During the occupation of Jiaozhou city the following year, German soldiers lived in the examination hall and temple.[101] Similar things went on inside the colony's borders. The Germans occupied a Taoist-Buddhist temple near the leasehold's boundary and used it as a customs house.[102] And while the Germans often described their use of the Qingdao *yamen* for official business (see fig. 7.11) as an act of necessity, it was clearly part of the symbolic mise-en-scène of the conquest and specifically of General Zhang's humiliation, which culminated in the latter's suicide attempt. Daily life in Qingdao assumed an aggressive quality. In one incident a colonial bureaucrat struck a Chinese man with a whip for not moving off the sidewalk to let him pass.[103] A Protestant

96. "Neue Störungen des Eisenbahnbaues," *Nachrichten aus Kiautschou, Beiblatt zum "Ostasiatischen Lloyd*," no. 17 (April 27, 1900): 95; "Aus dem Hinterlande," ibid., no. 6 (February 9, 1900): 36; "Die Unruhen in Kaumi," ibid., no. 7 (February 16, 1900): 39–40; "Zur Lage im Hinterlande," ibid., no. 8 (February 23, 1900): 45–46; and "Aus der Kolonie," ibid., no. 15 (April 13, 1900): 88.

97. Admiralstab der Marine 1903, p. 209; "Gefechte bei Kaumi," *Nachrichten aus Kiautschou, Beiblatt zum "Ostasiatischen Lloyd*," no. 44 (November 2, 1900): 210.

98. Mühlhahn 2000, pp. 129–39; Admiralstab der Marine 1903, p. 210. As Richard Wilhelm noted in his November 24, 1900, report on the destruction of Shawo, the Boxers did not instigate the movement, which was directly provoked by the construction of the railway (in Leutner 1997, p. 287).

99. Stichler 1989, p. 218.

100. See Mühlhahn 2000, p. 120, and the letter from the magistrate of Gaomi, Ge Zhitan, to the pro-Boxer Shandong governor, Yu Xian, from July 13, 1899, in Leutner 1997, p. 277.

101. "Aus der Kolonie," *Nachrichten aus Kiautschou, Beiblatt zum "Ostasiatischen Lloyd*," no. 11 (March 16, 1900): 65.

102. See S. Wilhelm 1956, p. 93, with a report on Richard Wilhelm's second trip into the interior during his first year in Kiaochow (1899–1900).

103. "Aus Tsingtau," *Deutsch-Asiatische Warte*, July 15, 1900, p. 2.

minister remarked that European children in Qingdao quickly learned to act like little "masters" toward the Chinese, and that "some who would never dream of striking another when at home in Europe are often unable to . . . stop themselves from occasionally using a whip on people."[104]

German Native Policy in Kiaochow, Compared

It may be useful to contrast German native policy in early Kiaochow with the Namibian and Samoan cases. Like the Ovaherero, and unlike the Samoans or the Khoikhoi, the Chinese were viewed first and foremost in terms of their potential economic contribution to the colony. In contrast to the Ovaherero, however, there was little interest in trying to refashion the Chinese culturally. As the official report (*Denkschrift*) on Kiaochow for 1899–1900 noted, "The guiding approach in native administration" was "to *habituate* the Chinese to the new conditions without effectively limiting the venerable autonomy of the family or their patriarchal living arrangements. *We will not intervene in private Chinese affairs or the internal governance of their communal affairs,* except to the extent required to assure public order and the security of the colony."[105] Thus, even though Max Weber and contemporary Sinologists were pointing to the Chinese family and Confucian ideology as impediments to development, there was no attempt by the colonial government to eliminate Confucianism or transform the arrangements of the Chinese family. Chinese culture was seen as so deeply embedded and so all encompassing that Germans could not really imagine remaking the Chinese as abject copies of themselves, in contrast to Southwest Africa.[106] Describing the Dabaodao district, a German navy priest wrote that "we don't try to change the way the Chinese go about living," although "we also won't let them do whatever they want to."[107] This was closer to a repressive than to a "productive," manipulative use of power. This approach to regulating a radically different culture characterized most of the German colonial interventions in Qingdao. As one of the colony's judges wrote in 1903, colonial law should "avoid disturbing the ancient, deeply rooted, simple legal traditions of the

104. Weicker 1908, pp. 125–26.

105. Kiaochow *Denkschrift* for 1899–1900, p. 27 (my emphasis).

106. This is my only disagreement with the excellent study by Mühlhahn (2000), who emphasizes the Germans' alleged efforts at "manipulative acculturation." The "cultural imperialism" that emerged after 1905 partook of a different imaginary, one that was not Sinophobic and not really colonial. "Acculturation" in this later period in, for instance, the Qingdao German-Chinese college, can no longer even be seen as particularly "manipulative."

107. Weicker 1908, p. 49.

natives as much as possible. Nothing contributes more to a fruitful and peaceful colonization than the maintenance of the old traditional customs and legal views of the people."[108] The main difference from Samoa, whose native policies were also oriented toward regulated difference, was the Kiaochow regime's overarching hostility to the Chinese. By kidnapping the Rizhao mandarins and sacking the Gaomi *shuyuan*, the Germans focused on the specific symbols that had been reviled by Sinophobes as the "many sorts of learning which these parts of the world never heard of" (in the words of Defoe). But nothing was proposed to take the place of this detested culture, which was seen as unmovable.

German Qingdao in the first period thus represents a regime of native policy premised on the absolute difference of the colonized. It was focused on the external aspects of behavior, using threats of violence and material incentives rather than ideological insinuation. This is not to deny that the subjectivity of colonized was influenced, willy nilly, by the presence of a colonial state. Chinese workers adjusted to German managers' demands, Chinese students adapted to their German teachers' expectations, Chinese merchants altered their ways of doing business, and the Chinese theaters tailored some of their repertoire to a European audience.[109] Other groups who can hardly have been immune to the foreign ideological formation include the "Chinese inspectors" under Schrameier's supervision, the Chinese policemen, the Chinese military companies in German uniforms who were trained and commanded by the navy, and the village elders who agreed to advise district commissioners about legal cases and Chinese law.[110] But these putative ideological changes were not the central focus of German policy. Equally important is the fact that the apprentices in the shipyard school and those in the public elementary schools took lessons in Chinese and Chinese history, rather than learning to recite the German equivalent of "nos ancêtres les Gaulois."[111] The Chinese businessmen in the colony sold Chinese goods; the actors performed Chinese

---

108. Köbner 1903, pp. 6–7.

109. Seelemann 1982, p. 425. See the account of German soldiers attending a Chinese theater in Qingdao, in Lindenberg 1900, vol. 2, pp. 364–65. Figure 7.21, though unidentified, seems to be from a performance at a Qingdao theater.

110. For photos of Germans training Chinese troops in Qingdao, see BA-MA-Freiburg, Nachlass Diederichs, vol. 45, p. 30r; and Lu and Lu 2005, p. 154.

111. "Nos ancêtres, les Gaulois" was a French colonialist slogan (and the title of an ironic poem by Leopold Sédar Senghor) according to which French colonial schools taught African children that they were descended from Celtic Gauls. This did not mean, of course, that French colonialism was trying to make Africans into Frenchmen; see Ha 2003.

plays. Without reintroducing the mind-body distinction that has been so successfully undermined in recent theories of social practice, we still need to acknowledge that the colonizers in Kiaochow were more concerned with what *they* saw as material practices and less oriented toward subjective transformations (Southwest Africa) or cultural reproduction (Samoa). Naturally, the Catholic and Protestant missions *were* focused on reshaping their Chinese followers' subjective and spiritual life. But these missions were not part of the colonial state. The Protestant Weimar Mission was more intimately connected to the colonial regime, but it actually avoided religious teaching (see below).

Of course, some Germans did claim that they were involved in a sort of civilizing mission in Kiaochow. One goal for the colony that was occasionally discussed was to lift China up, to contribute to its development, perhaps in order to make it a better trading partner for Europe. Some of those who accepted the thesis of Chinese stagnation believed that the solution was for China to adopt not just advanced European technology but also elements of European culture. Wilhelm Schrameier claimed that *everything* the Germans did in Kiaochow was aimed at "consciously influencing the Chinese."[112] An economic geographer who specialized in Kiaochow insisted that "the first German sailor entering a still undeveloped land" has already exercised an "educational influence on the population" by "broadcasting orderliness, cleanliness, and by using the German language."[113] According to a legal scholar, Kiaochow's achievements would "serve as an example to the outsiders"—that is, to the Chinese—"who will then [attempt to] attain an equally high cultural level."[114] A German minister hoped that Germany would "show China the paths that will lead contemporary Chinese culture to the superior Christian-Germanic culture."[115] And a German travel writer in 1914 claimed that the Germans had "habituated the Chinese in Kiaochow to orderliness, cleanliness, and morals in just a single decade."[116] But all of these quotes are from the period after 1905. It was only then that there emerged a serious program intended to "influence the spirit and character" of the Chinese in the colony. By that time the entire context of this project had changed, and those who believed China was culturally underdeveloped were less influential in Kiaochow politics.

112. Schrameier 1910, p. 809.
113. Wilhelm Berensmann, quoted in Mühlhahn 2000, p. 64.
114. Hövermann 1914, p. 2.
115. Weicker 1908, p. 110.
116. Schweitzer 1914, pp. 152–53.

Early Native Policy and the Haunting
of Sinophobia by Sinophilia

The central features of native policy in the first period, then, were rigorous segregation combined with aggressive hostility and a hands-off approach to cultural change. To account for this we need to consider the apotheosis of Sinophobia that occurred at the same time as the German occupation of Kiaochow. Germany was heavily involved in the joint expedition against the Yihetuan, contributing almost twenty-thousand troops to the allied forces and the "supreme commander," Count Alfred von Waldersee. The most infamous incident in the German campaign is Kaiser Wilhelm's July 1900 *Hunnenrede* (see chap. 1). Anxious to satisfy the kaiser's call to "take no prisoners," von Waldersee embarked on a series of harsh punitive expeditions against suspected Boxers and sympathizers in and around Beijing.[117] Kiaochow was involved in the anti-Boxer campaign on several levels. In addition to the expeditions against supposed Boxers in Shandong Province, discussed above, the Third Naval Battalion sent several contingents of marines to Beijing in June 1900.[118]

The views of China among many Germans stationed in Beijing and Qingdao during the second half of the 1890s echoed the kaiser's hostility. The new German envoy Baron Clemens von Ketteler was not predisposed to be as Sinophobic as his predecessor, von Heyking, given his background as a translator trainee in Beijing and as a diplomatic translator there and in Canton.[119] In May 1900, however, von Ketteler allegedly told the other European envoys that the Boxer uprising signaled the onset of China's partition. Given the hysterical atmosphere among those hoping for a second "scramble," von Ketteler was immediately identified as an imperialist Sinophobe. He was reprimanded by the German Foreign Office, which never seriously entertained the idea of Chinese partition. During the Boxers' siege of Beijing in 1900, before any Europeans had been killed, von Ketteler ordered German legation troops to open fire on a group of fifty to one hundred Boxers who were engaging in what the German press called "war dances" (*Kriegstänze*—presumably the martial arts from which the Boxers' name

---

117. Sharf and Harrington 2000, p. 211.

118. BA-MA-Freiburg, RM 3, vol. 6782, especially "Denkschrift: Lage im Hinterlande von Kiautschou," October 4, 1900, pp. 80–97; and BA-MA-Freiburg, RM 51, vol. 7. The first Qingdao contingent, led by Premierleutnant (First Lieutenant) Count von Soden, left the colony at the beginning of June 1900, and two further companies departed in the second half of June to assist Edward Seymour's troops in Tianjin (Stichler 1989, p. 172).

119. P. Fischer 1994.

was derived) near the legation building, and seven Chinese were killed.[120] Von Ketteler also took potshots at Boxers from the walls of the German compound and personally beat a seventeen-year-old Yihetuan supporter who was captured and locked up in the Legation.[121]

The descriptions of Chinese officials by the "conqueror" of Qingdao, Admiral Otto von Diederichs, were replete with racial slurs.[122] The admiral identified various examples of what he called "scoundrelish behavior and the simplemindedness and superstition that accompanies it," and of "the trickiness and unreliability of the yellow race."[123] Diederichs treated General Zhang Gaoyuan disdainfully as "a helpless weakling" and drew on the discourse of Oriental despotism in describing the "subservience" of the people of Jiaozhou and Jimo as a result of their habitual "fear" of the local magistrates.[124]

Western propaganda in the context of the anti-Boxer campaign completed the process of bringing the Chinese under the sign of the generic racial "native" at the precise moment when the German colonial regime was taking shape.[125] The official *Amtsblatt* (*Gazette*) for the Qingdao colony printed an article in 1901 that began with the words "there can hardly be a single human race that has a less romantic appearance than the Chinese."[126] The Chinese scholar and reformer Kang Youwei, who moved into Captain Liliencron's former house in Qingdao in 1925, recognized that the Chinese

120. "Aus der Kolonie," *Nachrichten aus Kiautschou, Beiblatt zum "Ostasiatischen Lloyd,"* no. 39 (September 28, 1900): 194.

121. Preston 1999, p. 64, quoting from the unpublished diary of an Australian correspondent for the *London Times*, George Morrison; also O'Connor 1974, pp. 75, 95–96; Michael 1986, pp. 149–51; and Felber and Rostek 1987, p. 20.

122. Diederichs's description of a visit to the Zongli Yamen was almost identical to those of von Heyking and E. Wolf 1901, pp. 52–55: "Five or six gentlemen sat with partially stupid facial expressions" ("Die Besetzung von Tsingtau am 14.XI.1897," BA-MA-Freiburg, Nachlass Diederichs, vol. 24, p. 11).

123. Admiral Otto von Diederichs, "Die Besetzung von Tsingtau am 14.XI.1897," BA-MA-Freiburg, Nachlass Diederichs, vol. 24, pp. 42, 45; see also ibid., pp. 39, 45, on the "double-dealing" or "forked-tonguedness" (*Doppelzüngigkeit*) of Chinese officials.

124. Ibid., p. 24. Diederichs had somewhat friendlier things to say about the local officials in neighboring villages; see his report "Lage an Kiautschou Bucht," from February 15, 1898, BA-MA-Freiburg, RM 3, vol. 6697, p. 229r.

125. Two striking examples of this are the coffee-table books on the allied campaign, Kürschner 1901 and *Deutschland in China* 1902. Despite their patriotic, militaristic style of presentation, however, neither of these books was entirely univocal (see below).

126. "Chinesische Redeblumen," *Amtsblatt für das Deutsche Kiautschou-Gebiet*, May 11, 1901, p. 161.

"had at least been a half-civilized nation in the eyes of the west" before their defeat by Japan, but that afterward Europeans "put us on the same level as the Negro slaves in Africa."[127] A German vaudeville play from this period called *Our Bluejackets in Jiaozhou* began with the words "here among these Kaffirs"—using the South African generic epithet for "blacks" to refer to the Chinese.[128] In another play called *Boxer*, members of the German expeditionary force capture a Chinese woman who speaks German and ask her whether she "might have been on display in the Panoptikum" in Berlin, since "the most savage sorts of people" could be seen there.[129] The eminent founder of cellular pathology, Rudolph Virchow, invited the members of the Berlin Society for Anthropology, Ethnology, and Ancient History to view a group of Chinese who were being displayed at the Schumann Circus in Berlin in 1905.[130] Viewing *"Naturvölker"* in zoos, circuses, and fairs was not unusual in this period; what was novel was the inclusion of Chinese.[131]

A magazine associated with the German Navy League, *Überall*, is revealing with respect to the image of China in this period, which combined garden-variety Sinophobia with extreme belligerence. A 1901 report on "shipping along the Chinese coast" opened with the observation that "the entire economic existence of the Chinese presents not only stasis but often even regression."[132] Discussing a "revolt of Chinese coolies" in Samoa, the paper warned that if the Chinese dared to even touch a single white colonist, "well-suited trees and solid hemp ropes" would be found for them. The article concluded that these events in Samoa were "characteristic of the cunning and insidiousness of the yellow race."[133] A photograph of two Chinese boys in a 1899 issue of *Überall* was captioned simply "Two German Subjects," even though there was no article on Kiaochow at all, suggesting that the Chinese per se were being imagined as German subjects.[134]

The theme of "pestilential filth" had been a mainstay of Sinophobia since the mid-nineteenth century, and this idea was closely tied to "racial"

127. Kang's "Fifth Petition to the Throne" following the occupation of Jiaozhou, translated by Mühlhahn (2000, p. 106). On Kang Youwei see Lo 1967; Xiao 1975; Zhen 1991.

128. Schmasow n.d., p. 6.

129. Hellborn n.d. (ca. 1900-1901), p. 6.

130. See "Chinesentruppe," *Zeitschrift für Ethnologie* 37 (1905): 445.

131. There is a huge and repetitive literature on the sordid *Völkerschauen*; for example, Benninghoff-Luhl 1986.

132. "Schifffahrtsverhältnisse an der chinesischen Küste," *Überall* 3, pt. 2 (1903): 1118.

133. "Samoa: Revolte der chinesische Kulis auf Samoa," *Überall* 10 (11, 1907-8): 811.

134. *Überall* 1 (3, 1899): 40.

distaste. Officials in Qingdao insisted that the segregation of the Chinese was motivated by hygienic concerns. The planners did not decide to create a system of sewage and running water for all Chinese residents of Qingdao, however, which presumably would have solved the main hygiene problems. This resembles the logic of the German's uprooting the Duala people in Cameroon from their ancestral district and moving them kilometers away. They argued that this was necessary to keep Germans from being bitten by the malarial mosquitoes that were thought to arise inevitably in the presence of Africans. The alternative of clearing the malarial swamps and letting the Duala remain in their homes was not seriously entertained.[135]

Sinophobes were both fascinated with and repelled by the Chinese body, and as in the Khoikhoi and Samoan cases, this ambivalence was sexualized (even if less explicitly so that in the two other cases). A memo by one of the colony's sanitary councilors justifying urban segregation veered off into a hallucinatory tableau of desire and deviance: "Close cohabitation in tight spaces, filth and vermin, and above all the disgusting sexual deviations indulged in especially by the Chinese male make such a measure absolutely necessary. Sodomy by inserting the penis into the cloacae of large geese and ducks . . . and also pederasty, sexual abuse of children of both sexes, and rape in its most shocking forms, are all on the agenda in all of China. . . . The Chinaman certainly excites our genuine admiration with his sedulousness and . . . with the power and agility of his beautiful, athletically built body. . . . But as soon as the sun sets, depravity takes over in the opium dens, the harbor gin shops, and the bordellos."[136] Unlike in the Samoan case, European gender stereotypes were less conventionally (or nonfetishistically) heterosexual in the Sinophobic worldview. Chinese women only rarely figured as lovers of Europeans in these fantasies; instead, Europeans focused on footbinding, reproducing shocking anatomical pictures of Chinese women's feet.[137] This literature contains the same mixture of the grotesque and the prurient found in the literature on Khoikhoi female sexuality. Freud argued in his essay on fetishism, written in the same period,

135. Eckert 1999; "Enteignung in Duala," BA-Berlin, RKA, vols. 4427-31.

136. Kronecker 1913, pp. 11-12.

137. See, for example, Welcker 1870, 1872; Stricker 1871; and Virchow 1903. British and French anthropologists were no less fascinated by footbinding. For psychoanalysis footbinding can be interpreted as a form of fetishism, which for Freud was not homosexual but an alternative way for men to fend off "the fright of castration at the sight of a female genital" without becoming homosexual as a result ([1927] 1963, p. 154). Freud interprets footbinding as "mutilating the female foot and then revering it like a fetish" (p. 157).

that heterosexual European men often unconsciously elided the foot or shoe with the female genitals. But in the case of footbinding the fetish function was disrupted, since the deformed foot gestured precisely toward that "genital mutilation" (female castration) that fetishism was supposed to disavow (according to Freud). Figure 7.9, published in the anthropological journal *Archiv für Anthropologie* in 1871, contributed an additional mutilation of its own, severing the leg above the ankle.

There were few precedents for a program of attempting to remake Chinese culture along the lines of the acculturation program in Southwest Africa. Geographer Georg Wegener insisted that there was simply "no possibility of understanding between the two races."[138] Ovaherero culture had also been described in the precolonial era as impenetrable, but the Germans seemed to believe that loss of land and cattle and the trauma of the genocide would dissolve Ovaherero culture and allow it to be remolded in more useful ways. By contrast, even the missionaries did not believe that Chinese culture was vulnerable to being forcibly transformed by external forces. The dogged resistance by the Chinese state and people to Western imperialism made projects of cultural substitution seem implausible. Chinese arrogance may have been a Sinophobic theme, but it indirectly indexed real practices of resistance. The German writer Alfons Paquet wrote that "even the lowest of these yellow-brown people carries with him like an amulet the consciousness and the instincts of his people's ancient culture."[139] Kiaochow's chief engineer ended his report about a reconnaissance trip in Shandong Province with a list of "prominent characteristics" of the Chinese, which included the fact that they "consider us to be barbarians." He concluded: "Each one of them is very aware of the Middle Kingdom's ancient culture."[140] Theories of Asiatic despotism convinced Diederichs that the local authorities in Shandong "possess[ed] and exercise[d] an absolute authority over the people that none of our military commanders could ever attain with his own troops." The Chinese were extremely unlikely to switch their allegiances.[141]

German interventions during the initial segregationist phase of colonial rule in Kiaochow were interlaced with, or undermined by, strains of

---

138. Wegener 1904, p. 54.

139. Pacquet 1911, p. vi.

140. A. Gaedertz, "Eine Rekognoszierungsreise in der Provinz Shantung (Schluss)," *Nachrichten aus Kiautschou, Beiblatt zum "Ostasiatischen Lloyd,"* no. 49 (September 9, 1899): 3.

141. Diederichs's report, "Lage an Kiautschou Bucht," February 15, 1898, BA-MA-Freiburg, RM 3, vol. 6697, p. 229r.

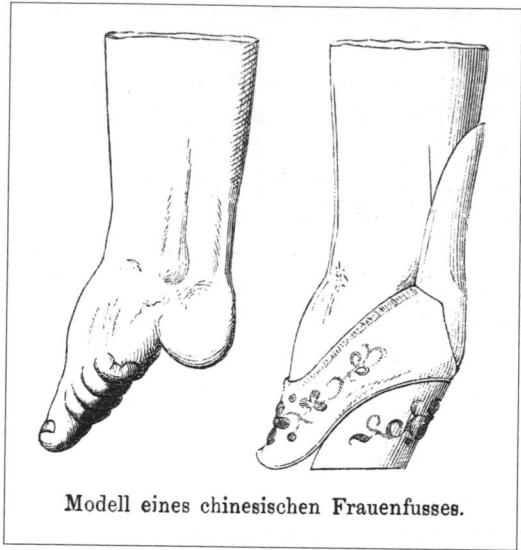

Modell eines chinesischen Frauenfusses.

FIGURE 7.9 Model of a Chinese woman's foot crippled
by footbinding. From Welcker 1870, p. 223.

classical Sinophilia. Even the actions of the conqueror of Qingdao were
haunted by Sinophilia. Admiral Diederichs asserted that Chinese workers,
though driven mainly by fear, nonetheless had "a refined sense of justice."[142]
The idea of a deeply rooted sense of justice putting limits on the ruling elite
had been a central theme of early Sinophilia. Diederichs defended the use
of flogging as punishment in an official report in February 1898 by referring to the authority of the "Chinese punitive specifications communicated
by the Bureaucrat Koo of Jiaozhou," suggesting at the very least a certain
desire for legitimacy in Chinese eyes.[143] Kiaochow's first German newspaper, the *Deutsch-Asiatische Warte*, attacked the colonial administration for its
alleged coddling of the Chinese and its "extreme sensitivity in favor of the
Chinese population."[144] And indeed, the colonial bureaucrat who struck a
Chinese with his whip for not moving from the sidewalk to let him pass,
mentioned above, was berated by the governor, Jaeschke, who happened to
be riding past on horseback at that moment. The *Deutsch-Asiatische Warte*
commented that this was "characteristic of the kid-glove treatment of the

142. Ibid.
143. Ibid., p. 229v.
144. Quoted in Seelemann 1982, pp. 81–82.

natives as it is wrongly instituted by the offices here."[145] Colonial policy was not all of a single piece, even in the first decade.

After 1904 or 1905, the forces associated with Sinophilia increasingly placed their stamp on native policy. Where the founders of the colony had failed to propose any project for remaking the Chinese soul, Sinophiles like Richard Wilhelm hoped to penetrate the "soul of China" (the title of his famous book) and to coax it out of its seclusion.

The Seminar for Oriental Languages and German Sinology as a Conduit for Sinophilia

Sinophile ideas were actively represented in the colony by the translators and by various graduates of the Seminar für Orientalische Sprachen (Seminar for Oriental Languages). This seminar was a language-training institute at the University of Berlin, founded in 1887 with the central purpose of educating officials for the foreign service.[146] Chinese was the language in which the largest number of translators graduated from the seminar before 1918. Although most of the Germans in the colony were associated with the navy, many of those bound for posts as district officials, translators, and other civil and military positions had studied at the seminar.[147] Academic Sinology, including the more pragmatic versions of it that proliferated at the Berlin seminar, was a breeding ground for the more moderate approach to China that increasingly set the tone for native policy in Kiaochow. Translators were present in the colonial administration from the beginning; translator Schrameier was the founder of the colony's native policy. As the Foreign Office and the German envoys in Beijing and Ji'nan shifted toward a friendlier stance toward China, the views of the translators, Sinologists, moderate missionaries, and other Sinophile groups in Kiaochow became increasingly influential in the day-to-day creation and implementation of native policy.

The seminar was significant not just because its students learned some Chinese but because it was not permeated by the Sinophobia that was

145. "Aus Tsingtau," *Deutsch-Asiatische Warte*, July 15, 1900, p. 2.

146. Sachau 1912; Ruland 1973, p. 54; Morgenroth 1990.

147. Hövermann 1914, p. 27. Lists of SOS graduates and their job placements are given in *Mitteilungen des Seminars für Orientalische Sprachen zu Berlin*, starting in 1899. Seelemann (1982) overemphasizes a programmatic split between a Sinophile Foreign Office and a Sinophobic navy. The German envoys von Brand, von Heyking, and von Ketteler all pushed a Sinophobic and imperialist line, but none of them came up through the navy. The change in policy that Seelemann attributes to the new German envoy to China Count Arthur von Rex (1906–11) cannot be traced to a policy line characteristic of the German foreign service per se.

standard in military and diplomatic circles at the turn of the century.[148] The seminar's mandate, as it evolved in the years after 1887, encompassed not just modern Asian languages but also Swahili and other African languages (and eventually European languages), as well as applied topics relevant to colonial service and trade, such as tropical hygiene, colonial law, administration, history, and missionary work. The seminar's journal, *Mitteilungen des Seminars für Orientalische Sprachen zu Berlin* (Communications of the Berlin Seminar for Oriental Languages, first issued in 1898) encompassed more than colonial and linguistic questions, just as the seminar's teachers lectured and wrote on a broader range of topics. Officially the journal's purview encompassed "literature, customs and mores, religion, legal views and institutions," the "general historical and cultural development of the specific peoples," and "art and culture." Although the editors specified that contributions were supposed to connect these themes to "trade, missions, and German colonialism," this guideline was not strictly adhered to.[149] Topics actually covered in the *Mitteilungen* ranged from the reorganization of the Chinese army to the work of the neo-Daoist philosopher Wang Chong.

The publications of most of the faculty, including Carl Arendt, the seminar's director from 1887 to 1902, "attempted to counter dominant prejudices and to evince understanding for China."[150] Arendt was a former translator and secretary at the German legation in Beijing. He lectured and published on modern Chinese history, edited the East Asian section of the *Mitteilungen*, and argued against the theory that the Chinese language lacked a grammar. Another typical figure at the seminar was Alfred Forke, who combined a respectful interest in Chinese philosophy and high culture with distaste for some of the more mundane aspects of everyday Chinese existence.[151] Forke's long account of a trip from Beijing to Xi'an and Luoyang in 1898, for

148. The renowned Chinese historian and Sinophobe J. J. M. de Groot was not part of the SOS, although he published in its journal. De Groot arrived in Berlin in 1912, taking up the first regular German university appointment in Sinology. An exception to the Sinophilia of the seminar's faculty was Wilhelm Schüler, who had been a missionary in Qingdao and Shanghai before receiving a teaching post at the seminar in 1914. Schüler's book on China and Shandong was published by the Qingdao branch of the German Colonial Society and contained no criticism of German colonialism; see Schüler 1912, pp. 347–63; and Leutner 1987, pp. 41–43.

149. *Mitteilungen des Seminars für Ostasiatische Sprachen zu Berlin* 1 (1, 1898): i, v.

150. Leutner 1987, p. 41.

151. Forke translated and commented on the *Lun Heng*, the main work of Han dynasty philosopher Wang Chong, in *Mitteilungen des Seminars für Orientalische Sprachen zu Berlin*, vols. 9–11. See Emmerich 1999.

instance, contained none of the deprecating comments about the Chinese or advice for dealing with the "natives" that peppered the travel narratives of von Richthofen. Forke "distanced himself" from the violent German occupation of Kiaochow and criticized "Christian conversion at the point of a gun."[152] Erich Haenisch, a student of J. J. M. de Groot and the first German Sinologist to write a *Habilitation* thesis, wrote extensively, sometimes in the *Mitteilungen*, on China in the Mongol (Yuan dynasty) and Manchu (Qing dynasty) periods and on the role of Confucianism in Chinese history.[153] The seminar also employed Chinese teachers and lecturers—perhaps one reason that de Groot scorned the institution.[154] One of these Chinese faculty members, Wang Ching Dao, published an article in the *Mitteilungen* on "the Confucian idea of the state and its relationship to constitutionalism."[155] It would be difficult to find a better example of early-twentieth-century transculturation in the German-Chinese milieu than this essay, in view of the role of German constitutional law (both directly and mediated through Japan) in the ongoing Chinese reforms of the era. Wang relied on German theorists such as Georg Jellinek, Hermann Rehm, and Hegel (although he criticized the latter's interpretation of China) and discussed the work of China specialists Karl Gützlaff, Richard Wilhelm, Max von Brant, and Johann Heinrich Plath.

Even before the creation of the Seminar for Oriental Languages, the typical experiences of German translators during their linguistic training in Beijing were conducive to Sinophilia. The German envoys or ministers, by contrast, socialized mainly with other European elites.[156] Each of the translator trainees had his own Chinese mandarin as a teacher, available to him throughout the day.[157] Wilhelm Schrameier arrived in Beijing in 1885 and worked as a translator at the German consulates in Hong Kong and

152. Leutner 1987, p. 43, citing an article by Forke from 1914.

153. Bauer 1967, p. 207; Haenisch 1905. In Haenisch's very professional work the entire debate between Sinophobes and Sinophiles has already been left behind.

154. On the hiring of these Chinese teachers, see BA-Berlin, DBC, vol. 656; for their names, see the *Mitteilungen*, vols. 7, 1 (1904: I–II); 8, 1 (1905: I–II); 11, 1 (1908: I–II); 14, 1 (1911: I–II); and 15, 1 (1912: I–II).

155. C. Wang 1913.

156. It is worth noting that German envoy Max von Brandt (1874–93), who served in Beijing before the recrudescence of Sinophobia at the end of the century, was less imbued with that ideology than his successors Gustav Schenck zu Schweinsberg (1893–96), Edmund von Heyking (1896–99), and Clemens von Ketteler (1899–1900). In the heat of the most Sinophobic and colonialist moment von Brandt published an interesting book entitled *Chinese Philosophy and State Confucianism* (1898).

157. According to the recollections of Otto Franke (1954, p. 47).

Canton and in the general consulate in Shanghai before taking up his post in the Kiaochow administration. According to Schrameier, the translator trainees in Beijing haunted the Chinese theaters and the antique stores, where merchants provided them with an "initial comprehensive introduction to Chinese art history."[158] Sinophilia had not been entirely suppressed. Such curiosity about Chinese culture would mark Schrameier and others like him as "subaltern" in the eyes of diplomats from the nobility and militarists like Kaiser Wilhelm.

Rapprochement: The Second Phase of German Colonialism in Kiaochow, 1905–14

A frivolous game with promises was played with China, which was treated . . . like a Negro state of secondary importance [wie einen Negerstaat zweiter Güte].
RICHARD WILHELM[159]

By 1905 new institutions were beginning to be superimposed on the original apartheid-like infrastructure in Qingdao. These new policies embodied a program of rapprochement, syncretism, and exchange between two civilizations conceptualized as different but relatively equal in value. Although Kiaochow was often criticized for its military character during the early years, Oskar Truppel presided over what was essentially a demilitarization of the colony and what he called "a balancing of the differing [Chinese and German] ways of thought" during his governorship (1901–11). This "balancing" took place largely against his will, but not against the wishes of the higher German authorities in Berlin and Beijing or many of the lower-level civil servants in Kiaochow.[160]

The expansion of the German military presence outside Kiaochow was linked to a sneering distaste for Chinese culture and a refusal to treat the Shandong provincial authorities as equals. When Shandong governor Zhou Fu announced his intention to visit Qingdao in 1902 Truppel's immediate response was that this was "barely believable."[161] But Zhou Fu did visit

158. Matzat 1985, p. 4.

159. Wilhelm 1928, p. 367.

160. For a representative depiction of Kiaochow as a militarized colony in the early period, see Bigelow 1898, p. 585. The quote is from a report signed by the acting governor rather than Truppel, but its content makes it clearly identifiable as the product of the latter (Imperial Government of Kiaochow to von Rex, BA-Berlin, DBC, vol. 1258, p. 217v).

161. Truppel to Mumm, December 24, 1902, BA-Berlin, R. 9208, vol. 1239, p. 5; quoted in Stichler 1989, p. 224.

Qingdao (and later moved to the colony). Richard Wilhelm recalled this event as having put an end to the "antagonistic atmosphere" by demonstrating "that more could be achieved on both sides by mutual trust and goodwill." The most important result, according to Wilhelm, was that "the two cultures came into contact."[162] Truppel soon reciprocated, visiting Zhou Fu in Ji'nan, and his visit was turned into a grand ceremonial event.[163] Soon after Zhou Fu's replacement as provincial governor in November 1904 by Hu Tinggan (who was replaced in turn by a young nationalist, Yang Shixiang, early in 1905), the German troops pulled back into Qingdao, abandoning their garrisons in Gaomi and Jiaozhou.[164] In 1910, a photograph appeared in the *Berliner Abend-Zeitung* with the caption "The children of the two governors playing together," which seemed put Governor Truppel and the Shandong governor Sun Baoqi on an equal footing (fig. 7.10).[165] Photographs were taken of German colonial governors meeting other Shandong governors and state officials in which they posed as equals.

The 1905 accord on the withdrawal of German troops back into the leasehold from the province happened concurrently with a German movement toward policies of cultivating "cultural-political relationships, especially with the educated Chinese upper strata."[166] In 1905 the colony's chief justice, Dr. Crusen, proclaimed in a public lecture in Qingdao that "the so-called fifty-kilometer zone in Shandong is not a [sphere of influence] and is destined to remain Chinese forever."[167] One of the other early signs of change had been the creation of the Chinese Committee in Qingdao in 1902.[168] Between 1902 and 1910 the twelve members of this committee were selected by Chinese merchants from the three provincial guilds (*huiguan*) active in Kiaochow: the Jiyan guild, representing merchants from Shandong and Tianjin, the Sanjiang guild, representing the lower Yangtzi

162. R. Wilhelm 1928, p. 166.

163. See Truppel, "Reise in das Innere Shantungs," June 1, 1903, Anlage 2 ("Aufenthalt in Tsinanfu"), BA-MA-Freiburg, Nachlass Truppel, vol. 19, pp. 12v–14v.

164. Schrecker 1971, pp. 166–69; Mühlhahn 2000, p. 131.

165. "Bilder vom Tage," *Tägliche Sonder-Beilage der Berliner Abend-Zeitung*, June 16, 1910, p. 3. On Truppel's relations with Zhou Fu, see BA-MA-Freiburg, Nachlass Truppel, vol. 33. On Sun Baoqi, who governed Shandong from 1909 to 1912, see Mühlhahn 2000, p. 473.

166. Stichler 1988, p. 117.

167. "Lokalnachrichten," *Tsingtauer Neueste Nachrichten* 2 (November 29, 1905): 2.

168. Kiaochow *Denkschrift* for 1901–2, p. 23. Stichler discusses the committee as part of the German administration in terms of "collaboration" and a "comprador" class; conversely, Mühlhahn 2000, pp. 271–73, includes it under the category of Chinese strategies of resistance. Both views are partially correct but incomplete.

FIGURE 7.10 Children of the German governor of Kiaochow and the Chinese governor of Shandong province playing together. From BA-MA-Freiburg, Nachlass Truppel, vol. 90, document 25. (Courtesy of BA-MA-Freiburg.)

region; and the Guangdong guild, made up of merchants from Canton.[169] After 1910 the governor himself selected four representatives (*Vertrauensmänner*) from these guilds—two from the Jiyan guild and one each from the Sanjiang and Guangdong guilds.[170] Although this was a step backward in terms of representativeness and Chinese influence, the idea was that the *Vertrauensmänner* would eventually become part of the advisory committee to the governor, which had hitherto consisted exclusively of Europeans.[171] A Chinese chamber of commerce was also created in 1909.[172]

In 1904 a colonial bank director publicly praised Truppel for making the Chinese "what they should be, namely, fully equal citizens [*Bürger*] of our colony."[173] This was certainly an exaggeration: the Chinese did not have equal rights, and the dualistic legal system remained in place until the end

169. Zhang Yufa 1986, pp. 835-36; F. Huang 1999, p. 104.

170. Mühlhahn 2000, p. 161; Hövermann 1914, pp. 26-27.

171. Mohr 1911, p. 21.

172. "Die chinesische Handelskammer in Tsingtau," *Tsingtauer Neueste Nachrichten* 6 (12 October 1909): 2.

173. "Festive Speech of Bank Director Homann on the Occasion of the Onset of Governor Truppel's Vacation, November 6, 1904," BA-MA-Freiburg, Nachlass Truppel, vol. 59, p. 3.

of the German colonial period. Still, the colony was moving in the direction of greater legal and cultural equality. When the Qing dynasty was toppled in the 1911 Xinhai revolution, many upper-class Chinese scholars and ex-officials streamed into Qingdao from around the country.[174] Several wealthy Chinese residents of Qingdao had German wives. Partly as a result of the fact that "racial mixing" was occurring at a high social class level, but also due to the liberalizing trend in German-Chinese relations, the ban on Chinese residence in the European district was partly lifted. After 1912 there were very few areas in Qingdao that were off limits to elite Chinese. Some rich Chinese began to vacation on Qingdao's beaches alongside European tourists.[175] In 1914, a law was passed stipulating that any Chinese could live in the city's European district with the permission of the governor and the approval of three-fourths of the members of the citizens' representative council.[176] Although mixed marriage was being banned and children of mixed marriages were being deprived of their German citizenship precisely at the same time in other German colonies, children of mixed Chinese and German heritage in Kiaochow retained the possibility of being treated legally as Germans (even if there was still discrimination in colonial civil society). Laws forbidding mixed marriage were never seriously entertained in Kiaochow. Instead, discussions of the topic of mixed marriage in the German East Asian press were focused on the Chinese government's ban on Chinese students marrying foreigners while studying abroad.[177] From the perspective of German colonialism in Africa or the Pacific, this reversal seemed incredible. Although some Germans living in Qingdao campaigned against the admission of qualified Chinese students to the German gymnasium, the colonial administration defended their presence, defying settlers, as in Samoa.[178]

German buildings also began to combine Chinese and European design elements, and a few were done in a fully Chinese style. During the early years of the colony any direct association of German and Chinese architecture was strictly a matter of temporary necessity or a gesture of symbolic

174. Schüler 1912, pp. 361–62; R. Wilhelm 1928, pp. 169ff.; *Kiautschou im Jahre 1911* (Tsingtau: Deutsch-chinesische Druckerei & Verlagsanstalt Walther Schmidt, 1911), p. 1.

175. Seelemann 1982, pp. 144, 158, 145, 209. The relocation of Chinese government officials to Qingdao is discussed in Meyer-Waldeck, "Monatsbericht für den Monat Januar 1913," February 21, 1913, BA-MA-Freiburg, RM 3, vol. 6765, pp. 325rv.

176. "Verordnung betr. Wohnen von Chinesen im Europäerviertel," *Amtsblatt für das Deutsche Kiautschou-Gebiet,* January 23, 1914, p. 17.

177. "Verbot von Mischehen," *Der Ostasiatischer Lloyd,* May 27, 1910, p. 534.

178. "Zur Schulfrage," *Tsingtauer Neueste Nachrichten* 2 (November 29, 1905): 1; 2 (December 2, 1905): 2.

FIGURE 7.II German officials preening in front of occupied Qingdao *yamen,* from Admiral Diederichs's photo album. From BA-MA-Freiburg, Nachlass Diederichs, vol. 45. (Courtesy of BA-MA-Freiburg.)

domination. Thus, the Qingdao *yamen* building was occupied (fig. 7.11) as a show of power and because the Germans initially wanted to concentrate their efforts on other construction projects, but the main German administrative building that was completed in 1906 was done in an almost completely German style (fig. 7.12).[179] Other aspects of early architecture were generically "colonial" or "Oriental" without being specifically Chinese.[180] The veranda, for instance, was a characteristic feature of German villas and public buildings in Qingdao.[181] The governor's mansion (fig. 7.13), completed in October 1907, had verandas whose exotic or decorative function was indicated by the fact that "some of them could not even be entered from the rooms behind them."[182]

The countryside villa of the colony's chief justice, Dr. Crusen, had a

179. The Prinz-Heinrich Hotel on the Kaiser-Wilhelm Ufer, built around 1900, was decorated on its eastern facade "with the Chinese character 'shou,' meaning long life" (Warner 1994, p. 268).

180. A Danish journalist who visited Qingdao in 1910 described the city's German villas as being built in a "German-Oriental style" ("Schanghai und Tsingtau," *Ostasiatischer Lloyd,* March 11, 1910, p. 253).

181. Weicker 1908, p. 47.

182. Lind 1988, pp. 100-101; see also Warner 1994, pp. 206-9.

FIGURE 7.12 (top) Headquarters of the German colonial administration (Gouvernements-Dienstgebäude), Qingdao, completed 1906. Photo by the author, 2005.

FIGURE 7.13 (bottom) German governor's residence, Qingdao (ca. 1910). From BA-MA-Freiburg, Nachlass Truppel, vol. 80. (Courtesy of BA-MA-Freiburg.)

small "Chinese temple" on its grounds.[183] A photo of the interior of another colonial judge's home from the period shows a Chinese-style standing-screen wall in one of the rooms.[184] A serious scholarly study of Chinese architecture was undertaken in 1906 by Ernst Boerschmann, who had first been sent to China in 1902 as a civil engineer for the German troops occupying Beijing. He spent a good deal of time in Qingdao. Boerschmann was given a leave of absence from the army to travel in China from 1906 to 1909, and his study was financed by the German and Prussian governments. He was convinced of the "greatness of Chinese culture" and set out to study the "most impressive buildings in the most important, religiously significant places and in the centers of spiritual and economic life, just as we would do in the study of our own culture." Boerschmann believed that religious and philosophical texts were the highest expression of China's culture and that they were "revealed in Chinese art, especially in architecture, with a precision that has not been attained by our own artistic creation."[185] The fact that German government agencies were now promoting the study of Chinese architecture rather than knocking down Chinese walls with cannonballs was part of a rather abrupt change in goals and prevailing ethnographic representations in this period.

The sheer presence of stylistic hybridity does not yet reveal the meaning to the Germans of the inclusion of Chinese architectural elements in Qingdao buildings. For example, the massive gargoylelike dragon above the main entrance of the governor's mansion (fig. 7.14) was perhaps meant to invoke "Viking" or European gothic dragons rather than Chinese ones.[186] It is not a repeated motif, however, but a singular one. Furthermore, the dragon seems to rise like a ship out of the pattern of waves carved into the granite eves, and it faces west rather than east.[187] This strengthens the sense of the dragon as being closer to Zheng He (the mythical Chinese navigator) than James Cook. These peculiarities of the design, combined with the very anomaly of including a dragon—whether European or Chinese—in a twentieth-century German structure, indicate that processes of transcultur-

183. BA-MA-Freiburg, Nachlass Truppel, vol. 79, p. 3v, photo "Partie auf dem Lauschan."

184. BA-MA-Freiburg, Nachlass Truppel, vol. 79, p. 17v, photo "Oberrichter Wilke und Frau in ihrem Zimmer."

185. Boerschmann 1911–14, vol. I, p. xiv.

186. Warner 1994, p. 206.

187. Town planning and architecture had been sensitive to issues of compass directions in China much longer than in Germany, of course. In the planning of Qingdao, Germany applied the grid pattern only to the Chinese districts; in the European district the course of streets and avenues conformed to the lay of the land and meandered in an effort to avoid the spread of windblown dust and also to make a non-Chinese impression.

FIGURE 7.14 (top left) Dragon on the roof of the German governor's residence, Qingdao. (Photo courtesy of Zhu Jianjun and Xiang Gu, 2005.)

FIGURE 7.15 (below) Painting in the German governor's residence, Qingdao, detail. Photo by the author, 2005.

FIGURE 7.16 (top right) Mecklenburghaus Convalescent Home, Kiaochow colony. From Lind 1998, p. 104.

ation had penetrated to the heart of the colonial state. Both of the mansion's architects were part of the colonial government and therefore responsible for the regime's self-presentation. One scroll-shaped painting inside the governor's residence seemed to show Qingdao in an earlier period, unsullied by European colonialism (fig. 7.15). The Mecklenburghaus Convalescent Home (fig. 7.16), built in 1903, combined Chinese roof elements and columns with German *Fachwerk*-style heavy wooden beams and stone.

A final example of architectural syncretism is the Tsingtau-Klub, completed in 1911, which contains a traditional "spirit wall" (*yingbi*, literally, "shadow wall") at the entrance (plate 10). Like bridges shaped in the zigzag form, these walls were believed to keep malevolent sprits at bay; more positively, the *yingbi* was a plastic expression of metaphysical ideas, of the "thought of eternity," also often represented by a mirror. The German wall

FIGURE 7.17 Spirit wall at Fayu temple on Putuoshan Island. From Boerschmann 1911–14, 1:41.

in question is made of blue porcelain tiles that recall the colors of the Temple of Heaven in Beijing and decorative walls inside the Forbidden City. The overall design of the Qingdao wall resembles that of traditional spirit walls such as the one in figure 7.17 from the Fa-Yu Temple on Putuoshan (普陀山) Island, with the larger mirrorlike image in the center flanked by symmetrical rows of smaller rectangular ornaments on both sides. Whereas the central images in the great spirit walls often depicted a "powerful mythical animal resembling a tiger in . . . extremely stylized and bizarre form," the German ghost wall inside the Tsingtau-Klub had a stylized German eagle at its center and a fireplace. The existence of a German "spirit wall" is more than ironic, since Chinese were prohibited from joining the Tsingtau-Klub until quite late, and also in light of the European predilection for knocking down Chinese walls as punishment for China's "decades of high-walled exclusion" of foreigners.[188]

188. On the Tsingtau-Klub wall see Warner 1994, p. 262; and Biener 2001, p. 105; neither author comments on the irony of the club's spirit wall. On the use and meaning of spirit walls in Chinese elite architecture, see Boerschmann 1911–14, vol. 1, pp. 41–45; and in vernacular architecture see Knapp 1989, p. 171. Seelemann 1982, p. 422, mentions the ban on Chinese membership in German clubs in Qingdao; the first quote is from Boerschmann 1911–14, vol. 1, p. 42; the second quote is from Hevia 1992, p. 315.

Other examples of the emerging approach to native policy were found in the sphere of education.[189] A "German-Chinese school" had already existed in the early years of the colony, but the classes were held in German and the aim was to accustom the Chinese students to "discipline" and to train translators for the navy and the government.[190] In 1905 the government opened the first of twenty-seven Chinese grammar schools in the colony.[191] Instruction was carried out by two groups: Chinese teachers who had gained a reputation in the villages for their Confucian learning and German missionaries from the General Evangelical-Protestant Missionary Association (Allgemeiner Evangelisch-Protestantischer Missionsverein), or "Weimar Mission."[192] This was one of three Protestant missions operating in Kiaochow, in addition to the Catholic Steyl Mission. The Weimar Mission was a liberal, nationalist, "high church" association, founded in 1884 by theology professors and pastors who wanted to "distance themselves consciously from the dominant 'Pietistic' strand of the [Protestant] missionary movement" in Germany.[193] Rather than emphasizing conversion to Christianity, the Weimar Mission pursued a classical Jesuit strategy of seeking influence through the educated Chinese elites. In practical terms this meant that the Weimar missionaries focused their teaching to the children of the higher Chinese social classes on secular topics, networked with Chinese literati, and translated "the best of European and American literature" into Chinese. The Chinese grammar schools in the colony relied on the standard five-year Chinese elementary school curriculum, supplemented by German language instruction during the last two years.[194] In a significant gesture of cultural reconciliation, given the fraught history of Christianity in China, the curriculum contained no religious material at all.[195]

The Weimar Mission's most significant activity in Kiaochow was the

189. See Zhang Yufa 1999 for an excellent overview of German schools in Qingdao; and Kreissler 1989, Y. Huang 1995, and Kim 2004 for more comprehensive studies.

190. "Pruefung in der Deutsch Chinesischen-Schule," *Nachrichten aus Kiautschou, Beiblatt zum "Ostasiatischen Lloyd,"* no. 19 (February 4, 1899): 2.

191. See the remarks by a former Chinese teacher in the colony (Luan Baode 1982), and the comments in "Denkschrift über Einrichtung chinesischer Schulen im Schutzgebiet," BA-Berlin, DBC, vol. 1258, p. 45v.

192. R. Wilhelm n.d.; Stichler 1989, p. 254.

193. Gründer 1982, p. 44; Mogk 1972, p. 161. Seelemann 1982 refers to the Weimar Mission appropriately as "high church."

194. Weicker 1908, p. 190; R. Wilhelm n.d., p. 8.

195. The government-run naval dockyards school trained Chinese apprentices, who were drawn from the provincial villages of Shandong. They were given instruction in Chinese and examined in technical matters as well as Chinese history and geography (Seelemann 1982, p. 376).

creation of the Qingdao German-Chinese Seminar (Deutsch-Chinesisches Seminar), a *gymnasium* for adolescent boys. The seminar was headed by Richard Wilhelm, the future Sinologist and Weimar Republic intellectual. The seminar trained Chinese teachers for the colony's elementary schools. Shandong governor Zhou Fu also decreed that graduates of the seminar could take the exam to enter the provincial university in Ji'nan.[196] The instructors for Chinese, math, physics, and chemistry classes were Chinese; Germans taught German language and history. The school gained an excellent reputation, and Chinese officials and wealthy families sent their sons there.[197] As in the grammar schools, there was no religious instruction and Christian holidays were not celebrated.[198]

Richard Wilhelm defended the idea of a mainly Chinese curriculum devoid of Christian teaching, arguing that cultural exchange should not be reduced to the simple transfer of European "machine culture" or even the "proven truths of European science," but should entail "an appropriation of our thinking and inner life, both religious and scientific," with all of its "contradictions and insufficiencies."[199] For Wilhelm, Chinese was "one of the most significant literary languages," a "cultural oeuvre and an educational means . . . of the highest sort," without which China's admirable "state and culture would be unthinkable." Rejecting the Sinophobic claim that Chinese was linguistically primitive, Wilhelm described the Chinese script as "the containers into which a highly gifted people has placed its entire mental labor and the best works of its soul for millennia." Just "a few of these characters taken together," he marveled, "express an entire worldview with wonderful simplicity." Wilhelm spoke approvingly of one "German in Shandong who stuck his young son into a Chinese village school, in which he learned the discourses of Confucius, the famous teacher of the Chinese, just like any Chinese youngster." The "enemy" in Wilhelm's view was "not Confucianism, but the alienation and despiritualization of Chinese humanity due to a superficial European education."[200] According to the recollections of one of the Chinese teachers at the seminar, Wilhelm often presided over early morning gatherings in which he discussed the

---

196. Kiaochow *Denkschrift* for 1905–6, p. 38; S. Wilhelm 1956, pp. 119–21.

197. Luan Baode 1982.

198. Gerber 2003, p. 174.

199. R. Wilhelm n.d., p. 10. As Leutner (1997, p. 431) points out, the idea that religious lessons should be voluntary was also accepted by Bishop Anzer and the Steyl missionaries when they set up their middle schools in Yanzhou and Jining in 1902. But the Catholic missions in Kiaochow and elsewhere remained committed to the goals of Christian instruction and conversion.

200. R. Wilhelm n.d., pp. 8–10.

ethical teachings of Confucius, Mencius, and Christianity. Wilhelm also elaborated an entire program of cultural synthesis and exchange that had a different accent from that of the more blatant "cultural imperialism" being proposed by figures like Karl Lamprecht and the former settlement commissary in Southwest Africa, Paul Rohrbach.[201] After being introduced to Chinese culture by Richard Wilhelm, Rohrbach helped create a *gymnasium* for girls in Qingdao, the "Schu-Fan" (Shufan) School in the Taixizhen district.[202] The Schu-Fan School's curriculum, like that of the German-Chinese Seminar for boys, was part Chinese and part German and was oriented toward the children of the local Chinese elite.[203]

The most dramatic illustration of the shift in native policy is the creation of the Qingdao German-Chinese college (deutsch-chinesische Hochschule).[204] The college was first proposed to the Navy Office in 1905 in a plan that was signed by the acting governor of Kiaochow but probably written by the commissary for Chinese affairs, Wilhelm Schrameier, who was influenced by discussions with Richard Wilhelm.[205] Schrameier envisioned

201. Luan Baode 1982. On "cultural imperialism" in Wilhelmine Germany see Bruch 1982; Kloosterhuis 1994; and Rohrbach 1910, 1912.

202. See Mogk 1972, p. 162; F. Huang 1999, pp. 170–71; Blumhardt n.d.; and the Schu-Fan School's first year's report, in BA-Berlin, DBC, vol. 1259, after p. 265. Rohrbach was employed briefly by the Weimar Mission as a propagandist (Mogk 1972, p. 162). Gründer (1982, p. 314) interprets both Rohrbach and Wilhelm as trying to extend German influence over China through schooling, medicine, and scientific pursuits. This is too sweeping, in my view, in light of Wilhelm's already skeptical approach to German colonialism in his November 24, 1900, report on the German devastation in the Gaomi region (reprinted in Leutner 1997, p. 287). Rohrbach, by contrast, did not hesitate to speak of the "yellow race" (1912, p. 23). Asking rhetorically whether the Chinese "are actually a *Kulturvolk* in the true and profound sense of the word," he answered that China was "'barbarous' in an objective sense." Rohrbach also endorsed the thesis of Chinese stagnation (1909a, pp. 3, 11). Such tropes are not found in Wilhelm's writings.

203. Blumhardt n.d.

204. The college has been discussed by Kreissler (1989, pp. 131–38); see also *Tsingtauer Neueste Nachrichten*, October 26, 1909, p. 2; and August 1, 1913, p. 2; Mou Le 1914; O. Franke 1911b, 1954; Schrecker 1971, pp. 244–45; Luan Baode 1982; Stichler 1989, pp. 252–91; and Mühlhahn 1999, 2000.

205. See Stichler 1989, p. 255; and Matzat 1998b, p. 80, for the assessment of the document's authorship. As Matzat points out, Acting Governor Jacobson was an "unknown lieutenant commander" who was replacing Commander Funk, who was himself representing the absent Governor Truppel. The memo's detailed discussion of European schools elsewhere in China makes it unlikely that anyone in Qingdao other than Schrameier could have written it, as do the nearly identical formulations in a memorandum signed by Schrameier in 1908 (BA-Berlin, DBC, vol. 1258, pp. 29–47). This issue of authorship supports my general argument about the social basis of the Sinophilic turn in native policy: Schrameier came from the translating corps, a milieu that was more respectful of China than the military. The fact that he had enough influence

a unified school system in the colony reaching from the elementary to the college level. His ultimate goal was for these schools to "influence the Chinese spirit and character in an all-encompassing manner and to become the mechanism for permeating the entire province, the Shandong hinterland that depends economically on Qingdao, with German knowledge and German spirit."[206] At this early stage of discussion the college was construed as having an entirely German curriculum; Chinese material would be treated in the elementary schools. The German envoy to China, Count Arthur von Rex, proposed the idea of a German-Chinese university for Qingdao in 1907, and Navy Secretary von Tirpitz immediately endorsed the idea of "an educational institution on a larger scale in the interest of our influence in China." Von Tirpitz broke with the segregationism that had hitherto prevailed in the colony and moved in the direction of cooperation with the Chinese government, writing:

> It seems particularly important for the viability and especially the desired political effectiveness of the planned educational institutions that from the start the Chinese central government as well as the most important provincial governors are enlightened about the goals and advantages of the planned institutions and thus become interested in the latter; that they allocate appropriate student material and as far as possible assume responsibility for the recognition of the examinations taken in Qingdao and the subsequent advancement of the students. In the same sense I would see it as admissible and even desirable that the responsible Chinese offices be involved in the creation of the curriculum, etc., from the start.

Von Tirpitz emphasized the need to include a law faculty in the proposed university, since he expected that "the most direct political influence" on China would emanate "precisely from this school."[207] At this early stage von Tirpitz also seems to have imagined the school's curriculum as entirely Western. A memo by Count von Rex in early 1908 concerning the strong demand for Western education in China noted that "the entire population wants to ~~civilize~~ modernize itself." The fact that the verb "civilize" was

---

to write a memo of this importance is indicative of the unacknowledged power of the translators and kindred groups within the local colonial state.

206. BA-Berlin, DBC, vol. 1241, pp. 198–219, reprinted in Leutner 1997, pp. 444–53; quote from p. 449.

207. All quotes from von Tirpitz to von Bülow, October 4, 1907, BA-Berlin, DBC, vol. 1258, pp. 3–41; and von Tirpitz, October 23, 1907, in ibid., p. 7. For von Rex's endorsement, see von Rex to von Bülow, May 5, 1907, BA-Berlin, R 901 (Foreign Office), vol. 38930, p. 3.

crossed out in the original memo suggests that von Rex had second thoughts about whether China was not in fact already "civilized."[208] This marked a significant difference from his predecessors von Ketteler and von Heyking, who had insisted that China was barbaric. The change in "ethnographic" perceptions was accompanying changes in native policy and was occurring at the highest levels of German government.

The initial aim guiding these discussions was to orient Chinese elites toward Germany. The timing on the German side corresponded to a more general movement toward ideas of a "cultural mission" to achieve German geopolitical ends. The German initiative was also related to ongoing reforms within the Chinese educational system that made such an intervention seem more plausible—specifically, the educational reforms written by education minister Zhang Zhidong that were introduced in 1904-5.[209] The ancient Beijing-centered system of repeated examinations of candidates' knowledge of classical texts to assess their qualification for state service was starting to give way to a nationwide system of universities that would each control their own admissions and grant academic degrees.

Many of the institutional aspects of von Tirpitz's original plan were eventually realized. But the equilibrium between German and Chinese elements in the school's actual constitution represented a shift in the direction of Chinese interests and some openness on the German side to cultural métissage. The contours of the college on its opening day in 1909 contained elements of the program of "cultural synthesis and exchange" championed by Richard Wilhelm and other German intellectuals at the time and reflected the reform ideas of Zhang Zhidong, who supported the project and whose office had conducted the negotiations with the Germans. During discussions with Germany in the months leading up to the official negotiations, Zhang Zhidong insisted that instruction in the "purely Chinese sciences" be carried out by Chinese teachers but also said that Chinese higher education in general should be "reorganized according to German models and rely on German teachers."[210] After the Hundred Days Reforms in 1898,

---

208. Memo of February 25, 1908, BA-Berlin, DBC, vol. 1258, p. 20v.

209. See Ayers 1971; Fairbank and Goldman 1998, pp. 242-44; F. Huang 1999, pp. 253-66. In later years a newspaper published at the German-Chinese college attributed the school's very existence to Zhang Zhidong, who had "called on the Chinese to 'Learn!'"; see "Die deutsch-chinesische Hochschule in Tsingtau," Der West-östliche Bote I (1, November 1913): 32.

210. Report from May 22, 1908, by Kiaochow governor Truppel on discussion with Zhang Zhidong on May 3, BA-Berlin, DCB, vol. 1258, p. 110v; Otto Franke to RMA, June 24, 1908, reporting on Zhang's counterproposal to the Germans at the onset of the official negotiations, ibid., p. 137.

Zhang Zhidong had coined the phrase "The old [i.e., Chinese] learning is the substance the new [Western] learning is the vehicle."[211] This was a specific adaptation of the Confucian slogan *tiyong* (體用), or "essence and practical use," from the reformist self-strengthening movement. This meant that "Chinese learning should remain the essence, but Western learning should be used for practical development."[212] The German-Chinese college in its final form corresponded much more closely to this Chinese project than had been the case in the original German plan: the mechanical arts and natural sciences were taught exclusively in the "Western" mode, while the cultural sciences—law and economics—were a mixture of Chinese and European approaches.[213]

The ability of the Chinese to codetermine the college's form and content also resulted from an evolution in German interests. The Germans wanted the Chinese to bear a large portion of the college's budget, and this gave Zhang more leverage in the negotiations. German geopolitical strategy was also beginning to favor a more accommodating approach to the Chinese government. The enhanced power of the translators and Sinologists in the colony and in German China policy more generally was reflected in the selection of Sinologist Otto Franke to conduct the negotiations over the German-Chinese college.[214] This assignment was significant in light of Franke's criticism of Baron von Heyking's aggressive style in his discussions with the Chinese government in 1897–98 concerning Kiaochow's annexation. Franke was given quite a bit of leeway in these negotiations and agreed to allow the Chinese authorities to select the students and the Chinese teachers for the school. When Zhang argued that the school should have a Chinese codirector, Franke responded that this contradicted his instructions, but the two sides agreed that the Chinese Educational Ministry could post a permanent representative at the school.[215] Franke endorsed the idea that the college's goal was not to transform its students into artificial

211. Stichler 1989, p. 274.

212. Spence 1990, p. 225.

213. See the report on Zhang's initial bargaining points in the memo of February 25, 1908, BA-Berlin, DBC, vol. 1258, p. 25r. These included the idea that "the Chinese lessons have to be presented according to the specifications of the [Chinese] Ministry of Education, which should also select the instructors."

214. See O. Franke 1954, pp. 121ff., and the documentation in BA-Berlin, DBC, vols. 1258–59.

215. This was Zhang Kai (Luan Baode 1982). See Franke's report to von Tirpitz, RMA, July 18, 1908, BA-Berlin, DBC, vol. 1258, pp. 158–65. Zhang's report of August 14, 1909, to the Chinese State Council is reprinted in Leutner 1997, pp. 461–64.

Germans or "characterless cultural hermaphrodites."[216] The blueprint that eventually emerged from these discussions included a mixed Chinese and European curriculum.[217] The Chinese side insisted that the school's official (and not too mellifluous) name would be Advanced School of Special Sciences of a Special Type (Hochschule für Spezialwissenschaften mit besonderem Charakter, or Tebie gaodeng zhuanmen xueteng). The inclusion of the adjective "special" (besonders/tebie) signaled that it was not going to be given the same status as the Imperial University in Beijing, but also that it was elevated in some respects above the other provincial Chinese universities.[218] Although the Germans had hoped that the degrees granted by the Qingdao college would be recognized as equivalent to those of the Imperial University, Franke conceded that graduates would have to go to Beijing to earn the highest literary degree qualifying them to become officials.[219] Governor Truppel objected vigorously to allowing the Chinese such influence over the school, but he was unable to change the agreed-upon plan.[220]

216. O. Franke 1911b, p. 204.

217. The final statutes were agreed upon in Beijing in August 1908; see *Tsingtauer Neueste Nachrichten*, October 26, 1909, p. 2. They were published in the *Amtsblatt für das Deutsche Kiautschou-Gebiet*, 1909, p. 205; and in Deutsch-chinesische Hochschule 1910, pp. 24–27.

218. Specifically, graduates who wanted to enter the Chinese civil service would still have to go to Beijing to take the national examination, but they would not have to take any additional courses there. See the statutes of the Qingdao college and accompanying memo from Otto Franke, August 7, 1908, BA-Berlin, DBC, vol. 1258, pp. 184–95. As with most aspects of the German colony, this reading of the college's name was also open to different interpretations on the Chinese and German sides. The Germans referred to the school simply as the "German-Chinese college," while the Chinese colloquially called it the Heilan University, after the name of the district in which the school was built (Leutner 1997, p. 470 n. 36). The city's official plaque on the main building of the college (which is currently occupied by the railway administration) calls it the Dehua Daxue, a direct translation of "German-Chinese University." The doubling of the word *special* in the school's full title also deserves comment. At the onset of negotiations the adjective "special" referred only to the sciences that would be taught there—Franke referred to the "University for Special Sciences" (Hochschule für Spezial-Wissenschaften); see Franke's report to RMA of June 24, 1908, BA-Berlin, DBC, vol. 1258, p. 138. By August 7 of that year, at Chinese insistence, the phrase "of a special type" had been added to the school's name; see von Rex to Zhang, August 7, 1908, BA-Berlin, DBC, vol. 1258, p. 182; also Zhang's report to the Chinese State Council, August 8, 1909, in Leutner 1997, p. 463.

219. See Franke to RMA, July 18, 1908, BA-Berlin, DBC, vol. 1258, p. 161; and Deutsch-chinesische Hochschule 1910, pp. 26–27.

220. See especially Truppel to von Rex, August 18, 1908, BA-Berlin, DBC, vol. 1258, pp. 215–17; and Truppel to von Rex, September 1, 1908, BA-Berlin, DBC, vol. 1259, pp. 35–36.

Franke received strong backing against Truppel from Admiral von Tirpitz and the German envoy in Beijing.[221]

When the Qingdao college finally opened in October 1909 it combined a general five- or six-year preparatory lower school with an advanced school for graduates of the *gymnasium*. Chinese courses at the lower-school level included language, literature, classics, geography, ethics, and history; at the college level, Chinese law and ethical philosophy were offered. Western disciplines taught at the lower school included German language, natural sciences, introductory philosophy (psychology, logic, and epistemology), and health lessons, based on Western rather than Chinese medicine. The upper school was divided into four specialized disciplines: law and political economy (*Staatswissenschaften*), natural sciences and engineering, agriculture and forestry, and medicine. Physics, chemistry, medicine, and engineering were all based mainly on Western science.[222] The law and political economy section, however, was more syncretic. Religious teaching, that is, European religion, was excluded from the curriculum, and religious "propaganda" was banned from the college.[223] In his internal comments on the first draft of the German proposal, Zhang Zhidong had commended the "absence of missionary activities" and recognized that "the fact that . . . Chinese knowledge will have an established place in the school's teaching already differentiates . . . the German school from others that have been created by foreigners."[224]

The German-Chinese college brought German and Chinese teachers together in a setting that suggested a civilizational exchange rather than colonialism encounter. According to the colony's official annual report, "young people [should] not lose touch with their own literature and culture. . . . The young men should be educated to love their fatherland . . . but also to appreciate German culture and to develop their country according to these values."[225] At the school's opening ceremony in 1909, speakers from both sides endorsed the idea of combining the best of their two cultures. A toast was

221. O. Franke 1954, pp. 121–22; Kreissler 1989, p. 134; and Stichler 1989, pp. 287–91.

222. Deutsch-chinesische Hochschule 1909, pp. 4–21; Deutsch-chinesische Hochschule 1910, pp. 6, 10. On the medical school see the report of December 15, 1912, by navy doctor Praefcke on the "current state and further expansion of the medical division," BA-MA-Freiburg, RM 3, vol. 7001, pp. 148–61. On the internal struggles in China between Chinese and Western medicine at this time see the brilliant dissertation by Lei (1999).

223. Deutsch-chinesische Hochschule 1910, p. 26.

224. Zhang Zhidong, report to Chinese State Council of August 14, 1909, in Leutner 1997, p. 463.

225. Kiaochow *Denkschrift* for 1907–8, pp. 10–12. See discussion of the school and the *Denkschrift* in *Tsingtauer Neueste Nachrichten*, August 22, 1908, p. 2.

FIGURE 7.18 Staff and students in front of German-Chinese university, Qingdao
(ca. 1910–11). From BA-MA-Freiburg, Nachlass Truppel, vol. 81. (Courtesy of BA-MA-
Freiburg.)

raised to the Chinese emperor, the "national anthem" of the Qing Empire
was sung, and the school's German director proclaimed that "all of the *cultural peoples [Kulturvölker]* are linked by a common bond" and should "share
their discoveries." Here the Chinese were unambiguously (re)inscribed into
the dominant pole of the German racial-anthropological binary. The imperial German and late Qing dynasty flags flew side by side in front of one of
the school's provisional buildings (fig. 7.18).[226]

The Germans set out to reshape China but ended up with a school that
more strongly resembled an open-ended cultural "joint venture."[227] In the
process, many Germans gained a clearer sense of the differences among
their aims in China. Richard Wilhelm and Otto Franke wanted China's
encounter with the West to take place on the basis of its own inherited
traditions. This pointed beyond colonialism altogether, since it no longer

226. "Die Eröffnung der Deutsch-Chinesischen Hochschule," *Tsingtauer Neueste Nachrichten,* October 26, 1909, pp. 6–7. The college's main teaching building was not completed until
1912, and this photo is from Truppel's photo album for 1910–11.

227. In fact, the plaque currently visible in front of the main building of the former college, placed there by the Qingdao Tourism Bureau's Cultural Relics Department in 2000,
calls the school a German-Chinese "joint-run program." Mühlhahn (2000, p. 254) emphasizes the *disciplinary* aspects of the German cultural schooling policy. As I argued above, this
is *not* specifically colonial; indeed, the model he applies here was proposed by Foucault in an
analysis of Europe. To call all disciplinary strategies colonial is to stretch that adjective to the
breaking point or to render it strictly metaphorical.

insisted on a rule of hierarchical difference. "Cultural imperialists" like Paul Rohrbach, by contrast, believed that influencing China would require a "reconstruction and reconstitution of Chinese culture through a synthesis of Confucian and Occidental cultural elements." Rather than building on Chinese tradition, this approach would necessitate an "internal confrontation with Confucianism."[228] Rohrbach's conception was compatible with a rule of hierarchical difference, although it would have represented a step away from the severe segregationism that dominated colonial policy in the initial period. Both cultural exchange and "internal confrontations" leading to a German-dominated synthesis required the colonizers to approach Chinese culture hermeneutically, even if the latter approach was compatible with continued colonial rule.

There is a difference between policy and implementation, however, and the college could have moved in several different directions. One of these was respectful exchange and translation, a process of bidirectional transculturation that would no longer privilege the European side. Another possibility was that the school would come to embody a bid for cultural hegemony and acculturation into a German-controlled synthesis. Finally, there might have developed syncretic cultural processes that actually favored Chinese teachers or nationalist reformers, as Zhang Zhidong hoped.

The activities in the college's Law and Economy Department suggest that several of these possibilities coexisted. On one level, this department conformed to the translation-and-exchange model championed by Otto Franke and Richard Wilhelm. The law students studied both Chinese and European law.[229] The department published the *German-Chinese Legal Journal* (*Deutsch-chinesische Rechtszeitung*), which carried a column by the Chinese chief judge of Shandong Province on important legal decisions from all over China.[230] At the same time, the Law and Economy Department published a series of Chinese translations of German law.[231] This section and its journal also began to promote a synthesis of Chinese and German forms. One of the school's law professors, Kurt Romberg, wrote that the Chinese "have created eternal values for all of humanity" in the area that "Kant

228. Rohrbach (1912), pp. 19–20. A more ambiguous figure is Alfons Paquet, discussed below.

229. See the Law School curriculum in Deutsch-chinesische Hochschule 1910, p. 10; also the memo by the Law Department of November 1911, in BA-Berlin, DBC, vol. 1259, p. 281.

230. See *Deutsch-chinesische Rechtszeitung* 1 (1, November 1911): 8, and the column "Gerichtsentscheidungen" in various issues.

231. These were called the *Chinesisch-deutsche Gesetzsammlung* and were published in Qingdao.

called practical reason" and that these were legal "treasures" that China "should not be allowed to keep for itself." Like Leibniz three hundred years earlier, he thus suggested that Europe had something to learn from China, that cultural exchange had to be reciprocal. What the West, and especially the supposedly less materialistic Germans, could offer China was "methodological techniques" and "legal forms." But these empty forms had to be "filled" with Chinese contents. This was a paraphrase of the *tiyong* principle, from the pen of a colonial German. Such syncretism would contribute to an "orderly state" and an effective legal system in China, Romberg concluded. And at this point, "consular jurisdiction and foreign barracks" would, he forecasted, become superfluous."[232] This demonstrated that the open-ended cultural processes unleashed by institutions like the German-Chinese college could move away from the rule of difference toward processes of transculturation that no longer privileged the colonizers.

An even more striking example of the erosion of hierarchical binarism was the Confucius Society (Konfuzius-Gesellschaft) founded by Richard Wilhelm. Although this was not an official government institution, Wilhelm played a central role in the colony's school system and was widely regarded as one of the most influential Germans in Kiaochow. The exalted stature of the society's Chinese members, many of whom were high-ranking ex-officials and scholars who had supported the Qing regime and who moved to Qingdao after 1911, meant that the club's activities had broader implications.[233] The goal of the Confucius Society was to stimulate intellectual discussions in which "German and Chinese culture and science can enter into fruitful exchange," according to Wilhelm. The society's guiding principle, which Wilhelm described as the only possible foundation for "genuine relations between the Orient and Occident," was an "exchange of the highest achievements of the spiritual heroes of both cultures." The challenge facing the society's Chinese members, in Wilhelm's view, was weighty: to rescue the traditional principles and treasures of Chinese cul-

232. Romberg (1911), pp. 23, 25. Romberg also insisted that the "culture" that Germany had to offer was not merely "a series of technical skills—which were in any case already partly familiar in China, even if they were not being used." In a veiled jab at American and British materialism, he asked whether "the crude behavior of the foreigners . . . [does not] do more to spoil ethical values than to create them among the Chinese who are chained to them?" Romberg concluded by comparing the struggle between Chinese neotraditionalists like Ku Hung-Ming (1911) and Kang Youwei and the Chinese "Western-oriented fanatics" to the "dispute between humanism and the so-called realists in Germany" (ibid., p. 26).

233. For a list of the members of Wilhelm's Confucius Society see Forsman 1979, pp. 102–3. These included Zhou Fu, the former Shandong governor.

ture, which were in great danger. Many of these treasures had been "crudely destroyed during the storms of the [1911] revolution." One of the society's central goals was therefore to create a library "for the collection of Chinese treasures," but World War I broke out just as the building was completed.[234] Unlike Augustin Krämer and other ethnologists and Orientalists at the time, Wilhelm did not pillage the most valuable artifacts of a culture under siege but instead tried to make sure they were protected in China.

Explaining the Shift in Native Policy

The period after 1905 represented a fairly dramatic shift in native policy, accompanied by more positive portrayals of the Chinese both in Germany and in Kiaochow. Before asking about the reasons for this development we need to consider the possibility that the colonial regime before 1904 was already based on mixed principles, despite its seemingly thoroughgoing racialism. The partial reliance on Chinese law in Chinese trials led inexorably to mixed legal forms, even if the people in charge were Germans.[235] The chief justice of Qingdao, Dr. Crusen, summarized the legal system as a "unique, half German and half Chinese form."[236] But allowing such cultural-political interpenetration, even within the repressive context of the law, could open the floodgates to uncontrollable cultural change. A legal dissertation written in 1911 defended the German reliance on Chinese law with reference to "the respect for an ancient culture that has shown a high degree of competence and development in all areas, including legal science."[237] What is remarkable here is not just the assumption that China was a developing rather than a stagnant country or the expression of respect, but the reappearance of the resonant Sinophile idea of an admirably *ancient* culture. This bears little resemblance to the arguments and emotions associated with German efforts to preserve customary law in Samoa or among the Namibian Rehoboth Basters. Such justifications for the preservation of Chinese elements

234. R. Wilhelm 1914, pp. 248, 251, 250; see also 1928, p. 179.

235. John Schrecker (1971, pp. 62–63) argues that the role of the district commissioner as practiced, especially in the rural district, was close to that of the Chinese *zhixian* (district magistrate), who also combined administrative and judicial functions. But the district commissioner in Germany's other colonies was also entrusted with "far-reaching powers" (Gann and Duignan 1977, p. 70), including judicial ones. Only a more careful investigation of this question would allow us to determine the extent to which the self-understanding of the rural district commissioner in Kiaochow was shaped by the local Chinese elite.

236. Crusen 1914, p. 134.

237. Karlowa 1911, p. 25.

in the colony's legal system had not been widespread when that system was first created. These elements were initially retained for more pragmatic reasons. The harsh penalties of Chinese law were seen as a useful deterrent. But even though legal syncretism did not necessarily reflect any real appreciation of Chinese culture, the daily activities of the district commissioners required that they immerse themselves in Chinese law, and this inevitably oriented them toward a more "hermeneutic" approach to the colonized culture.

The shift in official policy starting around 1904 did not correspond to any major events in the colony comparable to the 1894 and 1904 wars in Southwest Africa. Three main factors have been proposed as explanations: economic pressures, Chinese resistance, and German military and foreign policy considerations. The second and third are significant in accounting for the *timing* of the move away from the early regime of harsh segregationism, but they cannot explain the *form* of the policies that took its place. The two previous case studies in this book suggest that native policy was shaped by precolonial ethnographic imagery and symbolic competition among social groups within the colonial state. Let us first consider the factors emphasized in the existing secondary literature.

Economic considerations tell us very little about either the timing or the form of this shift. German capitalists in China criticized the Kiaochow colony as too militaristic and statist and called for its liberalization.[238] But this did not necessarily imply more liberal *native policies*. In fact, newspapers associated with German economic interests in China, like the *Ostasiatischer Lloyd* and the *Deutsch-Asiatische Warte,* more frequently criticized the Kiaochow government for its overly lax treatment of the Chinese. In any case, German residents had only "extremely limited possibilities of truly influencing the decisions of the governor" through the strictly advisory citizens' representative council.[239]

One might hypothesize that economic considerations influenced the changes in less direct ways. The Kiaochow colony had been evaluated by the navy and Foreign Office from the very beginning in terms of its economic potential, which referred above all to its contributions to trade. The navy's scorched earth policies in the colony's hinterland in 1899–1900 provoked protests by some German business interests that "Germany doesn't gain anything in the end if the railroad moves through wastelands devoid of human beings and steams past ruined towns and villages, proclaiming the

238. Mühlhahn 2000, p. 160.
239. Stichler 1989, p. 94.

'triumph of culture.'" If this continued, Germans would soon be the "most hated foreign devils."[240] Schrameier later recalled that the colonial government had reacted too harshly during the Boxer period and that the Chinese had nearly fled the colony, which would have been an economic disaster.[241] The point is that these policies were pursued nonetheless during the initial years. It is unclear why economic considerations should have become more important after 1904.

Another possible "economic" explanation would focus on the fact that trade within the colony was largely in Chinese hands.[242] The shift toward a more congenial native policy may have been related to the fact that the colony's economic life depended not just on attracting and retaining a Chinese labor force but also on promoting Chinese-owned businesses. Yet even these considerations could not specify whether the colonizers would pursue a policy of assimilation, guarantee a "separate but equal" status for the Chinese, or engage in some version of cultural synthesis. What changed after 1905 was more than simply a relaxation of earlier restrictions or an agreement to listen to the colony's Chinese residents.

All studies of Kiaochow have emphasized the impact of resistance and cooperation (or collaboration) on the colonial regime. The sheer presence of the Chinese state represented a crucial difference from the other German colonies. Starting with Yuan Shikai, governor of Shandong in 1900–1901 (and later the first president of the Republic of China, from 1912 to 1916), provincial authorities in Ji'nan worked with great success to contain the Germans in Kiaochow by undercutting German mining activities in the province, opening up Ji'nan as a "self-opened mart" (*zikai shangbu*), reminding the Germans of the colony's limited (ninety-nine-year) life expectancy and its status as "leasehold," and insisting on the equality of the "two governors." But previous studies have not connected resistance and collaboration

240. "Gefechte bei Kaumi," *Nachrichten aus Kiautschou, Beiblatt zum "Ostasiatischen Lloyd,"* no. 44 (November 2, 1900): 210; see also letter from Eugen Wolf to chancellor, April 11, 1899, PA-AA, vol. 18241 (no pagination).

241. Schrameier, "Ueber die Entwicklung und Bedeutung des Kiautschougebietes: Ein Rückblick," *Deutsch-chinesischer Verband 1914, Anlage zum Jahresbericht* (Berlin, 1915), p. 41 (BA-Berlin, DBC, vol. 655).

242. Seelemann 1982, p. 484; Mühlhahn 2000, p. 169. Klein (2004, p. 322) argues that Kiaochow's administrators decided to loosen the restrictions on Chinese residence in the European district because they were impressed by the financial power of the Chinese immigrants to Qingdao after 1911. This may help explain that particular decision, but it does not account for the broader shift in native policy after 1904.

to the transformation of native policy inside the colony.[243] Hans-Christian Stichler suggests that since the Boxers and other movements (including the 1911 Xinhai revolution) did not openly challenge the Kiaochow administration, the Germans basically had a free hand within the colony.[244] In several cases when the Chinese directly challenged policies inside the colony, they were unsuccessful. When the government created the Chinese Committee in 1902, for example, Chinese merchants asked to be allowed to work directly with Shandong provincial officials. This was vetoed by the German legation in Beijing.[245] In 1910, the Shandong governor asked Germany to help him conduct a census of the leasehold, again insinuating China's partial sovereignty over Kiaochow. The governor, Captain Meyer-Waldeck, responded that the Germans alone were responsible for this.[246]

This is not to suggest that Chinese resistance around native policy was always ineffective. When Sun Yat-sen came to Qingdao in 1912, the students at the German-Chinese college threatened to leave the school if they were not allowed to meet him on the school's premises. Local merchants threatened to leave the colony if they were not permitted to meet Sun. The Germans capitulated.[247] Chinese envoys to Samoa and Berlin were able to end the flogging of Chinese workers in Samoa, as noted earlier.

Native policy was also affected by the evolving profile of German *geopolitical* strategy. Both the navy and the Foreign Office were increasingly oriented toward improving relations with China in order to secure a possible ally as Germany became isolated inside Europe.[248] The result was an approach to China that resembled the Americans' "open door" policy, insofar as it backed away from any suggestion that Germany wanted to infringe

---

243. Schrecker (1971) and Mühlhahn (2000) frequently invoke Chinese resistance, but both authors locate it outside the colony proper. When discussing policies in the colony's schools and workplaces, Mühlhahn emphasizes Foucauldian discipline rather than resistance, and Schrecker emphasizes German efficiency.

244. Stichler 1989, p. 109.

245. Ibid., p. 107.

246. Seelemann 1982, pp. 452–53.

247. See local Chinese newspaper clippings sent by Consul Merklinghaus from Ji'nan to DBC, October 6, 1912, BA-Berlin, DBC, vol. 1259, pp. 257–79; and Kiaochow governor Meyer-Waldeck to DBC, October 26, 1912, ibid., pp. 282–87).

248. The 1905 Russo-Japanese War also made Germany more interested in finding alternative partners in the global periphery (Seelemann 1982, pp. 445–46; Stichler 1989, p. 234). According to Trumpener (1968, pp. 14–16), Germany was not actually seriously cultivating the Ottoman Empire as a "natural ally in the foreseeable future" before 1914, but the two countries were plunged into a hasty alliance on August 2.

on Chinese sovereignty.[249] This change in strategy led to an acute struggle over the direction of China policy between the administration of Kiaochow, on the one hand, and the Foreign Office, German legation, and secretary of the navy, on the other. The Foreign Ministry "moved rapidly to restrict the influence of the naval government in Qingdao to the Leasehold's borders," going so far as to set up a separate consulate in Ji'nan in order to create a counterweight to its own colony in the same province.[250] The aims of the movement for "cultural imperialism" tended to overlap with the new geopolitical strategic orientation when it came to China.

Geostrategic considerations thus influenced colonial native policy by urging powerful actors in the Foreign Office and the navy to censure Truppel when he resisted reforms and to shift power to a different set of Germans in Kiaochow. As a committed colonialist, Truppel recognized that granting the Chinese nearly equal status in running the college was, from a colonial standpoint, a "Begriffsverwirrung" (category mistake) and an "injury to German sovereignty in the protectorate."[251] He rebuked the navy and the Beijing legation, insisting that the time was "not yet ripe for China to jointly govern any aspect of the colony." A university jointly run by the Chinese could easily take on the character of a purely Chinese school. And the Chinese were not the colonizer's *partners* but rather "our charges [*Schutzgenossen*], our subjects."[252]

THE IMPORTANCE OF ORIENTALISM

If the first phase of colonial native policy was based on the Sinophobia that crystallized in the era leading up to 1897 and the Boxer uprising, the second phase fell back on a version of Sinophilia whose main contours had emerged in the seventeenth and eighteenth centuries. Indeed, Sinophilia made a powerful comeback more generally after 1900. This was generated partly by revulsion against Kaiser Wilhelm's populist anti-Asian slurs and

249. Indeed, Chancellor von Bülow had already used the expression "open door" (in English) in describing German aims in China during the height of the Boxer uprising (P. Fischer 1994, p. 351). On the interpretation of American imperialism as anticolonial and as epitomized by the "open door" approach see W. Williams 1959; Steinmetz 2005e.

250. Seelemann 1982, pp. 437, 440.

251. Truppel to RMA, August 31, 1908, BA-Berlin, DBC, vol. 1259, p. 53r, on "Chinesenschule."

252. Kiaochow Government [Truppel] to von Rex, August 18, 1908, BA-Berlin, DBC, vol. 1258, p. 215.

the atrocities committed in the German campaign against the Boxers. Venerable Sinophile tropes had been hovering just below the surface even in some of the most blatant examples of "yellow peril" discourse in the latter decades of the nineteenth century, as shown in the previous chapter. Karl May's *Et in terra pax*, the story that represented a complete reversal in that best-selling author's representation of China, appeared in a lavishly illustrated three-volume collection called *China* that was published in the immediate wake of the suppression of the Yihetuan. The second volume was given over entirely to a 450-page treatment of "The Troubles, 1900/1901" by a German lieutenant, detailing all aspects of the military expedition. The most notorious aspects of the Germans' intervention were celebrated here in patriotic style, including the participation of the gunboat *Iltis* in the destruction and storming of the Dagu fort at the mouth of the Beihe River in June 1900 and the "cleansing" (*Säuberung*) of Yihetuan supporters in Zhili Province outside Beijing by members of the East Asian Expeditionary Force.[253] The contributors to the first volume, which dealt with Chinese culture and history, were mainly missionaries, military officers, consuls, university professors, and a navy surveyor who had studied Jiaozhou Bay before the 1897 annexation and had published a crudely patriotic book on the colony. But the third volume, entitled "Narratives, etc., from and about China," included not only May's novel and other literary texts by Germans but also translations of Chinese novellas. In this respect the three-volume compilation resembled Du Halde's *Description de la Chine*, the pinnacle of Jesuit Sinophilia. Another coffee-table book on the campaign, *Deutschland in China*, included picturesque color images of Chinese scenes. An image of Count von Waldersee at his desk in the Beijing Winter Palace (plate 11) is an interesting example of the multivocality of discourse on China. On the one hand, this illustration is a record of official looting. Von Waldersee's usurpation of the place of the Chinese mandarin or empress resembles in this respect the occupation of the Qingdao *yamen* (fig. 7.11) and other instances of pillaging in the wake of imperialist invasions.[254] On the other hand, the image identifies von Waldersee with his Chinese envi-

253. The storming of the Dagu fort was condemned by European envoys in Beijing and by Social Democratic leader August Bebel in the German Reichstag as a "declaration of war" (Michael 1986, p. 151). Even some of the admirals of the powers present at a war council on June 15 voted against storming Dagu (Herrings 1903, p. 47). For a recent treatment of these campaigns see Hevia 1992.

254. Hevia 1992; Wong 2001, p. 143; Tong 2006.

ronment, turning him into a cryptomandarin and symbolically reversing the direction of usurpation. One visual axis connects von Waldersee's blue uniform and the large, blue, patterned vase behind him. There is a reverse echo of the figure-ground pattern of the medals and buttons adorning von Waldersee's uniform in the figure-ground pattern of blue decorations on the white vase. Some of the patches on the vase also resemble the iron cross on von Waldersee's chest. A second axis runs between the calligraphic tablet hanging on the upper-left-hand wall, von Waldersee's hands, and the open inkpot on the desk. This depiction of von Waldersee contrasts sharply with the image of the aggressive Teutonic "Hun" (e.g., fig. 6.13). Von Waldersee could even be confused with a Confucian scholar, leaning meditatively over his desk, his delicate hands engaged in an activity that recalls Chinese calligraphy.[255]

As the writings of Confucius and Mencius started to become better known in translation, some modern intellectuals followed Richard Wilhelm in abandoning imperialist claims to superiority. A book by the Chinese intellectual Ku Hung-Ming, *China's Defense against European Ideas,* appeared in German in 1911. Ku had studied in Edinburgh and Leipzig and had served as secretary-interpreter to Viceroy Zhang Zhidong. After the Xinhai revolution of 1911 he taught English literature at Beijing University.[256] *China's Defense* was translated into German by Richard Wilhelm and had an introduction by Alfons Paquet, the publicist, travel writer, playwright, and supporter of Martin Buber's version of Zionism, who had spent six months traveling in China, including Qingdao, and who had met Ku Hung-Ming in Shanghai.[257] As a guest of Shandong governor Zhou Fu in 1902, Ku had met members of the Kiaochow colony's delegation.[258] Ku was also part of Rich-

---

255. Of course, this image is also sensitive to the public presentation preferred by von Waldersee himself. The frontispiece of von Waldersee's published memoirs, for instance, depicts him holding an open book rather than a sword (Waldersee 1923, vol. 1).

256. L. Liu 1999a, p. 163.

257. Paquet 1911, pp. xi–xiv; 1912, pp. 290ff. Paquet wanted to turn Qingdao into a "place of self reflexion, of spiritual work, of thinking in the Far East" and called for a German at the head of the Beijing legation "with deep knowledge of China, both a statesman and an intellectual." Paquet stylized China as a "communistically organized empire" presenting a model for a German "synthesis of absolutism and socialism" as a European "middle empire," against the British and American systems (Paquet 1912, pp. 304, 317; 1914, pp. 59, 61; see also Koenen 2003, p. 685). In the 1920s Paquet wrote a number of plays, including the proto-Brechtian *Fahnen,* that were directed by Erwin Piscator at the Berlin Volksbühne.

258. Hauptmann von Scholler's report of April 21, 1902, on the "greeting deputation" sent to the Shandong governor in March 1902, BA-Berlin , DBC, vol. 1238, pp. 211–15.

ard Wilhelm's circle in Qingdao.[259] Later Ku was nominated by Wilhelm and others for the post of "first scholar" at a planned Richthofen Institute in Beijing.[260] As Paquet wrote in his introduction to one of Ku's collections of essays, the Chinese writer urged Europeans to acknowledge the connection between racism and the colonizer's "ecstasy of domination." According to Paquet, Ku described the Yihetuan as "misguided and betrayed, but still brave Boxer chaps [*brave Boxerburschen*]." Like Zhang Zhidong, Kang Youwei, and other nationalist reformers before 1911, Ku embraced Confucianism as a means of warding off imperialism (even though that tradition was personally foreign to him). Most significant in the present context was the fact that this description of the Boxers as "brave chaps" was published in Germany just a decade after Kaiser Wilhelm's "Hun speech" and the murder by Yihetuan sympathizers of Baron von Ketteler during the siege of Beijing.[261]

The main lineaments of native policies in Kiaochow thus resonated with traditional and reemerging Sinophilia. Just as Sinophobia had been a calculated and point-by-point refutation of Sinophilia, the new policies in Kiaochow seemed to be a deliberate reversal of those of the earlier period. They took for granted that China was an advanced civilization on a level equal to that of Europe. Opening these floodgates within a colonial context pointed beyond European claims to sovereignty and supremacy, beyond colonialism.

FANTASIES OF EXALTATION: SUBALTERN STUDIES ON THE SIDE OF THE COLONIZER

Wherever there was a German colony . . . the most varied occasions were useful for holding Germans together: *we passed over all class differences.*

ADMIRAL VON TIRPITZ[262]

The shift in native policy was thus propelled by economic and geopolitical considerations and by Chinese resistance; the first decade of the twentieth century also saw the (re)emergence of a distinctive strand of ethnographic discourse. This does not mean that elite class conflicts internal to

---

259. R. Wilhelm 1928, p. 183.

260. Communication by German legation in Beijing to chancellor, BA-Berlin, DBC, vol. 655, pp. 40–45, April 16, 1914.

261. Paquet 1911, pp. iv, vii.

262. Von Tirpitz 1919, vol. 1, p. 109 (my emphasis).

the colonial state field and imaginary identifications across the colonizer-colonized boundary were unimportant in China. If figures like Otto Franke and Richard Wilhelm had not been available, the powers in Berlin pressing for a more accommodating stance toward China would not have been able to change colonial practice in Kiaochow so readily.

The center of gravity of the ongoing creation and implementation of native policy was gradually relocated. The first period was dominated by the governors—Captains Carl Rosendahl, Jaeschke, and Truppel—and overseen by von Tirpitz and the navy. In the second period the focus moved from the top military personnel toward men who followed the translator career path within the German Foreign Office and toward navy personnel who had undergone preparation at the Seminar for Oriental Languages.[263] The most sensitive political positions for native policy in the colony were staffed by "philologists." Translator Wilhelm Schrameier was the colony's Chinese commissary for twelve years, from 1897 to 1909. The district commissioners in Qingdao and Licun, men like Heinrich Mootz and Emil Krebs, were former translator trainees who had gone through the language immersion training in Beijing.[264] The Kiaochow government paid a special bonus to "all military and civilian personnel who passed a language exam," and many of them spent some time at the Seminar for Oriental Languages in Berlin before shipping out to Qingdao, or took Chinese lessons once they were in the colony.[265] The Weimar Mission schools brought teachers to the colony who were overwhelmingly Sinophilic. Although some of the Germans who came to teach at the German-Chinese college were technical specialists with no special interest in China, others entered through the translating and Sinological paths. Sinologist Ferdinand Lessing, for example, taught at the college and directed its library's Chinese collection.[266] Lessing was a pioneer in the study of Mongolian culture and linguistics, Buddhism, and Chinese art.[267] He "studied law and Oriental languages in Berlin and earned a diploma in Chinese at the Seminar for Oriental Languages (1902–5) before going to China in 1907, after a brief stint at the [Berlin] Ethnological

263. Seelemann 1982, p. 361, also discusses a split between Sinophobes and Sinophiles in Kiaochow but sees the former as merchants and petty bureaucrats and the latter as administrators. Although this seems correct with regard to the German merchants, it does not capture the divisions among the colonial state's personnel.

264. Stichler 1989, pp. 107, 108 n. 1.

265. Weicker 1908, p. 111.

266. Deutsch-chinesische Hochschule 1910, p. 22.

267. Lessing and Walravens 2000.

Museum."[268] Lessing exemplifies the circulation between the Sinological milieus in Germany (especially Berlin) and official and semiofficial positions in Kiaochow.[269] He was also involved in a strike against the German-Chinese college when its director, Georg Keiper, tried to enforce a set of "school ordinances" drafted by Governor Truppel that these professors saw as infringing on their academic autonomy.[270] Essentially, this was the same intraelite class struggle as the fight between Theodor Leutwein and the von François and von Trotha contingent in Southwest Africa and between Solf and the settlers and navy officers in Samoa, except that the *Bildungsbürger* were never put in charge of the colony in Kiaochow.

Truppel's approach had fallen into disfavor with the navy and the Foreign Office by this time. Admiral von Tirpitz directly "criticized the behavior of Truppel, whose attempts to gain influence over the school triggered the conflict."[271] Truppel was a narrow-minded, traditional military man, but his personal papers show little evidence of the nasty racism of von Heyking or von Trotha. Rather, it was Truppel's stubborn commitment to the first model of colonial governance introduced in Kiaochow that made him fall into disfavor.[272]

The translators and "men on the spot" who were imbued with one or the other version of Sinophilia now began to shape policy at all levels. The centrality of culture and education to this new alignment in native policy reflects the increased importance of the *bildungsbürgerliche* fraction of the trichotimized German elite within Kiaochow policymaking. A German diplomat who was in Beijing from 1906 to 1908, Artur von Kemnitz, recalled this shift in the center of gravity of the colony's governance away from what he called the "more effective" consular service personnel to the "professionals" (*Fachleute*) and career translators, members of the translator career path (*Dolmetscherlaufbahn*). Von Kemnitz argued vehemently that "China hands" and "specialists" were "useful only as advisers" but that only "diplomats with comprehensive global experience" should be the "responsible bearers

---

268. Leutner 1987, p. 50.

269. Lessing taught at Beijing University and the Medical College in Mukden (Shenyang) before returning to Berlin in 1925 for an appointment at the SOS (Lessing and Walravens 2000). From 1935 until his retirement Lessing taught at the University of California in Berkeley.

270. Keiper to Betz, December 19, 1910, BA-Berlin, DBC, vol. 1259, p. 228.

271. Mühlhahn 2000, p. 249.

272. Truppel was elevated to the nobility by Kaiser Wilhelm shortly after his demission as governor in 1911 and became a member of the *Aufsichtsrat* (supervisory board) of the Shandong Railway Company the following year (Stichler 1989, p. 86).

of German policy."[273] Von Kemnitz accused the latter groups of having undergone a process of "Sinification" (*Verchinesung*) due to their "long stay in the country."[274] The examples of Governor Truppel and Sanitary Councilor Kronecker make it clear, however, that a long stay in China was not sufficient in and of itself to "Sinify" anyone. Instead, certain Europeans were already prepared to be Sinified before they arrived in China. In part this involved preparation in places like the Seminar for Oriental Languages, where Sinophile discourse could be internalized. Equally important were the symbolic and imaginary projects common to many members of the middling educated classes. For many German *Bildungsbürger* like Richard Wilhelm and Alfons Paquet the image of the Chinese mandarin whose learning put him in charge of a meritocratic but absolutist state possessed an almost irresistible appeal.

Officials who were more secure in their personal class position seemed to recognize the social aspirations that undergirded much of German Sinophilia. The extremely class-conscious von Heykings sneered at Germans who showed any interest in Chinese culture.[275] Otto Franke observed that elites in the Foreign Office wanted to have lawyers making the important decisions rather than the "subaltern spirits" who "worried about such irrelevant things as Oriental languages."[276] Wilhelm Schrameier's failure to be promoted to a higher position than Chinese commissary within the foreign service was attributed to the prejudice against translators.[277] Governor Truppel fulminated against "Sinified" German bureaucrats who threatened to undermine the hierarchical distinction between Chinese and Europeans. When the director of the Chinese Customs Office in Qingdao, Ernst Ohlmer, wrote a memo in 1905 calling for German cooperation with America and China in order to stave off Japanese expansion, Truppel accused Ohlmer of being "more Chinese than the Chinese bureaucrats."[278] This insinuation that translators and other go-betweens with the

273. Von Kemnitz to Foreign Office, March 12, 1917, and minute from March 2, 1917, both in PA-AA, R 2167, no pagination (Deutschland 135, Nr. 15). On the *Dolmetscherlaufbahn* see the 1888 "Notiz," reprinted in Sachau 1912, p. 51.

274. Von Kemnitz to Foreign Office, March 12, 1917, PA-AA, R 2167, no pagination (Deutschland 135, Nr. 15).

275. O. Franke 1954, p. 98.

276. Ibid., p. 68.

277. Stichler 1989, p. 156. Schrameier failed to be promoted to the new consular position in Ji'nan in 1904 (Matzat 1998, pp. 112-19).

278. Mühlhahn 2000, p. 163. See Schrecker 1971, pp. 75-77, for an explanation of the Imperial Maritime Customs Office and its role in Qingdao. The fact that a German was in charge

Chinese were prone to going native is indicative of the ongoing symbolic struggle among colonial Germans. The fact that Ohlmer was an arrivé from very modest background conditions, but one whose overall power as a customs official equaled Truppel's, fueled the flames.[279]

To understand the connections between individual social class "projects" and Sinophilia we can look more closely at two men involved in the shift after 1905, Otto Franke and Richard Wilhelm. Franke had graduated from the Berlin SOS seminar, published in its journal, and gone through the standard Foreign Office translator traineeship in Beijing. In 1909 he was appointed to the first German chair in Sinology at the Hamburg Colonial Institute (the precursor of Hamburg University, which was founded in 1919). Like the Berlin seminar, the Hamburg institute's curriculum involved the training of colonial administrators. After the war Franke held the prestigious Sinology Chair at Berlin University (1923-31). Franke was later called the "most prominent Sinologist in Germany."[280]

Franke resembled Wilhelm Solf in distancing himself explicitly from overt racism against the Chinese, which he suggested was the province of the traditional German elites. Not only did Franke's approach to cultural class distinction resemble Solf's; the two men's careers overlapped at numerous points. Both studied Sanskrit with the same professors at Göttingen and Kiel. In 1887, Franke met Solf again at the Seminar for Oriental Languages. A year later Franke began his career as a translator with the German consular service in China. Having heard Solf's story about his unpleasant interactions with von Heyking in Calcutta, Franke found himself working under the same man in 1896. As a translator during the negotiations over the annexation of Qingdao, Franke strongly disapproved of von Heyking's haughty manner, saying that the envoy scorned officials who were ignorant about China and exhibited an "artificially heightened race feeling." Like Solf, Franke preferred to associate with intellectuals, academics, and other Sinologists while he was abroad and later in his career.[281] During a posting to the German consul general in Shanghai, Franke attended sessions of the

---

of it was something the Germans had insisted on in the original leasehold negotiations, but Ohlmer was regarded suspiciously as "a representative of China" and as "a Chinese official" from the start (ibid., p. 77). During his time in China Ohlmer accumulated a significant collection of porcelain (see Wiesner 1981).

279. Stichler 1989, pp. 81-82.

280. Theunissen 1947, p. 277.

281. O. Franke 1911a, p. vi; 1954, p. 98. Franke later recalled having felt especially happy during a period spent with a "homogeneous circle" of journalists at a Cologne newspaper (1954, p. 113).

local branch of the Royal Asiatic Society, just as Solf had participated in the Bengal Asiatic Society while in India.

In addition to these symbolic distinction strategies oriented toward other Europeans, Franke seems to have cross-identified with Chinese elites. Except for some Catholic missionaries, few Germans dressed in traditional Chinese clothing after 1900. Identification took different forms. Franke recognized that the traditional Confucian ideas were so powerful that "even the first Christian missionaries who lived in China in the sixteenth and seventeenth centuries could not escape their influence." Like these "learned Jesuits," Franke himself seems to have been "overcome by the wisdom of Chinese antiquity."[282] He claimed to have been more interested in gaining the respect of "educated Chinese" than of other Germans.

Franke's pronounced ressentiment vis-à-vis German elites sheds a different light on this entire complex. In his memoirs Franke recalls his own proud refusal to follow the "typical custom of waiting indefinitely in the antechamber" in order to meet an official in the Prussian Ministry of Culture, and speculates that his pride cost him a teaching post in that case. Just a few pages earlier in his memoirs Franke reports on Prince Chun's refusal to perform three kowtows to Kaiser Wilhelm during his "atonement mission" to Berlin after the Boxer Rebellion. The requirement that Europeans perform the kowtow before the Chinese emperor had been a source of sharp conflict since the Macartney mission in 1793.[283] Franke's identification with Prince Chun seems to have been based on the same mixture of cultural pride and humiliation that he associated with the Chinese—a mixture that was also typical of the symbolic and imaginary identifications of German *Bildungsbürger* at the time.[284]

Richard Wilhelm (fig. 7.19) provides a second example of the uses of China by Wilhelmine *Bildungsbürger* in their symbolic class maneuvering. Wilhelm worked as a missionary and teacher in Kiaochow from 1899 to

---

282. O. Franke 1906, p. 163.

283. O. Franke 1954, p. 117. On the demand that Prince Chun perform a kowtow, see ibid., p. 111; and Hetze 1987. On the 1793 kowtow conflict during the Macartney mission, see E. Pritchard 1943; and Hevia 1995a.

284. Franke's memoirs were written before Germany's defeat in World War II but were not published until 1954, after his death in 1946. His narrative of Prince Chun's atonement mission may therefore have been overdetermined by the "humiliations" of Germany in the Versailles Treaty (just as Paul Rohrbach displaced the "devil's handwriting" onto that treaty), but there is no textual evidence for this reading either here or in his other post–World War I writing.

FIGURE 7.19 (left) Richard Wilhelm. Frontispiece from S. Wilhelm 1956.

FIGURE 7.20 (right) Lao Naixuan. From R. Wilhelm 1926, facing p. 160.

1919, and, like Franke, he became a renowned Sinologist in Germany in the 1920s. Most interesting in the present context is Wilhelm's profound identification with the imago of the Chinese scholar-gentleman. Like Solf and Franke, Richard Wilhelm staked out a distinguished class position that was defined by the possession of rare cultural knowledge and noble acquaintances which clearly differentiated him from the crass commercial bourgeoisie.[285] This symbolic effort was doubled by a set of imaginary identifications. Even if Wilhelm did not dress in traditional Chinese mandarin clothing—something that was already going out of fashion even among the Chinese literati with whom he liked to associate—he called those costumes "gorgeous" and "imposing."[286] Carl Jung thought that Wilhelm had

285. Wilhelm does not seem to have considered it necessary to distance himself from the German nobility. Unlike Franke and Solf he was not confronted in his daily missionary work with embittered aristocrats clinging to their last bastion of power in the military and foreign service.

286. R. Wilhlem 1928, p. 167.

acquired a Chinese habitus by the time he returned to Europe in 1920. Hermann Hesse insisted that "if you look at Wilhelm's picture for a longer period of time, you become aware of the fact that his friendly smile is very Asiatic . . . playfully expressing all of the nuances between archness and sarcasm, like the stories, legends, and anecdotes of the great wisemen of old China."[287] In his death notice for Wilhelm in 1930, Hesse called him "chinesisch-weise" (wise like a Chinaman) and "the mandarin, the most Chinese European of our era."[288] As Jung wrote, Wilhelm became "a pupil of a Chinese master of the old school and . . . an initiate in the psychology of Chinese yoga."[289] Wilhelm's enthusiasm for yoga was certainly unusual for a European male of his era. His recollections of Qingdao were filled with praise for friends like the former education minister in Ji'nan, with his "thorough mastery of Chinese literature," and for the other "distinguished representatives of the old culture" whom he met regularly after 1911.[290] One Qingdao acquaintance was especially important to Wilhelm: Lao Naixuan (fig. 7.20), a former magistrate and member of the Board of Education who moved to Qingdao and worked with Wilhelm on his famous translation of the Yi Jing.[291] Although Wilhelm's published account did not bother to give his mentor's biography or even his full name, referring simply to "my reverend master Lao," it did mention that Lao Naixuan's own teacher's family had been "closely related to the descendants of Confucius.[292] The implicit suggestion was that Wilhelm himself was an indirect intellectual descendant of Confucius. Like Bell and Anzer, Wilhelm received a mandarin button (fourth class) from the Chinese emperor and earned the rank of *Daotai* (circuit intendant). He compared his meetings with Chinese literati after 1911 to the "high-water marks in Chinese history when scholars and artists met, as, for instance, the meeting of the scholars in the Pavilion of the Orchards" described by the calligrapher-poet Wang Xizhi in the fourth century.[293] In his 1914 article on the Qingdao Confucius Society Wilhelm compared his own efforts to save treasures of Chinese art and literature

287. Hesse 1956, pp. 131-32.

288. Hesse 1930.

289. Jung 1966, p. 55. In 1930 Wilhelm was asked to lecture on yoga at a congress of German psychotherapists (ibid., p. 60).

290. R. Wilhelm 1928, pp. 169-70.

291. Ibid., pp. 180 ff. Lao Naixuan specialized in Chinese phonetics, dialects, and reform of the writing system (Cheng 1999). According to Wilhelm, Lao Naixuan was directed to him by Zhou Fu, the former governor of Shandong Province. See Xu Youchun 1991, 1170-71.

292. R. Wilhelm 1928, p. 181.

293. Ibid., p. 170.

from the ravages of the Chinese revolutionaries and foreign capitalism to the work of Confucius, who had toiled to preserve the "highest and worthiest products of the Chinese spirit" in the face of the "torrent of destruction" unleashed by the first Chinese emperor (the Qin king, Shi Huangdi), who burned the scholars' books and was also said to have buried the scholars alive.[294] Even more revealing of the cross-identifications at play was the fact that Wilhelm moved immediately from the historical repression of scholars by the Qin Emperor to the contemporary threat, which he identified as "the invasion of the crude, materialist sides of European-American civilization."[295]

Wilhelm's work and writing was enthusiastically devoted to "intellectual and spiritual exchange" and "synthesis." He was memorialized by Carl Jung as a "mind which created a bridge between East and West and gave to the Occident the precious heritage of a culture thousands of years old."[296] Wilhelm's Sinophilia stood firmly in the tradition of Jesuits like Schall von Bell and Du Halde, despite his Protestant background. His criticism of Europe was conservative, or, rather, a kind of conservative modernism. His aim vis-à-vis Europe was not to eliminate "machine culture" but to limit its claims to total hegemony.[297]

294. R. Wilhelm 1914, p. 249. But see Bodde 1986, pp. 71-72, 95-96, on this infamous and possibly mythical execution.

295. R. Wilhelm 1914, p. 249.

296. Jung 1966, p. 53. After returning to Germany in 1920, after twenty years in China, Wilhelm befriended Jung, Hesse, Buber, Keyserling, Paquet, and other Asia enthusiasts. He taught at Beijing University between 1922 and 1924, and from 1924 until his death in 1930 at the university in Frankfurt am Main, where he founded the Sinological Institute. His works on Chinese philosophy and his translations of the Yi Jing and other works into German are still valued and still in print. European views of China had come full circle by the 1920s; Jung had discovered that "our unconscious is full of Eastern symbolism," and he attacked even more vehemently than Wilhelm the "European materialism and cupidity" that were "flooding China" (Jung 1966, p. 59). Chinese thought, according to Jung, had "set in the soil of Europe a tender seedling, giving us a new intuition of life and its meaning, far removed from the tension and arrogance of the European will" (ibid., pp. 60-61). Kolonko (1997) attributes the entire shift in the "German view of China from negative to positive in the twenties" to Wilhelm's translations and writings. Judging by Hermann Hesse's own enthusiastic writings on China, the contents of his personal library, and his comments on Wilhelm's importance, this view is partly correct (Hsia 1974).

297. Despite the overwhelmingly positive assessments of Wilhelm by his intellectual contemporaries and in the present (e.g., Sun 2003), Wilhelm's belief that China and Europe belonged to two different historical periods (1928, pp. 234-35) was certainly oversimplified. China was also capable of producing its own "mechanical culture," for instance. Although Wilhelm may have led a sort of "double existence" (Gerber 2003, p. 174) as a member of both

FIGURE 7.21 Germans and Chinese, in a scene from colonial Qingdao. From BA-MA-Freiburg, Nachlass Truppel, N 224, vol. 80 (photo album), p. 29 recto. (Courtesy of BA-MA-Freiburg.)

Conclusion

The contours of the new native policies that were emerging in Kiaochow after 1905 can be explained in terms of the details of Sinophile discourse and the internal dynamics among different sectors of the colonizers, specifically, the symbolic and imaginary identifications of the middle-class translators and Sinological *Bildungsbürger*. The immediate impetus for this shift in policy was located at the level of global power alignments. The local result was that by 1914, native policy in Kiaochow had become a highly contradictory formation. On the one hand, social life was still largely segregated in the hospitals, schools, and clubs, and the legal system remained dualistic.[298] At the same time, there was some residential desegregation, economic life in the colony was increasingly dominated by the Chinese and Japanese, the schools were promoting cross-cultural exchange, and people like Richard Wilhelm were bridging the cultural gap, at least in the realm of high culture. The Tsingtau-Klub responded to criticism after 1906 by al-

---

the colonial and local Chinese elites, the fact that he retained a Chinese "boy" need not be seen as a contradiction, since service relations were hardly un-Chinese.

298. Seelemann 1982, p. 422.

lowing Chinese to play tennis there. Germans and Chinese attended local theatrical events together (fig. 7.21).[299]

If things had continued this way, Kiaochow might have eventually lost its colonial character altogether. The Japanese conquest of the colony in 1914 made this future unknowable. The Germans of Qingdao became prisoners of the East Asian state whose subjects had been elevated into the category of "white" in German colonial law.[300] As elsewhere in the Pacific and Africa, the German overseas empire ended almost as abruptly as it had started.

299. This unlabeled and undated photograph from Truppel's collection seems to represent a scene at a local Qingdao theater, possibly the one in Dabadao.

300. Krebs 1998.

EIGHT

Conclusion ɬ Colonial Afterlives

The aftereffects of the colonial period have been dispersed diffusely in German politics and culture up to the present day. Colonial advocacy groups succeeded in creating new streets named after the lost colonies and installing monuments to colonial heroes in German cities. The golden age of German colonial film was the 1930s and 1940s, with *Ohm Krüger* (1941) celebrating the Boers' struggle against the British in South Africa and *Carl Peters* (1941) rehabilitating the controversial founder of German East Africa. A burgeoning *Kolonialpolitsches Amt* (Office for Colonial Policy) in Nazi Germany was allowed to expand and draw up plans for reconquered colonial territories. In February 1943, after the defeat at Stalingrad, Hitler shut down that colonial office, putting a final end to any dreams of a renewed overseas German empire. In East Germany, colonial-imperialist agitation was suppressed after the war and monuments were dismantled, but in the west "only those colonial signs were removed that stemmed from the Nazi period," and several new monuments glorifying German colonialism were actually installed.[1] In contrast to France, however, there was not much debate or even interest in anticolonialism in Germany during the postwar decades of decolonization.[2] This was due to the "premature" loss of the German col-

---

1. Speitkamp 2000, p. 185; also J. Zeller 2000, p. 59.

2. The recent *banlieue* riots and colonial history controversy in France demonstrated the difference it makes when an immigrant minority population actually stems from the former colonies of the country in question. Thus, for example, former Algerian independence fighter Bachir Boumaza, whose contribution to the 1959 book *La gangrène* had described the torture methods employed by French colonial forces during the Algerian war, declared the French law of February 23, 2005, defending colonialism to be "morally equivalent to revisionist efforts concerning Nazism" ("Trois questions à Bachir Boumaza," *Le Monde*, June 11, 2005).

onies and the resulting absence of postcolonial immigrants, politicians, and intellectuals from those colonies in Germany, and also to the preoccupation on both sides of the German border after 1949 with the Nazi atrocities and communism.

The postwar German emphasis, especially in the West, on "coming to terms with the past," apologies, and reparations to victims of Nazism also seems to explain why Germany was the *first* metropolitan country to offer an official apology and a special aid package to Namibian communities grievously affected by modern colonial atrocities.[3] At the same time, British chancellor of the exchequer Gordon Brown used a visit to Tanzania in 2005 to reiterate his message that Britain must *stop* apologizing for its colonial past and the French government passed a law calling on teachers and textbooks to recognize "the positive role of the French overseas presence, especially in North Africa."[4] In one respect this divergence among European official positions on colonialism seems like a continuation of the discussions around the 1919 Versailles conference, with contemporary Germans internalizing the British depiction of them that was codified in the 1918 "Blue Book" on "the condition and the treatment of the natives tribes of South-West Africa" by Germany. German exceptionialism exists as a specifically postwar, post-Holocaust phenomenon, and it now encompasses colonial history, just as it permeated discussions of German unification in 1989–90 and more recent German participation in U.S.-led military missions.[5]

Turning to the aftereffects of colonialism, we can first note that much of Africa continues to suffer from the destruction wrought by European colonialism, while many residents of postcolonial Hong Kong have embraced laws and institutions imposed by their former British colonizers in

3. Steinmetz and Hell 2006.

4. See "La polémique sur la loi relative au 'rôle positif' de la colonisation enfle," *Le Monde*, August 12, 2005; Seamus Milne, "Comment and Analysis," *Guardian* (London), January 27, 2005. All of this European churning of colonial memory is taking place against a swirling debate on American "empire." In Michael Hanneke's film *Caché* (2005), for instance, a middle-class Parisian family's life is thrown into disarray by the return of the colonial repressed in the guise of an Algerian who had been orphaned by the death of his parents during the massacre of Algerian demonstrators in Paris in 1961 (Einaudi 2001; Joshua Cole 2003). This French drama unfolds as images of the U.S. war in Iraq flicker on the television screen.

5. This is not a critique of the German apology and foreign aid to Namibia, which indeed should become a model for European, Japanese, and U.S. treatment of former colonies (and for German treatment of its other former colonies, especially Tanzania). This should not stop us from trying to understand why it is that Germany, unlike other European countries, officially acknowledged its colonial crimes. On German exceptionalism as a postwar, post-Shoah culture, see Steinmetz 1997.

resisting some aspects of mainland Chinese rule.[6] Without gainsaying the symbolic violence perpetrated by even the mildest forms of colonial governance, the sheer variety of postcolonial legacies indicates that it would be misleading to lump all modern colonies together under a single description. If we turn specifically to the legacies of German colonialism, this variety is evident.

Southwest Africa was ruled after 1919 by British South Africa as a class C League of Nations mandate, as were Samoa, New Guinea and Nauru, and the islands of the German Pacific north of the equator. These colonies did not differ in any intrinsic way from the class B mandates of East Africa, Togo, Cameroon, and Ruanda-Urundi; the difference was that the class C mandates were all coveted by the British southern Dominion states (Australia, New Zealand, and South Africa) and that they "would escape virtually all the provisions of mandatory administration, except that of furnishing an annual report to the Permanent Mandates Commission."[7] They were defined as societies "not yet able to stand by themselves under the strenuous conditions of the modern world," in the words of Woodrow Wilson. Above all, such societies were said to be unable to build and sustain a state. In Carl Schmitt's summary, "people and countries unable to forge an organizational apparatus characteristic of a modern state are 'uncivilized'; as stated in Article 22 of the Geneva League of Nations: 'Under the strenuous conditions of the modern world' . . . they are unfit to govern themselves; they are made into colonies, protectorates, or in some other way into objects of protection and control by states able to perform this organizational-technical feat."[8]

Native policy in Southwest Africa after 1919 developed partly on the basis of South African precedent, but it also perpetuated some of the main premises of German rule. This was the only German colony in Africa where Germans were permitted to remain uninterruptedly in the territory even before the Weimar Republic joined the League of Nations in 1926.[9] Along

6. See Rodney [1972] 1981; B. Davidson 1992; and Bayart 1993. On the general problem of colonial continuities and discontinuities, see Mommsen and Osterhammel 1986.

7. Crozier 1979, p. 485; H. Hall 1967. Class A mandates consisted of the former Ottoman provinces of Iraq, Syria, Lebanon, and Palestine. The mandate colonies were subject to certain international controls intended to protect indigenous rights. See Callahan 1999; League of Nations 1922; and the article "Mandate" in *Encyclopaedia Britannica Online.*

8. Wilson's address to the third plenary session of the Paris Peace Conference, February 14, 1919, quoted in Callahan 1999, p. 35; Schmitt [1938] 1996, p. 47.

9. Germans also regained their status as "the largest single group of European settlers" in the East African mandate colony by 1930 (Callahan 1999, p. 135).

with this ongoing presence of German settlers, continuity was enhanced by the fact that some Union officials in the post-1918 colony were direct descendants of German colonial-era settlers and precolonial pioneers.[10] One lasting legacy of the German period was the destruction of communal land ownership and the creation of a system of privately owned land. Indeed, the distribution of land in contemporary Namibia remains "racially-weighted": almost 30 percent of the estimated six thousand farm units in Namibia are owned by Germans or by persons of German descent who speak German at home.[11] The 1921 report of the South African Native Reserves Commission recognized the existence of "six small reserves held by various communities under German treaty" and created new reservations for other racially defined groups, but it also acknowledged that the amount of land granted to autochthonous groups was "infinitesimal in comparison with the area occupied by Europeans or available for European occupation."[12] The Namibian government in recent years started to return some of the lands seized during the colonial era to Africans without resorting to violence.[13] But there has been little public discussion, to date, of the need to remove or historically contextualize the many public monuments to the German colonizers that loom over postcolonial Windhoek (see plate 12) and Swakopmund.[14]

Western Samoa was taken over by New Zealand in 1920 as a class C mandate. It regained its independence only in 1962. When the New Zealand rulers were confronted in 1926 by an anticolonial movement, the Mau, or "Strongly Held View," they departed from the Germans' relatively nonviolent approach. In 1929 they used machine guns against the rebels and killed a leading *matai* (chief) and unarmed supporters of the Mau. The New Zealanders also banned certain customs that the Germans had tried to preserve and regulate, like the fine mat *malaga*.[15] Other institutions that the Germans had introduced were retained, or have reemerged since Samoan independence. The New Zealanders adopted the German "Instructions to Samoan Officials" from 1913 and preserved the Land and Titles Court, which bal-

10. Silvester, Wallace, and Hayes 1998, p. 19. One descendant of German protocolonizers was Carl Hugo Linsingen Hahn, a.k.a. "Cocky" Hahn, grandson of Hugo Hahn, founder of the RMG mission to the Ovaherero (see chap. 2). Cocky Hahn was a South African colonial agent, the native commissioner in Ovamboland, from 1921 to 1946 (Hayes 1996).

11. W. Werner 1993, pp. 135, 156–57. On the history of German settlement in Namibia, which included renewed immigration after 1920 and between the late 1940s and 1955, see Schmidt-Lauber 1993.

12. W. Werner 1993, p. 143.

13. This issue has been covered extensively in the *Namibian* in recent years.

14. See Zeller 2000; Steinmetz and Hell 2006.

15. Field 1991, pp. 62–72.

anced custom against "Western" rational-legal modernity and often ruled in favor of the traditional concepts.[16] In Samoa, then, the period after German colonialism appears primarily as a deterioration, until independence. Nonetheless, the leading Samoan historian, Malama Meleisea, is harshly critical of the German era. The fiction of the country's leading writer, Albert Wendt, pays little heed to the German period, even though Wendt is of partly German descent.[17]

Contemporary Qingdao presents a distinctive "postcolonial" story insofar as the city and the Kiaochow colony were returned to China by the Washington Naval Conference of 1921-22 after being occupied along with the rest of Shandong by Japan starting in 1914. Sixteen years later Japan occupied Qingdao a second time, from 1938 to 1945.[18] During this period Qingdao was transformed into an important industrial development zone. Both before 1939 and after World War II the villas in the city's former European district were occupied by members of the Chinese political elite.[19] In 1984 Qingdao was designated as one of China's national economic development zones meant to encourage foreign investment, and the city became enmeshed in a dense web of connections to foreign investors.[20] The former "Bismarck barracks" that housed the German Third Naval Infantry before 1915 is now one of the main buildings on the central campus of Qingdao Oceanic University. Qingdao also reemerged as a beach resort, a role it had played during the German colonial era, when it was called the "Brighton of China," after the British seaside resort.[21] Today the city is marketed to tourists using the architectural remnants of German colonialism. Many of the German buildings are adorned with historical plaques installed by the Tourism and Cultural Relics Bureau and inscribed in Chinese, English, and German. These touristic presentations betray little anti-imperialist animus

16. For the 1913 German instructions, see NZNA AGCA XVII.A1, vol. 6, pp. 98–113. On the Land and Titles Court see Meleisea 1987a and chap. 5.

17. See Sharrad 2003.

18. Canning 1975. In 1945 the Guomintang (KMT) government allowed the U.S. Navy to use Qingdao as the headquarters of its western Pacific fleet. This lasted until 1949, when the Red Army took Qingdao.

19. Mao Zedong and Lin Biao were the most famous residents of the former German governor's mansion (fig. 7.13) after 1949. Since 1996 the mansion has functioned as a museum.

20. In 2004 there were 1,768 foreign-funded projects in Qingdao and total foreign investment was 10.56 billion dollars; 141 of these projects were German (information from http://www.china.ahk.de/gic/biznews/developmentzone/qdz.htm).

21. Jim Yardley, "Qingdao Journal: Look at the Sea of People (Actually, It's a Chinese Beach)," *New York Times*, national edition, July 30, 2004, p. A4. See also Tsingtauer Verkehrs-Ausschuss (1913).

but direct their accusations primarily at the Chinese Cultural Revolution.[22] When the Qingdao railway station was modernized and expanded in 1993, the architects placed an exact copy of the old German station on the entrance facade (fig. 7.1, *bottom*), incorporating and depoliticizing the colonial past rather than erasing or criticizing it.[23] Another legacy of the colonial period, the Tsingtao brewery (formerly the Germania Bräuerei), is familiar from Chinese restaurants around the world and is a looming presence in contemporary Qingdao (fig. 8.1). Despite these seemingly untroubled appropriations of the colonial past, many Chinese historians remain highly critical of the German period, recognizing the German conquest as the onset of a new stage of Western penetration and humiliation of the country.[24] Chinese intellectuals have been debating the need for a "decolonization of consciousness," a discussion similar to that taking place in countries where the colonial past has a more immediate presence. Some are reopening debate on the appropriateness for China of the forms of modernity that were initially introduced or imposed in the context of nineteenth-century imperialism.[25]

This leads us to the final question, which is whether there is not, in fact, a difference between China and the other colonies considered in this book, one that makes the precolonial and postcolonial periods—if not the period of direct Western and Japanese colonialism—somewhat anomalous. The heuristic fiction running through this book has been that ethnographic discourse has little realistic content, little indexical relationship to its purported object, not even a granule of indexical truth analogous to the *punctum* in every photograph, in Roland Barthes's analysis of that most realistic of representational genres.[26] This assumption has probably not damaged the explanation, since my aim has been to examine the effects of precolonial perceptions on colonial policy and not to trace their genesis or adequacy. This explanatory bracketing of the explanans, as it were, may nonetheless have created the impression that all European ethnographic representations were equally unrealistic. But the shifts in German colonial policy in Kiaochow raise some suspicions about this methodological premise. Over the course of a mere seventeen years of colonial rule, more and more Germans became

22. An exception is the former residence of Kang Youwei (see fig. 7.2, house at upper left). The current plaque (2005) in front of the building notes that Kang appealed "more than ten times for the return of sovereign rights to Qingdao" during the German occupation. On Kang and Kiaochow, see F. Huang 1999, pp. 266–79.

23. Warner 1994, pp. 222–23.

24. See, for example, the essays in Liu Shanzhang 1991. One colonial German who has escaped Chinese criticism is Richard Wilhelm (see Sun 2003).

25. See H. Wang 2003a, 2003b; L. Liu 2004.

26. Barthes 1981.

FIGURE 8.1 The former Germania (later Tsingtao) brewery at number 56 Dengzhou Lu (formerly Hauptmann-Müller-Straße), now the Qingdao beer museum. The slogan on the side of the museum reads, "Tsingtao beer can give you passion and happiness." Photo by the author, 2005.

China enthusiasts. Being encompassed by China, these Germans were following in the footsteps of earlier conquerors, including the Manchu rulers of the Qing empire.[27] Like the middle-class Sinologists in "German China," those earlier Asian "colonialists" had shifted from a hostile or indifferent approach to China to one of self-assimilation. The more a European like Richard Wilhelm entered into dialogue with the colonized, relinquishing claims to superiority, the more his understanding of China seemed to converge with that of his foreign interlocutors. The case of Kiaochow thus forces us to ask whether the discourse of Sinophilia, or certain strands of that discourse, was not, in fact, more adequate epistemologically than its ethnographic contenders, and if so, whether this epistemological realism was partly a function of the power of Chinese civilization to compel its observers to pay closer attention to its own self-interpretations. A further implication would be that each colony to some extent codetermined its own form of colonialism. But what was it about China that allowed it to exercise this powerful integrative pull on its would-be conquerors, and why did China differ in this respect from Samoa and Southwest Africa?

One answer has to do with comparative social complexity and political power, no matter how much such categories have fallen into disfavor. The earliest theorists of social differentiation, including Marx and Durkheim, and the early theorists of the development of non-Western states, were

27. M. Elliott 2001.

perhaps justified in distinguishing societies according to their levels of social and political complexity.[28] There is overwhelming evidence that stateless
societies are not only less complex institutionally, but also, as a result, less
powerful and effective. They have lower levels of the sorts of power sociologist Michael Mann calls "authoritative power" and "diffused power."[29]

There is plentiful evidence for the importance of social complexity and
social power in the comparison among these three cases. As a state, late
Qing China was able to force the Germans to withdraw into the narrower
borders of the colony after initially being caught off guard and allowing
them to penetrate Shandong. China staked out a position at the heart of the
colony in the Qingdao Customs Office and in the German-Chinese college.
Even if the Chinese were not able to determine single-handedly the cultural
exchanges that emerged after 1905, the fact that more and more Germans
wanted to interact with China on an equal basis was partly a function of
China itself. China's ancient literary and philosophical tradition, its capacity to generate a leisured and learned ruling class, proved extremely attractive to Europeans. The continuing political power of the Chinese state,
however diminished, played a part in this "conversion" of Europeans. The
fact that China had an independent system of schools, universities, and examinations made Europeans more likely to accept the Sinophile interpretation regardless of the actual contents of Chinese education. The Shandong
provincial government was able to stimulate the opening of Chinese-owned
mines and mining schools to compete with the Germans, recover railway
rights,[30] and mobilize an army that could effectively fight the Boxers in
Shandong Province, limiting the Germans' ability to deploy their own
troops there. The ability of provincial governors throughout China to defy
the Empress Dowager Cixi's command to support the Yihetuan was a sign
of a state in disarray, but the Shandong governor's ability to repress the Boxers *effectively* within his own sphere demonstrated that he still possessed
political and military resources backed by a fairly developed economy.[31]

China was relatively rich in these forms of sociocultural and state power,
and the other two colonies were relatively poor in them. The two attempts

28. E.g., Durkheim 1915. On differing degrees of stateness see Durkheim 1992, pp. 42–50.
29. Mann 1986–93, vol. 1, p. 8.
30. Lee 1977.
31. This argument about the Chinese difference does not necessitate any claim that *psychic* complexity or cultural excellence increases concurrently with social complexity. Such
a reductionist shortcut has been taken by social theorists in the past (e.g., Elias 1994), but it
is completely unjustified and has usually stemmed from unexamined racism. Any argument
that equates political, social, cultural, and psychic complexity involves a mixing of distinct
ontological levels.

by the Witbooi to drive the German colonizers into the sea were unsuccessful, as were the Samoans' efforts to organize an independent copramarketing company and bypass European traders. The "weapons of the weak" may have been able to revise and limit German colonial practice, but they were revealed time and again to be weak weapons. Any equalization of the profound unevenness of political and economic power among postcolonial states must take seriously the impact of material resources and political institutions and cannot restrict itself to correcting Orientalist or racial stereotypes.

But if this book has demonstrated one thing, it is that the "hard" structures of colonial states, economies, and societies are shaped by and consubstantial with ethnographic discourses, symbolic struggles among the colonizers, and psychic identifications across the colonial boundary. This book has also demonstrated that ethnographic discourse, colonial subjectivity, and the colonial state were less uniform and more internally complex and heterogeneous than has usually been argued. Except in the most extreme and unusual situations, European representations of non-Europeans were much more layered and fragmentary than theories of "Orientalism" have led us to believe. European ethnographic discourse tended to organize itself as a field, that is, as a conflictual symbolic space, which meant that opposing positions emerged almost automatically. Only in the most unusual circumstances, as in European representations of the nineteenth-century Namibian Ovaherero, did such discourse speak with a single voice. This does not mean that the core policies of the colonial state were not profoundly shaped by precolonial ethnographic discourse. These determinations were not simple ones, however, but were mediated through the structure of the colonial state field itself.

The colonial state, I have argued here, can best be understood as a kind of field, one that is structured around opposing principles and interests and around conflict over specific stakes. Actors in the field of the colonial state competed to accumulate ethnographic capital. This field's internal heterogeneity and the fact that a field is "a space of possibilities" with an "immense elasticity"[32] meant that colonial policy was never a smooth, continuous process but was prone to sudden shifts in direction. The relative autonomy of the colonial government from the metropolitan state and its independence from other fields in terms of its definition of symbolic capital meant that it was, in fact, a kind of state, even if political theorists have paid little attention to it.

Just as it is impossible to generalize about the contents of ethnographic

32. Pierre Bourdieu in Maître 1990, x, xii.

discourse or the policies of the colonial state, neither can one characterize the "mind of the colonizer" in general terms, except to say that it was as complex and internally contradictory as the subjectivity of the colonized. Europeans were divided by social class, and European psychic identifications rooted in the imaginary and the symbolic orders were responsible for discontinuous and sometimes incompatible perceptions and practices.

The argument that colonial policies were profoundly shaped by precolonial ethnographic discourse, by the configuration of the colonial state as a specific type of field, and by colonizers' identifications with the colonized across the racial-cultural boundary may be applied to other modern colonial empires, including the French, British, Belgian, and American ones. The account in this book may also be relevant for understanding metropolitan state fields, which were undoubtedly shaped by rulers' "ethnographic" perceptions of the masses and their perverse identifications across social class boundaries. Postcolonial criticism has shown how events and discourses rebound from colonies back into the metropoles. Such matrices of reverberation also exist in the realm of social and political theory.

APPENDIX 1

A Note on Sources and Procedures

Several methodological assumptions guide my analysis of precolonial ethnographic discourse, whose limits are more difficult to specify than colonial policy. First, this discourse analysis encompasses material produced in all major European languages. This procedure is necessary because of the fluid boundaries between German and non-German discourse during the period under investigation. During the sixteenth and seventeenth centuries the relevant literature on China was mainly written in Latin, although much of it was translated quickly (and often repeatedly) into German.[1] Seventeenth-century literature on the Cape Colony was mainly written in Dutch, but much of it was translated into German. The national origin of many of the DEIC employees who wrote about the Cape Colony was German. Furthermore, most of the German colonial officials who internalized these ethnographic images in the late nineteenth century were graduates of a German *gymnasium* and had advanced university degrees, which usually meant that they could read some foreign languages. In all overseas sites of precolonial

---

1. Travel narratives were translated from various European languages into German in collections like *Allgemeine Historie der Reisen zu Wasser und Lande* (Leipzig, 1749-50), *Allgemeine Unterhaltende Reise-Bibliothek oder Sammlung der besten und neuesten Reisebeschreibungen* (Berlin 1806-9); *Allgemeine Welt- und Menschenkunde* (1810), edited by Eduard Zimmermann; *Neue Bibliothek der wichtigsten Reisebeschreibungen zur Erweiterung der Erd- und Völkerkunde* (Weimar: Landes-Comptoir, 1815-33), edited by Friedrich Bertuch; *Bibliothek der neuesten und wichtigsten Reisebeschreibungen* (1800-1806); Johann Bernoulli's *Sammlung kurzer Reisebeschreibungen und anderer zur Erweiterung der Länder- und Menschenkenntniß dienender Nachrichten* (1781-84/85); *Magazin von merkwürdigen neuen Reisebeschreibungen aus fremden Sprachen übersetzt* (Berlin), edited by Reinhold Forster et al.; *Taschenbibliothek der neuesten unterhaltendsten Reisebeschreibungen* (1826-28); and *Taschenbuch der Reisen; oder Unterhaltende Darstellung der Entdeckungen des 18. Jh.*

ethnographic observation, Germans moved within a multilingual society in which English, Dutch, French, and any number of local languages were the media of daily communication. The artificiality of restricting an analysis of "German" ethnographic discourse to German-language sources is reinforced by the fact that many contributions by "German" authors were written or published in Latin or Dutch during the sixteenth and seventeenth centuries and in English during the eighteenth and nineteenth centuries. I therefore discuss the most influential non-German writings in each case (and occasionally reconstruct their history of translation into German).

Nevertheless, I retain a focus on German ethnographic sources. Germans were more likely to have read other German sources, ceteris paribus, especially in the more nationalistic nineteenth century. A book by the second German governor of Southwest Africa, for instance, refers *only* to recent German-language literature.[2] Ethnographic images were embedded in texts that did more than just represent the non-European Other; they also proposed a particular relationship between the non-Westerner and the European observer. Although the Germanness of the author rarely made much difference for the way in which the non-European was represented, ethnographic visions sometimes positioned the implicit European reader in nationally specific ways. The seventeenth-century account of China by Evert Ysbrants Ides, for instance, who led a semiofficial Russian mission to China in 1692–93, began by explaining that he had wanted to write the narrative because "only *Russians,* and no *German,* had hitherto travell'd thro' great *Tartary* to *China.*"[3] Nineteenth-century German texts that defended the flogging of Africans and Chinese pointed out that flogging had been practiced until recently in Prussia.[4]

My analysis of formations of ethnographic discourse draws on material from diverse sources and genres and includes visual representations as well as written ones. The scientific expeditions of the Enlightenment era, including Captain Cook's Pacific voyages and Lord Macartney's embassy to the Chinese emperor, often included painters and draftsmen in their entourage. One of the mainstays of overseas travel literature throughout the early modern and modern periods was the lavish use of illustrations. Visual material was also central to the scientific anthropology, craniometry, ethnology, and "race science" that developed in the nineteenth century. The chinoiserie

2. C. von François 1899.

3. Ides 1706, from "epistele dedicatory" (no pagination; italics in the original).

4. This is not to say that the German colonial administrators positioned themselves as creators of a superior "German" variant of colonialism; indeed (pace Zantop 1997), this was rarely the case in the colonies examined here.

mode of the eighteenth century meant that Europe was flooded with images of China. The textual genres included in this analysis include anthropology and ethnography,[5] missionary writings, philosophical and theoretical texts, and fiction. Ethnographic descriptions were also often proposed en passant, or in the margins of academic texts and novels set in Europe; yet as postcolonial cultural criticism has argued, marginal placement in a text does not necessarily indicate ideological insignificance. I include journals as well as books.[6]

My central aim in chapters 2, 4, and 6 is to reconstruct ideological formations of discourse concerning China and the Chinese, Samoans, Ovaherero, Khoikhoi, and the Reheboth Basters. This makes sense only to the extent that Europeans at the time perceived a given people as having a distinct and bounded ethnic, cultural, or "racial" existence. The unity that prevails within any given formation of ethnographic discourse is defined by the shared object (e.g. "the Ovaherero") and by a finite set of ways of talking about that object. The collections of statements grouped into discursive formations usually exhibit some level of structuration. In chapter 6, for example, I show that the same tropes were deployed in novels, theoretical treatises, travel narratives, and scientific accounts concerning China.

I make no assumption here that these discursive objects—ethnic groups, races, cultures—corresponded to real social entities. This is not to say that there was *not* a real object, such as "the Samoans" or "Ovaherero culture," but simply that ethnographic discourse was often based on misperceptions of the social world, and that some misperceptions involved the invention of ethnicities and races. Of course, ethnographic categories that are empirically incorrect may help to bring ethnic realities into closer correspondence with those categories. Such "looping effects" of social categories do not require that we revise our agnostic view of the relationship between the discursive object and the external object of discourse, or that we conclude that there is no difference between the two.[7] Medieval representations of races of giants or troglodytes could not conjure those discursive objects into existence, but European interventions in Southwest Africa may well have contributed to the salience of identities like Ovaherero or Berg Damara, just

5. In nineteenth-century Germany, *Anthropologie* usually referred to physical anthropology while *Ethnologie* meant cultural anthropology. I use *ethnography* and *ethnographic* throughout this book to refer to any image or text that claims to represent the character or culture of a given people or ethnos. It is not coterminous with disciplines of *Ethnologie* or *Anthropologie* in nineteenth-century Germany and is certainly not limited to professional anthropologists.

6. I read every available issue of the ethnographically related journals listed in the bibliography for the period through 1914.

7. Hacking 1995, 1999.

as German interventions in Rwanda before 1914 may have sharpened ethnic distinctions between Tutsi and Hutu.[8]

Having delimited the common features of a given formation of ethnographic discourse, I look for lines of internal variation. Ethnographic formations contain heterogeneous material that does not necessarily coalesce into a single unified argument or narrative or deploy a consistent set of tropes, even if it has a common object. Discursive formations vary in this regard: some contain numerous distinctive viewpoints or strands, others only one or two. Formations of ethnographic discourse also differ in terms of the extent to which they are dominated or hegemonized by a given strand. This is significant because the more homogeneous and hegemonized formations offered colonizers a smaller degree of cognitive latitude for thinking about the colonized. German discourse on China was more differentiated and less hegemonized by any one particular voice than was discourse about the Ovaherero, for instance. Just as I cannot deal with the complex determination of precolonial ethnographic representations, I do not spend much time on the problem of why certain strands were more powerful than others. It is evident, however, that the prestige of certain ethnographic visions depended partly on the reputation of their proponents and the power of the social classes with which they were conjuncturally associated. The presence of Leibniz among the champions of Chinese civilization, for instance, was important in balancing the scales against the prestigious China bashers of the late eighteenth and nineteenth centuries. Other ethnographic strands, such as the portrayal of the Khoikhoi as "noble savages," could be more easily attacked by demeaning the veracity or competence of their less distinguished proponents such as François Le Vaillant. Precolonial ethnographic discourse often had fieldlike characteristics, just like the colonial state. Nineteenth-century "ethnographers" faced off, just like Margaret Mead and Derek Freeman in our own time.

I reconstruct the entire historical trajectory of five discursive formations, concerning the Khoikhoi, Ovaherero, Reheboth Basters, Samoans, and Chinese, placing greatest emphasis on the decades immediately preceding colonization. Only by reconstructing the evolution of a discursive formation over the long (or longish) term can we grasp its internal structure. Important structural features of a discursive formation include the relative historical depth of each strand and the submerged persistence of strands from earlier periods that might be reawakened later. The five formations differed enormously in terms of their sheer historical depth. Europeans began

8. Bindseil 1988.

discussing the Khoikhoi at the end of the fifteenth century, when exploring and trading vessels began calling at the Cape of Good Hope. Descriptions of the Ovaherero began to congeal only with the founding of the Rhenish Mission in Hereroland during the 1840s. The shorter time frame in this case meant that German colonizers had a thinner stock of representations to draw upon when devising their colonial schemes than they had with some other populations. Representations of Samoa began with the visit by Lapérouse in 1787 and began thickening following the arrival of missionaries from the London Missionary Society in 1830. The structure of modern European discourse on China began to take shape in the sixteenth century, even if vague perceptions existed much earlier. The main options for European representations of China that were established by the middle of the eighteenth century remained in place until the early twentieth century.

As for the analysis of colonial policy in chapters 3, 5, and 7, it is relatively straightforward to determine the sorts of material that need to be considered. Relevant sources correspond to the political boundaries drawn by the colonial state itself. I rely on primary archival documents and printed sources generated by officials and personnel of these states and by the various German ministries, as well as the sparser documentation generated by African, Samoan, and Chinese organizations (some of which is included in the colonial archives themselves). The most important sources are the documents of the Colonial Department of the Foreign Office and later the Colonial Office; the Foreign Office; the navy and army; the German legation in Beijing; the local colonial state archives in Namibia, New Zealand (for Samoa), and Qingdao; the private papers of German officials and missionaries; and the mission archives.[9] I also read all of the German colonial journals for this period, some daily German newspapers, and all of the available newspapers from the colonies.

9. When the Colonial Office was created in 1907, the documents of the Colonial Department of the Foreign Office migrated with it and are kept separately in the Bundesarchiv in Berlin. The records of the pre-1914 Foreign Office, by contrast, are housed in the Politisches Archiv des Auswärtigen Amts, separate from the records of all the other federal-level departments. The military archives in Freiburg have the largest collection of documents from Kiaochow as well as military collections relating to colonial warfare elsewhere. The federal archives in Koblenz possess the personal papers of many former German officials. The Archiv- und Museumsstiftung in Wuppertal keeps the records of the Rhenish Missionary Society. See the bibliography for a full list of documents consulted.

Head Administrators of German Southwest Africa, Samoa, and Kiaochow

SOUTHWEST AFRICA

Imperial Commissaries (Kaiserliche Kommissare)
Dr. Heinrich Ernst Goering: May 1885–August 1890
Curt von François: March 1891–November 1893; *Landeshauptmann,*
    November 1893–March 15, 1894

Governors (Gouverneure)
Theodor Leutwein: March 15, 1894–April 18, 1898, *Landeshauptmann;* there-
    after *Gouverneur,* officially through August 19, 1905, but General Lothar
    von Trotha was effectively in charge of the colony from January to
    August 1905.
Dr. Friedrich von Lindequist: August 19, 1905–May 20, 1907
Bruno von Schuckmann: May 20, 1907–June 20, 1910
Dr. Theodor Seitz: August 28, 1910–1915

SAMOA

Governors
Dr. Wilhelm H. Solf: January 25, 1900–December 19, 1911
Dr. Erich Schultz, June 19, 1912–1914

KIAOCHOW

Governors
Captain Oskar Truppel: February–April 1898
Captain Carl Rosendahl, March 7, 1909 (actually began service April 16, 1898)–
    October 10, 1898
Captain Paul Jaeschke: February 19, 1899–January 27, 1901
Captain Oskar Truppel: February 20, 1901–August 17, 1911
Captain Alfred Meyer-Waldeck, August 19, 1911–1914

BIBLIOGRAPHY

MANUSCRIPT SOURCES CITED

I. Archival and Museum Foundation Wuppertal (Archiv- und Museumsstiftung Wuppertal), documents of the Rhenish Missionary Society (Rheinische Missionsgesellschaft, or RMG), precursor of the United Evangelical Mission (Vereinigte Evangelische Mission), Wuppertal, Germany

1.404: "Beitrag zur Missionsgeschichte des Witbooistammes," by missionary Johannes Olpp, for the archive of the mission, 1897 (given to the archive by Olpp in 1904); transcript (original in 2.597)

1.575: Missionary Hugo Hahn, correspondence files

1.577b: Missionary Hugo Hahn, correspondence files

1.594a: Missionary Peter Heinrich Brincker, correspondence files

1.616a: Missionary Friedrich Anton Judt, correspondence files

2.500a: Gibeon Station

2.580a: "Gibeon: Geschichte der Station und des Witbooischen Volksstammes," Übertragung von Aufzeichnungen von Jacob Knauer, 1863–67, und Johannes Olpp, 1868–79

2.589: "Rehoboth: Geschichte der Station und der Rehobother Bastards," Übertragung von Aufzeichnungen von Johann Christian Friedrich Heidmann, 1866–1902, und 1 Brief von Franz Heinrich Kleinschmidt, 1851

2.597: "Die Witboois: Ihre Geschichte in Kamerun," by missionary Johannes Olpp

2.604a–2.604e: Herero-Aufstand: Zeitungsausschnitte (Originale)

3.538b: Missionary Johann Christian Friedrich Heidmann, Unkorrigierte private Abschrift der Personalakte, von Richard Gottfried Vollmer, pt. 2

II. German Federal Archives (Bundesarchiv), Berlin Branch (BA-Berlin)

Records of the Imperial Colonial Office (Reichskolonialamt), R 1001

Vol. 1212: Landerwerbungen und Angebote in Deutsch-Südwestafrika, 1914–35

Vol. 1219: Kronland und Eingeborenen-Reservate in Südwestafrika

Vol. 1483, 1486, 1489: Militärische Expedition der Schutztruppe, Kämpfe gegen Witbooi

Vol. 2025: Abschriften von Verträgen mit Häuptlingen aus dem Gebiet DSWA, 1884-1903

Vol. 2089: Differenzen zwischen Generalleutnant von Trotha und Gouv. Leutwein bezgl. der Aufstände im DSWA im Jahre 1904

Vol. 2090: Deportation der Kriegsgefangenen aus DSWA in andere Kolonien

Vol. 2107: Entsendung einer bewaffneten Expedition gegen die Hereros— u. v. François

Vol. 2100: Das Herero Land, 1895-96

Vols. 2113-19: Aufstand der Hereros im Jahre 1904, vols. 3-9

Vol. 2123: Angelegenheiten des Rothen Volkes

Vol. 2124: Die Bastards von Rehoboth, 1886-1927

Vol. 2131: Die Kämpfe zwischen dem Nama u. d. Herero, 1892-93, vol. 4

Vols. 2133-34: Aufstand im Namaland 1904, vols. 1-2

Vols. 2138-40: Aufstand im Namalande im Jahre 1894, vols. 5-7

Vol. 2167: Bastards in Rietfontein (Philander), 1894-95

Vol. 2169: Bergdamaras, 1895-96; 1921-22

Vol. 2170: Die Bastarde von Grootfontein, vol. 1, 1896-98

Vol. 2171: Die Bastarde von Grootfontein, vol. 2, 1898-1939

Vol. 2174: Verhandlungen des Gouvernementrats in Windhuk, 1906

Vol. 2216: Enschädigungsansprüche SWA

Vols. 2759-60: Deutsche Schule auf Samoa, 1901-16

Vol. 3053: Allgemeine Verhältnisse auf den Samoa-Inseln, 1899

Vol. 3061: Allgemeine Verhältnisse auf den Samoa-Inseln, 1901

Vol. 3069: Unruhen in Samoa, 1909

Vol. 5432: Die Mischehen und die Rechtsverhältnisse der Mischlinge in Samoa, 1900-1920

Vol. 5588: Rechtsstellung der Angehörigen fremder farbiger Völker in Samoa, 1911-14

Vols. 6349-50: Für die Kolonialausstellung bestimmte Afrikaner der deutschen Kolonien, 1894-1907

Collection "Protectorate German Southwest Africa" ("Schutzgebiet Deutsch-Südwestafrika"), R 1002

Vol. 2591: Eingeborenenangelegenheiten, allgemeines, 1907-14

Vol. 2597: Eingeborenen der Inspektion

Records of the German Legation in China (Deutsche Botschaft China), R 9208

Vol. 655: Gründung eines Richthofen-Instituts für deutsche Chinaforschung, 1913-15

Vol. 1238-47: Pachtgebiet Kiautschou, 1901-16

Vol. 1258-60: Schulwesen in Tsingtau, 1907-16

Records of the Foreign Office (Auswärtiges Amt) in the Bundesarchiv, R 901

Vol. 38930: Akten betr. Deutsche Unterrichtsveranstaltungen für Chinesen in
Tsingtau, 1907-8

Collection of microfilmed copies of German colonial records for German Samoa
owned by New Zealand National Archives (NZNA); Archives of the German
Colonial Administration (AGCA)

Record no. VI, vols. 3-4: Gouvernmentsrat (Governing Council) 1909-13

Record no. VI 13, vols. 1-3: Rechtsverhältnisse der Mischlinge (Legal Conditions of
Half-Castes), 1903-13

Record no. VI 28, vol. 1: Station Süd-Upolu (Southern Upolu Station), 1914

Record no. XVII.A.1, vols. 1-6: Allgemeine Verwaltung und Rechtspflege (Government and Adminstration of Justice)

Record no. XVII.A.2, vols. 1-5: Samoan Affairs, Mataafa and the Malo

Record no. XVII.B, vols. 1-3: Samoan Affairs, District Administration, Malo in
Mulinuu

Record no. XVII.B.1, vols. 1-10: District Administration, Atua

Record no. XVII.B.2, vols 1-2: District Administration, Falealili

Record no. XVII.B.3, vols 1-2: District Administration, Vaa-o-Fonoti

Record no. XVII.B.5, vols. 1-3: District Administration, Aana and Manono

III. German Federal Archives (Bundesarchiv), Koblenz Branch (BA-Koblenz)

Papers of Wilhelm Solf, first governor of German Samoa (Nachlass Solf)

Vol. 16: Aus der Tätigkeit beim Generalkonsulat Kalkutta, 1889-91

Vol. 18: Munizipalpräsident in Apia (Samoa) 1899, vol. 1, Briefband

Vol. 20-32: Gouverneur von Samoa, 1900-1911

Vol. 34: Tagebuch über die Dienstreise Sr. Exzellenz des Herrn Staatssek. Dr. Solf
nach Südwest-, Süd-, u. Ostafrika, 27 Mai bis Okt 1912

IV. German Federal Archives–Military Archives (Bundesarchiv-Militärarchiv),
Freiburg Branch (BA-MA-Freiburg)

Imperial Navy Office (RMA: Reichs-Marine-Amt), RM 3

Vol. 6693: Bericht Kiautschou Bucht and Plan zur Besitz-Ergreifung, 1896-97

Vol. 6694: Denkschrift über die Besitzergreifung der Kiautschou-Bucht und Ver-
trag mit China

Vol. 6697: Berichte über Besetzung sowie Lage und Ereignisse in Kiautschou

Vol. 6765: Gouvernements-Tätigkeits-Berichte

Vol. 6782: Unruhen in China

Vol. 7001: Kiautschou-Neubauten für die deutsch-chinesische Hochschule

Kaiserliche Shutztruppen und sonstige deutsche Landstreitkaräfte in Übersee,
RM 53

Vol. 7: Tätigkeit in China, Lt. Pfleger und Olt. Fulda

Personal papers of Oskar von Truppel (Nachlass Truppel)
Vol. 19: Das innere Schantungs: Reisebericht d. Gouv. Truppel
Vol. 33: Privatdienstliche Korrespondenz Truppel mit dem Gouv. von Schantung, Tshoufu: Einlauf (Originale)
Vol. 59: Der Gouverneur von Kiautschou, Kapt. zur See Truppel, Festrede des Bankdirektors Homann anläßlich des Urlaubsantritts des Gouverneur's: Handschrift 6.11.1904
Vol. 62: Tsingtauer Werft: Ausbildung chinesischer Handwerker
Vol. 78: Unser Leben und Treiben in Tsingtau, vol. 2
Vol. 81: In Tsingtau, 1910-11

Personal papers of Otto von Diederichs (Nachlass Diederichs)
Vol. 24: "Die Besatzung von Tsingtau am 14.XI.1897" (written ca. 1908-00)

Personal papers of Berthold von Deimling (Nachlass Deimling)
Vols. 1-3: Lebenserinnerungen

V. Political Archives of the German Foreign Office (Politisches Archiv des Auswärtigen Amts)
Vols. 3905-6: Alwin Wilhelm Otto Franke, personnel documents (Personalia)
Vols. 13812-13: Wilhelm Schrameier, personnel documents
Vols. 2165-67: Die Gesandtschaft in Peking, 1886-1920 (Deutschland 135, Nr. 15)
Vols. 18239-41: Kiauschou und die deutschen Interessen in Schantung, 1899-1922 (China 22)

VI. National Archives of Namibia (NAN)
Zentralbureau des Kaiserlichen Gouvernements (ZBU), 1884-1915

PERIODICALS CONSULTED

Abhandlungen des Hamburgischen Kolonialinstituts (vols. 1 [1910]-43 [1921])
Amtsblatt für das Deutsche Kiautschou-Gebiet (vols. 1 [1900]-14 [1914])
Amtsblatt für das Schutzgebiet Deutsch-Südwestafrika (vols. 1 [1910]-5 [1914])
Annalen der Verbreitung des Glaubens (1863-1918)
Archiv für Anthropologie: Zeitschrift für Naturgeschichte und Urgeschichte des Menschen (1866-1914)
Das Ausland (vols. 3 [1830]-60 [1887])
Beiträge zur Kolonialpolitik- und Kolonialwirtschaft (vols. 1 [1899-1901]-5 [1903])
Berichte der Rheinischen Missionsgesellschaft (detailed titles and dates: *Jahresbericht der Rheinischen Missionsgesellschaft* [vols. 1 (1830)-49 (1877)], *Auszüge aus den Berichten und Briefe der Sendboten der Rheinischen Missionsgesellschaft* (1840-41 through 1842-43), *Monats-Berichte der Rheinischen Missionsgesellschaft* [vols. 1 (1843-44)-4 (1846-47)], *Berichte der Rheinischen Missionsgesellschaft* [vols. 5 (1847)-67 (1914)])
Cape Monthly Magazine (1857-81)

Correspondenzblatt der Deutschen Gesellschaft für Anthropologie, Ethnologie und Urgeschichte (vols. 1 [1870-71]-43 [1912])

Deutsch-Asiatische Warte (1898-1902)

Deutsch-Chinesiche Rechtszeitung (1911-14)

Deutsche Kolonialzeitung (vols. 1 [1884]-4 [1887] and 1 n.s. [1888]-39, n.s. [1922])

Die Deutschen Kolonien (Aus Fernen Landen) (1902-1907).

Die Deutschen Schutzgebiete in Afrika und der Südsee (1891-92 through 1912-13); earlier titles: *Die Entwicklung der Schutzgebiete* (1891-92 through 1893-94); and *Jahresbericht über die Entwicklung der dentschen Schutzgebieten in Afrika und der Südsee* (1894-95 through 1907-8).

Deutsches Kolonialblatt: Amtsblatt für die Schutzgebiete des Deutschen Reiches (vols. 1 [1890]-24 [1913])

Dongfang Zazhi [Eastern Miscellany] (Shanghai: Shangwu yin shu guan) (vols. 1 [1904]-10 [1914])

Der Ferne Osten/The East of Asia (vols. 1 [1902]-3 [1905-6])

Globus: Illustrierte Zeitschrift für Länder- und Völkerkunde: Chronik der Reisen und Geographische Zeitung (vols. 1 [1862]-98 [1910])

Journal des Museums Godeffroy (1873-1910)

Keetmanshooper Nachrichten (1910-11)

Keetmanshooper Zeitung (1912-13)

Kiautschou-Post (1908-14)

Koloniale Monatsblätter (1913-14)

Koloniale Rundschau (1909-12)

Koloniales Jahrbuch (vols. 1 [1888]-11 [1899])

Kolonial-Politisches Correspondenz (vols. 1 [1883]-3 [1887])

Kolonie und Heimat (vols. 1 [1907-8]-7 [1914])

Lüderitzbuchter Zeitung (1909-14)

Mitteilungen von Forschungsreisenden und Gelehrten aus den deutschen Schutzgebieten (vols. 1 [1888]-32 [1919])

Mitteilungen des Seminars für orientalische Sprachen (vols. 1 [1898]-16 [1913])

Nachrichten aus Kiautschou (1898-1900)

(Neues) Göttingisches Historisches Magazin (vols. 1 [1787]-8 [1791]); 1, n.s. [1792]-3, n.s. [1794]

O le Savali [The Messenger] (1905-14)

O le Sulu Samoa [The Samoan Torch] (1890-1914)

Der Ostasiatische Lloyd (1866-1917)

Petermanns Geographische Mittheilungen (vols. 1 [1855]-64 [1918])

Samoan Reporter (1845-62)

Samoanische Zeitung (vols. 1 [1901]-15 [1915])

Samoanisches Gouvernements-Blatt (vols. 3 [1900]-5 [1910])

Samoa Weekly Herald (1899-1900)

Der Tropenpflanzer (vols. 1 [1897]-16 [1912])

Tsingtauer Neueste Nachrichten (vols. 1 [1904]-11 [1914])

Überall (Organ des deutschen Flottenbundes) (vols. 1 [1898–99]–17 [1914–15])

Unterhaltungen aus der Länder- und Völkerkunde (vols. 1 [1817]–11 [1828])

Verhandlungen der Berliner Gesellschaft für Anthropologie, Ethnologie und Urgeschichte (1870–1914)

Verhandlungen der Gesellschaft für Erdkunde zu Berlin (vols. 1 [1873–74]–28 [1901])

Verordnungsblatt für das Kiautschougebiet (vols. 1 [1900]–15 [1914])

Der West-östliche Bote (1913–14)

Windhoeker Anzeiger/Deutsch Südwestafrikanische Zeitung (as *Windhoeker Zeitung*, 1898–1901; as *Deutsch Südwestafrikanische Zeitung*, 1901–14)

Zeitschrift der Gesellschaft für Erdkunde zu Berlin (vols. 1 [1866]–51 [1916])

Zeitschrift für Ethnologie (vols. 2 [1870]–47 [1915])

Zeitschrift für Kolonialpolitik, Kolonialrecht und Kolonialwirtschaft (vols. 6 [1904]–12 [1910])

PUBLISHED WORKS

Abraham, Nicolas, and Maria Torok. 1994. *The Shell and the Kernel*. Chicago: University of Chicago Press.

Abusch, Alexander. 1946. *Der Irrweg einer Nation*. Berlin: Aufbau-Verlag.

Ackerman, Gerald M. 1986. *Jean-Léon Gérôme*. London: Sotheby's Publications.

Adams, Julia. 1994. "The Familial State: Elite Family Practices and State-Making in the Early Modern Netherlands." *Theory and Society* 23 (4): 505–39.

Adams, Julia. 2005. *The Familial State: Ruling Families and Merchant Capitalism in Early Modern Europe*. Ithaca, N.Y.: Cornell University Press.

Administration of Western Samoa. 1925. *Handbook of Western Samoa*. Wellington, New Zealand: W. A. G. Skinner, Government Printer.

Admiralstab der Marine, ed. 1903. *Die Kaiserliche Marine während der Wirren in China, 1900–1901*. Berlin: Ernst Siegfried Mittler und Sohn.

Agnew, Vanessa. 1999a. "Ethnographic Transgressions and Confessions in Georg Forster's 'Voyage round the World.'" Pp. 304–15 in *Schwellen*, ed. Nicholas Saul, Daniel Steuer, Frank Möbus, and Birgit Illner. Würzberg: Königshausen and Neumann.

Agnew, Vanessa. 1999b. "Dissecting the Cannibal: Comparing the Function of the Autopsy Principle in the Diaries and Narratives of Captain Cook's Second Voyage." Pp. 50–60 in *Marginal Voices, Marginal Forms: Diaries in European Literature and History*, ed. Rachael Langford and Russell West. Amsterdam: Rodopi.

Albertini, Rudolph von. 1982. *European Colonial Rule, 1880–1940*. Westport, Conn.: Greenwood.

Alexander, J. E. [1838] 1967. *An Expedition of Discovery into the Interior of Africa*. 2 vols. Cape Town: Struik.

Alexander, N. E. 1981. "Jakob Marengo and Namibian History." *Social Dynamics* 7 (1): 1–7.

Allan, Charles Wilfrid. 1975. *Jesuits at the Court of Peking*. Arlington, Va.: University Publications of America.

Alloula, Malek. 1986. *The Colonial Harem*. Minneapolis: University of Minnesota Press.

Alnaes, Kirsten. 1989. "Living with the Past: The Songs of the Herero in Botswana." *Africa* 59 (3): 267-99.

Althusser, Louis. 1971a. "Freud and Lacan." Pp. 195-219 in *Lenin and Philosophy*, by Louis Althusser. London: NLB.

Althusser, Louis. 1971b. "Ideology and Ideological State Apparatuses." Pp. 121-72 in *Lenin and Philosophy*, by Louis Althusser,. London: NLB.

Althusser, Louis. 1996. "Correspondence with Jacques Lacan." Pp. 145-73 in *Writings on Psychoanalysis: Freud and Lacan*, ed. Olivier Corpet and François Matheron, trans. Jeffrey Mehlman. New York: Columbia University Press.

Alverdes, Hermann. 1906. *Mein Tagebuch aus Südwest*. Oldenburg: G. Stalling.

Amelung, Iwo. 1998. "Gegen die ausländischen Barbaren: Die 'Boxer' und ihr Mythos." Pp. 165-72 in Hinz and Lind 1998.

Andersson, Charles J. 1856. *Lake Ngami*. London: Hurst and Blackett.

Andersson, Charles J. [1861] 1968. *The Okavango River*. Cape Town, C. Struik.

Andersson, Charles J. [1875] 1969. *Notes of Travel in South Africa*. Cape Town, C. Struik.

Andersson, Charles J. 1987-89. *Diaries and Correspondence of Charles John Andersson*. 2 vols. Ed. Brigitte Lau. Windhoek: National Archives.

Anson, George. [1748] 1974. *A Voyage round the World in the Years MDCCXL, I, II, III, IV*. London: Oxford University Press.

Anzieu-Premmereur, Christine, and Victor Souffir. 2003. "Argument." *Revue française de psychanalyse* 66:1037-42.

Appiah, Kwame Anthony. 1992. *In My Father's House*. New York: Oxford University Press.

Appleton, W. W. 1951. *A Cycle of Cathay*. New York: Columbia University Press.

Apter, Andrew. 1999. "The Subvention of Tradition: A Genealogy of the Nigerian Durbar." Pp. 213-52 in Steinmetz 1999a.

Arbeitsausschuss der Deutschen Kolonial-Ausstellung, ed. 1896. *Deutschland und seine Kolonien im Jahre 1896: Amtlicher Bericht über die erste deutsche Kolonial-Ausstellung*. Berlin: Reimer.

Arendt, Carl. 1899-1900. "Synchronistische Regententabellen zur Geschichte der chinesischen Dynastien." *Mittheilungen des Seminars für Orientalische Sprachen zu Berlin* 2 (1): 152-250; 3 (1) 1-164.

Arendt, Hannah. 1945/1946. "Imperialism: Road to Suicide: The Political Origins and Use of Racism." *Commentary* 1:27-35.

Arendt, Hannah. [1950] 1958. *The Origins of Totalitarianism*. New York: World Publishing Co.

Arendt, Hannah. 1970. *On Violence*. New York: Harcourt, Brace and World.

Arrighi, Giovanni. 1994. *The Long Twentieth Century*. New York: Verso.

Asad, Talal. 1973. *Anthropology and the Colonial Encounter*. New York: Humanity Books.

Ashcroft, Bill, Gareth Griffiths, and Helen Tiffin, eds. 1989. *The Empire Writes Back: Theory and Practice in Post-colonial Literatures*. London: Routledge.

Auer, G. 1911. *In Südwestafrika gegen die Hereros: Nach den Kriegs-Tagebüchern des Obermatrosen G. Auer*. Ed. M. Unterbeck. 2nd ed. Berlin: Ernst Hoffmann & Co.

Aurich, Ursula. 1935. *China im Spiegel der deutschen Literatur des 18. Jahrhunderts*. Berlin: E. Ebering.

Austen, Ralph. 1977. "Duala versus Germans in Cameroon: Economic Dimensions of a Political Conflict." *Revue Française d'Histoire d'Outre-Mer* 237 (4): 477-97.

Austen, Ralph, and Jonathan Derrick. 1999. *Middlemen of the Cameroons Rivers: The Duala and Their Hinterland, c. 1600-1960*. Cambridge: Cambridge University Press.

Austen, Roger. 1991. *Genteel Pagan: The Double Life of Charles Warren Stoddard*. Amherst: University of Massachusetts Press.

Ayers, William. 1971. *Chang Chih-tung and Educational Reform in China*. Cambridge, Mass.: Harvard University Press.

Bade, Klaus. 1975. *Friedrich Fabri und der Imperialismus in der Bismarckzeit: Revolution, Depression, Expansion*. Freiburg: Atlantis.

Baessler, Arthur. 1895. *Südsee-Bilder*. Berlin: G. Reimer.

Baguet, M. A. 1891. *Les Iles Samoa*. Anvers: Imprimerie Veuvede Backer.

Bakhtin, M. M. 1981. *The Dialogic Imagination*. Austin: University of Texas Press.

Bargatzky, Thomas. 1997. "'The Kava Ceremony Is a Prophecy': An Interpretation of the Transition to Christianity in Samoa." Pp. 82-99 in *European Impact and Pacific Influence*, ed. Hermann Hiery and John Mackenzie. London: Tauris Academic Studies.

Barlow, Tani E. 1997. "Colonialism's Career in Postwar China Studies." Pp. 373-411 in *Formations of Colonial Modernity in East Asia*, ed. Tani Barlow. Durham, N.C.: Duke University Press.

Barradale, V. A. 1907. *Pearls of the Pacific: Being Sketches of Missionary Life and Work in Samoa and Other Islands in the South Seas*. London: London Missionary Society.

Barrow, John. 1801-4. *An Account of Travels into the Interior of Southern Africa in the Years 1797 and 1798*. London: T. Cadell, jun., and W. Davies.

Barrow, John. [1804] 1806. *Travels in China*. 2nd ed. London: T. Cadell and W. Davies.

Barrow, John. 1805. "John Barrow's, Esqs.—vormaligen Privatsekretärs des Grafen von Macartney, jetzigen Sekretärs der Admiralität—Reise durch China von Peking nach Canton im Gefolge der Großbrittannischen Gesandtschaft in den Jahren 1793 und 1794." *Archiv der neuesten und interessantesten Reisebeschreibungen*. Vienna: Anton Doll.

Barthes, Roland. 1981. *Camera Lucida: Reflections on Photography*. New York: Hill and Wang.

Bartlett, Robert. 1993. *The Making of Europe: Conquest, Colonization, and Cultural Change, 950-1350*. Princeton, N.J.: Princeton University Press.

Bastian, Adolf. 1871. *Die Völker des östlichen Asien: Studien und Reisen*, Vol. 6, *Reisen in China von Peking zur Mongolischen Grenze*. Jena: Hermann Costenoble.

Bastian, Adolf. 1883. *Inselgruppen in Oceanien: Reiseergebnisse und Studien*. Berlin: Ferdinand Dümmlers Verlagsbuchhandlung.

Bastian, Adolf. 1889. *Einiges aus Samoa und andern Inseln der Südsee*. Berlin: Ferdinand Dümmlers Verlagsbuchhandlung.

Bastian, Adolf. 1894. *Die samoanische Schöpfungs-Sage und Anschliessendes aus der Südsee*. Berlin: E. Felber.

Bauer, Wolfgang. 1967. "Erich Haenisch (1880-1966)." *Zeitschrift der Deutschen Morgenländischen Gesellschaft* 117 (2): 205-10.

Bayart, Jean-François. 1993. *The State in Africa: The Politics of the Belly*. London: Longman.

Bayer, Maximilian. 1906a. *Der Krieg in Südwestafrika und seine Bedeutung für die Entwickelung der Kolonie*. Leipzig: Engelmann.

Bayer, Maximilian. 1906b. *Die Nation der Bastards*. Koloniale Abhandlungen. Berlin: Süsserott.

Bayer, Maximilian. [1906] 1984. *The Rehobother Baster Nation of Namibia*. Basel: Basler Afrika Bibliographien.

Bayer, Maximilian. 1909. *Mit dem Hauptquartier in Südwestafrika*. Berlin: Wilhlem Weicher.

Bayer, Maximilian. 1911. *Im Kampfe gegen die Hereros: Bilder aus dem Feldzug in Südwest*. Cologne: Hermann & Friedrich Schaffstein.

Beaglehole, J. C., ed. 1955-67. *The Journals of Captain James Cook on His Voyages of Discovery*. Vol. 1, *The Voyage of the Endeavor, 1768-1771*. Vol. 2, *The Voyage of the Resolution and the Adventure, 1772-1775*. Vol. 3, *The Voyage of the Resolution and Discovery, 1776-1780*. Cambridge: Cambridge University Press.

Behm, A. 1859. "Das Amerikanische Polynesien." *Mitteilungen aus Justus Perthes' Geographischer Anstalt über wichtige neue Erforschungen auf dem Gesammtgebiete der Geographie von Dr. A. Petermann* 5:173-94.

Behme, Fr., and M. Krieger. 1906. *Führer durch Tsingtau und Umgebung*. 3rd ed. Wolfenbüttel: Heckners Verlag.

Beiderbecke, Heinrich. 1875. "Otyozondjupa." *Berichte der Rheinischen Missionsgesellschaft* 31 (9): 263-76.

Beiderbecke, Heinrich. 1924. *Life among the Hereros in Africa*. Trans. J. A. Weyl. New York: Ernst Kaufmann.

Bell, John. [1763] 1966. *Travels from St. Petersburgh in Russia, to Various Parts of Asia*. Edinburgh: Edinburgh University Press.

Bell, Michael, and Michael Gardiner. 1998. *Bakhtin and the Human Sciences: No Last Words*. Thousand Oaks, Calif.: Sage.

Belmessous, Saliha. 2005. "Assimilation and Racialism in Seventeenth and Eighteenth-Century French Colonial Policy." *American Historical Review* 110 (2): 322-49.

Benninghoff-Luhl, Sibylle. 1986. "Völkerschauen: Attraktion und Gefahr des Exotischen." *SOWI (Sozialwissenschaftliche Information)* 15 (4): 41–48.

Berensmann, Phil. 1904. "Wirtschaftsgeographie Schantungs unter besondere Berücksichtigung des Kiautschougebiets." *Zeitschrift für Kolonialpolitik, Kolonialrecht und Kolonialwirtschaft* 6 (8): 570–667.

Berg, Anton, ed. 1864–73. *Die preussische Expedition nach Ost-Asien; nach amtlichen Quellen.* Berlin: Verlag der Königlichen Geheimen Ober-Hofbuchdruckerei (R. V. Decker).

Berger, Willy R. 1990. *China-Bild und China-Mode im Europa der Aufklärung.* Cologne: Böhlau Verlag.

Bergesen, Albert, and Ronald Schoenberg. 1980. "Long Waves of Colonial Expansion and Contraction." Pp. 231–77 in *Studies of the Modern World-System,* ed. Albert Bergesen. New York: Academic Press.

Berghahn, Volker R. 1971. *Der Tirpitzplan.* Düsseldorf: Droste.

Berkhofer, Robert F. 1978. *The White Man's Indian: Images of the American Indian from Columbus to the Present.* New York: Knopf.

Berman, Bruce, and John Lonsdale. 1992. *Unhappy Valley: Conflict in Kenya and Africa.* London: James Currey.

Berman, Russell. 1998. *Enlightenment or Empire: Colonial Discourse in German Culture.* Lincoln: University of Nebraska Press.

Bernard, Henri. 1940. "Stumpf Kilian, un émule allemand du Père Ricci." *Monumenta Nipponica* 3 (1): 321–22.

Bertrand, Romain. 2005. *Etat colonial, noblesse et nationalisme à Java: La tradition parfaite.* Paris: Karthala.

Bhabha, Homi. 1994a. "Signs Taken for Wonders: Questions of Ambivalence and Authority under a Tree outside Delhi, May 1817." Pp. 102–22 in *The Location of Culture.* London: Routledge.

Bhabha, Homi. 1994b. "The Other Question: Stereotype, Discrimination and the Discourse of Colonialism." Pp. 66–84 in *The Location of Culture.* London: Routledge.

Bhabha, Homi. 1994c. "Of Mimicry and Man: The Ambivalence of Colonial Discourse." Pp. 85–92 in *The Location of Culture.* London: Routledge.

Bhabha, Homi. 2004. "Foreword." Pp. vii–xli in Fanon [1961] 2004.

Bhaskar, Roy. 1986. *Scientific Realism and Human Emancipation.* London: Verso.

Bieber, Horst. 1972. *Paul Rohrbach, ein konservativer Publizist und Kritiker der Weimarer Republik.* München-Pullach: Verlag Dokumentation.

Biener, Annette S. 2001. *Das deutsche Pachtgebiet Tsingtau in Schantung, 1897–1914.* Bonn: Selbstverlag des Herausagebers.

Bigelow, Poultney. 1898. "Germany's First Colony in China." *Harper's New Monthly Magazine* 100 (March): 577–90.

Bindseil, Reinhart. 1988. *Ruanda und Deutschland seit den Tagen Richard Kandts.* Berlin: Dietrich Reimer Verlag.

Bitterli, Urs. 1976. *Die "Wilden" und die "Zivilisierten."* Munich: Beck.

Bitterli, Urs. 1989. *Cultures in Conflict.* Stanford, Calif.: Stanford University Press.

Blackbourn, David, and Geoff Eley. 1985. *The Peculiarities of German History*. New York: Oxford University Press.

Blanton, Casey. 1995. *Picturing Paradise: Colonial Photography of Samoa, 1875–1925*. Daytona Beach, Fla.: Daytona Beach Community College.

Bleek, Wilhelm Heinrich Immanuel. 1864. *Reynard the Fox in South Africa; or, Hottentot Fables and Tales*. London: Trübner and Co.

Bley, Helmut. 1995. "Gewaltverhältnisse in Siedlergesellschaften des südlichen Afrika." Pp. 141–65 in *Siedler-Identität*, ed. Christof Dipper and Rudolf Hiestand. Frankfurt am Main: Peter Lang.

Bley, Helmut. [1971] 1996. *South-West Africa under German Rule, 1894–1914*. Evanston, Ill.: Northwestern University Press.

Bloch, Marc. 1953. *The Historian's Craft*. New York: Knopf.

Block, Fred. 1988. "Beyond Relative Autonomy: State Managers as Historical Subjects." Pp. 81–98 in *Revising State Theory*. Philadelphia: Temple University Press.

Blue, Gregory. 1999. "China and Western Social Thought in the Modern Period." Pp. 57–109 in *China and Historical Capitalism: Genealogies of Sinological Knowledge*, ed. Timothy Brook and Gregory Blue. Cambridge: Cambridge University Press.

Blumenbach, Johann Friedrich. 1865. *The Anthropological Treatises of Johann Friedrich Blumenbach*. Ed. Thomas Bendysche. London: Longman.

Blumhardt, Hanna. n.d. [ca. 1913]. "Unsere Schu-Fan-Mädchenschule in Tsingtau (China)." Pp. 11–15 in *Unsere Schulem in Tsingtau*, Flugschriften des Allgemeinen Evangelisch-Protestantischen Missionvereins. Görlitz: Buch- und Steindruckerei Hoffmann & Reiber.

Bochert, C. 1980. "The Witbois and the Germans in South West Africa: A Study of Their Interaction between 1863 and 1905." M.A. thesis, University of Natal.

Bodde, Derk. 1986. "The State and Empire of Ch'in." Pp. 20–102 in *The Cambridge History of China*, vol. 1, ed. Denis Twitchett and Michael Loewe. Cambridge: Cambridge University Press.

Böhr, E. 1876. "Die Samoa- oder Schiffer-Inseln." *Deutsche Rundschau* 6:426–34.

Boerschmann, Ernst. 1911–14. *Die Baukunst und religiöse Kultur der Chinesen*. 2 vols. Berlin, G. Reimer.

Bokhorst, Matthys. 1973a. "François Le Vaillant: His Life and Work." Pp. 1–28 in *François Le Vaillant, Traveller in South Africa, and His Collection of 165 Watercolor Paintings*, vol. 1, ed. Cape Town Library of Parliament. Cape Town: Library of Parliament.

Bokhorst, Matthys. 1973b. "An Art Historian's Appraisal of the Le Vaillant Collection." Pp. 99–122 in *François Le Vaillant, Traveller in South Africa, and His Collection of 165 Watercolor Paintings*, vol. 2, ed. Cape Town Library of Parliament. Cape Town: Library of Parliament.

Bollig, Michael, and Tjakazapi Janson Mbunguha. 1997. *When War Came the Cattle Slept: Himba Oral Traditions*. Cologne: R. Köppe.

Bolling, Frederick Andersen. 1678. *Oost-Indiske Reise-bog hvor udi befattis hans Reise til Oost-Indien etc. end og negotierne med de regierendis itzige Hollandske Herrers andtkomst, gage, promotion og politie udi O. I.* Copenhagen.

Boonzaier, Emile, Candy Malherbe, Andy Smith, and Penny Berens. 1996. *The Cape Herders: A History of the Khoikhoi of Southern Africa.* Cape Town: David Philip.

Bordwell, David. 1989. *Making Meaning: Inference and Rhetoric in the Interpretation of Cinema.* Cambridge, Mass.: Harvard University Press.

Bordwell, David, and Kristin Thompson. 1979. *Film Art: An Introduction.* Reading, Mass.: Addison-Wesley.

Botero, Giovanni. [1589] 1956. *The Reason of State.* Ed. and trans. P. D. and D. P. Waley. London: Routledge and Kegan Paul.

Bornemann, Fritz. 1977. *Johann Baptist Anzer bis zur Ankunft in Shantung 1880.* Rome: apud Collegium Verbi Divini.

Bougainville, Louis-Antoine de. [1769] 1970a. *News from New Cythera: A Report of Bougainville's Voyage, 1766-1769.* Ed. L. Davis Hammond. Minneapolis: University of Minnesota Press.

Bougainville, Louis-Antoine de. [1769] 1970b. *Relation de la découverte que vient de faire Mr. de Bougainville d'une Isle qu il a nommé La nouvelle Cythere.* In Bougainville [1769] 1970a.

Bougainville, Louis-Antoine de. [1772] 1967. *A Voyage round the World.* Amsterdam: N. Israel; New York: Da Capo Press.

Bourdieu, Pierre. [1972] 1977. *Outline of a Theory of Practice.* Cambridge: Cambridge University Press.

Bourdieu, Pierre. 1980. "Le mort saisit le vif: Les relations entre l'histoire réifée et l'histoire incorporée." *Actes de la recherche en sciences sociales* 32-33:3-14.

Bourdieu, Pierre. [1979] 1984. *Distinction.* Cambridge, Mass.: Harvard University Press.

Bourdieu, Pierre. 1985. "The Genesis of the Concepts of *Habitus* and *Field.*" *Sociocriticism* 2 (2): 11-24.

Bourdieu, Pierre. 1986. "The Forms of Capital." Pp. 241-58 in *Handbook of Theory and Research for the Sociology of Education,* ed. J. C. Richardson. New York: Greenwood Press.

Bourdieu, Pierre. 1987. "What Makes a Class? On the Theoretical and Practical Existence of Groups." *Berkeley Journal of Sociology* 32:1-18.

Bourdieu, Pierre. [1989] 1996. *The State Nobility: Elite Schools in the Field of Power.* Cambridge: Polity.

Bourdieu, Pierre. [1980] 1990. *The Logic of Practice.* Stanford, Calif.: Stanford University Press.

Bourdieu, Pierre. [1993] 1999. *The Weight of the World.* Stanford, Calif.: Stanford University Press.

Bourdieu, Pierre. [1997] 2000. *Pascalian Mediations.* Stanford, Calif.: Stanford University Press.

Bourdieu, Pierre. [1998] 2002. *Masculine Domination.* Cambridge: Polity.

Bourdieu, Pierre. 1999. "Rethinking the State: Genesis and Structure of the Bureaucratic Field." Pp. 53-75 in Steinmetz 1999a.

Bourdieu, Pierre, Jean-Claude Chamboredon, and Jean-Claude Passeron. [1968] 1991. *The Craft of Sociology*. Berlin: Walter de Gruyter.

Boyer, Jean Paul. 1979. *Hermann von Keyserling*. Lille: L'Atelier de reproduction des thèses.

Bradlow, Edna. 1989. "The 'Great Fear' at the Cape of Good Hope, 1851–52." *International Journal of African Historical Studies* 22 (3): 401–21.

Brandt, Max August Scipio von. 1898. *Die chinesische Philosophie und der Staats-Confucianismus*. Stuttgart: Strecker & Moser.

Brandt, Max August Scipio von. 1901. *Dreiunddreissig Jahre in Ost-Asien*. 3 vols. Leipzig: Wigand.

Braumann, Franz. 1985. "Einführung." Pp. 7–18 in *Als Kundschafter des Papstes nach China 1656–1664*, by Johannes Grueber. Stuttgart: Thienemann.

Braun, Georg. 1912. *Zur Frage der Rechtsgültigkeit der Mischehen in den deutschen Schutzgebieten*. Greifswald: J. Abel.

Braun, Martin. 1991. *Nichts menschliches soll mir fremd sein: Georg Forster und die frühe deutsche Völkerkunde vor dem Hintergrund der klassischen Kulturwissenschaften*. Bonn: Holos.

Brenner, Neil. 1999. "Global Cities, Glocal States: State-Scaling and the Making of Urban Governance in the European Union." Ph.D. diss., University of Chicago.

Brickman, Celia. 2003. *Aboriginal Populations in the Mind: Race and Primitivity in Psychoanalysis*. New York: Columbia University Press.

Bridgman, Jon M. 1981. *The Revolt of the Hereros*. Berkeley: University of California Press.

Bridgman, Jon, and Leslie J. Worley. 1995. "Genocide of the Hereros." Pp. 3–48 in *Genocide in the Twentieth Century*, ed. Samuel Totten, William S. Parsons, and Israel Charny. New York: Garland.

Brincker, P. H. 1899. "Die Eingeborenen Deutsch-Südwest-Afrikas nach Geschichte, Charakter, Sitten, Gebräuchen und Sprachen." *Mittheilungen des Seminars für Orientalische Sprachen zu Berlin* 2 (3): 125–39.

Britz, Rudolph G., Hartmut Lang, and Cornelia Limpricht. 1999. *A Concise History of the Rehoboth Basters until 1990*. Windhoek: Klaus Hess Publishers.

Brooks, Peter. [1976] 1995. *The Melodramatic Imagination: Balzac, Henry James, Melodrama, and the Mode of Excess*. New Haven, Conn.: Yale University Press.

Brown, Arthur Judson. 1904. *New Forces in Old China: An Unwelcome but Inevitable Awakening*. New York: F. H. Revell Co.

Brown, George. 1910. *Melanesians and Polynesians*. London: Macmillan and Co.

Brunner, Horst. 1967. *Die poetische Insel*. Stuttgart: Metzler.

Brunschwig, Henri. 1957. *L'expansion allemande outre-mer du XVe siècle à nos jours*. Paris: PUF.

Bryson, Norman. 1994. "Géricault and 'Masculinity.'" Pp. 228–59 in *Visual Culture: Images and Interpretations*, ed. Michael Ann Holly, Norman Bryson, and Keith Moxey. Hanover, N.H.: Wesleyan University Press.

Buck, Peter Henry. 1930. *Samoan Material Culture*. Museum Bulletin 75. Honolulu: Bernice P. Bishop Museum.

Buck-Morss, Susan. 2000. "Hegel and Haiti." *Critical Inquiry* 26 (Summer): 856–57.

Budack, Kuno Franz Robert Heinrich. 1972. "Die traditionelle politische Struktur der Khoe-Khoen in Südwestafrika." Ph.D. diss., University of Pretoria.

Budack, K. F. R. 1974. Der "'Bastardaufstand' in Deutsch-Südwestafrika." *Afrikanischer Heimatkalender* 44:39–64.

Budack, K. F. R. 1986. "Die Klassifikation der Khwe-Khwen (Naman) in Südwestafrika." Pp. 107–43 in *Contemporary Studies on Khoisan*, ed. Rainer Vossen and Klaus Keuthmann. Hamburg: Helmut Buske Verlag.

Budde, Hendrik, Christophe Müller-Hofstede, and Gereon Sievernich. 1985. *Europa und die Kaiser von China*. Frankfurt am Main: Insel Verlag.

Buecher-Verzeichnis der Kiautschou-Bibliothek. 1898. Berlin: Deutscher Verlag.

Bühler, Andreas Heinrich. 2003. *Der Namaaufstand gegen die deutsche Kolonialherrschaft in Namibia von 1904–1913*. Frankfurt am Main: IKO, Verlag für interkulturelle Kommunikation.

Bülow, Franz Joseph von. 1896. *Deutsch-Südwestafrika: Drei Jahre im Lande Hendrik Witboois*. Berlin: E. S. Mittler.

Bülow, Werner von. 1899. "Beiträge zur Ethnographie der Samoa-Inseln." *Internationales Archiv für Ethnographie* 12:66–75, 129–43.

Bülow, Werner von. 1903. "Die Verwaltung der Landgemeinden in Deutsch-Samoa." *Globus* 83 (24): 373–77.

Büttner, Carl Gotthilf. 1884. *Das Hinterland von Walfischbai und Angra Pequena*. Heidelberg: Carl Winter's Universitätsbuchhandlung.

Büttner, Carl Gotthilf. 1885a. "Die Missionsstation Otjimbingue in Damaraland." *Zeitschrift der Gesellschaft für Erdkunde zu Berlin* 20:39–56.

Büttner, Carl Gotthilf. 1885b. *Kolonialpolitik und Christentum in Südwestafrika*. Heidelberg: Carl Winter's Universitätsbuchhandlung.

Büttner, Carl Gotthilf. 1885c. *Ackerbau und Viehzucht in Süd-West-Afrika (Damara- und Gr. Namaqualand)*. Leipzig: Verlag von Edwin Schloemp.

Buffon, Georges Louis Leclerc, comte de. 1749. "Histoire naturelle de l'homme: Variétés dans l'espèce humaine." Pp. 371–530 in *Histoire naturelle, générale et particuliére*, vol. 3. Paris: L'Imprimerie royale.

Burchell, William. 1822–24. *Travels in the Interior of Southern Africa*. 2 vols. London: Printed for Longman, Hurst, Rees, Orme, and Brown.

Burgsdorff-Garath, Alhard von. 1982. *Der Hauptmann Henning von Burgsdorff: Vom tapferen Leben und Sterben des Bezirkshauptmanns von Gibeon*. Windhoek: John Meinert.

Butler, Judith. 1997. *The Psychic Life of Power*. Stanford, Calif.: Stanford University Press.

Cahen, Gaston. 1914. *Some Early Russo-Chinese Relations*. Shanghai: National Review Office.

Caillou, Alan. 1974. *South from Khartoum: The Story of Emin Pasha*. New York: Hawthorn Books.

Callahan, Michael D. 1999. *Mandates and Empire: The League of Nations and Africa, 1914-1931*. Brighton: Sussex Academic Press.

Camille, Michael. 1989. "The Devil's Writing: Diabolic Literacy in Medieval Art." Pp. 355-60 in *World Art*, vol. 2, ed. Irving Lavin. University Park, PA: Pennsylvania State University Press.

Campbell, John, Rev. 1814. *Travels in South Africa Undertaken at the Request of the Missionary Society*. London: Black, Parry.

Cannadine, David. 2001. *Ornamentalism: How the British Saw Their Empire*. Oxford: Oxford University Press.

Canning, Craig Noel. 1975. "The Japanese Occupation of Shantung during World War I." Ph.D. diss., Stanford University.

Cape Town Library of Parliament, ed. 1973. *François Le Vaillant, Traveller in South Africa, and His Collection of 165 Watercolor Paintings*. 2 vols. Cape Town: Library of Parliament.

Carcassonne, E. 1924. "La Chine dans 'L'esprit des lois.' " *Revue d'Histoire Littéraire de la France* 31 (2): 193-205.

Careri, Giovanni Francesco Gemelli. [1704] 1752. *A Voyage Round the World*. Vol. 4 of *A Collection of Voyages and Travels*, compiled and ed. Awnsham Churchill. London: A. and J. Churchill.

Carus, Carl Gustav. 1849. *Über ungleiche Befähigung der verschiedenen Menschheitsstämme für höhere geistige Entwickelungen*. Leipzig: F. A. Brockhaus.

Certeau, Michel de. 1986. *Heterologies: Discourse on the Other*. Minneapolis: University of Minnesota Press.

Césaire, Aimé. [1950] 2000. *Discourse on Colonialism*. New York: Monthly Review Press.

Chamisso, Adalbert von. 1986. *A Voyage around the World with the Romanzov Exploring Expedition in the Years 1815-1818, in the Brig* Rurik, *Captain Otto von Kotzebue*. Ed. and trans. Henry Kratz. Honolulu: University of Hawaii Press.

Chapman, J. [1868] 1971. *Travels in the Interior of South Africa, 1849-1863*. Cape Town: A. A. Balkema.

Charlot, Jean. 1958. *Choris and Kamehameha*. Honolulu: Bishop Museum Press.

Chateaubriand, François René de. [1802] 1961. *Atala and René*. New York: Signet.

Chatterjee, Partha. 1993. *The Nation and Its Fragments*. Princeton, N.J.: Princeton University Press.

Chen, Jitong [Tcheng-Ki-Tong]. 1890. *Bits of China*. London: Trischler and Co.

Chen, Jitong [Chen, Chi-tung]. 1892. *Mon pays—la Chine aujourd'hui*. Paris: G. Charpentier.

Cheng, Siu-kei. 1999. "Lao Naixuan (1843-1921) hanzi gaige lilun yanjiu" [Lao Naixuan (1843-1921) on the reformation of the Chinese writing system]. M.Phil. diss., University of Hong Kong.

Chiu, Fred Y. L. 1997. "Politics and the Body Social in Colonial Hong Kong." Pp. 295-322 in *Formations of Colonial Modernity in East Asia*, ed. Tani Barlow. Durham, N.C.: Duke University Press.

Choris, Louis. 1822. *Voyage pittoresque autour du monde, avec des portraits de sauvages d'Amérique, d'Asie, d'Afrique, et des îles du Grand océan; des paysages, des vues maritimes, et plusieurs objets d'histoire naturelle.* Paris, Impr. de Firmin Didot.

Choris, Louis. 1999. *Journal des Malers Ludwig York Choris.* Ed. Niklaus R. Schweizer. Berlin: Lang.

Christmann, Fr., and Richard Oberländer. 1873. *Ozeanien, die Inseln der Südsee.* Leipzig: O. Spamer.

Churchill, Llewella Pierce. 1902. *Samoa 'Uma.* New York: Forest and Stream Publishing Co.

Churchward, William. 1887. *My Consulate in Samoa.* London: Richard Bentley and Son.

Clarence-Smith, W. G., and R. Moorsom. 1975. "Underdevelopment and Class Formation in Ovamboland, 1815-1915." *Journal of African History* 16 (3): 365-81.

Clark, Geoffrey. 2003. "Dumont d'Urville's Oceania." *Journal of Pacific History* 38 (2): 155-61.

Clendinnen, Inga. 1987. *Ambivalent Conquests: Maya and Spaniard in Yucatan, 1517-1570.* Cambridge: Cambridge University Press.

Cocker, Mark. 1998. *Rivers of Blood, Rivers of Gold.* London: Jonathan Cape.

Coetzee, J. M. 1988. *White Writing.* New Haven, Conn.: Yale University Press.

Coetzee, J. M. 1997. *Boyhood: Scenes from Provincial Life.* New York: Penguin.

Cohen, Paul A. 1997. *History in Three Keys: The Boxers as Event, Experience, and Myth.* New York: Columbia University Press.

Cohn, Bernard S. 1981. "Anthropology and History in the 1980s: Toward a Rapprochement." *Journal of Interdisciplinary History* 12 (2): 227-52.

Cohn, Bernard S. 1983. "Representing Authority in Victorian India." Pp. 165-209 in *The Invention of Tradition,* ed. Eric Hobsbawm and Terence Ranger. Cambridge: Cambridge University Press.

Cole, Joshua. 2003. "Remembering the Battle of Paris: 17 October 1961 in French and Algerian Memory." *French Politics, Culture, and Society* 21 (3): 21-50.

Collani, Claudia von. 1989. "P. Kilian Stumpf SJ: Nachfolger des hl. Kilian in China." *Würzburger Diözesangeschichtsblätter* 51:545-67.

Collani, Claudia von. 1998. "Johann Adam Schall von Bell: Weltbild und Weltchronologie in der Chinamission im 17. Jahrhundert." Pp. 79-99 in Malek 1998, vol. 1.

Collani, Claudia von. 1992. "Koffler, Andreas Wolfgang." Pp. 299-300 in *Biographisch-Bibliographisches Kirchenlexikon,* ed. Friedrich Wilhelm Bautz. Hamm: Verlag Traugott Bautz.

Collier, Andrew. 1994. *Critical Realism: An Introduction to Roy Bhaskar's Philosophy.* New York: Verso.

Collier, Andrew. 2005. "Critical Realism." Pp. 327-45 in Steinmetz 2005.

Colvocoresses, George Musalas. [1852] 1855. *Four Years in the Government Exploring Expedition.* 5th ed. New York, J. M. Fairchild.

Comaroff, Jean, and John Comaroff. 1991-97. *Of Revelation and Revolution: Christi-*

anity, Colonialism, and Consciousness in South Africa. 2 vols. Chicago: University of Chicago Press.

Comaroff, John L. 1987. "Of Totemism and Ethnicity: Consciousness, Practice, and the Signs of Inequality." *Ethnos* 52:302-23.

Comaroff, John L. 1989. "Images of Empire, Contests of Conscience: Models of Colonial Domination in South Africa." *American Ethnologist* 16:661-85.

Commerson, Philibert. [1769] 1915. "Sur la découverte de la nouvelle isle de Cythère ou Taïti." Pp. 461-66 in *The Quest and Ocupation of Tahiti by Emissaries of Spain during the Years 1772-1776,* vol. 2, ed. Bolton Corney. London: Hakluyt Society.

Cook, James. 1777. *A Voyage towards the South Pole, and round the World. Performed in His Majesty's ships the Resolution and Adventure, in the Years 1772, 1773, 1774, and 1775.* London: W. Strahan and T. Cadell in the Strand.

Cook, James. 1955-67. See Beaglehole, J. C., ed., 1955-67.

Cooper, Fred. 1996. *Decolonization and African Society: The Labor Question in French and British Africa.* Cambridge: Cambridge University Press.

Cooper, H. Stonehewer. 1880. *Coral Lands.* 2 vols. London: Richard Bentley and Son.

Cooper, James Fenimore. [1826] 1986. *The Last of the Mohicans.* New York: Penguin.

Corcuff, Philippe, ed. 2004. *Pierre Bourdieu: Les champs de la critique.* Paris: Bibliothèque Centre Pompidou.

Cordier, Henri. 1901-2. *Histoire des relations de la Chine avec les puissances occidentales.* 3 vols. Paris: F. Alcan.

Cornell, Fred C. [1920] 1986. *The Glamour of Prospecting: Wanderings of a South African Prospector in Search of Copper, Gold, Emeralds, and Diamonds.* Ed. Douglas Cornell. Cape Town: David Philip.

Corr, Charles A. 1975. "Christian Wolff and Leibniz." *Journal of the History of Ideas* 36 (2, April-June): 241-62.

Corry, Stephen. 1975. "Ethnocide: A Report from Colombia." *Royal Anthropological Institute News,* no. 6 (January-February): 1-2.

Craig, Gordon A. 1955. *The Politics of the Prussian Army, 1650-1945.* Oxford: Oxford University Press.

Crips, Liliane. 1993. "Les avatars d'une utopie scientiste en Allemagne: Eugen Fischer (1874-1967) et l'hygiène raciale." *Le Mouvement Social,* no. 163:7-23.

Crothers, George D. 1940. *The German Elections of 1907.* New York: Columbia University Press.

Crozier, Andrew J. 1979. "The Establishment of the Mandates System, 1919-25: Some Problems Created by the Paris Peace Conference." *Journal of Contemporary History* 14 (3): 483-513.

Crusen, Georg. 1913. "Die rechtliche Stellung der Chinesen in Kiautschou." *Zeitschrift für Kolonialrecht* 15 (2): 4-17; (3): 47-57.

Crusen, Georg. 1914. "Moderne Gedanken im Chinesen-Strafrecht des Kiautschougebietes." *Mitteilungen der internationalen kriminalistischen Vereinigung* 21 (1): 134-42.

Cruz, Gaspar da. [1569] 1953. "Treatise in Which the Things of China Are Related at Great Length, with Their Peculiarities." Pp. 44–218 in *South China in the Sixteenth Century*, ed. C. R. Boxer. London: Hakluyt Society.

Cullinan, Patrick. 1978. "1818: M. François le Vaillant Recalls His Travels to the Interior Parts of Africa, 1780–1785." Pp. 43–46 in *Mantis Poets*, ed. Jack Cope. Cape Town: David Philip.

Cullinan, Patrick. 1992. *Robert Jacob Gordon, 1743–1795*. Cape Town: Struik Winchester.

Daalder, Ivo H., and James M. Lindsay. 2003. *America Unbound*. Washington: Brookings Institution Press.

Dabringhaus, Sabine. 1996. "Einleitung." Pp. 7–92 in *Nachricht von der britischen Gesandtschaftsreise nach China 1792–94*, by Johann Christian Hüttner. Sigmaringen: Jan Thorbecke Verlag.

Dalrymple, Alexander. 1770. *A historical collection of the several voyages and discoveries in the South Pacific ocean*. 2 vols. London: Printed for the author.

Damm, Hans. 1944. "Augustin Krämer †." *Ethnologischer Anzeiger* 4 (8): 496–99.

Dapper, Olfert. 1660. *Beschreibung von Africa*. Amsterdam: J. V. Meurs.

Dapper, Olfert. 1675. *Gedenkwürdige Verrichtung der Niederländischen Ost-Indischen Gesellschaft in dem Kaiserreich Taising oder Sina, durch ihre Zweyte Gesandtschaft an den Unter-König Singlamong und Feld-Herrn*. Amsterdam: J. V. Meurs.

Dapper, Olfert. 1676. *Beschreibung des Keyserthums Sina oder Taising*. Amsterdam: Jacob von Meurs.

Dauphiné, James. 1985. "Quelques aspects litteraires du mythe de Tahiti." *L'Information Littéraire* 37 (5): 198–204.

Davies, Joan H. 1942. "Palgrave and Damaraland." Pp. 91–203 in *Archives Year Book for South African History*, vol. 5, pt. 2.

Davidson, Basil. 1992. *The Black Man's Burden: Africa and the Curse of the Nation State*. New York: Times Books.

Davidson, J. W. 1967. *Samoa mo Samoa*. Melbourne: Oxford University Press.

Dedering, Tilman. 1988. "Problems of Pre-colonial Namibian Historiography." *South African Historical Journal* 20:95–104.

Dedering, Tilman. 1993a. "Hendrik Witbooi, the Prophet." *Kleio* 25:54–78.

Dedering, Tilman. 1993b. "The German-Herero War of 1904: Revisionism of Genocide or Imaginary Historiography?" *Journal of Southern African Studies* 19 (1): 80–88.

Dedering, Tilman. 1997. *Hate the Old and Follow the New: Khoekhoe and Missionaries in Early 19th-Century Namibia*. Stuttgart: Steiner.

Deeken, Richard. 1901. *Manuia Samoa! Samoanische Reiseskizzen und Beobachtungen*. Oldenburg: Gerhard Stalling.

Defoe, Daniel. [1705] 1840. *The Consolidator*. Pp. 205–413 in *The Novellas and Miscellaneous Works of Daniel Defoe*. Vol. 9. Oxford: Thomas Tegg.

Defoe, Daniel. 1719. *The Farther Adventures of Robinson Crusoe; Being the Second and Last Part of his Life, and of the Strange Surprizing Accounts of his Travels Round Three Parts of the Globe*. London: W. Taylor.

de Groot, J. J. M. 1892. *The Religious System of China*. Vol. 1. Leyden: E. J. Brill.

Dehergne, Joseph. 1973. *Répertoire des jésuites de Chine de 1552 à 1800*. Rome: Institutum historicum S.I.

Deimling, Berthold von. 1900. *Die Kolonie Kiautschou in den ersten beiden Jahren ihrer Entwickung*. Berlin: Trowitzsch & Sohn.

Deimling, Berthold von. 1930. *Aus der alten in die neue Zeit*. Berlin: Ullstein.

Delavignette, Robert. 1939. *Les vrais chefs de l'Empire*. Paris: Gallimard.

Demel, Walter. 1992. "Wie die Chinesen gelb wurden: Ein Beitrag zur Frühgeschichte der Rassentheorien." *Historische Zeitschrift* 255:625–66.

Dening, Greg. 1980. *Islands and Beaches*. Carlton: Melbourne University Press.

Dening, Greg. 1992. *Mr. Bligh's Bad Language*. Cambridge: Cambridge University Press.

Denis, Andrée. 1976. "La fortune littéraire et théâtrale de Kotzebue en France pendant la Révolution, le Consulat et l'Empire." Ph.D. diss., University of Paris IV. Lille: Reproduction des thèses.

"Denkschrift, betreffend das südwestafrikanische Schutzgebiet" (1893–94). 1895. Pp. 426–97 in *Stenographische Berichte über die Verhandlungen des Reichstages*, 9th legislative period, 3rd session 1894–95, Anlageband 1, vol. 162, document no. 89. Berlin: Julius Sittenfeld.

Denkschrift betreffend die Entwickelung des Kiautschou-Gebiets 1898–1909. Berlin: Reichsdruckerei.

"Denkschrift über Eingeborenen-Politik und Herero-Aufstand in Deutsch-Südwestafrika." 1904. Beilage zum *Deutschen Kolonialblatt*. Berlin: Mittler.

Denzler, Erwin. 1991. "Johannes Olpp, Missionar in Südwestafrika, Schriftsteller und Missionsprediger, 1837–1920." Pp. 135–70 in *Lebensbilder aus Schwaben und Franken*, ed. Gerhard Taddey. Stuttgart: W. Kohlhammer.

De Quincey, Thomas. [1821] 1950. *Confessions of an English Opium-Eater, Together with Selections from the Autobiography of Thomas De Quincey*. London: Cresset Press.

Deutsch-chinesische Hochschule. 1909. *Programm der deutsch-chinesischen Hochschule in Tsingtau*. Tsingtau [Qingdao].

Deutsch-chinesische Hochschule. 1910. *Programm der deutsch-chinesischen Hochschule in Tsingtau*. Tsingtau [Qingdao].

Deutschland in China, 1900–1901; bearbeitet von Teilnehmern an der Expedition, illustriert von Schlachtenmaler Rocholl. 1902. Düsseldorf: A. Bagel.

Dickinson, G. Lowes. 1901. *Letters from John Chinaman*. London: J. M. Dent and Sons.

Diderot, Denis. [1772] 1956. *Supplement to Bougainville's "Voyage"*. Pp. 179–228 in *"Rameau's Nephew" and Other Works*, trans. Jacques Barzun and Ralph H. Brown. New York: Bobbs-Merrill.

Diderot, Denis. [1819] 1876. "Voyage de Hollande." Pp. 363–471 in *Oeuvres Complètes de Diderot*, vol. 17, ed. J. Assézat and Maurice Tourneaux. Paris: Garnier Frères.

Dorsenne, Jean. [1926] 1996. "C'était le soir des dieux." Pp. 837–934 in *Polynésie*, ed. Alain Quella-Villéger. Paris: Omnibus.

Dove, Karl. 1896a. *Südwestafrika: Kriegs- und Friedensbilder aus der ersten deutschen Kolonie*. Berlin: Allgemeiner Verein für Deutsche Litteratur.

Dove, Karl. 1896b. *Deutsch-Südwestafrika. Petermanns Mitteilungen*, Ergänzungsheft 120. Gotha: Justus Perthes.

Dove, Karl. 1913a. *Die deutschen Kolonien*. Vol. 4, *Südwestafrika*. Leipzig: G. J. Goeschen'sche Verlagsbuchhandlung.

Dove, Karl. 1913b. *Deutsch-Südwestafrika*. 2nd ed. Süsserotts Kolonialbibliothek, vol. 5. Berlin: Süsserott.

Drechsler, Horst. [1966] 1980. *Let us Die Fighting: The Struggle of the Herero and Nama against German Imperialism (1884–1915)*. London: Zed Press.

Drechsler, Horst. 1984. *Aufstände in Südwestafrika: Der Kampf der Herero und Nama 1904 bis 1907 gegen die deutsche Kolonialherrschaft*. Berlin: Dietz Verlag.

Drechsler, Horst. 1996. *Südwestafrika unter deutscher Kolonialherrschaft*. Stuttgart: Franz Steiner Verlag.

Drießler, Heinrich. 1932. *Die Rheinische Mission in Südwestafrika*. Gütersloh: Bertelsmann.

Drygalski, Erich von. 1905. "Gedächtnisrede auf Ferdinand Freiherr von Richthofen." *Zeitschrift der Gesellschaft für Erdkunde zu Berlin* 40:681–97.

Du Halde, Jean-Baptiste. 1741. *The General History of China*. 4 vols. London: J. Watts.

Duhr, Joseph. 1936. *Un jésuite en chine: Adam Schall, astronome et conseiller impérial (1592–1666)*. Bruxelles: L'edition universelle.

Dumont d'Urville, J. 1832. "Sur les îles du grand océan." *Bulletin de la société de géographie* 105 (January): 1–21.

Dumont d'Urville, J. 1842–54. *Voyage au pole sud et dans l'Océanie sur les corvettes l'Astrolabe et la Zélée*. Paris: Gide.

Du Plessis, Johannes. 1911. *History of Christian Missions in South Africa*. London: Longmans, Green and Co.

Durchhardt, Heinz. 1986. "Afrika und die deutschen Kolonialprojekte der 2. Hälfte des 17. Jahrhunderts." *Archiv für Kulturgeschichte* 68 (1): 119–33.

Durham, Deborah. 1993. "Images of Culture: Being Herero in a Liberal Democracy (Botswana)." 2 vols. Ph.D. diss., University of Chicago.

Durham, Deborah. 1995. "The Lady in the Logo: Tribal Dress and Western Culture in a Southern African Community." Pp. 183–94 in *Dress and Ethnicity*, ed. Joanne B. Eicher. Oxford: Berg.

Durkheim, Émile. 1915. *Elementary Forms of the Religious Life*. New York: Macmillan.

Durkheim, Émile. 1992. *Professional Ethics and Civic Morals*. London: Routledge.

Duval, Eugène-Jean. 2002. *La révolte des sagaies: Madagascar 1947*. Paris: L'Harmattan.

Eckart, Wolfgang Uwe. 1997. *Medizin und Konolonialimperialismus: Deutschland, 1884–1945*. Paderborn: Schöningh.

Eckenbrecher, Margarethe Hopfer von. 1907. *Was Afrika mir gab und nahm: Erlebnisse einer deutschen Ansiedlerfrau im Südwestafrika*. Berlin: Ernst Siegfried Mittler und Sohn.

Eckert, Andreas. 1999. *Grundbesitz, Landkonflikte und kolonialer Wandel: Douala 1880 bis 1960*. Stuttgart: Steiner.

Eckert, Andreas. 2003. "Namibia: Ein deutscher Sonderweg in Afrika?" Pp. 226-36 in Zimmerer and Zeller 2003.

Edmond, Rod. 1997. *Representing the South Pacific: Colonial Discourse from Cook to Gauguin*. Cambridge: Cambridge University Press.

Eggeling, Heinrich von. 1909. *Anatommische Untersuchungen an den Köpfen von vier Hereros, einem Herero- und einem Hottentottenkinde*. Pp. 322-72 in Schultze 1909.

Ehlers, Otto. *Samoa, die Perle der Südsee*. 2nd ed. Berlin: Verlag von Hermann Paetel.

Einaudi, Jean-Luc. 2001. *Octobre 1961: Un massacre à Paris*. Paris: Fayard.

Einstein, Carl. 1915. *Negerplastik*. Leipzig: Verlag der Weißen Bücher.

Eirola, Martti. 1992. *The Ovambogefahr*. Rovaniemi: Ponjois-Suommen Historiallinen Yhdistys.

Eisenman, Stephen F. 1997. *Gauguin's Skirt*. London: Thames and Hudson.

Elbourne, Elizabeth. 1992. "Early Khoisan Uses of Mission Christianity." *Kronos* 19:3-27.

Elbourne, Elizabeth. 2000. "'Race,' Warfare, and Religion in Mid-Nineteenth-Century Southern Africa: The Khoikhoi Rebellion against the Cape Colony and its Issues, 1850-58." *Journal of African Cultural Studies* 13 (1): 17-42.

Elbourne, Elizabeth. 2002. *Blood Ground: Colonialism, Missions, and the Contest for Christianity in the Cape Colony and Britain, 1799-1853*. Montreal: McGill-Queen's University Press.

Elbourne, Elizabeth. 2003. "'The Fact so Often Disputed by the Black Man': Khoekhoe Citizenship at the Cape in the Early to Mid Nineteenth Century." *Citizenship Studies* 7 (4): 379-400.

Elias, Norbert. 1994. *The Civilizing Process*. Oxford: Blackwell.

Elliott, Mark C. 2001. *The Manchu Way: The Eight Banners and Ethnic Identity in Late Imperial China*. Stanford, Calif.: Stanford University Press.

Ellis, William. 1853. *Polynesian Researches during a Residence of Nearly Eight Years in the Society and Sandwich Islands*. London: Henry G. Bohn.

Elphick, Richard. [1975] 1985. *Khoikhoi and the Founding of White South Africa*. Johannesburg: Ravan Press.

Elphick, Richard. 1977. *Kraal and Castle: Khoikhoi and the Founding of White South Africa*. New Haven, Conn.: Yale University Press.

Emmerich, Reinhard. 1999. "'Ich fühle mich immer wieder angezogen von originellen und freien Geistern': Alfred Forke in Berlin (1867-1944)." Pp. 421-48 in *Chinawissenschaften, deutschsprachige Entwicklungen*, ed. Britta Jubin. Hamburg: Institut für Asienkunde.

Emmett, Tony. 1999. *Popular Resistance and the Roots of Nationalism in Namibia, 1915-1966*. Basel: P. Schlettwein Publishing.

Engel, Lothar. 1976. *Kolonialismus und Nationalismus im deutschen Protestantismus in Namibia 1907 bis 1945.* Frankfurt am Main: Herbert Lang.

Engelmann, Gerhard. 1988. *Ferdinand von Richthofen, 1833-1905. Albrecht Penck, 1858-1945: Zwei markante Geographen Berlins.* Stuttgart: Franz Steiner Verlag.

Engels, Friedrich. [1857] 1969. "Persia—China (June 5, 1857, *New York Daily Tribune*)." Pp. 184-90 in Marx 1969.

Erbar, Ralph. 1990. *Ein 'Platz an der Sonne'? Die Verwaltungs- und Wirtschaftsgeschichte der deutschen Kolonie Togo 1884-1914.* Stuttgart: Franz Steiner Verlag.

Erffa, B. H. A., Frh. von. 1905. *Reise- und Kriegsbilder von Deutsch-Südwest-Afrika.* Halle: Verlag der Buchhandlung des Waisenhauses.

Erichsen, Casper W. 2003. "Zwangsarbeit im Konzentrationslager auf der Haifischinsel." Pp. 80-85 in Zimmerer and Zeller 2003.

Erichsen, Casper W. 2004. "'The Angel of Death Has Descended Violently among Them': A Study of Namibia's Concentration Camps and Prisoners-of-War, 1904-08." M.A. thesis, University of Namibia.

Erskine, John Elphinstone. 1853. *Journal of a Cruise among the Islands of the Western Pacific.* London: John Murray.

Esherick, Joseph W. 1987. *The Origins of the Boxer Uprising.* Berkeley: University of California Press.

Esterhuyse, J. H. 1968. *South West Africa, 1880-1894.* Cape Town: C. Stuik.

Estermann, Carlos. 1981. *The Ethnography of Southwestern Angola.* Vol. 3, *The Herero People.* New York: Africana Publishing Co.

Estorff, Ludwig von. 1911. Kriegserlebnisse in Südwestafrika. *Militärwochenblatt,* Beiheft 3:79-101.

Estorff, Ludwig von. 1968. *Wanderungen und Kämpfe in Südwestafrika, Ostafrika und Südafrika.* Ed. Christoph-Friedrich Kutscher. Wiesbaden: Wiesbadener Kurier Verlag.

Étiemble. 1988. *L'Europe chinoise.* Vol. 2. Paris: Gallimard.

Eze, Emmanuel Chukwudi, ed. 1997. *Race and the Enlightenment.* London: Blackwell.

Fabian, Johannes. 1983. *Time and the Other. How Anthropology Makes Its Object.* New York: Columbia University Press.

Fabian, Johannes. 2000. *Out of Our Minds: Reason and Madness in the Exploration of Central Africa.* Berkeley: University of Califonia Press.

Fabri, Friedrich. 1884. *Deutsche Kolonialbestrebungen: Angra Pequena und Südwestafrika.* Elberfeld: R. L. Freidrichs.

Fabri, Friedrich. [1879] 1998. *Bedarf Deutschland der Kolonien?/Does Germany Need Colonies?* Ed. and trans. E. C. M. Breuning and M. E. Chamberlain. Lewiston, N.Y.: Edwin Mellen Press.

Fairbank, John King. [1953] 1969. *Trade and Diplomacy on the China Coast.* Stanford, Calif.: Standford University Press.

Fairbank, John King. 1986. *The Great Chinese Revolution, 1800-1985.* New York: Harper and Row.

Fairbank, John King, and Merle Goldman. 1998. *China: A New History*. Cambridge, Mass.: Harvard University Press.

Falkenberg, Rainer. 1984. *Der Kohlenbergbau in Boshan-xian, Shandong, im ersten Drittel des 20. Jahrhunderts*. Bonn: Selbstverlag des Herausgebers, W. Matzat.

Falkenberg, Rainer. 1986. "Luis Weiler's Briefe aus China (Dez. 1897–Aug. 1901): Materalien zur Entwicklung in Qingdao und zum Bau der Shandong-Bahn." Pp. 113–34 in Kuo and Leutner 1986.

Fang, Weigui. 1992. *Das Chinabild in der deutschen Literatur*. Frankfurt am Main: P. Lang.

Fanon, Frantz. [1952] 1967. *Black Skin, White Masks*. New York: Grove Weidenfeld.

Fanon, Frantz. [1961] 2004. *The Wretched of the Earth*. Trans. Richard Philcox. New York: Grove Press.

Felber, Roland. 1994. "Das Deutschlandbild Kang Youweis von der Hundert-tagereform 1898 bis zur Xinhai-Revolution 1911." Pp. 161–90 in Kuo and Leutner 1994.

Felber, Roland, and Horst Rostek. 1987. "Der 'Hunnenkrieg' Kaiser Wilhelms II: Imperialistische Intervention in China 1900/01." *Illustrierte historische Hefte*, no. 45:2–43.

Ferguson, Niall. 2003. "The Empire Slinks Back." *New York Times Magazine*, April 27, pp. 52–57.

Ferro, Marc. [1994] 1997. *Colonization: A Global History*. London: Routledge.

Field, Michael J. 1991. *Mau: Samoa's Struggle for Freedom*. Auckland: Polynesia Press.

Fieldhouse, D. K. 1966. *The Colonial Empires: A Comparative Survey from the Eighteenth Century*. New York: Dell.

Firth, Raymond. 2001. "The Creative Contribution of Indigenous People to Their Ethnography." *Journal of the Polynesian Society* 110 (3): 241–45.

Firth, Stewart. 1973. "German Recruitment and Employment of Labourers in the Western Pacific before the First World War." D.Phil. thesis, Oxford University.

Firth, Stewart, and Doug Munro. 1990. "German Regulation and Employment of Plantation Labour in Samoa, 1864–1914." Unpublished paper. Adelaide: Flinders University of South Australia.

Fisch, Maria. 1999. *The Caprivi Strip during the German Colonial Period, 1890 to 1914*. Windhoek: Out of Africa Publishers.

Fischer, Adolf. 1914. *Menschen und Tiere in Deutsch-Südwest*. Stuttgart: Deutsche Verlags-Anstalt.

Fischer, Eugen. 1909a. "Beobachtungen am Bastardvolk in Deutsch-Südwesta-frika." *Korrespondezblatt der Deutschen Anthropolgischen Gesellschaft* 40 (September–December): 75–77.

Fischer, Eugen. 1909b. "Das Rehobother Bastardvolk in Deutsch-Südwestafrika." *Die Umschau* 13 (December 18): 1047–51.

Fischer, Eugen. 1913. *Die Rehobother Bastards und das Bastardierungsproblem beim Menschen*. Jena: Verlag von Gustav Fischer.

Fischer, Eugen. 1914. *Das Problem der Rassenkreuzung beim Menschen*. Freiburg im Breisgau: Speyer & Kaerner, Universitätsbuchhandlung.

Fischer, Eugen. 1936-37. "Neue Rehobother Bastard-Studien." *Zeitschrift für Morphologie und Anthropologie* 36:127-39.

Fischer, Eugen. 1959. "Vor fünfzig Jahren in Südwestafrika: Zur Erforschung der menschlichen Erblehre." *Journal of the South West Africa Scientific Society* 13:43-52.

Fischer, Eugen. 1961. *Die Rehobother Bastards und das Bastardierungsproblem beim Menschen*. Graz: Akademische Druck- und Verlagsanstalt.

Fischer, Eugen, and Gerhard Kittel. 1943. *Das antike Weltjudentum*. Hamburg: Hanseatische Verlagsanstalt.

Fischer, Per. 1994. "Clemens von Ketteler: Ein Lebensbild aus amtlichen und privaten deutschen Quellen." Pp. 333-57 in Kuo and Leutner 1994.

Förster, E. Th. 1905. "Die Ursachen des Hereroaufstandes." Pp. 478-552 in *Krieg und Frieden im Hererolande: Auszeichnungen aus dem Kriegsjahre 1904*, ed. Conrad Rust. Oxford: L. A. Kittler.

Förster, Stig, Wolfgang J. Mommsen, and Ronald Robinson, eds. 1988. *Bismarck, Europe, and Africa: The Berlin Africa Conference 1884-1885 and the Onset of Partition*. Oxford: Oxford University Press.

Fontane, Theodor. [1894] 1967. *Effie Briest*. Harmondsworth: Penguin.

Forbes, David W. 1992. *Encounters with Paradise: Views of Hawaii and Its People, 1778-1941*. Honolulu: Honolulu Academy of Arts.

Forke, Alfred. 1898. "Von Peking nach Ch'ang-an und Lo-yang." *Mittheilungen des Seminars für Orientalische Sprachen zu Berlin* 1 (1): 1-126.

Forsman, Mary Catherine. 1979. "Richard Wilhelm and Sino-German Dialogue." B.A. thesis, Harvard College.

Forster, Georg. [1777] 2000. *A Voyage Round the World*. 2 vols. Ed. Nicholas Thomas and Oliver Berghof. Honolulu: University of Hawai'i Press.

Forster, Georg. [1786] 1974. "Noch etwas über die Menschenracen." Pp. 130-56 in *Georg Forsters Werke*, vol. 8. Berlin (East): Akademie-Verlag.

Forster, Georg. 1985a. "O-Taheiti." Pp. 35-71 in *Georg Forsters Werke*, vol. 5. Berlin (East): Akademie-Verlag.

Forster, Georg. 1985b. "Cook, der Entdecker." Pp. 191-302 in *Georg Forsters Werke*, vol. 5. Berlin (East): Akademie-Verlag.

Forster, Georg. 1985c. "Fragmente über Cooks letzte Reise." Pp. 72-92 in *Georg Forsters Werke*, vol. 5. Berlin (East): Akademie-Verlag.

Forster, Georg. 1985d. "Nachrichten von den Pelew-Inseln: Vorrede." Pp. 323-33 in *Georg Forsters Werke*, vol. 5. Berlin (East): Akademie-Verlag.

Forster, Johann Reinhold. [1778] 1996. *Observations Made during a Voyage round the World*. Ed. Nicholas Thomas, Harriet Guest, and Michael Dettelbach. Honolulu: University of Hawai'i Press.

Forster, Johann Reinhold. 1982. *The Resolution Journal of Johann Reinhold Forster, 1772-1775*. 4 vols. London: Hakluyt Society.

Foster, Sir William. 1934. "Extracts from a Journal Kept on Board the Hosiander, Begun by Ralph Standish and Continued by Ralph Croft, 3 February 1612 to 29 August 1613." Pp. 183–198 in *The Voyage of Thomas Best to the East Indies, 1612–14*, ed. Sir William Foster. London: Printed for the Hakluyt Society.

Foster, Sir William, ed. 1940. *The Voyages of Sir James Lancaster to Brazil and the East Indies, 1591–1603*. London: Hakluyt Society.

Foster, Sir William. 1943. *The Voyage of Sir Henry Middleton to the Moluccas*. London: Hakluyt Society.

Foucault, Michel. 1980. *The History of Sexuality: An Introduction*. New York: Vintage.

Fourny, Jean-François. 2000. "Bourdieu's Uneasy Psychoanalysis." *Substance* 29, no. 3 (93): 103–12.

François, Alfred von. 1905. *Der Hottentotten-Aufstand*. Berlin: Ernst Siegfried Mittler und Sohn.

François, Hugo von. 1895. *Nama und Damara*. Madgeburg: G. Baensch jun.

François, Curt von. 1899. *Deutsch-Südwestafrika: Geschichte der Kolonisation bis zum Ausbruch des Krieges mit Witbooi*. Berlin: Dietrich Reimer.

François, Curt von. 1972. *Ohne Schuß durch dick und dünn: Erste Erforschung des Togohinterlandes*. Idstein: Esch-Waldems (Eigenverlag).

Franke, Herbert. 1960. *Zur Biographie von Johann Heinrich Plath (1802–1874)*. Munich: Verlag der Bayerischen Akademie der Wissenschaften.

Franke, Otto. 1906. "Die politische Idee in der ostasiatischen Kulturwelt." Pp. 161–69 in *Verhandlungen des Deutschen Kolonialkongresses 1905*. Berlin: Dietrich Reimer.

Franke, Otto. 1911a. *Ostasiatische Neubildungen*. Hamburg: C. Boysen.

Franke, Otto. 1911b. "Die deutsch-chinesischen Hochschule in Tsingtau, ihre Vorgeschichte, ihre Einrichtung und ihre Aufgaben." Pp. 200–218 in O. Franke 1911a.

Franke, Otto. 1954. *Erinnerungen aus zwei Welten: Randglossen zur eigenen Lebensgeschichte*. Berlin: Walter de Gruyter & Co.

Franzius, Georg. [1899] n.d.. *Kiautschou: Deutschlands Erwerbung in Ostasien*. Berlin: Schall & Grund.

Freeman, Derek. 1964. "Some Observations on Kinship and Political Authority in Samoa." *American Anthropologist* 66 (3): 553–68.

Freeman, Michael. 1995. "Puritans and Pequots: The Question of Genocide." *The New England Quarterly* 68 (2): 278–93.

Freimut, Ernst. n.d. (1909). *Gedanken am Wege: Reiseplaudereien aus Deutsch-Südwestafrika*. Berlin: Deutscher Kolonial-Verlag.

Frenssen, Gustav. [1905] 1908. *Peter Moor's Journey to Southwest Africa*. Boston: Houghton Mifflin Co.

Freud, Sigmund. [1921] 1955. "Group Psychology and the Analysis of Ego." Pp. 67–143 in *The Standard Edition of the Complete Psychological Works of Sigmund Freud*, vol. 18, trans. and ed. James Strachey. London: Hogarth Press.

Freud, Sigmund. [1923] 1961. "The Ego and the Id." Pp. 3–66 in *The Standard Edition of the Complete Psychological Works of Sigmund Freud*, vol. 19, trans. and ed. James Strachey. London: Hogarth Press.

Freud, Sigmund. [1927] 1963. "Fetishism." Pp. 149–57 in *The Standard Edition of the Complete Psychological Works of Sigmund Freud*, vol. 21, trans. and ed. James Strachey. London: Hogarth Press.

Friedel, Ernest August. 1867. *Die Gründung preußisch-deutscher Colonien im Indischen und Großen Ocean mit besonderer Rücksicht auf das östliche Asien*. Berlin: Verlag von Albert Eichhoff.

Friederici, Georg. n.d. *Feldzugs-Erinnerungen aus China*. Berlin: Heilbrunn & Co.

Friedrichsmeyer, Sara, Sara Lennox, and Susanne Zantop, eds. 1998. *The Imperialist Imagination: German Colonialism and Its Legacy*. Ann Arbor: University of Michigan Press.

Fristoe, Ashby J. 1977. *The Samoan Archives*. Honolulu: University of Hawaii, Pacific Islands Study Program.

Fritsch, Gustav. 1872. *Die Eingeborenen Südafrikas, ethnographisch und anatomisch beschrieben*. Breslau: Hirt.

Fritsch, Gustav. 1880. "Die afrikanischen Buschmänner als Urrasse." *Zeitschrift für Ethnologie* 12:289–300.

Fryke, Christopher. [1700] 1929. "A Relation of a Voyage Made to the East Indies." Pp. 1–169 in *Voyages to the East Indies: Christopher Fryke and Christopher Schweitzer*, ed. C. Ernest Fayle. London: Cassell and Co.

Fuhrmann, Wolfgang. 2003. "Propaganda, Sciences, and Entertainment: German Colonial Cinematography: A Case Study in the History of Early Nonfiction Cinema." Ph.D. diss., University of Utrecht.

Furber, David Bruce. 2003. "Going East: Colonialism and German Life in Nazi-Occupied Poland." Ph.D. diss., State University of New York at Buffalo.

Gabelentz, Georg von der. 1888. *Confucius und seine Lehre*. Leipzig: F. A. Brockhaus.

Gahlings, Ute. 1992. *Sinn und Ursprung: Untersuchungen zum philosophischen Weg Hermann Graf Keyserlings*. Sankt Augustin: Academia Verlag.

Gahlings, Ute. 2000. "Keyserlings Begegnung mit China und Japan." Pp. 156–80 in *Hermann Graf Keyserling und Asien*, ed. Ute Gahlings and Klaus Jork. Biebelsheim: Edition Vidya.

Gailey, Christine Ward. 1994. "Politics, Colonialism, and the Mutable Color of Southern Pacific Peoples." *Transforming Anthropology* 5 (1–2): 34–40.

Gallagher, John, and Ronald Robinson. 1953. "The Imperialism of Free Trade." *Economic History Review* 6 (1): 1–15.

Galton, Francis. 1853. *The Narrative of an Explorer in Tropical South Africa*. London: J. Murray.

Gandhi, Leela. 1998. *Postcolonial Theory*. New York: Columbia University Press.

Gann, Lewis H. 1987. "Marginal Colonialism: The German Case." Pp. 1–17 in *Germans in the Tropics: Essays in German Colonial History*, ed. Arthur J. Knoll and Lewis H. Gann. New York: Greenwood Press.

Gann, Lewis H., and Peter Duignan. 1977. *The Rulers of German Africa, 1884-1914*. Stanford, Calif.: Stanford University Press.

Garnier, F. 1875. F. "Garnier's Schilderungen aus Yünnan." *Globus* 28 (22): 337-42.

Garrett, John. 1973. "The Conflict between the London Missionary Society and the Wesleyan Methodists in 19th Century Samoa." *Journal of Pacific History* 8:65-80.

Gauguin, Paul. 1919. *Noa-Noa*. Trans. O. F. Theis. New York: N. L. Brown.

Gaulejac, Vincent de. 2004. "De l'inconscient chez Freud à l'inconscient selon Bourdieu: Entre psychanalyse et socio-analyse." Pp. 75-86 in Corcuff 2004.

Gaydish, Jeffrey S. 2001. "Old Swakopmund Reexamined: German Labor Mobilization Practices in Colonial Namibia." M.A. thesis, Arizona State University.

Geary, Christraud M. 1988. *Images from Bamum*. Washington, D.C.: Published for the National Museum of African Art by the Smithsonian Institute Press.

Gell, Alfred. 1993. *Wrapping in Images: Tattooing in Polynesia*. Oxford: Oxford University Press.

Gemäldegalerie. 1975. *Katalog der ausgestellten Gemälde des 13.-18. Jahrhunderts*. Berlin: Mann.

Gentz. 1902-3. "Die rechtliche Stellung der Bastards in Deutsch-Südwestafrika." *Beiträge zur Kolonialpolitik und Kolonialwirtschaft* 4:90-92.

Gerber, Lydia. 2003. "Richard Wilhelms Missionsarbeit im deutschen Pachtgebiet Kiautschou, 1899-1914." Pp. 167-99 in Hirsch 2003.

Gerlach, Hans-Martin, and Siegfried Wollgast. 1979. "Christian Wolff: Ein hervorragender deutscher Philosoph der Aufklärung." *Deutsche Zeitschrift für Philosophie* 27 (10): 1239-47.

Gerland, Georg. 1868. *Über das Aussterben der Naturvölker*. Leipzig: Verlag von Friedrich Fleischer.

Gerstäcker, Friedrich. 1868. *Die Missionäre: Roman aus der Südsee*. 3rd ed. Jena: Hermann Costenoble.

Gerstäcker, Friedrich. 1885. *Tahiti: Roman aus der Südsee*. 5th ed. Jena: Hermann Costenoble.

Gessler, Bernhard. 2000. *Eugen Fischer (1874-1967): Leben und Werk des Freiburger Anatomen, Anthropologen und Rassenhygienikers bis 1927*. Frankfurt am Main: Peter Lang.

Gewald, Jan-Bart. 1998a. *Herero Heroes: A Socio-Political History of the Herero of Namibia, 1890-1923*. Athens: Ohio University Press.

Gewald, Jan-Bart. 1998b. "Herero Annual Parades: Commemorating to Create." Pp. 131-51 in *Afrikaner schreiben zurück*, ed. Heike Behrend and Thomas Geider. Cologne: Köppe.

Gewald, Jan-Bart. 2000. "Colonization, Genocide, and Resurgence: The Herero of Namibia, 1890-1933." Pp. 187-226 in *People, Cattle and Land*, ed. Michael Bollig and Jan-Bart Gewald. Cologne: R. Köppe

Gewald, Jan-Bart. 2003. "Kolonisierung, Völkermord und Wiederkehr: Die Herero von Namibia 1890-1923." Pp. 105-20 in Zimmerer and Zeller 2003.

Giddens, Anthony. 1985. *The Nation-State and Violence*. Cambridge: Polity Press.

Gifford, Prosser, and William Roger Louis. 1971. *France and Britain in Africa: Imperial Rivalry and Colonial Rule.* New Haven, Conn.: Yale University Press.

Gifford, Prosser, William Roger Louis, and Alison Smith. 1967. *Britain and Germany in Africa: Imperial Rivalry and Colonial Rule.* New Haven, Conn.: Yale University Press.

Gilman, Sander L. 1985. "Black Bodies, White Bodies: Toward an Iconography of Female Sexuality in Late Nineteenth-Century Art, Medicine, and Literature." Pp. 223-61 in *"Race," Writing, and Difference,* ed. Henry Louis Gates, Jr. Chicago: University of Chicago Press.

Gilson, R. P. 1970. *Samoa, 1830 to 1900.* Melbourne: Oxford University Press.

Given, James. 1990. *State and Society in Medieval Europe.* Ithaca, N.Y.: Cornell University Press.

Go, Julian. 2000. "Transcultured States: Elite Political Culture in Puerto Rico and the Philippines during US Colonial Rule (c. 1898-1912)." Ph.D. diss., University of Chicago.

Gobineau, Arthur, comte de. [1852] 1915. *The Inequality of Human Races.* New York: G. P. Putnam's Sons.

Godshall, Wilson Leon. 1929. *Tsingtau under Three Flags.* Shanghai: Commerical Press.

Goh, Daniel. 2005. "Ethnographic Empire: Imperial Culture and Colonial State Formation in Malaya and the Philippines, 1880-1940." Ph.D. diss., University of Michigan, Ann Arbor.

Goldblatt, Israel. 1971. *History of South West Africa from the Beginning of the 19th Century.* Cape Town: Juta and Co.

Gollwitzer, Heinz. 1962. *Die gelbe Gefahr: Geschichte eines Schlagwortes.* Göttingen: Vandenhoek & Ruprecht.

Goltz, Bogunil. 1858. *Der Mensch und die Leute: Zur Charakteristik der barbarischen und der civilisierten Nationen.* Berlin: Verlag von Fritz Duncker.

Gordon, Robert J. 1992. *The Bushman Myth.* Boulder, Colo.: Westview Press.

Gordon, Robert J. 1998. "Vagrancy, Law, and 'Shadow Knowledge': Internal Pacification, 1915-1939." Pp. 3-48 in Hayes, Silvester, Wallace, and Hartmann 1998.

Gothsch, Manfred. 1983. *Die deutsche Völkerkunde und ihr Verhältnis zum Kolonialismus.* Baden-Baden: Nomos.

Gould, Stephen Jay. 1996. *The Mismeasure of Man.* 2nd ed. New York: W. W. Norton and Co.

Grattan, F. J. H. [1948] 1985. *An Introduction to Samoan Custom.* Papakura, New Zealand: R. McMillan.

Gray, Frederic Charles. 1970. "Tahiti in French Literature from Bougainville to Pierre Loti." Ph.D. diss., University of Arizona.

Greenberg, Valerie D. 1988. "The Resistance of Effi Briest: An (Un)told Tale. *PMLA* 103 (5): 770-82.

Grentrup, Theodor. 1914. *Die Rassenmischehen in den deutschen Kolonien.* Paderborn: F. Schöningh.

Grevenbroek, Johannes Gulielmus de. [1695] 1933. "An Elegant and Accurate Account of the African Race Living Round the Cape of Good Hope Commonly Called Hottentots." Pp. 159-299 in *The Early Cape Hottentots, Described in the Writings of Olfert Dapper (1668), Willem ten Rhyne (1686) and Johannes Gulielmus de Grevenbrock (1695)*, ed. and trans. Isaac Schapera. Cape Town: Van Riebeeck Society.

Grimm, Hans. 1916. *Der Gang durch den Sand und andere Geschichten aus südafrikanischer Not*. Munich: Albert Langen.

Grössel, Wolfgang. 1891. *Justinianus von Weltz, der Vorkämpfer der lutherischen Mission*. Leipzig: Akademische Buchhandlung (W. Faber).

Grosrichard, Alain. 1998. *The Sultan's Court: European Fantasies of the East*. London: Verso.

Grosse, Pascal. 2006. "From Colonialism to National Socialism to Postcolonialism: Hannah Arendt's *Origins of Totalitarianism*." *Postcolonial Studies* 9 (1): 35-52.

Grosser Generalstab für Kriegsgeschichte. 1912. *Brandenburg-Preussen auf der Westküste von Afrika 1681 bis 1721*. Leipzig: Voigtländer.

Grothpeter. John J. 1994. *Historical Dictionary of Namibia*. Metuchen, N.J.: Scarecrow Press.

Grube, Wilhelm. 1910. *Religion und Kultus der Chinesen*. Leipzig: Rudolf Haupt.

Gruber, Alain. 1984. *Chinoiserie*. Bern: Abegg-Stiftung.

Grueber, Johannes. 1985. *Als Kundschafter des Papstes nach China 1656-1664: Die erste Durchquerung Tibets*. Stuttgart: Thienemann.

Gründer, Horst. 1982. *Christliche Mission und deutscher Imperialismus: Eine politische Geschichte*. Paderborn: Ferdinand Schöningh.

Gründer, Horst. 2004. *Geschichte der deutschen Kolonien*. 5th ed. Paderborn: Ferdinand Schöningh.

Grünfeld, Ernst. 1913. *Hafenkolonien und kolonieähnliche Verhältnisse in China, Japan und Korea: Eine kolonialpolitische Studie*. Jena: G. Fischer.

Guest, Harriet. 1992. "The Great Distinction: Figures of the Exotic in the Work of William Hodges." Pp. 296-341 in *New Feminist Discourses*. London: Routledge.

Gützlaff, Karl. 1834. *A Journal of Three Voyages*. London: Frederick Westley and A. H. Davis.

Gützlaff, Karl. 1838. *China Opened; or, A Display of the Topography, History, Customs, Manners, Arts, Manufacturies, etc*. 2 vols. London: Smith, Elder and Co.

Guy, Basil. 1963. *The French Image of China before and after Voltaire*. Geneva: Institut et Musée Voltaire.

Ha, Marie-Paule. 2003. "From 'Nos Ancêtres, les Gaulois' to 'Leur Culture Ancestrale': Symbolic Violence and the Politics of Colonial Schooling in Indochina." *French Colonial History* 3:101-18.

Habermas, Jürgen. [1981] 1984-87. *The Theory of Communicative Action*. Trans. Thomas McCarthy. Boston: Beacon Press.

Hacking, Ian. 1995. "The Looping Effects of Human Kinds." Pp. 351-96 in *Causal Cognition: A Multidisciplinary Approach*, ed. D. Sperber, D. Premack, and A. J. Premack. Oxford: Clarendon Press.

Hacking, Ian. 1999. *The Social Construction of What?* Cambridge, Mass.: Harvard University Press.

Haenisch, Erich. 1905. "Die Tafel des Yü." *Mitteilungen des Seminars für Orientalische Sprachen zu Berlin* 7 (1): 293-303.

Hahn, Carl Hugo. 1984-85. *Tagebücher, 1837-1860, Diaries: A Missionary in Nama- and Damaraland.* 5 vols. Ed. Brigitte Lau. Windhoek: Department of National Education.

Hahn, Emma Sarah. 1992. *The Letters of Emma Sarah Hahn, Pioneer Missionary among the Herero.* Ed. Dorothy Guedes. Windhoek: Namibia Scientific Society.

Hahn, Theophilus. 1867. "Die Nama-Hottentotten." *Globus* 12:238-42, 275-79,304-7, 332-36.

Hahn, Theophilus. 1868. "Ein Racenkampf im nordwestlichen Theile der Cap-Region." *Globus* 14:202-7, 245-48.

Hahn, Theophilus. 1869a. "Ein Brüderkrieg in Südwestafrika." *Globus* 16:236-38.

Hahn, Theophilus. 1869b. "Ein Racenkampf zwischen den Basutos und den holländischen Bauern in Südostafrika." *Globus* 15:13-17.

Hahn, Theophilus. 1870. "Beiträge zur Kunde der Hottentotten." Pp. 1-21 in *VI. und VII. Jahresbericht des Vereins für Erdkunde zu Dresden.* Dresden: G. Schönfeld's Buchhandlung.

Hahn, Theophilus. 1878. "The Graves of Heitsi-eibib: A Chapter on the Prehistoric Hottentot Race." *Cape Monthly Magazine* 16 (97): 257-65.

Hahn, Theophilus. 1881. *Tsuni-//Goam: The Supreme Being of the Khoi-Khoi.* London: Trubner.

Hale, Horatio. [1846] 1986. *Ethnography and Philology.* United States Exploring Expedition during the Years 1838, 1839, 1840, 1841, 1842. Ridgewood, N.J.: Gregg Press.

Hall, H. Duncan. 1967. "The British Commonwealth and the Founding of the League Mandate System." Pp. 345-68 in *Studies in International History,* ed. K. Bourne and D. C. Watt. Hamden, Conn.: Archon Books.

Hall, Stuart. 1983. "The Problem of Ideology: Marxism without Guarantees." Pp. 56-85 in *Marx 100 Years on,* ed. B. Matthews. London: Lawrence and Wishart.

Halm, Peter. 1952. "Der schreibende Teufel." Pp. 237-49 in *Cristianesimo e Ragion di Stato: L'Umanesimo e il Demoniaco nell'arte,* ed. Enrico Castelli. Rome: Fratelli Bocca Editori.

Hamilton, Andrew. 1998. "Nineteenth-Century French Missionaries and *Fa'a Samoa.*" *Journal of Pacific History* 33 (2): 163-77.

Hampe, Karl-Alexander. 2001. *Das Auswärtige Amt in Wilhelminischer Zeit.* Münster: Scriptorium.

Hanan, Patrick. 2000. "The Missionary Novels of Nineteenth-Century China." *Harvard Journal of Asiatic Studies* 60 (December): 413-43.

Hardt, Michael, and Antonio Negri. 2000. *Empire.* Cambridge, Mass.: Harvard University Press.

Harms, Volker. 1991. "'Südseebilder': Zur Ethnographiegeschichte einer Foto-Sammlung aus den Jahren 1890-1910." *Tribus: Jahrbuch des Linden-Museums* 40 (December):161-77.

Harms, Volker, ed. 1992. *Südseebilder*. Tübingen: Völkerkundliches Institut.

Harms, Volker. 2004. "Die ehemals private Südsee-Sammlung von Augustin Krämer in der Tübinger Universität: Eine sammlungsgeschichtliche und biographische Skizze." *TenDenZen* 11:51-60.

Harrison, Charles, Francis Frascina, and Gill Perry. 1993. *Primitivism, Cubism, Abstraction*. New Haven, Conn.: Yale University Press.

Hartig, Otto. 1913. "Pordenone, Odoric of." P. 281 in *The Catholic Encyclopedia*, vol. 12, ed. Charles G. Herbermann et al. New York: Encyclopedia Press.

Hartmann, Georg. 1904. *Die Zukunft Deutsch-Süd-West-Afrikas*. Berlin: Mittler & Sohn.

Hartmann, Georg. 1910. "Die Mischrassen in unseren Kolonien, besonders in Südwestafrika." Pp. 906-32 in *Verhandlungen des Deutschen Kolonialkongresses 1910*, ed. Redaktionsausschuss. Berlin: Dietrich Riemer.

Hartwig, Georg. [1861] 1871. *Die Inseln des Grossen Oceans im Natur- und Völkerleben*. Wiesbaden: Verlag von M. Bischkopff.

Harvey, David. 2003. *The New Imperialism*. Oxford: Oxford University Press.

Hassels, Michael. 1993. *Potsdamer Schlösser und Gärten: Bau-und Gartenkunst vom 17. bis 20. Jahrhundert*. Potsdam: Stiftung Schlösser und Gärten Potsdam-Sanssouci.

Hawkesworth, John. 1775. *An account of the voyages undertaken by the order of His present Majesty, for making discoveries in the southern hemisphere, and successively performed by Commodore Byron, Captain Wallis, Captain Carteret, and Captain Cook, in the Dolphin, the Swallow, and the Endeavour*. 2 vols. Dublin: Printed for James Williams.

Hayes, Patricia. 1996. "'Cocky' Hahn and the 'Black Venus': The Making of a Native Commissioner in South West Africa, 1915-46." *Gender and Society* 8 (3): 364-92.

Hayes, Patricia, Jeremy Silvester, Marion Wallace, and Wolfram Hartmann. 1998. *Namibia under South African Rule*. Oxford: James Currey.

Hedström, Peter, and Richard Swedberg. 1998. "Social Mechanisms: An Introductory Essay." Pp. 1-31 in *Social Mechanisms*, ed. Peter Hedström and Richard Swedberg. Cambridge: Cambridge University Press.

Heermann, Ingrid. 1987. *Mythos Tahiti*. Berlin: D. Reimer.

Hegel, Georg Wilhelm Friedrich. [1807] 1910. *Phenomenology of Mind*. London: S. Sonnenscheinand Co.

Hegel, Georg Wilhelm Friedrich. 1956. *The Philosophy of History*. New York: Dover Publications.

Hegel, Georg Wilhelm Friedrich. 1983. *Hegel and the Human Spirit*. Trans. and ed. Leo Rauch. Detroit: Wayne State University Press.

Hegel, Georg Wilhelm Friedrich. 1984-87. *The Philosophy of Religion*. 2 vols. Berkeley, Calif.: University of California Press.

Heidegger, Martin. [1927] 1996. *Being and Time*. Trans. Joan Stambaugh. Albany: State University of New York Press.

Hell, Julia. 1992. "Wilhelm Raabes *Stopfkuchen*: Der ungleichzeitige Bürger." *Jahrbuch der Raabe-Gesellschaft*, pp. 165–93.

Hell, Julia. 1997. *Post-Fascist Fantasies: Psychoanalysis, History, and the Literature of East Germany*. Durham, N.C.: Duke University Press.

Hell, Julia. 2002. "The Melodrama of Illegal Identifications; or, Post-Holocaust Authorship in Uwe Johnson's *Jahrestage: Aus dem Leben von Gesine Cresspahl*." *Monatshefte* 94 (Summer): 209–29.

Hellborn, R. n.d. [ca. 1900–1901]. *Boxer: Militärischer Schwank mit Gesang in einem Akt*. Landsberg an der Warthe: Volger & Klein.

Hempenstall, Peter J. 1973. "Indigenous Resistance to German Rule in the Pacific Colonies of Samoa, Ponape and New Guinea, 1884 to 1914." D.Phil. thesis, Magdalen College, Oxford.

Hempenstall, Peter J. 1978. *Pacific Islanders under German Rule*. Canberra: Australian National University Presses.

Hempenstall, Peter J. 1987. "The Neglected Empire: The Superstructure of the Colonial State in German Melanesia." Pp. 93–117 in *Germans in the Tropics: Essays in German Colonial History*, ed. Arthur J. Knoll and Lewis H. Gann. New York: Greenwood Press.

Hempenstall, Peter J., and Paula T. Mochida. 2005. *The Lost Man: Wilhelm Solf in German History*. Wiesbaden: Harrassowitz.

Henderson, W. O. 1993. *The German Colonial Empire, 1884–1919*. London: Cass.

Hendrickson, Anne Alfhild Bell. 1992. "Historical Idioms of Identity Construction among the Ovaherero in Southern Africa." Ph.D. diss., New York University.

Hengst, Karl. 1981. *Jesuiten an Universitäten und Jesuitenuniversitäten*. Paderborn: Schöningh.

Henniger, Julius. 1971. "Ein Beitrag zur Kenntnis der Herstellungsweise 'feiner Matten' in Samoa." *Baessler-Archiv*, n.s., 19:29–45.

Henrichsen, Dag. 1997. "Herrschaft und Identifikation im vorkolonialen Zentralnamibia: Das Herero- und Damaraland im 19. Jahrhundert." Ph.D. diss., Universität Hamburg.

Henrichsen, Dag. 2000. "*Ozongombe, Omavita* and *Ozondjembo:* The Process of (Re-)Pastoralization amonst Herero in Pre-colonial 19th Century Central Namibia." Pp. 149–85 in *People, Cattle and Land*, ed. Michael Bollig and Jan-Bart Gewald. Cologne: R. Köppe.

Henrichsen, Dag. 2004. "*Ozombambuse* and *Ovasolondate:* Everyday Military Life and African Service in German South West Africa." Pp. 161–84 in *Hues between Black and White: Historical Photography from Colonial Namibia 1860s to 1915*, ed. Wolfram Hartmann. Windhoek: Out of Africa Publishers.

Henry, Teuira. 1928. *Ancient Tahiti*. Honolulu: Bernice Pauahi Bishop Museum.

Herbert, Thomas. 1677. *Some Years Travels into Divers Parts of Africa, and Asia the Great*. 4th impression. London: Printed by R. Everingham for R. Scot, T. Basset, J. Wright, and R. Chiswell.

Herbst, Wilhelm. 1872–76. *Johann Heinrich Voss.* 3 vols. Leipzig: B. G. Teubner.

Herder, Johann Gottfried. [1784] 1985. *Ideen zur Philosophie der Geschichte der Menscheit.* Wiesbaden: Fourier Verlag.

Hermann, R[udolf] A. 1906. "Mischehen und Grundeigentum in Deutsch-Südwestafrika. *Zeitschrift für Kolonialpolitik, Kolonialrecht und Kolonialwirtschaft* 8:134–41.

Herport, Albrecht. [1669] 1930. *Reise nach Java, Formosa, Vorder-Indien und Ceylon 1659-1668.* The Hague: Martinius Nijhoff. Reprint of the author's *Ost-Indianische Reiß-Beschreibung* (Bern: G. Sonnleiter, 1669).

Herrings, Joseph. 1903. *Taku: Die deutsche Reichsmarine im Kampf und Sieg.* Berlin: J. Medinger.

Hesse, Hermann. 1956. "Über Richard Wilhelm." Pp. 131–34 in *60 Jahre Eugen Diederichs Verlag: Ein Almanach.* Düsseldorf: Eugen Diederichs Verlag.

Hesse, Hermann. 1930. "Richard Wilhelm's letztes Werk." *Der Bücherwurm* 15 (11): 302.

Hetze, Stefanie. 1987. "Feindbild und Exotik: Prinz Chun zur 'Sühnemission' in Berlin." Pp. 79–88 in Kuo 1987.

Hevia, James L. 1992. "Leaving a Brand on China: Missionary Discourse in the Wake of the Boxer Movement." *Modern China* 18 (July):304–32.

Hevia, James L. 1995a. "The Scandal of Inequality: *Koutou* as Signifer." *Positions* 3 (1): 97–118.

Hevia, James L. 1995b. *Cherishing Men from Afar: Qing Guest Ritual and the Macartney Embassy of 1793.* Durham, N.C.: Duke University Press.

Hevia, James L. 2003. *English Lessons: The Pedagogy of Imperialism in Nineteenth-Century China.* Durham, N.C.: Duke University Press.

Heyking, Elisabeth von. 1926. *Tagebücher aus vier Weltteilen, 1886-1904.* Ed. Grete Litzmann. Leipzig: Koehler & Amelang.

Heywood, Annemarie, Brigitte Lau, and Rajmund Ohly. 1992. *Warriors, Leaders, Sages, and Outcasts in the Namibian Past: Narratives Collected from Herero Sources for the Michael Scott Oral Records Project (MSORP), 1985-6.* Windhoek: MSORP.

Hiery, Hermann J. 1995. *Das deutsche Reich in der Südsee (1900-1921).* Göttingen: Vandenhoeck.

Hiery, Hermann. 2005. *Bilder aus der deutschen Südsee: Fotografien 1884-1914.* Paderborn: Ferdinand Schöningh.

Hiery, Hermann, ed. 2001. *Die deutsche Südsee 1884-1914.* 2nd ed. Paderborn: Ferdinand Schöningh.

Hiery, Hermann, and Hans-Martin Hinz, eds. 1999. *Alltagsleben und Kulturaustausch. Deutsche und Chinesen in Tsingtau 1897-1914.* Wolfratshausen: Edition Minerva Hermann Farnung.

Hillebrecht, Werner. 2003. "Die Nama und der Krieg im Süden." Pp. 121–33 in Zimmerer and Zeller 2003.

Hinz, Hans-Martin, and Christoph Lind, eds. 1998. *Tsingtau: Ein Kapitel deutscher Kolonialgeschichte in China 1897-1914.* Berlin: Deutsches Historisches Museum.

Hirsch, Klaus. 2003. *Richard Wilhelm, Botschafter zweier Welten*. Frankfurt am Main: IKO-Verlag für Interkulturelle Kommunikation.

Hjarnø, Jan. 1979-80. "Social Reproduction: Towards an Understanding of Aboriginal Samoa." *Folk: Dansk Etnografisk Tidsskrift* 21-22:72-123.

Hoare, Michael Edward. 1976. *The Tactless Philosopher: Johann Reinhold Forster (1729-98)*. Melbourne: Hawthorn Press.

Hochschild, Adam. 1999. *King Leopold's Ghost*. New York: Mariner Books.

Hoernelé, Winifred. 1985. *"The Social Organization of the Nama" and Other Essays by Winifred Hoernelé*. Ed. Peter Carstens. Johannesburg: Witwatersrand University Press.

Hövermann, Otto. 1914. *Kiautschou, Verwaltung und Gerichtsbarkeit*. Tübingen: J. C. B. Mohr.

Hoffmann, Hermann Edler von. 1907. *Einführung in das deutsche Kolonialrecht*. Leipzig: G. J. Göschen'sche Verlagshandlung.

Hoffmann, Hermann Edler von. 1911. *Einführung in das deutsche Kolonialrecht*. Leipzig: G. J. Göschen'sche Verlagshandlung.

Hoffmeister, Hermann. 1882. *Völkerkunde, oder Ethnographie und Ethnologie*. Berlin: Verlag von Kogge & Fritze.

Holmes, Jeanette R. 1967. "Aboriginal and Modern Samoa: A Study of Cultural Change Based on London Missionary Society Journals, 1830-1840." M.A. thesis, Wichita State University.

Holmes, Lowell D. 1969. "Samoan Oratory." *Journal of American Folklore* 82 (326): 342-52.

Holub, Emil. [1881] 1970. *Seven Years in South Africa: Travels, Researches, and Hunting Adventures, between the Diamond-Fields and the Zambesi (1872-79)*. Detroit: Negro History Press.

Honneth, Axel. 1995. *The Struggle for Recognition*. Cambridge: Polity Press.

Hordern, Charles, and Major Henry Fitz Maurice Stacke. 1941. *Military Operations: East Africa*. Vol. 1. London: H. M. Stationery Office.

Hsia, Adrian. 1974. *Hermann Hesse und China*. Frankfurt am Main: Suhrkamp.

Hsia, Adrian. 1985. *Deutsche Denker über China*. Frankfurt am Main: Insel Verlag.

Hua, Meng. 2000. "The Chinese Genesis of the Term 'Foreign Devil.'" Pp. 26-37 in *Images of Westerners in Chinese and Japanese Literature*, ed. Hua Meng and Sukehiro Hirakawa. Amsterdam: Rodopi.

Huang, Fuh-teh. 1999. *Qingdao: Chinesen unter deutscher Herrschaft 1897-1914*. Bochum: Projekt.

Huang, Yi. 1995. *Der deutsche Einfluss auf die Entwicklung des chinesischen Bildungswesens von 1871 bis 1918*. Frankfurt am Main: P. Lang.

Huard, P. 1953. "La diffusion de l'anatomie européenne dans quelques secteurs de l'Asie." *Archives Internationales d'Histoire des Sciences* 6:266-78.

Hubatsch, Walther. 1955. *Die Ära Tirpitz*. Göttingen: Musterschmidt.

Huc, Evariste Régis. [1855] 1970. *The Chinese Empire, Forming a Sequel to the Work Entitled "Recollections of a Journey through Tartary and Thibet."* 2 vols. 2nd ed. Port Washington, N.Y.: Kennikat Press.

Hucker, Charles O. 1966. *The Censorial System of Ming China*. Stanford, Calif.: Stanford University Press.

Hübner, Joseph Alexander. 1886. *A travers l'empire britannique (1883-1884)*. 2 vols. Paris: Hachette.

Hull, Isabel V. 2005. *Absolute Destruction: Military Culture and the Practices of War in Imperial Germany*. Ithaca, N.Y.: Cornell University Press.

Hulme, Peter. 1986. *Colonial Encounters: Europe and the Native Caribbean, 1492-1797*. London: Methuen.

Huntington, Samuel P. 1996. *The Clash of Civilizations and the Remaking of World Order*. New York: Simon and Schuster.

Huntington, Samuel P., and Jorge Dominguez. 1975. "Political Development." Pp. 1-114 in *Handbook of Political Science*, vol. 3, ed. Fred Greenstein and Nelson Polsby. Reading, Mass.: Addison-Wesley Publishing Co.

Huonder, Anton. 1899. *Deutsche Jesuitenmissionäre des 17. und 18. Jahrhunderts*. Freiburg: Herder'sche Verlagsbuchhandlung.

Hyrkkanen, Markku. 1986. *Sozialistische Kolonialpolitik: Eduard Bernsteins Stellung zur Kolonialpolitk und zum Imperialismus 1882-1914*. Helsinki: SHS.

Iannaccone, Isaia. 1998. *Johann Schreck Terrentius*. Naples: Istituto Universitario Orientale, Dipartimeno Di Studi Asiatici.

Ides, Evert Ysbrants. 1706. *Three Years Travels from Moscow over-land to China*. London: Freeman.

Iliffe, John. 1967. "The Organization of the Maji-Maji Rebellion." *Journal of African History* 8:495-512.

Iliffe, John. 1979. *A Modern History of Tanganyika*. Cambridge: Cambridge University Press.

Inden, Ronald. 1986. "Orientalist Constructions of India." *Modern Asian Studies* 20 (3): 401-46.

Irle, J. 1906. *Die Herero*. Gütersloh: Bertelsmann.

Isbrand, Everard, and Adam Brand. 1698. *A journal of the embassy . . . over land into China . . . in the years 1693, 1694, and 1695*. London: D. Brown and T. Goodwin.

Ivison, Douglas. 1997. "Outhouses of the European Soul: Imperialism in Thomas Pynchon." *Pynchon Notes* 40-41 (Spring-Fall): 134-43.

Jacob, Yves. 1995. *Dumont d'Urville: Le dernier grand marin de découvertes*. Grenoble: Editions Glénat.

Jacobs, Hans. 1995. *Reisen und Bürgertum: Eine Analyse deutscher Reiseberichte aus China im 19. Jh.* Berlin: Koster.

Jacoby, Russell. 1983. *The Repression of Psychoanalysis: Otto Fenichel and the Political Freudians*. New York: Basic Books.

Jandesek, Reinhold. 1992. *Das fremde China: Berichte europäischer Reisender des späten Mittelalters und der frühen Neuzeit*. Pfaffenweiler: Centaurus-Verlagsgesellschaft.

JanMohamed, Abdul R. 1985. "The Economy of Manichean Allegory: The Function of Racial Difference in Colonialist Literature." Pp. 78-106 in *"Race," Writing, and Difference*, ed. Henry Louis Gates, Jr. Chicago: University of Chicago Press.

Jarry, Madeleine. 1981. *Chinoiserie.* New York: Venfore Press.

Jenkins, Richard. 1992. *Pierre Bourdieu.* London: Routledge.

Jennings, Francis. 1975. *The Invasion of America.* New York: Norton.

Jennings, M. 1977. "Tutivillus: The Literary Career of the Recording Demon." *Studies in Philology* 74 (5): 1–91.

Jod, Petrus. 1961–62. "Das Witbooi-Volk und die Gründung Gibeons." *Journal of the South West Africa Scientific Society* 16:81–98.

Johnson, Chalmers. 2004. *The Sorrows of Empire.* New York: Henry Holt.

Jones, David Martin. 2001. *The Image of China in Western Social and Political Thought.* New York: Palgrave.

Joppien, Rüdiger. 1979. "The Artistic Bequest of Captain Cook's Voyages: Popular Imagery in European Costume Books of the Late Eighteenth Century and Early Nineteenth Centuries." Pp. 187–210 in *Captain James Cook and His Times,* ed. Robin Fisher and Hugh Johnson. Vancouver: Douglas and McIntyre.

Joppien, Rüdiger, and Bernard Smith. 1985–88. *The Art of Captain Cook's Voyages.* 3 vols. in 4. New Haven, Conn.: Yale University Press.

Julien, Philippe. 1994. *Jacques Lacan's Return to Freud: The Real, the Symbolic, and the Imaginary.* New York: New York University Press.

Jung, Carl. 1966. "Richard Wilhelm: In Memoriam." Pp. 53–62 in *The Spirit in Man, Art, and Literature.* New York: Pantheon Books.

Justi, Johann Heinrich Gottlob von. [1762] 1978. *Vergleichungen der europäischen mit den asiatischen und anderen vermeintlich barbarischen Regierungen, in drei Büchern verfaßt.* Königstein: Scriptor Verlag.

Kämpchen, Martin. 1999. *Rabindranath Tagore in Germany.* Shimla: Indian Institute of Advanced Study, Rashtrapati Nivas.

Kang Youwei. 1986. *Wuxu bianfa qianhou* [Before and after the 1898 Reform]. Shanghai: Shanghai renmin chubanshe.

Karlowa, Hans. 1911. "Die Strafgerichtbarkeit über die Eingeborenen in den deutschen Kolonien." Ph.D. diss., Heidelberg University. Borna-Leipzig: Buchdruckerei Robert Noske.

Kaufmann, Sepp. 1968. "Zur Frage der Herkunft P. Johann Gruebers." *Archivum Historicum Societatis Iesu* 37:427–41.

Keane, Webb. 2005. "Estrangement, Intimacy, and the Objects of Anthropology." Pp. 59–88 in Steinmetz 2005f.

Keate, George. 1788. *An Account of the Pelew islands.* London: G. Nicol.

Keesing, Felix M. 1934. *Modern Samoa.* Stanford, Calif.: Stanford University Press.

Keesing, Felix M. 1937. "The Taupo System of Samoa: A Study of Institutional Change." *Oceania* 8 (1): 1–14.

Keesing, Felix M. 1956. *Elite Communication in Samoa.* Stanford, Calif.: Stanford University Press.

Kehr, Eckart. 1977. "The Genesis of the Prussian Reserve Officer." Pp. 97–108 in *Economic Interest, Militarism, and Foreign Policy,* ed. Gordon A. Craig. Berkeley: University of California Press.

Kennan, George F. 1951. *American Diplomacy, 1900–1950*. Chicago: University of Chicago Press.

Kennedy, P. M. 1974. *The Samoan Tangle*. Dublin: Irish University Press.

Kennedy, Reginald Frank. 1975. *Catalogue of Prints in the Africana Museum and in Books in the Strange Collection of Africana in the Johannesburg Public Library up to 1870*. Johannesburg: Africana Museum.

Keyserling, Hermann Graf von. 1925. *The Travel Diary of a Philosopher*. London: J. Cape.

Kienetz, Alvin. 1976. "Nineteenth-Century South West Africa as a German Settlement Colony." Ph.D. diss., University of Minnesota.

Kienetz, Alvin. 1977. "The Key Role of the Orlam Migrations in the Early Europeanization of South-West Africa (Namibia)." *International Journal of African Historical Studies* 10 (4): 553–72.

Kiernan, Victor G. 1980. "Europe in the Colonial Mirror." *History of European Ideas* 1 (1): 39–61.

Kim, Chun-Shik. 2004. *Deutscher Kulturimperialismus in China: Deutsches Kolonialschulwesen in Kiautschou (China) 1898–1914*. Stuttgart: F. Steiner.

King, Anthony. 1990. *Urbanism, Colonialism, and the World Economy*. London: Routlege.

Kirby, William C. 1984. *Germany and Republican China*. Stanford, Calif.: Stanford University Press.

Kircher, Athanasius. 1670. *La Chine d'Athanase Kirchere de la Compagnie de Jesus*. Amsterdam: Jean Jansson A Waesberge.

Kirchhoff, Alfred. 1880. *Die Südseeinseln und der deutsche Südseehandel*. Heidelberg: Winter's Universitätsbuchhandlung.

Kirk, Tony. 1973. "Progress and Decline in the Kat River Settlement, 1829–1854." *Journal of African History* 14 (3): 411–28.

Kjæret, Kristin, and Kristian Stokke. 2003. "Rehoboth Baster, Namibian or Namibian Baster? An Analysis of National Discourses in Rehoboth, Namibia." *Nations and Nationalism* 9 (4): 579–600.

Klein, Thoralf. 2004. "Rasse—Kultur—soziale Stellung: Konzeptionen des 'Eingeborenen' und koloniale Segregation in Kiautschou." Pp. 304–28 in *Rassenmischehen, Mischlinge, Rassentrennung: Zur Politik der Rasse im deutschen Kolonialreich*, ed. Frank Becker. Stuttgart: F. Steiner.

Klein-Arendt, Reinhard. 2001. "Die Nachrichtenübermittlung in den deutschen Südseekolonien." Pp. 177–97 in Hiery 2001.

Kleist, Heinrich von. [1811] 1978. "The Betrothal in St. Domingo." Pp. 231–69 in *"The Marquise of O"—and Other Stories*. London: Penguin.

Klemm, Gustav. 1843–52. *Allgemeine Cultur-Geschichte der Menschheit*. 10 vols. Leipzig: B. G. Teubner.

Klemm, Gustav. 1847. *China, das Reich der Mitte*. Leipzig: B. G. Teubner.

Kley, Edwin J. van. 1971. "Europe's 'Discovery' of China and the Writing of World History." *American Historical Review* 76:358–85.

Kloosterhuis, Jürgen. 1994. *Friedliche Imperialisten: Deutsche Auslandsvereine und auswärtige Kulturpolitik, 1906–1918.* Frankfurt am Main: P. Lang.

Knapp, Ronald G. 1989. *China's Vernacular Architecture.* Honolulu: University of Hawai'i Press.

Knappe, Wilhelm. 1906. *Deutsche Kulturbestrebungen in China.* Berlin: Hermann Paetel.

Knoll, Arthur J. 1978. *Togo under Imperial Germany, 1884–1914: A Case Study in Colonial Rule.* Stanford, Calif.: Hoover Institution Press.

Ko, Dorothy. 2002. "Footbinding as Female Inscription." Pp. 147–77 in *Rethinking Confucianism: Past and Present in China, Japan, Korea, and Vietnam,* ed. Benjamin A. Elman, John B. Duncan, and Herman Ooms. Los Angeles: UCLA Asian Pacific Monograph Series.

Köbner, Otto. 1903. *Die Organisation der Rechtspflege in den Kolonien.* Berlin: Ernst Siegfried Mittler und Sohn.

Köbner, Otto, and Johannes Gerstmeyer. 1908. *Die deutsche Kolonial-Gesetzgebung.* Vol. 11. Berlin: Ernst Siegfried Mittler und Sohn.

Kögler, P. Ignatii [Ignaz]. [1717] 1726. "Brief P. P. Ignatii Kögler." P. 23 in *Allerhand so lehr- als geist-reiche Brief, Schriften und Reis-Beschreibungen,* vol. 1, no. 7, ed., Josef Stöcklein and Peter Probst.

Koenen, Gerd. 2003. "'Rom oder Moskau': Deutschland, der Westen und die Revolutionierung Russlands 1914–1924." Ph.D. diss., Universität Tübingen.

Kössler, Reinhart. 2003. "'A Luta Continua': Strategische Orientierung und Erinnerungspolitik am Beispiel des 'Heroes Day' der Witbooi in Gibeon." Pp. 180–91 in Zimmerer and Zeller 2003.

Kössler, Reinhart. 2005. *In Search of Survival and Dignity: Two Traditional Communities in Southern Namibia under South African Rule.* Windhoek: Gamsberg Macmillan.

Kolb, Peter. 1731. *The Present State of the Cape of Good-Hope.* 2nd ed. London: W. Innys and R. Manby.

Kolb, Peter. 1979. *Unter Hottentotten: 1705–1713.* Ed. Werner Jopp. Tübingen: Horst Erdmann Verlag.

Kolonko, Petra. 1997. "Wie die Hunnen es den Chinesen zeigten." *Frankfurter Allgemeine Zeitung,* March 8.

Komander, Gerhild H. M. 1994. *Das chinesische Haus im Park Sanssouci.* Berlin: JUP Industrie- und Presseklischee.

Kopytoff, Igor. 1986. "The Cultural Biography of Things: Commoditization as Process." Pp. 64–91 in *The Social Life of Things: Commodities in Cultural Perspective,* ed. Arjun Appadurai. Cambridge: Cambridge University Press.

Kotzebue, August von. [1789] 1800a. *The East Indian.* Pp. 2–88 in *The Dramatic Works of Baron Kotzebue,* vol. 2, trans. Charles Smith. New York: Stephen Stephens.

Kotzebue, August von. [1789] 1800b. *The Virgin of the Sun.* Pp. 1–62 in *The Dramatic Works of Baron Kotzebue,* vol. 2, trans. Charles Smith. New York: Stephen Stephens.

Kotzebue, August von. [1791] 1840. *Bruder Moritz, der Sonderling, oder: Die Colonie für die Pelew-Islend*. Pp. 73-186 in *Theater von August von Kotzebue*, vol. 3. Leipzig: Verlag von Eduard Kummer.

Kotzebue, August von. [1795] 1800. *Pizarro; or, The Spaniards in Peru*. Pp. 000-000 in *The Dramatic Works of Baron Kotzebue*, trans. Charles Smith. New York: Stephen Stephens.

Kotzebue, August von. [1796] 1840. *Die Negersklaven*. Pp. 155-244 in *Theater von August von Kotzebue*, vol. 5. Leipzig: Verlag von Eduard Kummer.

Kotzebue, August von. [1797] 1800. *La Peyrouse: A Comedy, in Two Acts*. Trans. Charles Smith. New York: Charles Smith and S. Stephens.

Kotzebue, August von. 1841. *La Peyrouse: Ein Schauspiel*. Pp. 29-62 in *Theater von August von Kotzebue*, vol. 37. Leipzig: Verlag von Eduard Kummer.

Krämer, Augustin. 1899. "Die samoanische Königsfrage im Hinblick auf die letzten Ereignisse zu Apia." *Globus* 75 (12): 185-89.

Krämer, Augustin. 1902. "Die Chinesengefahr in den deutschen Südsee-Kolonien." *Deutsche Kolonialzeitung* 19 (4): 30-31.

Krämer, Augustin. 1902-3. *Die Samoa-Inseln*. Stuttgart: E. Schweizerbartsche Verlagsbuchhandlung.

Krämer, Augustin. 1903. "Wechselbeziehungen ethnographischer und geographischer Forschung, nebst einige Bemerkungen zur Kartographie der Südsee." *Globus* 84 (23): 362-64.

Krämer, Augustin. 1904. "Zur Frage der Deportation der Hereros." *Deutsche Kolonialzeitung* 21 (21): 202-3.

Krämer, Augustin. 1906. *Hawaii, Ostmikronesien, und Samoa*. Stuttgart: Verlag von Strecker & Schröder.

Krämer, Augustin. 1908. "Studienreise nach den Zentral- und Westkarolinien." *Mitteilungen aus den deutschen Schutzgebieten* 21 (3): 169-86.

Krämer, Augustin. 1909a. "Gouvernementale Übergriffe in ethnographische Arbeitsgebiete und Mittel zur Abhilfe." *Globus* 96 (17): 264-66.

Krämer, Augustin. 1909b. "Samoa." Pp. 119-38 in *Die deutschen Kolonien*, vol. 2, ed. Kurd Schwabe. Berlin: Weller & Hüttich.

Krämer, Augustin. 1914. "Palau als Naturschutzpark." *Deutsche Kolonialzeitung* 31 (10): 159-61.

Krämer, Augustin. 1917. *Palau. Ergebnisse der Südsee-Expedition 1908-1910*, vol. II B 3, pt. 1. Hamburg, L. Friederichsen & Co.

Krämer, Augustin. 1923. *Salamasina: Bilder aus altsamoanischer Kultur und Geschichte*. Stuttgart: Strecker und Schröder.

Krämer, Augustin. 1994-95. *The Samoa Islands*. Honolulu: University of Hawai'i Press.

Krämer, Augustin, and Hans Nevermann. 1938. *Ralik-Ratak (Marshall-Inseln)*. Hamburg: Friederichsen, De Gruyter & Co.

Krämer-Bannow, Elisabeth. 1913. "Menschenschutz in unseren Kolonien." *Kosmos: Handweiser für Naturfreunde; Natur- und Heimatschutz* 10 (9): 353-60.

Krämer-Bannow, Elisabeth. n.d. [ca. 1913]. "Heimatschutz in die deutschen Kolonien!" *Dürer-Bund: Flugschrift zur Ausdruckskultur*, no. 117, pp. 1–7.

Krämer-Bannow, Elisabeth, and Augustin Krämer. 1916. *Bei kunstsinnigen Kannibalen der Südsee: Wanderungen auf Neu-Mecklenburg 1908–1909*. Berlin: D. Reimer.

Kraft, Rudolf. 1976. *Emin Pascha: Ein deutscher Arzt als Gouverneur von Äquatoria*. Darmstadt: Turris-Verlag.

Krammer, Otto. 1988. *Bildungswesen und Gegenreformation*. Würzburg: Gesellschaft für Deutsche Studentengeschichte, Archivverein der Markomannia.

Krebs, Gerhard. 1998. "Der Chor der Gefangenen: Die Verteidiger von Tsingtau in japanischen Lagern." Pp. 196–202 in Hinz and Lind 1998.

Kreissler, Françoise. 1989. *L'action culturelle allemande en Chine*. Paris: Edition de la Maison des Sciences de l'Homme.

Kretzschmar, E. 1853. *Südafrikanische Skizzen*. Leipzig: Verlag der J. C. Hinrichs'schen Buchhandlung.

Kreyher, J. 1863. *Die preussische Expedition nach Ostasien in den Jahren 1859–1862: Reisebilder aus Japan, China und Siam*. Hamburg: Rauheshaus.

Kriegk, Georg Ludwig. 1854. *Die Völkerstämme und ihre Zweige*. New ed. Frankfurt am Main: Heinrich Ludwig Brönner.

Kriegsgeschichtliche Abteilung I des Grossen Generalstabs. 1906–7. *Die Kämpfe der deutschen Truppen in Südwestafrika*. 2 vols. Berlin: Ernst Siegfried Mittler und Sohn.

Kristeva, Julia. 1982. *Powers of Horror*. New York: Columbia University Press.

Krönlein, Johann Georg. 1852. "Krönlein über Bersaba." *Berichte der Rheinischen Missionsgesellschaft* 9 (20): 314–19.

Kronecker, Franz. 1913. *Fünfzehn Jahre Kiautschou: Eine kolonialmedizinische Studie*. Berlin: J. Goldschmidt.

Krosigk, Klaus-Henning von. 1998. *Der Garten zu Britz*. Berlin: Hellmich PrePress & Print.

Krüger, Gesine. 1998. "Der deutsche Kolonialkrieg 1904–1907: Unterwerfung und Eigen-Sinn der Herero." Pp. 10–26 in *Überleben in Kriegen in Afrika*, ed. Helmut Bley and Gesine Krüger. Leipzig: Leipziger Universitätsbuchhandlung.

Krüger, Gesine. 1999. *Kriegsbewältigung und Kriegsbewußtsein*. Göttingen: Vandenhoeck & Ruprecht.

Krüger, Gesine. 2003. "Das goldene Zeitalter der Viehzüchter: Namibia im 19. Jahrhundert." Pp. 13–25 in Zimmerer and Zeller 2003.

Krusenstern, Adam Johann von. [1813] 1969. *Voyage round the World in the Years 1803, 1804, 1805, and 1806*. N. Israel/Da Capo.

Ku, Hung-Ming [Gu Hongming]. 1901. *Papers from a Viceroy's Yamen*. Shanghai: Shanghai Mercury.

Ku, Hung-Ming [Gu Hongming]. 1911. *Chinas Verteidigung gegen europäische Ideen*. Jena: E. Diederichs.

Küas, Richard. 1939. *Togo-Erinnerungen*. Berlin: Wegweiser-Verlag.

Külz, Wilhelm. 1909. *Deutsch-Südafrika im 25. Jahre deutscher Schutzherrschaft.* Berlin: W. Süsserott.

Kuepers, Jacobus Joannes Antonius Mathias. 1974. *China und die katholische Mission in Süd-Shantung 1882-1900: Die Geschichte einer Konfrontation.* Steyl: Drukkerij van het Missiehuis Steyl.

Kürschner, Joseph, ed. 1901. *China.* 3 vols. Leipzig: Zieger.

Kuo, Heng-yü, ed. 1986. *Von der Kolonialpolitik zur Kooperation: Studien zur Geschichte der deutsch-chinesischen Beziehungen.* Munich: Minerva.

Kuo, Heng-yü, ed. 1987. *Berlin und China.* Berlin: Colloquium Verlag.

Kuo, Heng-yü, and Mechthild Leutner, eds. 1986. *Beiträge zu den deutsch-chinesischen Beziehungen.* Munich: Minerva Publikation.

Kuo, Heng-yü, and Mechthild Leutner, eds. 1991. *Deutsch-chinesischen Beziehungen vom. 19. Jahrhundert bis zur Gegenwart.* Munich: Minerva Publikation.

Kuo, Heng-yü, and Mechthild Leutner, eds. 1994. *Deutschland und China.* Munich: Minerva Publikation.

Labisch, Alfons. 1986. "Hygiene ist Moral—Moral ist Hygiene." Pp. 265-85 in *Soziale Sicherheit und soziale Disziplinierung,* ed. Christoph Sachße and Florian Tennstedt. Frankfurt am Main: Suhrkamp.

Lacan, Jacques. [1949] 1977. "The Mirror Stage as Formative of the Function of the I." Pp. 1-7 in *Ecrits.* New York: Norton.

Lacan, Jacques. 1991. *The Seminar of Jacques Lacan.* Bk. 1, *Freud's Papers on Technique, 1953-1954.* New York: W. W. Norton and Co.

Lach, Donald F. 1953. "The Sinophilism of Christian Wolff (1679-1754)." *Journal of the History of Ideas* 14 (October): 561-74.

Lach, Donald F., and Edwin Kley. 1965-93. *Asia in the Making of Europe.* 4 vols. in 9. Chicago: University of Chicago Press.

Laclau, Ernesto, and Chantal Mouffe. 1985. *Hegemony and Socialist Strategy.* London: Verso.

Lafond de Lurcy, Gabriel. 1845. "Quelques semaines dans les archipels de Samoa et Viti." *Bulletin de la Société de Géographie,* ser. 3, 3 (January): 1-30.

Lagache, Daniel. 1961. "La psychanalyse et la structure de la personnalité." *La Psychanalyse* 6:5-58.

Laitin, David D. 1986. *Hegemony and Culture: Politics and Religious Change among the Yoruba.* Chicago: University of Chicago Press.

Lange, Lorenz . [1722] 1968. "Journal of Laurence Lange's Travels to China." Pp. 3-40 in *The Present State of Russia,* by Friedrich Christian Weber, vol. 2. London: Cass.

Langhansz, Christoph. 1705. *Neue Ost-Indische Reise, worinnen umständlich beschrieben werden unterschiedene Küsten und Inseln in Ost-Indien* . . . Leipzig: Michael Rohrlachs.

Lapérouse, Jean-François de Galaup, comte de. 1799. *Voyage de La Pérouse autour du monde,* Vol. 2. Ed. M. L. A. Milet-Mureau. London: A. Hamilton.

La Pérouse, Jean-François de Galaup, comte de. 1994–95. *The Journal of Jean-François de Galaup de la Pérouse, 1785–1788*. Trans. and ed. John Dunmore. London: Hakluyt Society.

Laplanche J., and J.-B. Pontalis. 1973. *The Language of Psychoanalysis*. New York: W. W. Norton and Co.

Larrimore, Mark. 2000. "Orientalism and Antivoluntarism in the History of Ethics: On Christian Wolff's *Oratorio de Sinarum philosophica practica*." *Journal of Religious Ethics* 28 (2): 189–219.

Laske, Friedrich. 1909. *Der ostasiatische Einfluss auf die Baukunst des Abendlandes, vornehmlich Deutschlands, im 18. Jahrhundert*. Berlin: W. Ernst.

Lau, Brigitte. 1979. "A Critique of the Historical Sources and Historiography Relating to the 'Damaras' in Pre-colonial Namibia." B.A. thesis, University of Cape Town.

Lau, Brigitta [*sic*]. 1981. "'Thank God the Germans Came': Vedder and Namibian History." Pp. 24–53 in *Africa Seminar: Collected Papers*, vol. 2, ed. K. Gottschalk and C. Saunders. Cape Town: Centre for African Studies.

Lau, Brigitte. 1987a. "The Emergence of Kommando Politics in Namaland, southern Namibia, 1800–1870." M.A. thesis, University of Cape Town.

Lau, Brigitte. 1987b. *Southern and Central Namibia in Jonker Afrikaner's Time*. Windhoek: National Archives.

Lau, Brigitte. 1995a. "Concerning the Hendrik Witbooi Papers." Pp. 17–37 in *History and Historiography*, ed. Annemarie Heywood. Windhoek: Discourse/ MSORP.

Lau, Brigitte. 1995b. "Uncertain Histories: The Herero-German War of 1904." Pp. 39–52 in *History and Historiography*, ed. Annemarie Heywood. Windhoek: Discourse/MSORP.

Laux, Claire. 2000. *Les théocraties missionaries en Polynésie (Tahiti, Hawaii, Cook, Tonga, Gambier, Wallis et Futuna) au XIXe siècle*. Paris: L'Harmattan.

Lawson, Tony. 1998. "Economic Science without Experimentation/Abstraction." Pp. 144–85 in *Critical Realism, Essential Readings*, ed. Roy Bhaskar, Andrew Collier, Tony Lawson, Margaret Archer, and Alan Norrie. London: Routledge.

Lawson, Tony. 1999. "Feminism, Realism, and Universalism." *Feminist Economics* 5 (2): 25–59.

League of Nations. 1922. *Statut national des habitants des territoires sous mandats B et C*. Lausanne: Imp. Réunies.

Leclerc, Gerard. 1972. *Anthropologie et colonialisme*. Paris: Fayard.

Le Cour Grandmaison, Olivier. 2005. *Coloniser, exterminer: Sur la guerre et l'état colonial*. Paris: Fayard.

Lee, En-Hah. 1977. *China's Quest for Railway Autonomy, 1904–1911: A Study of the Chinese Railway-Rights Recovery Movement*. Singapore: Singapore University Press.

Lefebvre, Henri. 2003. "Space and the State." Pp. 84–100 in *State/Space: A Reader*, ed. Bob Jessop, Martin Jones, Neil Brenner, and Gordon Macleod. London: Blackwell.

Legassick, Martin. 1979. "The Northern Frontier to c. 1820: The Rise and Decline of the Griqua People." Pp. 358-420 in *The Shaping of South African Society, 1652-1820*, ed. Richard Elphick and Hermann Giliomee. Middletown, Conn.: Wesleyan University Press.

Legère, Karsten. 1988. "C. G. Büttner und die 'Zeitschrift für afrikanische Sprachen.'" *Asien, Afrika, Lateinamerika* 16 (6): 1036-48.

Lehmann, F. Rudolf. 1951. "Die Häuptlings-Erbfolgeordnung der Herero." *Zeitschrift für Ethnographie* 27:94-102.

Lehner, Georg. 2002. *Österreich-Ungarn und der "Boxeraufstand" in China*. Innsbruck: StudienVerlag.

Lei, Xianglin. 1999. "When Chinese Medicine Encountered the State, 1910-1949." Ph.D. diss., University of Chicago.

Leiris, Michel. 1950. "L'ethnographie devant le colonialisme." *Les temps modernes*, no. 58:357-74.

Leibniz, Gottfried Wilhelm. 1990. *Leibniz korrespondiert mit China*. Ed. Rita Widmaier. Frankfurt am Main: Vittorio Klostermann.

Leibniz, Gottfried Wilhelm. 1994. *Writings on China*. Ed. Daniel J. Cook and Henry Rosemont, Jr. Chicago: Open Court.

Lemkin, Raphaël. 1944. *Axis Rule in Occupied Europe*. Washington, D.C.: Carnegie Endowment for International Peace, Division of International Law.

Lepsius, Johannes, Albrecht Mendelssohn Bartholdy, and Friedrich Thimme, eds. 1922-27. *Die Grosse Politik der europäischen Kabinette 1871-1914*. 40 vols. Berlin: Deutsche Verlagsgesellschaft für Politik.

Lessing, Ferdinand, and Hartmut Walravens. 2000. *Ferdinand Lessing (1882-1961)*. Osnabrück: Zeller.

Lesson, Pierre Adolphe. 1880-84. *Les Polynésiens*. Paris: Ernest Leroux.

Leupold, Bernd. 1998. "Chinesen unter deutschem Recht: Das Justizwesen im Schutzgebiet." Pp. 143-45 in Hinz and Lind 1998.

Leutner, Mechthild. 1987. "Sinologie in Berlin: Die Durchsetzung einer wissenschaftliche Disziplin zur Erschließund und zum Verständnis Chinas." Pp. 31-56 in Kuo 1987.

Leutner, Mechthild, ed. 1997. *Musterkolonie Kiautschou*. Berlin: Akademie Verlag.

Leutwein, Paul. 1909. *Du weitest Deine Brust. Der Blick wird freier*. Berlin: Deutscher Kolonial-Verlag.

Leutwein, Paul. 1934. *Theodor Leutwein, der Eroberer Deutsch-Südwestafrikas*. Lübeck: Coleman.

Leutwein, Theodor. 1894. "Ueber die letzten Kämpfe mit Hendrik Witbooi." *Militärwochenblatt*, Beilage zu Nr. 97, November 17, pp. 2565-76.

Leutwein, Theodor. 1898. *Deutsch-Südwestafrika: Vortrag*. Berlin: Abteilung Berlin-Charlottenburg der deutschen Kolonialgesellschaft.

Leutwein, Theodor. 1898-99. "Die Kämpfe der Kaiserlichen Schutztruppe in Deutsch-Südwestafrika in den Jahren 1894-1896, sowie die sich hieraus uns ergebenden Lehren: Vortrag." *Militärwochenblatt*, Beiheft 1:1-30.

Leutwein, Theodor. 1907a. *Elf Jahre Gouverneur in Deutsch-Südwestafrika*. Berlin: Ernst Siegfried Mittler und Sohn.

Leutwein, Theodor. 1907b. "Der Aufstand in Deutsch-Südwestafrika und die Schutzverträge." *Deutsche Revue* 35:102–14.

Leutwein, Theodor. 1909. "Die Rassenfrage in den Kolonien." *Die Umschau* 13 (15): 311–14.

Leutwein, Theodor. 1912. *Die Kämpfe mit Hendrik Witbooi 1894 und Witbois Ende*. Voigtländers Quellenbücher, vol. 5. Leipzig: Voigtländer.

Le Vaillant, François. 1790. *Travels from the Cape of Good Hope into the Interior Parts of Africa*. London: William Lane.

Le Vaillant, François. 1796. *New Travels into the Interior parts of Africa by the Way of the Cape of Good Hope*. London: G. G. and J. Robinson.

Levi, Margaret. 1981. "A Predatory Theory of Rule." *Politics and Society* 10 (4): 431–66.

Levy, Steven T., and Lawrence B. Inderbitzin. 2001. "Fantasy and Psychoanalytic Discourse." *International Journal of Psychoanalysis* 82:795–803.

Li, Changke. 1992. *Der China-Roman in der deutschen Literatur 1890–1930*. Regensburg: S. Roderer Verlag.

Lichtenstein, Hinrich. [1811–12] 1967. *Reisen im südlichen Afrika in den Jahren 1803, 1804, 1805 und 1806*. 2 vols. Stuttgart: F. A. Brockhaus.

Liebersohn, Harry. 1999. "Images of Monarchy: Kamehameha I and the Art of Louis Choris." Pp. 44–64 in *Double Vision: Art Histories and Colonial Histories in the Pacific*, ed. Nicholas Thomas and Diane Losche. Cambridge: Cambridge University Press.

Liebersohn, Harry. 2003. "Coming of Age in the Pacific: German Ethnography from Chamisso to Krämer." Pp. 31–46 in *Worldly Provincialism: German Anthropology in the Age of Empire*, ed. H. Glenn Penny and Matti Bunzl. Ann Arbor: University of Michigan Press.

Lind, Christoph. 1998. "Heimatliches Idyll und kolonialer Herrschaftsanspruch: Architektur in Tsingtau." Pp. 96–105 in Hinz and Lind 1998.

Lindenberg, Paul. 1900. *Um die Erde in Wort und Bild*. Berlin: F. Dümmler.

Lindqvist, Sven. 1996. *"Exterminate All the Brutes."* New York: New Press.

Lindsay, Hugh Hamilton, and Friedrich August Gützlaff. 1833. *Report of Proceedings on a Voyage to the Northern Ports of China in the Ship Lord Amherst*. London: B. Fellowes.

Linné [Linnaeus]. [1735] 1806. *A General System of Nature*. 7 vols. London: Lackington.

Linnekin, Jocelyn. 1990. "Fine Mats and Money: Contending Exchange Paradigms in Colonial Samoa." *Anthropological Quarterly* 63 (October):1–13.

Linnekin, Jocelyn. 1991a. "Ignoble Savages and Other European Visions: The La Perouse Affair in Samoan History." *Journal of Pacific History* 26 (1): 3–26.

Linnekin, Jocelyn. 1991b. "Structural History and Political Economy: The Contact Encounter in Hawai'i and Samoa." *History and Anthropology* 5:205–32.

LiPuma, Edward, and Benjamin Lee. 2005. "Financial Derivatives and the Rise of Circulation." *Economy and Society* 34 (3): 404-27.

Liu, Jianhui. 2005. "Inherited Urban Memories: The Formation of Modern Urban Space in Dalian and Its Transformations." Paper delivered at the conference "Comparative Modernisms: Empire, Aesthetics, and History," Tsinghua University, Beijing, August 3-6.

Liu, Lydia. 1999a. "The Desire for the Sovereign and the Logic of Reciprocity in the Family of Nations." *Diacritics* 29 (4): 150-77.

Liu, Lydia. 1999b. "Legislating the Universal: The Circulation of International Law in the Nineteenth Century." Pp. 127-64 in *Tokens of Exchange*, ed. Lydia Liu. Durham, N.C.: Duke University Press.

Liu, Lydia. 2004. *The Clash of Empires*. Cambridge, Mass.: Harvard University Press.

Liu Shanzhang and Zhou Quan, eds. 1991. *Zhong De guanxi shi wencong* [Collected Essays on the History of Chinese-German Relations]. Qingdao Shi: Qingdao chu ban she.

Liu, Xinwu. 1986. "Die Forschungsreisen Ferdinand von Richthofens in China." Pp. 9-33 in Kuo 1986.

Lloyd, Christopher. 1970. *Mr. Barrow of the Admiralty*. London: Collins.

Lloyd, Jill. 1991. *German Expressionism: Primitivism and Modernity*. New Haven, Conn.: Yale University Press.

Lo, Jung-pang. 1967. *K'ang Yu-wei*. Tucson: Published for the Association for Asian Studies by University of Arizona Press.

Lodewycksz, Willem. 1915. *De eerste schipvaart der Nederlanders naar Oost-Indië onder Cornelis de Houtman, 1595-1597*. Bk. 1. Ed. G. P. Rouffaer and J. W. Ijzerman. Werken uitgegeven door de Linschoten-vereeniging, vol. 7. The Hague: M. Nijhoff.

Löbbecke, Robert. 1982. *Ein Westfale in China*. Ed. Götz Bettge. Münster: Westfälisches Archivamt.

Lösch, Niels C. 1997. *Rasse als Konstrukt: Leben und Werk Eugen Fischers*. Frankfurt am Main: Peter Lang.

Loh-Loh, John. 1982. "The Image of China in the Literature of Wilhelmine Germany." Ph.D. diss., University of Pittsburgh.

Lonsdale, John. 1981. "States and Social Processes in Africa: A Historiographical Survey." *African Studies Review* 24 (2-3): 139-225.

Loth, Heinrich. 1963. *Die christliche Mission in Südwestafrika*. Berlin: Akademie-Verlag.

Loti, Pierre. [1879] 1976. *The Marriage of Loti*. Honolulu: University Press of Hawaii.

Louis, William Roger. 1963. *Ruanda-Urundi, 1884-1919*. Oxford: Clarendon Press.

Louis, William Roger. 1967. *Great Britain and Germany's Lost Colonies, 1914-1919*. Oxford: Clarendon Press.

Love, Jacob Wainwright. 1991. *Samoan Variations*. New York: Garland Publishing.

Lovejoy, Arthur O. [1936] 1964. *The Great Chain of Being.* Cambridge, Mass.: Harvard University Press.

Lovejoy, Arthur O. 1955. "The Supposed Primitivism of Rousseau's *Discourse on Inequality.*" Pp. 14–37 in *Essays in the History of Ideas.* New York: Braziller.

Loveman, Mara. 2001. "Nation-State Building, 'Race,' and the Production of Official Statistics: Brazil in Comparative Perspective." Ph.D. diss., University of California, Los Angeles.

Lovett, Richard. 1899. *The History of the London Missionary Society, 1795–1895.* London: H. Frowde.

Lu, May, and David Lu. 2005. *Qingdao Old Postcards.* Qingdao: Qingdao Publishing House.

Luan Baode. 1982. "Deguoren zai Qingdao ban jiaoyu de pianduan huiyi" [Fragments of Memories of the Schools Founded by the Germans in Qingdao]. Pp. 223–30 in *Wenshi ziliao xuanji* [Selected Materials on History and Literature], vol. 1. Ji'nan.

Ludloff, R. F. 1891. *Nach Deutsch-Namaland (Südwestafrika): Reisebriefe von Dr. R. Ludloff.* Berlin: Ditz'sche Hofbuchdruckerei.

Lüderitz, Adolf. 1945. *Die Erschließung von Deutsch-Südwest-Afrika durch Adolf Lüderitz: Akten, Briefe und Denkschriften.* Ed. C. A. Lüderitz. Oldenburg: Gerhard Stalling.

Luhmann, Niklas. 1989. *Ecological Communication.* Chicago: University of Chicago Press.

Lukács, Georg. [1954] 1973. *Die Zerstörung der Vernunft.* Darmstadt: Luchterhand.

Lundtofte, Henrik. 2003. "'I believe that the nation as such must be annihilated . . .': The Radicalization of the German Suppression of the Herero Rising in 1904." Pp. 15–53 in *Genocide,* ed. Steven L. B. Jensen and Gwynneth Llewellyn. Copenhagen: Danish Center for Holocaust and Genocide Studies.

Luschan, Felix von. 1906. "Bericht über eine Reise in Südafrika." *Verhandlungen der Berliner Gesellschaft für Anthropologie, Ethnologie und Urgeschichte* 38:863–66.

Luschan, Felix von. [1909] 1911. "Anthropological View of Race." Pp. 13–24 in *Papers on Inter-racial Problems,* ed. G. Spiller. London: P. S. King.

Maas, Otto. 1932. "Die Franziskanermission in China während des 18. Jahrhunderts." *Zeitschrift für Missionswissenschaft und Religionswissenschaft* 22:225–49.

Macartney, George Macartney, Earl. 1962. *An Embassy to China.* Ed. J. L. Cranmer-Byng. London: Longmans.

Macey, David. 2000. *Frantz Fanon: A Biography.* New York: Picador.

Mack Smith, Denis. 1976. *Mussolini's Roman Empire.* New York: Viking Press.

Magalhaes, Gabriel de. 1688. *A New History of China Containing a Description of the Most Considerable Particulars of that Vast Empire.* London: Thomas Newborough.

Mageo, Jeanette Marie. 1988. "Mālosi: A Psychological Explantion of Mead's and Freeman's Work and of Samoan Aggression." *Pacific Studies* 11 (2): 25–65.

Mageo, Jeanette Marie. 1994. "Hairdos and Don't's: Symbolism and Sexual History in Samoa." *Man,* n.s., 29 (2): 407–32.

Mageo, Jeanette Marie. 1998. *Theorizing Self in Samoa*. Ann Arbor: University of Michigan Press.

Maître, Jacques, 1994. "Avant-propos avec Pierre Bourdieu." Pp. v–xxii in *L'autobiographie d'un paranoïaque*. Paris: Anthropos.

Malek, Roman, ed. 1998. *Western Learning and Christianity in China*. Sankt Augustin: China-Zentrum.

Mandair, Arvind. 2006. "Hegel's Excess: Indology, Historical Difference, and the Post-secular Turn of Theory." *Postcolonial Studies* 9 (1): 15–34.

Mandeville, John. 1983. *The Travels of Sir John Mandeville*. London: Penguin.

Mann, Kristin, and Richard Roberts, eds. *Law in Colonial Africa*. Portsmouth, N.H.: Heinemann.

Mann, Michael. 1986–93. *The Sources of Social Power*. 2 vols. New York: Cambridge University Press.

Mann, Michael. 2003. *Incoherent Empire*. New York: Verso.

Marais, Johannes S. [1939] 1957. *The Cape Coloured People, 1652–1937*. Johannesburg: Witwatersrand University Press.

Marchal, Jules. 1996. *L'état libre du Congo*. 2 vols. Borgloon: Bellings.

Margueron, Daniel. 1989. *Tahiti dans toute sa littérature: Essai sur Tahiti et ses îles dans la littérature française de la découverte à nos jours*. Paris: L'Harmattan.

Marin, Aylic [Édouard Petit]. 1888. *En Océanie*. Paris: Charles Bayle.

Maron, Hermann. 1863. *Japan und China: Reiseskizzen entworfen während der preussischen Expedition nach Ost-Asien*. Berlin: Druck und Verlag von O. Janke.

Marques, A. 1889. *Iles Samoa*. Lisbon: Imprimerie nationale.

Marsack, C. C. 1958. *Notes on the Practices of the Court and the Principles Adopted in the Hearing of Cases affecting (1) Samoan Matai Titles; and (2) Land Held according to Customs and Usages of Western Samoa*. Apia: Land and Titles Court.

Marshall, P. J. 1993. "Britain and China in the Late Eighteenth Century." Pp. 11–29 in *Ritual and Diplomacy: The Macartney Mission to China, 1792–1794*, ed. Robert A. Bickers. London: British Association for Chinese Studies and Wellsweep.

Martin, Bernd. 1988. "The Prussian Expedition to the Far East (1860–1862)." *Newsletter for Modern Chinese History* 6:38–52.

Martin, Bernd. 1991. "Die preußische Ostasienexpedition in China: Zur Vorgeschichte der Freundschafts-, Handels- und Schiffahrts-Vertrages vom 2. September 1861." Pp. 209–40 in Kuo and Leutner 1991.

Martin, Bernd. 1994. "'Governement Jiaozhou': Forschungsstand und Archivebestände zum deutschen Pachtgebiet Qingdao (Tsingtao) 1897–1914." Pp. 375–97 in Kuo and Leutner 1994.

Martin, Peter. 1993. *Schwarze Teufel, edle Mohren*. Hamburg: Junius.

Martini, Martinus. 1654a. *Bellum tartaricum: Or, The Conquest of the Great and most Renowned Empire of China, by the Invasion of the Tartars*. London: J. Crook.

Martini, Martinus. 1654b. *Zeitung auss der newen Welt oder Chinesischen Königreichen*. Augsburg: Andream Aperger.

Marx, Christoph. 1999. "'Die im Dunkeln sieht man nicht': Kriegsgefangenen im Burenkrieg 1899-1902." Pp. 255-76 in *In der Hand des Feindes,* ed. Rüdiger Overmans. Cologne: Böhlau.

Marx, Karl. 1969a. *Karl Marx on Colonialism and Modernization.* Ed. Schlomo Avineri. Garden City, N.Y.: Anchor Books.

Marx, Karl. 1969b. "Chinese Affairs (July 7, 1862, *Die Presse*)." Pp. 442-44 in K. Marx 1969a.

Marx, Karl. 1969c. "Revolution in China and in Europe (June 14, 1853, *New York Daily Tribune*)." Pp. 67-75 in K. Marx 1969a.

Marx, Karl. 1977. *Capital.* Vol. I. Trans. Ben Fowkes. New York: Vintage Books.

Marx, Karl, and Friedrich Engels. 1972. *On Colonialism.* New York: International.

Mather, Cotton. [1692] 1950. *On Witchcraft.* Mount Vernon, N.Y.: Peter Pauper Press.

Matzat, Wilhelm. 1985. *Die Tsingtauer Landordung des Chinesenkommissars Wilhelm Schrameier.* Bonn: Selbstverlag des Herausgebers.

Matzat, Wilhelm. 1986. "Wilhelm Schrameier und die Landordnung in Qingdao." Pp. 33-65 in Kuo and Leutner 1986.

Matzat, Wilhelm. 1998a. "Alltagsleben im Schutzgebiet: Zivilisten und Militärs, Chinesen und Deutsche." Pp. 106-20 in Hinz and Lind 1998.

Matzat, Wilhelm. 1998b. *Neue Materialien zu den Aktivitäten des Chinesenkommissars Wilhelm Schrameier in Tsingtau.* Bonn: Selbstverlag des Herausgebers.

Maugham, W. Somerset. 1977. "Mackintosh." Pp. 144-74 in *Collected Short Stories.* New York: Penguin.

Maukisch, Heinrich Eduard. 1836. *Reise in die Ferne oder Vater Reinhold's Mittheilungen über die Erde und ihre Bewohner.* Leipzig: Verlag von J. G. Taubert.

Mauss, Marcel. 1967. *The Gift.* New York: W. W. Norton.

May, Karl. 1889. *Der blaurote Methusalem.* Wien: Verlag Carl Ueberreuter.

May, Karl. 1901. *Et in terra pax.* Pp. 1-288 in Kürschner 1901, vol. 3.

May, Karl. [1894] 1954. *Am stillen Ozean.* Wien: Verlag Carl Ueberreuter.

McClintock, Anne. 1995. *Imperial Leather.* London: Routledge.

McGregor, G. D. L., and H. H. P. Häberling. 1991. *Die Eingeborenen-Passmarken in Deutsch Südwest Afrika: The Native Pass Tokens of German South West Africa.* Windhoek: G. D. L. McGregor, 1991.

McKiernan, Gerald. 1954. *The Narrative and Journal of Gerald McKiernan in South West Africa, 1874-1879.* Cape Town: Van Riebeeck Society.

McMurray, Jonathan S. 2001. *Distant Ties: Germany, the Ottoman Empire, and the Construction of the Baghdad Railway.* Westport, Conn.: Praeger.

Mead, Margaret. [1928] 1973. *Coming of Age in Samoa.* New York: William Morrow.

Mead, Margaret. 1972. *Blackberry Winter.* New York: William Morrow.

Meade, Herbert George Philip, and Sir Robert Henry Meade. 1871. *A Ride through the Disturbed Districts of New Zealand: Together with Some Accounts of the South Sea Islands: Being Selections from the Journals and Letters of Lieut. the Hon. Herbert Meade, R.N.: Edited by His Brother.* 2nd ed. London: John Murray.

Meinecke, Carl E. 1875-76. *Die Inseln des Stillen Oceans*. 2 vols. Leipzig: Verlag von Paul Frohberg.

Meine Kriegs-Erlebnisse in Deutsch-Süd-West-Afrika: Von einem Offizier der Schutztruppe. 1907. Minden in Westfalen: Wilhelm Köhler.

Meiners, Christoph. 1778. *Abhandlungen Sinesischer Jesuiten*. Leipzig: In der Weygandschen Buchhandlung.

Meiners, Christoph. 1795-96. *Betrachtungen über die Fruchtbarkeit, oder Unfruchtbarkeit, über den vormahligen und gegenwärtigen Zustand der vornehmsten Länder in Asien*. 2 vols. Lübeck: Bohn und Compagnie.

Meiners, Christoph. 1811-15. *Untersuchungen über die Verschiedenheiten der Menschenarten*. 3 vols. Tübingen: J. B. Cotta.

Meister, Friedrich. 1903. *Hung Li Tscheng oder der Drache am gelben Meer*. Berlin: Brandus'sche Buchhandlung.

Meister, Friedrich. 1904. *Muhrero rikrera! (Nimm dich in acht, Herero!), oder die Schiffsfähnriche*. Leipzig: Verlag von Abel & Müller.

Meister, Georg. 1692. *Die orientalisch-indianische Kunst und Lustgärtner*. Dresden: C. Hekel.

Melber, Henning. 1985. "Namibia: The German Roots of Apartheid." *Race and Class* 27 (1): 63-77.

Meleisea, Malama. 1980. "We Want the Forest, yet Fear the Spirits: Culture and Change in Western Samoa." *Pacific Perspectives* 9 (1): 21-29.

Meleisea, Malama. 1987a. *The Making of Modern Samoa*. Suva, Fiji: Institute of Pacific Studies of the University of the South Pacific.

Meleisea, Malama. 1987b. *Lagaga: A Short History of Western Samoa*. Suva, Fiji: University of the South Pacific.

Meleisea, Malama. 1992. *Change and Adaptations in Western Samoa*. Christchurch, New Zealand: Macmillan Brown Centre.

Meleisea, Malama. 1999. "The Postmodern Legacy of a Premodern Warrior Goddess in Modern Samoa." Pp. 55-60 in *Voyages and Beaches: Pacific Encounters, 1769-1840*, ed. Alex Calder, Jonathan Lamb, and Bridget Orr. Honolulu: University of Hawai'i Press.

Melville, Herman. [1846] 1996. *Typee*. New York: Penguin.

Memmi, Albert. [1965] 1991. *The Colonizer and the Colonized*. Boston: Beacon Press.

Mendoza, Juan Gonzalez de. 1853. *The History of the Great and Mighty Kingdom of China*. 2 vols. London: Hakluyt Society.

Mentzel, Christian. 1696. *Kurtze chinesische Chronologia oder Zeit-Register*. Berlin: Johann Michael Rüdiger.

Menzel, Gustav. 1992. *C. G. Büttner*. Wuppertal: Verlag der Vereinigten Evangelischen Mission.

Menzel, Gustav. 2000. *Wiederstand und Gottesfurcht: Hendrik Witbooi—eine Biographie in zeitgenössischen Quellen*. Cologne: Rüdiger Köppe Verlag.

Merensky, Alexander. 1875a. "Vortrag über die Hottentotten." *Verhandlungen der Berliner Gesellschaft für Anthropologie, Ethnologie und Urgeschichte* 7:18-24.

Merensky, Alexander. 1875b. *Beiträge zur Kenntnis Südafrikas*. Berlin: Verlag des Missionshauses.

Merensky, Alexander. [1886] 1912. *Wie erzieht man am besten den Neger zur Plangenarbeit?* Berlin: Süsserott.

Merensky, Alexander. [1899] 1996. *Erinnerungen aus dem Missionsleben in Transvaal (Südafrika), 1859 bis 1882*. Ed. Ulrich van der Heyden. Berlin: Edition Ost.

Merensky, Alexander. 1906. "Die äthiopische Bewegung unter den eingeborenen Christen Südafrikas." Pp. 538–52 in *Verhandlungen des Deutschen Kolonialkongresses 1905 zu Berlin am 5., 6., und 7. Oktober 1905*, ed. Redaktionsausschuss. Berlin: Dietrich Reimer.

Mergner, Gottfried. 1988. "Solidarität mit den 'Wilden'? Das Verhältnis der deutschen Sozialdemokratie zu den afrikanischen Widerstandskämpfen in den ehemaligen deutschen Kolonien um die Jahrhundertwende. Pp. 68–86 in *Internationalism in the Labor Movement 1830–1940*, ed. Frits van Holthoon and Marcel van der Linden. Leiden: Brill.

Merians, Linda E. 1998. "'Hottentot': The Emergence of an Early Modern Racist Epithet." *Shakespeare Studies* 26:123–44.

Meyer, Thomas, and Alfred von Kiderlen-Wächter. 1996. *Endlich eine Tat, eine befreiende Tat . . .* Husum: Matthiesen.

Michael, M. 1986. "Zur Entsendung einer deutschen Expeditionstruppe nach China während des Boxeraufstandes." Pp. 141–61 in Kuo 1986.

Michaelis, Rainer. 1999. *Fridericiana: Christian Bernhardt Rode (1725–1797)*. Berlin: Staatliche Museen zu Berlin.

Mielke, Andreas. 1993. *Laokoon und die Hottentotten, oder, Über die Grenzen von Reisebeschreibung und Satire*. Baden Baden: Koerner.

Miles, William F. S. 1994. *Hausaland Divided*. Ithaca, N.Y.: Cornell University Press.

Minamiki, George. 1985. *The Chinese Rites Controversy*. Chicago: Loyola University Press.

Mitchell, Timothy. 1988. *Colonizing Egypt*. Berkeley: University of California Press.

Mitchell, Timothy. 1991. "The Limits of the State: Beyond Statist Approaches and their Critics." *American Political Science Review* 85 (1): 77–96.

Mitchell, Timothy. 2002. "McJihad: Islam in the U.S. Global Order." *Social Text* 20, no. 4 (73): 1–18.

Moerenhout, J.-A. 1837. *Voyages aux îles du Grand océan*. Paris: A. Bertrand.

Moffat, Robert. 1842. *Missionary Labours and Scenes in Southern Africa*. London: J. Snow.

Mogk, Walter. 1972. *Paul Rohrbach und das "Größere Deutschland."* Munich: W. Goldmann.

Mohr, F. W. 1911. *Handbuch für das Schutzgebiet Kiautschou*. Leipzig: Köhler.

Moi, Toril. 1994. *Simone de Beauvoir: The Making of an Intellectual Woman*. Oxford: Blackwell.

Moltke, Helmuth Johannes Ludwig von. 1922. *Erinnerungen, Briefe, Dokumente, 1877–1916*. Stuttgart: Der Kommende Tag.

Mommsen, Wolfgang J., and Jürgen Osterhammel, eds. 1986. *Imperialism and After*. London: Allen and Unwin.

Mommsen, Wolfgang J., and J. A. de Moor, eds. *European Expansion and Law*. Oxford: Berg.

Montaigne, Michel de. [1580] 1958a. "On Experience." Pp. 343–406 in *Essays*. Harmondsworth: Penguin.

Montaigne, Michel de. [1580] 1958b. "On Cannibals." Pp. 105–18 in *Essays*. Harmondsworth: Penguin.

Montanus, Arnoldus. 1671. *Atlas Chinensis*. London: T. Johnson.

Montesquieu, Charles-Louis Secondat, baron de. 1949. *The Spirit of the Laws*. New York: Hafner Publishing Company.

Moodie, Donald, ed. and trans. [1838] 1960. *The Record; or, A Series of Official Papers Relative to the Condition and Treatment of the Native Tribes of South Africa*. Amsterdam: A. A. Balkema.

Moorehead, Alan. [1966] 2000. *The Fatal Impact*. New York: Barnes and Noble Books.

Moors, H. J. 1986. *Some Recollections of Early Samoa*. N.p.: Western Samoa Historical and Cultural Trust.

Mootz, Heinrich. 1901. *Die Namen der Orte in Deutsch-Schantung*. 2nd ed. Tsingtau: Missionsdruckerei.

Morgenroth, Wolfgang. 1990. "Das Seminar für orientalische Sprachen in der Wissenschaftstradition der Sektion Asienwissenschaften der Humboldt Universität zu Berlin." Pp. 6–30 in *Das "Seminar für Orientalische Sprachen" in der Wissenschaftstradition der Sektion Asienwissenschaften der Humboldt-Universität zu Berlin*, ed. Hannelore Bernhardt. Berlin: Humboldt-Universität.

Moritz, Eduard. 1912. "Die ältesten Reiseberichte über Deutsch-Südwestafrika." Pt. 1. *Mitteilungen aus den deutschen Schutzgebieten* 25 (4): 161–268.

Moritz, Eduard. 1916. "Die ältesten Reiseberichte über Deutsch-Südwestafrika." Pt. 2. *Mitteilungen aus den deutschen Schutzgebieten* 29 (4): 136–253.

Moritz, Eduard. 1918. "Die ältesten Reiseberichte über Deutsch-Südwestafrika." Pt. 3. *Mitteilungen aus den deutschen Schutzgebieten* 31 (1): 60–143.

Moses, John A. 1972. "The Solf Regime in Samoa: Ideal and Reality." *New Zealand Journal of History* 6 (1): 42–56.

Moses, John A. 1977. "The Coolie Labour Question and German Colonial Policy in Samoa, 1900–14." Pp. 234–62 in *Germany in the Pacific and Far East, 1870–1914*, ed. John A. Moses and Paul M. Kennedy. St. Lucia: University of Queensland Press.

Mosse, George L. 1985. *Toward the Final Solution*. Madison: University of Wisconsin Press.

Mossop, E. E., ed. and trans. 1935. *The Journal of Hendrik Jacob Wikar (1779)*. Cape Town: Van Riebeeck Society.

Mossop, E. E., ed. 1947. *The Journals of Brink and Rhenius, being the Journal of Carel Frederik Brink of the Journey into Great Namaqualand (1761-2) made by Captain Hendrik Hop and the Journal of Ensign Johannes Tobias Rhenius (1724)*. Cape Town: Van Riebeeck Society.

Mou Le. 1914. *Qingdao Quanshu* [Qingdao Encyclopedia]. 2nd ed. N.p. [Qingdao].

Mucchielli, Laurent. 1996. "Autour des 'Instructions sur les Boschimans' d'Henri Thulié." Pp. 201-41 in *Le terrain des sciences humaines*, ed. Claude Blanckaert. Paris: Editions L'Harmattan.

Mühlhahn, Klaus. 1999. "Der Alltag an der Hochschule in Qingdao: Deutsche, Chinesen und die universitäre Bildung." Pp. 182-97 in Hiery 1999.

Mühlhahn, Klaus. 2000. *Herrschaft und Widerstand in der "Musterkolonie" Kiautschou*. Munich: R. Oldenbourg.

Mühlmann, Wilhelm Emil. 1955. *Arioi und Mamaia*. Wiesbaden: Franz Steiner Verlag.

Muel-Dreyfus, Francine. 2003. "Une écoute sociologique de la psychanalyse." Pp. 227-35 in *Travailler avec Bourdieu*, ed. Pierre Encrevé and Rose Marie Lagrave. Paris: Flammarion.

Müller, Friedrich. 1873. *Allgemeine Ethnographie*. Wien: Alfred Hölder.

Müller, Fritz. 1962. *Kolonien unter der Peitsche*. Berlin: Rütten und Loening.

Müller, Karl, and Adolf Schulze. 1932. *Zwei Hundert Jahre Brüdermission*. 2 vols. Herrnhut: Missionsbuchhandlung.

Mungello, David. 1982. "Die Schrift T'ien-hsüeh chuan-kai als eine Zwischenformulierung der jesuitische Anpassungsmethode im 17. Jahrhundert." *China Mission Studies (1550-1800) Bulletin* 4:24-39.

Mungello, David. 1985. *Curious Land: Jesuit Accomodation and the Origins of Sinology*. Stuttgart: Franz Steiner Verlag.

Mungello, David. 1999. *The Great Encounter of China and the West, 1500-1800*. Lanham: Rowman and Littlefield Publishers.

Munro, Doug, and Stewart Firth. 1990. "German Labour Policy and the Partition of the Western Pacific: The View from Samoa." *Journal of Pacific History* 25 (1): 85-102.

Murray, Archibald Wright. 1863. *Missions in Western Polynesia*. London: John Snow.

Murray, Archibald Wright. 1876. *Forty Years' Mission Work in Polynesia and New Guinea, from 1835 to 1875*. London: James Nisbet and Co.

Naber, E. E., ed. 1930-32. *Reisebeschreibungen von deutschen Beamten und Kriegsleuten im Dienst der Niederländischen West- und Ost-Indischen Kompagnien 1602-1797*. 12 vols. The Hague: Martinus Nijhoff.

Nachtwei, Winfried. 1976. *Namibia: Von der antikolonialen Revolte zum nationalen Befreiungskampf*. Mannheim: Sendler.

Naundorf, Gert. 1975. "Würzburger Chinabeziehungen: Bericht und Bermerkungen." *Zeitschrift für Missionswissenschaft und Religionsgeschichte* 59:127-32.

Naundorf, Gert. 1975-76. "Ignaz Köglers S.J. Elogium für Kilian Stumpf (1720)." *Zeitschrift für Missionswissenschaft* 59:269-85; 60:29-50.

Navarrete, Domingo Fernández. [1676] 1962. *An Account of the Empire of China, Historical, Political, Moral and Religious*. Pp. 1–396 in *The Travels and Controversies of Friar Domingo Navarrete, 1618–1686*, 2 vols., ed. J. S. Cummins. Cambridge: Cambridge University Press.

Netanyahu, Benzion. 1995. *The Origins of the Inquisition in Fifteenth Century Spain*. New York: Random House.

Newbury, Colin W. 1980. *Tahiti Nui*. Honolulu: University Press of Hawaii.

Nieuhof, Johann. [1669] 1972. *An Embassy from the East India Company of the United Provinces, to the Grand Tartar Cham, Emperor of China*. Menston, UK: Scolar Press.

Nightingale, Thomas. 1835. *Oceanic Sketches*. London: James Cochrane and Co.

Nitsche, Georg. 1913. *Ovamboland*. Kiel: Donath.

Noyes, John. 1992. *Colonial Space*. Chur: Harwood Academic Publishers.

Nuhn, Walter. 1989. *Sturm über Südwest*. Stuttgart: Bernard & Graefe Verlag.

Obermüller, Julius. 1889. *Samoa: Zur Geschichte der deutschen Colonie in der Süd-See mit besonderer Rücksicht auf die Kämpfe um dieselben und die Ereignisse von 1888–1889*. Leipzig: Eduard Heinrich Mayer.

O'Connor, Richard. 1974. *The Boxer Rebellion*. London: Hale.

Odhiambo, Atieno, and John Lonsdale, eds. 2003. *Mau Mau and Nationhood*. Oxford: James Currey.

Odorico, da Pordenone. n.d. [1933]. *De Venise á Pekin au Moyen Age*. Paris: Téqui.

Offe, Claus. 1984. "Theses on the Theory of the State." Pp. 119–29 in *Contradictions of the Welfare State*, ed. John Keane. Cambridge, Mass.: MIT Press.

Olearius, Adami. 1696. *Des Welt-berühmten Adami Olearii colligirte und viel vermehrte Reise-Beschreibungen*. Hamburg: In Verlegung Zacharias Hertein und Thomas von Wiering.

Oliver, Douglas L. 1974. *Ancient Tahitian Society*. Honolulu: University Press of Hawaii.

Ollivier, Isabel, trans. 1985. *Extracts from Journals Relating to the Visit to New Zealand in May–July 1772 of the French Ships the* Mascarin *and the* Marquis de Castries *under the Command of M.-J. Marion du Fresne*. Wellington: Alexander Turnbull Library Endowment Trust with Indosuez New Zealand.

Olusoga, David Adetayo. 2004. *Genocide and the Second Reich*. London: BBC.

Oosthuizen, G. J. J. 1996. "Die hantering van minderheidsgroepe in Duits-Suidwes-Afrika: Die Rehoboth-Basters, 1884–1915." *Kleio* 27:99–119.

Ortner, Sherry. 1999. "Introduction." Pp. 1–13 in *The Fate of "Culture": Geertz and Beyond*, ed. Sherry Ortner. Berkeley: University of California Press.

Osterhammel, Jürgen. 1987. "Forschungsreise und Kolonialprogramm: Ferdinand von Richthofen und die Erschließung Chinas im 19. Jh." *Archiv für Kulturgeschichte* 69:150–97.

Osterhammel, Jürgen. 1995. *Kolonialismus*. Munich: C. H. Beck.

Osterhammel, Jürgen. 1998. *Die Entzauberung Asiens*. Munich: C. H. Beck.

Ostwald, Thomas. 1976. *Friedrich Gerstäcker: Leben und Werk*. Brunswick: Graff.

Otaheitische Gemälde. 1803. Bremen: Bei Carl Seiffert.

Padel, John. 1986. "Ego in Current Thinking." Pp. 154–72 in *The British School of Psychoanalysis,* ed. Gregorio Kohon. London: Free Association Books.

Palgrave, William Coates. [1877] 1969. *Report of Mr. Palgrave, Special Commisioner* [sic] *of His Mission to Damaraland and Great Namaqualand.* Pretoria, State Library.

Palmer, Alison. 2000. *Colonial Genocide.* Adelaide: Crawford House.

Papin, Bernard. 1984. "L'utopie tahitienne du *Supplement au voyage de Bougainville* ou le 'modèle idéal' en politique." *L'information littéraire* 36 (3): 102–5.

Panzergrau, Kurt. 1998. *Die Bildung und Erziehung der Eingeborenen Südwestafrikas (Hereroland und Gross-Namaqualand) durch die Rheinische Missionsgesellschaft von 1842–1914.* Munich: Akademischer Verlag.

Paquet, Alfons. 1911. "Vorwort." Pp. i–xiv in Ku 1911.

Paquet, Alfons. 1912. *Li, oder Im neuen Osten.* Frankfurt am Main: Rütten & Loening.

Paquet, Alfons. 1914. "Der Kaisergedanke." *Der neue Merkur* 1:45–62.

Park, Young Hai. 1974. "La carrière scénique de *L'Orphelin de la Chine.*" *Studies on Voltaire and the Eighteenth Century* 120:93–137.

Parkinson, Sydney. 1773. *A Journal of a Voyage to the South Seas, in His Majesty's Ship, the Endeavour.* Ed. Stanfield Parkinson. London: Printed for S. Parkinson.

Passarge, Siegfried. 1997. *The Kalahari Ethnographies (1896–1898) of Siegfried Passarge.* Cologne: Rüdiger Köppe.

Pauw, Cornelius de. 1774. *Philosophische Untersuchungen ueber die Aegypter und Chineser.* Berlin: Georg Jacob Decker.

Pearson, Patrick. 1986. "The History and Social Structure of the Rehoboth Baster Community of Namibia." M.A. thesis, University of the Witwatersrand.

Pennington, Renee and Henry Hardpenning. 1991. "How Many Refugees Were There? History and Population Change among the Herero and Mbanderu of Northwestern Botswana." *Botswana Notes and Records* 23:209–21.

Penn, Nigel. 1999. *Rogues, Rebels, and Runaways: Eighteenth-Century Cape Characters.* Cape Town: David Philip.

Penny, H. Glenn. 2002. *Objects of Culture.* Chapel Hill: University of North Carolina Press.

Peschel, Oscar. 1867. "Die Rückwirkung der Ländergestaltung auf die menschliche Gesittung." Pt. 1. *Das Ausland* 40 (39): 913–18.

Peschel, Oscar. 1876. *The Races of Man, and Their Geographical Distribution.* New York: D. Appleton and Co.

Philip, The Rev. John. [1828] 1969. *Researches in South Africa.* New York: Negro Universities Press.

Philippi, Hans. 1985. "Das deutsche diplomatische Korps 1871–1914." Pp. 41–80 in *Das Diplomatische Korps 1871–1945,* ed. Klaus Schwabe. Boppard am Rhein: Harald Boldt Verlag.

Phillips, Charles. 1890. *Samoa, Past and Present*. London: J. Snow.

Pieper, Rudolf. 1900. *Unkraut, Knospen und Blüten aus dem "blumigen Reich der Mitte."* Steyl: Missionsdruckerei.

Pigulla, Andreas. 1996. *China in der deutschen Weltgeschichtsschreibung vom 18. Jh. bis zum Gegenwart*. Wiesbaden: Harrasowitz Verlag.

Plath, Johann Heinrich. 1857. "China und die Chinesen." Pp. 430–64 in *Deutsches Staats-Wörterbuch*, vol. 2, ed. Johann Caspar Bluntschli and Karl Ludwig Theodor Brater. Stuttgart: Expedition des Staats-Wörterbuchs.

Plath, Johann Heinrich. 1864. *Verfassung und Verwaltung China's unter den drei ersten Dynastieen*. Munich: Verlag der k. Akademie.

Plath, Johann Heinrich. 1869. *China vor 4000 Jahren*. Munich: Akademische Buchdruckerei von F. Straub.

Poewe, Karla O. 1985. *The Namibian Herero*. Lewiston, N.Y.: E. Mellen Press.

Polo, Marco. 1993. *The Travels of Marco Polo*. New York: Dover.

Pollock, Sheldon. 2000. "Indology, Power, and the Case of Germany." Pp. 302–23 in *Orientalism: A Reader*, ed. A. L. Macfie. New York: New York University Press.

Pomeau, Réné. 1963. "Introduction." Pp. i–lxvi in Voltaire 1963.

Pomeranz, Kenneth. 2000. *The Great Divergence*. Princeton, N.J.: Princeton University Press.

Pommerin, Reiner. 1979. *Sterilisierung der Rheinlandbastarde*. Düsseldorf: Droste.

Pons, Philippe. [1999] 2002. *Macao*. London: Reaktion.

Pool, Gerhardus. 1976. "Die Herero-Opstand, 1904–1907." Ph.D. diss., University of Stellenbosch.

Pool, Gerhard. 1991. *Samuel Maharero*. Windhoek: Gamsberg Macmillan Publishers.

Poulantzas, Nicos. 1975. *Classes in Contemporary Capitalism*. London: New Left Books.

Poulantzas, Nicos. 1978. *Political Power and Social Classes*. New York: Verso.

Poulton, Leslee. 1988. "O Tahiti: Fiction and Reality in Four French Writers." Ph.D. diss., Indiana University.

Povinelli, Elisabeth. 2002. *The Cunning of Recognition*. Durham, N.C.: Duke University Press.

Pratt, Mary Louise. 1992. *Imperial Eyes*. London: Routledge.

Prein, Philipp. 1994. "Guns and Top Hats: African Resistance in German South West Africa, 1907–1915." *Journal of Southern African Studies* 20 (1): 99–121.

Preradovich, Nikolaus von. 1955. *Die Führungsschichten in Österreich und Preußen (1804–1918)*. Wiesbaden: Franz Steiner.

Preston, Diana. 1999. *Besieged in Peking*. London: Constable.

Pritchard, Earl H. 1943. "The Kowtow in the Macartney Embassy to China in 1793." *The Far Eastern Quarterly* 2 (February):163–203.

Pritchard, W. J. 1866. *Polynesian Remembrances; or, Life in the South Pacific Islands*. London: Chapman and Hall.

Proctor, Robert. 1988. "From Anthropologie to Rassenkunde in the German Anthropological Tradition." Pp. 138–79 in *Bones, Bodies, Behavior,* ed. George Stocking. Madison: University of Wisconsin Press.

Purchas, Samuel. [1625] 2004. "The first Voyage made to East-India by Master Iames Lancaster, now Knight, for the Merchants of *London,* Anno, *1600.* With foure tall Shippes, (to wit) the *Dragon,* the *Hector,* the *Ascension* and *Susan,* and a Victualler called the *Guest.*" Pp. 148–64 in *Purchas his Pilgrims: In Fiue Bookes,* bk. 3, pt. 1, chap. 3. Ann Arbor, Mich.: Early English Books Online Text Creation Partnership.

Pynchon, Thomas. 1963. *V., a Novel.* Philadelphia: Lippincott.

Pynchon, Thomas. 1973. *Gravity's Rainbow.* New York: Viking Press.

Pytlik, Anna. 1997. *Träume im Tropenlicht: Forscherinnen auf Reisen.* Reutlingen: Coyote.

Quartey, Seth. 2004. "Missionary Practices: German-Speaking Missionaries between the Home Committee and Colonial Environment in the Gold Coast (West Africa), 1828–1895." Ph.D. diss., University of Michigan.

Quatrefages de Bréau, Jean Louis Armand de. 1864. *Les Polynésiens et leurs migrations.* Paris: A. Bertrand.

Quatrefages de Bréau, Jean Louis Armand de. 1879. *The Human Species.* New York: D. Appleton and Co.

Quesnay, François. [1767] 1946. *China a Model for Europe (Despotism in China).* Ed. and trans. Lewis A. Maverick. San Antonio, Tex.: Paul Anderson Co.

Quilley, Geoff, and John Bonehill, eds. 2004. *William Hodges 1744–1797: The Art of Exploration.* New Haven, Conn.: Yale University Press for the National Maritime Museum, Greenwich.

Raabe, Wilhelm. [1881] 1983. *Tubby Schaumann.* Pp. 155–311 in *Novels,* ed. Volkmar Sander. New York: Continuum.

Rabemananjara, Raymond William. 2000. *Madagascar: L'affaire de mars 1947.* Paris: L'Harmattan.

Rabinow, Paul. 1989. *French Modern.* Cambridge, Mass.: MIT Press.

Rada, Martín de. 1953. "The Relation of Fr. Martín de Rada, O.E.S.A." Pp. 241–310 in *South China in the Sixteenth Century,* ed. C. R. Boxer. London: Hakluyt Society.

Rai, Satya M. 2000. "The Jallianwala Bagh Tragedy: Its Impact on the Political Awakening and Thinking in India." Pp. 25–37 in *Jallianwala Bagh Massacre,* ed. V. N. Datta and S. Settar. Delhi: Pragati Publications and Indian Council of Historical Research.

Ranke, Johannes. 1894–1900. *Der Mensch.* 2nd ed. 2 vols. Leipzig: Bibliographisches Institut.

Rasmussen, Holger. 1972. "Der schreibende Teufel in Nordeuropa." Pp. 455–64 in *Festschrift Matthias Zender,* ed. Edith Ennen and Günter Wiegelmann. Bonn: Ludwig Röhrscheied Verlag.

Rassool, Ciraj and Patricia Hayes. 2001. "Science and the Spectacle: /Khanako's South Africa, 1936-1937." Paper presented at the conference "Reimagining South Africa and the Political Imagination of South Africans," University of Michigan.

Ratenhof, Udo. 1985. *Die Chinapolitik des Deutschen Reiches 1871 bis 1945*. Boppard am Rhein: Harald Boldt Verlag.

Ratzel, Friedrich. 1882-91. *Anthropo-Geographie*. 2 vols. Stuttgart: Verlag von J. Engelhorn.

Raven-Hart, Rowland, ed. and trans. 1967. *Before Van Riebeeck*. Cape Town: C. Struik.

Raven-Hart, Rowland, ed. and trans. 1971. *Cape Good Hope, 1652-1702*. 2 vols. Cape Town: A. A. Balkema.

Read, James, Jr. 1852. *The Kat River Settlement in 1851*. Cape Town: A. S. Robertson.

Reichwein, Adolf. 1925. *China and Europe*. New York: Knopf.

Reil, Sebald. 1978. *Kilian Stumpf, 1655-1720*. Münster: Aschendorff.

Reinbothe, Roswitha. 1992. *Kulturexport und Wirtschaftsmacht*. Frankfurt am Main: Verlag für Interkulturelle Kommunikation.

Reinhard, Wolfgang. 1978. "'Sozialimperialismus' oder 'Entkolonialiserung der Historie'? Kolonialkrise und 'Hottentottenwahlen' 1904-1907." *Historisches Jahrbuch* 97-98:384-417.

Reinhard, Wolfgang. 1988. "Eingeborenenpolitik in Südwestafrika 1842 bis 1915: Der deutsche Weg zur Apartheid." Pp. 543-56 in *Historische Blickpunkte*, ed. Sabina Weiss. Innsbruck: Institut für Sprachwissenschaft.

Reinhard, Wolfgang. 1996. *Kleine Geschichte des Kolonialismus*. Stuttgart: Alfred Kroeber.

Renan, Ernest. [1871] 1874. *La réforme intellectuelle et morale*. Paris: Michel Lévy Frères.

Rennie, David Field. 1865. *Peking and the Pekingese during the First Year of the British Embassy at Peking*. London: J. Murray.

Ricci, Matteo, Nicholas Trigault, and and Paulus Welser. 1617. *Historia von Einfuerung der christlichen Religion in dass grosse Königreich China durch die Societet Jesu*. Augsburg: A. Hierat von Creollen.

Richthofen, Ferdinand Freiherr von. 1870. "Schreiben des Freiherrn Ferdinand von Richthofen über seine Reisen zur Grenze von Korea und in der Provinz Hunan." *Zeitschrift der Gesellschaft für Erdkunde zu Berlin* 5:317-39.

Richthofen, Ferdinand Freiherr von. 1871. "Aus brieflichen Mittheilungen des Freiherrn Ferdinand v. Richthofen." *Zeitschrift der Gesellschaft für Erdkunde zu Berlin*, ser. 3, 6:151-58.

Richthofen, Ferdinand Freiherr von. 1873. "Über die Ursachen der Gleichförmigkeit des chinesischen Racentypus und seiner örtlicher Schwankungen." *Verhandlungen der Berliner Gesellschaft für Anthropologie, Ethnologie und Urgeschichte* 5:37-48.

Richthofen, Ferdinand Freiherr von. 1873–74a. "Ueber die neuesten Versuche zur Oeffnung direkter Handlungswege nach dem südwestlichen China." *Verhandlungen der Gesellschaft für Erdkunde zu Berlin* 1 (4): 58–63.

Richthofen, Ferdinand Freiherr von. 1873–74b. "Über den natürlichsten Weg für eine Eisenbahnverbindung zwischen China und Europa." *Verhandlungen der Gesellschaft für Erdkunde zu Berlin* 1 (4): 115–26.

Richthofen, Ferdinand Freiherr von. 1875. *Letters to the Shanghai General Chamber of Commerce*. Shanghai.

Richthofen, Ferdinand Freiherr von. 1877–1912. *China*. 5 vols. Berlin: Dietrich Reimer.

Richthofen, Ferdinand Freiherr von. 1897. *Kiautschou, seine Weltstellung und voraussichtliche Bedeutung*. Berlin: Verlag von Georg Stilke.

Richthofen, Ferdinand Freiherr von. 1898. *Schantung und seine Eingangspforte Kiautschou*. Berlin: Dietrich Reimer.

Richthofen, Ferdinand Freiherr von. 1902. *Chrysanthemum und Drache*. Berlin: Fred. Dümmlers Verlagsbuchhandlung.

Richthofen, Ferdinand Freiherr von. 1907. *Ferdinand von Richthofen's Tagebücher aus China*. 2 vols. Berlin: Dietrich Reimer.

Ringer, Fritz. 1969. *The Decline of the German Mandarins*. Cambridge, Mass.: Harvard University Press.

Rinke, Stefan H. 1992. *Zwischen Weltpolitik und Monroe Doktrin*. Stuttgart: H.-D. Heinz.

Ritter, Br. 1868. "Der Stand der Hereró-Mission im Jahre 1867." *Berichte der Rheinischen Missionsgesellschaft*, 24 (11): 330–44.

Rivinius, Karl J. 1979. *Die katholische Mission in Süd-Schantung*. St. Augustin: Steyler Verlag.

Rivinius, Karl Josef. 1987. *Weltlicher Schutz und Mission: Das deutsche Protektorat über die katholische Mission von Süd-Shantung*. Cologne: Bohlau.

Robinson, Ronald. 1986. "The Excentric Idea of Imperialism, with or without Empire." Pp. 267–89 in Mommsen and Osterhammel 1986.

Robinson, Ronald. 1972. "Non-European Foundations of European Imperialism: Sketch for a Theory of Collaboration." Pp. 117–40 in *Studies in the Theory of Imperialism*, ed. Roger Owen and Bob Sutcliffe. London: Longman.

Rodney, Walter. [1972] 1981. *How Europe Underdeveloped Africa*. Rev. ed. Washington, D.C.: Howard University Press.

Rohden, L. von. 1888. *Geschichte der Rheinischen Missions-Gesellschaft*. 3rd ed. Barmen: D. B. Wiemann.

Rohlfs, Gerhard. 1874. *Quer durch Afrika*. Leipzig: F. A. Brockhaus.

Rohlfs, Gerhard. 1884. *Angra Pequena*. Bielefeld: Verlag von Velhagen & Klaßing.

Rohrbach, Paul. 1907. *Südwestafrika*. Berlin: Buchverlag der "Hilfe."

Rohrbach, Paul. 1909a. *Deutsch-chinesische Studien*. Berlin: Verlag von Georg Stilke.

Rohrbach, Paul. 1909b. *Aus Südwest-Afrikas schweren Tagen*. Berlin: Wilhelm Weicher.

Rohrbach, Paul. 1912. *Deutschland in China voran!* Berlin-Schöneberg: Protestantischer Schriftenvertrieb.

Rohrbach, Paul. 1953. *Um des Teufels Handschrift.* Hamburg: H. Dulk.

Romberg, Kurt. 1911. "Ku Hung Ming." *Deutsch-chinesische Rechtszeitung* I (1): 22–26.

Rose, Cowper. 1829. *Four Years in Southern Africa.* London: Henry Colburn and Richard Bentley.

Rose, Ernst. 1981. *Blick nach Osten.* Frankfurt am Main: Peter Lang.

Rose, Jacqueline. 1998. *States of Fantasy.* Oxford: Oxford University Press.

Ross, Robert. 1999. *Status and Respectability in the Cape Colony, 1750–1870: A Tragedy of Manners.* Cambridge: Cambridge University Press.

Roth, Markus. 2004. "'Pioneers of the East': The District Chiefs (*Kreishauptleute*) in the Government-General in a Comparative Perspective." Paper presented at the annual meeting of the Council of European Studies, Chicago.

Rothberg, Michael. 2004. "The Work of Testimony in the Age of Decolonization: *Chonicle of a Summer,* Cinema Verité, and the Emergence of the Holocaust Survivor." *PMLA* 119 (5): 1231–46.

Rouffaer, Gerrit Pieter. 1925. *De eerste Schipvaart der Nederlanders naar Oost Indië onder Cornelis de Houtman, 1595-1597.* Vol. 2. The Hague: M. Nijhoff.

Rousseau, Jean-Jacques. [1750] 1975. "Discourse . . . on the Question Posed by the Academy: Has the Restoration of the Arts and Sciences Been Conducive to the Purification of Morals?" Pp. 203–30 in *The Essential Rousseau,* ed. Lowell Bair. New York: Meridian.

Rousseau, Jean-Jacques. [1755] 1988. "Discourse on the Origin and Foundations of Inequality among Men." Pp. 3–57 in *Rousseau's Political Writings,* ed. Alan Ritter. New York: W. W. Norton and Co.

Rowbotham, Arnold H. 1932. "Voltaire, Sinophile." *PMLA* 47 (December):1050–65.

Rubin, William. 1984. *Primtivism in 20th Century Art.* New York: Museum of Modern Art.

Ruland, Bernd. 1973. *Deutsche Botschaft Peking.* Bayreuth: Hestia.

Rust, Conrad. 1905. *Krieg und Frieden im Hererolande: Aufzeichnungen aus dem Kriegsjahre 1904.* Leipzig: L. A. Kittler.

Saada, Emmanuelle. 2002. "Race and Sociological Reason in the Republic: Inquiries on the *Métis* in the French Empire (1908-37)." *International Sociology* 17 (3): 361–91.

Sachau, Eduard. 1912. *Denkschrift über das Seminar für orientalische Sprachen an der Königlichen Friedrich-Wilhelms-Universität zu Berlin von 1887 bis 1912.* Berlin: Reichsdrückerei.

Sahlins, Marshall D. 1958. *Social Stratification in Polynesia.* Seattle: University of Washington Press.

Sahlins, Marshall. 1976. *The Use and Abuse of Biology.* Ann Arbor: University of Michigan Press.

Sahlins, Marshall. 1981. *Historical Metaphors and Mythical Realities.* Ann Arbor: University of Michigan Press.

Sahlins, Marshall. 1993. "Goodbye to *Tristes Tropes:* Ethnography in the Context of Modern World History." *Journal of Modern History* 65 (March): 1–25.

Said, Edward. 1978. *Orientalism.* New York: Vintage.

Said, Edward. 1993. *Culture and Imperialism.* New York: Knopf.

Salesa, Damon Ieremia. 1997. "'Troublesome Half-Castes': Tales of a Samoan Borderland." M.A. thesis, University of Auckland.

Salesa, Damon Ieremia. 2003. "'Travel-Happy' Samoa: Colonialism, Samoan Migration and a 'Brown Pacific.'" *New Zealand Journal of History* 37 (2): 171–88.

Salzmann, Erich von. 1905. *Im Kampfe gegen die Herero.* Berlin: D. Reimer.

Sander, Ludwig. 1912. *Geschichte der Deutschen Kolonial-Gesellschaft für Südwest-Afrika von ihrer Gründung bis zum Jahre 1910.* Berlin, D. Reimer.

Santner, Eric L. 1996. *My Own Private Germany.* Princeton, N.J.: Princeton University Press.

Sartre, Jean-Paul. 2001. *Colonialism and Neocolonialism.* London: Routledge.

Saussure, Ferdinand de. [1915] 1986. *Course in General Linguistics.* La Salle, Ill.: Open Court.

Schall von Bell, Johann Adam. 1834. *Geschichte der chinesischen Mission.* Vienna: Druck und Verlag der Mechitaristen-Congregations-Buchhandlung.

Schapera, Isaac. "General Introduction." Pp. i–xv in *The Early Cape Hottentots, Described in the Writings of Olfert Dapper (1668), Willem ten Rhyne (1686) and Johannes Gulielmus de Grevenbrock (1695),* ed. and trans. Isaac Schapera. Cape Town: Van Riebeeck Society.

Scherer, James A., ed. and trans. 1969. *Justinian Welz.* Grand Rapids, Mich.: Eerdmans.

Scheulen, Peter. 1998. *Die "Eingeborenen" Deutsch-Südwestafrikas.* Cologne: Rüdiger Köppe Verlag.

Schinz, Hans. 1891. *Deutsch-Südwest-Afrika: Forschungsreisen durch die deutschen Schutzgebiete Groß-Nama- und Hereroland, nach dem Kunene, dem Ngami-See und der Kalaχari, 1884–1887.* Oldenburg: Schulzesche Hof-Buchhandlung und Hof-Buchdruckeri.

Schleip, Dietrich. 1989. "Ozeanistische Ethnographie und koloniale Praxis: Das Beispiel Augustin Krämer." *Tribus. Jahrbuch des Linden-Museums* 38 (December): 121–48.

Schlettwein, C. 1907. *Der Farmer in Deutsch-Südwest-Afrika.* Wismar: Hinstorff'sche Verlagsbuchhandlung.

Schlyter, Herman. 1946. *Karl Gützlaff als Missionar in China.* Lund: C. W. K. Gleerup.

Schlyter, Herman. 1976. *Der China-Missionar Karl Gützlaff und seine Heimatbasis.* Klippan: Ljungbergs Boktryckeri.

Schmasow, Alfred. n.d. [ca. 1899–1900]. *Unsere Blaujacken in Kiautschou: Schwank in 1 Akt.* Landsberg an der Warthe: Volger & Klein.

Schmidt, Georg. 1981. *Das Tagebuch und die Briefe von Georg Schmidt, dem ersten*

Missionar in Südafrika (1737-1744). Bellville: Die Wes-Kaaplandse Instituut Vir Historiese Navorsing.

Schmidt, Gustav. 1989. *Der europäische Imperialismus*. Munich: Oldenbourg.

Schmidt, Vera. 1976. *Die deutsche Eisenbahnpolitik in Shantung 1898-1914*. Wiesbaden: Otto Harrassowitz.

Schmidt-Lauber, Brigitta. 1993. *Die abhängigen Herren*. Münster: Lit Verlag.

Schmidt-Lauber, Brigitta. 1998. *Die verkehrte Hautfarbe*. Berlin: D. Reimer.

Schmitt, Carl. [1922] 1985. *Political Theology*. Cambridge, Mass.: MIT Press.

Schmitt, Carl. [1938] 1996. *The Leviathan in the State Theory of Thomas Hobbes*. Westport, Conn.: Greenwood Press.

Schmitt, Carl. [1950] 2003. *The Nomos of the Earth*. Trans. and annotated by G. L. Ulmen. New York: Telos Press.

Schmitt-Egner, Peter. 1975. *Kolonialismus und Faschismus*. Giessen: Achenbach.

Schmitz, Oscar A. H. 1924. "Zur Einführung." Pp. 1-5 in *Der Geist des chinesichen Volkes*, by Ku Hung-Ming. Jena: E. Diederichs.

Schmuhl, Hans-Walter. 1987. *Rassenhygiene, Nationalsozialismus, Euthanasie*. Göttingen: Vandenhoeck & Ruprecht.

Schnabel, Johann Gottfried. 1902. *Die Insel Felsenburg*. Berlin: B. Behr's Verlag.

Schnee, Heinrich, ed. 1920. *Deutsches Kolonial-Lexikon*. Leipzig: Quelle und Meyer.

Schneider, Jost. 1998. "Literatur und Wissenschaft bei Georg Forster." *Études Germaniques* 53 (4): 673-86.

Schneider-Christians, Dorothee. 1992. "Die alte Religion und das Christentum Samoas." Ph.D. diss., Bonn University.

Schnitzler, Arthur. 1989. "Boxeraufstand." Pp. 90-94 in *Der blinde Geronimo und sein Bruder*. Frankfurt am Main: Fischer.

Schoeffel, Penelope. 1987. "Rank, Gender, and Politics in Ancient Samoa: The Geneaology of Salamāsina O Le Tafaifā." *Journal of Pacific History* 22:174-93.

Schoeffel, Penelope. 1999. "Samoan Exchange and 'Fine Mats': An Historical Reconsideration." *Journal of the Polynesian Society* 108 (2): 117-48.

Schott, Peter. 1992. "Die Stigmen des Bösen: Kulturgeschichtliche Wurzeln der Ausmerze-Ideologie." Pp. 9-22 in *Wissenschaft auf Irrwegen: Biologismus, Rassenhygiene, Eugenik*, ed. Peter Propping and Heinz Schott. Bonn: Bouvier.

Schott, Wilhelm. 1826-32. *Werke des tschinesischen Weisen Kung-fu-dsü und seiner Schüler*. Halle: Regner.

Schott, Wilhelm. 1830. "China." Pp. 159-76 in *Allgemeine Encyclopädie der Wissenschaften und Künste*, vol. 21, ed. J. S. Ersch and J. G. Gruber. Leipzig: Gleditsch.

Schott, Wilhelm. 1857. *Über die chinesische Verskunst*. Berlin: Druckerei der Königlichen Akademie der Wissenschaften.

Schrameier, Wilhelm Ludwig. 1910. "Reformbestrebungen in China und deutsche Kultureinflüsse." *Dokumente des Fortschritts* 3 (11): 803-10.

Schrameier, Wilhelm Ludwig. 1914. *Aus Kiautschous Verwaltung: Die Land-, Steuer- und Zollpolitik des Kiautschougebietes*. Jena: G. Fischer.

Schrecker, J. E. 1971. *Imperialism and Chinese Nationalism*. Cambridge, Mass.: Harvard University Press.

Schröder, Hans-Christoph. 1968. *Sozialismus und Imperialismus: Die Auseinandersetzung der deutschen Sozialdemokratie mit dem Imperialismusproblem und der "Weltpolitik" vor 1914*. Hannover: Verlag fur Literatur und Zeitgeschehen.

Schröder, Hans-Christoph. 1973. *Sozialistische Imperialismusdeutung: Studien zu ihrer Geschichte*. Göttingen: Vandenhoeck & Ruprecht.

Schück, Richard. 1889. *Brandenburg-Preussens Kolonial-Politik under dem Grossen Kurfürsten und seinen Nachfolgern (1647–1721)*. Leipzig: F. W. Grunow.

Schüler, Wilhelm. 1912. *Abriß der neuren Geschichte Chinas unter besonderer Berücksichtigung der Provinz Shantung*. Berlin: Karl Curtius.

Schulte-Althoff, Franz-Josef. 1985. "Rassenmischung im kolonialen System: Zur deutschen Kolonialpolitik im letzten Jahrzehnt vor dem Ersten Weltkrieg." *Historisches Jahrbuch* 105:52–94.

Schultz [Schultz-Ewerth], Erich. 1905. *Die wichtigsten Grundsaetze des samoanischen Familien- und Erbrechts*. Apia: Verlag von E. Luebke.

Schultz [Schultz-Ewerth], Erich. 1911. "The Most Important Principles of Samoan Family Law." *Journal of the Polynesian Society* 20:43–53.

Schultz-Ewerth, Erich. 1924. "Samoanisches Recht." *Blätter für vergleichende Rechtswissenschaft und Volkswirtschaftslehre* 18 (7–9): 83–134.

Schultz-Ewerth, Erich. 1926. *Erinnerungen an Samoa*. Berlin: August Scherl.

Schultze, Leonhard. 1907. *Aus Namaland und Kalahari*. Jena: Gustav Fischer.

Schultze, Leonhard, ed. 1909. *Zoologische und anthropologische Ergebnisse einer Forschungsreise im westlichen und zentralen Südafrika ausgeführt in den Jahren 1903–1905*. Vol. 3. Denkschriften der medicinisch-naturwissenschaftlichen Gesellschaft zu Jena, vol. 15. Jena: Gustav Fischer.

Schultze, Leonhard. 1910. "Südwestafrika." Pp. 129–298 in *Das deutsche Kolonialreich*, vol. 2, ed. Hans Meyer. Leipzig: Bibliographisches Institut.

Schuster, Ingrid. 1988. *Vorbilder und Zerrbilder*. Frankfurt am Main: Peter Lang.

Schwabe, Klaus. 1982. *Das diplomatische Korps 1871–1945*. Boppard am Rhein: Harald Boldt Verlag.

Schwabe, Kurd. 1899. *Mit Schwert und Pflug in Deutsch-Südwestafrika*. Berlin: Mittler.

Schwabe, Kurd. 1905. "Deutsch-Südwestafrika: Historisch-geographische, militärische und wirtschaftliche Studien." *Militärwochenblatt*, Beiheft 6:213–40.

Schwabe, Kurd. 1907. *Der Krieg in Deutsch-Südwestafrika*. Berlin: Verlag von C. A. Weller.

Schwabe, Kurd. 1910. *Im deutschen Diamantenlande*. Berlin: Ernst Siegfried Mittler & Sohn.

Schwabe, Kurd, and Paul Leutwein. 1926. "Deutsch-Südwestafrika." Pp. 105–68 in *Die deutschen Kolonien*, vol. 1, ed. Kurd Schwabe and Paul Leutwein. 2nd ed. Berlin: Verlagsanstalt für Farben-Photographie Carl Weller.

Schwartz, Theodore. 1983. "Anthropology: A Quaint Science." *American Anthropologist*, n.s., 85 (4): 919-29.

Schweiger-Lerchenfeld, Armand, Freiherr von. 1901. "Der Chinese und chinesisches Leben." Pp. 84-156 in Kürschner 1901, vol. 1.

Schweitzer, Georg. 1914. *China im neuen Gewande*. Berlin: Karl Siegismund.

Scott, David. 1995. "Colonial Governmentality." *Social Text*, no. 43:191-220.

Scott, James C. 1985. *Weapons of the Weak*. New Haven, Conn.: Yale University Press.

Scott, Paul. [1953] 2005. *Six Days in Marapore*. Chicago: University of Chicago Press.

Sebald, Peter. 1988. *Togo 1884-1914*. Berlin: Akademie-Verlag.

Secretariat of the United Nations. 1955. "The Rehoboth Community of South West Africa." *African Studies* 14 (4): 175-200.

Seeberg, Karl-Martin. 1989. *Der Maji-Maji-Krieg gegen die deutsche Kolonialherrschaft*. Berlin: Dietrich Reimer Verlag.

Seed, David. 1982. "Pynchon's Herero." *Pynchon Notes* 10 (October): 37-44.

Seelemann, Dirk Alexander. 1982. "The Social and Economic Development of the Kiaochou Leasehold (Shantung, China) under German Administration, 1897-1914." Ph.D. diss., University of Toronto.

Seidel, D. 1898. *Deutschlands erste Kolonie: Gesammelte Erfahrungen und Erlebnisse während eines Aufenthaltes von neun Jahren in Deutsch-Südwest-Afrika*. Hamburg: O. W. C. Busch.

Selden, Elizabeth. 1942. "China in German Poetry from 1773 to 1833." *University of California Publications in Modern Philology* 25 (3): 141-316.

Sellier, Walter. 1901. "Kotzebue in England." Ph.D. diss., University of Leipzig. Leipzig: O. Fischer.

Selmeci, Andreas, and Dag Henrichsen. 1995. *Das Schwarzkommando*. Bielefeld: Aisthesis Verlag.

Sergi, Sergio. 1909. *Cerebra Hererica*. Pp. 1-322 in Schultze 1909.

Sewell, William, Jr. 1967. "Marc Bloch and the Logic of Comparative History." *History and Theory* 16 (2): 208-18.

Sewell, William, Jr. 1985. "Ideologies and Social Revolutions: Reflections on the French Case." *Journal of Modern History* 57 (March): 57-85.

Sewell, William, Jr. 1996. "Three Temporalities: Toward an Eventful Sociology." Pp. 245-80 in *The Historic Turn in the Human Sciences*, ed. Terrence J. McDonald. Ann Arbor: University of Michigan Press.

Shaffer, J. Robert. 2000. *American Samoa*. Honolulu: Island Heritage Pub.

Shandongsheng lishi xuehui, ed. 1961. *Shandong jindaishi ziliao* [Materials on the Modern History of Shangong]. 3 vols. Jinan: Shandong Renmin Chubanshe.

Shankman, Paul. 2001. "Interethnic Unions and the Regulation of Sex in Colonial Samoa, 1830-1945." *Journal of the Polynesian Society* 110 (2): 119-47.

Sharf, Frederic A., and Peter Harrington. 2000. *China 1900: The Eyewitnesses Speak*. London: Greenhill Books.

Sharrad, Paul. 2003. *Albert Wendt and Pacific Literature*. Manchester: Manchester University Press.

Shaw, Margaret. 1973. "Hottentots, Bushmen and Bantu." Pp. 127–51 in *François Le Vaillant, Traveller in South Africa, and His Collection of 165 Watercolor Paintings*, vol. 1, ed. Cape Town Library of Parliament, South Africa. Cape Town: Library of Parliament.

Shore, Bradd. 1982. *Sala'ilua: A Samoan Mystery*. New York: Columbia University Press.

Sieg, Katrin. 1998. "Ethnic Drag and National Identity: Multicultural Crises, Crossings, and Interventions." Pp. 295–319 in *The Imperialist Imagination: German Colonialism and Its Legacies*, ed. Sara Friedrichsmeyer, Sara Lennox, and Susanne Zantop. Ann Arbor: University of Michigan Press.

Siep, Ludwig. 1979. *Anerkennung als Prinzip der praktischen Philosophie*. Freiburg [Breisgau]: Alber.

Silverman, Kaja. 1992. *Male Subjectivity at the Margins*. New York: Routledge.

Silvester, Jeremy. 2000. "Assembling and Resembling: Herero History in Vaalgras, Southern Namibia." Pp. 473–95 in *People, Cattle and Land*, ed. Michael Bollig and Jan-Bart Gewald. Cologne: R. Köppe.

Silvester, Jeremy, and Jan-Bart Gewald. 2003. *Words Cannot Be Found: German Colonial Rule in Namibia: An Annotated Reprint of the 1918 Blue Book*. Leiden: Brill.

Silvester, Jeremy, Marion Wallace, and Patricia Hayes. 1998. "'Trees Never Meet': Mobility and Containment: An Overview, 1915–1946." Pp. 3–48 in Hayes, Silvester, Wallace, and Hartmann 1998.

Skocpol, Theda. 1979. *States and Social Revolutions*. Cambridge: Cambridge University Press.

Skotnes, Pippa. 1996. *Miscast*. Cape Town: University of Cape Town Press.

Smith, Adam. [1776] 1954. *The Wealth of Nations*. New York: Dutton.

Smith, Bernard. 1985. *European Vision and the South Pacific*. 2nd ed. New Haven, Conn.: Yale University Press.

Smith, Bernard. 1992. *Imagining the Pacific*. New Haven, Conn.: Yale University Press.

Smith, Woodruff D. 1978. *The German Colonial Empire*. Chapel Hill: University of North Carolina Press.

Soemmering, Samuel Thomas von. 1785. *Ueber die körperliche Verschiedenheit des Negers vom Europäer*. Frankfurt am Main: Varrentrapp Sohn und Wenner.

Soesemann, Bernd. 1976. "Die sog. Hunnenrede Wilhelms II." *Historische Zeitschrift* 222 (2): 342–58.

Solf, Wilhelm. 1886. "Kaçmîr-Recension der Pancâçikâ." Ph.D. diss., University of Halle.

Solf, Wilhelm. 1908. *Eingeborene und Ansiedler auf Samoa*. N.p.

Solf, Wilhelm, King George II of Tonga, and Hamilton Hunter. [1907] 1983. *The Cyclopedia of Samoa, Tonga, Tahiti, and the Cook Islands (Illustrated)*. Papakura, New Zealand: R. McMillan.

Somerville, William. 1979. *William Somerville's Narrative of His Journeys to the Eastern Cape Frontier and to Lattakoe, 1799-1802*. Cape Town: Van Riebeeck Society.

Sonnenberg, Else von. 1905. *Wie es am Waterberg zuging*. Berlin: Wilhelm Süsserott.

Sparrman, Anders. [1785] 1975. *A Voyage to the Cape of Good Hope*. 2 vols. Ed. V. S. Forbes. Cape Town: Van Riebeeck Society.

Speck von Sternburg, Hermann. 1979. "Report to German Chancellor, Dec. 16 1895, from Beijing, Imperial German Consulate." Pp. 109-31 in *Die katholische Mission in Süd-Schantung*, ed. Karl J. Rivinius. St. Augustin: Steyler Verlag.

Spectator Germanicus. 1913. "Eingeborenensorgen in Deutschsüdwest." *Süddeutsche Monatshefte* 10, pt. 2:249-53.

Speitkamp, Winfried. 2000. "Kolonialherrschaft und Denkmal: Afrikanische und deutsche Erinnerungskultur im Konflikt." Pp. 165-90 in *Architektur und Erinnerung*, ed. Wolfram Martini. Göttingen: Vandenhoeck & Ruprecht.

Spence, Jonathan D. 1990. *The Search for Modern China*. New York: W. W. Norton.

Spence, Jonathan D. 1998. *The Chan's Great Continent*. New York: W. W. Norton.

Spierenburg, Pieter. 1987. "From Amsterdam to Auburn: An Explanation for the Rise of the Prison in Seventeenth-Century Holland and Nineteenth-Century America." *Journal of Social History* 20 (3): 439-61.

Spiess, Gustav. 1864. *Die Preussische Expedition nach Ostasien während der Jahre 1860-1862*. Berlin: O. Spamer.

Spivak, Gayatri. 1988. *In Other Worlds*. New York: Routledge.

Spoehr, Florence Mann. 1963. *White Falcon: The House of Godeffroy and Its Commercial and Scientific Role in the Pacific*. Palo Alto, Calif.: Pacific Books.

Spraul, Gunter. 1988. "Der 'Völkermord' an den Herero." *Geschichte in Wissenschaft und Unterricht* 12:713-39.

Stair, John B. [1897] 1983. *Old Samoa; or, Flotsam and Jetsam from the Pacific Ocean*. Papkura, New Zealand: R. McMillan.

Stals, E. L. P. 1963. *Kurt Streitwolf*. Pretoria: Perskor.

Stannard, David E. 1992. *American Holocaust*. New York: Oxford University Press.

Staunton, George. 1797. *An Authentic Account of an Embassy from the King of Great Britain to the Emperor of China*. London: G. Nicol.

Steinmetz, George. 1992. "Reflections on the Role of Social Narratives in Working-Class Formation." *Social Science History* 16 (3, Fall): 489-516.

Steinmetz, George. 1993. *Regulating the Social: The Welfare State and Local Politics in Imperial Germany*. Princeton, N.J.: Princeton University Press.

Steinmetz, George. 1997. "German Exceptionalism and the Origins of Nazism: The Career of a Concept." Pp. 251-84 in *Stalinism and Nazism*, ed. Ian Kershaw and Moshe Lewin. Cambridge: Cambridge University Press.

Steinmetz, George. 1998. "Critical Realism and Historical Sociology." *Comparative Studies in Society and History* 39 (4): 170-86.

Steinmetz, George, ed. 1999a. *State/Culture: Historical Studies of the State in the Social Sciences*. Ithaca, N.Y.: Cornell University Press.

Steinmetz, George. 1999b. "Culture and the State." Pp. 1-49 in Steinmetz 1999a.

Steinmetz, George. 2002. "Precoloniality and Colonial Subjectivity: Ethnographic Discourse and Native Policy in German Overseas Imperialism, 1780s–1914." *Political Power and Social Theory* 15:135–228.

Steinmetz, George. 2003a. "The State of Emergency and the Revival of American Imperialism: Toward an Authoritarian Post-Fordism." *Public Culture* 15 (2): 323–45.

Steinmetz, George. 2003b. "'The Devil's Handwriting': Precolonial Discourse, Ethnographic Acuity and Cross-Identification in German Colonialism." *Comparative Studies in Society and History* 45 (1): 41–95.

Steinmetz, George. 2004a. "Odious Comparisons? Incommensurability, the Case Study, and 'Small N's.'" *Sociological Theory* 22 (1): 371–400.

Steinmetz, George. 2004b. "The Uncontrollable Afterlives of Ethnography: Lessons from German 'Salvage Colonialism' for a New Age of Empire." *Ethnography* 5 (3): 247–83.

Steinmetz, George. 2005a. "Bourdieu and the Psychoanalytic Theory of the Subject." Paper prepared for the conference "Bourdieuian Theory and Historical Analysis," Yale University, April 29–May 1.

Steinmetz, George. 2005b. "Von der 'Eingeborenenpolitik' zur Vernichtungsstrategie: Deutsch-Südwestafrika, 1904." *Peripherie: Zeitschrift für Politik und Ökonomie der Dritten Welt* 96:195–227.

Steinmetz, George. 2005c. "Empire, Imperialism, or Colonialism? From Windhoek to Washington, by Way of Basra." Pp. 135–56 in *Lessons of Empire,* ed. Craig Calhoun, Fred Cooper, and Kevin Moore. New York: New Press.

Steinmetz, George. 2005d. "The Epistemological Unconscious of U.S. Sociology and the Transition to Post-Fordism: The Case of Historical Sociology." Pp. 109–57 in *ReMaking Modernity,* ed. Julia Adams, Elisabeth Clemens, and Ann Orloff. Durham, N.C.: Duke University Press.

Steinmetz, George. 2005e. "Return to Empire: The New U.S. Imperialism in Theoretical and Historical Perspective." *Sociological Theory* 23 (4): 339–67.

Steinmetz, George, ed. 2005f. *The Politics of Method in the Human Sciences: Positivism and Its Epistemological Others.* Durham, N.C.: Duke University Press.

Steinmetz, George. 2006a. "Decolonizing German Theory: An Introduction." *Postcolonial Studies* 9 (1): 3–13.

Steinmetz, George. 2006b. "Bourdieu's Disavowal of Lacan: Psychoanalytic Theory and the Concepts of "Habitus" and 'Symbolic Capital.'" *Constellations* 13 (4): 445–464.

Steinmetz, George, and Julia Hell. 2006. "The Visual Archive of Colonialism: Germany and Namibia." *Public Culture* 18 (1): 147–83.

Steinmetz, George. 2007. "American Sociology before and after World War Two: The (Temporary) Settling of a Disciplinary Field." Pp. 314–366 in *Sociology in America: A History,* ed. Craig Calhoun. Chicago: University of Chicago Press.

Stenz, Georg. 1899. *Erlebnisse eines Missionars in China.* Trier: Paulinus-Druckerei.

Stenz, George M. [Georg]. 1924. *Twenty-Five Years in China (1893-1918)*. Techy, Ill.: Mission Press.

Stevenson, Robert Louis. [1890] 1998. *In the South Seas*. London: Penguin.

Stevenson, Robert Louis. [1892] 1996. *A Footnote to History: Eight Years of Trouble in Samoa*. Honolulu: University of Hawai'i Press.

Stevenson, Robert Louis. 1895. *Vailima Letters*. Chicago: Stone and Kimball.

Stevenson, Robert Louis. 1996. *South Sea Tales*. London: Penguin.

Stichler, Hans-Christian. 1988. "Die Orte Gaomi und Jiaozhou während der deutschen Kolonialherrschaft in China: Über einen wichtigen Abschnitt der Geschichte deutscher Chinapolitik Anfang des 20. Jahrhunderts." *Wissenschaftliche Zeitschrift der Humboldt-Universität. Reihe Gesellschaftswissenschaften* 37 (2): 109-20.

Stichler, Hans-Christian. 1989. "Das Gouvernement Jiaozhou und die deutsche Kolonialpolitik in Shandong 1897-1909: Ein Beitrag zur geschichte der deutsch-chinesischen Beziehungen." Ph.D. diss., Humboldt University Berlin.

Stockenstrom, Andries. 1854. *Light and Shade: As Shown in the Character of the Hottentots of the Kat River Settlement, and in the Conduct of the Colonial Government towards Them*. Cape Town: Saul Solomon.

Stocking, George, Jr. 1973. "From Chronology to Ethnology: James Cowles Prichard and British Anthropology, 1800-1850." Pp. ix-cx in *Researches into the Physical History of Man*, by James Cowles Prichard, ed. George W. Stocking, Jr. Chicago: University of Chicago Press.

Stocking, George, Jr. 1987. *Victorian Anthropology*. New York: Free Press.

Stocking, George Jr. 1991. "Colonial Situations." Pp. 3-8 in *Colonial Situations: Essays on the Contextualization of Ethnographic Knowledge*, ed. George Stocking. Madison: University of Wisconsin Press.

Stoddard, Charles Warren. 1874. *Summer Cruising in the South Seas*. London: Chatto and Windus.

Stoddart, Brian, and Keith A. P. Sandiford, eds. 1998. *The Imperial Game: Cricket, Culture, and Society*. Manchester: Manchester University Press.

Stoecker, Helmuth. 1958. *Deutschland und China im 19. Jahrhundert*. Berlin: Rütten & Loening.

Stoler, Ann Laura. 1989. "Rethinking Colonial Categories: European Communities and the Boundaries of Rule." *Comparative Studies in Society and History* 31 (1): 134-61.

Stoler, Ann Laura. 1997. *Race and the Education of Desire*. Durham, N.C.: Duke University Press.

Stoler, Ann Laura. 2001. "Tense and Tender Ties: The Politics of Comparison in North American History and (Post)Colonial Studies." *Journal of American History* 88 (December): 829-65.

Stoler, Ann Laura. 2002. *Carnal Knowledge and Imperial Power*. Berkeley: University of California Press.

Stoler, Ann Laura. 2006. "On Degrees of Imperial Sovereignty." *Public Culture* 18 (1): 125–46.

Strassberger, Elfriede. 1969. *The Rhenish Mission Society in South Africa, 1830–1950*. Cape Town: C. Struik.

Streit, Robert, and Johannes Dindinger. 1931. *Bibliotheca missionum*. Vol. 6. Aachen: Verlag Franziskus Xaverius Missionsverein.

Streitwolf, Kurt. 1911. *Der Caprivizipfel*. Süsserotts Kolonialbibliothek, vol. 21. Berlin: Süsserott.

Stricker, Wilhelm. 1871. "Der Fuss der Chinesinnen." *Archiv für Anthropologie* 4 (3): 241–43.

Stuebel, Oskar. 1896. *Samoanische Texte: Unter Beihülfe von Eingeborenen gesammelt und übersetzt*. Berlin: F. W. K. Müller.

Sturma, Michael. 2002. *South Sea Maidens: Western Fantasy and Sexual Politics in the South Pacific*. Westport, Conn.: Greenwood Press.

Sudholt, Gerd. 1975. *Die deutsche Eingeborenenpolitik in Südwestafrika: Von den Anfängen bis 1904*. Hildesheim: G. Olms.

Sullivan, Michael. 1997. *The Meeting of Eastern and Western Art*. Rev. ed. Berkeley: University of California Press.

Sun, Lixin. 2003. "Richard Wilhelms Vorstellung über den Kulturaustausch zwischen China und dem Westen." Pp. 85–101 in Hirsch 2003.

Sundermeier, Theo. 1968. "Die Kolonisationsidee Carl Hugo Hahns." *Afrikanischer Heimatkalender*, pp. 43–53.

Sundermeier, Theo, Heinrich Tjituka, and Brigitte Lau. 1985. *The Mbanderu*. Windhoek: MSORP.

Sunseri, Thaddeus R. 1993. "A Social History of Cotton Production in German East Africa, 1884–1915." Ph.D. diss. University of Minnesota.

Suskind, Ron. 2004. "Without a Doubt." *New York Times Magazine*, October 17, 2004, pp. 44–51, 64, 102.

Szpilka, Jaime. 1999. "Some Reflections of Identification." *International Journal of Psychoanalysis* 80:1175–87.

Taillemite, Etienne. *Bougainville et ses compagnons autour du monde 1766–1769*. 2 vols. Paris: Imprimerie nationale.

Taylor, Peter J. 2003. "The State as Container: Territoriality in the Modern World System." Pp. 101–13 in *State/Space*, ed. Neil Brenner, Bob Jessop, Martin Jones, and Gordon Macleod. London: Blackwell.

Tcherkézoff, Serge. 2001. *Le mythe occidental de la sexualité polynésienne: Margaret Mead, Derek Freeman et Samoa*. Paris: Presses universitaires de France.

Tcherkézoff, Serge. 2003. "A Long and Unfortunate Voyage toward the 'Invention' of the Melanesia/Polynesia Distinction, 1595–1832." *Journal of Pacific History* 38 (2): 175–96.

Temple, Sir William. 1814. *The Works of Sir William Temple*. 4 vols. London: F. C. and J. Rivington.

Terry, Edward. 1655. *A Voyage to East-India: Wherein Some Things are Taken Notice of in Our Passage Thither, but Many More in Our Abode There, Within that Rich and Most Spacious Empire of the Great Mogol.* London: Printed by T. W. for J. Martin, and J. Allstrye.

Theroux, Paul. 1993. *The Happy Isles of Oceania.* New York: Ballantine Books.

Theunissen, Beatus. 1947. "Otto Franke: In Memoriam." *Monumenta Serica* 12:277–96.

Thévenot, Melchisédec. 1676. *China and France, or, Two treatises.* London: Printed by T. N. for Samuel Lowndes.

Theweleit, Klaus. [1977–78] 1987–89. *Male Fantasies.* Minneapolis: University of Minnesota Press.

Thomas, Nicholas. 1994. *Colonialism's Culture: Anthropology, Travel, and Government.* Princeton, N.J.: Princeton University Press.

Thomas, Nicholas. 1997. "Melanesians and Polynesians: Ethnic Typifications inside and outside Anthropology." Pp. 133–55 in *In Oceania.* Durham, N.C.: Duke University Press.

Thomas, Nicholas. 2002. "Dumont d'Urville's Anthropology." Pp. 53–70 in *Lure of the Southern Seas,* ed. Susan Hunt, Nicholas Thomas, and Martin Terry. Sydney: Historic Houses Trust of New South Wales.

Thomas, Nicholas, and Oliver Berghof. 2000. "Introduction." Pp. xix–xliii in Georg Forster [1777] 2000, vol. 1.

Thompson, George. [1827] 1967–68. *Travels and Adventures in Southern Africa.* 2 vols. Cape Town: Van Riebeeck Society.

Thoreau, Henry David. 1949. *Journal.* Vol. 9. Boston: Houghton Mifflin.

Tiessen, Ernst. 1906. "Die Schriften Ferdinand Frh. v. Richthofens." Pp. 1–18 in *Ferdinand Frh. v. Richthofen,* ed. Erich V. Drygalski. Leipzig: W. Weicher.

Tilly, Charles. 1985. "War Making and State Making as Organized Crime." Pp. 167–91 in *Bringing the State Back In,* ed. Dietrich Rueschmayer, Peter B. Evans, and Theda Skocpol. New York: Cambridge University Press.

Tilly, Charles. 1990. *Coercion, Capital, and European States, AD 990–1990.* Cambridge: Blackwell.

Timkowski, George [Timkovski, Egor Fedorovich]. 1827. *Travels of the Russian Mission through Mongolia to China.* London: Longman.

Timm, Uwe. [1978] 2003. *Morenga.* New York: New Directions.

Tindall, B. A. 1856. *Two Lectures on Great Namaqualand and Its Inhabitants.* Cape Town: G. J. Pike's Printing Office.

Tindall, Benjamin Arthur, ed. 1959. *The Journal of Joseph Tindall, Missionary in South West Africa, 1839–55.* Cape Town: Van Riebeeck Society.

Tirpitz, Alfred von. 1919. *My Memoirs.* New York: Dodd, Mead, and Co.

Tocqueville, Alexis de. [1835–40] 1945. *Democracy in America.* New York: Vintage Books.

Todorov, Tzvetan. 1984. *The Conquest of America.* New York: Harper and Row.

Todorov, Tzvetan. 1993. *On Human Diversity: Nationalism, Racism, and Exoticism in French Thought*. Cambridge, Mass.: Harvard University Press.

Tom, Nancy. 1986. *The Chinese in Western Samoa, 1875-1975*. Apia, Western Samoa: Western Samoa Historical and Cultural Trust.

Tong, Q. S. 2006. "The Aesthetic of Imperial Ruins: The Elgins and John Bowring. *Boundary 2* 33 (1): 123-50.

Totten, Samuel, William S. Parsons, and Israel Charny, eds. 1995. *Genocide in the Twentieth Century*. New York: Garland.

Townsend, Mary E. 1930. *The Rise and Fall of Germany's Colonial Empire, 1884-1918*. New York: Macmillan.

Trautmann, Thomas R. 1977. *Aryans and British India*. Berkeley: University of California Press.

Treue, Wolfgang. 1976. *Die Jaluit-Gesellschaft auf den Marshall-Inseln 1887-1914*. Berlin: Duncker & Humblot.

Trigault, Nicolas, and Matteo Ricci. [1615] 1953. *China in the Sixteenth Century: The Journals of Matthew Ricci, 1583-1610*. Trans. Louis J. Gallagher, S.J. New York: Random House.

Tronnier, Richard. 1904. "Die Durchquerung Tibets seitens der Jesuiten Johannes Grueber und Albert de Dorville im Jahre 1661." *Zeitschrift der Gesellschaft für Erdkunde zu Berlin* 39:328-61.

Trotha, Trutz von. 1988. "Zur Entstehung von Recht: Deutsche Kolonial-herrschaft und Recht im 'Schutzgebiet Togo,' 1884-1914." *Rechtshistorisches Journal* 7:317-46.

Trotha, Trutz von. 1990. "Stationen: Ein Beitrag zur Theorie der Staatsentstehung auf der Grundlage der deutschen Kolonialherrschaft über Togo in Westafrika, 1884-1914." Pp. 197-218 in *Macht und Recht: Festschrift Heinrich Popitz*, ed. Hans Oswald. Opladen: Westdeutscher Verlag.

Trotha, Trutz von. 1994. *Koloniale Herrschaft*. Tübingen: J. C. B. Mohr.

Trouillot, Michel-Rolph. 1991. "Anthropology and the Savage Slot: The Poetics and Politics of Otherness." Pp. 18-44 in *Recapturing Anthropology: Working in the Present*, ed. Richard Fox. Santa Fe: School of American Research Press.

Trumpener, Ulrich. 1968. *Germany and the Ottoman Empire, 1914-1918*. Princeton, N.J.: Princeton University Press.

Trumpener, Ulrich. 1975. "German Officers in the Ottoman Empire, 1880-1918: Some Comments on Their Backgrounds, Functions, and Accomplishments." Pp. 30-43 in *Germany and the Middle East, 1835-1939*, ed. Jehuda L. Wallach. Tel-Aviv: Tel-Aviv University.

Tscharner, Eduard Horst von. 1939. *China in der deutschen Dichtung bis zur Klassik*. Munich: E. Reinhardt.

Tsingtauer Verkehrs-Ausschuss. 1913. *Tsingtau: Ein Führer durch das deutsche Schutzgebiet in Ostasien: The "Brighton of China."* Tsingtau: A. Haupt.

Turner, George. 1861. *Nineteen Years in Polynesia*. London: John Snow.

Turner, George. 1884. *Samoa, a Hundred Years Ago and Long Before*. London: Macmillan and Co.

Tyszka, Fritz von. 1904. *Dr. Solf und Samoa*. Berlin: Deutscher Kolonial-Verlag.

Union of South Africa. 1918. *Report on the Natives of South-West Africa and Their Treatment by Germany*. London: H.M.S.O.

Union of South Africa. 1927. *Report of the Rehoboth Commission*. Cape Town: Cape Times.

Universität Hamburg, Allgemeiner Studentenausschuss. 1969. *Das Permanente Kolonialinstitut: 50 Jahre Hamburger Universität*. Hamburg: Allgemeiner Studentenausschuss.

Unverzagt, Georg Johann. 1725. *Die Gesantschaft Ihro Kayserlichen Majest. von Gross-Russland an den sinesischen Kayser*. Lübeck: Johann Christian Schmidt.

Väth, Alfons. 1991. *Johann Adam Schall von Bell*. Speyer: Nettetal.

Van der Heyden, Ulrich. 2001. *Rote Adler an Afrikas Küste*. Berlin: Selignow.

Vangroenweghe, Daniel. 1986. *Du sang sur les lianes*. Bruxelles: Didier Hatier.

Vedder, Heinrich. [1938] 1966. *South West Africa in Early Times*. London: Frank Cass and Co.

Vedder, Heinrich. 1955. *Kurze Geschichten aus einem langen Leben*. 2nd ed. Wuppertal-Barmen: Verlag der Rheinischen Missions-Gesellschaft.

Verwaltung der Staatlichen Schlösser und Gärten. 1973. *Charlottenburg Palace*. 3rd ed. Berlin: Verwaltung der Staatlichen Schlösser und Gärten.

Viehe, Gottlieb. 1876. "Religiöse Anschauungen und Gebräuche der Hereró." *Berichte der Rheinischen Missionsgesellschaft* 32 (4): 82–109.

Viehe, Gottlieb. 1879. "Einige Gebräuche der Ovaherero nach der Geburt eines Kindes." *Berichte der Rheinischen Missionsgesellschaft* 35 (12): 372–78.

Vierkandt, Alfred. 1896. *Naturvölker und Kulturvölker*. Leipzig: Duncker & Humblot.

Vigne, Randolph. 1973. *A Dwelling Place of Our Own: The Story of the Namibian Nation*. London: International Defence and Aid Fund.

Virchow, Hans. 1903. "Das Skelett eines verkrüppelten Chinesinnen-Fusses." *Zeitschrift für Ethnologie* 35:266–314.

Voeltz, Richard A. 1988. *German Colonialism and the South West Africa Company, 1884–1914*. Athens: Ohio University, Center for International Studies.

Vogel, Johann Wilhelm. 1716. *Zehen-Jährige, jetzo auffs neue revidirt- und vermehrte Ost-Indianische Reise-Beschreibung in III Theile abgetheilet*. Altenburg: Johann Ludwig Richter.

Volk, Winfried. 1934. *Die Entdeckung Tahitis und das Wunschbild der seligen Insel in der deutschen Literatur*. Heidelberg: Kranz und Heinrichmöller.

Volosinov, V. N. 1985. *Marxism and the Philosophy of Language*. Cambridge, Mass.: Harvard University Press.

Voltaire. [1755] 1877. *L'orphelin de la Chine: Tragédie*. Pp. 289–358 in *Oeuvres complètes*, vol. 5. Paris: Garnier Frères.

Voltaire. [1764] 1879. "De la chine (Dictionnaire philosophique II)." Pp. 449–58 in *Oeuvres complètes*, vol. 18. Paris: Garnier Frères.

Voltaire. [1766] 1879. "Commentaire sur le livre des délits et des peines par un avocat de province." Pp. 530–77 in *Oeuvres complètes*, vol. 25. Paris: Garnier Frères.

Voltaire. [1776] 1879a. "Entretiens chinoises." Pp. 19–34 in *Oeuvres complètes*, vol. 27. Paris: Garnier Frères.

Voltaire. [1776] 1879b. "Lettres chinoises, indiennes, et tartars à M. Pauw par un bénédictin." Pp. 452–98 in *Oeuvres complètes*, vol. 29. Paris: Garnier Frères.

Voltaire. 1879a. "Dieu et les hommes par le Docteur Obern." Pp. 129–248 in *Oeuvres complètes*, vol. 28. Paris: Garnier Frères.

Voltaire. 1879b. "Fanatisme." Pp. 73–87 in *Oeuvres Complètes*, vol. 19. Paris: Garnier Frères.

Voltaire. 1963. *Essai sur les moeurs et l'esprit des nations.* 2 vols. Paris: Editions Garnier Frères.

Vom Bruch, Rüdiger. 1982. *Weltpolitik als Kulturmission: Auswärtige Kulturpolitik und Bildungsbürgertum in Deutschland am Vorabend des Ersten Weltkrieges.* Paderborn: F. Schöningh.

Wätjen, Hermann. 1943. "Die deutsche Handelsschifffahrt in chinesischen Gewässern um die Mitte des 19. Jahrhunderts." *Hansische Geschichtsblätter* 67–68:222–50.

Wagner, Guenther. 1954. "Some Economic Aspects of Herero Life." *African Studies* 13 (nos. 3–4): 117–30.

Waldersee, Alfred Heinrich Karl Ludwig von. 1923. *Denkwürdigkeiten des General-Feldmarschalls Alfred Grafen von Waldersee.* 3 vols. Ed. Heinrich Otto Meissner. Stuttgart: Deutsche Verlags-Anstalt.

Wallace, Marion. 2003. "'Making Tradition': Healing, History and Ethnic Identity among Otjiherero-Speakers in Namibia, c. 1850–1950." *Journal of Southern African Studies* 29 (2): 355–72.

Wallenkampf, Arnold Valentin. 1969. "The Herero Rebellion in South West Africa, 1904–1906: A Study in German Colonialism." Ph.D. diss., University of California, Los Angeles.

Walther, Daniel Joseph. 2002. *Creating Germans Abroad: Cultural Policies and National Identity in Namibia.* Athens: Ohio University Press.

Wang, Ching Dao. 1913. "Die Staatsidee des Konfuzius und ihre Beziehung zur konstitutionelle Verfassung." *Mitteilungen des Seminars für Orientalische Sprachen zu Berlin* 16 (1): 1–49.

Wang, Hui. 2003a. "The 1989 Social Movement and the Historical Roots of China's Neoliberalism." Pp. 41–115 in *China's New Order*, ed. Theodor Huters. Cambridge, Mass.: Harvard University Press.

Wang, Hui. 2003b. "Contemporary Chinese Thought and the Question of Modernity (1997)." Pp. 139–87 in *China's New Order*, ed. Theodor Huters. Cambridge, Mass.: Harvard University Press.

Wareham, Evelyn. 2002. *Race and Realpolitik: The Politics of Colonisation in German Samoa*. Frankfurt am Main: Peter Lang.

Warner, Torsten. 1994. *Deutsche Architektur in China*. Berlin: Ernst & Sohn.

Warren, Bill. 1980. *Imperialism, Pioneer of Capitalism*. London: NLB.

Watson, Robert Mackenzie. 1918. *History of Samoa*. Wellington: Whitcombe and Tombs.

Webb, John. 1669. *An Historical Essay Endeavoring a Probability that the Language of the Empire of China is the Primitive Language*. London: Printed for Nath. Brook.

Weber, Eugen Joseph. 1976. *Peasants into Frenchmen: The Modernization of Rural France, 1870-1914*. Stanford, Calif.: Stanford University Press.

Weber, Max. [1895] 1989. "The National State and Economic Policy." Pp. 188-209 in *Reading Weber*, ed. Keith Tribe. London: Routledge.

Weber, Max. [1919] 1958. "Science as a Vocation." Pp. 77-128 in *From Max Weber: Essays in Sociology*, ed. Hans Gerth and C. Wright Mills. Oxford: Oxford University Press.

Weber, Max. 1964. *The Religion of China: Confucianism and Taoism*. Ed. and trans. Hans H. Gerth. New York: Free Press.

Weber, Max. 1978. *Economy and Society*. 2 vols. Berkeley: University of California Press.

Wege, Fritz. 1969. "Die Anfänge der Herausbildung einer Arbeiterklasse in Südwestafrika unter der deutschen Kolonialherrschaft." *Jahrbuch für Wirtschaftsgeschichte* 10 (1): 183-221.

Wege, Fritz. 1971. "Zur sozialen Lage der Arbeiter Namibias unter der deutschen Kolonialherrschaft in den Jahren vor dem ersten Weltkrieg." *Jahrbuch für Wirtschaftsgeschichte* 12 (3): 201-18.

Wegener, Georg. 1902. *Zur Kriegszeit durch China 1900/1901*. 2nd ed. Berlin: Allgemeiner Verein für Deutsche Litteratur.

Wegener, Georg. 1904. "Der Chinese als fremde Arbeiter." *Velhagen und Klasings Monatshefte* 19 (2): 49-54.

Wehler, Hans-Ulrich. 1972. "Industrial Growth and Early German Imperialism." Pp. 71-92 in *Studies in the Theory of Imperialism*, ed. Bob Sutcliffe. London: Longman.

Wehler, Hans-Ulrich. 1984. *Bismarck und der Imperialismus*. 2nd ed. Frankfurt am Main: Suhrkamp.

Weicker, Hans. 1908. *Kiautschou, das deutsche Schutzgebiet in Ostasien*. Berlin: Alfred Schall.

Weindling, Paul. 1989. *Health, Race, and German Politics between National Unification and Nazism, 1870-1945*. Cambridge: Cambridge University Press.

Weingart, Peter, Jürgen Kroll, and Kurt Bayertz. 1988. *Rasse, Blut und Gene: Geschichte der Eugenik und Rassenhygiene in Deutschland*. Frankfurt am Main: Suhrkamp.

Weiss, Sheila Faith. 1990. "The Race Hygiene Movement in Germany, 1904–1945." Pp. 8–68 in *The Wellborn Science: Eugenics in Germany, France, and Russia*, ed. Mark B. Adams. New York: Oxford University Press.

Welcker, H. 1870. "Über die künstliche Verkrüppelung der Füsse der Chinesinnen." *Archiv für Anthropologie* 4 (3): 221–32.

Welcker, H. 1872. "Die Füsse der Chinesinnen." *Archiv für Anthropologie* 5 (2): 133–52.

Werner, B. von. 1889. *Ein deutsches Kriegsschiff in der Südsee*. Leipzig: Brockhaus.

Werner, Reinhold. 1873. *Die preussische Expedition nach China, Japan, und Siam in den jahren 1860, 1861 und 1862: Reisebriefe*. 2nd ed. Leipzig: Brockhaus.

Werner, Wolfgang. 1990. "'Playing Soldiers': The Truppenspieler Movement among the Herero of Namibia, 1915 to ca. 1945." *Journal of Southern African Studies* 16 (3): 476–502.

Werner, Wolfgang. 1993. "A Brief History of Land Dispossession in Namibia." *Journal of Southern African Studies* 19 (1): 135–46.

Werner, Wolfgang. 1998. *No One Will Become Rich: Economy and Society in the Herero Reserves in Namibia, 1915–1946*. Basel: Schlettwein.

Wessels, Cornelius. 1940. "New Documents Relating to the Journey of Fr. John Grueber." *Archivum Historicum Societatis Iesu* 9:281–302.

Wiesner, Ulrich. 1981. *Chinesisches Porzellan: Die Ohlmer'sche Sammlung im Roemer-Museum, Hildesheim*. Mainz am Rhein: Verlag Philipp von Zabern.

Wiethoff, Bodo. 1971. "Das Chinabild J. G. Herders." Pp. 666–79 in *Asien: Tradition und Fortschritt*, ed. Lydia Brüll and Ulrich Kemper. Wiesbaden: O. Harrassowitz.

Wildenthal, Lora. 2001. *German Women for Empire, 1884–1945*. Durham, N.C.: Duke University Press.

Wilder, Gary. 2005. *The French Imperial Nation-State: Negritude and Colonial Humanism between the Two World Wars*. Chicago: University of Chicago Press.

Wildhaber, Robert. 1955. *Das Sündenregister auf der Kuhhaut*. Helsinki: Suomalainen Tiedeakatemia.

Wilhelm, Richard. 1914. "Aus unserer Arbeit (Konfuziusgesellschaft)." *Zeitschrift für Missionskunde und Religionswissenschaft* 8:248–51.

Wilhelm, Richard. 1924. *I Ging: Das Buch der Wandlungen*. Jena, Eugen Diederichs.

Wilhelm, Richard. 1926. *Die Seele Chinas*. Berlin: R. Hobbing.

Wilhelm, Richard. 1928. *The Soul of China*. New York: Harcourt, Brace and Co.

Wilhelm, Richard. n.d. [1913]. "Unser Deutsch-Chinesisches Seminar in Tsingtau (China)." Pp. 3–11 in *Unsere Schulem in Tsingtau*. Görlitz: Buch- und Steindruckerei Hoffmann & Reiber.

Wilhelm, Salome Blumhardt. 1956. *Richard Wilhelm, der geistige Mittler zwischen China und Europa*. Düsseldorf: E. Diederichs.

Wilkes, Charles. 1845. *Narrative of the United States Exploring Expedition during the Years 1838, 1839, 1840, 1841, 1842*. 5 vols. Philadelphia: Lea and Blanchard.

Willeke, Bernward H. 1947. "Franciscan Missions in Shantung, China." *Franciscan Studies* 7:171–87.

Willeke, Bernward H. 1974. "Würzburg und die Chinamission im 17. und 18. Jahrhundert." Pp. 417–29 in *Aus Reformation und Gegenreformation: Festschrift für Theobald Freudenberger*. Würzburg: Bischöfl. Ordinariatsarchiv.

Williams, John. 1837. *A Narrative of Missionary Enterprises in the South Sea Islands*. 1st U.S. ed. New York: D. Appleton and Co.

Williams, John. 1984. *The Samoan Journals of John Williams, 1830 and 1832*. Ed. Richard M. Moyle. Canberra: Australian National University Press.

Williams, William Appleman. 1959. *The Tragedy of American Diplomacy*. Cleveland: World Pub. Co.

Wilson, James. [1799] 1966. *A Missionary Voyage to the Southern Pacific Ocean, 1796–1798*. Graz: Akademische Druck- und Verlagsanstalt.

Winckelmann, Johann. [1776] 1968. *History of Ancient Art*. New York: Frederick Ungar Publishing Co.

Witbooi, Hendrik. 1996. *The Hendrik Witbooi Papers*. Trans. Annmarie Heywood and Eben Maasdorp. Windhoek: National Archives of Namibia.

Wittgenstein, Ludwig. 1969. *On Certainty*. Ed. G. E. M. Anscombe and G. H. von Wright. Trans. Denis Paul and G. E. M. Anscombe. New York: Harper.

Witt, Peter-Christian. 1973. "Reichsfinanzen und Rüstungspolitik 1898–1914." Pp. 146–77 in *Marine und Marinepolitik im kaiserlichen Deutschland 1871–1914*, ed. Herbert Schottelius and Wilhelm Deist. Düsseldorf: Droste.

Wohltmann, Ferdinand. 1903. *Vortrag zu den Lichtbildern der Deutschen Kolonialgesellschaft über Kultur- und Vegatationsbilder aus Samoa*. Berlin: Deutsche Kolonialgesellschaft.

Wolf, Eugen. 1901. *Meine Wanderungen: Im innern Chinas*. Stuttgart: Deutsche Verlags-Anstalt.

Wolff, Christian. [1721] 1975. *Vernünfftige Gedancken von dem gesellschafftlichen Leben der Menschen und Insonderheit dem gemeinen Wesen*. Hildesheim: G. Olms.

Wolff, Christian. [1726] 1740. "Rede von der Sittenlehre der Sineser." Pp. 1–320 in *Gesammelte kleine philosophische Schriften*, vol. 6. Halle: Renger.

Wolff, Christian. [1745] 1995. *Natürliche Gottesgelahrheit*. Vol. 1, pt. 23, no. 2, 2, of *Gesammelte Werke*. Halle: Renger.

Woltmann, Ludwig. 1903. *Politische Anthropologie: Eine Untersuchung über den Einfluss der Descendenztheorie auf die Lehre von der politischen Entwicklung der Völker*. Eisenach: Thüringische Verlags-Anstalt.

Wong, Young-tsu. 2001. *Paradise Lost: The Imperial Garden Yuanming Yuan*. Honoulu: University of Hawai'i Press.

Wood, Frances. 1998. *No Dogs and Not Many Chinese: Treaty Port Life in China, 1843–1943*. London: John Murray.

Wright, Erik Olin. 1979. *Class, Crisis and the State*. London: Verso.

Wright, Gwendolyn. 1991. *The Politics of Design in French Colonial Urbanism*. Chicago: University of Chicago Press.

Wright, John L. 1982. *Libya: A Modern History*. London: Croom Helm.

Wurffbain, Johann Sigmund. [1686] 1930–32. *Reise nach den Molukken und Vorder-Indien 1632–1646*. 2 vols. The Hague: Martinus Nijhoff.

Xiao Gongquan. 1975. *A Modern China and a New World: K'ang Yu-wei, Reformer and Utopian, 1858–1927*. Seattle: University of Washington Press.

Xu Jian. 1999. "Die deutsche Kulturpolitik in China und ihre Auswirkungen in den Jahren 1897 bis 1914." Pp. 152–56 in Hiery and Hinz 1999.

Xu Youchun. 1991. *Mingguo renwu da cidian* [Who's Who in the Republican Period]. Beijing: Hebei renmin chubanshe.

Yarnall, James L. 1998. *Recreation and Idleness: The Pacific Travels of John La Farge*. New York: Vance Jordon Fine Art.

Yearwood, Peter J. 1990. "Great Britain and the Partition of Africa." *Journal of Commonwealth and Imperial History* 18:316–41.

Young, Crawford. 1994. *The African Colonial State in Comparative Perspective*. New Haven, Conn.: Yale University Press.

Young, Robert J. C. 2001. *Postcolonialism: An Historical Introduction*. Oxford: Blackwell Publishers.

Yuan Rongsou. [1928] 1969. *Jiao'ao zhi* [Jiao'ao Chronicle]. 3 vols. Taibei: Wenhai chubanshe.

Zachariä, Friedrich Wilhelm. 1778. "Tayti oder die glückliche Insel." Pp. 137–74 in *Poetische Schriften*, vol. 4. Reuttlingen: Johann Georg Fleischhauer.

Zantop, Susanne. 1997. *Colonial Fantasies: Conquest, Family, and Nation in Precolonial Germany, 1770–1870*. Durham, N.C.: Duke University Press.

Zecchini, Laurent. 2005. "Le mystère du sort de Lapérouse demeure." *Le Monde*, May 25, p. 23.

Zeidler, Heinrich Friedrich Bernhard. 1914. "Beiträge zur Anthropologie der Herero." Ph.D. diss., Friedrich-Wilhelms-Universität Berlin. Stuttgart: E. Schweizbart'sche Verlagsbuchhandlung.

Zeller, Eduard. 1862. "Wolff's Vertreibung aus Halle: Der Kampf des Pietismus mit der Philosophie." *Preussische Jahrbücher* 10:47–72.

Zeller, Joachim. 2000. *Kolonialdenkmäler und Geschichtsbewußtsein*. Frankfurt am Main: IKO.

Zeller, Joachim. 2003. "'Ombepera i koza: Die Kälte tötet mich': Zur Geschichte des Konzentrationslagers in Swakopmund (1904–1908)." Pp. 64–79 in Zimmerer and Zeller 2003.

Zhang Shufeng. 1991. "Li Hongzhang yu Jiaozhouwan" [Li Hongzhang and Jiaozhou Bay]. Pp. 66–80 in Liu Shanzhang and Zhou Quan 1991.

Zhang Yufa. 1982. *Zhongguo xiandaihua de quyu yanjiu: Shandong sheng (1860–1916)* [Modernization in China, Regional Research: Shandong Province (1860–1916)]. Taibei: Academia Sinica.

Zhang Yufa. 1986. "Qingdao de shiliquan" [Qingdao's Sphere of Influence].

Pp. 801–38 in *Jindai Zhongguo quyushi yantaohui lunwenji* [Proceedings of the Conference on Regional Studies of Modern China], ed. Zhongyang yanjiuyuan jindaishi yanjiusuo. Taibei: Academia Sinica.

Zhang Yufa. 1999. "Erzieungswesen in Qingdao in der Ära der deutschen Besetzung: Ansichten einese chinesischen Wissenschaftlers." Pp. 210–22 in Hiery and Hinz 1999.

Zhen Dahu. 1991. "Kang Youwei and the Jiaozhou Incident." Pp. 93–103 in Liu Shanzhang, Zhou Quan zhu bian 1991.

Zhu Maodou. 1994. "Deutsche Truppeneinsätze in Shandong nach dem Abschluß des 'Jiaoao-Pachtvertrags.'" Pp. 309–32 in Kuo and Leutner 1994.

Zimmerer, Jürgen. 1999. "Kriegsgefangene im Koloialkrieg: Der Krieg gegen die Herero und Nama in Deutsch-Südwestafrika (1904-1907)." Pp. 277–94 in *In der Hand des Feindes*, ed. Rüdiger Overmans. Cologne: Böhlau.

Zimmerer, Jürgen. 2001. *Deutsche Herrschaft über Afrikaner: Staatlicher Machtanspruch und Wirklichkeit im kolonialen Namibia*. 2nd ed. Münster: Lit.

Zimmerer, Jürgen. 2003. "Krieg, KZ und Völkermord in Südwestafrika: Der erste deutsche Genozid." In Zimmerer and Zeller 2003.

Zimmerer, Jürgen, and Joachim Zeller, ed. 2003. *Völkermord in Deutsch-Südwestafrika: Der Kolonialkrieg (1904-1908) in Namibia und seine Folgen*. Berlin: Links.

Zimmerman, Andrew. 2001. *Anthropology and Antihumanism in Imperial Germany*. Chicago: University of Chicago Press.

Zimmerman, Andrew. 2006. "Decolonizing Weber." *Postcolonial Studies* 9 (1): 53–79.

Zinoman, Peter. 2001. *The Colonial Bastille: A History of Imprisonment in Vietnam, 1862–1940*. Berkeley: University of California Press.

Žižek, Slavoj. 1989. *The Sublime Object of Ideology*. New York: Verso.

Zwergern, von. 1911. "Aus Deutsch-Südwestafrika." Pt. 1, "Zur Bastardfrage." *Frankfurter Zeitung*, no. 208 (July 29).

INDEX

A

A'ana ('Upolu, Samoa), xxxii map 3,
    312n295
abjection, 83, 86, 90
*Account of Travels into the Interior of
    South Africa* (Barrow, John), xxii,
    100–101
Adams, Julia, 23n75
Adelung, Johann Christoph, 403
Adler, Alfred, 51
"Africans," representations of, 10n31,
    60, 79–89, 82n32, 82n34, 92, 101,
    108, 120n190, 177–78, 189, 198,
    246, 261n66, 386n122, 387, 387 fig.
    6.4, 389, 401, 422n281, 463. *See also*
    race, discourse on
Afrikaner (//Aixa//ain) Orlams,
    7n16, 8, 110–11, 111n140, 115n168,
    131, 149; "War of Liberation" of
    Ovaherero from the Afrikaners
    (1863), 8, 111, 131. *See also* Orlams
Afrikaner (Dutch settler descendants),
    163–64
Afrikaner, Jan Jonker (son of Jonker
    Afrikaner), 112n144, 118, 122,
    127n224, 149
Afrikaner, Jonker, 110–11, 111n140,
    112n144, 115n161, 118, 132n249
agency of the colonized
—cooperation: as determinant of

native policy, xix, 2, 27, 35–36,
    66–67, 214–15, 231, 237–38, 268,
    319, 332, 356–58, 470–72, 471n168,
    492–93; examples of, 122, 138–39,
    157–59, 164–65, 177, 214–15,
    219–28, 319
—as determinant of ethnographic
    discourse, 67n227, 88–89, 104–5,
    120–21, 129–34, 177–79, 356–58,
    362–63, 439–42, 465, 492–93, 515
—resistance: Chinese, 362–63, 408–9,
    430, 439–42, 454–57, 465, 493;
    as determinant of native policy,
    xix, 2, 27, 66–67, 131–32, 355–58,
    147, 151, 153, 171–72, 179, 437,
    439–42, 465, 470–72, 471n168,
    491–93, 493n243, 497; Ovaherero,
    183, 191–93; Polynesian, 281;
    Rehobother, 238–39, 239n426;
    Samoan, 289, 299, 327–30, 356–58;
    Witbooi, 147–52, 169–70, 176.
    See also Boxers (Yihetuan): Boxer
    Rebellion; Dadao Hui (Big Knife
    Society, China); Herero and Nama
    wars; Kat River rebellion of 1851
    (Cape Colony); Lafoga 'Oloa,
    Samoan uprising (1904); Mau a
    Pule, Samoan uprising (1908–9);
    Witbooi (/Khobesin) Orlams:
    uprisings